ANNIBALE FANTOLI

GALILEO

FOR COPERNICANISM AND FOR THE CHURCH

Whether in reaching such a decision it is advisable to consider, ponder, and examine what he [Copernicus] writes is something that I have done my best to show in an essay of mine. I hope the blessed God has granted me this, for I have no other aim but the honor of the Holy Church and do not direct my small labors to any other goal. (Galileo to Dini, 23 March 1615)

Translation by George V. Coyne, S.J.

Second Edition, Revised and Corrected

Originally published in Italian under the title *Galileo per il Copernicanesimo e per la Chiesa*

© First English Edition, Copyright 1994 Vatican Observatory Foundation

© Second English Edition, Copyright 1996 Vatican Observatory Foundation

Camera-ready copy prepared by Francesco Rossi

Published by the Vatican Observatory Publications

Distributed (except in Italy and the Vatican City State) by:
    The University of Notre Dame Press
    Notre Dame, Indiana 46656
    USA

Distributed in Italy and the Vatican City State by:
    Libreria Editrice Vaticana
    V-00120 Città del Vaticano
    Vatican City State
    Rome, Italy

ISBN 0-268-01032-3

for Teruko

CONTENTS

PRESENTATION   XI

PREFACE   XV

FOREWORD TO THE ENGLISH EDITION   XVIII

EDITORIAL NOTE   1

INTRODUCTION: FROM THE TRADITIONAL WORLDVIEW TO THE THEORY OF COPERNICUS

1. From Aristotelian Cosmology to the System of Ptolemy   1

2. The Encounter with Christianity and the Medieval Synthesis   12

3. The "Copernican Revolution" and the Reaction of the Theologians   19

4. The Reaction of the Astronomers. The System of Tycho Brahe   28

5. The World of Copernicus Expanded to the Infinite. Giordano Bruno   34

CONTENTS

CHAPTER 1: GALILEO ENTERS ON STAGE. FROM HIS BIRTH TO HIS YEARS IN PADUA

1. Family Milieu and Early Education   47

2. "Conversion" to Euclid and Archimedes   50

3. Mathematics Teacher at Pisa. The Sources of his Teaching   54

4. The Pisan *De Motu* and Galileo's First Orientation Towards Copernicus   58

5. The Beginning of his Teaching Career at Padua   63

6. The First Idea of a Possible "Proof" of Copernicanism   68

7. The *Nova* of 1604 and a New Attempt at a "Proof" of Copernicanism   74

8. Private Teaching and Activities in Technical Matters   82

9. Friends and Family Affairs   84

CHAPTER 2: THE TELESCOPIC DISCOVERIES. THE BEGINNING AND GROWTH OF THE CONTROVERSIES

1. The Making of the Telescope and the First Astronomical Discoveries   107

2. The *Sidereus Nuncius* and the Plan to Return to Florence   110

3. The Reactions to the *Sidereus Nuncius* and the Return to Florence   114

4. The Beginning of the Controversies about
    Scripture. Galileo's Trip to Rome   124

5. The Dispute about Floating Bodies. The "League"
    against Galileo is Born   135

6. The Sunspots and the Beginning of the
    Controversy with Scheiner   138

CHAPTER 3:   EPILOGUE TO THE SCRIPTURAL
             CONTROVERSY. THE *DE REVOLUTIONIBUS*
             IS LISTED ON THE INDEX

1. The Theologians Begin to Intervene in the
    Copernican Controversy   169

2. The *Letter to Castelli*. The Reaction of the
    Dominicans in Florence   173

3. Foscarini and Bellarmine on the Copernican
    Question   182

4. Galileo's Response. The *Letter to Christina
    of Lorraine*   189

5. The Dominican, Caccini, Accuses Galileo
    before the Holy Office   209

6. Galileo Goes to Rome to Defend Copernicanism   211

7. The Intervention of the Holy Office. The *De
    Revolutionibus* is Placed on the *Index*   215

8. Rumors of an Abjuration by Galileo. Bellarmine's
    Testimony for Galileo. Some Final Remarks   227

CHAPTER 4:   THE CONTROVERSY ABOUT COMETS AND
              THE ASSAYER. MAFFEO BARBERINI IS
              ELECTED POPE

1. The Three Comets of 1618 and the *Disputatio
   Astronomica* of Grassi   271

2. The Response of Galileo. The *Discourse on
   the Comets*   276

3. Grassi's Response. The *Libra Astronomica*   280

4. *The Assayer* is Born. Maffeo Barberini is
   Elected Pope   283

5. A New Response of Grassi. *The Ratio
   Ponderum Librae et Simbellae*   296

CHAPTER 5:   THE RESUMPTION OF THE COPERNICAN
              PROGRAM. THE *DIALOGUE* IS PUBLISHED

1. A New Trip of Galileo to Rome and Conversations
   with Urban VIII   319

2. The *Letter to Ingoli*   323

3. *The Assayer* denounced by a "Pious Person" to
   the Holy Office   327

4. A Return to the *Discourse on the Ebb and
   Flow of the Sea*   328

5. The *Rosa Ursina* of Scheiner and the Completion
   of the *Dialogue*   330

6. Galileo in Rome. The Events Surrounding the
   Permission to Print the *Dialogue*   335

7. The *Dialogue Concerning the Two Chief World
   Systems*   343

CHAPTER 6: THE STORM BREAKS LOOSE. THE TRIAL
AND CONDEMNATION OF GALILEO

1. The *Dialogue* Arrives in Rome. The Reactions
    against it Begin   389

2. Urban VIII Becomes Aware of the Contents
    of the *Dialogue*. The First Dispositions are
    Taken against the Book   392

3. The Charges against the *Dialogue* are Specified   397

4. The Discovery of the Injunction of Segizzi to
    Galileo and the Answer of the Commission
    Appointed to Examine the *Dialogue*   402

5. Galileo is Summoned to Rome by the Holy Office   404

6. Beginning of the Trial and Galileo's Defense   419

7. The Extra-Judicial Attempt by the Commissary
    Maculano   426

8. The Condemnation and Abjuration of Galileo   436

9. Some final Considerations on the Condemnation
    of Galileo   446

CHAPTER 7: THE "GALILEO AFFAIR" FROM THE TRIAL'S
END UNTIL TODAY

1. Galileo Returns to Florence. The *Two New
    Sciences* are Published in Holland   487

2. Galileo's Last Years and his Death. The Plan
    for a Mausoleum in his Honor is Put Aside   489

3. The Mausoleum is Finally Built. The Holy
   Office Allows a Conditional Reprinting of
   the *Dialogue*   493

4. The Decree of 1616 is Omitted in the New
   Edition of the *Index of Forbidden Books*.
   The Settele Case   496

5. The Galilean Dispute in the XIX Century
   and the "Opening" of the Vatican Archives
   to Scholars   499

6. The *Galileo* of Pio Paschini and Vatican
   Council II   503

7. John Paul II and the Frank Recognition of the
   Errors of the Past   507

BIBLIOGRAPHY   533

INDEX OF NAMES   553

PRESENTATION

It is a great privilege for me to be able to present this work of Annibale Fantoli which is the seventh publication and volume three in the series, *Studi Galileiani*. The series began in 1981 as an initiative of the Working Group on Science and Epistemology of the so-called Galileo Commission which had been constituted in that year by Pope John Paul II. On 31 October 1992 in a solemn discourse given on the occasion of the Plenary Meeting of the Pontifical Academy of Sciences before the assembled College of Cardinals and Diplomatic Corps the Pope concluded the work of that Commission. The reason why I consider it a rare privilege to present this work is the fact that, in my opinion, it responds in an exemplary way to the wish expressed by John Paul II in 1979 when he said:

> . . . I hope that theologians, scholars and historians, animated by a spirit of sincere collaboration, will study the Galileo case more deeply and, in loyal recognition of wrongs from whatever side they come, will dispel the mistrust that still opposes, in many minds, a fruitful concord between science and faith, between the Church and the world.[1]

In this work, based on a quite broad examination of the pertinent studies published thus far, Fantoli presents us with what seems to me to be the most up to date, in-depth study of the Galileo affair. Through a critical analysis of both the principal historical sources and of the most recent studies on Galileo this work aims to reconstruct the history of the ideas which were the principal factors in defining the Galileo affair.

In this historical reconstruction it becomes clear that Fantoli has a remarkable ability to identify objectively and honestly "the wrongs from whatever side they originated". This book is the result of more than twenty-five years of study on Galileo. The author began these studies as a Jesuit teacher at Sophia University in Tokyo and he has carried them out since then with a profound and enduring love for both the Church and for historical truth. In this he very much resembles Galileo who, as both the subtitle, *For Copernicanism and For the Church*, and the background cover pictures indicate, at the same time as he fought to promote Copernicanism, wished to affirm that he was doing so selflessly or, as he himself said:

> Whether in reaching such a decision it is advisable to consider, ponder, and examine what he [Copernicus] writes is something that I have done my best to show in an essay of mine. I hope the blessed God has granted me this, for I have no other aim but the honor of the Holy Church and do not direct my small labors to any other goal. (Galileo to Dini, 23 March 1615)[2]

And so it happens that those very words which, according to the author, summarize the guiding principles for all of Galileo's activity, also define the criteria which guided the author's dedication to a deeper understanding of the historical events. This is not an apologetic work in which the author takes sides. It is rather a sincere effort at an objective analysis whose purpose is to contribute to the good of both science and the Church.

Each of us lives out his life in a given historical period. We, both readers and author, have the good fortune to live at a time when the dialogue between science, philosophy and theology has a great deal of support. Galileo was less fortunate. In his time such a dialogue was not possible and, although he fought on behalf of both the Church and science, he was in the end forced to side publicly with the Church. With the passage of time Galileo has been proven right. Fantoli has succeeded in showing quite clearly the special meaning of this posthumous victory. Galileo conducted a strange battle; he felt obliged to wage the battle on both fronts: on behalf of the Copernican system and in support of

Holy Scripture. But, after a temporary defeat, history has awarded him the triumphs he deserved on both fronts, although several centuries separated the one triumph from the other.

The frank admission by John Paul II of the tragic mistake committed by Galileo's judges has raised for many people the question as to whether we might still see in the future another Galileo case. I would answer this question by recalling a passage from a letter written by Cardinal Newman on 28 May 1876 to his friend Mivart in regard to those who at that time in the name of the faith were against any form of evolutionism:

> No one but will incur the jealous narrowness of those who think no latitude of opinion, reasoning or thought is allowable in theological questions. Those who would not allow Galileo to reason 300 years ago will not allow any one else now. The past is no lesson for them for the present and the future; and their notion of stability in faith is ever to be repeating errors and then repeating retractions of them.[3]

No confession of a mistake, however sincere, can as such guarantee that other mistakes will not occur. Only a spirit of true dialogue between science and faith can minimize the risk that this could happen. Again we might recall the words of John Paul II:

> For too long a time they [science and religion] have been at arm's length. . . As such it [theology] must be in vital exchange today with science just as it has always been with philosophy and other forms of learning. . . Theology is not to incorporate indifferently each new philosophical or scientific theory. As these findings become part of the intellectual culture of the time, however, theologians must understand them and test their value in bringing out from Christian belief some of the possibilities which have not yet been realized.[4]

This work of Fantoli shows dramatically how, when all is said and done, it was truly a lack of dialogue which brought

about that tragic mistake which caused so much suffering to
Galileo and seriously damaged the Church. In that regard,
this work makes a new, and I would say special, contribution
to the much desired and growing dialogue between science and
faith. If it is true that the past teaches us about the future,
then this work of Fantoli will serve as a lesson to us that only
humility and freedom of spirit can cultivate in the human
spirit the ability to recognize the truth under whatever guise
it comes to us. Such an ability is essential if we are to avoid
perpetrating other Galileo cases.

As translator of this work I wish to express my profound
gratitude to Sabino Maffeo, S.J. and Martin F. McCarthy, S.J.
for their careful reading of this English edition and for their
suggestions both for many substantial improvements in it and
also for several modifications and additions to what was
presented in the Italian edition.

George V. Coyne, S.J.
Director of the Vatican Observatory

NOTES

[1] *Discourses of the Popes from Pius XI to John Paul II to the
Pontifical Academy of Sciences, 1936-1986* (Pontificia Academia
Scientiarum: Vatican City 1986) p. 153.
[2] Favaro, V, 299-300; trans. by Finocchiaro 1989, 62.
[3] Newman to Mivart 1876 June 5, *Letters and Diaries* XXVII,
71.
[4] Message of John Paul II to the Director of the Vatican
Observatory, in *Physics, Philosophy and Theology: A Common Quest
for Understanding*, eds. R.J. Russell, W.R. Stoeger and G.V. Coyne
(Vatican Observatory, University of Notre Dame Press:Notre Dame,
IN, 1988) p. M10.

PREFACE

It was more than twenty-five years ago, while I was preparing a course on Galileo at Sophia University in Tokyo, that the first thought to write this book came to me. This long period of incubation provided me the opportunity to apply myself to a deeper and more extensive treatment of many details which I had left at the beginning in a quite sketchy state. It is my hope that this has helped me to avoid the shoals on which so many, even very recent, Galilean studies have become bogged down. However, I leave it to the reader to judge whether I have succeeded in that endeavor.

I do not pretend with this book to make any original contribution in the specialized field of the history of science, nor in that of the history of western ideas, even though one must take account of those fields in so far as they provide presuppositions required for an understanding of the Galileo affair. In fact, I have found it necessary to review those presuppositions for the reader, in an altogether schematic way, in the Introduction which follows.

Nor is it my intention in this book to present a complete biography of Galileo. My aim is rather to highlight the many different factors (conceptual, ideological and religious) which were present in an influential way in the various stages of Galileo's life and to show the complex dialectical interplay among them which will progressively lead to the conflict between Galileo's Copernicanism and contemporary philosophers and theologians, and, at the end, to his conflict with the Church.

Galileo certainly did not wish this last conflict to occur. On the contrary, as I hope will become clear in this book, one of Galileo's principal motives in his works was to assure that Copernicus' view, even if not positively accepted by the

Church, would at least not be too hastily condemned by her. This shows that for Galileo it was never a question of choosing between Copernicanism on the one hand and the Church on the other; at the same time it reveals that the saddest aspect of the whole drama was the fact the Galileo was faced with an injunction to choose the part of the Church and *against* Copernicanism. As a matter of fact, however, even after he had read and signed the document of abjuration, Galileo remained unwavering in his attitude, looking now with more patience and farsightedness at a Church which would in the end have made a more correct judgement. Galileo was, therefore, neither a free-thinker who rose up against the "obscurantism" of the Church, nor a man weakened by the trial and condemnation to the point that he preferred to remain on the side of the Church even at the expense of abandoning his new view of the universe.

This to my mind justifies my choice of the subtitle: *For Copernicanism and for the Church.*

To avoid making the text too dense with scholarly details I have consigned to the notes the discussion of many controversial issues and my critical evaluation of the opinions of many of the best known Galilean scholars. Not infrequently my own examination of the material has led me to conclusions different than theirs. But this does not at all detract, I must emphasize this right at the start, from my high regard for them and my appreciation for their great accomplishments.

Many other notes have been added in order to furnish new information and at times unpublished documents which will help to understand the Galileo affair and the principal characters, both persons and institutions, involved in it.

Due to this choice of distributing the material, the notes are numerous and, at times, quite detailed. Even though I am well aware that to consult these notes will cause interruptions in the reading of the text itself and will, therefore, seriously test the reader's patience, I do suggest that as far as possible the notes be consulted. In fact, the notes complement the text, sometimes in an essential way, and provide the reasons for certain conclusions which might otherwise appear to be completely gratuitous.

As is always the case with the publication of a book of historical research, this work would never have seen the light of day without the help, advice and criticism of many during the course of my redrafting of it over these twenty-five years. Although I could not possibly remember all of them, I wish to thank His Eminence, Cardinal Joseph Ratzinger, Prefect of the Congregation for the Doctrine of the Faith, for having allowed me to consult some documents concerning Galileo in the archives of the old Holy Office. I am also grateful to Father Innocenzo Mariani, the archivist of that Congregation, for all of the help he gave me in those researches. My gratitude goes also to Professor Carlo Maccagni of the *Domus Galilaeana* at Pisa for the generous help he gave me in the initial stages of this work. I express my thanks to both Father Vincenzo Monachino, S.J., at one time dean of the Faculty of Church History and currently archivist of the Pontifical Gregorian University, for having permitted me free access to the correspondence of Clavius and other Jesuits, contemporaries of Galileo, and to Father Giacomo Martina, S.J., professor of Church History at the same University, for his constant readiness to provide me copies of articles from journals and books which were otherwise difficult to find.

With respect to the final stages of the revisions of the text and of the preparation for publication I am most grateful in the first place to Father George Coyne, S.J., Director of the Vatican Observatory, who very kindly considered this work of mine and judged it in a positive light. I am truly honored that he has decided to publish it in the series: *Studi Galileiani*. My deepest gratitude also goes to Father Sabino Maffeo, S.J. who tirelessly and patiently read and reread the text and pointed out many typographical errors and other mistakes which had escaped me. He also suggested many changes in style and in certain expressions and he obtained for me in a timely fashion the most recent publications to have appeared on the topics contained in this book. I must also thank Juan Casanovas, S.J. and Saverio Corradino, S.J. of the same Observatory for their constructive critiques which have helped to improve various arguments.

I am very much in debt to Professor Olaf Pedersen, emeritus professor of the History of Science at the University of Aarhus, Denmark, who also read the text and made important suggestions to me concerning it.

Finally, I wish in a special way to thank my wife, Teruko, who was always at my side as I labored on this book, supporting me with her affection, her understanding and her patience and who, with her loving impatience, urged me on, and in fact compelled me, to publish.

FOREWORD TO THE ENGLISH EDITION

It is for me a source of great satisfaction to see this English version of my book come to the light of day only one year after the publication of the Italian edition. In the first place I wish to express my profound gratitude to Father George V. Coyne, S.J., Director of the Vatican Observatory, who, after having seen to the publication of my original work in the Vatican Observatory series, *Studi Galileiani*, then also took upon himself the task of this translation and, despite his many other obligations, has brought it to completion in such a brief period of time. In addition to him I also wish to thank Father Sabino Maffeo, S.J. and Father Martin F. McCarthy, S.J., also of the Vatican Observatory, for their precious and tireless help to me in the search for further sources of information and in textual improvements in the Italian edition with a view also to this translation. Alongside them my sincere gratitude goes also to those readers of the Italian version who, by reason of their comments and constructive criticisms, have allowed me to make many further corrections, changes and additions, which it has been possible to include in this English edition. In this regard I especially want to thank Professors Ugo Baldini of the University "G. D'Annunzio" of Chieti, Richard J. Blackwell of St. Louis University, Jerzy Dobrzycki of the Institute for the History of Science of Warsaw, Paolo Maffei of the University of Perugia, and the Fathers P.N. Mayaud, S.J. and P. Millefiorini, S.J. Thanks to the collaboration of all these persons the current English version offers, I hope, an improved text with respect to the original Italian edition.

Victoria, British Columbia, Canada
12 April 1994

Annibale Fantoli

PREFACE TO THE SECOND REVISED EDITION

This second edition of my book has been required by the fact that in just over one year since its release the first edition went out of print. This was undoubtedly due to the fact that in reviewing the book many Galileo scholars passed a very positive judgment upon it. First of all I would like to extend my most sincere thanks to them. It goes without saying that my gratitude also goes to them for their critical observations. These criticisms, together with my own personal reflections and with new data furnished by more recent and often very valuable studies, have allowed me to broaden and to update my treatment of the material and in some cases to revise my judgment, even on some points of considerable importance. This has happened especially with regard to the final stage of Galileo's trial and the evaluation of the reasons for his condemnation. I have also given further attention to the question of Galileo's "Juvenilia" and to the treatment of the Letter to Christina of Lorraine. I hope that this further work on my book will have succeeded not only in increasing the number of pages but also in improving the content.

As with the first edition, this Second Revised Edition would never have seen the light of day without the tireless, accurate and patient work of Father George V. Coyne, S.J., Director of the Vatican Observatory. Yet again he has found the time to provide prompt translations of many new texts. Once more I extend to him my most sincere thanks. I am also deeply grateful to Father Sabino Maffeo, S.J., also of the Vatican Observatory, for his precious collaboration in bringing to my attention a number of new publications and then having furnished me in a timely manner much new information, as well as for having patiently carried out the task of integrating the new texts into the previous edition. Without his very generous help and his constructive criticism it would have been impossible to realize many of the improvements in this second edition.

Victoria, British Columbia, Canada
Autumn 1995

Annibale Fantoli

EDITORIAL NOTE:

The following criteria have been used in referring to the scholarly source material:

- For references to the National Edition of the Works of Galileo (*Edizione Nazionale delle Opere di Galileo*), edited by A. Favaro, the volume is indicated by a Roman numeral, followed by the page number in Arabic numerals. The source for the English translation is indicated after this. Where no such source is indicated, the translation is by G.V. Coyne, S.J.

- A complete Bibliography of all sources referred to is given at the end of the book where the sources are listed in alphabetical order by the surname of the principal author/editor and, under each author, in chronological order by the year of publication. In the text reference to the sources in the Bibliography are made by placing the surname of the author, the year and the page number (e.g. Drake 1978, 252).

INTRODUCTION

FROM THE TRADITIONAL WORLDVIEW TO THE THEORY OF COPERNICUS

The whole drama of Galileo's life begins and develops against the background of the conflict between a worldview still prevalent in his days, the one of Aristotle and Ptolemy, adopted by the Church in the Middle Ages, and the new concept of the world whose starting point is marked by the publication of Copernicus' *De Revolutionibus*. In order, therefore, to evaluate correctly this drama and the factors which determined its conclusion it seems necessary in this Introduction to review, albeit in a very schematic way, the genesis and the characteristics of these two contrasting worldviews and also the harbingers of the open contrasts which were coming and which would reach their climax with the condemnation and abjuration of Galileo.

1.   *From Aristotelian cosmology to the system of Ptolemy*

What is often referred to as the "Aristotelian-Ptolemaic system" actually comes from the blending of two profoundly different conceptions of the world. The view worked out by the great Greek philosopher Aristotle is an attempt to explain the world from a physical point of view (the so-called philosophy of nature). The other view, developed some five hundred years later by the famous Greek geographer and astronomer, Ptolemy, presents instead, at least in its original thrust, an attempt at a purely mathematical explanation of the motion of the heavenly bodies.

According to Aristotle (384-321 B.C.) the Universe is of finite dimensions and consists of two clearly distinct parts: the world of heavenly bodies and that of the sublunar bodies. The latter are made up of four elements (earth, water, air, and fire), which by this time were commonly held by the Greeks, and they are distinguished into the heavy elements (earth and water) and the light elements (air and fire), which are endowed respectively with different natural rectilinear motions: the former from on high to down low and the latter from down low to on high. The termination point of these motions is referred to as the "natural place" of the element. Once there they no longer move. It follows that the sublunar world is subdivided into a central sphere, the "natural place" of the element earth, and three other spherical shells, the natural places respectively of water, air and fire.

The position of the Earth (formed mainly, although not exclusively,[1] of the element earth) at the center of the universe and its immobility there, are for Aristotle the necessary consequences of this theory of natural motion and places, and they are "confirmed", as the theory itself, by sense experience.

As to the world of the heavenly bodies, which move in an interminable, and therefore natural, circular motion (this too based on sense experience), it cannot be made up of the four elements (which, as we know, have natural rectilinear motions), but rather of a fifth element, exclusively heavenly, the "ether" endowed, as a matter of fact, with natural circular motion.

Because this element is unique and has a circular motion, in contrast to the natural rectilinear motion of the four sublunar elements, it can go continuously in the same direction and so there is no possibility of a motion in the opposite direction and, therefore, no possibility of an "opposition", the ultimate cause of change. Therefore, in contrast to the earthly bodies, the heavenly bodies are immutable (that is, they cannot be generated and cannot corrupt). Again, for Aristotle, this is confirmed by age old observations. All apparent phenomena of changes in the heavens (such as the appearance of *novae* and of comets) must be interpreted in a "meteorological" sense as happening in the Earth's atmosphere.

With respect to the location and motions of these heavenly bodies, Aristotle, who was not an astronomer, accepted Eudoxus' theory of concentric spheres[2] which were designed to explain the complex motions of the planets, especially the retrograde motions and the stationary states (see Figures 1 and 2). Although Eudoxus' position on the precise nature of these spheres is not known, Aristotle gave them a physical meaning and considered them to be material spheres made of ether[3].

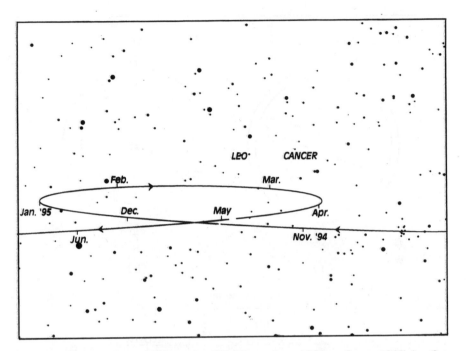

Fig. 1. The motion of Mars during November 1994 - June 1995 in the constellations of Cancer and Leo. The path of the planet is along the line on which are indicated the position of the planet at the beginning of each month from November 1994 to June 1995. We note that Mars travels so that, although its motion in general is direct, that is, to the east (left) among the stars, there is a time from about 1 January to 30 March 1995 when it moves westward (right) in a retrograde motion. The retrograde motions of Mars always have approximately this form and duration but they do not always occur on the same dates or in the same part of the sky. (Image processed by computer program: *Dance of the Planets*).

In the sublunar world, the existence of a movement is explained (within the context of the theory of the four causes: material, formal, efficient and final) either as the attraction to its natural place (in the case of natural motion) or as the result of actions of the various bodies upon one another (in the case of violent motion).

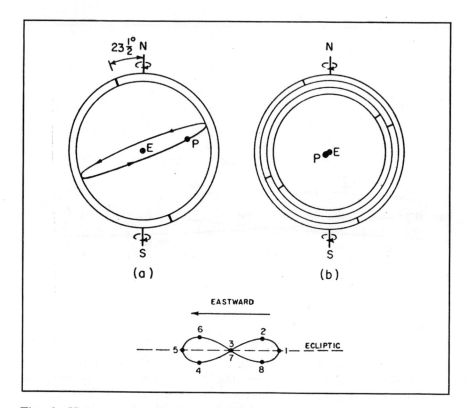

Fig. 2. Homocentric spheres. In the two-sphere system (a) the outer sphere produces the daily rotation and the inner sphere moves the planet (Sun or Moon) with a regular velocity eastward about the ecliptic. In the four-sphere system (b) the planet P lies out of the plane of the page approximately on a line which goes from the Earth E to the eye of the reader. The two inner spheres generate a knot-like motion shown at the bottom of the figure, while the two outer spheres produce the daily motion and the mean displacement of the planet eastward. (From Kuhn 1971, 57-58).

But in the heavenly world? Although at first he adhered to it, Aristotle later on discarded the Platonic idea of a world "soul", the autonomous principle of motion. Being at the same time unaware (as were all of the other Greeks) of the principle of inertia, Aristotle came to find the cause of heavenly motions, as is well known, in the application on a cosmic scale of the principle of final causality. According to him, all of the heavenly bodies in the end are moved by a "first unmovable mover" who must, that is, have in himself the ultimate cause of motion, as pure energy, pure activity, with no passivity, and who, therefore, must be immaterial[4] and perfect: God. On the other hand, God could not move as an efficient cause (in Aristotelian physics to every action of an efficient cause their is a corresponding reaction on it by the body which is moved and this implies an inevitable passivity in the very agent himself). God must, therefore, act as the *final* cause of motion, that is, as the object desired, the object "loved".

It is also known that, in order to justify this desire or love in material bodies such as the stars and the planets, Aristotle had to assume in the sphere of the fixed stars and in the lower spheres of the planets the existence of a whole series of "first immovable movers", immaterial but finite (later on called "intelligences" and which, in medieval Christian thought were often identified with the angels). As they were capable of knowledge and of love, they communicated their desire for union with God, the perfect being and the end of all things, to the sphere in which they existed, and thus they gave it its circular motion, always poised towards its eternally unobtainable goal.

This is undoubtedly a grandiose cosmological synthesis which can explain why Aristotle will exercise such a fascination, as we shall see, in Arabic and medieval Christian thought, and even up to the time of Galileo.

But it did not take too long for its weak point to become known. This was the theory of concentric spheres which, as we know, Aristotle took from Eudoxus (409-365 B.C.) and Callippus (370?-300? B.C.) and to which he attributed a physical meaning. With time this theory seemed less and less able to "save the appearances" in the sky, such as that of the variation during the year in the apparent brightness of the planets, and so the theory of Ptolemy replaced it.

It is well known that the development of this new mathematical explanation of the motions of the heavenly bodies became possible by the enormous advancements of Greek astronomy fostered by its relationship to Babylonian astronomy[5] in the Hellenistic period. This applies both at the level of observations and at that of the mathematical theory of the eccentrics and epicycles, especially with Apollonius (262-190 B.C.) and afterwards with the great astronomer, Hipparchus (? - 120 B.C.).

The first complete explanation of all the heavenly motions, even from a quantitative point of view on the basis of a rigorous mathematical treatment, was given by Ptolemy (active about the year 130 A.D.) with the system which he presented in what is without a doubt the greatest astronomical work of antiquity, the *Syntaxis* (later named by the Arabs the *Almagest*).[6]

In the footsteps of Aristotle, Hipparchus and the greater majority of his predecessors, Ptolemy also affirmed the immobility of the Earth. He supports this position by bringing to bear the traditional arguments from common experience, as well as those based upon the physics of Aristotle which, in general, he accepts.

But with respect to the theory of the concentric spheres Ptolemy differs very definitely with Aristotle. Instead he proposes a purely mathematical explanation of the motion of the planets in which he reiterates and improves that already proposed by Hipparchus.

This explanation is based upon three fundamental principles:

1. *The principle of eccentric motions*: The Earth is not at the center of the planetary orbits but in an eccentric position with respect to them as shown in Figure 3. This principle easily explained both the annual variation in the brightness of the planets and the apparent variation in their velocity (in particular, the fact that the four seasons were of unequal length).

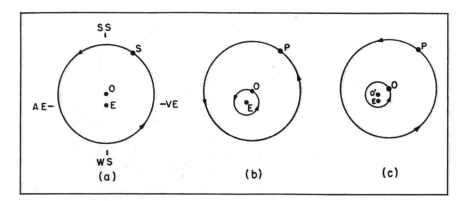

Fig. 3. (a) Simple eccentric motion: the circular motion of the Sun about the Earth is not centered on the Earth, but it is *eccentric* with respect to it; (b) eccentric on a deferent: while the Planet describes a circle centered on O, the point O rotates in turn on another circle (the *deferent*) centered on the Earth; (c) eccentric on an eccentric: in this case even the center of the *deferent* does not coincide with the Earth, but is eccentric with respect to it. (From Kuhn 1971, 69).

2. *The principle of the epicycles*: This is used to explain the stationary states and the retrograde motion of the planets. To accomplish this, the motion of each planet is made up of two or more component circular motions. Each planet revolves on a circle (the *epicycle*) whose center in turn revolves on a larger circle (the *deferent*) whose center in turn could eventually revolve on still a further *deferent*, and so on. The resultant geometrical trajectory (*epicycloid*), composed of these two or more circular motions, accounted for the "stationary states" and the "retrograde" motions (see Figure 4). But there were still other irregularities which had to be explained. To this end Ptolemy introduced a third principle.

3. *The Principle of the equant*: This is illustrated in Figure 5. This principle, which was introduced to account for the annual variation in the angular velocities of the planets, was contrary to the traditional principle of explaining the celestial motions by a combination of uniform circular motions.

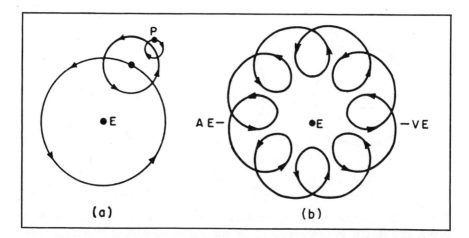

Fig. 4. Epicycle on an epicycle on a deferent (a) and (b) the typical trajectory in space generated by this system of composite circles. For simplicity a trajectory is designed which closes on itself regularly but this is not true for the actual motion of the planets. (From Kuhn 1971, 68).

Copernicus himself will vehemently criticize Ptolemy on this point. But the principle of the equant, together with the other two principles finally allowed the preparation of tables for the positions of the celestial objects which were in adequate agreement with the observations. In particular, the principle of the epicycles proved to be enormously flexible. By appropriate variations in the radius of the epicycle, as well as in the direction and velocity of the planets motion about it, and by introducing supplementary epicycles for each planet, it was possible at will to correct the errors in the orbits which had been calculated previously. As a result, the system of Ptolemy remained "for more than 1400 years the Alpha and Omega of theoretical astronomy".[7]

Even though Ptolemy did not limit himself to the construction of this mathematical theory and tried afterwards in his book, *Hypothesis on the Planets*,[8] to give some physical meaning to it, the immense influence of the *Syntaxis* had the effect of aggravating still further the existing situation of a "divorce" between the points of view of the "philosophers of nature" and those of the "professional astronomers".

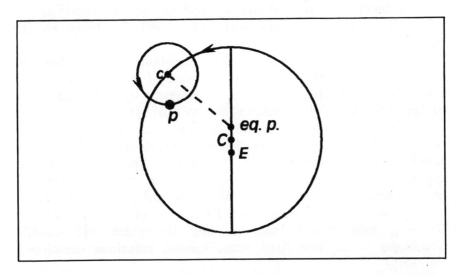

Fig. 5. The planet moves with a uniform circular motion on the epicycle (the small circle) while the epicycle's center c moves along the deferent (the large circle) with an angular velocity which is constant not with respect to the center C of the deferent but with respect to an eccentric point, called the "equant point", located symmetrically opposite to the Earth's position which is also eccentric.

While the former purported to understand *the structure of the physical world* and the *cause* of the motions of the celestial objects, the latter limited themselves to the formulation of *mathematical constructs* which could be used to *calculate* the celestial motions and did not worry too much about establishing a "realistic" justification for these constructs.

In this summary description of Greek cosmology we should make a mention, at least, of the theories of the Earth's motion. Even though, as I have already noted, Aristotle and the majority of the great Greek astronomers had opted for a geocentric cosmology, there was no lack of a variety of geokinetic conceptions within the wider circle of Greek thinking. One such was the idea of the combined motion of the Earth and an anti-

Earth about a central fire (not to be confused with the Sun) which had been worked out by Philolaus (about 475 B.C.) within the context of the Pythagorean school.[9] In a further modification of this theory the central fire as well as the hypothesis of an anti-earth were done away with, which left the earth at the center of the universe.

But the idea (also implied in Philolaus' system) that the earth rotated on its own axis in twenty-four hours was left untouched. This idea was taken up later on by a contemporary of Aristotle, Heraclides Ponticus (388 to 310? B.C.).[10]

Less than a century later a true heliocentric theory was formulated by Aristarchus of Samos (310-230 B.C.). On the one hand, the Sun becomes for Aristarchus the center of the movements of all of the planets, including the Earth. On the other hand, the Earth, in addition to the movement of its revolution about the Sun, keeps its motion of daily rotation on its own axis, which Philolaus and Heraclides had already attributed to it. The fixed stars instead remained completely immobile.

The work in which Aristarchus explained his astronomical system has been lost. But there are numerous witnesses in antiquity, the most important of them being Archimedes,[11] a younger contemporary of Aristarchus, who testify without a doubt as to how he had arrived at those fundamental affirmations which Copernicus would make his own 1800 years later.

The fact remains, however, that despite the existence of these diverse theories of the movement of the Earth, they did not succeed, except for rare exceptions, among the Greeks. The reasons for this failure are many. In addition to those based on common experience (the lack of any sense perception of this motion, the non existence of a whole series of phenomena which would result from such a motion, such as a violent wind, and the westward shift in the point of impact of an object thrown upwards) there were those, at least for the Aristotelians, which derived from the theory of natural places and motions of the four elements. On the basis of this theory both of the motions of the Earth were eliminated *a priori*, because they required a *natural rotational* motion of the material particles which made up the

Earth about its center and not rectilinear to it. It is just for this reason that Aristotle himself had rejected the theory of the motion of the Earth proposed by the Pythagorean Philolaus.

But even apart from these objections of common sense and of Aristotelian physics against the movement of the Earth, there was still a real astronomical difficulty. In fact, if there existed a motion of the Earth, one should be able to note in the course of the year a shift in the position of the fixed stars on the celestial sphere, the so-called phenomenon of "stellar parallax" (Figure 6), a phenomenon which instead was not observed.

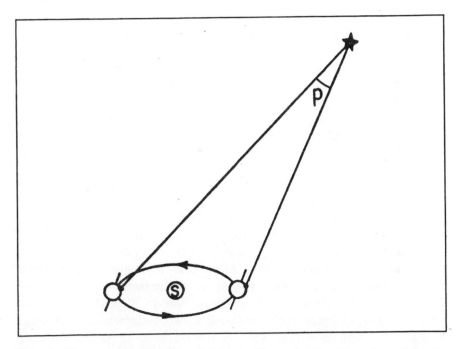

Fig. 6. The annual parallax of a star. Since the line from an observer on the Earth to a fixed star does not remain constantly parallel to itself as the Earth moves along its orbit, the apparent position of the star on the celestial sphere should change by an angle p in the course of six months. (From Kuhn 1971, 162).

It seems that this argument, independent of Aristotelian physics, was taken into consideration by Aristarchus himself who would have explained the lack of stellar parallax as due to the enormous dimensions of the universe and thus to the huge distances of the fixed stars from the Earth. Compared to such distances the diameter of the Earth's orbit about the Sun was of negligible size, so that the parallax was practically zero and thus not observable.

On the other hand, Aristarchus had not succeeded in providing a mathematical formulation for his system, whereas such a formulation, as we know, was the great final result obtained by Greek geostatic astronomy. It was only natural, therefore, that Aristarchus' conception was completely eclipsed by the success of the Ptolemaic system and that it remained such, even in the Middle Ages, both in the world of Arabian culture as in that of Western European Christendom.

2.   *The encounter with Christianity and the medieval synthesis*

As is known the problem of the relationship between the biblical image of the world, as it appears in the creation narratives of *Genesis* and in other texts of the Old Testament (see Fig. 7), and the philosophical and astronomical concepts of the Greeks was a central problem for Christianity right from the first phase of its development. Alongside intransigent tendencies which rejected any possibility of a compromise between the Christian faith, founded on a literal sense of the Bible, and Greek culture,[12] there had appeared an attitude which was more conciliatory and positive. This could be seen especially among the Christian thinkers of the so-called School of Alexandria and it was taken up and became more significant under the Greek and Latin Fathers of the Church.

As to the greatest of the Latin Fathers, St. Augustine (354-430 A.D.), on the one hand his initial interest in philosophy changed with time after his conversion (387 A.D.) into an increasingly critical attitude towards Greek philosophy in which,

Fig. 7. The image of the world according to the Bible. 1. Waters above the firmament; 2. storage of snow; 3. storage of hail; 4. rooms of the winds; 5. the firmament; 6. cataracts; 7. the pillars of heaven; 8. the pillars of the Earth; 9. fountains of the abyss; 10. center of the Earth; 11. the subterranean waters; 12. the rivers of the underworld. (From Jacobs 1975, 69).

as he put it, shafts of light and truth are obscured by numerous contradictions and errors. On the other hand, his judgment of

Greek science, and in particular of astronomy, remained relatively more positive, even after his conversion.

But what was one to think when the conclusions of Greek science, such as those in the area of cosmology, seemed to contradict Holy Scripture? In his various writings St. Augustine responds to this question in generic terms by observing that "we do not read in the Gospel that the Lord said: I will send you the Paraclete to teach you how the Sun and the Moon move. Because he wished to make them Christians, not mathematicians".[13] And he added that not even the "sacred writers" intended to teach anything about "the form and figure of the heavens" or about any other scientific questions since "they were not useful for salvation".[14]

This invitation to be prudent becomes more specific later on in many texts of Augustine, which will be employed in the Middle Ages, and later by Galileo himself (especially in the *Letter to Christina of Lorraine*) to warn against giving hasty judgments on the basis of biblical texts. Otherwise, it could happen that, once such scientific affirmations were proven, Scripture would be scorned by non-believers and their way to heaven would be blocked.[15]

But together with these invitations to prudence there is also in Augustine's writings, we might say even predominantly so, an invitation to prefer "those matters which concern salvation" to scientific research.[16] In fact, although he is not hostile to Greek science and is prepared to accept its sphere of validity, St. Augustine judges that scientific research is not necessary to the believer who can dedicate his intellectual energies much more profitably to matters of faith.[17]

All of these tendencies which had taken shape in the Patristic period could not at that time be deepened because of the profound cultural crisis which accompanied the progressive disintegration of the Roman Empire in the West. A noteworthy negative factor was the loss of the knowledge of Greek which, accompanied by the scarcity of Latin translations of the treasures of Greek philosophy and science, brought about an almost total disappearance of their knowledge in the High Middle Ages.[18]

The rediscovery of Greek philosophy and science, beginning in the 12th century came about, as is known, through Arabic thought,[19] in which the assimilation of Greek culture had occurred a long time before. This Arabic mediation functioned not only in the area of linguistics by the translation of Greek works into Arabic and then into Latin, but also, and in a more lasting way, through the great commentaries, especially those of Avicenna (980-1087 A.D.) and of Averroes (1126-1198 A.D.),[20] which in their Latin translations were indispensable for the assimilation of the difficult philosophical and scientific texts of antiquity.

This assimilation and the subsequent synthesis of the Greek and Christian cultures came about, as is known, through Medieval Scholasticism which flourished in those new centers of knowledge, or "schools" *par excellence*, the *universitates studiorum*.

I will here limit myself to considerations of the position towards the Greek view of the world of the greatest exponent of scholasticism, St. Thomas Aquinas (1225-1274 A.D.).[21]

First of all, his attitude towards Greek philosophy in general is completely different from that of St. Augustine. For Aquinas it was certainly not a waste of time to pursue philosophy, above all because philosophy, and especially that of Aristotle, once appropriate corrections were made, such as that concerning the eternity of the world, could be used to establish the rationality of the premises upon which theological affirmations relied. But beyond this interest for philosophy as the *ancilla theologiae* on the part of St. Thomas, the theologian, there was also his interest as a philosopher as such, even a "natural philosopher". His great commentaries on the *Libri Physicorum* and on the *De Coelo* of Aristotle are the best proof of this, as is the fact that he made his own the principal tenets of this latter work.[22]

It is precisely this conviction that the conclusions of the *De Coelo* are certain that leads St. Thomas, as well as the other medieval scholastics, to give an answer to the question as to the interpretation of descriptions of the world given in Genesis and in other Scriptural passages. Aquinas, following St. Augustine in this, repeatedly emphasizes the fact that the Scriptures frequently use expressions adapted to the ability to understand of the people of that time, without it being necessary to hold those expressions "as they sound" to be matters of faith.[23] He is, of course, convinced that each and every word of the Bible is true, but there are cases where that truth need not be made to coincide *sic et simpliciter* with the common and immediate meaning of each word.

The whole treatment given by Aquinas in the first part of the *Summa Theologiae* concerning the meaning of the words of the creation as given in *Genesis*[24] is an illustration of this principle and at the same time it is a proof of the ingenuity and inventive spirit (which to us moderns sometimes gives the impression of real intellectual acrobatics) with which he succeeds in finding a meaning for a biblical expression which is compatible with what are for him the certain conclusions of Aristotelian philosophy.

I must make a very important remark here. St. Thomas, like the other medieval scholastics, does not use faith (which for him is of a higher order) as a tool to constrain the conclusions of Greek natural philosophy. On the contrary, he shows that he is intellectually open to the extent that he can accept those conclusions, once they seem to be certain, and, in light of them, revise the traditional interpretation of the creation accounts and of other biblical passages. To be specific, it was not at all the "compatibility" of the geocentrism of Aristotle with the biblical description of the world that led the scholastics to prefer it to the ancient theories of the motion of the Earth.[25]

As it was, that "compatibility" relied upon one point only, that of the immobility of the Earth. For everything else, between the primitive biblical view of the world and that of Aristotle (including the concept itself of "Earth") there was an abyss, and the Christian intellectuals of the Middle Ages were well aware of this. The fact that they had the courage to cross that abyss was due, I repeat, to their conviction that the Aristotelian cosmology was undoubtedly *true*.

Granted all of his admiration for Aristotle, St. Thomas naturally could not ignore or underestimate the deficiencies in Aristotle's theory of homocentric spheres and the superiority, in so far as astronomy is concerned, of the theory of Ptolemy. The very fact that the "rediscovery" of Aristotelian philosophy happened at the same time as a sufficient knowledge of the content and the techniques of calculation of the *Almagest* was attained had contributed to making ever more evident the dilemma, present also in Arabic philosophy, of choosing between the Aristotelian physical homocentric spheres and the mathematical deferents and epicycles of Ptolemy.[26]

The existence of this dilemma in St. Thomas' thought is particularly evident in his commentary on *De Coelo* and in the *Summa Theologiae*.[27] In this later work, as a good philosopher, he emphasizes the fundamental difference between a hypothesis in natural philosophy which with sufficient reasons can be proven true, and a purely mathematical hypothesis which cannot be proven true but which may, nonetheless, be able to provide a sufficiently exact description of the phenomena. And St. Thomas presents, as an example of a merely mathematical theory, that of Ptolemy in which "a system of deferents and epicycles is introduced, because this hypothesis allows one to account for our sense experience of the celestial motions." But he immediately adds: "But this does not provide sufficient proof [of the truth of Ptolemy's hypothesis] because there might be another hypothesis which could just as well account for the same phenomena".[28]

It is right here that we find the dilemma faced by Aquinas and all of the intellectuals of the Middle Ages. The system of the Aristotelian world, as a physical conception, was founded on principles, which according to the medieval scholastics could be established beyond any doubt. Nonetheless, it could not account for important celestial phenomena, whereas the method of Ptolemy with its deferents and epicycles could do so. But what was the physical foundation for such a hypothesis? The attempt made by Ptolemy himself in his book, *Hypothesis on the Planets*, to assure such a physical foundation, an attempt which was repeated by the Arab Ibn Al Aytam (965-1039 A.D.), who was known later on in Europe with the name Alhazen (see Figure 8), would not have been able to satisfy St. Thomas, had he known of it. It implied, as a matter of fact, physical movements about a different center than the Earth without any explanation of the cause of such movements which would be able to replace the

explanation of Aristotle, which for Aquinas was the only true
one.

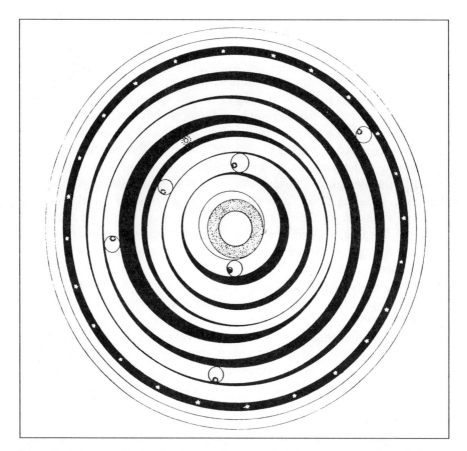

Fig. 8. The system of solid spheres of Alhazen, reproduced in a
cosmological plan of the XVth century (Reconstructed in de Santillana
1955, 68).

As to the other "astronomical hypothesis" of which Aquinas
speaks in the text cited above, one which was just as able to
account for the celestial phenomenon as was that of Ptolemy, it
is only presented here as a pure possibility without any
reference to a concrete theory. Since he made no claim to be an

astronomer (and indeed showed no interest in astronomy), St. Thomas limits himself in this passage to noting that in the area of mathematical representations of physical phenomena there can be two such which are perfectly equivalent without there being any possibility to decide which of them is the true one. This is because, I repeat, a purely mathematical theory cannot be verifiable on the physical plane of the philosophy of nature. When the discussion reverted to this plane (which was by and far the one which he preferred and the one where he undoubtedly felt himself most at ease) St. Thomas could have no hesitation. Even with the unresolved problem of the celestial motions,[29] the natural philosophy of Aristotle was as a whole the only true philosophy and such it would always be because it was founded upon indisputable philosophical principles. As we will see, this will also be the position of the Aristotelians at the time of Copernicus and Galileo.[30]

3.   *The "Copernican revolution" and the reaction of the theologians*

The appearance of the great work of Copernicus, *De Revolutionibus Orbium Coelestium*,[31] was not something absolutely new as to the ideas of geokineticism and heliocentrism when we consider the existence of his Greek predecessors. Nonetheless, the complete mathematical explanation of the idea contained therein made it an absolute novelty on a scientific plane. Also, considering the vastness of the synthesis, the *De Revolutionibus* is without comparison to any preceding work except for the *Almagest* of Ptolemy.

I will limit myself here to recall briefly the principal affirmations of the great Polish astronomer (1473-1543).[32] In order to "save the appearances" Copernicus held that it was sufficient to put the Sun instead of the Earth at the center of the universe. He attributed three motions to the Earth: a diurnal rotation on its own axis (which would explain the apparent diurnal motion of the heavenly bodies around the Earth); the revolution about the Sun (which would explain the apparent motion of the Sun along the ecliptic [Fig. 9a], the changes of the seasons [Fig. 9b], the complicated apparent motion of the

planets during the year   [Fig. 10]; the precession of the
terrestrial axis which was necessary, according to Copernicus, to
insure the constant inclination of 23.5 degrees of this axis with
respect to the perpendicular to the plane of the ecliptic.[33]

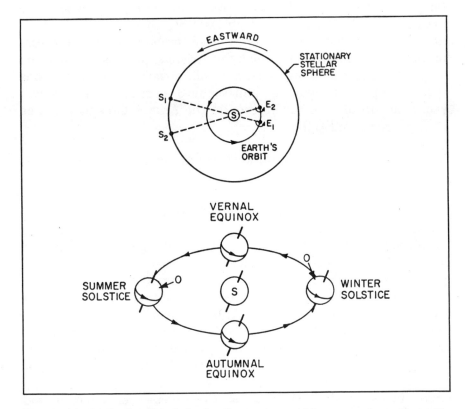

Fig. 9. (a) While the Earth in its Copernican orbit moves from E_1 to E_2,
the apparent position of the central Sun, seen against the sphere of the
stars, varies from S_1 to S_2. (b) The annual motion of the Earth in its
Copernican orbit. At every instant the axis of the Earth is kept parallel
to itself or to a fixed line drawn through the Sun. Consequently an
observer O at noontime at mean north latitudes sees the sun much
closer to one's vertical at summer solstice than at the winter one.
(From Kuhn 1971, 160-161).

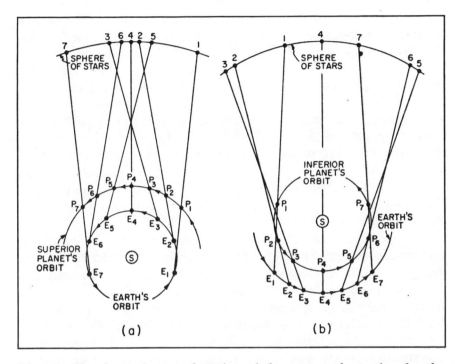

Fig. 10. The Copernican explanation of the retrograde motion for the superior planets (a) and for the inferior planets (b). In each drawing while the Earth moves from **E**1 to **E**$_7$, the planet moves from P_1 to P_7. At the same time the apparent position of the planet on the sphere of the stars moves from 1 to 7. Corresponding to the stretch in which the two planets overtake one another there is the westward retrograde motion from 3 to 5, short in the first case, longer in the second. (From Kuhn 1971, 165).

These fundamental ideas (together with answers to the traditional objections to the movement of the Earth, including the lack of an observed parallax[34]) are contained in the first book of the *De Revolutionibus*, which is dedicated to non-specialists, while the other five books contain a mathematical treatment of the theory intended for astronomers.

Even though it was revolutionary in its fundamental assertions, the Copernican theory remained faithful to tradition with respect to the idea of the spherical form of the universe and the circularity of celestial motions. This was, of course, a tradition which had never been questioned in the 2000 years of western astronomical and philosophical thinking,[35] and Copernicus, therefore, accepted it without the shadow of a doubt. But such an acceptance inevitably caused him to introduce the corrections provided by eccentrics and epicycles, with the result that the advantage that his theory had of a greater simplicity as compared to that of Ptolemy, a point emphasized by Copernicus in the first book of the *De Revolutionibus*, lost for the most part all of its force in the successive mathematical development. Thus to the seven concentric spheres for the motions of the planets, of which Copernicus had spoken at the beginning of his work, a large number of epicycles was added, only a bit less than those required by Ptolemy.

Copernicus was also forced to take from the Alexandrian astronomer the principle of eccentric motions in order to explain the increase in the apparent velocity of the Sun through the signs of the zodiac in wintertime, so that the Copernican system, speaking rigorously, was no longer heliocentric.

In conclusion, the explanation of Copernicus with its fundamental hypotheses had undeniable virtues of simplicity in a qualitative sense and unquestionable advantages over that of Ptolemy in its description of the motions of the inferior planets (Mercury and Venus) as well as that of the Moon. But in a quantitative sense, that is as a mathematical theory for computing planetary motions, it did not, in general, prove to be sensibly more accurate than that of Ptolemy. As we will see, this is the reason that it did not succeed in gaining the acceptance of the greater part of contemporary astronomers and those who came afterwards up to the time of Kepler and Galileo.

But there is more to it than that. If the system of Copernicus was to be interpreted not only as a mathematical theory, but as a physical explanation of the make-up of the world, it was obviously in contradiction with the fundamental principles of Aristotelian cosmology, such as that of the motions and natural places of the four elements, from which is deduced the immobility of the Earth at the center of the Universe, and that of the radical distinction between the Earth and heavenly bodies.

Copernicus certainly sensed the weight of these difficulties and feared a critical reaction from the Aristotelians, to whom for the most part the teaching of natural philosophy in Europe had been entrusted up until this time. And the reactions would be even stronger since, in addition to vague reasons of convenience in support of his theory,[36] he had sketched a theory of gravity which was in sharp contrast with that of Aristotle.[37] This was undoubtedly the fundamental reason for the protracted hesitation to publish his work.[38]

As a matter of fact, however, these feared reactions on the part of the Aristotelian philosophers never really materialized, at least with the strength that he feared. One reason for this is that, as we shall see, the majority of astronomers of the second half of the 16th century did not accept his theory and so for the Aristotelians there did not even arise the problem of a real threat to their philosophy.

But the "Notice to the Reader", which the editor of the *De Revolutionibus*, the Protestant Andreas Osiander,[39] had, unknown to Copernicus, placed at the beginning of the book, undoubtedly influenced this situation of relative tranquillity. In this notice Osiander asserted that the theory proposed in the book ought to be considered to be a pure mathematical hypothesis and not as an explanation of the real structure of the universe. As a mathematical theory, adds Osiander, it was no more probable than those of the ancients, but it was presented because it contained marvelous hypotheses and also because it had the virtue of being simple. But, repeated Osiander, as far as hypotheses go, no one should look for any certainty from astronomy because it is not capable of providing such certainties. As you see, this was the old thesis that the fields of competence of natural philosophy and of astronomical theories are to be kept totally distinct.

Osiander's reason for this notice was not only to turn aside the expected reactions of the philosophers, but also, perhaps even above all, to prevent a sharpening of the criticisms against the new theory from the perspective of Scripture. These had been surfacing for some time among Protestant theologians, such as the famous Melanchthon.[40]

Copernicus was spared the sadness of seeing his true intentions thus betrayed. Having already suffered a cerebral paralysis months before, he was by then near death when a copy of the *De Revolutionibus* was placed in his hands.[41]

Osiander's intervention probably had a certain effect among Protestant theologians, even though it would not have led the better informed astray. However that might be, the criticisms arising among the Reformers, even though they continued, never reached the point of becoming an official position, considering that the Protestant movement lacked a centralized structure endowed with an authority comparable to that of the Catholic Church.

But what was the reaction of the Catholic Church to the Copernican system? In Catholic writings which treat of the Galileo problem it is generally held that among Catholics, in contrast to the Protestants, the attitude was marked by a certain moderation, one might even say impartiality, and that the Church's prohibition of the *De Revolutionibus* and later the condemnation of Galileo were due to the excessive and intemperate zeal of Galileo whereby he tried to make Church authorities accept a theory for which there were until that time no convincing proofs.

Let us recall briefly the facts which support this thesis. There is, first of all, the fact that at the time of the announcement of the project to reform the Julian calendar, given by Pope Leo X during the Fifth Lateran Council (1512-1517), Copernicus was among the astronomers "of renown"[42] to whom an invitation was extended to collaborate in the reform project. Copernicus himself recalls this in the preface he dedicated to Paul III at the beginning of the *De Revolutionibus*. This seems to show that there were not yet any suspicions about the general content of his ideas as being contrary to Sacred Scripture.

There is also the fact that later on (in 1533) Pope Clement VII accompanied by four other prelates received in the Vatican Gardens "an explanation of the opinions of Copernicus on the movement of the Earth", provided by Johann Albrecht of Widmanstadt (1500-1577).[43] On that occasion the Pope rewarded him with a gift of a precious Greek manuscript. This indicates that at least he was pleased with the explanation.[44]

After the death of Clement VII, Widmanstadt entered into the service of Nicholas Schönberg (1472-1537), who had been a confidant of the deceased Pontiff and who was later on appointed a cardinal by Paul III (1539-1549). Under Widmanstadt's influence Schönberg became interested in the ideas of Copernicus to the extent that he requested Theodoric of Radzyn to have copied at his expense at Fronbork all of the writings of Copernicus and to have them sent to Rome. Later on he also exhorted Copernicus in a letter addressed to him in 1536 to publish his writings. Copernicus inserted this letter in the introductory material to the De Revolutionibus.

A further confirmation of this attitude within the Church, which was not only not contrary to, but at times even explicitly favorable to, the new astronomical ideas, is found in the task undertaken by Copernicus' old colleague, the canon Tiedemann Giese, who later on had become Bishop of Chelmo, to persuade him to publish the De Revolutionibus. After its printing with the "Notice to the Reader" by Osiander, Giese will protest in the strongest terms possible the arbitrary initiative of Osiander, seeing it as a betrayal of the true ideas of Copernicus which he had always shared.

Finally, the fact that Copernicus should wish to dedicate his work to the reigning Pope Paul III and thus protect it from possible attacks by his calumniators, as Copernicus himself writes in his dedication, shows that he must have nourished a trust in the Pope's openness of mind. In contrast to this trust he condemned the ignorance of those who, although they had no expertise in mathematics, should wish nevertheless to judge the case and, arguing from the malicious distortion of some Scriptural passage, would perhaps dare to complain with attacks on his work.

As a matter of fact, the Church did not take, either at that time or at any time before 1616, any measures against the De Revolutionibus. This fact is commonly interpreted by Catholic authors as showing that Copernicus' trust was well-founded. Recent studies,[45] however, seem to indicate that the silence of Paul III and his immediate successors should not be interpreted

as an impartial withholding of judgement, and even less as an
approval of the theory of Copernicus. In fact, from what the
Dominican Giovanni Maria Tolosani (about 1470-1549) said in
his treatise, *De Purissima Veritate Sacrae Scripturae*,[46] the
Master of the Sacred Palace, Bartolomeo Spina, who was also a
Dominican, had intended to condemn the work of Copernicus but
he was prevented from doing so by sickness followed by his
death. Tolosani's statement appears to be trustworthy. Because
of the close relationship which existed between him and Spina,
he should have been well informed. And according to his own
statement at the beginning of the appendix to the treatise I have
referred to, he wrote it so that the intent of his friend,
frustrated by his death, would be realized, namely, he wished to
denounce the errors into which Copernicus had fallen. On the
other hand, it is altogether credible that Paul III, having once
received the work of Copernicus dedicated to him, gave it to
Spina, his trusted advisor, with the intention of subscribing to
his judgement. After the death of Spina it is likely that his
successor had neither the time nor the wish to take up the
matter. As to Paul III, even if we suppose that he had had some
preliminary negative judgement on the *De Revolutionibus* from
Spina, he was by this time so occupied by the deliberations of
the Council of Trent (1545-1563) which had just begun and so
preoccupied by the serious religious problems of those times that
he had no time to dedicate to the question concerning
Copernicus. At any rate, it was a question which, given that he
was even aware of it, must have seemed to him a good deal less
important than the problems brought to bear by the Protestant
movement.

These same circumstances must have had a great deal to
do with the official silence of the Church with respect to the
Copernican theory during the next seven decades. On the other
hand, since this theory had not been widely accepted by the
astronomers themselves, Catholic authorities must have judged
that it did not pose a real danger such as to require doctrinal
statements.

From what I have just reviewed, the silence of the Catholic
Church with respect to Copernicanism up until the beginning
of the 17th century, seems to have a quite less positive meaning

than has been supposed in the past. And that appears to be confirmed by the position taken by individual Catholic theologians of that time. Of course, there were some theologians who lined up in favor of Copernicanism. Above all, as we have seen, there was Bishop Giese to whom, together with the Protestant Rheticus, goes the credit for having persuaded Copernicus to publish the *De Revolutionibus*. Both Giese and Rheticus were, of course, aware of the criticisms levelled against the theory on the basis of Scriptural texts concerning the immobility of the Earth and the motion of the Sun and they had purposely written responses to these objections from Scripture. While Giese's response has been lost, that of Rheticus, published in a XVII century book, has been recently rediscovered.[47] Another response is contained in the *Commentary on the Book of Job* which was published in 1584 at Toledo and later in Rome (1591) by the Augustinian Diego de Zuñiga, a professor of theology at the University of Osuna. The author examines in that work the passage: "He shook the Earth and moved it from its place, causing its pillars to tremble" (Job, 9,6). According to Diego de Zuñiga it was much simpler to interpret that passage by relying on the opinion of the Pythagoreans "which in our days Copernicus has demonstrated". The other passages which speak of the movement of the Sun reflect, added Zuñiga, the common manner of speaking (used at times even by Copernicus and his followers) but, in fact, they refer to the movement of the Earth.[48]

As we shall see, this book will be involved in the Index listing by the Catholic Church of the *De Revolutionibus* in 1616. But up until the assumption of the rigid doctrinal position expressed by the Index prohibition, it does not seem that Diego de Zuñiga's opinion created any problems for him.[49]

Alongside of these men who were open-minded or even outright supporters of the new world-view, there were others, even among Catholics, who took a hostile attitude. There was, for example, Spina whom I have already quoted, and even a clearer case with his friend Tolosani. In the appendix to his treatise *De Veritate Sacrae Scripturae*, composed, as Tolosani himself admits, with the aim of realizing the intent pursued by his dead friend Spina (that is, to show up the errors of Copernicus), Tolosani severely criticizes Copernicus in detail. As to philosophy he accuses him of the crassest ignorance of the natural philosophy arguments already championed by Aristotle against the Pythagorean theory of the motion of the Earth. As to theology, he declares that the theory of Copernicus "contradicts Sacred Scripture which declares that the Heaven stands on high while the Earth rests below". Tolosani finishes with a warning which unfortunately will prove to be prophetic:

> The Pythagorean theory [and by implication the Copernican] could easily give rise to quarrels between the Catholic interpreters of Sacred Scripture and those who would obstinately embrace such beliefs. I have written this little work in order to prevent such a scandal from occurring.[50]

4.   *The reaction of the astronomers. The system of Tycho Brahe*

About four or five hundred copies of the *De Revolutionibus* were printed, but it was certainly not a great publishing success. The second edition came out only 23 years later (1566) and the third only 51 years after that. Without a doubt, it would be totally wrong to assert that the work went unnoticed by astronomers.[51] But, as we have already seen, the theory of Copernicus presented no decisive advantages, at least in a general sense, over that of Ptolemy, even if we limit ourselves to the point of view of the calculation of planetary motions. And it was this point of view which dominated among the astronomers of that time. It is true that Erasmus Reinhold (1511-1553) used the tables of the *De Revolutionibus* for the construction of his *Tabulae Prutenicae* (1551) which replaced the by then antiquated *Tabulae Alphonsinae*. But, given the scarcity of more recent observations, including those of Copernicus himself, Reinhold had to put in also the data from the *Almagest*, so that his *Tabulae* at the end were not much more accurate than the *Alphonsinae* which were by then three centuries old. Nonetheless, his tables undoubtedly constituted some progress and were generally accepted, so that they helped to spread the fame of Copernicus. It is, however, symptomatic that Reinhold himself was careful not to affirm anything about the physical significance of the Copernican theory, perhaps also because he was a professor at Wittenberg, where the influence of Melanchthon was still felt.

Undoubtedly, the continuation of the rigid religious influence of Protestantism right up until the beginning of the 17th century had an influence on the fact that other astronomers such as Kaspar Peucer, the author of *Hypotheses astronomicae* (1571), and Nicholas Müller, who was in charge of the third edition of the *De Revolutionibus* in 1617, distanced themselves from Copernicanism as a physical theory. And so in Germany for the time being those who supported the theory of Copernicus remained few. There stands out among these Michael Mästlin (1550-1631) to whom we should probably give credit for having introduced the Copernican ideas to his great disciple, Johannes Kepler (1571-1630).

Before its acceptance in Germany the Copernican system found sympathetic adherents in England such as Robert Record (1510-1558), the greatest English mathematician of his time, and the great William Gilbert (1544-1603), author of the *De Magnete* (1600). Still more clearly in favor of Copernicanism was Thomas Digges (?-1595) in his work *Alae seu scalae mathematicae* (1572) and later in the appendix to the meteorological study *Prognostication everlasting*, a work of his father, Leonard, published by him in 1592.

To these more or less declared supporters of Copernicus we should add Pierre de la Ramée (Latin name Petrus Ramus, 1515-1572) in France and Giovanni Battista Benedetti (1530-1590) in Italy, and, more than anyone else, Giordano Bruno to whom I will return at the end of this Introduction. But, apart from this narrow group who promoted the ideas of Copernicus, the greater majority of astronomers and of intellectuals during the seven decades after the death of the great Polish astronomer proved to be skeptical or even outright contrary to his ideas.

But the clearest proof of this lack of acceptance of the Copernican theory among the astronomers of those times is undoubtedly given by the work of the most famous of them, Tycho Brahe (1546-1601). The great merit of this Danish astronomer consists in having realized that, in order to construct an adequate theory for the motions of the planets, it was necessary to have available a great number of observations with an accuracy much greater than that obtained previously. He accomplished this by using instruments much larger and of greater accuracy than those employed up until that time. He did this at the center for astronomical observations, unrivalled in Europe, which he had constructed by himself on the little island of "Uraniborg". In this way Brahe collected an enormous quantity of data on the positions of the planets and of the fixed stars. This data will be used later by Kepler and will lead him to the discovery of the three laws for the orbits of the planets, which made a decisive contribution to overcoming the traditional view of the world.

Brahe's merit is, however, not only to be found in the collection of observations, as precious as it might be. In 1572, when he was just at the beginning of his activity as an astronomer, a *nova* appeared in the constellation of Cassiopeia and it immediately became a topic of lively debate between the astronomers and the supporters of the Aristotelian natural philosophy, who, on the basis of the principle of the incorruptibility of the heavens, tried to interpret it as a meteorological phenomenon. The exact observations of Brahe, however, showed that the phenomenon of parallax was not observable and that, therefore, the *nova* was certainly further out than the Moon and probably belonged to the sphere of the fixed stars or was rather close to it. But these results were published by Brahe with the title *De Nova stella* (1573) in an extremely limited number of copies and distributed to a select group of his correspondents. It will be only after the posthumous edition of is work, *Progymnasmata* (1602), that Brahe's conclusions will have circulated more widely and will have begun to arouse discussion among Aristotelian philosophers. It is true that in the meantime the Jesuit mathematician Clavius had arrived at the same conclusions as Brahe, most probably independently, and had published them in the 1585 edition of his commentary on the *Sphere* of Sacrobosco.[52] But Clavius, like Brahe, was not able to give a plausible explanation of the phenomenon of the *nova* as belonging to the sphere of the fixed stars and so the Aristotelian philosophers, at least those knowledgeable of their statements, were able to ignore them and uphold the "orthodox" explanation of the *nova* as an atmospheric phenomenon. They were all the more successful in this as the *nova* had rapidly disappeared thus making it impossible to check on it any longer.

But the numerous comets that appeared between 1577 and 1596 gave a new and stronger shock to the Aristotelian view. Given that the authority of Brahe as an observer was established by now, it became increasingly difficult to question his results which proved that the comets too belonged to the celestial world and not to the sublunar one. This, as a celestial "novelty", thus gave the lie to the immutability of the world of the heavenly bodies. Furthermore, the probability that they moved along "oval" orbits[53] about the Sun indicated that they should cross without hindrance some of the solid spheres postulated by the Aristotelian cosmology. The most obvious conclusion was to deny the existence of such spheres.

Although Tycho Brahe had thus contributed to the questioning of the fundamental astronomical concepts of Aristotle, he was, nevertheless, not able to bring himself to the point of making his own the theory of Copernicus. This was due more to the fact that his accurate observations did not succeed in revealing any effect of parallax among the fixed stars than to Scriptural arguments or to the traditional difficulties of common experience against the movement of the Earth; all of this we have seen. Surely he knew the answer of Aristarchus, which was taken up by Copernicus, of the enormous distances of the fixed stars which made it impossible to measure parallax, even though it existed. But Tycho saw a great difficulty against this assumption of the immensity of space.[54] Before the discovery of the telescope and of its use for astronomical observations the phenomenon of the diffraction of light coming from a star was unknown. This causes a brighter star to appear to have a larger diameter. As a result, the apparent diameter was considered to be the true one. Now, if one admitted the immense stellar distances to which Copernicus subscribed, the stars would have had to have dimensions enormously greater than those of the Sun and that appeared with reason to Tycho to be unlikely.[55]

For all of these reasons the Danish astronomer, even though convinced that the Aristotelian view of the world could not be upheld and despite his great esteem for Copernicus, was not able to embrace the Copernican theory. Instead, he developed a new world system which, while it incorporated some simplifying elements of Copernicus, still kept the Earth immobile at the center of the universe with the Moon and the Sun turning about it. On the other hand, the Sun becomes the center of the rotation of the other five planets, all of them from west to east. Moreover, all of the seven planets participate in the daily motion of the sphere of the fixed stars, from east to west (see Fig. 11).

Of course, even Tycho Brahe kept to the unquestioned tradition held to that time of circular motions and was, therefore, forced to use epicycles, eccentrics and equants in order to make his theory fit the observations. This is what Ptolemy had done and, apart from the equants, also Copernicus. From the point of view of mathematics, the system of Tycho Brahe was almost exactly equal to that of Copernicus, but by leaving the Earth immobile at the center of the world it had the advantage of being able to avoid all of the problems which arose in the theory of Copernicus, in particular the lack of parallax. Because of this it found a certain favor among the astronomers of those times, at least those who limited themselves to the plane of mathematical hypotheses and did not care, as in the case of the Ptolemaic theory, about the problem of thinking up a physical mechanism which would be able to produce the particular planetary motions which were required.

On the other hand, this problem existed for those who did not accept a complete divorce between mathematics and natural philosophy. Tycho's system appeared to them to be an attempt at a mathematical compromise which was not able to answer the questions about physics which the Danish astronomer himself had raised with his conclusions about the *nova* of 1572 and about the comets. As we will see, it was especially this last reason which made Galileo always extremely critical of the system of Tycho and caused him to refuse to consider it as a true third possibility among the "two chief world systems", that is, the one of Aristotle and Ptolemy on the one hand and that of Copernicus on the other.

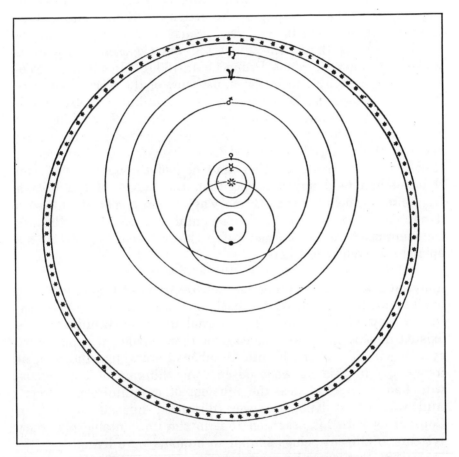

Fig. 11. The system of Tycho Brahe. The Earth is again at the center of a rotating sphere of stars, and the Sun and the Moon move in their old Ptolemaic orbits. On the other hand the planets are fixed on epicycles whose common center is the Sun. (From Dreyer 1953, 364).

5.   *The world of Copernicus expanded to the infinite.*
      Giordano Bruno

During the period which extends from the death of
Copernicus to the beginning of the activity of Kepler and Galileo
the most outstanding figure (also because of the tragic ending to
his life) among those who supported the Copernican theory is
without a doubt Giordano Bruno (1548-1600).[56] Inspired by Neo-
Platonic philosophy and by Cusanus' view of the world (see Note
35), Bruno asserts the existence of an infinite nature which
possesses an infinite dynamism. It is difficult at times to
recognize in this concept of nature a sufficient distinction
between the material world and God. Even though Bruno never
took a clear monistic position, and denied throughout the trial
that he had held any such position, the judges of the Roman
Inquisition concluded that Bruno was in fact a monist and so a
dangerous heretic. The fundamental reason for Bruno's
condemnation to be burned, after he refused to retract his
opinions, certainly lies here.[57]

But it is also true that Bruno had specified his view of
material reality by adopting the heliocentrism of Copernicus and
boldly transforming it, on the basis of the atomism of Lucretius,
into a view of an infinite and eternal universe. Infinite worlds
existed in this universe and each of them made up a planetary
system with one of the infinite number of stars, like the Sun, at
its center. In this he went beyond the thinking of Copernicus,
who had refused to face the problem of an infinite universe.[58]
And without a doubt he even distanced himself more from
Copernicus with his assertion that in the uncountable planetary
systems intelligent beings similar to humans were living.

This last assertion certainly constituted a further reason
for condemning Bruno.[59] Even though the acts of Bruno's trial
have been lost, what we have said is clear from the still existing
documents and especially from the Trial Summary compiled in
March 1598. A copy of this, prepared for the use of the Assessor
of the Holy Office, Marcello Filonardi, is still extant.[60] We also
know from these same documents that his adherence to the

Copernican idea of the motion of the earth was also included among the "censures" which were presented to Bruno and to which he had to respond in the course of the interrogations in the final phase of the trial. We do not know whether this censure was included later on in the eight heretical propositions which, at the suggestion of one of the consultors of the Holy Office, the Jesuit Robert Bellarmine, were extracted from the acts of the trial and from Bruno's works and which were delivered to him on 18 January 1599 so that he would abjure them. But the existence of this censure is a clear indication of how seriously preoccupied Church authorities were with Copernicanism because of its opposition to statements in the Sacred Scriptures.[61] The possibility that the Copernican theory could be radically extended, as Bruno had done, must have made their preoccupation even more profound.

As we shall see, Galileo arrived in the Venetian Republic at almost the same time as Bruno was expelled from it. As Bruno set out on what would become the tragic conclusion of his own life, Galileo must have sensed the overwhelming shadow of danger cast over the Copernican theory by Bruno who, although a bright intellectual, had never been a scientist, and even less an astronomer.[62] It is not, therefore, without significance that Galileo never made mention of Bruno in his writings in contrast to Kepler who, by temperament and interests, was undoubtedly, much less removed from Bruno than was Galileo.

This shadow cast by the ideas of Bruno was all the more foreboding because the intellectual climate within Catholic culture was becoming ever more rigid as the Counter-reformation gradually had brought about a strengthening of the Catholic Church's control on opinions which seemed in some way to be related to the faith.

Precisely in order to make this control more effective, Paul III had in 1542 established the Holy Office (or Roman Inquisition).[63] Bruno was a famous victim of this increasingly rigid doctrinal control and of the Roman Inquisition which had become its tool. The second, no less renowned, victim will be Galileo.

NOTES

[1] The four elements never exist in a pure state but they have a constant tendency to change among themselves and to unite to form composites.

[2] On the system of Eudoxus see Neugebauer 1969, 151 ff. and Pedersen and Pihl 1974, 74 ff. The system of Eudoxus included a total of 27 spheres (three each for the Sun and the Moon, four for each of the other five planets, and one for the fixed stars). More spheres were added by Callippus, a disciple of Eudoxus.

[3] Since he did not permit the existence of a vacuum, Aristotle had to introduce many other "compensatory" spheres so as to neutralize the perturbations caused by the motion of spheres which were in immediate contact with one another.

[4] In fact, matter necessarily implies passivity.

[5] See Neugebauer 1969, 145 ff.

[6] For a detailed exposition of the Ptolemaic system see Neugebauer 1969, 191 ff. and Pedersen and Pihl 1974, 88 ff.

[7] Dreyer 1953, 202.

[8] See Pedersen and Pihl 1974, 100 ff.

[9] As the Earth moved about the central fire, the inhabited hemisphere always faced away from the fire (which was, therefore, invisible). This implied a rotation of the Earth on its own axis.

[10] The Neo-Platonic Calcidius (first half of the IV century A.D.), in his commentary on the Plato's *Timaeus* seems to attribute to Heraclides the theory of the rotation of Venus about the Sun. Martianus Capella (IV-V century A.D.) adds Mercury to Venus. See the texts in Cohen and Drabkin 1975, 107. Heraclides became known in the Middle Ages through these two authors. But their testimonies are of quite dubious value.

[11] See the text in Cohen and Drabkin 1975, 108-109.

[12] Such, for example, is the position expressed by the Christian apologete Tertullian (about 200 A.D.) in his *Apologeticus* and later on in *Ad Nationes*. A century later another apologete Lactantius (240-320) in his *De Divinis Institutionibus* (III, 24) took aim particularly at the theory of the sphericity of the Earth and proposed instead that the Biblical conception was the only true one. Copernicus will quote him with very critical words in the Preface to *De Revolutionibus*.

[13] *De Actis cum Felice Manichaeo*, I, 2.

[14] *De Genesi ad Litteram*, II, 9.

[15] See, for example, *De Genesi ad Litteram*, I, 18, 19, 21. The quotations from St. Thomas are found in *Summa Theologiae*, Pars I, q.68 and ff.

[16] *De Genesi ad Litteram*, II, 9.

[17] It is usual also to ask what we are to believe from Scripture about the form and figure of the heavens. Many, as a matter of fact, discuss quite a bit those matters which our [sacred] authors paid no attention to and which as to eternal life are of no value to those who are familiar with them. Moreover, they spend a lot of time (which is even worse) which should be spent on heavenly matters. What difference does it make to me if the heavens, like a sphere completely wrap around the Earth, or whether, like a vault, they cover only the top part of it? *De Genesi ad Litteram*, II, 9.

[18] See Crombie 1969, Vol. I, 29 ff.

[19] See Crombie 1969, 51 ff. On the mediating role of Arabian astronomy see Pedersen and Pihl 1974, 174 ff. and Pedersen 1978, 303 ff.

[20] On Averroes see Wallace 1978b, 91 ff.

[21] On the cosmology of St. Thomas Aquinas see Wallace 1978b, Note 20.

[22] On the cosmological view of St. Thomas Aquinas see Litt 1963.

[23] See, for example, *Summa Theologiae*, Pars I, q.68, art. 3; q.70, art. 1.

[24] *Summa Theologiae*, Pars I, q.65-70.

[25] In his commentary on the *De Coelo* of Aristotle, Book II, Lectio XI, 39 (3) St. Thomas had himself rejected the theory of the Pythagoreans on the motion of the Earth, as well as that of "Heraclitus Ponticus and Aristarchus". As we see, in this passage, which is the only place in which he mentions Aristarchus, he associates him with Heraclides (whom he calls "Heraclitus") and thus shows that he did not know that there existed in Greek thought a theory which was completely heliocentric. But, as I have already said, even if he had known of its existence, he would certainly have rejected such a theory as, above all else, philosophically absurd. There is no doubt that St. Thomas, with all of his openness, remained a medieval thinker. Also, if he had had to face the problem of heliocentrism, he would most likely have looked upon it as also contradictory to Sacred Scripture. But, I must repeat that his judgement about its irreconcilability with the Bible would have depended on his judgment that it contradicted physical truth. If Aristarchus' theory had been accepted as true by the Greeks, there is no doubt that St. Thomas, based on the guiding principles we already know, would not have seen in it any opposition to Sacred Scripture. We will find this position again in the judgment

the consultors to the Holy Office will give in 1616 on the movement of the Earth: "absurd in philosophy and formally heretical". The firmness of their judgement of heresy (that is, opposed to Holy Scripture) will depend on the firmness that it was philosophically wrong.

[26] See Grant 1978, 280 ff.

[27] For the Thomistic texts see Litt 1963, 342 ff.

[28] *Summa Theologiae*, Pars I, q.32, art. 1.

[29] The Aristotelian treatise on the motion of the sublunar world had undergone serious criticisms beginning with Joannes Philoponus (VI century A.D.). Such criticisms will appear again in more detail during the medieval period. See Pedersen and Pihl 1974, 229 ff. But St. Thomas' attention was concentrated on the motion of the planets.

[30] Even though there was unanimous acceptance of Greek-Hellenistic geocentrism by Christian intellectuals in the Middle Ages, the possibility of a rotation of the Earth on its own axis was not excluded from consideration by many Scholastic thinkers, at least in theoretical discussions. This happened in the climate of greater freedom from Aristotelianism which was favored by the condemnation, brought about by the Bishop of Paris, Etienne Tempier in 1277, three years after the death of St. Thomas Aquinas, of 219 philosophical propositions considered to be contrary to the Christian faith (see Grant 1979, 26-29). The considerations in this respect which are contained in the *Quaestiones de Coelo et Mundo* (Questions on Heaven and Earth) of Jean Buridan (1295?-1358) are of particular interest and even more so the ones found in the *Livre du Ciel et du Monde* (Book on Heaven and Earth) of Nicole Oresme, the Bishop of Lisieux (1325-1382). See Crombie 1969, 88-95; Dijksterhuis 1969, 216-219; Grant 1979, 64-70. In his work Oresme examines the usual arguments against the Earth's motion, those drawn from "experience" as well as well as from Aristotelian philosophy and Sacred Scripture, and he shows that they are not probative by proposing considerations which in some way anticipate those which will be given by Copernicus and by Galileo himself. To be specific, as to the miracle of the Sun's standing still referred to in Joshua X, 12-14, Oresme states that in the Joshua narration the Bible is employing a common manner of speaking but that it is much simpler, in fact, to think of the Earth remaining still rather than that the whole complex heavenly mechanism to which the Sun belongs would do so. Oresme then passes to arguments in favor of the Earth's rotation and in agreement with Buridan he first of all invokes the principle of the relativity of motion whereby the daily motion of the heavenly bodies can be explained as due either to their own real motion or to the rotation of the Earth on its axis. Still in agreement with Buridan he then states that it is simpler and more

convincing to admit this motion of the Earth rather than the enormously fast motion of the heavenly bodies resulting from the rotation in twenty-four hours of the sphere of the fixed stars which drags them along with it. It is likewise more reasonable that the Earth, which is formed of the four less noble elements, be moving and the heavens, which is formed of the noble element, ether, be at rest, since it is nobler to be at rest than in motion. After this whole series of arguments in favor of the Earth's motion Oresme's conclusion cannot but surprise us. In fact, he writes:

> And still they maintain and I [also] believe that the heavens move and that the Earth does not: because "God fixed the Earth in a way that it could not move" (Psalm 92); [and this] despite reasons to the contrary, because they constitute *persuasive* arguments which do not *evidently* prove. (italics are the author's)

This completely unexpected conclusion is due undoubtedly to his fear of putting himself in opposition to the common interpretation of theologians which was founded upon the collection of texts from the Bible which speak of the immobility of the Earth as does the text quoted by Oresme himself above. It would be wrong to try to see the scorching Scriptural polemics against the Earth's motion at the time of Galileo already there in Oresme's time. But there is no doubt that Oresme, as a bishop, must have in a special way felt a responsibility to the Church and preferred "to have respect for the majesty of the Catholic faith", as he himself declares at the end of his book, rather than to hold as fundamental a hypothesis for which there existed "persuasive arguments" but not evident proofs.

[31] As is well known, the word *orbium* does not refer to celestial bodies but to the spheres which also in the Copernican system control the movements of the planets and the stars.

[32] On the Copernican system see Pedersen and Pihl 1974, 299 ff.

[33] The movement of precession postulated by Copernicus in the *De revolutionibus* includes two components. The first (an annual conical rotation of the Earth's axis) is introduced by Copernicus to assure the constant orientation of the Earth's axis during its annual motion of revolution (see *De revolutionibus*, Book I, Chapter XI and for an explanation Kuhn 1971, 163-164). All later astronomers, including Kepler and Galileo, will, with reason, deny that such a component is necessary. The other component, instead, is intended to explain the physical mechanism of the precession of the equinoxes as due precisely to this second, very slow, conical motion of the Earth's axis (see *De*

revolutionibus, Book III). The merit thus goes to Copernicus for having been the first to provide the correct explanation of the precessional changes of stellar coordinates, which up until that time had been attributed to a conical rotation of the axis of the sphere of the fixed stars.

[34] As Aristarchus had already done, Copernicus explained the lack of parallax as due to the enormous dimensions of the universe. See *De revolutionibus* L.I, c.5.

[35] Cusanus (Nikolaus von Kues, 1401-1464) was the only exception. In his famous work, *De Docta Ignorantia,* he had denied the Aristotelian concept of a finite world and substituted it with a "mathematical" one, consisting of a universe which was unlimited and thus without a center. On the other hand, in the wake of Plato and the Neo-Platonists, he had asserted that perfect circles do not exist in nature. It was only in this sense that he had denied the circularity of the celestial motions. And the negation of the existence of a center had relativized all of these "imperfect" motions. But Cusanus was not an astronomer and his view of the world remained on a purely speculative plane, even though he had a considerable influence on many intellectuals, such as Giordano Bruno.

[36] An example is that described in Book I, Chapter 10:

> At the center of all there is the Sun, as on a throne. In this beautiful temple [of the universe] how could we place this luminary in a better position from which it can brighten at one and the same time the entire universe? It is rightly called the Lamp, the Mind, the Ruler of the universe. Trismegistus called it the visible God and the *Electra* of Sophocles the all-foreseeing one. And, in fact, thus is the Sun, as if on its royal throne, governing the family of stars which surround it.

For the source of this conception of the Sun see A. Koyré 1974, 63 ff.

[37] See Pedersen and Pihl 1974, 317-18.

[38] In the Preface to the *De Revolutionibus* Copernicus is insistent about the fact that his work is meant for mathematicians, not in the sense that it was purely a mathematical hypothesis, but in the sense that it could not at the beginning be understood except by mathematicians. Once accepted by them, it would in the end also be welcomed (at least this was Copernicus's hope) also by philosophers.

[39] Osiander, a well known preacher but with interests also in mathematics and astronomy, assumed in its final phases responsibility for the publication of *De Revolutionibus* in place of Rheticus. On the

whole question of the "Notice" of Osiander see Rosen 1971, 403 ff. and 1984, 192 ff.

[40] It appears that Luther himself (1483-1546) while he was at Wittenberg, which had become the center of the Reformation, had declared in table conversation with friends: "That mad man [Copernicus] wants to turn upside down all astronomical knowledge, but as Scripture tells us, Joshua ordered the Sun and not the Earth to stand still" (Luther, Tischreden, ed. Weimar, Vol. II, 419). For a "sweetened" version of these words of Luther see Norlind 1953, 273 ff. The text of this version is quoted again by Rosen 1984, 182-83. As to Melanchthon (Philipp Schwarzerd, called Melanchthon, 1497-1560), a close friend and collaborator of Luther, he was a dominant figure at the University of Wittenberg. Even quite a few years after the death of Copernicus, he still continued to oppose his ideas. See his *Initia doctrinae physicae*, Wittenberg, 1549, 60 ff.

[41] This circumstance is not a pious legend. It is, in fact, reported by the close friend of Copernicus, Bishop Giese. See Rosen 1971, 274 (890).

[42] Between 1511 and 1513 he had had distributed in manuscript a first draft of his system, the *Commentariolus*, and this helped to make known the author's ideas.

[43] Widmanstadt, vice-chancellor of Austria and private secretary to the Pope, had probably received his information on the Copernican theory from Theodoric of Radzyn, who at that time represented at Rome the chapter of Warmia, to which Copernicus as a canon also belonged. The Greek codex given to him by the Pope contained the treatise, *De sensu et sensibili* (On sensation and sensible objects) by the famous commentator on Aristotle, Alexander of Aphrodisias, who flourished in about 200 A.D. Widmanstadt annotated the codex with the words: "The Supreme Pontiff Clement VII gave me this codex in Rome in the year 1533 after I had explained to him the opinion of Copernicus on the motion of the Earth in the Vatican gardens in the presence of Cardinals Francesco Orsini and Giuseppe Salviati, of Giovanni Pietro, vescovo di Viterbo, and of the doctor, Matteo Curzio".

[44] It should not seem strange that a Pope, who was the nephew of Lorenzo dei Medici and a patron of Renaissance culture, should find the new ideas to be no less interesting than the treasures of antiquity.

[45] See Garin 1971, 85 ff. and 1973, 31 ff. The article of Rosen 1975 is based upon these studies of Garin.

[46] The treatise was finished in 1544 but remained in manuscript form. The appendix, entitled *De Coelo supremo immobili et terra infima et stabili, coeterisque coelis et elementis intermediis mobilibus*, was composed two years later. Tolosani belonged to the Monastery of St.

Mark in Florence. This explains how another Dominican of the same monastery, Tommaso Caccini, who, as we shall see will become one of the fiercest adversaries of Galileo, had the opportunity about 60 years later to read this treatise. A note in the margin of Tolosani's manuscript testifies to this fact. See Blackwell 1991, 24, note 32. This appendix has been edited by Garin 1973.

[47] See Hooykaas 1984.

[48] See Paschini 1965, 295-96. The essential parts of the text of the *Commentaria* are reproduced by Barone 1983. He also mentions that the same ideas that the Copernican doctrine could be reconciled with Sacred Scripture were taken up again by de Zuñiga in Chapter 5 of the fourth book of his *Physica*, published in Toledo in 1597 (Barone 1983, 329); see also Vernet 1972.

[49] Zuñiga's opinion had, however, been criticized by the Jesuit theologian J. Pineda in his *Commentaria in Job* (1597-1601). See Grisar 1882, 26 ff.

[50] Even Clavius, the famous Jesuit mathematician of those days (I will speak of him later), who played an important role in the calendar reform which took place in 1582, in his *Opera Mathematica* (Mainz, 1611-12), Volume III passes a negative sentence, even though a moderate one, on the Copernican system. Clavius had a great respect for the mathematical talents of Copernicus, but he, nonetheless, ventured the opinion that: "many errors and absurdities are contained in [his] position". And after giving some examples of them he concluded: "All of that is contrary to the common teaching of the philosophers and astronomers and it seems to contradict that which the Holy Scripture teaches in many places". As Lattis 1994, 139 comments, this is the only instance where Clavius puts the teaching of Copernicanism in direct opposition to that of Sacred Scripture. And even in this instance by using the expression "seems to contradict" he refrains from placing a categorical theological judgment. For a careful analysis of Clavius' position with respect to Copernicanism see Lattis 1994, Chapter 5.

[51] Koestler 1959, 194, calls the *De Revolutionibus* "the book which nobody read". But such a characterization is unjustified, even though, with the exception of Book I, this work of Copernicus is not easy reading. However, at least the astronomers read it.

[52] On Clavius see Note 50 above. For Clavius' position on the *nova* see Lattis 1994, 147 ff. In addition to Clavius, and like him independently of Brahe, Michael Mästlin had also arrived at the same conclusions as Brahe on the *nova* of 1572.

[53] In the history of western astronomical thought Tycho is the first to have upheld this probability of a celestial motion different from a circular one.

[54] On the further reason based on the supposed absence of stationary points and retrogressions in the cometary orbits about the Sun see Shea 1972, 86-87.

[55] It seems that Tycho was the first to raise this difficulty. See Dreyer 1953, 360-61.

[56] After having left the Dominican order, which he had entered when he was seventeen, in order to avoid a trial for his ideas which were considered heretical by his Dominican superiors (1576), Bruno went for many years wandering about in Switzerland, France, England and later in Germany, almost constantly at the center of polemics and the object of condemnations for his philosophical and theological concepts. Finally he accepted the invitation of the Venetian patrician, Giovanni Mocenigo, and returned to Italy in 1591. He stayed in the house of his host in Venice and hoped to obtain the chair of mathematics at Padua, which was instead assigned, as we will see, to Galileo one year later. Accusations for holding heretical ideas were brought against him in the following year by Mocenigo himself. Bruno was subjected to a first trial under the Venetian Inquisition and after that in 1593 he was consigned to the Roman Inquisition. After a new trial which stretched out for seven years, Bruno in the end refused to retract his ideas and he was condemned to be burned at the stake as an impenitent and pertinacious heretic.

[57] Alongside the philosophical reasons for Bruno's condemnation there were also without a doubt the theological ones. Mocenigo and other Venetians had accused Bruno of denying the dogma of the Trinity (he identified the Holy Spirit with the "world soul"), the divinity of Christ, Eucharistic transubstantiation, the existence and eternity of hell, the virginity of Mary, the cult of the saints, the authority of Sacred Scripture and the Church Fathers, etc. But Bruno had constantly denied that there was any basis to these accusations and had confessed only to having had serious doubts about the Trinity and the divinity of Christ, doubts to which he had professed repentance. In the end the accusations remained unproven. As the trial finished, however, Bruno's obstinate impenitence with respect to his philosophical and cosmological concepts will constitute for the judges a proof of the reality also of his theological errors. These will, therefore, be inserted as an integral part of the sentence of condemnation. See Firpo 1993, 103, 108 ff. for an opinion contrary to what Mercati 1942, 8 asserts on the preponderance of theological motives in the condemnation. The sentence of condemnation is preserved only in a

partial copy addressed to the Governor of Rome. Except for transubstantiation it contains none of the points of accusation (Firpo 1993, 339-344). But nine days later fourteen of the points of accusation were recalled by memory by the converted Protestant Kaspar Schoppe, an eyewitness of the solemn public reading of the sentence of condemnation (Firpo 1993, 103-104).

[58] In Book I, Chapter VIII of the *De Revolutionibus* Copernicus had mentioned the problem as to whether the universe was infinite or not, but he prudently avoided entering into the case saying that: "Let us leave to the discussion of philosophers [to decide] whether the world is finite or infinite".

[59] If in fact an infinite multitude of intelligent beings existed, how were we to interpret the Christian doctrine of the redemptive death of Christ which took place once and for all (*semel et pro omnibus*)?

[60] If they had not been destroyed beforehand, the acts of the trial of Bruno were lost as a result of the subsequent transfer of the Roman archives to France at the time of Napoleon I. We will have the opportunity to speak about this in Chapter 7. However, twenty-six excerpts of the minutes of the Holy Office concerning Bruno were recovered and published by Monsignor Enrico Carusi in 1925 and in this way additions were made to the incomplete copy of the sentence of condemnation and the few other documents that were previously known. Then in 1940 Monsignor Angelo Mercati searched out the Summary of Bruno's trial in the personal archives of Pius IX and he published it two years later (see Mercati 1942). Still more documents were discovered by Luigi Firpo and published posthumously with all the previous documents (Firpo 1993). This publication, therefore, provides today the fundamental starting point for all research on the trial and condemnation of Bruno. For the history of the Summary see Firpo 1993, 87-88 and for text of the same see Firpo 1993, 247-304. The accusation of having upheld the eternity of the universe and the infinity of worlds is already found in the deposition of Mocenigo in Venice (Firpo 1993, 143). It will be included among the censures compiled by the Roman inquisitors (see censures VI and IX reproduced in Firpo 1993, 267-273, together with Bruno's responses).

[61] As we will see, Bellarmine will also have an important part to play in the first phase of the Galileo affair. His role in Bruno's trial has frequently been exaggerated. See Firpo 1993, 91 ff. As Firpo notes, Bellarmine took part in the trial, as a consultor of the Holy Office, only from February 1597 on "when the interrogations and the censures had already been made". It is true that the compilation of the eight heretical theses to be presented to Bruno for his abjuration came about as a result of Bellarmine's proposal and was accomplished by himself

and the commissary of the Holy Office, Alberto Tragagliolo. But still the purpose of this undertaking of Bellarmine was to bring to a rapid conclusion a trial which had already been stretched out over many years. And certainly the conclusion sought by Bellarmine was Bruno's abjuration and not his death by burning at the stake. Nonetheless, after being elected cardinal in March 1599 and becoming immediately thereafter a member of the Holy Office, he participated in the final session of Bruno's trial. On Bellarmine's role in the condemnation of Bruno see Le Bachelet 1923, 193-210 and Blackwell 1991, 47 ff. The censure on the motion of the earth is found in the Summary as a part of censure **XXXIV** (see Firpo 1993, 302-303). From Bruno's response we see that in opposition to his idea they quoted the verse from the Bible: *Terra autem stat in aeternum* (but the Earth remains in eternity); and against the immobility of the Sun the other verse: *Sol oritur et occidit* (the Sun rises and sets). As we shall see, both of these Biblical verses will also be used by Galileo's adversaries. And Bruno's answer follows the same line of thought as that which Galileo will use fifteen years later. It is obviously unthinkable that such a reply could satisfy Bruno's judges. According to Firpo 1993, 97-98, even though the affirmation of the Earth's motion was probably not included in the eight theses to be abjured, which were composed by Bellarmine and Tragagliolo (they were lost except for the first which concerned the denial of transubstantiation), it was most likely included in the second and more detailed text of abjuration which was presented to Bruno in September 1599. As we will have the opportunity to see more clearly when we treat of Galileo's trial, since there existed no dogmatic definition by the Catholic Church against the affirmation of the mobility of the earth and of the immobility of the Sun, such an affirmation could not be considered to be heretical in the strict theological meaning of the term. And in his defense Bruno had insisted on this very point. But the affirmation was, nonetheless, considered by theologians as certainly opposed to Sacred Scripture and to the teaching of the Church Fathers and it was, therefore, considered as heretical in the wider "inquisitorial" sense. And so Bruno was requested (as will happen later to Galileo) to abjure it.

[62] Bruno's knowledge of the Copernican system was totally superficial and even contained gross errors. See McMullin 1987, 55-74.

[63] More complete information on the Holy Office (or the Congregation of the Roman and Universal Inquisition) and also on the Congregation of the Index (established in 1571 by Pius V), as well as on the duties of the Master of the Sacred Palace, may be found in Brandmüller and Greipl 1992, 47 ff.

CHAPTER 1

GALILEO ENTERS ON STAGE: FROM HIS BIRTH TO HIS YEARS IN PADUA

1. *Family milieu and early education*

On 7 December 1592 the new professor of mathematics at the University of Padua, Galileo Galilei, gave his first lecture in the Great Hall before a large audience. Who was this professor who had not yet turned thirty?

Galileo was born on 15 February 1564 at Pisa in the Grand Duchy of Tuscany. During the second half of the XVII century Italy was divided into numerous independent states with various forms of government. The Grand Duchy of Tuscany was ruled by a powerful family of merchants and bankers, the Medici. The capital was Florence, at that time one of the richest cities of Europe and one which in the Middle Ages and especially in the Renaissance, had contributed in a unique way to the culture and art of the Western world.

Galileo's family also had ancient roots in Florence. The original family name, Buonaiuti, had been changed at the beginning of the XV century into that of Galilei.[1] The family had taken an active part in the stormy political life of Florence but there had been a constant decline in its fortunes, and at the time of Galileo's birth the economic situation of the Galilei was strained.

It appears that Galileo's father, Vincenzio (1520?-1591), was residing in Pisa for trading. But rather than to that profession, Vincenzio dedicated his best energies during his lifetime to music. He was a skillful lute player, but even more than that he was the exponent of the new musical theories which were being developed within the group of the *Camerata Fiorentina*.[2] Various treatises of his on musical theory are still preserved. The most important among them is his *Dialogo della musica antica e della moderna* which was widely distributed in Europe and which was quoted with high praise by Kepler himself. These works are important not only for the musical theory of the Renaissance, but also because they contributed to the development of experimental science.[3] The knowledge of mathematics together with the employment of experimental science which are implicitly contained in these writings are of particular interest for evaluating the influence which the family atmosphere had upon the young Galileo.

As a typical Renaissance man, Vincenzio shows, in addition to his knowledge of music and mathematics, a quite broad culture and a good mastery of the classical languages. Moreover, from his works he makes it abundantly clear that he possessed a wit which could at times turn into a biting sarcasm. He also showed an independent judgement which led him to reject the principle of authority which was at the basis of much of the knowledge of that age.

There is no doubt that, besides his versatile genius and his artistic talents, Galileo inherited from his father that propensity for mathematics and for the experimental method which were fundamental to his scientific work. He also inherited his independent and argumentative spirit, intolerant of being imposed upon from outside, especially as regards intellectual activity.

On the other hand from his mother, Giulia Ammannati (1538-1620) who possessed "a sharp and quarrelsome character, he perhaps acquired a certain polemical aggressiveness, a certain impatience which breaks out in sudden fits of anger and expresses itself in diatribes and lashing derision. These won him an increasing number of enemies and will contribute to much of his misfortune".[4]

After Galileo Vincenzio had two other sons and three or four daughters by Giulia. Only Virginia, Michelangelo, and Livia survived. Just as their mother, they will have an influence on Galileo's life especially by causing him interminable economic worries during the major part of his life.

Galileo received his early education from the age of ten at Pisa. After the family came back to Florence, he spent a brief period of study at the monastery of Vallombrosa, about thirty kilometers east of the city.[5] As he matured Galileo gave increasingly clear indications of his great intellectual talents and this led his father to direct him towards the medical profession.

Undoubtedly Vincenzio was dreaming that his son (and thus also the whole family) would have a future more promising than the difficult economic situation in which they then found themselves.

Thus for his medical studies Galileo had to return to Pisa where he registered for courses at the university in September of 1581. The University of Pisa had alternating periods of growth and of decadence over a period of two hundred years during which the ancient seafaring Republic, having lost its independence in 1406, became subject to the rule of Florence. The strategy of the Medici was to seek to sooth the hatred that the people of Pisa continued to harbor against the people of Florence and that led them to favor the University of Pisa at the expense of the one at Florence, where there remained only the chairs of letters and of philosophy. But, despite the great efforts of the Grand Duke Cosimo I (1519-1574) to raise the standards, the University of Pisa was passing through difficult times when Galileo entered there.

On the faculty of medicine there were still some teachers of great renown, such as Andrea Cesalpino (1519-1603), whose name is linked to the studies of the circulation of the blood and to the first attempts at botanical classification. But, even if Galileo followed his classes, the courses which he had to attend were as a whole certainly not capable of awakening in him an interest in medicine.

As in the other European universities of that time, medical studies at Pisa were based upon the teaching of the famous Greek doctor Galen (129-199 A.D.). Galen was not only the most famous doctor in the Roman Empire of his time, but, thanks to the large quantity of medical and philosophical writings which he left, he also later on exercised an enormous influence in the Byzantine Empire, in the Arab world, and then in the Latin medieval world.[6] Such an influence was still the dominant one in university instruction in the second half of the XVI century despite the development of the new medical science which was taking place at that time.

It was thus through Galen that the medical students were introduced to their material. And alongside him the basis of their professional formation was furnished by the philosophy and the natural science of Aristotle together with the study of Euclid and an introduction to astronomy (based on the *Sphaera* of Sacrobosco and the *Theorica Planetarum*).[7]

The oldest biographies of Galileo, such as those of Viviani and Gherardini[8] make an important point of the fact that Galileo showed quite a lack of enthusiasm, in fact of any interest at all, for the courses which he had to follow, even though at the same time they state that the young student on his own part dedicated himself to the study "of Aristotle, of Plato and of the other ancient philosophers" (XIX, 603). And this interest for philosophy will persist, as we shall see, throughout Galileo's life.

2.   *"Conversion" to Euclid and Archimedes*

While he was attending his second year at the university at the beginning of 1583, Galileo had a meeting with the mathematician Ostilio Ricci (1540-1603) and this had a decisive influence upon his future career.[9] At that time Ricci was a tutor in mathematics to the pages of the Grand Duke and he was then in Pisa with the Duke's court.[10] From what Galileo himself asserted towards the end of his life it was Ricci who introduced him to the study of the geometry of Euclid and afterwards to the mechanics of Archimedes.

Thus the fascinating world of clear, rigorous mathematical deduction and of the science of Archimedes was opened to the young Galileo. Here the solution to problems in mechanics was derived not from abstract metaphysical principles but from contact with physical experience. It was above all Archimedes, with his experimental-mathematical approach, who most fascinated the young student, not only because it opened up to him a whole field of research unknown to him up until that time, but also because it showed him a method of solving problems which he will perfect and make his own.

Of course, it would be over simplistic to see this "conversion" to Euclid and Archimedes as the result of a simple encounter with a mathematician such as Ricci who, all things considered, was not of any great stature. Without a doubt the influence of his father during his childhood and adolescence had predisposed Galileo to make the later choices which he did with the knowledge of the road he was taking, once it was clearly indicated to him. Be that as it may, he was by now decided to dedicate all of his energies to the study of mathematics, of mechanics, and of natural philosophy, rather than to the pursuit of medicine.

This new direction taken by his son was surely a hard blow to accept for Vincenzio.[11] But after a useless attempt to dissuade Galileo, his father finally gave in to him and allowed him to return to Florence in the Spring of 1585 without having completed his medical studies.

During this four year stay of his in Florence Galileo deepened his knowledge of Euclid and especially of Archimedes. We have a proof of the influence exercised by Archimedes on Galileo in his first scientific work, written in Italian and entitled *La Bilancetta* (The Little Balance). It described a method for determining the specific weight of an object by using an instrument similar to the hydrostatic scale in use up until our time. Even though Galileo did not claim originality for his method it included an ingenious device to increase the accuracy of the measurements. This work was distributed in manuscript form among friends and acquaintances and it was received with interest and so helped to throw light upon the talent of this young student.[12]

It was also under the inspiration of Archimedes that he demonstrated some theorems on the barycenter of parabolic conic figures of revolution probably during the period 1586-1587. He circulated this work in manuscript form and published it fifty years later as an appendix to the *Discorsi*.[13] The theme had already been dealt with in a book by Federico Commandino (1509-1575) published in 1565. With this work Galileo also gave proof of his talent both in theory and in practical matters and he was praised by scholars even from outside of Italy.

Among the people to whom Galileo had sent copies of these demonstrations (or at least the fundamental theorem) there was the Jesuit Clavius, of whom I have already spoken in the Introduction, and he merits special attention here. Christoph Clau (Clavius in Latin) was born in Bamberg, Germany in 1537. At the age of 18 he entered the Society of Jesus (the Jesuits) which had just recently been founded. He studied at Coimbra in Portugal and he became a professor of mathematics at the

Roman College (1564).[14] During his many years of teaching at
this famous school of the Jesuits in Rome Clavius published
various treatises of mathematics and astronomy which had a
wide circulation and, as we have already seen, he played an
important role in the reform of the calendar which was carried
out under Pope Gregory XIII (1582). At the same time, he
proceeded with the founding at the Roman College of a school of
mathematicians and astronomers, mostly Jesuit, which had a
noteworthy influence in Europe and, even more so, in the Orient
where the Jesuits had opened missions in India, China and
Japan.[15]

Posterity, truly enough, considered the title of "Euclid the
Second", attributed to him by his contemporaries, to be
exaggerated. (Actually Clavius' value was more in his abilities
as a clear popularizer of mathematics and traditional astronomy
than as an original thinker.) But the fact remains that at the
time of Galileo he was considered as one of the greatest living
mathematicians. Galileo himself shared that opinion.

In this regard it is interesting to note that the first letter
of Galileo which has been preserved is precisely the one which
he sent on 8 January 1588 to this mathematician of the Roman
College (X, 22-23). At the beginning of that letter Galileo wrote:
"I think it is about time to break the silence I have had in
regard to Your Reverence ever since I left Rome". It is from
these words that we learn of the first trip made by Galileo to
Rome not long before, in the summer of 1587.

In all probability the principal purpose of that trip was to
obtain letters of recommendation for his application to the chair
of mathematics at the University of Bologna. Galileo had already
had a brief teaching experience in Siena in 1585-1586 and he
had to his credit the two works of which I have already spoken.
But mathematicians much better known and with much more
experience than he had were seeking the chair at Bologna.
Galileo was, therefore, well aware that he had to obtain
authoritative support, which he could have above all from Rome,
since Bologna at that time was part of the Papal States. A proof
of this appears to be had in a letter written in support of Galileo
by Cardinal Enrico Caetani to the Senate in Bologna in
February 1588 (X, 27-27).

A recommendation from the famous Clavius would also have helped Galileo a great deal and this appears to have been the principal purpose of his visit to the Jesuit at the Roman College. Galileo left him a copy of that theorem of his which formed the basis of his other theorems on the barycenters.[16] So there was born at that time a relationship based upon a deep esteem for one another which will remain unfailing right up until the death of Clavius (1612). It is no wonder that Galileo, still a very young man, should be full of admiration for that Jesuit who had by then arrived at the height of his fame.[17] What is rather surprising is the fact that Clavius, as famous and as loaded with work as he was, had found the time to respond immediately on 16 January to the above-mentioned letter of Galileo of 8 January, a letter from one who was thirty years his junior and who had just begun his scientific career. Moreover, this same mathematician of the Roman College was well known for making much more famous personages wait, often in vain.[18] Even his second answer on March 5 to a subsequent letter from Galileo will be just as fast. And in neither of them is there any note of paternalism or condescendence. On the contrary Clavius does not hesitate to confess frankly that he is not able to give more complete answers to the questions Galileo had addressed to him because he is "at this moment far removed from such speculations" (X, 24).

For the time being the correspondence ends there. It will be Clavius who will write again to Galileo sixteen years later in 1604. And Galileo will not answer until 1610. But these long periods of silence will not cool the cordial relationship and esteem they have for one another.

The demonstration of the theorems of the barycenter of the parabolic cones of revolution also gained for Galileo, in addition to the esteem of Clavius, that of a famous scholar in mechanics of those times, Guidobaldo del Monte (1545-1607). He had been a disciple of Commandino and Galileo had sent him his basic theorem. Without a doubt del Monte was struck by the capabilities of this young correspondent and from that time on he never ceased to help him, not only with respect to studies in which they had a common interest but also with respect to his career as a professor.

In addition to his devotion to the study of mathematics and physics (without neglecting to deepen his knowledge of the Latin classics and of the most famous Italian poets[19]) Galileo certainly did not belittle the problem of finding a stable university teaching position, which could provide him and his family greater financial security. We have already seen how he had considered a chair of mathematics to teach afternoon courses at Bologna. But , despite influential recommendations and even an attempt to hide his very young age,[20] the authorities at the University of Bologna gave preference to the 33 year old G. Antonio Magini, who had already published several books and was, therefore, much better known than Galileo. Thus in August 1588 Magini took up that chair which he would hold until his death in 1617.

At about the same time as his try for the University of Bologna, it appears that Galileo had also thought of the University of Padua, where the chair of mathematics had been vacant since January 1588. At any rate it is certain that right from the beginning of 1588 he tried the University of Pisa and then Florence, probably hoping to obtain the same lectureship in mathematics that had been held by his teacher, Ostilio Ricci. But, despite the high recommendations of his friend Guidobaldo del Monte, both attempts failed. But a year later the incumbent in the chair of mathematics at Pisa, Filippo Fantoni, left after a long teaching career. Thanks again to the intervention of Guidobaldo del Monte with the Grand Duke Ferdinand, Galileo was able to obtain that chair in July 1589. Thus he returned as a professor to the same university he had left when he was still a student just about four years previously.

3.   *Mathematics teacher at Pisa. The sources of his teaching*

Galileo's assignment was for three years and the salary was quite small. But Galileo undoubtedly must have considered Pisa only as a first step on his way to chairs of greater splendor. And if the salary was small, he hoped no doubt to augment it by giving private lessons.

His predecessor Fantoni had taught his courses in a two-year cycle beginning in the first year with the first book of

Euclid's *Elements* and Sacrobosco's *Sphere* (the usual "classical" treatise on the fundamentals of Ptolemaic astronomy) and then going on in the next year to the fifth book of the *Elements* and the *Theorica Planetarum* (Theory of the Planets; this was also a well known medieval treatise on planetary motions according to the system of Ptolemy). As we know from a *rotulus* (list of courses) of the University of Pisa, Galileo also taught astronomy in addition to Euclid. We learn from him that he was proceeding with the composition of a commentary on the *Almagest*, which should have been published after a short time, but which, as a matter of fact, never saw the light of day. (see I, 314).[21]

As happens to all young professors at the beginning of their teaching career, Galileo undoubtedly had to face the problem of preparing his lectures. Was he, therefore, happy enough to make use of the texts which Fantoni must have employed or did he wish to prepare, at least for the astronomical material, his own summaries? And if he followed the latter course, what material did he use for his compilations?

Up until thirty years ago there was no satisfactory answer to this question. But a long series of subsequent research on the collection of Galilean manuscripts, already published in part by Antonio Favaro in the first volume of the National Edition of Galileo's Works, has allowed us to set up a whole new approach to the problem.

The manuscripts which with we are concerned are kept in the *Collezione Galileiana* of the National Library in Florence and are divided into three groups. The first group (Ms 27) contains questions of logic based on Aristotle's treatise *Posteriores Analytici*. The second (Ms 46) contains questions connected with Aristotle's *De Coelo* and *De Generatione* plus some notes on motion. The third (Ms 71) contains the sketch of a dialogue and some treatises on motion, called (apparently by Galileo himself) *De Motu Antiquiora*[22], in order to distinguish these considerations on local motion from those which he composed in his time at Padua.

Favaro in the National Edition has almost entirely[23] omitted the first group of manuscripts which he considered to have no particular value. The second group, except for the notes on motion, was published with the title, *Juvenilia*, and its

composition is assigned to the period when Galileo was a student
at Pisa. According to Favaro, these are the result of notes taken
by Galileo while he was following the lectures of Francesco
Buonamici and other professors. To the third group Favaro gives
the title *De Motu* (adding to it the notes on motion from MS
46).[24]

The research to which I have alluded above, carried out by
Carugo and Crombie, Fredette and Wallace,[25] still shows,
however, that the first two groups of manuscripts (except for the
annotations on motion in MS 46) have a strict dependence on
texts of the Jesuit professors of the Roman College, while the
third (which contains the first attempts of Galileo to establish a
new science of motion) shows a greater independence, even
though concepts appear there which clearly come from the texts
just mentioned.

These results, rightly considered to be among the most
important obtained during the last decades in the area of Galileo
studies, have highlighted a fact which up until now had not been
known to even the most established Galileo scholars, namely, the
connection between the first phases in the development of
Galileo's thought and the climate of philosophical and scientific
thinking at the Roman College. Thus it has become clear that it
was rather through this contact with the Roman College than
through the supposed influence of Buonamici during his years of
study at Pisa that Galileo came into contact with the
Aristotelian and medieval way of questioning in natural
philosophy. It was a conceptual approach which was further
developed in the Jesuit teaching of natural philosophy at the
Roman College. The Jesuits undoubtedly followed Aristotle in
philosophy and Ptolemy in astronomy but with a greater
openness of mind than their counterparts in the various
European Universities.

The dating of these manuscripts is still open to debate. If
we accept Wallace's dating, they would, as a matter of fact, go
back to the period of Galileo's teaching at Pisa. According to
Wallace Galileo's trip to Rome in 1587 to meet Clavius provided
him perhaps with the opportunity to make a first contact with
the philosophy professors of the Roman College and thus he
became aware of the superior level of their teaching as compared

to that which he had received at Pisa. On the other hand, his subsequent correspondence with Clavius must have persuaded Galileo of the need first of all to deepen his knowledge of logic.[26] It was, therefore, probably through Clavius that Galileo came to possess the *annotationes* put together for the academic year 1587-1588 by Paolo della Valle or Valla from the Latin Vallus (1561-1622), a young professor of logic at the Roman College. In fact, Galileo had found in them a complete theory of the process of demonstration (necessary premises, types of proof, the various levels of certitude of the results thus achieved), based on the *Posteriores Analytici* of Aristotle. These must have seemed to him to be all the more necessary for the work he was taking up as a teacher and researcher since he was well aware of not having acquired this basic knowledge during the years of his university studies. And this, still following Wallace, would explain the care with which he edited his lecture outlines based on these notes,[27] almost certainly between the end of 1588 and partway into 1589. Once convinced of the superior quality of the teaching of logic at the Roman College as compared to that at Pisa, Galileo would have become persuaded that it would be important to have sent to him (with all probability again by Clavius) the notes of the other courses in natural philosophy which were related to the other topics which he was about to deal with or which he had already begun to teach.

According to Carugo and Crombie, however, the date for the manuscript MS 27 (the one, that is, of Galileo's notes on logic) should be changed to a date not earlier than 1597[28] and the other known manuscripts of Galileo contained in MS 46 should be most probably assigned a later date. Even later dates should be probably assigned to the writings on motion contained in MS 71.[29]

Even though the dating proposed by Carugo and Crombie for the notes on logic appears to be the easiest to defend, it does not appear to me to be proven beyond all doubt.[30] Even less convincing is in my opinion the assignment of later dates to all of the other manuscripts of Galileo.[31] In the absence, therefore, of more cogent arguments, I lean, as do most scholars of Galileo, towards the dating of at least the manuscripts, MS 46 and 71, to the period of Galileo's career in Pisa. It is true that only the composition of the *Tractatio de Coelo* in MS 46 can be, strictly speaking, justified by the need to teach astronomy at the University of Pisa. As I have already mentioned, Galileo had to expound to the students the *Sphere* of Sacrobosco and nothing could be more natural for him than to use Father Clavius' commentary on this work. In fact, important passages from Clavius are brought into the *Tractatio de Coelo*. As to the other writings found in MS 46 (the *Tractatio prima de Mundo*, the *Tractatus de alteratione* and the *Tractatus de elementis*) their content has to do undoubtedly with philosophy and, therefore, they have no direct relationship to Galileo's teaching. But we know already of the deep interest in philosophy which Galileo cultivated beginning with the period of his studies in Pisa and we will see how, even in later years, he will prefer to be considered a philosopher rather than a mathematician. Even though in his role as a young teacher of mathematics he had to avoid stepping into the field of philosophy in which his colleagues taught, nothing forbade him from taking the initiative to deepen his knowledge of natural philosophy by beginning with the tracts composed by the Jesuits of the Roman College.[32]

4.   *The Pisan* De Motu *and Galileo's first orientation towards Copernicus*

     From that period as a young teacher Galileo's thinking was taking a direction much more towards natural philosophy than towards pure mathematics. This is shown by his first pieces of research on motion, almost all of them contained in MS 71[33] which, as I have already noted, I will consider, as long as cogent arguments to the contrary are not available, to belong to Galileo's time in Pisa.
     The aim of the present book does not permit me to spend more time on these first researches of Galileo in kinematics and dynamics. I limit myself to noting that there is present in them, at least as a point of departure, a criticism of certain aspects of the Aristotelian theory of motion. Such criticism was already present in medieval thought and was further developed in the XVI century in the teaching of natural philosophy at the Roman College[34] and, in a way that was at least partially new, in the

studies in mechanics of Tartaglia, Benedetti, and Guidobaldo del Monte[35]. But in this field Galileo proves to be much more independent of his sources than he was in the compilations of logic in MS 27 and in those of natural philosophy in MS 46. He shows that he is altogether capable of proposing new questions and solutions which, even if they are not satisfactory or are even completely erroneous, nevertheless constitute the first stage in the construction of a new science of motion.

Particularly noteworthy for our purposes is the question introduced in the second part of the tract *De Motu Antiquiora*, also called for the sake of greater clarity "Pisan *De motu*"[36] on the rotation of material spheres. Galileo begins with the Aristotelian distinction between "*moto naturale*" (natural motion) and "*moto forzato*" (forced motion), with which we are familiar. He defines the first as a body's motion towards its natural place and the second as motion away from the natural place. In the case of a material sphere rotating about the center of the universe, its motion, neither towards nor away from the center, is neither natural nor forced and would, therefore, once begun continue indefinitely.

As we know, Aristotle had excluded the possibility of a rotation of the Earth on its own axis precisely because it would have been a forced motion and, therefore, could not have continued indefinitely. In substance Galileo asserts here that the dichotomy, natural-forced, is not perfect. A third possibility exists, that of a motion which, in another passage of the same tract, he calls "neutral". Therefore, he seems to suggest that it is possible to speak of a rotation of the Earth on its own axis. Does this mean that Galileo was already at this time (about 1591) tending towards Copernicanism?

As we have already noted, Galileo had read the *Almagest* (he had also made progress on a commentary to it) and most probably also the *De Revolutionibus* of Copernicus[37] in preparation for his astronomy teaching. It is very likely that this latter book had made a deep impression on him and that he had, therefore, begun to think about a physical justification for the Copernican system.[38] Still moving, as he was, in the ambit of the Aristotelian doctrine of natural places and motions, Galileo had come in the "Pisan *De motu*" to find a "physical"

justification for the rotation of the earth on its own axis. But the
further step required in the approach to a complete acceptance
of Copernicanism, namely, the "physical" justification for the
revolution of the Earth about the Sun, could not be realized on
the basis of the Galilean theory of "neutral" motions.[39]

Relying on these facts, Drake has recently taken the view
that Galileo in his teaching period at Pisa, after having studied
Copernicus and under his influence, went first from a previous
Ptolemaic position to one like that of Tycho Brahe (although he
did not know it as Brahe's) and then to a kind of "semi-
Copernicanism" where the Earth was no longer motionless but
had a daily rotational motion and the Sun was at the center of
the motion of all of the other planets.[40] His "conversion" to
Copernicanism, according to Drake, would not have happened
until quite a bit later when he was at Padua and a definitive
"conversion" would have happened only after his discovery of
the phases of Venus at the end of 1610.

We will have another opportunity to return to Galileo's
adherence (which Drake considers to have been only a passing
one) to Copernicanism during his time at Padua. As to his time
at Pisa, Drake is certainly correct in my opinion when he asserts
that from that period Galileo started to move towards
Copernicanism, having taken his first steps in that direction
with the discovery that, within the ambit of the Aristotelian
theory of natural places and motions (which Galileo still
accepted), it was possible to speak in a physical sense of a
rotation of the Earth, still thought to be at the center of the
world. But it is difficult to accept the idea that Galileo went
beyond this position and assumed (as to the further idea of the
Sun as the center of all of the planetary motions except that of
the Earth) a purely mathematical approach which would have
led him unknowingly, once Tycho Brahe's position was
surpassed, to a semi-Copernicanism.[41]

Galileo was not, it seems to me, the kind of person to be
satisfied even momentarily with a hybrid position, a compromise
between physics and mathematics, such as the one which Drake
apparently wishes to attribute to him. Throughout all of his
later work in cosmology Galileo will refuse to accept world
systems which do not have a physical meaning. And this was

also the fundamental reason for his deep aversion for Tycho Brahe's system once he became familiar with it. This well thought out intellectual aversion (which will, however, often degenerate into an unjustified lack of appreciation for the merits of the great Danish astronomer) would be difficult to understand if Galileo had really gone through a phase where he accepted Tycho's system. The same holds for semi-Copernicanism which, as best I can fathom, Galileo never mentions.

It is more likely that about 1590 Galileo would have been deeply impressed upon reading Copernicus and became convinced *intuitively* of the superiority of the heliocentric theory over the one of Aristotle and Ptolemy. And he must have begun from that time on to look for physical arguments to prove heliocentrism. But, since he was still maneuvering within the perspective of the physical conception of Aristotle of natural places and motions, he was at that time only able to come to a justification of the rotation of the Earth at the center of the world. Galileo knew very well that to accept Copernicanism one had to place the Sun more or less where the Earth was and assign to the Earth, in addition to rotation on its own axis, a further motion of revolution about the Sun, not to speak of even a third motion of the Earth's axis which we know Copernicus introduced. For the present he was certainly not prepared to extend his theory of "neutral" motions to all of the motions required by the Copernican system. Galileo must have sensed, again *intuitively*, that it was necessary to construct a new theory of motion which was completely detached from that of Aristotle. Undoubtedly, this gave further impetus to those studies of motion which he had already undertaken and which he will continue, as we shall see, during his years at Padua. For the present, however, Galileo was in the dark. In all probability he preferred to stop there with no plans to construct at that time his own world system to replace that of Copernicus which he was not yet able to prove. Thus, for him during his years at Pisa there was to be no system of Tycho and no semi-Copernican system. He would just wait until things became clearer, even though he would lean towards thinking that the truth stood on the side of Copernicus.[42]

Let us turn now to his teaching at the University of Pisa. The first biographers of Galileo spoke of the bitter arguments and clashes between the new professor of mathematics and his colleagues who taught Aristotelian philosophy. In particular, Viviani asserts:

> . . . and then, to the great discomfort of all the philosophers, through experiences and sound demonstrations and arguments, a great many conclusions of Aristotle on the subject of motion were shown by him to be false . . . he showing this by repeated experiments [esperienze] made from the height of the Leaning Tower of Pisa in the presence of other professors and all the students. (XIX, 606; trans. by Drake 1978, 19-20).

This account of Viviani has been taken up by later biographers of Galileo and they have embellished it with details, with the result that discredit has been cast on the authenticity of these "experiments" of Galileo at the Tower of Pisa. And many modern biographers consider the account to be pure legend. Recently, however, Drake has supported the credibility of Viviani's account and asserted that Galileo could really have wanted to give demonstrations of something with which he was already familiar on the basis of the conclusions he had drawn from his studies on motion. For the moment the conclusions were restricted to bodies with the same specific weight which fall in a surrounding medium such as air.[43]

Even putting aside the historicity of these experiments of Galileo, his critical attitude towards the theory of motion of Aristotle would not have gone unnoticed by teachers of Aristotelian philosophy. And this certainly did not in general help to maintain good relationships between Galileo and these philosophers.[44] Also his open-minded attitude with respect to certain academic customs, as wearing the toga,[45] would not have endeared him to his colleagues. Furthermore, Galileo had given an unfavorable opinion about a mechanism invented for the harbor at Leghorn by the illegitimate son of the Grand Duke, Giovanni de' Medici, thus gaining the hatred of that illustrious personage.

And so, having come to the third year of his teaching (1592), the prospects for an extension of his contract with the university were scarce. Furthermore, with the death of his father, Vincenzio, in June of the previous year Galileo, as the first-born son, found himself with the responsibility for the economic well-being of the family. With the quite meager salary which he received and without prospects for any sensible increase in the near future (even should his contract be renewed) the young professor undoubtedly must have become convinced of the need to look for a position in another university.

As I have already noted, Galileo had for some time aspired to teach at the most prestigious Italian university of that epoch, Padua, where the chair of mathematics had been vacant since 1588. Once again Galileo had recourse to the help of his friends. Guidobaldo del Monte and the Genovese G.V. Pinelli (1535-1601), who was living at that time at Padua and had great influence in the cultural circles of the Republic of Venice, gave their weighty support to the application of Galileo. During the first part of September Galileo himself went to Venice so that he might become known to persons in authority in the Venetian Republic on which the University of Padua depended. The impression he made must have been a good one because on the 26th of that month Galileo received an appointment to professor of mathematics with a four-year contract, renewable for another two years at the pleasure of the Doge and with a salary of 180 florins.

Since he was a subject of the Grand Duke of Tuscany, Galileo had to get his permission to go to Padua. The Grand Duke, perhaps convinced that it would be no great loss to allow the young and not yet very well known professor to take up service in the Venetian Republic, granted him permission with no difficulty. A little later, towards the end of the year 1592, Galileo arrived at Padua.

5.   *The beginning of his teaching career at Padua*

. Galileo was twenty-eight years old when he began teaching at Padua and he stayed in that city for eighteen years up until 1610. Thus, it was a long stay and Galileo will later write of it as the best period of his whole life (XVIII, 209). Undoubtedly, this happy experience of Galileo was noticeably influenced by the atmosphere of political and intellectual freedom, of fine manners and of open hospitality which were characteristic of the Republic of Venice to which Padua belonged.

The Venetian Republic was still, towards the end of the XVI century, the only State in Italy which could boast a completely independent political life and it was one of the richest in all of Europe. Long centuries of maritime trade, wise economic policies, and an efficient form of government, whereby the power of the Doge, elected by a large number of noble families, was tempered by the "Council of the Ten" and by the Senate, had favored the accumulation of immense wealth. Indeed, the first signs of decadence, which will become patently clear beginning with the first decades of the following century, were already present. The continuing expansion of the Turkish Empire and the competition in trade with France, and progressively with England, were little by little creating a crisis for the strong net of business relationships with the Near East which Venice had established over centuries. On the other hand, the discovery of America (1492) and the opening of sea routes to the Orient with the circumnavigation of Africa were slowly but persistently displacing the Mediterranean from the central position for European trade which it had held previously.

But Venice still showed enough vitality and initiative to confront these growing difficulties. Thus, that Venetian Republic, in whose territory Galileo began his new work,[46] was still the powerful, glorious and very rich "Serenissima".

In importance Padua was the second city of the Republic to whose territory it had been annexed in 1405. Even though it was politically a subject of Venice, it enjoyed sufficient autonomy and was a populous and rich city, favored by its position at the center of the routes which linked Venice to the rest of the Italian and European states. Also its mild climate and abundance of water allowed an intense growth in agriculture.

But, without a doubt, that which made Padua famous, not only in Italy but in all of Europe, was its university. The "Studium" of Padua had been founded when the city was a commune in 1222 and was, therefore, one of the oldest of

Europe. After it came under the control of the Venetian Republic, the University of Padua had gradually become one of the most renowned centers of European culture. At the time of Galileo it was passing through a certain crisis due to the rise of new universities in Europe with the result that the number of students attending the school at Padua was on the decrease.[47] But it still remained as an important center and academic activity stayed at a high level, thanks to the high standards for the choice of professors, to the excellent libraries and to the generous financial support provided by the Venetian Republic.

That which undoubtedly contributed to the renown of the University of Padua was a profound sense of respect for freedom of opinion and of teaching. This, of course, did not stem the tide of lively discussions, but they were always tempered by the innate Venetian sense of good manners. This traditional spirit of tolerance made it possible, among other things, for the Protestant students to pursue their studies without interference, even though that was an age of severe religious contention. And this tolerance was strongly supported by the Venetian Republic. The Republic certainly did not compromise when it came to matters considered to be unequivocally heretical. Six months before Galileo's arrival in Padua, Giordano Bruno had been imprisoned, as we have seen, in the Inquisition prisons in Venice precisely because he was suspected of heresy. But even in that case, it took months of negotiations before the Venetian Republic condescended to the request to have Bruno consigned to the Roman Inquisition. And the final decision in this matter (7 January 1593) was undoubtedly determined more by the conviction on the part of the authorities of the Republic that his opinions were really and gravely heretical than by the fact that he was not a citizen of Venice.

But when it came to matters where opinions were not clearly heretical, especially in the case of teachers at the University of Padua, the Republic was firmly dedicated to the defense of the freedom of opinion of those who came under suspicion. A case in point is that of the famous Aristotelian professor, Cesare Cremonini (1550-1631), whose treatment is in clear contrast with that accorded to Giordano Bruno. Despite the outright accusation of atheism, he not only succeeded in avoiding any condemnation, but he was constantly held in greatest esteem by the Republic and he carried out his teaching without interference up until the time of his death.[48]

At Padua Cremonini was the most authoritative exponent of the so-called "Paduan Averroism"[49] which was looked upon with great suspicion by the theology professors who judged it as tending to be contrary to the faith. But, despite the polemics and the accusations, the Aristotelian Averroists continued to have a great influence on the University of Padua at the time that Galileo taught there. Their influence was most felt in the field of natural philosophy and Galileo must have had to watch out for reactions from his Aristotelian colleagues. As I have noted, the University of Padua was much more open than that of Pisa. While, therefore, there may not have existed at Padua the danger of being opposed as he was at Pisa, there was the problem of the loss of prestige as a professor, should he have expressed too forthrightly his criticism of an Aristotelianism which still enjoyed such great authority. Prudence was, therefore, required and Galileo was well aware of that fact.

But if at Padua, as in a large number of European universities of those days, Aristotelianism was the accepted theoretical basis for the natural sciences, a flourishing experimental tradition also existed at the very core of the medical school at Padua. Towards the middle of the XVI century one of its most famous professors had been the Belgian Andreas Vesalius (1514-1564) who had carried out the dissection of cadavers during his lectures on anatomy. At the time of Galileo, the tradition of the practical study of anatomy had been brought to life by the famous anatomist, physiologist and embryologist, Gerolamo Fabrizio di Acquapendente (1533-1619) who became Galileo's personal physician.[50]

As I have said, Galileo held his inaugural lecture on 7 December 1592 and on the 13th of the same month he began his ordinary lectures which, according to Viviani, were attended by a great number of students (XIX, 628). Although it might be a bit exaggerated, it is certain that the time for the lectures in mathematics (three o'clock in the afternoon) was arranged so as to accommodate the attendance of both the students of philosophy and those in medicine (X, 264) and, therefore, the number of those who took the course must have been noteworthy.

We do not know exactly what Galileo taught in his first year. But the matter treated in subsequent years is well known. Thus in 1593-1594 he taught the *Sphaera* (as usual the treatise of Sacrobosco) and the *Elements* of Euclid; in 1594-1595 the fifth book of Euclid and the *Theoricae Planetarum* (the theory of the planets according to Ptolemy); in 1597-1598 the *Almagest* of Ptolemy; in 1598-1599 the *Elements* of Euclid and the *Quaestiones Mechanicae*, at that time attributed to Aristotle; in 1599-1600 and in 1603-1604 again the *Sphaera* of Euclid; in 1604-1605 again the *Theoricae Planetarum* (XIX, 118-120).

As we see, geometry and astronomy were at the center of his teaching which stayed at a modest and completely traditional level. This was also due to the fact that Galileo had among his students, as I have already said, the medical students for whom the study of astronomy was principally directed to supplying them the fundamental notions for the practice of astrology. In fact, despite the new experimental tendencies in medicine, every respectable doctor of those days had to be able to compile horoscopes.[51]

At any rate, Galileo's treatment of astronomy was restricted to the mathematical aspects of that science. The philosophical or "cosmological" aspects belonged to the professors of philosophy, who treated it in their commentaries on the *De Coelo* of Aristotle.

At Padua, just as at Pisa, Galileo taught (in public as well as in private lectures) Ptolemaic astronomy, as is proven by the *Trattato della Sfera o Cosmografia* of which there remain various copies written by the disciples of Galileo (one of whom claims to have had an original written by Galileo himself). This *Trattato della Sfera*, which was published in 1656 after the death of Galileo, is a further reworking of the tract *De Mundo*, composed while he was at Pisa, and just like the latter it betrays an undeniable dependence on the *In Sphaeram Joannis de Sacro Bosco Commentarius* written by Clavius.[52]

This public and private teaching of Ptolemaic astronomy does not at all imply that Galileo had put aside his preference for Copernicanism. He continued to consider it to be more

probable than the system of Ptolemy, even if, in the absence of
proofs, he preferred to keep a prudent reserve.[53]

6.   *The first idea of a possible "proof" of Copernicanism*

        Truly enough, the idea of a possible proof of Copernicanism
had come to Galileo already during the first years of his stay in
Padua. In fact, it was in all probability about 1595 that Galileo
began to think of an explanation of the phenomenon of the tides
(which were much more obvious in the upper Adriatic, and in
particular at Venice, than in the Tyrrhenian and the rest of the
Mediterranean) as an effect of the double movement of the
rotation of the Earth as claimed by the theory of Copernicus.[54]
The point of departure for this concept, which Galileo will
develop further in succeeding decades to the point of making it
the central theme of the *Dialogue,* can be traced, as Drake
has   made   clear,[55] in a succinct summary of it given in a
notebook of the Servite, Paolo Sarpi (1552-1623). Sarpi, a friend
of Galileo right from his first days in the Venetian Republic, was
most probably not a Copernican. His mention of the double
movement of the Earth, as a source of the tidal motions, should
not, therefore, be seen as an expression of his own personal
conviction. Rather Sarpi must have put down the argument just
as it had been communicated to him by Galileo.[56]
        Was this sudden intuition,[57] that it might be possible to
explain the tidal movements in terms of Copernicanism,
sufficient in itself to have made Galileo a thorough-going
Copernican? Drake says yes and thus he would set 1595 as
Galileo's "conversion" to Copernicanism. But it seems to me that
Galileo by temperament did not tend to sudden conversions.
Without a doubt, he knew that he would have to work more
seriously on the Copernican explanation of the phenomenon of
the tides before he would have a convincing proof. And, in fact,
this work will continue at intervals until he completes the
Dialogue in 1632. That first sketch of the theory, which he had
settled upon about 1595, must certainly have convinced him that
Copernicanism was highly probable. But a complete and
definitive adherence to heliocentrism by Galileo will occur only

later and not on the basis of the theory of the tides, but as the result of his discoveries with the telescope.

That Galileo by now considered the system of Copernicus to be much more probable than that of Aristotle-Ptolemy is confirmed by a letter which he sent in May 1597 to his old colleague at Pisa, Jacopo Mazzoni. At the beginning of that year Mazzoni had published a book entitled *In universam Platonis et Aristotelis philosophiam*, which included an argument against Copernicus. After having read the book Galileo judged the argument to be erroneous and explained his opinion in a frank manner to Mazzoni:

> But to tell the truth . . . I have been left . . . confused and intimidated upon seeing Your Most Worthy Excellency so resolute and frank in opposing the opinion of the Pythagoreans and of Copernicus concerning the motion and location of the Earth; . . . and Your Excellency's reasoning has made me prick up my ears all the more since I have held the very opinion to be much more probable than that of Aristotle and Ptolemy and I have some feelings on this and other matters that flow from it. (II, 198)

As the letter proceeded Galileo went on to criticize the argument which Mazzoni had championed against Copernicus.

In this text Galileo speaks of Copernicanism as "much more probable" than the system of Aristotle-Ptolemy. And he adds that he has "*qualche umore*" (namely, some idea not altogether clear but which remains for the present only as a "feeling") as to the motion and location of the Earth and as to other arguments that flow from it (very likely an allusion to his theory of the tides). Certainly, it can be accepted that Galileo, so as not to hurt his friend, wanted to soften his expressions in support of the theory of Copernicus. But it seems to me that the way Galileo expresses himself indicates quite well the degree to which he was also persuaded of the truth of that theory.

An apparently more explicit declaration of Copernicanism is found in a second letter sent by Galileo in August of that same year 1597 to Kepler, who the year before had published his *Mysterium Cosmographicum*. Two copies of this work were brought to Italy by a friend, Paul Hamberger, and delivered by

him to Galileo. That must have happened through the initiative
of Hamberger himself, because at that time Kepler knew nothing
of Galileo. However that might be, Galileo felt the need to thank
Kepler for his book and so he wrote him the aforementioned
letter in which he says:

> To now I have only seen the preface of the book, but from
> it I have come to know in some fashion the way you think;
> and I am certainly delighted to have such a companion in
> the search for the truth. And, in truth, it is something to
> be pitied that there are so few lovers of the truth who do
> not pursue a degraded way of philosophizing. But now is
> not the moment to deplore the miseries of our times but
> we should rather compliment you for the marvelous
> discoveries you have made in confirmation of the truth.
> Therefore, I can only add that I promise to read your book
> with pleasure and with the certainty to find therein most
> wonderful things. And I will do this all the more willingly
> since I have already for many years come to accept the
> Copernican opinion and with this hypothesis have been
> able to explain many natural phenomena, which under the
> current hypotheses remain unexplainable. I have written
> down many proofs and have undone the contrary
> arguments, but I have not yet dared to make these known
> because I have been frightened by the fate of our master
> Copernicus, who, although he gained an immortal fame
> among some, with an infinite number of others (how
> numerous are the stupid ones) he has been pushed aside
> and scorned. I would certainly not hesitate to put my
> thoughts out there, if there were more people around like
> you, but since there are not, I will forbear doing so. (X,
> 68).

As we see, Galileo seems in his letter to distinguish two
stages: the one whereby he had arrived many years ago at an
opinion concerning Copernicanism and the one which led to the
explanation, on the basis of that former opinion, of many
"natural phenomena". If these last words, as is highly probable,
refer to the theory of the tides, which goes back to two years
previous, his having come many years before to an opinion
concerning Copernicanism must have occurred quite a bit earlier.

But we have already seen how in his time at Pisa he had probably already begun to tend towards Copernicanism. Galileo's statement, therefore, in this letter to Kepler seems to refer precisely to the time of his teaching at Pisa.

We must note, however, the cautious way in which Galileo expresses himself also in this text: "Copernican opinion" and "this hypothesis". And this squares with what he had declared in the letter to Mazzoni where he also points to the Copernican theory as an "opinion of . . . Copernicus" and he describes it as "much more probable" than that of Aristotle and Ptolemy.

In conclusion, it appears that Galileo's tendency towards Copernicanism, which, with his reading of the *De Revolutionibus*, had begun more as an instinctive preference than a reasoned one, became progressively stronger. This was due first to his discovery at Pisa that it was possible to speak of a rotational motion of the Earth (in the way I have explained) and then at Padua with the idea that Copernicanism might be confirmed with the phenomenon of the tides. But Galileo was well aware that the elements in favor of Copernicanism, which he had dimly foreseen, still remained in the state of initial hints which would require a great deal more work. In order to come to a full acceptance of the Copernican vision of the world Galileo would have to detach himself completely from Aristotle's theory of natural places and motions in such wise as to be able to speak not only of a rotational motion of the Earth on its own axis at the center of the world, but also of a motion of revolution about a Sun which then became the new center, at least approximately, of the world. And that implied creating a new theory of motion. As to the idea of the tides, Galileo was well aware of the need to deepen it so that he could transform it into a scientific argument in favor of Copernicanism. For the present he could only describe the Copernican theory as an "opinion" and think of it as "much more probable" than the traditional view of the world. To have certainty Galileo would still have to wait many years, until the end of his stay at Padua.

As we have seen, in his letter to Kepler Galileo underlines the fact that his public silence with respect to his Copernican "convictions" was due to a fear of being mocked and spurned. It is likely that he would have especially feared such treatment on the part of his colleagues who were professors of philosophy. To speak in public, or even more so in his classroom lectures, in favor of Copernicanism without being able to bring forth convincing proofs would have provoked the most severe criticism on the part of those teachers of philosophy who enjoyed (as did Cremonini) great prestige and who would have been able to throw a bad light on the young professor before the academic authorities and thus perhaps compromise his position at Padua. And this Galileo had to avoid at all costs.

This posture of Galileo, whereby he publicly taught Ptolemaic astronomy but in his heart already professed Copernican ideas, has often been criticized, generally by authors not well disposed towards Galileo.[58] But, leaving aside the fact that such criticism is too facile in ignoring the practical reasons which I have mentioned previously, it seems to miss the deeper meaning of this silence of Galileo's. In my opinion his silence is also, even above all else, a proof of the seriousness of Galileo in his scientific work. Contrary to what has been so many times repeated by his detractors, by temperament Galileo was far from the kind of person who would throw himself without reflecting into the defense of new ideas. Even after he saw intuitively the truth of a theory, scientific rigor kept him from drawing hasty conclusions. Later on we will have the opportunity to see how Galileo often resisted the urgings of friends who considered him to be too prudent and would have wanted him to take a position too hurriedly. And we have already seen that even at Padua he was aware that he did not yet have sufficient "proofs" to motivate him to accept Copernicanism unconditionally.

Kepler replied two months later in October 1597 to Galileo's letter. He was happy, he wrote, that this correspondence had begun and he encouraged Galileo to proceed courageously and he also suggested to him that he eventually publish his writings in favor of Copernicanism in Germany, should he find it difficult to do so in Italy. And he asked Galileo to carry out careful measurements to detect, if possible, the parallax of two fixed stars which he had indicated, supposing that Galileo would have precise instruments available to him.

On the other hand Kepler did not ask him for any details about the "natural phenomena" in support of the Copernican theory to which Galileo had made reference. With remarkable perspicacity he had intuited that it was, as a matter of fact, the phenomenon of the tides, as we know from a letter he wrote in March of the following year to a friend of his in Munich (X, 72).[59]

Galileo never answered this letter of Kepler. His enthusiasm for the *Mysterium Cosmographicum* must have waned considerably after he had read the first pages. Kepler's abstruse style and his way of permeating his thoughts with concepts which did not seem to have much to do with science, at least as Galileo understood science, must have made him in a certain way uneasy with the German astronomer and he will remain uneasy in this respect throughout his life.[60] Even afterwards, when they again take up correspondence after a silence of thirteen years, Kepler will be consistently the one who shows a greater readiness to carry on their relationship than does Galileo. The only exception is the period which follows immediately upon the publication of the *Sidereus Nuncius*, and we will see why that is so.

Another letter which Galileo never answered is the one sent to him by Tycho Brahe in May of 1600, three years after that of Kepler. As we know from a preceding letter of Brahe, written in January of that same year of 1600 to Vincenzo Pinelli (X, 78-79), Brahe's son-in-law and disciple, Francesco Tengnagel, had gone to Italy in the autumn of 1599 hoping to meet Pinelli himself at Padua, but without success. Instead he met Galileo at that time and, according to Brahe, Galileo had given indications that he intended to write to the Danish astronomer. Brahe added the words: ". . . if at that time he had written to me (as he had promised) he would not have found me reluctant to respond. He may still want to write to me at some other time". But, since Galileo made no move to write, Brahe decided to take the initiative. From this letter of 4 May 1600 (X, 79-80) we now know that Galileo told Tengnagel that he had read Brahe's work, *Epistolarum astronomicarum libri* (published four years previously) and that he wanted to talk to him about it. On his part Brahe was continuing to make reference to his astronomical system by underlining the advantages that it had with respect to both the Ptolemaic and Copernican systems and he invited

Galileo to discuss with him any point that he might find interesting.

Why is it that Galileo never answered this letter which, coming from the most famous astronomer of that time, should have flattered him? According to Favaro these two letters of Brahe, as well as the ones sent at the same time to Magini and to Clavius, were written with the intention of attracting some support, even some praise, from eminent Catholic astronomers and mathematicians in order to strengthen his position with the Catholic Emperor. After all, even though a famous astronomer, Brahe was a Protestant. According to Favaro Galileo must have seen through this maneuver of Brahe and decided, therefore, not to respond. But perhaps Galileo's assertions to Tengnagel had been dictated out of simple courtesy and he had never really had any intention of setting up a correspondence with the author of a world system which must have seemed to him to be a compromise without any real physical significance.[61] We will have many opportunities to reconsider this instinctive intellectual aversion of Galileo for Brahe's ideas. This is only the first manifestation of it and over the years it will continuously grow deeper. Not infrequently it will lead him to forget or even to underestimate the great worth of the Danish astronomer.

7.   *The Nova of 1604 and a new attempt at a «proof» of Copernicanism*

It was only in 1604 that Galileo first publicly expressed a criticism of Aristotelian cosmology, disproving, although perhaps in an indirect way, the Aristotelian theory of the incorruptibility of the heavens. In that year there was observed throughout Europe a "new star", called for its position in the sky *Stella Nova Serpentarii*, and it created an enormous interest of the kind that since time immemorial was associated with the appearance of unusual celestial phenomena. The interest was first of all a practical one, in the sense of astrology, because portents in the sky were looked upon as warning signs of very important, and generally ill-omened, events on the Earth such as wars, earthquakes and epidemics. But there was also a speculative interest among specialists and educated people. In fact, as we have already seen with the *nova* of 1572, the appearance of a *nova* caused a serious problem in terms of the Aristotelian doctrine of the incorruptibility of the heavens. The *nova* of 1604 remained visible for a year and a half and was observed by the most famous astronomers and astrologers in Europe, including Kepler.[62] The *nova* was seen for the first time at Padua on 10 October 1604, but Galileo personally observed it only on 28 October (II, 279). Right away the correspondence between him and his friends becomes full of news with respect to this phenomenon in the skies as we can see from the replies sent to him by his friends. Unfortunately, the letters of Galileo have been lost, except for one letter written in January 1605 but left in the form of an incomplete rough draft (X, 134-135). In a short while we will return to speak of this document and of its importance for Galileo's thinking at this period.

At that same time, Clavius again took up affairs with Galileo and sent him his *Geometria Practica* which had been published at Rome in that very year. With it he included a letter in which he excused himself for his long silence and showed his wish to continue their past friendship. He then asked Galileo if he had observed the *nova* and requested that he would send him any data he might have on it (X, 120-121).[63]

Considering the great public interest Galileo could not refrain from taking up the argument on his own account. He probably did so with three lectures in November, but all that remains of them is the beginning and a fragment towards the end. Added to these are some notes on the observations and studies carried out by Galileo in that period together with some material on opinions about the *nova* of 1572, especially those of Tycho Brahe. But the rough draft of a letter of Galileo, which I have referred to above, and the reports of the lectures given by him, contained in some books published at that time (among them is one by Galileo himself using a pseudonym) allow us to reconstruct with sufficient verisimilitude the content of the lectures themselves.

Relying on his own observations as well as on those of his correspondents in other cities, Galileo had substantially asserted that, since no parallax effect had been noted during the period of the observations of the *nova*, it must lie "much higher than the Moon's sphere" (X, 134).[64]

As we know, the observations of Tycho Brahe and of many other astronomers at the time of the *nova* of 1572 made it clear that there was no parallax and thus they had already shown, at least to anyone open to accept their results, that the Aristotelian doctrine of the incorruptibility of the heavens could not be upheld. As I have already noted, Galileo in preparing his lectures had very diligently gathered together the names of these astronomers and their opinions, quoting especially Tycho Brahe by referring undoubtedly to his book, *Astronomiae instauratae progymnasmata* which appeared posthumously at Prague in 1602 (II, 283-284).

Galileo did not deal in his lectures with the Copernican question because there was no direct connection between it and the interpretation of the *nova*. But, for sure, even if he did not mention it in public he must have thought to himself of this relationship. Some indication of this is given by the fact that among the materials which he assembled for his lectures Galileo also puts a quote of the Latin philosopher Seneca where the opinion of the Pythagoreans and of Aristarchus on the motion of the Earth is given.[65]

We do not know how much these public lectures of Galileo contributed to heating up the discussions which were already taking place concerning the *nova*. On the one hand, there were the Aristotelians, who wanted to reduce it to being a meteorological phenomenon, and then there were the opponents who argued for its heavenly nature.[66] Among the die-hard defenders of Aristotle's position at Padua Cremonini stood out. He was almost certainly the inspiration, if not personally the author, of the *Discorso intorno alla Nuova Stella* (Discourse on the *Nova*), which was published at Padua in 1605 under the name of Antonio Lorenzini. The work criticized, among other things, the use of arguments drawn from the lack of parallax, which Galileo had used to deduce that the *nova* had to be located well beyond the sphere of the moon. According to Lorenzini-Cremonini one could not apply to the celestial realm either a method, such as that of the parallax, based on sense experience or mathematical rules which were valid only for earthly phenomena. In fact those procedures contradicted the most fundamental (and thus undeniable) philosophical principles which proved the essential difference between the realm of the Earth and that of the heavens.[67]

Galileo was probably aware of the true authorship of the *Discorso* and he hurried to join in the fun by responding with his own *Dialogo* written in the dialect of Padua under the pseudonym of Cecco di Ronchitti (II, 309-334).[68] In this *Dialogo* he expresses his reservations about the Aristotelian notions of the distinction between the realm of the Earth and that of the heavens, of the incorruptibility of heavenly bodies, and of the impossibility of a natural circular motion of the four elements. In this respect he made reference to the opinion of "some men of letters who claim that the Earth goes round and round like a mill stone" (II, 322).[69] Then the *Dialogo* deals at length with parallax showing that its use is also legitimate with respect to celestial objects and it distinguishes three different types of parallax. This last distinction seems in a special way to be linked to an attempt to interpret the phenomena connected with the *nova* in a Copernican sense.[70] This appears to be confirmed by two inserts which are contained in the *Dialogo* and are favorable to Copernicanism.[71]

But in what way had Galileo seen this relationship between Copernican theory and the *nova*? Drake proposes the following interpretation.[72] Because the *nova* had continuously diminished in brightness since Galileo had first begun to observe it,[73] he hypothesized that this was due to the progressive movement of the *nova* away from the Earth. And that motion must have been along the line of sight of the observer, because that was the only way that the lack of parallax could be explained. Now, if this decrease in the apparent brightness of the *nova* had continued for six months when the Earth, in the Copernican system, would have been in the opposite part of its orbit about the Sun, the parallax effect would have been large enough to be observed.[74] Such a measurement would have confirmed the movement of the Earth and would have been an undeniable proof of Copernicanism. According to Drake, Galileo was confident of a positive outcome to his suggestion and thus

would have added the two insertions I have mentioned in favor
of Copernicanism.[75]

The importance which Galileo attributed to the *nova* as a
way of proving Copernicanism seems to be confirmed by the
draft of the letter of January 1605 which I have recalled above.
In it Galileo begs pardon of his correspondent (probably
Girolamo Mercuriale) for having failed to send him a copy of the
three public lectures and he explains why, by the fact that he
had in the meantime considered expanding the discussion of the
nova. Here is his own explanation:

> Because I too, among so many others, have had the idea to
> submit to the judgement of the public what I think not
> only about the location and motion of this light but also
> about its substance and its origin and because I believe I
> have found an opinion which contains no obvious
> contradictions and which, therefore, might be true, it has
> been necessary for me, so that I might be sure of myself,
> to go ahead slowly and await the return of this star in the
> east after its separation from the Sun, and to observe
> again very diligently what changes it might have
> undergone both in its location as well as in its visible
> brightness and the quality of its light; and continuing my
> speculations about this marvel, I have finally come to
> believe that I could know something more than what ends
> in mere conjecture. And because this fantasy of mine draws
> out, or rather puts forth, most weighty consequences and
> conclusions, I have resolved to change my lessons in one
> part of the discourse, which I am now elaborating in
> regard to this material. (X, 134-135).

Undoubtedly the phrase,"most weighty consequences and
conclusions", is an allusion to a proof of Copernicanism[76] which
at that time, when Galileo was still intent in writing down the
"discourse" mentioned above, must have been seen by him as an
extraordinary possibility which could make its author famous.

Why is it that this letter was never finished (the last words
are those given above) and thus never sent to the addressee?
And why is it that the "discourse" promised by Galileo in that
letter was never published? Is it possible that Galileo had in the
meantime begun to have doubts? The much awaited parallax

effect was never seen. On the other hand Galileo was never truly certain "about the location and motion of this light" nor "about its substance and its origin", despite his statements in the letter.[77] For all of these reasons he had continued to seek information on the *nova* as seen in the letters he sent at that time to his correspondents in Verona (see X, 122 ff.).

The *Dialogo di Cecco* was reprinted at Verona probably about the middle of 1605. Drake emphasizes the fact that in that reprinting almost nothing is modified with respect to the original text except for two insertions which change from being in favor of Copernicanism to being against it.[78] According to Drake it is likely that such changes were made by Galileo himself. And, based on this supposition, he deduces that in the meantime Galileo, not having been able to discover any parallax effect for the *nova*, had very likely lost faith in Copernicanism[79] and had gone back to the semi-Copernican phase to which he, still according to Drake, had arrived during his time at Pisa.

I must admit that these conclusions of Drake do not appear to me to be sufficiently warranted. First of all, it would be necessary to prove that the changes inserted in the reprint of the *Dialogo* are really the work of Galileo. Drake admits that there is no real proof, but he still thinks it most likely. Secondly, even if Galileo is responsible for the changes, that would not necessarily prove a loss of faith in Copernicanism. Admitting that he had hoped to obtain a proof of the Copernican theory by discovering a parallax for the *nova*, the failure to do so must surely have been disheartening for Galileo. And perhaps he felt the need for a greater reserve in his statements. The changes in the reprint of the *Dialogo* could thus be explained as a "rhetorical" expedient to avoid the possible criticism of having previously attempted a Copernican interpretation of that heavenly phenomenon.[80]

On the other hand, if our conclusion is correct about the stage at which Galileo's thought had arrived at this time of his stay at Padua, then at the time that the *nova* appeared he still considered Copernicanism to be only "more probable" than the system of Aristotle and Ptolemy, but not outright proven. It, therefore, seems to be a bit too strong to speak of a "faith" in Copernicanism which he would have lost in the sequel. Without a doubt the failure in his attempt to use the *nova* as a proof of Copernicanism had left him perplexed. In this regard Drake finds it curious that from this failure Galileo did not draw the conclusion that the *nova* was located in the sphere of the fixed stars (thus explaining the absence of a measurable parallax) and so would have retreated from the idea that its decrease in brightness was due to its increasing distance from the Earth.[81] It seems to me that the last explanation was the least fanciful for that time[82] and that once Galileo had that idea he would have found it rather difficult to put it aside. Faced with the lack of a parallax, he now preferred an intermediate solution placing the *nova*, ever since its first appearance, quite a bit higher than all of the planets. This enormous distance, even ignoring any increase in it due to further separation from the Earth, was sufficient to explain the lack of parallax. This seems to be confirmed much later on by Galileo in his *Dialogue* when, in regard precisely to this *nova* of 1604, and also to that of 1572, he has Salviati say: "they are without any contradiction most high above all of the planets" (VII, 76 and 82).

To conclude, it seems to me that at the end of his attempt to give a Copernican interpretation to the phenomenon of the *nova* Galileo was disappointed in his great expectation of finding a clamorous proof of the Earth's movement. But he was not disillusioned with respect to the Copernican theory and, therefore, had no need to go back to a supposed semi-Copernican phase in his thinking, a phase which I do not think he ever had anyway.[83] As before, for Galileo the Copernican theory remained much more probable than the view of Aristotle and Ptolemy. And, lacking a true and proper astronomical proof, there still remained the possibility of a proof based on the phenomenon of the tides. Galileo would have to wait and he knew how to do so, as he will show many other times in his life.

On the other hand, even if Copernicanism was not yet proven, there was a parallel path which one could and must pursue, that of demonstrating the untenability of the Aristotelian view of the world right at its foundation, natural philosophy. Even if his first studies at Pisa on the motion of bodies had not yet implied radical doubts about that natural philosophy, his further studies at Padua had brought Galileo to the growing conviction that as a whole the natural philosophy of Aristotle was showing itself to be unacceptable. An indication of the path he is following is given by the *Dialogo di Cecco Ronchitti* where he questions the distinction between the heavenly world and that of the Earth and suggests that the first is composed of the same four elements as the second and is, therefore, just as changeable. This way of making the world and all it contains homogeneous has a more radical implication, the denial of the whole Aristotelian theory of natural places and motions, thus making possible circular motion about centers different than that of the Earth. And once having admitted that the four elements which composed the Earth were also common among all of the planets, the Sun and the fixed stars, to imagine the Earth as part of the planetary system then ceased to be as obviously absurd a supposition as it was in the context of the Aristotelian view of the world. Thus this new natural philosophy, to which Galileo's path was leading, was beginning to provide the fundamental presuppositions of the Copernican theory which its author, as we have seen, was not in a position to make explicit, nor perhaps even to have contemplated.

It is also for this reason, even especially so, that Galileo, convinced that there could be no other true "system of the world" other than that of Aristotle-Ptolemy and that of Copernicus, will carry along throughout his life two complementary programs of research: that of a direct proof of Copernicanism and that of constructing a new "natural philosophy", opposed to that of Aristotle, which would lay the foundations in physics for Copernicanism and thus open the way for its acceptance.[84]

Since he lacked for the present a direct proof of Copernicanism, Galileo must have felt that it was all the more important to continue his studies of motion, which in fact during this period at Padua developed well beyond his first attempts at Pisa, bringing him to conclusions which he will take up again in a systematic way in his *Discorsi* of 1638. Of particular importance are his studies on the isochronism of the oscillations of a pendulum[85] and those on falling bodies.[86]

8.   *Private teaching and activities in technical matters*

    But Galileo's scientific activity at Padua was not limited
only to the field of theoretical studies. As I have already
remarked, Galileo had both the temperament and the kind of
education which led him to combine speculative interests with
practical and technical ones. To this natural propensity there
was the further consideration that he had to teach privately in
order to increase his income in view of the burdens, sometimes
weighty ones, that came from his family. In these lessons
attended by many students, in addition to the teaching of the
Sphaera or *Cosmographia* (of which I have already spoken) and
of arithmetic and geometry, Galileo treated questions to do with
the techniques for fortifications and on military architecture, as
well as topics in optics and mechanics.[87] Galileo had the notes
for these courses distributed for student use in manuscript form.
    Galileo's interest in technical matters must have been
encouraged by his frequent visits to the famous Arsenal in
Venice where some of Europe's most competent shipbuilders
were working on the constructions of marine vessels.[88] The value
which Galileo placed on the technical and experimental aspects
of science is also proven by the fact that he constructed at his
home in Padua a small shop where he conducted experiments
and constructed instruments such as square rules, compasses,
and marine direction finders.[89]
    Among these instruments we should especially remember
the geometrical military compass, because of its originality as
well as for the polemics that it aroused. It was a particular type
of ruled calculator. Such instruments were well known and used
at that time, but the one which Galileo made by employing a
new, very practical idea enjoyed great success. Since it was being
ever more widely used, in 1606 Galileo published a small work
entitled, *Le operazioni del compasso geometrico e militare* (The
Operation of the Geometrical and Military Compass), in which
he explained how to use the instrument. The work was dedicated
to the young prince, Cosimo de' Medici, the son of Ferdinand,
the Grand Duke of Tuscany.
    This   publication   was   impugned   by   the   Milanese
Baldassarre Capra[90] with a booklet written in Latin a few

months later in which he claimed precedence over the instrument for himself and his own mathematics tutor, Simon Mayr. Galileo, aware of the intention of Capra to discredit him before the authorities of the University of Padua and thus seriously threaten his academic career, replied immediately bringing legal action against him for plagiary. The judgement was totally in Galileo's favor and Capra was publicly condemned. But Galileo felt it necessary to respond also in writing to the work of Capra, lest it would get circulated without a sufficient distribution of the condemnation. In this long work, entitled *Difesa contro alle calunnie et imposture di Baldessar Capra* (A defense against the calumnies and impostures of Baldessar Capra, II, 515-601) Galileo gave a first taste of the polemical power, at times implacable, that his prose could generate.

Another field of practical interest for Galileo during his years at Padua was that of the construction of magnets. After the publication of the fundamental work *De Magnete* of the Englishman William Gilbert (1600), interest in magnetism had led to a real mania for the collection of magnets. Along with his great admiration for the English scientist Galileo also showed widespread reservations with respect to many of his ideas. The concepts of "attraction" and of a "magnetic fluid" seemed especially to be leftover ideas from magic rather than true scientific concepts.[91] These reservations, however, did not keep him from developing a deep interest in the phenomena of magnetism. Galileo once again showed his mechanical talents by resolving the problem of ways to get armatures which could increase the force of the magnet. And so he produced magnets of great power, some of which he succeeded in selling for no small profit.

As a final note on the technical work of Galileo during these years I mention the construction of an apparatus for indicating temperature (thermoscope) which took place between the end of 1606 and the beginning of 1607. Even though it was quite imperfect it bears witness to the very widespread scientific interests of Galileo and, at the same time, to the awareness he had gained of the importance of measuring instruments in scientific research.

But without a doubt the most important instrument by far to come out of Galileo's shop was the telescope, whose construction was the result of his technical skills put at the service of his interest in observations and which allowed him to realize the most spectacular phase of his scientific activity. But I will speak of this in the following chapter.

9.   *Friends and family affairs*

The discussion thus far of the activity of Galileo at Padua is certainly not adequate to describe in sufficient detail all of the various experiences, both happy and sad, which were part of this period in his life. I wish to dwell for a moment on two points in particular which are important in any evaluation of the richness of Galileo as a human being. These are his friendships and the vicissitudes of his family.

We have already alluded to the cordial general atmosphere that characterized the relationships among the professors at the University of Padua, even among those who held quite diverse opinions. We have a typical example in the friendship of Galileo with Cesare Cremonini. Despite the irreconcilable contrasts as to their philosophical ideas, they were of mutual help to one another in difficult times. More important, without a doubt, was the friendship between Galileo and Paolo Sarpi (1552-1623). Sarpi entered the Order of Servites as a very young man and he had held important offices while being very active in areas of theology and politics. He had sided with the Republic of Venice in the serious issues that had arisen between the Republic and Pope Paul V.[92] Sarpi also had a deep interest in science which he had studied and in which he had acquired a reputation far superior, it seems, to his actual abilities. Galileo himself had a great admiration for him. I have already mentioned the probability that about 1595 Galileo had explained to Sarpi his first idea of a proof of the movement of the Earth based on the phenomenon of the tides. It is likewise important to recall the significant letter that Galileo wrote to him in 1604 with respect to the law of falling bodies. These friendly relationships with Sarpi carried over naturally to similar relationships with Sarpi's most faithful disciple and his successor as consultor to the

Venetian Republic for theological questions, Father Fulgenzio Micanzio (1570-1654).

Given the position taken by Sarpi and Micanzio in the dispute between the Republic and the Pope, it was inevitable that they would find themselves more and more in opposition to the Jesuits, the defenders of Papal authority. The influence that this anti-Jesuit attitude of Galileo's friends might have had on him during his period at Padua is difficult to evaluate. According to Favaro,[93] at any rate, right from the beginning of his work at Padua Galileo personally witnessed the polemics between the university authorities and the Jesuits, who were trying to establish a center for higher studies in the same city of Padua. But all of the reconstruction and interpretation of the facts of the case given by Favaro, an admittedly great historian of Galileo, seem to be influenced by the spirit of his times and, therefore, must be reevaluated.[94] At any rate, as Favaro himself admitted, it does not seem that Galileo had anything to do with the movement against the Jesuits which, again according to Favaro, was headed by Cremonini.

After the expulsion of the Jesuits from the Republic of Venice (1606) anti-Jesuit sentiments must have continued to grow and even other friends of Galileo, especially Sagredo, were not sparing in their darts of ridicule against the "Rocco Berlinzone" (a nickname applied to the Jesuits by their adversaries). By temperament Galileo would perhaps not have felt much sympathy for the Jesuits and he probably joined his friends in the gibes and jokes, and even the criticisms, against them.[95]   But he certainly at the same time maintained an esteem for the culture and the preparation in the sciences of the members of this religious order, especially of Clavius and his followers. On the other hand, others of Galileo's friends, such as Pinelli and Paolo Gualdo, were ardent supporters of the Jesuits and they undoubtedly must have helped Galileo preserve a sufficient equanimity with respect to that religious order.[96]

We have already mentioned Sagredo. Without a doubt, Gian Francesco Sagredo (1571-1620) was for Galileo the dearest friend he had of all of those of his time at Padua. Galileo immortalized his name in the *Dialogo sopra i due Massimi Sistemi* (Dialogue on the Two Chief World Systems) and afterwards in his *Discorsi e Dimostrazioni Matematiche intorno a' due nuove scienze attenenti alla Meccanica e ai movimenti locali* (Discourses and Mathematical Demonstrations about two new sciences belonging to Mechanics and local motions). Despite the many public offices he held, Sagredo nourished a lively interest for science and technology and he often brought friends together at his home on the Grand Canal in Venice to discuss a wide variety of topics.

Galileo's extremely rich personality, the acuteness and unfettered nature of his ideas, the brilliance of his conversation, all of these not only attracted to him friends and admirers from among the more educated and influential persons in the Republic of Venice, but also won him many enthusiastic disciples who often remained loyal to him for all of their lives. As we have seen Galileo did not neglect private teaching, which at that time was widespread at Padua as in other European universities. Undoubtedly there was a financial motive involved. But his own disciples and the numerous boarding students who lived at his house bear witness to the fact that he never showed a wish to profit from these lessons with the sole intention of making money. On the contrary, his generous hospitality and the cordial atmosphere he was able to set up in their regard left a profound impression upon those young people who came from practically all parts of Europe.[97] Particularly noteworthy among these disciples is Benedetto Castelli. He was born at Brescia about 1580 and became a Benedictine monk. Castelli began his stay at Padua in 1602 and he studied with Galileo from 1604 to 1606. As he himself will recall some years later in a letter to Galileo, he was encouraged by Galileo to take up the study of geometry and philosophy (X, 482). The meeting between the two of them at Padua signalled the beginning of a deep and faithful friendship which would not dwindle even in the most difficult moments of Galileo's life.

Galileo found another devoted student in the person of the young Prince Cosimo, son of the Grand Duke of Tuscany, Ferdinand. Even though he lived at Padua, Galileo never had the intention of distancing himself forever from his native land. On the contrary, he returned to Florence regularly during the summer vacations, unless he was prevented from doing so by some important business. During these stays at Florence, at least from 1605 on, he had begun to teach mathematics to the young prince and was given hospitality by his mother, the Grand Duchess Christina of Lorraine (X, 215 and 217). The lessons to the prince included instructions in the use of the "geometric and military compass" and that explains the dedication to Cosimo of the booklet written by Galileo on that matter. Thus a relationship of esteem and friendship grew between Galileo and his illustrious disciple, who was destined to succeed quite soon to his father as the Grand Duke of Tuscany. This relationship will have a profound influence on developments to come in Galileo's life.

As to family affairs during his time at Padua they were marked by continuing economic worries for the care of his mother, brother, and sisters. His sister Virginia married in 1591 and Livia ten years later. In both cases Galileo had to take upon himself the grave burden of the dowries and this absorbed for many years the greater part of his income.

At Padua Galileo had a long relationship with a Venetian woman, Marina Gamba, whom, however, he did not marry, nor did he, for appearances sake, live with her. Galileo had three children by Marina Gamba: Virginia in 1600, Livia in 1601 and Vincenzio in 1606. When, as we will see, he left Padua in 1610, he did not take Marina with him. As a matter of fact her presence at Florence would not have failed to create problems for him in his new role of mathematician and philosopher of the Grand Duke. Since, however, his son Vincenzio was still quite little, Galileo left him with his mother, but he took Virginia with him. Livia was already with her grandmother at Florence. According to Favaro this separation between Marina Gamba and Galileo took place in a friendly fashion and Galileo kept up correspondence with her and with Giovanni Bartolucci, whom Marina later married. She continued to have charge of Vincenzio for many years.[98] Recent studies, however, have shown that Favaro fell into error by confusing Marina Gamba with a totally different person, Marina Bartolucci.[99] The first Marina would have died a few years after the departure of Galileo. In his application of February 1619 to the Grand Duke Cosimo II for the legitimization of his son Galileo asserts that the mother of

Vincenzio, Marina Gamba, was "unmarried [at the time of Vincenzio's birth], never married later on and by now deceased" (XII, 441). It is likely that Vincenzio was entrusted to Marina Bartolucci after the death of his mother.

Thus amidst sad and happy events, theoretical studies and technical activities, hours of teaching and those of relaxation,[100] the first seventeen years of Galileo's stay at Padua passed by. Those were years that, without a doubt, must have seemed to him, by now 45 years old, rich both in what was accomplished and in the promising future. But not even in his wildest dreams would he have been able to imagine what the last year of his days in Padua had in store for him. There was to be a decisive turn of events in his own life and, in many respects, in the history of Western thought. It was to bring Galileo indisputable fame, but it will also act as a prologue to the unfolding drama of the second, briefer but much more intense, part of his existence.

NOTES

[1] In the first half of the XV century a member of the family, Galileo, had been a well known doctor and had held important public offices. The inscription on his tomb, still visible in the Church of the Holy Cross in Florence, remembers him as: "*Magister Galileus Galileis, olim Buonaiutis*". Therefore, the family name "Galilei" must have replaced that of "Buonaiuti" during the second half of the XIV century. It is likely that the name "Galileo" was given to his firstborn son by Vincenzio with the intention of recalling that illustrious ancestor. We will see how, as his son grew, Vincenzio dreamt that he would follow the same profession. For the genealogical tree of Galileo see XIX, 15.

[2] The *Camerata Fiorentina* was made up of a group of *literati* and musicians who met in the house of Count Giovanni Bardi in Florence. It was within this group that the theory of "drama in music" was formulated. It was based upon the incorrect opinion that ancient Greek tragedy was sung. The Italian melodrama developed at a later stage from that theory.

[3] See Drake 1970a.

[4] Flora 1953, X.

[5] According to the reports of an abbot of that monastery, Diego Franchi, who died in 1652, Galileo had even been a novice. But it

appears that his father, not at all happy with his son's presumed vocation, used the excuse of an illness of the eyes to bring him back home.

⁶ There remain about 120 treatises which bear his name. They are included in the Latin-Greek edition of C.G. Kuhn (22 Volumes: Leipzig, 1821-33).

⁷ See Wallace 1984a, 220. The *Sphaera* was a medieval treatise composed by the Englishman John Holywood (from which the name Sacrobosco) who taught astronomy at Paris towards the middle of the XIII century. It appears that the *Theorica Planetarum* was written by an unknown author between 1260 and 1280 with the purpose of correcting the defects of the last volume of the *Sphaera*. For the content of these two treatises see Pedersen and Pihl 1974, 252-253. At the time of Galileo the professor of mathematics was Fantoni; for the material taught by him see Wallace 1984a, 93.

⁸ Vincenzio Viviani was born at Florence in 1622. He was recommended to Galileo by the Grand Duke Ferdinand II because of his propensity for mathematics and he lived with Galileo at Arcetri as his disciple and helper from 1639 until Galileo's death. After the death of Evangelista Torricelli (1647) he was appointed mathematician to the Grand Duke. He published many books on mathematics and he contributed to the first (partial) edition of the works of Galileo (1655-1656). At the invitation of Prince Leopoldo of Tuscany he wrote the *Racconto istorico della vita del Sig.r Galileo Galilei* (1654). Upon his death (1703) he left in his will a sum of money for the construction of a burial monument to Galileo in the Church of the Holy Cross in Florence. Niccolò Gherardini was born about 1600. He had a degree in law. He lived in Rome at the time of the 1633 trial of Galileo and tried to be of help to him. When he moved close to Florence, he remained in contact with Galileo and in the course of various conversations with him he gathered biographical information which later on he made available in writing to Viviani for the book which I mentioned above. He died in 1678. The *Racconto istorico* is found in XIX, 597-632. The biographical information of Gherardini, under the title *Vita di Galileo*, is found in the same volume, 633-646. For a quite dismal picture of university instruction at Pisa in Galileo's time see Garin 1965, 124-125.

⁹ It seems that Ricci was a disciple of the famous algebraist Nicolò Tartaglia (1500-1557), the author of the first translation into a modern language (Italian) of the *Elements* of Euclid (1543). In that same year Tartaglia had also published a selection of texts of Archimedes: *On Bodies in Water* and *On the Equilibrium of Plane Figures*. Undoubtedly Ricci must have introduced Galileo to these texts of Archimedes and Galileo will make use of them, as we shall see, in

his first writings on hydrostatics and on the barycenter of solid bodies, as well as in his later writings on motion.

[10] The Grand Duke generally moved with his court to Pisa from Christmas to Easter. This custom was also part of the strategy of conciliation of the Medici with respect to the people of Pisa.

[11] Drake asserts that Vincenzio had threatened not to support his son for another year at Pisa with the consequence that Galileo had composed during that period a collection of courses under the title of *De Universo* with the hope of being able to teach natural philosophy and thus have secure financial support (see Drake 1990, 44). We will have an occasion to come back to these affirmations of Drake, which do not appear to be convincing.

[12] *La Bilancetta* was first published in 1644. It is found in I, 215-220.

[13] These theorems are found in I, 187-208.

[14] The Roman College began in 1551 as "a school of grammar, humanities and Christian doctrine" in a modest house in Rome. It grew very rapidly into a university center which rivalled the University of Rome (*La Sapienza*). In 1583 it was moved to an imposing edifice which had been constructed during the pontificate of Gregory XIII. See Villoslada 1954.

[15] See D'Elia 1960. On the Jesuit mathematicians see MacDonnell 1989.

[16] In a copy of the treatise *In Sphaeram* of Clavius (1570 edition), kept in the library of the diocesan seminary in Padua, there appears the following note on a fly-leaf: "Father Christopher Clavius began to explain to me the Sphere at Tivoli on 19 August 1578". Since an important copy of the *Dialogo*, the property of Galileo himself, is preserved in that same library (see Bellinati 1984, 127) in addition to other books of his it was logical to ask the question, as does Bellinati, as to whether the copy of the *In Sphaeram* had not also belonged to him, and, furthermore, whether the note in question had been written by him. Thanks to the kindness of Monsignor Bellinati I have been able to examine a photostatic copy of the note. But even after a careful comparison of the script with that of the first letter known of Galileo, of which I have spoken above, and with numerous other handwritten texts of Galileo I have not been able to come to a certain conclusion with respect to the authorship. The difficulty of attributing it to Galileo is complicated by the fact that one would have to suppose that Galileo made a mistake in writing 1578 instead of 1587. (In 1578 he would have been only 14 years old). It also seems improbable that Galileo would have spent some days at Tivoli at the time of his visit to Rome and that he would have received from Clavius such a special favor. In

fact, if such were the case, a mention of it ought to have been made by Galileo in the above-mentioned letter to Clavius. It seems more likely that the copy had originally belonged to one of the Jesuit disciples of Clavius who was with him in August 1578 in the vacation house which in fact the Roman College owned at Tivoli. Father Colpo of the Historical Institute of the Society of Jesus in Rome has kindly communicated to me this latter information. In order to explain that that copy later belonged to Galileo, it would be sufficient to suppose that, having been returned to Clavius, it was given by him to Galileo when the latter visited Rome in 1587. If we accept this hypothesis (putting aside the question as to whether the note is in Galileo's handwriting), one can obtain a confirmation of the year in which Galileo composed his first summary of astronomy (*Tractatio de Mundo et de Coelo*), which clearly depends, as a matter of fact, on the *In Sphaeram* of Clavius. See Note 31 to follow.

[17] On the respect which Galileo had for Clavius, see the words with which, in the letter I have mentioned above, he subjects himself to the opinion of the Jesuit mathematician.

[18] One such personage was Tycho Brahe who sent a long letter to Clavius in January 1600 and never received an answer from him. See Norlind 1954.

[19] His familiarity with the *Divine Comedy* of Dante is shown by his two lectures *Circa la figura, sito e grandezza dell'inferno di Dante* (On the figure, location and dimensions of Dante's Inferno) given by Galileo in 1587-1588 at the Florentine Academy. In those lectures Galileo defends the hypothesis, put forth in the last years of the XV century by Antonio Manetti, about the place, dimensions and form of the Inferno of Dante. He showed that he had a complete knowledge of the text as well as the mathematical skills to solve the problems which were implicit in Manetti's interpretation. See the text of these lectures in IX, 31-57.

[20] The application in the name of Galileo speaks of him as "a youth about 26 years old". He was actually only 23.

[21] According to Drake this would have been the time when Galileo studied both the *Almagest* and the *De Revolutionibus* of Copernicus (see Drake 1990, 51). Galileo never finished this work on the *Almagest* perhaps because in the meantime, as we will see, he was changing direction towards Copernicanism.

[22] See I, 245 *Avvertimento*.

[23] There is only a brief description and extract in IX, 291-292. According to Favaro Galileo would have written these questions on logic when he was at Vallombrosa (see IX, 279).

[24] Today these are called *De Motu Antiquiora* or "Pisan *De Motu*". Both the *Juvenilia* and the *De Motu* are found in Volume I of the National Edition.

[25] The studies under discussion were begun almost simultaneously in the late 1960s by A. Carugo and A.C. Crombie, by F. Fredette and by W. Wallace. Carugo and Crombie 1983 have shown how the *Tractatus de alteratione*, the *Tractatus de elementis* and the *Tractatio prima de Mundo*, all contained in MS 46, are based on works published by two Jesuit professors at the Roman College, Benito Pereira (1576) and Francisco de Toledo (1579 and 1581), while important parts of the *Tractatio de Coelo*, which also belongs to MS 46, come from the second edition (1581) of Clavius' *In Sphaeram Johannis de Sacro Bosco commentarius*. Subsequently Carugo has shown that there exists an obvious, at times even word for word, correspondence of the *Disputationes* (a commentary on the *Analytici Posteriores* of Aristotle), contained in MS 27, with the treatise, *Additamenta ad F. Toleti Commentaria una cum Quaestionibus in Aristotelis Logicam* (1597), of Ludovico Carbone, an alumnus of the Roman College. For his part F. Fredette dedicated his attention to the sources and to the sequence of composition of MS 46. As to Wallace, his research confirmed the previous results of Carugo and Crombie on the relationship of MS 47 and MS 71 to the printed works of Pereira, de Toledo and Clavius, but he also made clear that other possible sources for those manuscripts might be found in the *annotationes* (hand-written lecture notes taken by students as dictated by the philosophy professors of the Roman College) which still exist. As to MS 27, Wallace has highlighted how Carbone was accused by the Jesuit Paolo della Valle (in his Preface to the two volumes of his *Logica*, published in 1622) of having copied straight out the *annotationes* of his course in logic at the Roman College (1587-1588), changing only the order and that without acumen. Wallace, relying on these statements of della Valle, thinks that Galileo might have used the original *annotationes* of della Valle instead of those of Carbone which came ten years later. This would allow putting the composition of MS 27 at about 1589-1590 and that of MS 71 and MS 46 at about 1590-1591. Undoubtedly this dating would have the advantage of coinciding with the one placed at an old date by an unknown hand on the booklet containing MS 71: "about the year 1590" (I, 9.).

[26] Galileo must have sensed this lack of an adequate knowledge of logic at the time that Clavius and Guidobaldo del Monte were questioning him on the theorem of the barycenter which he had sent to them. See Wallace 1984a, 91 ff. and 224-225. Galileo himself, as

Wallace 1984a, 227 notes, is very critical of the way in which logic was taught during his studies at Pisa (see I, 285).

[27] Galileo did not simply limit himself to copying these notes by changing the words to suit his needs and summarizing the text of Valla. He rather also introduces, here and there, variations which are extremely interesting from the point of view of the development of his thought towards Copernicanism. See Wallace 1984b, 31 ff.

[28] As we have already mentioned in Note 25, Carugo and Crombie base their argument on the fact that MS 27 shows an undeniable agreement with Carbone's text , published in 1597. They do not accept Wallace's supposition about Galileo's use of the *annotationes* of della Valle which no longer exist and they comment that it is much simpler to suppose that Galileo had made use of a printed text which was, therefore, easily found, rather than of *annotationes* which it would have been much more difficult for him to obtain.

[29] See A. Carugo and A.C. Crombie 1983, p. 58 ff.

[30] Wallace's supposition that Galileo used the *annotationes* (hand-written notes) of della Valle instead of Carbone's printed work might appear to be gratuitous, since the *annotationes* have been lost. But, besides the resemblance in their content, the fact that there exist differences in the ordering of the texts between Carbone's and that of MS 27 while the ordering of the latter coincides with that of the *Logica* of della Valle (see, for example, Wallace 1986, 12-13) agrees with della Valle statements about the disordered plagiarism of Carbone and seems, therefore, to make the hypothesis of a direct use by Galileo of della Valle's *annotationes* less implausible. For sure, there is no trace whatsoever in Galileo's correspondence with Clavius of the dispatch of such *annotationes* nor of others by Clavius. But Galileo could have obtained the *annotationes* in other ways (see Wallace 1981, 240, Note 69). Recent studies by U. Baldini make quite plausible the hypothesis that della Valle, who taught theology at Padua from 1590 to 1600 and then philosophy at Venice from 1600 to 1602 or 1603, could have had contacts, as did other Jesuits, with the circle of Vincenzo Pinelli who lived at Padua from 1558 until his death in 1601. As we shall see Galileo also frequented that circle. So, if he had not had them before from Clavius, he could have obtained the *annotationes* on logic directly from della Valle at the beginning of his time in Padua (Baldini 1992, 369 ff.).

[31] The attribution to MS 71 of a date later than that for MS 27, thus placing MS 71 in Galileo's teaching period at Padua, is based on the supposition that in the composition of his writings he followed the traditional order whereby the material on logic came before that of natural philosophy (the material, in fact, of MS 71). But such a

supposition is open to discussion and moreover requires putting off for almost ten years the composition of the notes which, at least as to the *Tractatio de Coelo*, would have instead been very useful beginning right from the time of his astronomy instruction at Pisa. And there still remains the fact of the old dating of MS 71, "about the year 1590" (see Note 25), which I do not think should be neglected. There is also the dating offered by Galileo himself for the composition, at least, of the *Tractatio Prima de Mundo* (I, 27). In his computation in that *Tractatio* of the time from the creation of the world to the year in which he is writing Galileo states in the final part that from the birth of Christ to the destruction of Jerusalem 74 years had gone by and he adds: "*illinc usque ad praesens tempus 1510*" (from then up to the present time 1510 [years]). If we take this statement literally, MS 71, or at least the *Tractatio Prima de Mundo*, would go back right to the year 1584, as Favaro contends (I, 11-12). For an attempt to interpret these statements of Galileo so as to take this writing also back to about the year 1590 see Wallace 1981, 219-225. Moreover, as to the even later date of MS 46, this is brought forth only as an hypothesis by Carugo and Crombie, based upon the relationship which that manuscript is said by them to have with *La Bilancetta* and with *Le Meccaniche* of Galileo. But besides the difficulty, which these authors recognize, of coming to satisfactory conclusions on the dating of these two works, the statement of the problem of the motion of falling bodies given in MS 46 and the solutions proposed therein seem to me to indicate a beginning stage in Galileo's thought, before his time in Padua. The majority of Galilean scholars are also of this opinion (see, for example, Drake 1990, 47 ff.). For a critique of the chronology proposed by Carugo and Crombie 1983 of Galileo's writings see Wisan 1984.

[32] On the various possible factors that motivated Galileo to compose these notes in natural philosophy see Wallace 1984a, 94 ff. As for the interest of Galileo not only for natural philosophy, but also for philosophy in general, we have already recalled at the beginning of this chapter the testimony of his oldest biographers, Viviani and Gherardini. A clear confirmation of it is contained in the letter which Galileo will write in May 1610 to Vinta, the Grand Duke's Secretary of State, with the purpose of being appointed as mathematician to the Grand Duke: "finally, as to the title and the description of my service, I would wish that, in addition to the name of mathematician, Your Highness would add that of philosopher, since I can claim to have studied more years of philosophy, than months of pure mathematics" (X, 353). Of course, Galileo was referring here, first of all, to natural philosophy, which we call science today. But in those days science was intimately associated with philosophy in general and Galileo would certainly not have shared

the idea of science divorced from philosophy or even in outright opposition to it, an attitude which is so frequently found among contemporary scientists.

[33] Ms 46 contains in the last eight pages an extended series of "Pensieri e Frammenti" (Thoughts and Fragments, Favaro) or "Memoranda" (Drake) on motion which show a close relationship to the questions on motion in Ms 71. They are found in I, 409-419. According to Drake 1990, 50, these "Memoranda" go back to 1587.

[34] The notes from the courses in natural philosophy of the professors of the Roman College which Galileo possessed also contained problems on motion, which ordinarily followed upon the treatise on generation. See Wallace 1984a, 149 ff.

[35] See Drake and Drabkin 1969.

[36] See Drake 1990, 53. This tract is found in I, 251-340.

[37] In the "Pisan De Motu" (I, 326) Galileo quotes the De Revolutionibus of Copernicus with respect to a mathematical problem. This seems, as a matter of fact, to indicate that he had read that work carefully.

[38] In the Tractatio de Coelo (I, 47-50) Galileo had described the reasons for not accepting the Copernican system. These were based upon the teaching of the Jesuits at the Roman College and, in particular, Clavius. However, he apparently wishes in this text to avoid taking too definitive a position on the matter and simply asserts: Haec opinio [of Aristarchus and Copernicus] adversatur communi philosophorum astronomorumque sententiae, et rationi Terram in medio mundi consistere suadenti (This opinion is contrary to the common opinion of philosophers and astronomers and contradicts the reason which leads us to believe that the Earth is at the center of the world). The words: Haec . . . sententiae, are taken verbatim from the In Sphaeram Ioannis de Sacro Bosco Commentarius written by Clavius (1570 or 1581 edition). But, while Clavius promised with additional words to give a "demonstration" of why a heliocentric system was to be rejected, Galileo prefers to speak of the "reason which leads us to believe". See Wallace 1984b, 36.

[39] In fact, this theory presupposed that the Earth was at the center of the universe and was no longer valid in the case of a motion of revolution about the Sun.

[40] See Drake 1987 and also Drake 1990, 56-57.

[41] In fact, at this stage of his thought Galileo was not prepared to give a "physical" justification for the motion of the planets about the Sun (which, in neither Tycho's position nor in that of a semi-Copernicanism, is at the center where instead we have the Earth). In

neither of these two systems of the world could the motion of the planets be considered to be "neutral".

[42] As we shall see, he will say in 1597 that he had accepted the opinion of Copernicus "already for many years", in all probability with reference to his teaching period at Pisa.

[43] See Drake 1978, 19-21. Drake even holds the possibility that Viviani had heard the story which he recounts from Galileo's own lips during the last years of his life. But for a different interpretation of Viviani's account see Segre 1989, 435-451. A thesis like that of Drake is held by Wallace 1986, 26.

[44] An exception is had in the friendship between Galileo and Iacopo Mazzoni (1548-1598) who had become a teacher of philosophy at Pisa a year before Galileo. Undoubtedly Galileo must have been fascinated by the enormous learning of his colleague. In a letter to his father of 16 November 1590 (X, 44-45) Galileo mentions Mazzoni. In 1597 Galileo will send to him an important letter which I will deal with later.

[45] He gives witness of this attitude in his satirical writing, *Contra il portar la toga* (Against wearing the toga; IX, 213-223).

[46] See Bulferetti 1964, 25-28.

[47] From a manuscript in the University Library of Padua we find the following data on the number of students in the second half of the XVI century: 1561, 1210; 1562, 470; 1563, 541; 1564, 727; 1565, 720. See Favaro 1966-1968, Vol. I, 51, note 1.

[48] The accusations of heresy, of having, that is, denied the immortality of the soul, and even of atheism pursued Cremonini for practically his whole career as a teacher at the University of Padua. They brought about in 1599 at Padua a first trial which ended with a simple admonition. In 1604 they were repeated, together with a charge for different reasons against Galileo (see Note 80), and they even arrived in Rome at the Holy Office where the prefect at that time was Cardinal Camillo Borghese, who the year after was elected Pope with the name Paul V. The Holy Office began to take action four years later in 1608. From that time on the charges, trials and self-defenses of Cremonini began to multiply and in 1623 they led to the listing on the Index of his treatise *De Coelo*. In the face of everything the Venetian Republic kept its faith in Cremonini unchanged. For an up to date treatment of the affairs of Cremonini accompanied by some new documentation see Poppi 1993.

[49] On Aristotelianism at Padua see Kristeller 1965, Vol. II, 11 ff. He prefers to characterize it, rather than as "Averroistic" or "Alexandrian", as a "lay Aristotelianism" because it tended to be interested in logic and natural philosophy much more than in

metaphysics and its relationship to theology. Cremonini was, as a matter of fact, a teacher of natural philosophy.

[50] In the history of medicine his name is linked to the construction of the first anatomic theater in the world and also to the fact of having had as one of his disciples the founder of modern physiology, the Englishman William Harvey (1578-1657), who received his academic degree from Padua in 1602.

[51] As a matter of fact, this was also a task for astronomers. Galileo and Kepler prepared horoscopes (almost always in order to augment the meager income which they received from the profession of mathematician). Copernicus is a rare exception in this respect.

[52] The *Trattato della Sfera* is found in II, 211-255. For its dependence on Clavius see Wallace 1984a, 255 ff.

[53] On the other hand this prudent reserve did not mean that Galileo kept completely quiet on Copernicanism. This is shown by the *Trattato della Sfera* itself. With respect to the motion of the Earth he asserts:

> The present question is worthy of consideration, since there has been no lack of the greatest philosophers and mathematicians, who, once having taken the Earth as a star, made it mobile. Nevertheless, following the opinion of Aristotle and Ptolemy, we will adduce those reasons by which we can believe it to be completely stable. (II, 233).

After having given the reasons why the Earth could not have a rectilinear motion, Galileo considers the possibility of it having circular motion:

> But that it could have a circular motion is more than likely and so some have been led to believe it. They were moved to accept it principally by their opinion that it is almost impossible that the whole universe, with the exception of the Earth, would revolve from east to west and return to the east within the space of 24 hours; so they believed that the Earth within that time would more probably take a turn from west to east" (II, 233).

In the following part of this text, Galileo restricts himself to adducing the contrary arguments of Ptolemy without expressing his personal opinion. See for this matter Drake 1978, 54.

[54] On the third movement of the Earth (the precession of its axis), which Copernicus postulated and Galileo deemed not necessary, see the Introduction, Note 33.

[55] The explanation given here follows that of Drake 1978, 36 ff. and 1990, 71 ff.

[56] This seems to be confirmed by the assertion of the biographer of Sarpi, Micanzio, that Sarpi had his own theory of the tides based on a single movement of the Earth. See Drake 1978, 37 and 1990, 72.

[57] On the origin of this intuition see Drake 1978, 37.

[58] See, for example, Koestler 1959, 362-363.

[59] Kepler, however, asserts in this letter that an explanation of the tides must be found on the basis of the moon's attraction. On the meaning of this position of Kepler, which will be criticized by Galileo later on in the *Dialogue,* see Drake 1978, 41-42.

[60] A reflection of this uneasiness is discernible in Galileo's words about Kepler in the *Dialogue.*

[61] On the correspondence of Tycho Brahe with Magini and on the other reasons which might have driven Brahe to write just a little more than a year before his death to Clavius and to Galileo in addition to Magini see Norlind 1953.

[62] Kepler speaks of it in his work, *De Stella Nova in pede Serpentarii.* Following Tycho Brahe Kepler held that the *nova* was composed of material that had condensed in that part of the sphere of the fixed stars and had afterwards, when the star had disappeared, spread out in that same sphere. See Dreyer 1953, 412.

[63] On the occasion of the appearance of the *nova* a conference was held at the Roman College (probably by the young mathematician and disciple of Clavius, Odo Van Maelcote) and the position was taken that, contrary to Aristotle, it was a phenomenon in the world above the moon. See Baldini 1992, 155-171.

[64] In the draft of the letter Galileo had written:

> . . . because for me to simply demonstrate that the location of the new star is and always has been much higher than the sphere of the moon, which was the principal aim of my lectures, is such an easy task and so obvious and common that in my opinion it is not worth getting out of the teaching chair. But it was necessary for me to deal with it for the sake of the young scholars and the many others in attendance who needed to understand geometrical demonstrations, trite and all too familiar for those trained in the study of astronomy. (X, 134).

[65] Seneca wrote in his *Naturalium Quaestionum,* VII, c.2. See II, 283:

> It will be fitting to discuss this also so that we may know whether the world turns with the Earth standing still or whether the Earth moves and the world stands still. In

fact there were some who thought that we were unconsciously carried along in motion by nature and that the rising and setting of the stars is not caused by the movement of the heavens but that it is we ourselves who rise and set. It is worth pondering so that we might know in what situation we really are, that is whether the place assigned us by fate moves very slowly or very speedily and whether God leads the universe around us or us around the Universe.

In the reprinting of the *Edizione Nazionale delle Opere di Galileo* (1968) two drawings by Galileo (II, 621-622) were added. These undoubtedly refer to the *nova* and show clearly the Copernican position taken by Galileo. The words written by Galileo to explain the second of these drawings are reproduced in II, 280, lines 7-9.

[66] This dispute had already begun two years earlier on the occasion of the posthumous publication of the work, *Astronomiae Instauratae Progymnasmata*, of Tycho Brahe in which he asserted, against the basic ideas of Aristotelian cosmology, that neither the incorruptibility of the heavens nor the existence of the celestial spheres could be upheld. This publication had finally begun to provoke a reaction from the philosophers who had largely ignored, even deliberately, the problems raised by the *nova* of 1572.

[67] For a discussion of this point of view of Cremonini see Drake 1978, 106-108.

[68] The draft in the Paduan dialect was the work of Spinelli, a friend of Galileo. But Galileo himself was a passionate devotee of that dialect. See Favaro's comments on this in II, 272. At the same time as this response of Galileo another one appeared, the work of Baldessar Capra from Milan, who was at that time in Padua and was the first one to observe the *nova* on 10 October together with his mathematics tutor, the German Simon Mayr, and a mutual friend. In his *Consideratione Astronomica* (Astronomical Considerations, II, 287-305) Capra declared himself in agreement with what Galileo had said in his lectures concerning the position of the *nova* "in the sphere of the fixed stars". But he was not sparing in his stinging criticisms, even though amidst ceremonious praises, of Galileo, the mathematics professor at the University of Padua, whom he accuses of having been imprecise in describing his observations in his public lectures. Capra added that Galileo's inexactness should be excused especially considering that "one can see already from his writings a not too marked attention to matters mathematical" (II, 292-293). Although wounded in his pride,

Galileo limited himself to the addition of some marginal comments in his copy of the *Consideratione* and he said nothing publicly.

[69] As one can see we are dealing here with a nod towards the motion of the Earth on its own axis, linked, as we know, to the possibility of a "neutral" circular motion of the four elements and their composites.

[70] See Drake 1978, 108-109.

[71] See II, 318, 30-33 and II, 322, 1-3. The words of these inserts are given in note 78. More than explicitly favorable to Copernicanism they seem to favor, respectively, the immobility of the sphere of the fixed stars and the rotational motion of the Earth on its own axis.

[72] See Drake 1978, 109-110 and 1990, 131-132. In the latter work Drake modifies his former opinions.

[73] In the introduction to his public lectures, which has been preserved, Galileo admits that the *nova* had, at the beginning, been increasing in apparent brightness. See II, 277-278. But in the *Dialogo* Galileo asserts, contrary to the declarations of Lorenzini-Cremonini with which his previous statements agreed, that the *nova* had been continuously decreasing: " . . . as for me, I know that the first time that I saw it, it appeared to be extremely bright and then it continued to decrease, so to speak, in brightness" (II, 320). It may be that Galileo had interpreted the initial increase in brightness as associated with the process whereby the *nova* came to be (see Note 74). Once born the *nova* had continuously departed in the direction of the fixed stars and so Galileo was entitled to speak only of a progressive decrease in its brightness.

[74] Obviously all of this reasoning based on the separation of the *nova* from the Earth presupposed that it was not in the sphere of the fixed stars, the boundary of the universe beyond which it was impossible to proceed. In fact, Galileo, seeing that the *nova* had been first observed at the time of the conjunction of Mars and Jupiter and in that part of the sky, must have thought that it had, as a matter of fact, been formed there. The whole argument on the possibility of observing a parallax in confirmation of the Copernican theory depends on that supposition.

[75] See Notes 71 and 78.

[76] In the two drawings mentioned by Galileo and reproduced in II, 621-622 (see Note 65) we have a further confirmation of the fact that the "fantasy" referred to by Galileo in this letter is a Copernican explanation of the phenomenon of the *nova*.

[77] In the *Dialogo* Matteo, who speaks for Galileo, says:

Who, pray tell me, has told him [Lorenzini] that this new star is a real star? Sure it is a bright object, but it is not a star. Even I up until now have called it a star, because, even though it is not one, it appears to be a star like the others. (II, 317).

Matteo's interlocutor, Natale, shows himself (with all good reason) stupefied: "What then is it"? And Matteo answers:

What do I know about it? It's enough that it is not a star, properly so called: and the other stars have never been corrupted, because they are stars, and heaven needs them, for its own reasons: but not this one, which has come and must also go away. (II, 317).

Undoubtedly Galileo had thought of various possibilities as to the "substance and origin" of the "star". Often (as in the letter to Mercuriale) he calls it "light". And in the *Dialogo* he had aired the possibility that "it had originated in the air and then it had gone on rising further up" (II, 317). By now there was no difference in Galileo's mind between the realm of the Earth and that of the heavens and so something born in the air could very well have risen well beyond the sphere of the Moon, even to Mars, Jupiter and beyond. As we will see, Galileo will take up this idea again 13 years later in his sketch of a possible explanation for the phenomenon of comets.

[78] In the original edition of the *Dialogo* in Padua Galileo had said with respect to the opinion that the sphere of the fixed stars did not move: " . . . there are many (*even some capable people*) who believe that it does not move" (II, 318; italics by the author). In the reprinted edition of Verona this is changed to:

. . . a retort could be made by saying this *lie* that heaven did not move not even before it [the *nova*] was born and by quoting as *false* witnesses those of the *Pitarielli* and of the *coperchio di canne* [cane lids], who are lettered people who want to have it [the *nova*] in this way (II, 318).

And in the margin one reads: "He [the author] hints [here] at the Pythagoreans & the Copernicans [*coperchio di canne*]". In the second excerpt in the original edition favorable to Copernicanism, with respect to the natural motion of the elements, which according to Aristotle could not be circular, one reads:

And if I should say the contrary that they also go around? And truly there is no lack of learned people who say that the earth goes round and round like a mill-stone! (II, 321-322).

In the reprinted edition of Verona this insert is also corrected with the addition after the phrase "learned people" of the words "even though they are queer".

[79] See Drake 1978, 110.

[80] Furthermore, the cancellation in the reprinted edition of Verona of the references to the *Dialogo* of Lorenzini-Cremonini, which were contained in the original edition of Padua, could have been motivated by prudence. Galileo had many enemies at Padua and the *Consideratione* of Capra, with its stinging expressions critical of Galileo, was, in fact, an expression of such opposition. Galileo had every reason for not wishing to worsen this opposition, also in view of his reappointment to the chair of mathematics, which was at that moment held in suspense. The preceding "reconfirmation" of Galileo (four years of a "fixed contract" plus two years of an "extension" [at the Doge's discretion]) had terminated in September of 1604 and the subsequent contract would occur only in August of 1606 (see Favaro 1966-1968 Vol. II, 157 and 200). Considering the uncertainty of his position and of a salary increase which he had requested (see X, 105), Galileo had even momentarily considered transferring to the service of Duke Vincenzo Gonzaga at Mantua (see X, 106-107). A further motive for prudence on Galileo's part was perhaps due to an accusation made in his regard to the Inquisition at Padua in April 1604 by a certain Silvestro Pagnoni who had lived in Galileo's house for almost two years working probably as an amanuensis up to January of that year. Pagnoni accused Galileo not only of practicing judiciary astrology but also of firmly believing in it. He also stated that he had never seen him go to Mass, that by the words of his mother he never went to confession or to communion, that he had relations with a "Venetian Marina" [Marina Gamba] and that he read the letters [scandalous!] of Aretino [Pietro Aretino, 1492-1556]. To the question about the company which Galileo kept, he responded that he was seen "with Cremonini almost everyday" (see Poppi 1993, 51-54). This accusation, like that against Cremonini a few days before, was considered to be of no value by the Venetian authorities (see Poppi 1993, 51-54) but it seems that Galileo, once he had become aware of it, felt it necessary to be more cautious. Even though he still occasionally made horoscopes (X, 152-153, 216, 224, 226, 269, 272) it appears that he avoided doing them for pay. In fact, the notes on income gained from horoscopes which are found in the *Ricordi Autografi* (Autographical Remembrances) for 1603 disappear for the following years (XIX, 153-158). As to the *Lettere* of Aretino which had been prohibited, together with other works of his, not long after his death in 1556, Galileo must have gotten rid of them

(supposing that they were his property) because they are no longer found in his library (see Favaro 1886b, 219-293).

[81] See Drake 1990, 132.

[82] Just think, for example, of the explanation given by Tycho Brahe for the nova of 1572, followed by Kepler for that of 1604. See Note 62. Even though Galileo would admit changes in the realm of the heavens and, therefore, in the sphere of the fixed stars, it appears that he had had difficulty in imagining that the "fixed stars" could change. See the text from the Dialogue quoted in Note 77. And so the hypothesis of a "light" of an unspecified nature, whose brightness decreased as a result of its moving away from the zone between Mars and Jupiter where it originated, remained as the most plausible.

[83] On the other hand the two notes added to the reprinted edition at Verona of the Dialogue were against the immobility of the sphere of the fixed stars and against the rotation of the Earth (which was the condition for the former immobility). That is, those notes were not only against Copernicanism but also against semi-Copernicanism. How then would Galileo have been able to go back to a semi-Copernican position once the Copernican "proof" had failed?

[84] There is no better demonstration of the complementarity of these two research programs of Galileo than the Dialogo of 1632 where the discussion of physics is developed just as much as that of astronomy. As we will see, the definitive systematic presentation of his studies on motion in the Discorsi of 1638 after the failure of his Copernican program establishes a further decisive proof of this complementarity.

[85] See, for example, the letter to Guidobaldo del Monte of 20 November 1602 (X, 97-100). It appears that Galileo had begun to think of the isochronism of the oscillations of a pendulum right from the time of his teaching at Pisa (the first idea, in fact, might even go back to the time of his university studies in Pisa). But the first reference made by Galileo himself to these matters occurs in this letter. Even though Galileo was probably not the first to pay attention to this phenomenon, to him without a doubt goes the merit for having drawn the attention of scholars to it and thus having prepared the way for the conclusions of Christian Huygens.

[86] See the letter to Paolo Sarpi of 16 October 1604 (X, 115-116). For a thorough discussion of these studies on motion during Galileo's period at Padua see Drake 1978, 55 ff. and for a more recent and updated treatment see Drake 1990, 9-129.

[87] See Breve Instruzione all'Architettura Militare (Brief Instruction on Military Architecture, II, 15-75), which goes back to the

beginning of his stay at Padua, and the *Trattato di Fortificazione*
(Treatise on Fortifications, II, 77-146), composed a little later.

[88] The inspiration which Galileo drew for his studies from the
frequent visits to the Arsenal is highlighted by him at the beginning
of the *Discorsi* of 1638.

[89] In addition to its scientific interest, there were surely also
financial reasons which motivated this activity of Galileo. In fact, the
sale of these instruments must have helped to augment the ever
insufficient income of Galileo.

[90] See Note 68.

[91] Galileo always nurtured a strong dislike for the concept of
"attraction". It was this that led him to deny that the phenomenon of
the tides could be explained by attraction by the Moon, as many others,
including Kepler, had proposed.

[92] This controversy, which became famous as the "Contesa
dell'Interdetto" (The Interdict Dispute), began in December 1605. The
immediate cause of it was the passage by the Venetian Republic of
laws which placed limits on Church property and the referral to civil
courts of ecclesiastics guilty of common offenses. Pope Paul V had seen
in all of this a violation of ecclesiastical privilege and in April 1606 he
had enjoined the Republic to revoke those laws and provisions under
the pain of an interdict binding on all of the territory of the Republic
and of excommunication for the members of the Senate. On 6 May the
Republic had replied with a public announcement of the Doge in which
the act of the Pope was declared to have been "published against the
form of any natural reason and against the teaching of the divine
Scriptures, of the holy Fathers and the sacred canons . . ., unjust and
unmerited but even more . . . null and of no force, and thus invalid,
void and an illegitimate fulmination". See Cozzi 1979, 166. The
interdict, fulminated by Paul V, lasted until April of the following year
when an agreement was reached which scored a success, although not
so exploited, for the Republic's position. See again Cozzi 1979, 170-171.
During the whole dispute Sarpi had upheld with theological reasons the
Republic's position, while Cardinal Bellarmine had fought back in
support of the Holy See's rights.

[93] See Favaro 1966-1968, Vol. I, Chapter III.

[94] See C. Bellinati 1991.

[95] There is undoubtedly a certain ironic tone in the letter where
Galileo commented on the departure of the Jesuits upon their expulsion
from the Republic of Venice:

Last evening at two o'clock in the morning the Jesuit
Fathers were sent away with two boats, which were to lead

them that night out of the state. They all left with a
Crucifix hung on their necks and a lighted candle in their
hands. . . I believe that they will have also left Padua and
the rest of the state, with much weeping and pain of the
many ladies who are devoted to them. (X, 158).

[96] It was in Pinelli's house, as a matter of fact, that
Galileo first met Cardinal Bellarmine and Cardinal Baronio on their
visit to Venice.

[97] For details on the private teaching of Galileo at Padua see
Favaro 1966-1968, Vol. I, 139-164.

[98] See Favaro 1966-1968, Vol. II, 366.

[99] See C.Bellinati 1991.

[100] Galileo frequently spent times of relaxation in the company
of his friends either at Venice or in one of the lovely villas in the
environs of Padua. According to Viviani (XIX, 624-625) it would have
been precisely during one of these excursions to a villa near Padua that
Galileo contracted a kind of rheumatism that will plague him often
during the rest of his life.

CHAPTER 2

THE TELESCOPIC DISCOVERIES

THE BEGINNING AND GROWTH OF THE CONTROVERSIES

1. *The making of the telescope and the first astronomical discoveries*

For two reasons the year 1609 marks a decisive turn of events in the history of astronomy. The first consists in the publication of the *Astronomia Nova* of Kepler. The second is the beginning of observational astronomy with Galileo's use of the telescope. These two events, completely independent from one another, will be of fundamental importance for eliminating the old view of the world.

Kepler's book contained the formulation of the first two laws of planetary motions.[1] By basing his calculations on the numerous precise measurements of Tycho Brahe, Kepler, after many years of painful attempts at determining the orbit of Mars, finally came to the conclusion that it was not circular but elliptical and that the Sun was located at one of the foci of the ellipse. He subsequently extended this discovery to the orbits of the other planets. Alongside this first law of elliptical orbits Kepler formulated a second one which took account of the variable velocity of the planets in their motion about the Sun.

Thus by doing away with the "dogma" of the circularity of the motions of heavenly bodies, which, as we have seen, was accepted without discussion even by Copernicus, Kepler substantially improved the Copernican system. In fact, on the basis of these two laws the introduction of eccentrics and epicycles became superfluous and the simplicity of the Copernican conception finally became lucidly clear.

Due, however, to Kepler's temperament and his interests, the *Astronomia Nova* contained, alongside brilliant intuitions and rigorous mathematical deductions, a whole complex of considerations which weighed the work down and, considering also its convoluted Latin style, made it difficult to understand. Galileo, who must have already felt quite ill at ease with his reading of the *Mysterium Cosmographicum*, probably never read the *Astronomia Nova* or, if he did, was not prepared to appreciate its value. Consequently, he will, for the rest of his life, be attached to the traditional concept of circular motion and epicycles.[2] On the other hand, it is also true that without the development of a new dynamics it was impossible to draw out the fundamental importance of Kepler's laws, which, as a matter of fact, escaped the notice of most of his contemporaries, including the Jesuits. It will be precisely this development which will provide Newton the possibility of understanding the significance of Kepler's laws and thus lead him to the formulation of the principle of universal gravity and then to the complete physical explanation of the Copernican system.

It was precisely while Galileo remained "conservative" as to the mathematical theory of the motion of the planets that he showed a completely different intellectual openness to the results to be drawn from the revolutionary discoveries he was making with his use of the telescope for astronomical observations.

As we know Galileo was neither the inventor of the telescope nor the first to have the idea of using it for celestial observations. Even if we ignore the much disputed topic as to whether the first telescopes were made in Italy or in England[3] beginning with the end of the XVIth century, it is certain that in 1608 the Dutchman, Hans Lippershey, tried to obtain a patent for a telescope which he made and printed information on this instrument was circulated in Europe. A copy of such information fell into the hands of Paolo Sarpi at Venice in November 1608 and he wrote various letters to obtain confirmation and further details about the invention. Sarpi obtained an answer on these matters from Jacques Badouère who had studied with Galileo at Padua in 1597.

According to the reconstruction of the facts proposed by Drake,[4] Galileo, while he was at Venice toward the end of July 1609, most likely received precisely from Sarpi, if not the first information, at least the more precise details about the telescope. Right in that interval of time a stranger arrived in Padua with a telescope which he intended to sell to the Venetian Republic.

Still following Drake's reconstruction, it would have been this event which brought Galileo to the decision to try to make a similar instrument on his own. Given his previous experience in the construction of lenses and the technical level reached by his laboratory for the construction of instruments, Galileo must have felt almost certain that he would succeed. Upon his return to Padua, he went immediately to work spurred on by the prospect of being able to make a better telescope than the one possessed by the stranger (who in the meantime had arrived in Venice) and, therefore, with better possibilities of making a sale to the Venetian Republic. After some days Galileo would have informed Sarpi that, after many tries, he had succeeded in unlocking the "secret" of the telescope. Convinced of his friend's success, Sarpi would have persuaded the authorities in Venice to turn down the stranger's offer.

However that might be, Galileo went, in fact, to Venice towards the end of August with an instrument which was quite superior to any made up until that time. Upon his presentation of the use of the instrument to several important dignitaries of Venice, Galileo immediately received, as an official recognition of the worth of his "invention"[5] the appointment to a professorship for life and a salary increase from 520 to 1000 florins per year.[6]

Even though his principal motive in making the telescope was without a doubt the "commercial" one (he was always besieged by economic problems), it was certainly due to his taking up this technology that the telescope passed from the level of being little more than a curiosity to becoming an instrument of exceptional scientific value. Furthermore, to Galileo goes the merit of having shown for the first time this scientific (and not only practical) value of the telescope by using it for the observations of celestial objects.

As I have noted above, even with respect to such observations Galileo cannot lay claim to an absolute priority for the idea. Someone came before him, beginning in 1608 if not earlier,[7] but what was involved at that time were observations done by amateurs and reported as curiosities whose importance was not realized. In 1609 the Englishman, Thomas Harriot had attempted to draw a map of the Moon, before Galileo had thought of using the telescope for astronomical purposes.[8] But it was Galileo who understood with a true scientist's intuition the enormous importance of what he was observing.

The first celestial discoveries, which occurred about autumn of 1609, led Galileo to make telescopes ever more powerful. So in November of that same year he succeeded in making one with a 20 times magnification. It will be this instrument which will allow him from December on to carry out more accurate observations of the Moon and which will bring him in January 1610 to the most extraordinary of his discoveries, the satellites of Jupiter.

2.   *The* Sidereus Nuncius *and the plan to return to Florence*

The truly revolutionary importance of the results obtained led Galileo to cut short any hesitation in spreading the news to the educated community of Europe. And so the *Sidereus Nuncius* (Starry Message)[9] was born. It was published in March of that same year and was written in Latin precisely with a view to its distribution throughout Europe.[10] Galileo was even able to include the very latest observations, made at the beginning of that same month.

In this little book of only about sixty pages, which Galileo had dedicated to his former pupil, who by now had become Grand Duke under the name of Cosimo II de' Medici, there were described first of all the observations of the Moon, which proved that the lunar surface was mountainous just like the surface of the Earth.[11]

A second sensational discovery concerned the so-called "fixed stars". An enormous number of otherwise invisible stars, if one observed only with the naked eye, came into view with the telescope. And the "Milky Way", whose nature had been debated since antiquity, was seen to be made up of myriads of stars. The same proved to be the case for certain "nebulae".

But by far the most important result, according to Galileo himself, was the discovery of four planets which revolved around Jupiter. After having provided a detailed report on the observations which he had carried out on them Galileo concluded:

Here we have a valid and excellent argument for quieting the doubts of those who, while accepting with tranquil mind the revolutions of the planets about the sun in the Copernican system, are mightily disturbed to have the moon alone revolve about the earth and accompany it in an annual rotation about the sun. Some have believed that this structure of the universe should be thus rejected as impossible. (III, Part One, 95).

In these words we undoubtedly have the explanation for the extraordinary interest which Galileo attributed to his discoveries. As we have seen in the previous chapter, he had already for many years been persuaded that the Copernican view of the world was by far more probable than the one of Aristotle-Ptolemy. But he was not yet able to justify *physically* this conviction which he had. Now, however, with the telescopic discoveries, a new and completely unexpected way was opening up for him to search for just such a justification. It was the physical way of "sense experience", provided, as a matter of fact, by the new observational instrument.

It had already allowed him to confirm that on two fundamental points the system of Aristotle-Ptolemy could not be upheld. The first point was that of the essential difference (as asserted in that system) between heavenly bodies, including the Moon, and terrestrial bodies. The existence of mountains and valleys and even, perhaps, of lunar seas (as Galileo had at first thought) showed that the moon was essentially composed of the same material as the Earth.

The second was that of the Earth as the unique center of all celestial motions. The discovery of Jupiter's satellites showed that the motions of heavenly bodies could have centers different than that of the Earth. For sure, this last-mentioned discovery was no less consistent with the system of Tycho Brahe than it was with that of Copernicus. But even in these circumstances, Galileo gave no sign of having taken into consideration, even for a moment, the system of the Danish astronomer which will always be for him, as I have emphasized many times already, a purely mathematical compromise without any possibility of a physical justification.[12]

The importance of these discoveries for the Copernican system did not escape Galileo and it was precisely then that he began to conceive the project (as he announced in the *Sidereus Nuncius* itself) of much more extensive work on a "system of the world", which should finally give a comprehensive view of the reasons why the dilemma: the system of Aristotle-Ptolemy or that of Copernicus, could be, in fact should be, resolved in favor of the latter.[13] This "system of the world" was announced to appear "in a short while", but, as a matter of fact, it will not appear until 22 years later and it will be the famous *Dialogue*.

From now on this project will occupy Galileo's thinking and it will determine the future course of his life. As he faced the vastness of such a program of work, with the conviction that he had a "mission" to carry out,[14] Galileo was asking himself in an increasingly urgent manner whether he should accept the appointment for life at the University of Padua with the two-fold increase in salary promised him by the Venetian Republic. He certainly did not underestimate the many positive aspects of his long stay in the territory of the *Serenissima*. On the other hand, teaching took up precious time and even more time was lost with his private lessons and his care for the students to whom he provided lodging in his home. And it was precisely time which was necessary to Galileo at this moment. He needed all the time possible to dedicate to his mission to study Copernicanism. Furthermore, although he obviously could not speak about it, there was another reason for giving up his work as a teacher. Certain as he was by now of the truth of Copernicanism, it would have been increasingly difficult for him to continue to teach the traditional astronomy (as he would have had to do for reasons of prudence).

In a situation like this the idea of moving to Florence must have come spontaneously to his mind. As we have already seen, Galileo had never broken off his relations with Tuscany or with the Medici family. In recent years he had gone back regularly in the summertime to Florence as a mathematics teacher to the young prince, Cosimo, and this had given him the opportunity to improve relationships with the family of the Grand Duke, Ferdinand I, for, as we have seen, those relationships had in the past not always been the best. Just a little more than a year earlier Ferdinand I had died and his son, just turned eighteen, succeeded him. Given the great admiration that Cosimo had always had for Galileo, the latter must have seen in the new situation providential circumstances which would allow him to solve his problem. As we will see, his idea was to obtain from the new Grand Duke a position of mathematician for life with the same salary which the Venetian Republic had decreed for him, but without any teaching obligations. And this would have left him free to dedicate all of his time to scientific research.

There is no doubt that it was with the purpose of preparing the terrain that Galileo had dedicated the *Sidereus Nuncius* to Cosimo II and had given the name of "Medicean satellites" to the four satellites of Jupiter. Furthermore, in homage to the Grand Duke he had sent, together with a copy of the book, also the telescope which he had used for his observations, and he also promised to come soon on a visit during which he himself would have shown to Cosimo II "things of infinite amazement" (X, 302).

In fact, Galileo went to Florence during the first part of April and then proceeded to Pisa where the court of the Grand Duke was at that time. Doubtlessly that visit, added to the previous most gracious acts of homage by Galileo, contributed to strengthening even more the relations between him and his former disciple. Thus Galileo must have concluded that there was no use to interposing any further delays. When he returned to Padua at the end of that same month, he sent off on 7 May a long letter to the Grand Duke's Secretary of State, Belisario Vinta, explaining to him the reasons why he was inclined to leave his teaching post at Padua. It was substantially the wish to dedicate himself completely to scientific research, and in that regard he reported to Vinta the results he had thus far obtained and his future plans. Concerning these latter he wrote that he must bring to completion certain works described as:

> . . . principally two books on the system and constitution of the universe - an immense conception full of philosophy, astronomy, and geometry; three books on local motion, an entirely new science, no one else, ancient or modern, having discovered some of the very many admirable

properties that I demonstrate to exist in natural and forced
motions, whence I may reasonably call this a new science
discovered by me from its first principles; three books on
mechanics, two pertaining to the principles and foundations
and one on its problems . . . (X, 351-352; trans. by Drake,
1978, 160)[15]

In order to carry out this program, Galileo asked whether
it would not have been possible to obtain from the Grand Duke
an assignment which would exempt him from any teaching
obligations.[16]

There is no better indication of the true motivation for
Galileo's decision than this letter. It was certainly not a question
of improving his own financial situation. Galileo, although
accused many times of greediness, shows clearly that he put
pecuniary considerations in second place. If it were merely a
question of money, it would have been better for him to remain
at Padua. The true motive was a scientific one. He wished to be
certain that he would have enough time to dedicate to the very
extensive program he had already begun and to whose
completion he attached the utmost urgency. The great works
which will one day see the light of day, the *Dialogue* and the
Discourses, are already sketched out in this letter, a fact which
indicates how serious, extensive and far-seeing was Galileo's
research program.

The negotiations went forward expeditiously and already on
10 July Cosimo II appointed Galileo "Principal Mathematician
of the University of Pisa and Principal Mathematician and
Philosopher to the Grand Duke of Tuscany", with an annual
salary of 1000 *scudi* and without the obligation of residing in
Pisa or teaching. It was a lifetime appointment.

3.   *The reactions to the* Sidereus Nuncius *and the return to*
      Florence

By this time Galileo was certain of the outcome of the
negotiations and on 15 June he had already resigned from the
chair of mathematics at Padua. The Venetian Republic sought
uselessly to retain him by offering him even further increases in

salary. But Galileo had already decided and his departure took place on 2 August.

Despite promises made to his friends and repeated invitations extended by them, Galileo will never return again to Padua. He was undoubtedly aware that this brusque breakoff of relationships with the Republic had wounded the Venetian authorities, who were certain that they had always dealt with Galileo in the best way possible.

Before following Galileo in his new life in Florence, we should pause to consider the reactions raised by the publication of the *Sidereus Nuncius*. The 500 copies printed at that time were sold in one week, a fact which by itself shows the enormous interest generated by the book.[17] In addition to sending copies to the Grand Duke and to his friend, Castelli, Galileo sent a copy of the book to the Tuscan Ambassador to the Court of the Emperor of the Holy Roman Empire and King of Germany in Prague with the request that he would have Kepler read it, since, as mathematician of the Emperor, he also lived in that city. On 19 April the Ambassador responded to Galileo that Kepler was very pleased with the book, but that he was not able to check Galileo's observations because the telescope that was available to him was imperfect (X, 318-319). On that same day Kepler also sent a long letter to Galileo. After having lamented Galileo's silence, which had lasted for 12 years, and the fact that Galileo had not sent him his opinion on *Astronomia Nova*, Kepler declared that he was convinced of the truth of Galileo's observations and of the correctness of the conclusions contained in the *Sidereus Nuncius*, although he was cautious in the way he expressed himself, since he had not been able personally to verify everything (X, 319-340). A little later Kepler had that letter printed with some modifications. He gave it the title: *Dissertatio cum Nuncio Sidereo* and dedicated it to the Tuscan Ambassador.

If Kepler's position, however prudent, was clearly favorable to Galileo, there were not lacking reactions that were just as hostile. Such, for instance, was the reaction of Magini, who, as we know, was professor of mathematics at Bologna and a renowned astronomer. On his return trip from Florence (24-25 April) Galileo had purposely visited him with the obvious intention of winning the support of this influential professor. But, despite the external politeness, the meeting was not positive. In fact, right from the first news of the astronomical discoveries of Galileo, Magini had assumed a distinctly negative attitude. In addition to being a show of jealousy, his hostility probably flowed from a refusal to accept discoveries which were on the way to undermining the foundations of the astronomical science which Magini had taught until then and in which he had acquired his reputation.

A little before the visit of Galileo, in response to a request by the Elector of Cologne (to whom Galileo had sent a copy of the *Sidereus Nuncius*) to tell him what he thought of the book, Magini had expressed his conviction that both the telescope and the book were nothing other than a trick, and that in any case he had the intention of acquiring a telescope so that he could ascertain everything (X, 345).

At almost the same time Magini wrote to Kepler to request in turn his opinion on Jupiter's satellites (X, 341). On 10 May Kepler answered him with a letter which, for its brevity and dryness, was in contrast with what he had written to Galileo. Kepler limited himself to sending to Magini the *Dissertatio cum Nuncio Sidereo* with the additional remark:

> Accept this and excuse me. Both of us [Galileo and himself] are Copernicans. Like seeks like company. Still I think that if you read it [the *Dissertatio*] attentively you will notice that I have been sufficiently cautious and have recalled him [Galileo] to his very own principles. (X, 353).

But Magini was obviously not able to agree easily with the *Dissertatio*. After having written again to Kepler to give him news of Galileo's visit to Bologna, which I have recalled above, and of the failure of Galileo's attempts to show Jupiter's satellites "to more than twenty very learned persons" present that night at his home (X, 359), Magini continued his campaign against Galileo by alerting the most famous mathematicians of Europe to the latter's alleged discoveries.

Even more openly hostile to Galileo was the reaction of the Bohemian, Martin Horky, who at that time was studying mathematics and medicine at the University of Bologna. He was living in Magini's house and was said to be his disciple. Already in March Horky had sent the *Sidereus Nuncius* to Kepler (even though it appears that Kepler had not received it) and asked his opinion. He was convinced, most probably under the influence of Magini, that the discoveries of Galileo were false and he planned to write against him and his four planets (X, 311). On 27 April in a subsequent letter to Kepler (X, 342-343) Horky also gave him the news of Galileo's visit to Bologna, tracing out a repugnant picture of the physical appearance of Galileo and asserting that he, as well as the numerous others present at that night's observations, were convinced that "the instrument deceived".

In fact Horky wrote the promised book and it came out towards the end of June 1610 with the title: *Brevissima peregrinatio contra Nuncium Sidereum* (A very short excursion against the Starry Message, III, Part I, 129-145). In it Horky attacked Galileo and denied the reality of his discoveries with a tone which shocked even Magini, who chased him out of the house.[18] Kepler, to whom Horky had sent a copy of the pamphlet, also strongly condemned the behavior of the young student and suggested to him that he return to his homeland as soon as possible (X, 419). At the same time Kepler wrote to Galileo on 9 August and encouraged him not to be worried by the stupidities which Horky had written. He also gave Galileo permission to publish this letter if he thought it would be useful (X, 417).

But Horky was not about to give up. Besides seeing that the work was distributed in various European countries, he did not neglect to distribute it also in Italy. He even sent copies of it to Paolo Sarpi and to people in Florence. One of these latter copies was seen by one of Galileo's correspondents, A. Sartini, in the hands of the Aristotelian philosopher, Ludovico delle Colombe (1565-?; X, 398)[19] whom, as we will see quite soon, will become one of the leaders of the anti-Galilean faction in that city. Another copy fell into the hands of Francesco Sizzi, who at just that time was writing a book against Galileo's discoveries. I will speak of this shortly.

As we have seen, Kepler had shown that he substantially agreed with Galileo, but he was not able to check the discoveries himself because he did not have a proper telescope. This kept him from being completely sure of Galileo's discoveries. As he himself had admitted in the letter of 9 August quoted above, the telescope which he had made was not adequate (X, 414). Therefore, he urged Galileo to see to it that others too would be able to confirm his discoveries and so silence his opponents.

On 19 August Galileo answered Kepler and complained about the fact that the most famous of the professors of the University of Padua had outright refused to look through the telescope, despite the fact that he had proposed that they do so "an infinite number of times" (X, 423).[20] But he added that, despite this opposition of the philosophers, the truth of the discoveries had been recognized by many others.

Finally on 30 August Kepler was able to use the telescope which Galileo had sent to the Elector Archbishop of Cologne. After having conducted accurate observations for many days (up until 9 September) Kepler, by this time thoroughly certain that Galileo's discoveries were true, had printed a booklet with the title: *Narratio de observatis a .se quatuor Jovis Satellitibus erronibus, quos Galilaeus Galilaeus Mathematicus Florentinus iure inventionis Medicea Sidera nuncupavit* (A Description of the observations of the four satellites going about Jupiter, which were called by the Florentine Mathematician Galileo Galilei, by his right of having discovered them, the Medicean Stars, III, Part I, 181-188). It contained a full recognition of Galileo's discoveries. Obviously, this definitive stand taken by Kepler in his favor gave great delight to Galileo as he himself stated in a letter of 1 October to the Ambassador of the Grand Duke of Tuscany in Prague (X, 439). The latter showed this letter to Kepler, who wrote again to Galileo on 25 October to tell him that the day before Horky on his way back to Italy had come to visit him, certain to be praised for the victory he claimed to have won in the dispute with Galileo. But Kepler told Galileo that he had strongly reproached Horky and made it clear to him that he was not of his opinion (X, 457 ff.).

As for Galileo, following the advice of Kepler and also because he was busy with the negotiations for his transfer and

then with the move itself, did not answer Horky's *Peregrinatio.*
Instead a reply was given by one of his disciples, the Scotsman
Wedderburn (1584-1651), who was still at Padua and wrote a
refutation of Horky with the title: *Quatuor problematum contra
Nuntium Sidereum Confutatio* (A Refutation of four problems
raised against the Starry Message, III, Part I, 149-178). This
was read and approved by Kepler as we know from a letter of
31 December 1610 which he wrote to Galileo (X, 506-508).[21]

After these repeated interventions of such an authoritative
astronomer as Kepler and the distribution of the telescopes made
by Galileo, which permitted a direct check of his observations,
the opposition, at least in the scientific sector, was on the wane.
Thus Martin Hasdale was able to write to Galileo from Prague
at the end of 1610 that his discoveries were no longer disputed
in that city and that even Horky was by now convinced of his
error, and that he bitterly regretted having printed that book
which had caused him to lose his reputation.[22]

In the meantime, a little before his departure from Padua,
Galileo had made on 25 July 1610 a new discovery, this time
with respect to the planet Saturn. He made mention of it in a
confidential way to the Secretary of State, Vinta, in a letter of
30 July:

> . . . the star of Saturn is not alone but is a composite of
> three, which almost touch one another, nor do they move
> with respect to one another nor change, and they are
> located in a line along the length of the zodiac, the one in
> the middle being about three times larger than the ones at
> each side. (X, 410).

An announcement of the discovery, in the form of a
cryptogram (to prevent anyone from appropriating the priority
of the discovery) was given by Galileo to the Tuscan Ambassador
at Prague. Because the latter was not able, not even with the
help of Kepler, to decipher the cryptogram, Galileo sent him the
explanation on 13 November and indicated his wish to know
what Kepler thought of it (X, 474).

When he arrived in Florence Galileo took up the
observations as soon as he could. Probably during the first days
of October he began to observe also the planet Venus and thus

discovered as the days went by that this planet showed the phenomenon of phases as the moon does.[23]

Galileo immediately understood the fundamental importance of this discovery which could in no way be put into agreement with the astronomy of Aristotle-Ptolemy but proved, as it did, that Venus revolved around the Sun. As possible explanations there remained those of Tycho Brahe and of Copernicus. For Galileo who, as I have emphasized many times, refused to recognize the theory of Brahe as a true alternative to Copernicanism, the only choice was the latter one. The phases of Venus, therefore, constituted for Galileo the first incontrovertible proof of Copernicanism. This conviction of Galileo's is evident from the letter I have just quoted,[24] whereby on 11 December 1610 he reported the discovery, as usual, to the Tuscan Ambassador at Prague.

Meanwhile, towards the end of 1610 another precious support in favor of Galileo's discoveries came to him from the Jesuits of the Roman College and in particular in the person of Clavius. Previously, they had appeared skeptical of Galileo's observations. He had sought to put an end to their skepticism, since he knew quite well how much their opinion counted in the scientific circles of that time. On 17 September Galileo broke a long silence which, on his part, had lasted for 22 years and informed Clavius of his move to Florence and gave him details of his observations. He tried to convince his friend, who was by now quite old, that the weakness of the telescope at Clavius' disposal and the way of using it were the reasons why he could not confirm the discoveries (X, 431-432). But Clavius was not convinced.[25]

Galileo tried an indirect campaign of persuasion by showing Jupiter's satellites to the Jesuits in Florence, who were convinced, according to what he himself reported in a letter of 17 December to his friend in Padua, Paolo Gualdo (X, 484). Obviously, Galileo was hoping that the Jesuits in Florence would not have failed to inform those in Rome of what they had seen with their own eyes.

But there was no need for that. Towards the end of November, by reason of new observations probably made with a better telescope, Clavius had begun to change his mind with respect to Galileo's discoveries. Galileo's friend, Santini, gave him the first word of this from Venice on 4 December:

> Now I can report that Father Clavius in Rome finally writes me that they have observed Jupiter; and I will put below the observations copied right from his letter. (X 479-480).

Clavius had admitted to having observed stars about Jupiter, but he was not sure whether or not they were planets. But at the beginning of December the Jesuit's last doubts collapsed completely and on 17 December he himself so informed Galileo. After having announced to him that he and other Jesuits had seen very clearly the Medicean planets, he added: "Truly Your Lordship deserves much praise since you are the first to have observed this" (X, 484).

As to the news of Galileo's observations of Saturn, which Clavius had received from Santini, the Jesuit mathematician added:

> This [the existence which Galileo had noted of two little stars next to the central one] we have not yet been able to observe; we have only noted with the instrument that Saturn seems to be oblong in this way ◯◯◯. Continue please, Your Lordship, to observe; perhaps you will discover other new things about the other planets. On the Moon, I am very much surprised by its inequality and its roughness when it is not full. (X, 485).

Galileo was, of course, very pleased with Clavius' letter and on 30 December he thus began his answer to him:

> Your Reverence's letter has pleased me all the more since it was so much desired but unexpected; and having received it when I was indisposed and almost confined to bed, it has in large measure lifted me from my illness, since it has brought me the acquisition of so good a witness to the truth of my observations; who once adduced by me has gained some of the unbelievers; but the most obstinate still persist and consider Your Reverence's letter to be either fictitious or to be written

out of sympathy for me, and, to put it the way it is, they are waiting for me to find a way to make at least one of four Medicean planets come down from heaven to earth to certify that they exist and to clear up any doubts. (X, 499).

Galileo added information on the discovery of the phases of Venus and emphasized the extremely important consequences which could be derived from it:

And now you can see, my Lord, how we have ascertained that Venus (and indubitably Mercury will do the same) goes about the Sun, the center without any doubt of the principal revolutions of all the planets. Furthermore we are certain of how those planets are of themselves dark and they shine only by illumination from the Sun (which I do not believe happens, from some of my observations, in the case of the fixed stars); and how this system of planets exists in a different way than has been commonly held. (X, 500).

In this letter to Clavius Galileo had alluded to his poor health. In fact, Galileo, having by then been accustomed to a better climate during those many years in Padua, very much resented the more humid winters in Florence and he spent a great deal of his time in bed. But in January he was able to enjoy some relief from his ills thanks to the hospitality of his friend, Filippo Salviati[26], at the latter's villa outside of Florence where the air was much better.

During that stay Galileo received a letter from Naples from the Dominican Tommaso Campanella[27] who had read the *Sidereus Nuncius* and praised Galileo for having "purged men's eyes and having shown a new heaven and a new Earth on the Moon" (XI, 23). With his acumen Campanella had already intuited the revolutionary nature of the discoveries of Galileo and the use that could be made of them, at least against the world view of the system of Aristotle-Ptolemy.[28] At this time, as well as in the following period, Galileo will, however, maintain a certain reserve towards this Dominican intellectual, whose strange ideas on cosmology he certainly did not share,[29] as he did not those of Bruno.

As opposition in the scientific field was thus slowly losing vigor, due to the positions taken by such authoritative persons as Kepler and Clavius, the same could not be said of the opposition from the philosophical front. We have already seen that Galileo was not able to convince his philosopher colleagues, like Cremonini, at Padua. The latter was convinced that the authority of Aristotle in natural philosophy (and that of Plutarch on the deceptive nature of lenses) was enough to exclude a *priori* any possibility that the presumed discoveries of Galileo were other than an optical illusion, pure and simple. As a friend of Galileo, Paolo Gualdo (X, 100), informed him in May 1611 from Padua, Cremonini also had plans to write various refutations of the assertions of Galileo, but without naming the author (obviously out of respect for the friendship between them, although their opinions on philosophy differed). In the same letter Gualdo added some advice for Galileo:

> As to the matter of the Earth turning around, I have found hitherto no philosopher or astrologer who is willing to subscribe to the opinion of Your Honor, and much less would a theologian wish to do so; be pleased therefore to consider carefully before you publish this opinion assertively, for many things can be uttered by way of disputation which it is not wise to assert, especially when the contrary opinion is held by everyone, imbibed, so to speak, since the foundation of the world . . . It seems to me that you have acquired glory with the observation of the moon, of the four Planets, and similar things, without taking on the defense of something so contrary to the intelligence and the capacity of men, since there are very few who know what the signs and the aspects of the heavens mean (XI, 100-101).

As a priest, Gualdo had particularly in mind the difficulties that could have arisen in areas of theology, if Galileo took too open a position in favor of Copernicanism, and he thus advised him to be prudent. Gualdo's words were prophetic. As we will see in the following parts of this book, the arguments against Galileo (and at the same time against Copernicus) will move progressively towards the theological plane, as the possibility of refuting Galileo's discoveries on a scientific plane, as well as their consequences with respect to Aristotelian philosophy, will gradually diminish.

4.   *The beginning of the controversies about Scripture.*
      Galileo's trip to Rome

We have a first example of this turn of events, one of great consequence, in the controversies begun in Florence by the Aristotelian philosopher, Ludovico delle Colombe, whom I have mentioned above. Between the end of 1610 and the beginning of 1611 he distributed a dissertation in manuscript form with the title: *Di Ludovico delle Colombe contro il moto della terra* (From Ludovico delle Colombe against the motion of the earth).[30] It is fundamentally an attack against the hypothesis of Copernicus. After having brought to bear the "scientific" arguments against it, delle Colombe enters into the objections from Scripture and at the end quotes the words of the theologian de Pineda in his *Commentary on the Book of Job* (IX, 6):

> Others call this opinion, taken up from the mouth of those ancient philosophers from Copernicus to Clelio Calcagnino, mad, senseless, rash, and dangerous for the faith and [directed] to give a show of nice cleverness rather than to any advantage or utility in philosophy and in astrology. (III, Part I, 290).

Of course, delle Colombe was thinking of the literal sense of the Biblical passages, such as the one from the Book of Job on the basis of which de Pineda had attacked Copernicanism. In this regard he wrote:

> Could those poor fellows [namely, the promoters of the Copernican theory] perhaps have recourse to an interpretation of Scripture different than the literal sense? Definitely not, because all theologians, without

exception, say that when Scripture can be understood literally, it ought never be interpreted differently. (III, Part I, 290).

As we see, delle Colombe did not limit himself to attacking Copernicanism from the point of view of "natural philosophy". He had added an "argument" from Scripture based on the literal sense of the Biblical passages in which the author speaks of the motion of the Sun and the stability of the Earth. This is the kind of argument which, unfortunately, will become the norm in the disputes against Copernicanism and against Galileo and which will continue to grow during the coming years.

Galileo read this dissertation of delle Colombe carefully and commented upon it. Of course, it had remained in the form of a manuscript and, therefore, had a limited distribution and possible influence. It was full of errors and odd attempts at giving explanations.[31] But the fact that delle Colombe had drawn Scripture onto the stage no doubt worried Galileo as being a dangerous precedent.

A second attack against Galileo, this time more explicit came from another Florentine, Francesco Sizzi (1585?-1618) with a book published in Venice in 1611 with the title: *Dianoia astronomica, optica, physica* (III, Part I, 203-250). Sizzi, who was in communication with Magini and Horky, did not stop at criticizing Galileo from the point of view of traditional philosophy, but he ventured, as had delle Colombe, onto Scriptural territory and asserted among other things that the planets could not be more than seven, since there were seven arms to the candelabra of the Temple of Jerusalem.[32]

In the meantime the idea of a trip by Galileo to Rome was becoming more concrete. He was convinced of the importance of his discoveries for Copernicanism and undoubtedly trusted that they would provide him the possibility to obtain from Church authorities, if not a full recognition of heliocentrism, at least an open and balanced view of it.[33] On the other hand, such an attitude would have been useful as a counterbalance to the opposition (eventually it could have even silenced it) which had begun to appear, not only on the philosophical plane, but also, and even more dangerously, on the plane of Scripture. To this end it was important for him to be sure that he had the support of the Jesuits of the Roman College and in particular of Father Clavius, since their opinion in the area of science carried a great deal of weight among the Roman authorities.

It was also important for the Jesuits to have Galileo in Rome. In addition to Clavius, who was by now old and approaching the end of his life, but was nonetheless full of interest for anything that had to do with astronomy, there were the Jesuits of his school, such as Christoph Grienberger (1561-1636) from the Tyrol and Odo Van Maelcote (1572-1615). They had taken up the telescopic observations and were expecting with great interest Galileo's arrival in Rome.[34]

Galileo finally left Florence on 23 March 1611 and he arrived in Rome six days later. He stopped at the Tuscan Embassy. The day after his arrival he went to the Roman College where he had a long and cordial visit with Father Clavius and with his disciples, Grienberger and Odo Van Maelcote (XI, 79). The fact that Galileo had gone first of all to the Roman College confirms the importance he placed on his relationship with the Jesuits. Right after this he dedicated his time to meeting persons in authority so that he could try to convince them of the truth of his discoveries with the help of practical demonstrations with the telescope. Undoubtedly, the impression made on the Roman circles must have been a strong one, even though, as usual, there were contrasting opinions. A proof of this is given by the fact that one of the most authoritative theologians of the time, Cardinal Robert Bellarmine[35], felt the need to have clear ideas about these matters. Bellarmine, as we know, had already met Galileo many years earlier at Padua in the house of Pinelli, and, probably at the request of Galileo, was supposed to meet him again or perhaps had already seen him. Bellarmine took the obvious step of consulting the mathematicians among his fellow religious at the Roman College with a letter addressed to them on 19 April. In it Bellarmine posed five precise questions: 1) were there really a multitude of stars invisible to the naked eye; 2) was Saturn really composed of three stars together; 3) did Venus really have phases like the Moon; 4) was the lunar surface really rough and uneven; 5) did Jupiter really have four satellites revolving around it (XI, 87-88).

The reply of 24 April, signed by Clavius, Grienberger, Maelcote and Lembo, confirmed the reality of Galileo's discoveries. Only as regards the fourth question was there a report of a difference of opinion among the consultants:

> . . . it seems to Father Clavius more probable that the surface [of the Moon] is not unequal, but rather that the lunar body is not uniformly dense and that it has parts that are more dense and parts more rarified, as are ordinary spots, which one sees with natural vision. Others think that the surface is truly unequal: but up until now we are not certain enough about this that we could affirm it without a doubt. (XI, 92-93).

As we see, we are dealing with a profoundly honest answer, even though one notes in Clavius' case that he is influenced by philosophical worries of an Aristotelian mold which prevented him from accepting unconditionally the discoveries with respect to the Moon. Galileo himself retreated from trying to persuade Clavius. As he wrote in a letter of 16 July:

> . . . it would have been little less than a sacrilege to tire and trouble with discourses and comments an old man so venerable for his age, doctrine and goodness; he has with so many and such illustrious efforts gained an immortal reputation and so it means little to his glory that in this particular case alone he trespasses and remains with a false opinion on a matter on which it is easy to be convinced. (XI, 151).[36]

Were there other reasons, besides his own personal desire to be informed, for the questions which Bellarmine placed before the mathematicians of the Roman College? Among Galilean scholars, there have not been lacking, nor are they lacking at the present time, those who tend to present Bellarmine as one who right from the beginning was suspicious of Galileo and not well disposed towards him. In particular, de Santillana, who, as we will see, makes Bellarmine out to be the one who orchestrated placing Copernicus on the Index in 1616, tends to draw a picture of the aging Jesuit Cardinal as an authoritarian and suspicious person whose whole effort was to catch in error the scholar who had come to disturb the intellectual peace of the Catholic world, just as Giordano Bruno had done before him.[37]

On the basis of the documents of that epoch which are available it does not seem, however, that Bellarmine of set purpose harbored such a hostility towards Galileo. We already know the immediate purpose of Bellarmine's letter to the Jesuits of the Roman College. The tone of this letter does not show any hostility towards Galileo.

> I am aware that Your Reverences have news of the new celestial observations of a worthy mathematician by means of an instrument called a cannon or an ocular; and moreover I have seen, by means of the same instrument, some very marvelous things about the Moon and Venus.[38] But I wish you to do me the favor of telling me sincerely your opinion . . . I want to know this because I hear various opinions being spoken about this matter; and since Your Reverences are occupied with the mathematical sciences, you will easily be able to tell me whether these new inventions are well-founded or whether they are apparent and not true. (XI, 87-88).

In fact, Bellarmine met Galileo (before or after his letter to the Jesuits of the Roman College) during Galileo's stay in Rome and he spoke with him about Copernicanism, as the Cardinal himself will recall four years later in a context which will show once again that there was no hostility towards the Florentine scholar (XII, 151).

To support his thesis de Santillana mentions the meeting of the Holy Office held on 17 May while, as a matter of fact, Galileo was in Rome. At the bottom of the minutes of the arguments dealt with and of the decisions taken the following note is added: "To see whether in the trial of Cesare Cremonini mention is made of Galileo, professor of philosophy and of mathematics" (XIX, 275). From these minutes we understand that Bellarmine was among the seven cardinals present at the meeting. According to de Santillana it would have been precisely Bellarmine to have had added the above-mentioned note on the possible implication of Galileo in Cremonini's trial. Now, it is obvious that they must have spoken at that meeting of the discoveries and statements of Galileo, which were precisely at that time making such news in Rome. And some worries about those new astronomical ideas must have been expressed by one or other, or perhaps by many, of those present at the meeting.

But who took the initiative to see that a search be done at Padua concerning Galileo's involvement with Cremonini? In the minutes Bellarmine is named in the third place, so he was not responsible for the meeting. There is no mention in the minutes of any particular intervention of the Jesuit Cardinal. It is certainly possible that he did intervene. But there is no documentation which supports that conclusion as de Santillana would like to have it appear.[39]

On the other hand, Bellarmine, just like the others present at the meeting, certainly must have been worried about the theological repercussions of Galileo's discoveries. In the trial of Giordano Bruno, towards the end of which, as we already know, Bellarmine played an important role, there emerged, as we have seen, the theological problem created by the statement by Bruno that there existed an infinite number of worlds. Now the discoveries of Galileo had uncovered the existence of an enormous number of stars invisible to the naked eye, a fact which perhaps recalled to Bellarmine's mind the specter of Bruno. On this point it does not appear to be sheer chance that Bellarmine's first question to the mathematicians of the Roman College concerns precisely the "multitude of fixed stars".

But even apart from this, Bellarmine must have felt very deeply the problem of reconciling Copernicanism, by now a clearly professed position of Galileo, with the Scripture texts which spoke instead of the motion of the Sun and the immobility of the Earth. This problem must have arisen frequently in the course of the heated discussions to which Galileo was committed at that time with Churchmen and the educated Romans,[40] as had happened at Florence with the writings of delle Colombe and Sizzi. Certainly, in comparison to them Bellarmine was of a completely different intellectual standing. And, as we will see in the following chapter, he did not exclude *a priori* the possibility of reconciling Copernicanism with Holy Scripture (even though he considered such a reconciliation to be extremely improbable). What must have worried him, as well as the other cardinals of the Holy Office, was the zeal for Copernicanism shown by Galileo during his stay in Rome. He was undoubtedly a scientist of great value, but as a layperson he was incompetent in theological matters.[41] Was there not perhaps a danger that, precisely for that reason, he would underestimate the seriousness of the Scriptural problems connected with Copernicanism? Or might he not outright claim to provide solutions respecting these problems, a task which belonged exclusively to theologians (whose doctrines were in turn submitted to the judgment of ecclesiastical authorities)?

That such a concern existed among these authorities and, therefore, also for Bellarmine seems to be confirmed by the statement which the Cardinal is supposed to have made to the Tuscan Ambassador, Guicciardini, right after Galileo finished his stay in Rome: "If he [Galileo] had stayed here too much longer, they could not have failed to come to some justification of his affairs (XII, 207)".[42] It is precisely to these Roman authorities that reference is made with the phrase "they could not have failed to".

There is no doubt that there was concern. But, at least at the highest levels of ecclesiastical authority, it was limited to the area of the proceedings of the Holy Office which were bound to the strictest secrecy. Externally there were no leaks. And Galileo with a warm recommendation from the Grand Duke of Tuscany could, therefore, be honored in public, at least as a scientist. So he was received in audience by Pope Paul V, who gave him special treatment and did not allow him to remain kneeling in his presence, as was the custom at that time. A similar respect was shown to him as a scientist by various personalities in the Church who were most respected in Rome, among whom there was Cardinal Maffeo Barberini, who later on, when he becomes Pope Urban VIII, will play a very important part in the Galilean drama.

A public recognition of the esteem in which he was held was given by his admission on 25 April 1611 as the sixth member of the *Accademia dei Lincei* which had been founded eight years earlier by the young prince Federico Cesi (1583-1630) in order to promote the study of the natural sciences. This event marked the beginning of a deep and enduring friendship between Cesi and Galileo which will last up until the premature death of the prince. And Galileo considered it to be a great honor to have become one of the first members of this Academy and he often signed himself: "Galileo Galilei, Linceo".[43]

But without a doubt another event of no less importance for Galileo during his stay in Rome was the academic assembly held in his honor at the Roman College towards the middle of May with the presence of numerous cardinals and other personages in the world of Rome. The official talk with the expressive title: *Nuncius Sidereus Collegii Romani*, was given by the Belgian Jesuit, Odo Van Maelcote.[44] After recalling Galileo's discoveries, Maelcote brought forth as a confirmation of them the observations made by the astronomers of the Roman College, even if he left it to the listeners to draw their own conclusions concerning these matters.

Given the importance which Galileo attributed to the opinion of the astronomers of the Roman College, it is certainly strange that he does not mention at all this academic assembly in his letters of those times. Perhaps Galileo had hoped that Clavius and especially his disciples would have taken a more open position. And he was probably unhappy with various nuances of Maelcote's talk, such as the omission in the quotation of the long title of Galileo's *Sidereus Nuncius* of the words with respect to the telescope: "discovered by him a little while ago"; or the allusion to the discovery of the oval form of Saturn and of the phases of Venus as made by the Jesuit astronomers before they had been noticed by Galileo.[45]

It would, however, be wrong to see in the cautious statements of Maelcote an indication of coolness towards Galileo.[46] Without a doubt such caution was inspired by the attitude of Clavius. He was by now convinced that the system of Ptolemy could no longer be upheld as appears clearly from the words found in Volume III of the second edition of his *Opera Mathematica* which had just come out that year. After having recognized the value of Galileo's discoveries, which he described by quoting the *Sidereus Nuncius,* Clavius concluded: "Since that is the way things are, let the astronomers see how they can manage the celestial orbs, in such a way that they are able to save the phenomena".[47]

But these words did not necessarily signify the acceptance of the Copernican system. If we are to believe it, there is the testimony of the Jesuit Athanasius Kircher, which is found in a letter of September 1633 from Niccolò Fabri di Peiresc to Pierre Gassendi:

> Clavius, and with him the other Jesuits, would not have disapproved the opinion of Copernicus, in fact, they would not have been very far from it. They would, however, have been "pushed and obliged to write in favor of the common opinions of Aristotle". (XV, 254).

To what is Kircher referring with the words in quotation marks? From the documents in our possession there is no indication that the Superior General of the Jesuits at that time, Claudio Acquaviva (1543-1615), had issued any special orders concerning the posture to be taken by Jesuits with respect to the Copernican doctrine. But soon after the academic assembly in honor of Galileo at the Roman College Acquaviva had sent out on 24 May 1611 a circular letter to all Jesuit professors in which he recommended that they maintain "uniformity of doctrine". Undoubtedly that implied fidelity to Aristotelian doctrine. That doctrine had already been set as the basis for the teaching of philosophy in the *Constitutions* composed by the founder of the Jesuits, Ignatius of Loyola (1491-1556). And it had been reconfirmed as such in the *Ratio Studiorum* which was issued by Acquaviva in 1599 and which ratified the principles for the studies and for the teaching of Jesuits.[48]

Certainly, we must exclude that the reason for Acquaviva's circular letter was the problem of Copernicanism. Even if the philosophy professors, who had participated in the academic assembly at the Roman College in Galileo's honor, did not appear to be in agreement with the all too positive appreciation of Galileo's discoveries rendered by Maelcote from the point of view of science,[49] it does not seem likely that they could in such a short period of time have provoked the circular letter of Acquaviva. On the other hand Acquaviva's motive was much broader and embraced the fields of theological research as well as those of philosophy.[50]

But the fact remains that Clavius and the other Jesuits of the Roman College knew well the decrees of the *Constitutions* and later of the *Ratio Studiorum* on Aristotelian doctrine which will immediately afterwards be repeated, as we have seen, by the circular letter of Acquaviva. And that, without a doubt, made them cautious in accepting thoroughly Galileo's conclusions.

An important component of their circumspection is, therefore, surely given by the ideal of obedience "in some ways blind" that the founder of the Jesuits speaks of in the *Constitutions*.[51] But a second component, linked to the preceding one, is to be seen in the difficulty, at the same time both intellectual and psychological, of accepting revolutionary ideas in the field of cosmology, ideas which were not yet supported by a new "natural philosophy". To accept Copernicanism meant, as I have emphasized many times, denying a large part of the Aristotelian natural philosophy. But what natural philosophy could one call upon to substantiate the claim that the Sun and not the Earth must be at the center of the world system? It was also this knowledge of the physical problem which existed at the foundation of the new astronomical ideas which made the Jesuits hesitant.

Furthermore, there was the "theological" component and, to be more precise, the "Scriptural" component. Certainly the Jesuits had also given consideration to the difficulties against heliocentrism   deriving from Scripture. These kinds of considerations were becoming always more important, as a result of the heated debates between Galileo and his antagonists during his stay in Rome. Undoubtedly, the influence of Bellarmine, the most authoritative Jesuit theologian, did not fail to have an impact on the prudent hesitation of the Jesuits. As I have already stated, even if he was not irreconcilably opposed to Copernicanism, Bellarmine was very troubled by the theological problems it implied and such concerns of his were inevitably reflected in the position of the Jesuit astronomers.

Given this situation should we not surmise that Clavius and the other Jesuit astronomers were taking a direction from that time on towards the astronomical compromise of Tycho Brahe? Maelcote had mentioned him in his discourse at the Roman College and had defined him as the "incomparable astronomer" (a further reason, as I have noted, for Galileo's resentment). But the reference made was to his merits as a tireless observer, without any mention of his system. And yet it would have been quite natural to do so with respect to the phases of Venus, a phenomenon which could be explained in Tycho's system just as well as in that of Copernicus.

As to Clavius, he had received, as I have already stated, a long letter from Tycho Brahe at the beginning of 1600 (that is, one year before the death of the Danish astronomer),[52] but he had not responded. On the contrary, in a letter to Magini he had remarked that Brahe was "confusing all of astronomy, because he wants to have Mars lower than the Sun".[53] It appears, therefore, that Clavius did not have much sympathy for Tycho Brahe's system, even if he did have a great respect for his qualities as an observer. There is little doubt that, given the influence of Clavius on his brother Jesuits, they would also not have tended, at that time, towards the ideas of the Danish astronomer. In fact, from the correspondence of the circle of Clavius' disciples,[54] the tendency towards the system of Copernicus as opposed to that of Tycho Brahe is quite clear.[55] This is true, at least in certain cases, even in the first years after 1616. It will be especially after the condemnation of Galileo in 1633 that the Jesuits, although reluctantly, will opt for the system of Brahe.

Galileo departed for Florence on 4 June 1611. Undoubtedly, he must have been satisfied with his trip to Rome, which had given him the opportunity to gain the respect of many of the most important personages in the ecclesiastical and scientific circles of Rome.[56]

Even if his admirers did not always follow him right to the end, especially as far as openly Copernican conclusions, Galileo must have been convinced that he had built a sufficiently solid basis from which to launch his Copernican program. For him the most important factor was that the Church authorities and the Pope himself had given him a great show of respect. That must have justified his trust that his most ardent adversaries would little by little be forced into silence. Without a doubt Galileo overestimated the significance of such a show of respect, as we have already had occasion to notice. And the events to come will do nothing but put the lie to his optimism.

5.   The dispute about floating bodies. The "League" against Galileo is born.

A little after his return to Florence Galileo found himself involved in a dispute which will further sharpen the contrast between him and the Aristotelians. This dispute began during the summer of 1611 from a discussion which Galileo had with two professors of the University of Pisa with respect to ice floating on water. According to the two professors, who drew their conclusions on the theory of Aristotle, ice was denser than water (because condensation is a property of coldness). If it floated on water, that was due to its wide, flat shape which produced a resistance to submersion.

Contrary to this statement, Galileo maintained instead, on the basis of the theory of Archimedes, that it was the greater or lesser density of a body with respect to water that caused it to sink or to float. Consequently ice must be less dense than water. A few days later, Ludovico delle Colombe, who, as we have seen, had already shown himself to be an

adversary of Galileo in astronomical matters, took up a
position in the ranks of the Aristotelian professors by claiming
that he was able to carry out experiments which would prove
that it was the shape of a body which determined whether it
would float or not on water.

Thus there was born the plan to hold a public debate
between him and Galileo. But Galileo, at the suggestion of the
Grand Duke, preferred to put in writing a résumé of the
discussions that had been held up until that time.[57] On 2
October of that same year, on the occasion of a dinner given
by the Grand Duke to honor Cardinals Ferdinando Gonzaga
and Maffeo Barberini, who were passing through Florence at
that time, Galileo was invited by Cosimo II to speak in
support of his theory, while the new philosophy professor of
the University of Pisa, Flaminio Papazzoni, would have
defended the Aristotelian position. During the debate Cardinal
Gonzaga took the position of Papazzoni, while Cardinal
Barberini supported that of Galileo. The public debate ended
with Galileo the victor and he decided to replace the
manuscript which he had already sketched out with a true
and proper treatise on hydrostatics. The composition of the
treatise, obstructed by a serious illness which struck Galileo
right after the debate, was only completed the following
spring, while he was absent from Florence at the villa of his
friend, Salviati. The treatise was published a little later under
the title: *Discorso intorno alle cose che stanno in su l'acqua o
che in quella si muovono* (Discourse on objects which rest on
water or which move in it) and it was dedicated to Cosimo II.
Even though this first published work of Galileo on a topic in
physics did not provoke the same reaction as the *Sidereus
Nuncius* (the subject matter naturally determined that), it,
nonetheless, did not fail to arouse a great deal of interest
because of the variety of the topics treated and the
conclusions which could appear to be paradoxical, but which
were verifiable with simple experiments which could be
performed by anyone interested enough in these matters.[58] In
the introduction to this work Galileo alluded to the problem
of the determination of the period of rotation of the four
satellites of Jupiter and he proposed an explanation for the

phenomenon of the sunspots which he had begun to observe, at least in a systematic way, while he was in Rome. I will speak of this in the following section.

The *Discourse* had a great success; so before the end of that year Galileo had a second edition printed with various additions and clarifications. But the work's success provoked not only letters of consent but also of fiery opposition. Among the opponents we should remember Ludovico delle Colombe who towards the end of that same year composed a work dedicated to Giovanni de' Medici with the title: *Discorso apologetico d'intorno al discorso di Galileo Galilei* (An apologetic discourse concerning the discourse of Galileo Galilei, IV, 311-369).[59]

So as not to make the contrasts more bitter, Galileo preferred to offer no direct response to these writings but he entrusted the task of responding to his friend, Castelli, who had in the meantime obtained the chair of mathematics at the University of Pisa and was in that city.[60] But, despite Galileo's prudence, this argument with delle Colombe and the other Aristotelians only served to create a deeper division between them and gave a further push to the formation in Florence of an organized group against Galileo. The members of this group will become known among Galileo's friends as the "*colombi*" (pigeons), an obvious allusion to the most fiery of their exponents (Ludovico delle Colombe).

The first indication of the existence of the anti-Galilean group is found in a letter addressed to Galileo in December 1611 in which there is mention of meetings of Galileo's adversaries in the house of the Archbishop of Florence, Marzimedici, with the intent of fighting the ideas on the motion of the Earth and other Galilean theories (XI, 241-242). But the fact that these adversaries would have formed an outright "league" probably came to be known by Galileo through a letter of Tolomeo Nozzolini which had been brought to his attention.[61] Later on we will have the opportunity to see the influence of this group of relentless conservatives on developments in the Galileo affair.

6.   *The sunspots and the beginning of the controversy with*
      Scheiner

Another dispute, under certain aspects even more serious
because of its future developments, was the one in which
Galileo became embroiled with the Jesuit Christoph Scheiner
(1573-1650), a professor of mathematics at Ingolstadt, with
respect to the priority of the "discovery" of the sunspots.

In fact, the sunspots were not discovered in the XVII
century. Since they can be quite large, they are, in fact,
visible at times to the naked eye by looking at the Sun
towards sunset or through smoked glass. The spots had, as a
matter of fact, been already observed in the Greek-Roman
world, as well as in China.[62] However, they were generally
interpreted as due to the motion of planets that were in
conjunction with the Sun. Even in 1607 Kepler, upon
observing one of such "spots", took it to be Mercury.[63]
Generally speaking, the reason for such an interpretation was
that the Sun, since it was a perfect and incorruptible body,
could not have actual spots and imperfections on its surface.[64]

What, on the other hand, came to be realized for the first
time in the XVII century, especially through the work of
Galileo and later through that of Scheiner, was the
interpretation of these spots as phenomena which occurred on
the Sun's surface. This then led to the truly scientific study
of them.

On the basis of a great deal of evidence, including the
testimony of Galileo himself,[65] it seems that the first
observations to determine the nature of the spots were made
by Galileo at Padua in July-August 1610. He then made
further observations at Florence and in Rome during his visit
there. But at that time Galileo made no mention in writing of
these observations, perhaps because he had not attributed any
special importance to them.

On the other hand, the first publication on the sunspots
was done by a Dutchman, Johann Fabricius (1577-1613) and
came out at Wittenberg in 1611. In that work Fabricius stated
that the spots were neither clouds nor comets but that they
belonged to the solar surface. By studying their motion

Fabricius deduced the likelihood that the Sun was rotating on its own axis.[66]

As to Scheiner, on the basis of what he himself states (V, 25), his first observations of sunspots occurred in March-April 1611, while together with his Jesuit assistant, Cysat, he was intent upon measuring the relative size of the Sun's diameter with respect to that of the Moon. To do such measurements he observed the Sun late in the afternoon when its brightness was diminished by absorption in the Earth's atmosphere. This, as a matter of fact, helped them to discover the sunspots.[67]

However, from the beginning not even Scheiner gave particular attention to the phenomenon. But his interest was all of a sudden awakened in October of that same year[68] and on 12 November Scheiner wrote a letter to Mark Welser in Augusta,[69] providing him with the results of his observations. Welser, who had already been in correspondence with Galileo since October of the previous year but without knowing of his observations of the sunspots, informed one of his German friends who lived in Rome and had become a member of the *Accademia dei Lincei*, Johannes Faber, of the discoveries of Scheiner and asked him whether observations in this regard had also been carried out at Rome. When Federico Cesi came to know of this letter of Welser to Faber, he informed Galileo of it on 3 December (XI, 236). A little later Faber himself passed on the information to Galileo (XI, 238-239).

On 12 and 26 December Scheiner sent two other letters to Welser on his observations and subsequently he published them, together with the first letter, under the title: *Tres epistolae de maculis solaribus ad Marcum Welserium* (Three letters to Mark Welser on the sunspots). Upon the recommendation of his provincial superior (worried about the possible reactions to such a publication) Scheiner had chosen a pseudonym: "Apelles post tabulam latens" (Apelles hidden behind the painting).[70] In these letters Scheiner denied that the spots belonged to the solar surface and he proposed the hypothesis that they were "wandering stars" (that is, minor planets) different from Mercury and Venus.

As we already know, because of poor health conditions Galileo was at that time outside of Florence. It was, therefore, with some delay that he received a copy of Scheiner's publication sent to him by Welser in January 1612 with a request for his opinion on the matters raised (XI, 257). Thus, Galileo's response came only four months later (V, 94-113). In this long letter to Welser Galileo explains that the reason for his silence was, even more than the sickness from which he had just recovered, the lack of a sufficient number of continuous observations and, therefore, of a demonstration "more certain and tangible". Galileo continued by saying that, given the reactions to his previous discoveries, he feared that an error, "even a venial one" would have been ascribed to him as a most capital offense "by the enemies of the truth whose number was infinite".

Upon examining the three letters of "Apelle", Galileo stated that he was in agreement with the latter in judging the spots to be a real phenomenon (that is, not an illusion created by the eye or by a lens). But he criticized the reasons given by Apelle for his conclusion that the spots could not be on the body of the Sun. After having noted that they were not a permanent phenomenon, Galileo considered the statement of Apelle that they were neither clouds nor comets, but stars. Since the spots did not keep the same spherical shape, but were produced and then dissolved, and did not appear to have a periodic movement about the Sun, Galileo concluded that the name "stars" was not appropriate. Rather, they should have been called "clouds", contiguous to the surface of the Sun.

Taken as a whole Galileo's response was prudent. Obviously, he was not yet sure of himself, given the newness and the difficulty of the material under study. But altogether he nourished fond hopes:

> . . . that this new thing will turn out to be of admirable service in tuning for me some reed in this great discordant organ of our philosophy - an instrument on which I think I see many organists wearing themselves out trying vainly to get the whole thing in perfect harmony. Vainly, because they leave or rather preserve three or four of the principal reeds in discord, making it

quite impossible for the others to respond in perfect tune (V, 113; trans. by Drake 1957, 103)[71].

Although he had had to contradict his conclusions, Galileo had shown himself to be very courteous towards Apelle (whose true identity he did not yet know) and he had not spared praising him. On 1 June 1612 Welser thanked Galileo for his letter and proposed to have it printed by making a contact with Sagredo who had had it delivered to him. Sagredo on his part had already seen to the distribution of Galileo's letter among friends and Galileo had done the same.[72] In particular, he had sent to Cardinal Maffeo Barberini his answer to Welser together with the three letters of Apelle. And the Cardinal had answered praising him for the perspicacity of his genius and concluding that the opinion rejected by Galileo could not be true (XI, 325).

But Galileo, having learned from previous experiences, wanted to arm himself against possible difficulties from Scripture with respect to the sunspots. So he asked the opinion of Cardinal Carlo Conti about these matters. The cardinal answered in July 1612 and stated that Scripture did not support the Aristotelian theory of the incorruptibility of the heavens but that, on the contrary, the common opinion of the Fathers of the Church was that the heavens were corruptible. As to the circular motion of the Earth, Conti stated that it was not very consistent with Scripture and that, therefore, the Copernican hypothesis could be reconciled with Scripture only if one held that the *Bible* spoke the ordinary language of the common people, a thing, however, which (the cardinal added) "should not be admitted unless it is really necessary" (XI, 355). Despite his personal caution, Conti did not hesitate to inform Galileo in complete honesty of the existence of Diego de Zuñiga's opinion in support of the possibility of a reconciliation between Scripture and Copernicanism.

In the meantime Scheiner continued his observations and sent three new letters to Welser, which he then published in 1612, using his pseudonym and the title: *Accuratior Disquisitio* (A more accurate discourse, V, 37-70). Scheiner substantially repeated his theory that the sunspots were produced by planets revolving about the Sun (among them was Venus, which according to him established the truth of the system of Tycho Brahe). With respect to this planet, Scheiner later noted incidentally that its phases had been observed in Rome "almost at the same time" at which Galileo had observed them "in various cities in Italy" (V. 46), a veiled attempt perhaps to dispute the priority of the discovery by Galileo. Such a remark had nothing to do with the problem of the sunspots. It seems to show, together with his statement as to having discovered a fifth satellite of Jupiter (impossible for the telescopes of that epoch), as well as having claimed to have been the first to have shown the motion of Venus about the Sun (he had not), the beginning of a certain animosity of Scheiner towards Galileo.

In the meantime, Galileo had prepared a second letter addressed to Welser, completed in August and sent off the 21st of that month to Sagredo at Venice with the request to have it forwarded to the addressee, as had happened with the previous letter. Sagredo kept it in order to copy it and have it distributed. Welser finally received it during the first days of October and he wrote to Galileo with the repeated proposal to have it published and he told him that he would make sure that "Apelle" knew of it. With this new letter Galileo (who knew nothing yet of the three new letters of Apelle to Welser) intended to complete and make more precise the statements contained in his first letter. Relying on numerous new observations, he said that he was certain that the spots were not stars, but that they were close to the solar surface or at a distance from it which could not be detected. In addition to the growth and dissolution proper to each spot, they showed a motion in common in the course of which each kept its own latitude. From this Galileo deduced the rotation of the Sun on its own axis and the fact that it was a sphere. Surely, he added, the fact that the spots belonged to the Sun's surface implied abandoning the Aristotelian theory of the Sun's incorruptibility, as well as that of other celestial bodies. But, continued Galileo, Aristotle himself, if he were alive at the time, would have rather concluded in support of the corruptibility of the heavens (V, 138-139).

For his part Welser, before he received the second letter of Galileo, had sent him on 28 September a copy of the *Accuratior Disquisitio* of "Apelle". Thus, having just finished the second letter, Galileo felt obliged to send a third in order to answer the new publication of Apelle. The probability that the latter was a Jesuit was suggested a little later to Galileo by his friend Cigoli in a letter of 19 October (XI, 418) and it was subsequently confirmed by Cesi who insisted, as had Cigoli, that Galileo would decide to have his response to Welser published and so prevent that the "unnamed Jesuit" would be able to usurp the priority of the discoveries.

And thus, also through the intervention of Galileo's friends, the atmosphere was little by little being soured. Already in his letter to Cesi of 4 November Galileo shows how the statements of these friends of his had begun to have their effect on him. Alluding to the third letter of Welser, still being prepared, Galileo wrote:

> . . . but not for this should you [Cesi] be worried that much will be usurped because I hope to make it clear how foolishly this matter has been dealt with by the G. [*Gesuita*, Jesuit] to whom I wish to show such resentment as is fitting. (XI, 426).

This third letter of Galileo to Welser was finished on 1 December (V, 186-249).[73] In it Galileo states that above all it was a waste of energy to look for an understanding of the essence of terrestrial and celestial substances and that it was, therefore, necessary to restrict oneself to the study of the "affections" or the properties of bodies. Galileo applied this investigatory principle to the sunspots and declared that it was necessary to limit oneself to researching their properties, such as, their location, motion, form, mutability, production and decomposition. Once such properties were understood it would become possible "to philosophize better about the other more controversial conditions of the natural substances" (V, 188).[74]

Galileo then stated that he had read with interest the *Accuratior Disquisitio* of Apelle, but he added that on various points he was not in agreement with the author. The first point of difference was with respect to the proof given by Apelle for the revolution of Venus about the Sun. Galileo considered that the argument was not sufficiently established. He insisted that the real conclusive proof was the one which he had supplied in his first letter to Welser (that is, the one which was derived from the phenomenon of the planet's phases), a proof which Apelle on the other hand only cited in third place.

Going on to evaluate what Apelle was saying about the sunspots themselves, Galileo rejected the principle whereby Apelle denied that they were part of the solar surface, namely, the Aristotelian principle of the hardness and immutability of the Sun. On the contrary, Galileo showed, by a geometrical argument based on the very diagrams of Apelle, that the spots could not be located at any significant distance from the Sun. Galileo enunciated his hope that with these proofs Apelle would finally come to agree with his opinion and admit also the motion of the Sun on its own axis (which, as a matter of fact, was derived on the basis of Galileo's explanation of the spots).

Finally, after having rejected Apelle's theory that the Moon was more brilliant than glass, as well as his claim to have discovered a fifth satellite of Jupiter, Galileo disproved the explanation that the spots came from conglomerations in the form of clouds of very small stars. According to Apelle that was the explanation for the non-spherical but irregular aspect of the spots themselves.[75] Since these little "stars" could not be fixed stars (they changed their positions with respect to one another) they must have been minor planets. But how then could one explain, asked Galileo, the fact that, although they possessed different velocities, they were able to stay together for a long enough time to give the impression of spots?

At the end of his letter Galileo showed that he was convinced that he had

> . . . demonstrated that the sunspots are neither stars nor hard materials, and they are not located at a distance from the sun but are produced and dissolved upon it in a manner not unlike that of clouds and vapors and other luminous objects around the earth. (V, 236).

The three letters of Galileo to Welser were published in March 1613 under the editorship of the *Accademia dei Lincei* with the title: *Istoria e dimostrazioni intorno alle macchie solari* (A history and some demonstrations with respect to the sunspots) and it was dedicated to Galileo's great friend, Filippo Salviati. The book was supplied with a preface written by the librarian of the *Accademia dei Lincei*, Angelo de Filiis. In a polemical tone it claimed priority for Galileo's discoveries and, in particular, for the discovery of sunspots. When Galileo looked over it before it was printed, it must have made him uneasy with the foreboding that, by putting him in open argument with Scheiner, it ran the risk of damaging his relationship with the Jesuits. Although indirectly, this preoccupation of Galileo is documented in the responses he addressed to Cesi and Cigoli (XI, 483, 485), who insisted that he maintain his claim to priority even though in a subtler tone than that of de Filiis' original text (see V, 84-86). But Galileo's foreboding was correct and this preface, despite the fact that it was toned down, provoked protests on the part of the Jesuits of the Roman College and at the same time caused a first cooling off of the relationships between them and Galileo, relationships which up until that time, as we have seen, had been more than cordial. As to Scheiner he must have been profoundly resentful, even though he preferred for the moment to remain silent. Was he perhaps still prepared to distinguish the posture of de Filiis from Galileo's? Galileo had never, in fact, in his three letters to Welser touched upon the question of priority for the discovery of sunspots. It is difficult to give an answer. At any rate Scheiner will not hesitate many years later, as we shall see, at the time of his composition of the *Rosa Ursina*, his most important work, to make his resentment towards Angelo de Filiis quite obvious.

Galileo knew by now that "Apelle" was a Jesuit. But he did not come to know that it was Father Scheiner until March of the following year, 1614. On 19 January 1613 Scheiner had written to Magini to thank him for his favorable judgment on his publications and he asked him at the same time not to let his true name be known until the right moment had arrived (XI, 461-462). The Jesuit, Giuseppe Biancani, also wrote to Magini on 17 May 1613 and asserted the priority of Scheiner's discoveries over those of Galileo (XI, 509). In that same year another Jesuit, François D'Aguilon, published at Antwerp a treatise on optics in which he maintained that the sunspots had been first seen by Scheiner.[76] It was only later that Cesi, who had come to know of that latter work, informed Galileo of it (1 March 1614; XII, 29).

But despite the fact that Galileo's friends as usual showed themselves severe towards Scheiner and the Jesuits in general, it was important for Galileo not to ruin his relationships with them, particularly with Father Grienberger, who had succeeded, after Clavius' death in 1612, to the chair of first mathematician at the Roman College. In fact, in December 1614 Galileo wrote to his friend Gualdo in Rome:

> Do me the favor at your first opportunity to give my respects to Father Granbergiero [Grienberger] and assure him that I am a true and affectionate servant and admirer of his goodness and his virtue; and ask him, as I am asking Your Lordship, that he would let me have a copy, as soon as it arrives, of the writing of that fictitious Apelle, who has, however, now been unmasked. (XII, 115).[77]

This new writing to which Galileo alludes had appeared in that same year at Ingolstadt under the title: *Disquisitiones mathematicae de controversiis et novitatibus astronomicis* (Mathematical discourses on astronomical controversies and new discoveries). The title page listed a certain Locher Boius as author but it made clear that the disquisitions had been held under the direction of Father Christoph Scheiner, of whom Boius was evidently a disciple. In this work geocentrism was reasserted and the traditional difficulties both of an astronomical and a Scriptural nature were brought up against Copernicanism. After mentioning the recent discoveries with the telescope, with high praise for Galileo, especially for his discovery of Jupiter's satellites and those (presumed ones) of Saturn, the work added that, following such discoveries, Clavius and Magini had changed their system of the heavens. The book then went on to speak of the sunspots and it showed a further evolution in Scheiner's thought which, with respect to many points, had become closer to Galileo's opinions.

In February 1615 Scheiner himself sent a copy of this little work to Galileo with the expectation that he would receive in turn some of the latter's publications (XII, 137-138). In the accompanying letter, the German Jesuit mentioned that he knew that Galileo tended towards Copernicanism and he added:

> Nonetheless I, or rather my disciple, are not persons who wish to avoid being criticized by persons more learned than us; therefore, even though I do not think that in such questions one should uphold one's opinion vehemently, I hold that one can do no less than to consider the reasons adduced [by others] in order to arrive at the truth.

As we will see, Scheiner subsequently continued his interest in the sunspots. For the period that we are now involved with we will limit ourselves to recalling the appearance in 1615 of his new booklet of 34 pages entitled *Sol ellipticus*. He sent a copy to Galileo and asked for his opinion about it (XII, 170-171).

Thus for the present the controversy between Galileo and Scheiner over the sunspots comes to an end. As I have already noted, even though it had been kept at the level of formal courtesy, it did not fail to provoke a certain cooling off of the relationships between the Jesuits and Galileo. It seems important to repeat that the change was not due, at least at the beginning, to any attitude of Galileo, but rather to some statements with a polemical flavor on the part of Scheiner and to the reactions that they provoked on the part of Galileo's friends (and through them on Galileo himself). But Angelo de Filiis' preface, I repeat, must have already profoundly embittered Scheiner. Even if we admit that he was still prepared at that time to distinguish the posture of de Filiis from Galileo's, he had good reason later on to change his opinion. As we shall see, that will occur at the time of the *Discourse on the comets* where Guiducci, one of Galileo's disciples, will once more, writing under the direct "inspiration" of his master, take up against Scheiner the accusation that he had pretended to usurp Galileo's priority for the discovery of the sunspots. Scheiner, knowing the true author behind these statements, will be profoundly offended, and justifiably so. And his resentment will only increase after he reads the sharply worded sentences written, this time by Galileo himself, in *The Assayer* and interpreted by Scheiner as being directed to him.[78] Some years later we will have Scheiner's response in the *Rosa Ursina* and this will signal the complete break in a relationship which, as we have seen, had begun in an atmosphere of mutual esteem.

For the moment, despite the unfortunate statements of de Filiis, the differences had been kept on the plane of ideas. Galileo was convinced that the sunspots were a fundamental proof against Aristotelian cosmology which was founded, as we know, upon the "dogma" of the incorruptibility of heavenly bodies and thus also of the Sun. It will only be later on that Galileo will note that the movement of the spots on the Sun's surface is not rectilinear but in ellipses. He will deduce from this that the Sun's axis of rotation is not perpendicular to the plane of the ecliptic (as he had maintained in his letter to Welser) and from this phenomenon he will draw a confirmation of the Copernican system.[79]

NOTES

[1] The third law which, in a certain sense, is the most important one as it brings together the movements of all of the planets, will be

published by Kepler in a following work, the *Harmonices Mundi* (1619).

[2] The *Astronomia Nova* was printed in a very limited number of copies and Kepler did not send one to Galileo. This should not to be considered odd given the fact that Galileo had never answered Kepler's letter of 1597, thus provoking a break in their correspondence which will last until 1610. The works of Kepler, on the other hand, were then, and remained even afterwards, very difficult to find in bookstores (see Bucciantini 1995, 104). Still Galileo received from his friend Cesi on 21 July 1612 (XI, 366) an indication of Kepler's theory of elliptical orbits. With respect to Galileo's refusal to consider this theory see Drake 1978, 190 and Field 1984, especially 214-215.

[3] Drake asserts that Giovan Battista della Porta or Marcantonio de Dominis, who were involved in optics, would have been the ones to have constructed the first rudimentary types of telescopes. See Drake 1970b, 156. According to de Waard 1907 the first telescope would have been constructed by an Italian artisan in 1590. The Dutch were also artisans and they made the first telescopes known by using a long-focus lens as an objective and a short-focus one for the ocular. As to the lenses themselves, the first converging ones were discovered about 1280, but we do not know when diverging lenses were first made. Ronan 1991 states that the invention of the first rudimentary reflecting telescope was by Leonard Digges in England (between 1540 and 1559) and that the use of it for astronomical observations is to be attributed to his son Thomas (whom we have cited in the Introduction as one of the first followers of Copernicanism in England). According to Ronan, it would have been the discovery in this way of an enormous number of fixed stars - more than thirty years before Galileo - which brought Thomas Digges to state that the universe was infinite. Ronan also claims that Leonard and Thomas Digges had also experimented with lenses. It is not possible for me at this time to evaluate these claims which have aroused much interest in the press both in England and in Italy. Even if Thomas Digges had truly carried out these observations quite a bit before Galileo, the fact remains that such discoveries were unknown and had no scientific impact for more than four decades, while those of Galileo have made a fundamental contribution to the evolution of scientific thought in the western world.

[4] See Drake 1978, 138 ff. For further details see Drake 1970b, 140-148.

[5] Involved here, above all, was the military value, a fact which Galileo did not fail to make evident.

[6] A florin was the equivalent of 3.54 grams of pure gold. As we know Galileo began his teaching with a salary of 180 florins a year. That was increased to 320 florins in 1599 and to 520 in 1607. The increase to 1000 florins represented, therefore, almost twice what he had received during the last years. XIX, 123-124.

[7] In the Notice arrived from the La Haye, to which Pierre de l'Estoile alludes in his *Mémoires-Journaux* dated 18 November 1608, we read: " . . . even the stars which usually do not appear to our view, can be seen with this instrument". This text is in Danjon and Couder 1935, 597. It is quoted by Ronchi in Delorme 1968, 163. Ronchi himself thinks that Galileo would possibly have had news of this "Notice" through the answer of Badouère to Sarpi. And it would be precisely this news which would have aroused his interest as an astronomer in the instrument. As to the observations and astronomical discoveries of Thomas Digges (see Note 3), carried out thirty years earlier, Galileo, as all others in Europe, had no way of knowing about them at that time.

[8] See Drake 1978, 154.

[9] Not "Starry Messenger". See the point made by Galileo himself in VI, 388-389.

[10] The *Sidereus Nuncius* is found in III, Part I, 53-96.

[11] It was not really a question of a discovery, but rather of the confirmation of an opinion held since antiquity, as Kepler notes in his *Dissertatio cum Nuncio Sidereo* (III, Part I, 112 ff.). Beginning in 1609 Kepler himself had tried to produce a description of lunar geography in his writing: *Somnium, sive astronomia lunaris* (Dream or lunar astronomy), which was published in 1634, four years after his death, and which has been translated into English with the title, *Kepler's Dream* (see Lear 1965). We have here a book which we would today call "science fiction", but it is full of very interesting scientific considerations.

[12] In his dedication of the *Sidereus Nuncius* to the Grand Duke Cosimo II, Galileo, when speaking of the Jupiter's satellites, had said that they revolved about the planet with a large velocity and completed with the planet itself a revolution about the Sun, "the world's center", in 12 years (III, Part I, 56). In his English translation of the *Sidereus Nuncius* Drake made the following comment: "This is the first published intimation by Galileo that he accepted the Copernican system" (Drake 1957, 24). Twenty years later the same author seems to want to eliminate even this simple "intimation" by Galileo. In fact he writes:

He did not, however, declare in the *Starry Messenger* [Message] that the earth was a planet. What he said in his dedication to Cosimo de' Medici was that the stars Galileo had named after him went around Jupiter just "as all planets go around the sun"-a statement as compatible with the Tychonic as with Copernican astronomy. (Drake 1978, 157).

But Drake's quote of that same place is incomplete and omits the final and most important words: "center of the world". As Drake knows all too well, in the system of Brahe the Sun is not at the center of the *world*. It, therefore, is my opinion that this passage is certainly Copernican, all the more so if we accept that, in any case, Galileo never considered the system of Brahe as a true third possibility, in addition to those of Ptolemy and Copernicus. Of course, Galileo does not list the Earth as one of the planets, but that is implicitly asserted if the Sun is the "center of the world". As for that, the assertion that the Earth is a planet and revolves about the Sun occurs, admittedly as an insert, in the *Sidereus Nuncius* itself, in an excerpt given in Note 13 to follow.

[13] In the *Sidereus Nuncius* at the end of his account of the lunar discoveries Galileo wrote:

> But let these few indications of the argument suffice; we will speak of them at greater length in our "System of the World" where with many arguments and experiments the reflection of sunlight brought about by the Earth will be shown most validly to those who go on saying that it should be excluded from the list of the wandering heavenly objects especially because it does not have motion and light; and we will show that it revolves and is brighter than the Moon and is not the bilge of earthly sordidness and ugliness; this we will confirm with infinite natural reasons. (III, Part I, 75).

We have here the first affirmation by Galileo of the motion of the Earth. Of course, it is only a passing remark and refers to a future work. But its significance did not escape his adversaries.

[14] In the *Sidereus Nuncius* Galileo speaks of "a telescope I invented after receiving the illumination of Divine grace" (III, Part I, 60). That appears to indicate precisely his conviction that he had a mission entrusted to him by God. I must immediately add, however, that this conviction will never change Galileo into an "ardent enthusiast" or into an intemperate "Copernican zealot" who

would have the sole intention of forcing the Church to accept Copernicanism, as certain of his biographers have wanted to depict him.

[15] In his most recent work Drake asserts that Galileo had already written this *De systemate mundi* in 1600-1601. See Drake 1990, 80. Drake adds:

> There was never more than a single original manuscript of *De systemate mundi*, which Galileo destroyed later in 1632 when he was ordered to Rome to stand trial for publishing the *Dialogue*. It would have been seriously incriminating at that time should an unequivocally Copernican manuscript have been found among his papers by the inquisitors.

With all due respect to Drake for his competence in Galilean studies, I must confess that these assertions do not seem to me to be sufficiently well-founded. Certainly the studies on motion and on mechanics, which Galileo had carried forward during his time in Pisa and especially in Padua, were a preparation for such a work which Galileo had already then begun to think about, as Viviani states explicitly. But that work was not yet written at the time of the printing of the *Sidereus Nuncius*, where it was announced that it would soon appear (III, Part I, 75 and 96). And the writing of it, as well as other works, is given precisely in the text we are examining as one of the principal reasons why Galileo considered returning to Florence. Even two years later, at the time of the publication of the *Discorso intorno alle cose che stanno in su l'acqua* (Discourse on floating bodies), Galileo recognized that he had not yet been able to realize the projected work "which many are waiting for and which, according to my purpose expressed in the Astronomical *Avvertimento* I should have already put forth . . . " (IV, 63). To me it seems, in agreement with what Favaro claims in the introductory note prefixed to the *Dialogue* of 1632 (VII, 3), as also with all the biographers of Galileo, that this latter work is none other than the realization, after many delays, for reasons which will become clear later in this book, of his early plans for a work on the "System of the World". Since the manuscript of the *De systemate mundi* postulated by him is not to be found, Drake is forced to put forth a hypothesis that it was destroyed by Galileo towards the end of 1632 for fear that the inquisitors would break into his house. But this is a rather unlikely hypothesis. Even if we suppose that the Florentine inquisitors would have been able to use police methods with a man who, like Galileo, was under the protection of the Grand Duke and that Galileo would have feared them, such a break-in never, as a matter of fact, occurred. And there was no need for it, because the *Dialogue*, in the judgment of the experts whom the Roman Inquisition questioned, was unequivocally Copernican and there was, therefore, no need for further proofs to incriminate him.

[16] Later on in the same letter Galileo expressed a desire to have, in addition to the title of Mathematician, also that of Philosopher of the Grand Duke. See the text quoted in Note 32 of Chapter 1. Biagioli 1993 attributes great importance to this request of Galileo's. According to this author the purpose of Galileo's request was to raise his socio-cultural *status* so that it would be possible for him to beat back *as a philosopher*, and, therefore, on an equal footing, the objections which were levelled against him by the Aristotelian philosophers. Biagioli attributes even more importance to the choice of the Grand Duke of Tuscany as a "patron", a choice which would not only have changed Galileo into a "courtier" but which would have definitively motivated and oriented all of his subsequent activity. Thus it would have contributed in a determinative way to the formation of his identity as a scientist. In particular, according to Biagioli, Galileo would not have come to a full acceptance of Copernicanism except after he saw that its defense would assure him the position of strength which was essential for maintaining and reinforcing his client connections with his Medici patrons. While I agree with Biagioli on the importance which the title of philosopher had for Galileo (even though in his request there was something deeper than just a search for socio-cultural *status*, namely, he was *really* convinced that he was more a "philosopher" than a mathematician), I do not feel that I can accept Biagioli's attempt to use patronage as the key to interpret all of Galileo's scientific activity. Indubitably the client-patron relationship (studied by Biagioli through a thorough examination of the primary and secondary sources which is of great interest and value) was a pervasive reality in the social and cultural life of 16th century Europe. And Galileo could not exempt himself from it and, as a matter of fact, he accepted it and made use of it just as all of his contemporaries did. Whoever is familiar to some extent with the works of Galileo and above all with his correspondence cannot ignore this aspect of his life. But, I repeat, it is one thing to highlight the conditions which influenced, both positively and negatively, the practice of science in a culture of absolutism; it is another thing to claim that one has singled out among those conditions the determining factor of Galileo's scientific activity. Should we demythologize the usual picture of Galileo as a "pure scientist"? Yes,

I agree that we should. But the desire to see him now, at least prevalently, as a "courtier", seems to me to be an unwarranted impoverishment of a personality so rich and independent as that of Galileo.

[17] Galileo had the intention of doing a second enlarged edition in Italian; but it never appeared. Instead there was simply a reprinting of the *Sidereus Nuncius* at Frankfurt, Germany in that same year.

[18] Even though Magini carried forward on his own account a kind of campaign against Galileo, he preferred to keep up the appearances and show himself to be his friend. On the other hand, Horky himself admitted that he had written the book without Magini's knowledge.

[19] Ludovico delle Colombe had already written a *Discourse* on the *nova* of 1604. This came out in 1606 in Florence. In it the author, as any good Aristotelian, had maintained that the *nova* was, in fact, not a new star, but that it had always existed in the sky. A sharp criticism of these assertions of delle Colombe appeared in Florence in that same year with the title: *Considerations of Alimberto Mauri on some passages in the Discourse of Ludovico delle Colombe with respect to the star which appeared in 1604*. Delle Colombe retorted to this writing two years later with a new little work: *Pleasant and curious replies of Ludovico delle Colombe*. Delle Colombe suspected that Galileo might have had a part to play in Mauri's work. But then he rethought the affair and on 24 June 1607 had written to Galileo himself with a profession of friendship (X, 176-177). According to Drake 1978, 117-120, Galileo would have been the only, true author of the *Considerations*.

[20] Among these professors there was even Cremonini.

[21] In this letter Kepler promises to send Galileo a copy of his treatise in optics, *Dioptricae*, which came out the following year at Augsburg. It gives for the first time the real theory of Galileo's telescope and it proposes a telescope with a convex ocular. This will henceforth be called "Keplerian" and one will be made by the Jesuit Scheiner, the very year of Kepler's death (1630).

[22] The German, Martin Hasdale (about 1570-?) had stayed for a long time at Padua and Venice and had become a friend of Sarpi and of Galileo. Upon his return to Germany, he lived in Prague, where he enjoyed the favor of Rudolph II. After the latter's death he was imprisoned and subsequently retired to private life.

[23] It has recently been argued that the discovery of the phases of Venus had been accomplished by Galileo as the result of an idea given to him by his friend Castelli. In fact, on 5 December the latter

had written to Galileo and told him that, if the Copernican system were true, the phases of Venus should be observed (and also, at least partially, those of Mars). He asked Galileo whether he had made any such observations (X, 481-483). Galileo would have only then begun the observations of Venus, claiming later on (see his letter of 30 December in response to Castelli [X, 499] and the one to Clavius [X, 503]) that he had begun the observations three months before. But contrary to this hypothesis is the fact that already on 11 December Galileo had written to Giuliano de' Medici in Prague and told him among other matters:

> Meanwhile I am sending you the cipher [*cifera*] of another particular newly observed by me, which brings with itself a resolution of very great controversies in astronomy, and in particular contains in itself a powerful argument for the Pythagorean and Copernican arrangements; and in due time I will publish the interpretation [of this cipher], and other particulars. (X, 483).

These words certainly refer to the phases of Venus. Drake 1990, 137 emphasizes that it is extremely improbable that Castelli's letter of 5 December, sent from Brescia (where Castelli lived at that time) to Milan, where it was to be forwarded to Florence, could have reached Galileo in only five days. On the other hand - I might add - even if that had occurred, Galileo would have had only one night available to make the necessary checks with his telescope before sending off his ciphered message to Prague. Of course, one could answer that Galileo, having grasped immediately the correctness of Castelli's remark and in order to be certain of having the priority also for this discovery, had taken recourse in the expedient of sending the news in ciphered form, so that he would have the necessary time to calmly carry out the verification (in his mind he was sure of succeeding). It appears, however, that all of these suppositions in order to support such a hypothesis make it extremely weak, not to say completely improbable.

[24] See Note 23. Kepler, who was always on the lookout for more convincing proofs of the Copernican system, showed a great, although quite general, interest in the news and in a letter to Galileo of 9 January 1611 put forth his interpretation of the anagram (XI, 15-16). Its solution was sent by Galileo on 1 January 1611 to the Tuscan Ambassador in Prague. In the letter Galileo asserted:

. . . that Venus must necessarily orbit around the sun, as
do also Mercury and all the other planets-something
indeed believed by the Pythagoreans, Copernicus, Kepler,
and myself, but not sensibly proved as it is now in [the
case of] Venus and Mercury. (XI, 11-12).

As to Mercury, one could only make an inference, since that planet
was not magnified enough with the telescope available to Galileo.

[25] A friend of Galileo, the painter Ludovico Cardi, called *Cigoli*
(1559-1613), wrote to him from Rome in October 1610:

. . . and Clavius among the others, the head of them all,
said to a friend of mine about the four stars, that he was
laughing about them and that it will be necessary to
make a telescope which would make them and then show
them and that Galileo should keep his opinion and he
will keep his own. (X, 442)

Galileo certainly must have felt irritated by these ironic remarks of
Clavius. One senses an echo of this irritation even two months later
in a letter sent to Paolo Sarpi (12 February 1611, XII, 47).

[26] Filippo Salviati (1582-1614) had been a disciple of Galileo at
Padua and had subsequently continued scientific researches
undertaken by him at that time. Galileo will immortalize this friend
of his, as the Venetian Sagredo, in his two most famous works, the
Dialogue and the *Discourses*.

[27] Tommaso Campanella (1568-1639), a Calabrian, had entered
the Dominican Order at a very young age. Accusations were first
brought against him for his philosophical opinions and then for his
political activity against Spain, which at that time ruled over
Southern Italy. He was condemned to life imprisonment in Naples in
1603. More than 20 years later at the intervention of Urban VIII he
was transferred to Rome to the Inquisition prisons and was freed in
1629, but later on he had to seek refuge in France because of further
accusations of anti-Spanish activity. He died at Paris in the
Dominican monastery of Saint Honoré. On the beginnings of the
relationship between Galileo and Campanella and for a detailed
analysis of this long letter of Campanella to Galileo, see Ernst 1984,
256-258.

[28] Even though he admired Galileo, Campanella never adhered
to Copernicanism. In 1628 he will write to Urban VIII:

Do not think Your Beatitude that I am with Copernicus
. . . heaven does not move as Copernicus thinks, nor
Ptolemy, nor as Aristotle, nor as Plato and the others,

but as God wishes. (Trans. from quote by Paschini 1965, 33).

Later on we will see that this was too, as a matter of fact, the opinion of Urban VIII.

[29] On Campanella's ideas in cosmology see, for example, Yates 1969, Chapter XX: *Giordano Bruno and Tommaso Campanella*.

[30] This dissertation is found in III, Part I, 253-290.

[31] Delle Colombe, like any good Aristotelian, had tried to reconcile the data from the telescopic observations with the Aristotelian theory of the Moon as a perfect sphere by asserting that the valleys and mountains on the Moon were covered with a transparent glassy substance, which would thus allow the Moon to keep a perfectly spherical form. In this regard Galileo commented ironically: " . . . the imagination is truly beautiful . . . what is missing is that it is neither demonstrated nor demonstrable (XI, 142)". Delle Colombe came to know of the response of the Jesuits of the Roman College to Bellarmine (see my mention of it later on in the text) and, happy to hear that not even Clavius wished to accept a real roughness on the lunar surface, wrote him a letter (XI, 118) in which he claimed that the theses of Clavius were identical to his own. But when Galileo was informed of this letter, while he criticized the opinion of delle Colombe with the words cited above, he denied that Clavius agreed with the Florentine Aristotelian (XI, 151). On the other hand it appears that little by little Clavius became less reticent in his admission that the lunar surface was rough. One of his students at the Roman College, Father Saint-Vicent, wrote, in fact, on 23 July: "We hold that it is more than likely that the spots of the Moon cannot be explained with rarefactions and densities" (XI, 163). Although he was convinced that the manuscript of delle Colombe had no scientific value, Galileo read it carefully and added his own comments, at times quite extensive ones, as that given above.

[32] XI, 213. This implied that he denied the existence of the four Medicean Planets, which would have brought the number of planets from seven to eleven.

[33] The reasons for such a trip are clearly expressed in a letter of Galileo to the Secretary of State, Vinta, on 15 January 1611 (X, 27).

[34] Galileo knew and respected Father Grienberger. In his letter to Clavius of 30 December 1610 he had written:

> . . . and continue in your graciousness to me . . . as also
> that you would obtain for me the favor of the other

Father Christoph [Grienberger as a matter of fact], your
disciple, most esteemed by me for the reports I have of
his great merit in mathematics. (X, 502).

[35] On Robert Bellarmine see the profile drawn of him by de
Santillana 1960, Chapter V: *Saint Robert Bellarmine*. On the
philosophical and theological concepts of Bellarmine see also
Blackwell 1991, Chapter 2 and ff. and the most recent work of
Baldini 1992, 286-341. The best biography of Bellarmine by a
Catholic author is still the one of Brodrick 1961: *Robert Bellarmine,
Saint and Scholar*.

[36] As de Santillana 1960, 62 remarks the difficulty of accepting
the new discoveries due to the influence of preconceived ideas is
found even in persons of the stature of Kepler who confessed to
Galileo regarding the phases of Venus

For me your observation is unexpected. Because of the
great brilliance of Venus, I held that it shone with its
own light, so that now I go on reflecting about what
surface this planet could be endowed with. It would be
strange that Cintia [Venus] was not all golden, or as I
once wrote, of pure amber.

[37] See de Santillana 1960, 182 ff.

[38] These words could indicate that Bellarmine had already met
Galileo and had carried out those observations under his guidance
and with his telescope.

[39] Drake seems to follow de Santillana here. He says:

Before Galileo left Rome, Bellarmine asked the Venetian
Inquisition whether Galileo was implicated in proceedings
against Cremonini. (Drake 1978, 487, Note 20).

As we have seen, in the text of the minutes (quoted by Drake himself
in the note in question) neither Bellarmine nor the Inquisition in
Venice are mentioned.

[40] As we know, objections from Scripture against Copernicanism
were nothing new, even in Catholic circles, since they manifested
themselves right after the appearance of the *De Revolutionibus*.

[41] From the Middle Ages on, theological teaching was
monopolized by the clergy and especially by the religious orders. The
layperson's role was to show a deferential acceptance of such
teaching. Ignatius of Loyola himself, the founder of the Jesuits, while
he was still a simple layperson, a short while after his "conversion"
was imprisoned by the Spanish religious authorities for having dared

to teach the doctrine and practical asceticism of the "Spiritual Exercises".

[42] This report by Guicciardini of Bellarmines's statement is, however, to be taken with a certain grain of salt, since the Ambassador of the Grand Duke was not very well disposed to Galileo, as we will have the opportunity to witness later on.

[43] The *Accademia dei Lincei* (Academy of the Lynxes, 1603) was one of the first scientific academies to appear in Europe. It was followed by the Florentine *Accademia del Cimento* (Academy of Scientific Endeavor, 1652), by the Royal Society (1662) and by the *Académie des sciences* (1666). For a history of the *Accademia dei Lincei* see Gabrieli (1938-1942). Redondi 1987, 41 ff. offers a very interesting picture, though at times quite subjective, of the cultural program and the activity of the members of the Academy. For a "reappraisal" of it see Westfall 1989, 86 ff. Likewise interesting (though again rather subjective) is the description given by Biagioli 1993, 291 ff.

[44] This talk is found in III, Part I, 293-298. On Maelcote see Baldini 1992, 178, Note 9. Baldini recalls that Maelcote later on wrote two letters to Kepler in 1612 and 1614 in which he announced his admiration for the works of the German astronomer with special reference to the *Astronomia Nova*. For his part Kepler answered him in 1613.

[45] At the beginning of his discourse Maelcote had said that Galileo was "*inter astronomos nostri temporis et celeberrimos et foelicissimos merito numerandus*" [to be rightfully numbered among the most celebrated and happy astronomers of our time] (III, Part I, 293). Now the word *foelicissimus* (like the English word "happy") also has the meaning of "fortunate" and Galileo must, to his displeasure, have certainly interpreted it in that sense. An echo of his resentment can be noted eight years later in the *Discourse on the Comets* about which I will have the opportunity to speak later. In it Galileo puts in the mouth of the declared author of the *Discourse* (Guiducci) the following words:

> And since, virtuous Listeners, from what has been discussed so far, the road has, I believe, been made easier for philosophizing better about the conclusions examined by me than has been done by Tycho and by his followers, I do not wish to continue extending them a helping hand to disentangle themselves from yet a more serious development, in which this Tycho now finds himself and in which he seeks help if not from someone

> more valiant, *at least from a more fortunate*
> *mathematician.* (VI, 102; italics by the author).

Even the words "if not from someone more valiant" seem to be
dictated by the resentment which Galileo must have experienced in
hearing Tycho Brahe called by Maelcote "incomparable astronomer".
See the rest of my main text.

[46] The impression of their contemporaries was quite different,
as attested to by the Notice of 18 May 1611:

> On Friday evening of last week in the Roman College in
> the presence of cardinals and of his promoter, the
> Marquis di Monticello, a recital was given of a Latin ode
> in honor of Mister Galileo Galilei, mathematician of the
> Grand Duke, wherein the new observation of the new
> planets unknown to the ancient philosophers facilitated
> by improvements in the telescopes found by the
> Napoletan Porta was praised and exalted right to the
> stars; whence that Galileo with this public demonstration
> will go back to Florence most consoled and one might say
> crowned by the universal consent of this university.
> (Orbaan 1920, 284; quoted by Paschini 1965, 225).

[47] *Opera Mathematica*, Mainz, 1611, Vol. III, 775. This change
in Clavius' opinion is given great importance by Kepler in his
dedicatory letter to his book: *Epitome Astronomiae Copernicanae.*

[48] *Constitutiones Societatis Jesu*, P. IV, Chapter XIV, N. 3:

> In logic, natural and moral philosophy and metaphysics,
> the doctrine of Aristotle should be followed, as also in the
> other liberal arts. (trans. by Ganss 1970, 220).

Such legislative norms will be repeated by the law-making bodies of
the Society of Jesus, in particular in Decree 41 of the Fifth General
Congregation (1593-1594) where one reads:

> In matters of any importance philosophy professors
> should not deviate from the views of Aristotle, unless his
> view happens to be contrary to a teaching which is
> accepted everywhere in the schools, or especially if his
> view is contrary to orthodox faith. (*Institutum Societatis
> Jesu*, 1893 [Florence] II, 273; trans. by Blackwell 1991,
> 141).

This passage will be cited in 1599 in the *Ratio Studiorum Societatis
Jesu*, Chapter IX, No. 2 (Rules for professors of philosophy).

Needless to say such decrees of the *Constitutions* of the Jesuits had nothing to do with Copernicanism. At the time that Ignatius had written the *Constitutions*, the *De Revolutionibus* of Copernicus had been out for just about ten years and, as we have seen, the repercussions it had in the field of philosophy were minimal. The insistence on the doctrine of Aristotle was determined exclusively by the conviction that it furnished a solid basis for philosophy and, therefore, when appropriately modified, for the so-called "preambles of the faith". The same holds true for the subsequent provisions, including those of the *Ratio Studiorum*, all of which came before the development of the Copernican controversy as a result of the telescopic discoveries. As to the letter of Father Acquaviva, even though, as I have already said, it was almost certainly not motivated as to its philosophical content by the academic assembly held at the Roman College, it probably manifested the first preoccupations of Jesuit superiors in view of the discoveries by Galileo. During the course of the previous year those discoveries had already created a great sensation and found acceptance among the mathematicians of the Roman College. On the principle of uniformity (and solidity) of doctrine as found in the *Constitutions of the Society of Jesus* and in the letters of the General Superiors see Baldini 1992, 78 ff. See also Blackwell 1991, 137 ff. For an English version of the *Ratio Studiorum* see Fitzpatrick 1933. As to the Latin text of the 1611 letter of Father Acquaviva see: *Epistolae selectae praepositorum generalium ad superiores Societatis* (Selected letters of the General Superiors to the superiors of the Society [of Jesus]; Rome: Typis Polyglottis Vaticanis, 1911, 207-209).

[49] Grégoire de Saint-Vincent, one of the most worthwhile Jesuit mathematicians of that time, who was present at the academic assembly, recalled 50 years later in a letter to C. Huygens the welcome given to Galileo at the Roman College and added that the statements of the Jesuit astronomers on the motion of Venus about the Sun was accompanied by murmurs on the part of their philosopher colleagues. See Paschini 1965, 226.

[50] For more details on these matters see Blackwell 1991, 137 ff.

[51] There exists an enormous literature concerning the "blind obedience" of the Jesuits. Often a caricature is given of it, rather than an objective presentation. In fact, when the founder of the Jesuits, Ignatius of Loyola, had sketched out in the *Constitutions* the ideal of obedience for the new religious order, he had spoken of obedience "in a certain way blind" (*caeca quaedam oboedientia*; see the *Constitutions*, P. IV, Chapter I, N. 1). The meaning of this

expression is further explained in the famous *Letter on Obedience*. The highest level of obedience, states St. Ignatius, implies not only the assent of the will, but also that of the intellect, "in so far as the devout will can bend the intellect". Certainly, St. Ignatius adds immediately, the intelligence is not free as the will is and its assent carries it spontaneously towards that which appears to it to be true. "However, in certain cases, *when, that is, the intellect is not constrained by the evidence of the known truth*, it may tend, by reason of the will, in one direction or the other. *And when this case is presented*, whoever professes obedience should lean towards the will of the superior." (*Epistula de virtute oboedientiae*, 1553; italics are the author's). As we can see from these words, that which was required of the Jesuits through obedience was not the sacrifice of intelligence *tout-court* or the abdication of intellectual responsibility, as de Santillana, for example, claims. In the case where a Jesuit was faced with an *evident certainty*, no superior could demand that he assent to something contrary. The Jesuit astronomers of the Roman College themselves had shown that they were not slaves of an unconditionally blind obedience, when at the end they had accepted Galileo's discoveries, motivated, as a matter of fact, by the "evidence of the known truth". And yet this implied, without a doubt, that they were thereby not faithful in a matter of great importance to the tenets of Aristotelianism.

[52] See Note 18 of Chapter I.

[53] See Favaro 1886a, 214.

[54] See in the Archives of the Pontifical Gregorian University, *Corrispondenza di Clavio*, codices 529-530. A substantial part of these manuscripts have been published by Baldini and Napolitani 1992. Of equal importance is the codex 534, still unpublished, which contains the correspondence of Grienberger.

[55] One of the most explicit supporters of the Copernican ideas among the Jesuits was without a doubt Father Wenceslaus Kirwitzer, a professor at the Jesuit college in Graz. In December 1614 he wrote to Father Grienberger stating that the Ptolemaic system was completely false. We do not know Grienberger's response, but it must not have been contrary to Kirwitzer's expectations, since the latter wrote him again in June 1615 with an open profession of the conviction that he had by now acquired that the Copernican system was true. Subsequently Kirwitzer went as a missionary to China, where he died prematurely in 1626. See D'Elia 1960, 25-28.

[56] A testimony to this respect is given in the letter sent by Cardinal del Monte to Cosimo II (XI, 119).

[57] The notes prepared by Galileo for the written résumé are found in IV, 30-51. For further details see Drake 1978, 169-170. Biagioli 1993, 159-209 attributes great importance to this dispute about floating bodies and he sees in it a concrete example of Galileo's scientific activity as having its source and motivation in his role as philosopher at the court of the Grand Duke.

[58] This *Discourse* is found in IV, 51-141. For a summary of its contents see Drake 1978, 177-179.

[59] In this same volume IV of the *National Edition* there are gathered together other writings relative to the discussion of bodies which float on water.

[60] These writings of Castelli are found in IV, 245-286, 449-691, 693-789.

[61] This letter of 22 September 1612 was addressed to the Archbishop of Florence, Alessandro Marzimedici, and was very favorable to Galileo. Marzimedici, who does not seem to have been ill-disposed towards Galileo, allowed the letter to pass into the hands of the latter's friends. Thus it happened that Galileo came to know of it. It is found in IV, 289-293. Galileo answered Nozzolini in January of the following year (IV, 297-310).

[62] See Dame 1968, 191.

[63] Kepler 1941, Vol. IV, 79-98: *Phaenomenon singulare seu Mercurius in Sole.*

[64] Galileo himself alludes to such a prejudice (founded, as we know, on the Aristotle's theory in the *De Coelo*). See V, 138. Giordano Bruno, instead, had correctly interpreted the meaning of the sunspots and even came to the point of deducing from them the rotation of the Sun. See Michel 1965, particularly 402-403.

[65] For a detailed analysis of the sources see Dame 1968, 192-194. On the other hand, Drake gives January 1611 as the time of the first observations.

[66] See Favaro 1887, 35-89. Before Fabricius and perhaps also before Galileo, the spots would have been observed by the English mathematician and astronomer, Thomas Harriot (1560-1621). But his observations only became known in 1784 and were published only in 1833. See Favaro 1919.

[67] Drake writes:

Apelles declared that he had first seen apparent spots on the sun about May 1611, a date in accord with Paul Guldin's recollection that he had sent word of sunspots to Scheiner from Rome during Galileo's visit there. (Drake 1978, 182)

But there is no reason to doubt the sincerity of Scheiner's statements which were made when the dispute with Galileo over the priority of the "discovery" of the sunspots had not yet begun. On the other hand, Scheiner speaks (he wrote his first letter on 12 November 1611) of the discovery as having taken place seven or eight months before, that is, perhaps as early as the month of April, or even in March. And the month of March will be clearly given by him much later in his major work, the *Rosa Ursina*.

[68] On this Drake comments that the answer given by Galileo to his friend Cigoli on the sunspots was already known in Rome. Galileo had already understood the importance of this phenomenon for proving the rotation of the Sun. It may have been that the Jesuits in Rome, informed by Cigoli, had in turn passed on the information to Scheiner. But it might also have happened that Scheiner had obtained his information from the observations carried out by Fabricius (see Dame 1968, 196).

[69] Markus Welser was born at Augsburg in 1558 and had studied at Padua, Paris and Rome. As a banker and business man he had close relationships with the Jesuits. He was elected a member of the *Accademia dei Lincei* in the very year he died (1614).

[70] Apelles (4th century B.C.) was regarded, even in Scheiner's time, as the greatest painter of antiquity. Did Scheiner imply with the choice of this pseudonym that his work was a very valuable "work of art"? As to the use of pseudonyms they were recommended by Jesuit superiors of those times for authors of books whose subject matter was apt to give rise to disputes. The precise intention was to avoid that the Order itself would get officially involved in the disputes. This is clear from what Scheiner himself will state many years later in the *Rosa Ursina*:

> The Reverend Father Theodor Buseo, at that time Provincial of the Province of Upper Germany, was pleased with the new phenomenon [of the sunspots] but he did not think it would be opportune that my name should appear in this unexpected, and for many suspect, material. (*Rosa Ursina*, "Ad Lectorem" [To the reader], XIII).

Scheiner's Provincial was probably thinking of the problems which could arise with the most intransigent Aristotelians because of the hypothesis of a large number of small planets introduced to explain the phenomenon of the sunspots. On the other hand I think we can exclude, in this initial stage of the question, any worry about a possible argument with Galileo.

[71] One of the "untuned organ pipes" which could be and should be tuned right away was the theory of the incorruptible heavens. The phenomenon of the *novae* had, as we know, already established an argument against this incorruptibility. Now the sunspots, which Galileo considered "contiguous to the surface of the body of the sun, where they continuously are born and die, like as a matter of fact the clouds about the Earth" (Letter to Cesi of 12 May 1612; XI 296), are another irrefutable proof, according to Galileo, of the incorrectness of the Aristotelian theory. His certainty that the sunspots were on the solar surface became even stronger some days later (see the subsequent letter to Cesi of 26 May; XI, 301).

[72] The Aristotelians made their reactions known quite soon. Among them there was, as usual, Cremonini, who, according to what Gualdo had written to Galileo, had outright refused to read the letter for fear that he would "have to refrain from giving that complete faith in his philosophy which he had done up until now" (XI, 320).

[73] For a detailed examination of this letter see Dame 1968, 235-243.

[74] We already have in germ in these comments of Galileo the methodological position which he will present in more detail in *The Assayer*.

[75] This opinion was also shared by the Jesuits in Rome according to what Cesi told Galileo on 14 September (XI, 395). The only, but important, exception to this was Grienberger. As Faber wrote to Galileo at the end of November:

> Eight days ago Father Grünberger [sic] was in my house and he told me that he had not yet seen the most recent little work of Apelle [*Accuratior Disquisitio*]: but truly, even though he knows that he is a Jesuit, he agrees much more with Your Lordship than with Apelle, since it seems to him that the arguments with which Your Lordship rejects the foundation that they are not [sic] stars are very effective. However, as an obedient son he does not dare to express his opinion. (XI, 434).

We are obviously dealing here with the admission of the corruptibility of the Sun, which was contrary to Aristotelianism and, therefore, against the legislation on such matters then in force in the Society of Jesus. I have already mentioned that legislation (see Note 48) which had been stressed again just one year before in the letter of the General Superior, Father Acquaviva.

[76] Such statements (as well as those of Father Cysat who had assisted Scheiner during his first observations) seem to be in good faith, either because the previous observations of Galileo were not known or the chronology was not exactly established.

[77] These expressions of esteem by Galileo for Father Grienberger were a reciprocation of those which the Jesuit had shown towards Galileo when he spoke to Gualdo and which Gualdo had passed on to Galileo in his letter to him of 20 November (XII, 112). The fact that in Grienberger's case, in contrast with that of other Jesuits, the dispute over the sunspots had not damaged his esteem for Galileo is, for that matter, already clear from the declarations made by the Jesuit mathematician six months before to the young Florentine, Giovanni Bardi. Bardi was studying at that time at the Roman College and he spoke thus of Grienberger to Galileo:

> I asked him [Grienberger] what he thought of this book [on the sunspots] which he had already seen; and he said [it was] very good, and that in many things, as well for this [book] as for that other one on floating bodies, he [Grienberger] sided with Your Lordship [Galileo]. (XI, 512).

These words of Grienberger must have led Bardi a year later to propose to Grienberger, as a topic for a public disputation which had been assigned to him on a natural philosophy problem, the question of floating bodies for which he would adopt the position of Galileo. While accepting this proposal Grienberger showed that he was in complete agreement with Galileo's theory and then he himself took part in the disputation with some experiments (XII, 76 and 78). When Bardi wrote to Galileo about it, he added:

> Father Grienberger told me that if he had not been obliged to respect Aristotle (with whom, by order of the General, the Jesuits cannot disagree in any way but rather are obliged always to defend) he would have spoken more positively about this position [of Galileo] because he finds himself very satisfied with it. He also told me that he was not surprised that Aristotle's theory was against this one [of Galileo] because he [Aristotle] is clearly also wrong in regard to what you [Galileo] once told me about those two weights falling faster or slower. (XII, 76).

As we see in this case too Grienberger justified his reticence by alleging the orders of Father General Acquaviva. In fact, Acquaviva had returned to the argument about fidelity to Aristotle in a new letter of December 1613. See *Epistolae selectae praepositorum generalium ad superiores Societatis* (Selected letters of the General Superiors to the superiors of the Society [of Jesus]; Rome: Typis Polyglottis Vaticanis, 1911, 209-215). And it was impossible, only six months after this letter, for Grienberger not to feel the weight of those repeated prescriptions of his General Superior.

[78] At the beginning of *The Assayer* Galileo states:

> How many men attack my *Letters on Sunspots* and under what disguises! The material contained therein ought to have opened to the mind's eye much room for admirable speculation; instead it met with scorn and derision. Many people disbelieved it or failed to appreciate it. Others, not wanting to agree with my ideas, advanced ridiculous and impossible opinions against me; and some, overwhelmed and convinced by my arguments, attempted to rob me of that glory which was mine, pretending not to have seen my writings and trying to represent themselves as the original discoverers of these impressive marvels. (V, 214; trans by Drake 1957, 232).

And Scheiner will state in the *Rosa Ursina* (p. 2): "Haec . . . pleraque in Apellem digitum manifestum intendere videntur" (the major part of these [words] appear to be clearly directed to Apelle). Scheiner's opinion has been shared by the majority of Galileo scholars. Still, Drake maintains that it is clearly a matter of an equivocation, even though understandable after all that "Guiducci" had written in the *Discourse on the comets* (see Drake 1970b, 188 ff). Drake notes, correctly I think, that Galileo could not have possibly been alluding to Scheiner with the words, "trying to represent themselves as the original discoverers" in the last sentence of the quotation above. Drake states:

> As a matter of fact, Scheiner's letters on this subject preceded and were the publicly acknowledged reason for Galileo's own first writings about sunspots. And to Galileo's first letter, before it was published, Scheiner wrote a published reply. (Drake 1970b, 189).

According to Drake Scheiner's equivocation originated from the fact that he ignored that others had written about the sunspots and Galileo intended an allusion to them (thus the use of the plural expression in the phrase cited above). In particular, the accusation of representing himself as "discoverer" would most probably refer to the work published in 1619 in Latin by the Frenchman, Jean Du Pont de Tarde (1561-1636) under the title *Borbonia Sydera* and then translated into French in 1623. In November 1614 Tarde had visited Galileo in Florence (see XII, 117) and Galileo had shown him the sunspots and had spoken to him of the dispute with Scheiner. Afterwards Galileo sent Tarde a copy of his letters on the sunspots. However that might be, the responsibility, at least for the phrases contained in the *Discourse on the comets* of Guiducci and thus of the first unequivocal break with Scheiner, falls on Galileo's shoulders.

[79] As Favaro 1919, 32 ff. comments, Cigoli, as early as 23 September 1611, had communicated to Galileo that a Roman observer of the sunspots, Passignano, had seen them move along "spiral lines" (XI, 212). More precise information on the periodic change in the trajectories followed by the sunspots came to Galileo in April 1613 by means of the Dominican, Orazio Morandi, from the same Sizzi who in his *Dianoia* had, as we have already seen, attacked the *Starry Message*. At that time Sizzi was at Paris and, under the influence of a group of supporters of science, he had aligned himself on the side of Galileo in the argument over floating bodies and he had also dedicated himself to the study of sunspots. But at that time Galileo was not yet aware of the importance of the observations given by Sizzi to Morandi (XI, 491-493). It will only be in the *Dialogue* that Galileo will use this phenomenon as a proof in support of the motion of the Earth. See Drake 1970b, 183-184 and 1978, 209-210, 311.

CHAPTER 3

EPILOGUE TO THE SCRIPTURAL CONTROVERSY:

THE *DE REVOLUTIONIBUS* IS LISTED ON THE INDEX

1. *The theologians begin to intervene in the Copernican controversy*

We have already seen that the fundamental reason for Galileo's return to Florence from Padua had been the wish to be able to be completely free to devote himself to his research and observations without the obligation of teaching. For that same reason of having greater freedom Galileo, immediately after his return to Florence, had considered having his two daughters, Virginia and Livia, enter the convent. Considering the ideas of those times, they would have encountered difficulty in getting married. But, since they were still too young, Galileo's intentions could be carried out only between the end of 1613 and the beginning of 1614. After their admittance into the Monastery of St. Matthew at Arcetri near Florence, Virginia and Livia pronounced their solemn vows and took the names, respectively, of Maria Celeste and Arcangela. While the latter never came to accept in complete peace the egoistic decision of her father, Virginia, now known as "Suor Celeste", will always remain close to him with her affectionate care even, in fact above all, in the most difficult moments of his life.[1]

However, despite all of his planning, Galileo's strictly scientific activity after his return to Florence seems to get less as the years go by. This fact has been interpreted by some scholars as the result of a deliberate choice by Galileo who would have decided to go over from purely scientific research to the field of "cultural propaganda" in support of Copernicanism.[2] But rather than a deliberate choice, it seems to me that this fact depended on the way events developed as they drew Galileo more and more into controversies with his adversaries. This polemical climate, which, with its ups and downs of victories and moments of deep bitterness, required an enormous quantity of time and energy, could not help but make it difficult to continue any in-depth scientific work which required concentration and adequate tranquility.[3]

As we have already seen, in March 1613 the *Letters on Sunspots* were printed at Rome with the title: *Istoria e Dimostrazioni intorno alle Macchie Solari* (A History and Some Demonstrations Concerning Sunspots). The book was issued by the *Accademia dei Lincei* with the *Imprimatur,* that is, a permission to publish which was granted by Church authorities on the basis of favorable judgements by censors, whose task it was to determine whether books, which dealt with matters thought to be connected with Christian beliefs, were "orthodox" or not. In this case the censors' judgement on the book was very positive (see V, 74). But difficulties were not lacking in the first phases of the censors' review as regards the statement contained in the second letter to Welser whereby the incorruptibility of the heavens was said to be "not only false but erroneous and repugnant to those truths of Sacred Scripture about which there could be no doubt" (V, 138-139). As we know, Galileo had based this statement on the answer he had received on this matter from Cardinal Conti, but the reviser had remained immovable in his request to abolish this reference and any other reference to Sacred Scripture (see XI, 428-429). And so the passage had to be removed. On the other hand the reviser had not objected at all to having a clear statement about Copernicanism in the third letter to Welser, probably because it appeared in a marginal note and did not, therefore, constitute a true and proper profession of Copernicanism.[4]

It is perhaps the failure of the Church authorities to intervene as regards this last mentioned point that led Galileo to put aside the prudence that he had shown up to that moment. From now on he will carry on ever more decisively his "activity in favor of the Copernican system" with his disciples and friends at his side. By acting in this way Galileo showed that he had not yet taken sufficient account of the importance of the reviser's intervention in the *Istoria.* This intervention betrayed the preoccupation already existing in Rome since the time of

Galileo's visit there, and as we know even quite a bit before that, with respect to the new view of the world which had Galileo as its champion and which appeared to the large majority of theologians to be irreconcilable with Sacred Scripture. This preoccupation will only grow as the actions of the "galileisti" in favor of Copernicanism slowly develop, driving not a few of the theologians to join up with the Aristotelian philosophers and the conservative astronomers. This intervention of the theologians in the debate on Copernicanism, with the consequent displacement of its center of gravity from the area of natural philosophy and of astronomy to that of Scriptural theology, is the new element characterizing the period which follows upon the publication of the *Istoria* and it is pregnant with consequences for the future.

A first indication of this state of mind among theologians occurred a little more than a year before. In the course of a conversation[5] which had taken place among a group of Florentine intellectuals on 1 November 1612 the Dominican, Niccolò Lorini, had attacked the Copernican ideas as being contrary to Scripture. When Galileo, who for health reasons was at that time outside of Florence in the villa of his friend Salviati, learned of what had happened, he was very resentful and he sent a protest letter to Lorini. This letter has been lost. But we have the response of Lorini himself written on 5 November. The Dominican showed his surprise at being accused of discussing philosophical questions by whomsoever. But he admitted that he had made a reference, without any special involvement, to the "opinion of [that] Ipernicus, or whatever his name is", and he stated that it "appears to be against Holy Scripture" (XI, 427; trans. by Drake 1978, 197).

This answer must have made Galileo laugh for he wrote to Cesi the following January and spoke of:

> . . . an incompetent conversationalist who has decided to oppose the mobility of the earth. But this good fellow is so unfamiliar with the founder of that doctrine that he calls him 'Ipernicus' (trans. by Langford 1966, 51). Now Your Excellency can see how and from whom poor philosophy is jolted. (XI, 461).

Galileo must obviously have been convinced that he did not have much to fear from adversaries like this. But he was wrong. A little more than a year later, still at the court of the Grand Duke who was then at Pisa, something of much greater importance in the theological-biblical development of the Copernican controversy took place. Benedetto Castelli gave Galileo the news in a letter of 14 December (XI, 605-606). Two days before Castelli had taken part in a lunch offered by the Grand Duke together with Cosimo Boscaglia, a philosophy professor at the University of Pisa who enjoyed the esteem and protection of the Medici family.

Castelli, in response to a question of the Grand Duke, had spoken of the observations of the Medicean planets, which he had carried out the night before. The Grand Duke's mother, Christina of Lorraine, joined in the discussion about the planets and even Boscaglia, when asked, admitted that they were real and not a trick of the telescope. Boscaglia also admitted that Galileo's discoveries were true, but he added that "only the motion of the Earth seemed incredible and could not be true, all the more so since Holy Scripture was clearly against this opinion". They took up the discussion again after lunch. Christina appeared to take sides with Boscaglia on the question of the Earth's motion, while the Grand Duke Cosimo and the Grand Duchess, together with someone else, took sides with Castelli. The latter, speaking as a theologian, had blunted the Biblical arguments of Boscaglia and had reduced him to silence according to Castelli's own statement.

Castelli's report was optimistic but undoubtedly Galileo became very concerned about this Scriptural development in the discussion. He saw that his adversaries, since they could no longer deny the reality of his discoveries, were proceeding ever more to dig themselves in behind the bastion of Scripture. It was the last bulwark, but the one most to be feared, because it could nullify Galileo's plan to have Copernicanism accepted or at least considered without preconceptions in the Catholic world of that time. This was all the more true as the discussion continued to move from a narrow lineup of "specialists" to the much wider group of "educated" Catholics.

On the other hand it was of the utmost importance that the anti-Copernican (at the same time anti-Galilean) propaganda cease at the Grand Duke's court, even more so since the Grand Duchess Mother, Christina, could be vulnerable to such propaganda despite all of Castelli's optimism.[6] Galileo, therefore, on 21 December hastened to write a long letter to Castelli in which he treated explicitly and in depth the relationships between science and the *Bible* (V, 281-288).

2.   The Letter to Castelli. *The reaction of the Dominicans in Florence*

In the first place Galileo admitted in his letter that Sacred Scripture could not lie or deceive, but he immediately added that its interpreters and expositors could err in various ways; the most serious error would be if they should wish to stop at the pure meaning of the words. In fact, in such a case, one would wind up by attributing to God human forms and feelings like anger, repentance, and hate. Given, therefore, the possibility, even the necessity, of interpreting Scripture in a non-literal way, continued Galileo, "it seems to me that, in disputes about scientific matters it [Scripture] should be brought in only as a last resort" (V, 282). In fact, Galileo explained that both Holy Scripture (since it was dictated by the Holy Spirit) and nature (which faithfully carried out the divine orders) came from the Divine Word. But while Scripture had to be adapted to the common ability to understand and, therefore, had to use words and ways of speaking which, if taken in their literal sense, are far from the truth, nature, since it is "inexorable and unchangeable" and not at all concerned that its recondite reasoning and ways of acting be exposed to human abilities, "never transgresses the limits of the laws imposed upon it". Therefore, whatever "sense experience" puts before our eyes or whatever "necessary demonstrations" allow us to conclude should not be called in doubt on the basis of Scriptural citations which, taken in the literal sense, would seem to say something different.

In other words, since two truths (which come from the same Divine Word, the source of all truth) can never be in contradiction, once we are sure (in the way described above) of certain "natural effects", theologians should make every effort to find the true sense of the Scriptural passages which are related to those effects, so as to find agreement between the two truths. And Galileo added:

> And who wants to set bounds to the human mind? Who wants to assert that everything is known to the world? Hence, apart from articles concerning salvation and the establishment of the Faith, against the solidity of which there is no danger that anyone may ever raise a more valid and efficacious doctrine, it would perhaps be a very good counsel never to add more [articles of faith] without necessity. And if that is so, how much greater disorder [it would be] to add new articles at the request of persons who, beside the fact that we do not know whether they speak inspired by divine power, are clearly seen to be completely devoid of the information that would be required - I will not say to disprove, but - to understand the demonstrations with which the most acute sciences proceed in confirming some of their conclusions. (V, 284).

And Galileo concluded the, so to speak, doctrinal part of his letter with the following words:

> I would believe that the authority of Holy Writ had only the aim of persuading men of those articles and propositions which, being necessary for our salvation and overriding all human reason, could not be made credible by any other science, or by other means than the mouth of the Holy Ghost itself. But I do not think it necessary that the same God who has given us our senses, reason, and intelligence wished us to abandon their use, giving us by some other means the information that we could gain through them - and especially in matters of which only a minimal part, and in partial conclusions, is to be read in Scripture . . . (V, 284; trans. by Drake 1978, 226).

Galileo, therefore, was criticizing the posture of those who in discussions of questions to do with nature "which are not directly of the faith" start from Scriptural citations and often interpret them badly. And to conclude he proposed his own interpretation of the passage from the *Book of Joshua* which had been central to the discussions at the court of the Grand Duke.[7] After receiving this letter, Castelli, perhaps without even noting what he was doing, provided the opportunity to have copies made of it and these wound up in the hands of the opponents. Obviously that was not the kind of thing to help calm the waters.

The tension which had been building up during all of 1614 finally exploded clamorously with a sermon which another Dominican, Tommaso Caccini, gave on 21 December 1614 in the Church of *Santa Maria Novella* in Florence. According to a version which circulated in that city quite a bit later, Caccini would have begun his sermon with the words in Latin from the book of the *Acts of the Apostles* (1, 11): "*Viri Galilaei, quid statis adspicientes in coelum?*" ("Men of Galilee, what are you looking for in the sky"), with an obvious allusion to Galileo and his followers, the "*Galileisti*".[8]

Caccini had stated in his sermon that mathematics was a diabolic art and that mathematicians, as disseminators of heresies, should be driven from all of the states (XII, 130). As we see, it was a question of a fundamental attack against Copernicanism and its Galilean promoters with a defense of the literal sense of the extract from the *Book of Joshua*, which made up the sermon's theme.

Another Dominican, Luigi Maraffi, a great friend of Galileo, when he heard of the sermon wrote to him from Rome on 10 January 1615 to show his regret that a member of his Order had shown such "madness and ignorance" (XII, 127).

Galileo would have liked to have gone right to the bottom of the affair by requesting atonement from Caccini. But when he asked Cesi's opinion, he was advised to give up the idea because it would not have helped at all and could, on the contrary, have had serious consequences. In fact, Cesi added:

> ... as to Copernicus' opinion, Bellarmine himself who is one of the heads in the congregation concerning these matters [i.e., the Congregation of the Holy Office and that of the Index] has told me that he holds it to be heretical and that

the motion of the earth is without any doubt against Scripture.

If, therefore, with the heating up of the controversy, a response on the affair should have been requested of the Congregation of the Index, the book of Copernicus would have been prohibited. Cesi, therefore, proposed an indirect retort, for example by some mathematician at Pisa or Florence, since Caccini had in general offended mathematicians, or by some form of punishment determined by the archbishop of Florence (XII, 129-131).[9]

In the end, Galileo and his friends preferred to let the matter drop. But their opponents were not of the same mind. Lorini (who himself had deprecated the tone of the sermon of his religious companion Caccini) came a little later to possess a copy of the letter of Galileo to Castelli and he discussed it with other Dominicans of the monastery of St. Mark in Florence. While Lorini a little more than two years earlier had shown that he nourished no great interest in "Ipernicus", now the situation took a new course. In the *Letter to Castelli* Galileo had entered into theological matters and had pretended, even though he was only a simple scientist, to deal with matters of Biblical interpretation. That was extremely serious (the other fathers also agreed) because it set up an example of the kind of private interpretation of Holy Scripture which the Catholic Church had condemned.[10] Lorini felt that he was obliged "in conscience" to alert the Roman ecclesiastical authorities to the matter. On 7 February 1615 he sent a copy of the *Letter to Castelli* to Cardinal Paolo Sfondrati, Prefect of the Congregation of the Index,[11] so that it could be examined (XIX, 297-298).[12] In the accompanying letter, which Lorini had wished to be kept secret so that it would not be "taken as a court deposition", Galileo is not directly mentioned but it speaks of the "Galileisti" as the authors of the *Letter to Castelli*. After saying that the letter supported the Copernican position, Lorini added that it contained propositions which all the Fathers of the monastery of St. Mark considered to be:

. . . either suspect or rash: for example, that certain ways of speaking in Holy Scripture are inappropriate; that in disputes about natural effects the same Scripture holds the last place; that its expositors are often wrong in their interpretations; that the same Scripture must not meddle with anything else but matters concerning faith; and that, in questions about natural phenomena, philosophical or astronomical argument has more force than the sacred or divine one. Your Most Illustrious Lordship can see these propositions underlined by me in the above mentioned letter, of which I send you a faithful copy (XIX, 297; trans. by Finocchiaro 1989, 134).

Was, in fact, this copy sent by Lorini the "faithful copy" of Galileo's original? Favaro denied this and following him so did all other historians of Galileo. They have shown the importance of the discrepancies (in general completely in Galileo's disfavor) between this copy and the one which Favaro considered to be, on the whole, the closest to Galileo's original which has been lost. Favaro, therefore, inserted this one with some variations in Volume V of the National Edition.[13] However, Mauro Pesce has recently reexamined the question and has arrived at the conclusion that, in fact, the copy sent by Lorini was a faithful copy of the original *Letter to Castelli*.[14] As Galileo himself stated (V, 292) he wrote this letter with a "running pen", i.e. hastily, and did not, therefore, have time to refine certain statements, especially as regards Scripture.

On the other hand, Galileo had an inkling of Lorini's action and of the fact that other Dominicans of St. Mark's monastery, among them Caccini, had gone to Rome in order to bring to a head with the Roman authorities the accusations that the exposition in the *Letter to Castelli* was contrary to doctrinal orthodoxy. Galileo was obviously worried and he revised the *Letter*, still according to Pesce, by softening some of the expressions and by giving a more cautious rendering to the various statements which touched upon theology. It was, in fact, such a revised copy which he sent on 16 February to his friend Monsignor Piero Dini with the statement:

> . . . upon his return from Pisa the same Father [Lorini]
> who a few years ago expressed complaints in private
> conversation has hit me again. He has come across, I do
> not know how, a copy of a letter which about a year ago I
> wrote to the Father Mathematician of Pisa in connection
> with the use of sacred authorities in scientific disputes and
> the interpretation of Joshua's passage, and so they are
> making an uproar about it; from what I hear, they find
> many heresies in it and, in short, they have opened a new
> front to tear me to pieces. However, because I have not
> received the least sign of scruples from anyone else who
> has seen this letter, I suspect that perhaps whoever
> transcribed it may have inadvertently changed some word;
> such a change, together with a little inclination toward
> censure, may make things look very different from my
> intention. I hear that some of these Fathers, especially the
> same one who had complained earlier, have come there to
> try something else with his copy of this letter of mine, and
> so I did not consider it inappropriate to send you a copy of
> it in the correct version as I wrote it.[15] I ask you to do me
> the favor of reading it along with the Jesuit Father
> Grienberger a distinguished mathematician and a very
> good friend and patron of mine, and, if you deem it
> appropriate, of having it somehow come into the hands of
> the Most Illustrious Cardinal Bellarmine. The latter is the
> one whom these Dominican Fathers seem to want to rally
> around, with the hope of bringing about at least the
> condemnation of Copernicus's book, opinion, and doctrine.
> (V, 291-292; trans. by Finocchiaro 1989, 55).

Obviously, Galileo was still counting on the Jesuits to help
him in this delicate predicament. In fact, in a postscript to the
letter to Dini he added:

> I think the most immediate remedy would be to approach
> the Jesuit Fathers, as those whose knowledge is much
> above the common education of friars. (V, 295; trans. by
> Finocchiaro 1989, 58).

Galileo hoped that this superior education of theirs would
have driven them, if not to align themselves with him in favor
of Copernicanism, at least to react against the intemperance of

the ignoramuses. Since the *Letter* was not printed and, therefore, did not come under the competency of the Congregation of the Index, but still concerned questions connected with the Catholic faith, Cardinal Sfondrati sent it, together with the accusatory letter of Lorini, to Cardinal Millino, Secretary of the Holy Office. It was probably the latter Cardinal who requested a consultor to examine it. The consultor had difficulties with only three of the statements in the *Letter* (and, in fact, they concerned precisely phrases which were present in Lorini's copy, but not in the one sent by Galileo to Dini). But he added that two of the statements could be understood in the correct sense and: "For the rest, though it sometimes uses improper words, it does not diverge from the pathways of Catholic expression" (XIX, 305, trans. by Finocchiaro 1989, 136).

A few days later on February 25 during a meeting of the Holy Office the letter of Lorini to Cardinal Sfondrati was read and in all likelihood also the opinion of the consultor of the Holy Office on the *Letter to Castelli*. As we have seen this opinion was not unfavorable to Galileo but had pointed out some manners of speaking which were improper and which "sounded bad when they were used with regard to Holy Scripture". Therefore, the Holy Office wanted to go deeper into the matters. Since Lorini had sent only a copy, the Holy Office wanted to have the original, in order to formulate a definitive judgment. And since the letter had been sent to Castelli, who was then living in Pisa, the request for the original was sent on to the Archbishop and inquisitor of that city (XIX, 276).

Dini spoke of Galileo's fears to their common friend, Giovanni Ciampoli (XII, 144)[16] and the latter wrote in turn to Galileo on 28 February in a reassuring tone and stated that the influential Dominican Father Maraffi was "more than ever a servant" of Galileo and that the other Dominicans of influence in Rome did not nourish hostile feelings against him. He then added that he had spoken to Cardinal Maffeo Barberini "who, as you know from experience, has always admired your competency" and he continued:

. . . [the Cardinal] told me only yesterday evening that with respect to these opinions he would like greater

caution in not going beyond the arguments used by
Ptolemy and Copernicus, and finally in not exceeding the
bounds of physics and mathematics. For to explain the
Scriptures is claimed by theologians as their field, and if
new things are brought in even though to be admired for
their ingenuity, not everyone has the dispassionate faculty
of taking them just as they are said. One man amplifies,
the next one alters, and what came from the author's own
mouth becomes so transformed in spreading that he will no
longer recognize it as his own (XII, 146).

Dini's reply to Galileo came a little later. He wrote that he
had had many copies made of the *Letter to Castelli* and that he
had given a copy to Grienberger to whom he also read the letter
which Galileo had sent him on 16 February. And he added: "And
I did the same with many others, including the Most Illustrious
Bellarmine with whom I spoke at length of the things which
Your Excellency writes" (XII, 151). Despite the ambiguity of this
last phrase, it seems that one could conclude from it that Dini
delivered to the Cardinal a copy of the letter of Galileo to
Castelli.[17]

As to Bellarmine's reaction, Dini made reference to the fact
that the Cardinal excluded the possibility that things would end
with the prohibition of Copernicus, but that, in the worst case,
notes would have been added to the *De Revolutionibus* so as to
present the doctrine as a pure mathematical expedient. And
Bellarmine suggested that, for the sake of prudence, Galileo
should speak in the same manner. According to the Cardinal,
against the immobility of the Sun there was especially the
phrase from Psalm 18, 6 (according to the Vulgate): "Exultavit
ut gigas ad currendam viam, etc.", that is, the Sun "exulted like
a giant which prepares to run its course". Dini had replied that
this phrase could be interpreted as a common way of speaking,
but the Cardinal had said that: ". . . this is not something to
jump into, just as one ought not to jump hurriedly into
condemning any one of these opinions" (XII, 151; trans. by
Finocchiaro 1989, 59). And Dini continued:

And if you should have put together in your essay any
interpretation to the purpose, he will gladly look them

over. Now since I know that you will remember to submit yourself to the decisions of the holy Church as you have declared to me and to others, it will be a great help to you. (XII, 151).[18]

Dini added that, since Bellarmine had said that he would have spoken of the matter with Father Grienberger, he had also wished to see the latter, who admitted to him that he would have preferred that Galileo:

> . . . first carry out his demonstrations and then get involved in discussing the Scripture. . . In regard to the arguments advanced in favor of your position, the said Father thinks they are more plausible than true, since he is worried about other passages of the Holy Writ (XII, 151-152; trans. by Finocchiaro 1989, 59).

Galileo answered Dini on 23 March with a second important letter in which he offered a retort to each point raised in the comments of Bellarmine and Grienberger. Against the conviction, still commonly held at that time, that Copernicus had only proposed a mathematical hypothesis, Galileo made it clear that Copernicus was convinced of the mobility of the Earth as a real fact. According to Galileo it was necessary to either accept or reject Copernicanism without any possibility of a compromise (which would occur, as a matter of fact, if one wished to accept it as a pure mathematical hypothesis). And Galileo added:

> Whether in reaching such a decision it is advisable to consider, ponder, and examine what he [Copernicus] writes is something that I have done my best to show in an essay of mine . . . for I have no other aim but the honor of the Holy Church and do not direct my small labors to any other goal. . . Indeed, out of the same zeal, I am in the process of collecting all of Copernicus's reasons and making them clearly intelligible to many people, for in his works they are very difficult; and I am adding to them many more considerations, always based on celestial observations, on sensory experiences, and on the support of physical effects (V, 299-300; trans. by Finocchiaro 1989, 62).

The first writing to which Galileo here makes reference is the *Letter to Christina of Lorraine* (the Grand Duchess Mother) which Galileo was preparing precisely at that time. The second is most likely the *Discourse on the ebb and flow of the sea* which, after further elaborations and additions during a long gestation period, will one day become the famous *Dialogue*.

At the end of his letter Galileo answers the Scriptural argument, to which Bellarmine had alluded, by proposing an exegesis of Psalm 18, 6 which was certainly not done in a way as to win the Cardinal's sympathy.[19] And this was undoubtedly the reason why Dini, after having consulted Cesi, did not in the end have this letter read to Bellarmine (XII, 175).

3.   *Foscarini and Bellarmine on the Copernican question*

Without a doubt Galileo was encouraged in his Copernican campaign as well as in the composition of his *Letter to Christina of Lorraine* by the publication of a work by the Carmelite theologian, Antonio Foscarini.[20] This publication was entitled: *Letter of the Reverend Father Master Antonio Foscarini, Carmelite, on the opinion of the Pythagoreans and of Copernicus concerning the mobility of the Earth and the stability of the Sun and the new Pythagorean system of the world, etc.* It reproduced a letter sent by Foscarini himself to the Superior General of the Carmelites. On 7 March Cesi had sent a copy to Galileo with an accompanying letter in which he commented:

> . . . a work which certainly could not have appeared at a
> better time, unless to increase the fury of our adversaries
> is damaging, which I do not believe (XII, 150; trans. by
> Drake 1957, 154).[21]

In his work Foscarini gave importance above all to the inadequacy and unlikelihood of the system of Ptolemy. He then spoke of Galileo's discoveries thanks to which the Copernican hypothesis now appeared to be more acceptable since it was simpler and fit the observations better.[22] Then when he confronted the problem of the Scripture difficulties against the motion of the Earth, Foscarini substantially maintained that, since the truth is one, the truth of Scripture could not be contrary to the truth of the Copernican system (if one admitted that the latter could be proven). It should, therefore, be possible, continued Foscarini, to reconcile those Scriptural passages which were causing difficulty with Copernicanism. Foscarini went on to consider those passages which he gathered into six classes and he proposed six exegetical principles which, according to the Carmelite Father, would remove the difficulties in question.[23]

Foscarini had sent a copy of his publication to Cardinal Bellarmine with a request for his opinion on the matter. Bellarmine answered him on 12 April 1615 with the following letter:

My Reverend Father,

I have read with interest the letter in Italian and the essay in Latin which your Paternity sent to me; I thank you for one and for the other and confess that they are all full of intelligence and erudition. You ask for my opinion, and so I shall give it to you, but very briefly, since now you have little time for reading and I for writing.

First I say that it seems to me that your Paternity and Mr. Galileo are proceeding prudently by limiting yourselves to speaking suppositionally and not absolutely, as I have always believed that Copernicus spoke. For there is no danger in saying that, by assuming the Earth moves and the sun stands still, one saves all of the appearances better than by postulating eccentrics and epicycles; and that is sufficient for the mathematician. However, it is different to want to affirm that in reality the sun is at the center of the world and only turns on itself, without moving from east to west, and the earth is in the third heaven and revolves with great speed around the sun; this is a very dangerous thing, likely not only to irritate all scholastic philosophers and theologians, but also to harm the Holy Faith by rendering Holy Scripture false. For Your Paternity has well shown many ways of interpreting Holy Scripture, but has not applied them to particular cases; without a doubt you would have encountered very great difficulties if you had wanted to interpret all those passages you yourself cited.

Second, I say that, as you know, the Council [of Trent] prohibits interpreting Scripture against the common consensus of the Holy Fathers; and if Your Paternity wants to read not only the Holy Fathers, but also the modern commentaries on Genesis, the Psalms, Ecclesiastes, and Joshua, you will find all agreeing in the literal interpretation that the sun is in heaven and turns around the earth with great speed, and that the earth is very far from heaven and sits motionless at the center of the world. Consider now, with your sense of prudence, whether the church can tolerate giving Scripture a meaning contrary to the Holy Fathers and to all the Greek and Latin commentators. Nor can one answer that this is not a matter of faith, since it is not a matter of faith "as regards the topic,", it is a matter of faith "as regards the speaker"; and so it would be heretical to say that Abraham did not have two children and Jacob twelve, as well as to say that Christ was not born of a virgin, because both are said by the Holy Spirit through the mouth of the prophets and the apostles.

Third, I say that if there were a true demonstration that the sun is at the center of the world and the earth in the third heaven, and that the sun does not circle the earth but the earth circles the sun, then one would have to proceed with great care in explaining the Scriptures that appear contrary; and say rather that we do not understand them than that what is demonstrated is false. But I will not believe that there is such a demonstration, until it is shown me. Nor is it the same to demonstrate that by supposing the sun to be at the center and the earth in heaven one can save the appearances, and to demonstrate that in truth the sun is at the center and the earth in the heaven; for I believe the first demonstration may be available, but I have very great doubts about the second, and in case of doubt one must not abandon the Holy Scripture as interpreted by the Holy Fathers. I add that the one who wrote, "The sun also riseth, and the sun goeth down, and hasteth to his place where he arose," was Solomon, who not only spoke inspired by God, but was a man above all others wise and learned in the human sciences and in the knowledge of created things; he received all this wisdom from God; therefore it is not likely that he was affirming something that was contrary to truth already demonstrated or capable of being demonstrated. Now, suppose you say that Solomon speaks in accordance with appearances, since it seems to us that the sun moves (while the earth does so), just as to someone who moves away from the seashore on a ship it looks like the shore is moving, I shall answer that when someone moves away from the shore, although it appears to him that the shore is moving away from him, nevertheless he knows that it is an error and corrects it, seeing clearly that the ship moves and not the shore; but in regard to the sun and the earth, no wise man has any need to correct the error, since he clearly experiences that the earth stands still and that the eye is not in error when it judges that the sun moves, as it also is not in error when it judges that the moon and the stars move. And this is enough for now.

With this I greet dearly Your Paternity, and I pray to God to grant you all your wishes.

At home, 12 April 1615.

To Your Very Reverend Paternity.

As a Brother,
Cardinal Bellarmine
(XII, 171-172; trans. by Finocchiaro 1989, 67-69)

There is no doubt that Bellarmine's answer was a private one. But considering the prestige of the Cardinal in the world of theology of that time, it carried a great deal of weight and could be taken as an indication of the posture of the Church as it faced the Copernican problem.

There is a great deal of contrast among Galilean scholars in their judgment on this response of Bellarmine. In fact, they range from exaltation of the "truly scientific" mentality of the Cardinal (who would thus have given a lesson in scientific methodology to Galileo)[24] to the most harsh criticism of the narrow-mindedness, so it is claimed, of the famous Jesuit.

The fact is that Bellarmine was neither a positivist *ante litteram* nor an obscurantist by set purpose. The abundant information which we possess on his life and his works show him to be a man with a brilliant and argumentative intellect, open-minded, especially at the beginning of his teaching career at Louvain.[25] But the fact that the major part of his life had been dedicated to the polemic with the Protestants for the defense of the Catholic faith provoked undoubtedly a progressive hardening of his positions, an unshakable conviction of the definitive value of the philosophical-theological synthesis realized by Catholic thought and, therefore, an instinctive concern for the new ideas which at times seemed to undermine the foundations of an edifice which had been so solidly constructed. Since he was a theologian trained to go back to the origins of so many erroneous positions (or at least held to be such) and to foresee the most far-off consequences which might derive from them,[26] he was in no position to assume a posture of indifference in face of the problem posed by the Copernican ideas.

On the other hand, the fact itself of having spent so many years of his life and so much energy in the controversies with the Protestants, which were centered upon the literal meaning of the Bible and on the value of "tradition", had brought Bellarmine (perhaps without his even being aware of it) to extend the field of truths to be believed on the basis of faith well beyond that of matters concerning "faith and morals" of which the Council of Trent had spoken. That is evident in his response to Foscarini (see point number 2). According to Bellarmine, one seeks in vain to escape the difficulty represented by "the common consensus of the Holy Fathers", one of the sources of "tradition", on the interpretation *ad litteram* (that is, according to the literal sense) of Biblical statements about the motion of the Sun and the immobility of the Earth by declaring that "this is not a matter of faith". And the Cardinal explained his reason: "If it is not a matter of faith *ex parte objecti*" (that is, considering the object), "it is a matter of faith *ex parte dicentis*" (that is, considering who it is that speaks, the Holy Spirit). Now, the Council of Trent had spoken of matters of faith only in the first of these two cases: when, that is, one dealt with an *object* concerning faith or morals, thus implicitly admitting that there could be objects of Biblical statements which did not concern the previous and which, therefore, need not be accepted with an assent of faith. As we see, Bellarmine went quite beyond this. If his principle is accepted, every single word of Scripture would acquire the same value, because it is the word of the Holy Spirit himself. And thus, according to Bellarmine's example, it was just as much to be believed on faith that Christ was born of a virgin as to believe that Abraham had two sons; or, I might add, that the Sun moves.[27]

Once this principle was enunciated, the discussion was finished. The following third point of Bellarmine's answer to Foscarini would appear, therefore, to be altogether superfluous. If Scripture statements on the motion of the Sun are "matters of faith" in the sense indicated by Bellarmine, they constituted truths which could not be doubted and which could never be overturned by whatever progress science might make. How, therefore, could Bellarmine concede, right at the beginning of this third point, that, should there have been a true demonstration that the Sun is at the center of the world and that the Earth revolved around it, it would be necessary "to say rather that we do not understand [Scripture] than to say that what is demonstrated is false"? Had not the possibility that Scripture had not been well understood been excluded by the whole reasoning gone through in the second point? And how was it that such a possibility could return now even as a very remote and practically impossible eventuality? Was Bellarmine himself perhaps aware that the widening of matters of faith which he had worked out in the previous point was the fruit of a personal conviction of his and that it went beyond the doctrine formulated up until that time by the Catholic Church? Or did he perhaps wish to demonstrate, in a manner independent of the preceding theological consideration, that *even from a philosophical point of view* the Copernican hypothesis could not be upheld?

Whatever the case might be, Bellarmine immediately added: "But I will not believe that there is such a demonstration until it is shown to me". Here Galileo and Foscarini would have found themselves in complete agreement with the Cardinal. But their assent would have ended there, because immediately after that Bellarmine confessed that he was "extremely doubtful" that such a demonstration could ever be given. The basis for such skepticism here is now no longer of a theological nature but a *philosophical* one. It is enough to read over the last passage of the *Letter* which begins with the words: "And even if one should say that Solomon spoke according to appearances . . .". It is clear: even if Bellarmine states in theory that, if there should be a true proof, one would have to rethink the situation, he seems, in fact, to deny the possibility of such a demonstration on the basis of a *philosophical certainty founded on the evidence of common experience*: "because we clearly experience that the earth stays still".[28]

To conclude, despite the kind tenor and moderate manner of expressing himself, Bellarmine had in his response clearly denied the ideas put forth by Foscarini and by Galileo himself with respect to possibility of reconciling Copernicanism with Scripture. It was a denial based, as we have seen, both on theological reasons and on a philosophical consideration of "good sense". Thus, speaking concretely, Bellarmine had left but one way open: that of considering Copernicanism as a mere mathematical hypothesis. But it was precisely that which Galileo had always refused to do.

Bellarmine's response to Foscarini was also known to Galileo who wrote a very detailed comment on the matter. (V, 364-370).[29]

As to the advice given indirectly to Galileo by Grienberger, that is, to furnish convincing scientific demonstrations first of all and then to enter into the Scripture problems, Galileo commented in a letter to Dini of May 1615:

> To me the surest and swiftest way to prove that the position of Copernicus is not contrary to Scripture would be to give a host of proofs that it is true and that the contrary cannot be maintained at all; thus, since no two truths can contradict one another, this and the Bible must be perfectly harmonious. But how can I do this, and not be merely wasting my time when those Peripatetics who must be convinced show themselves incapable of following even the simplest and easiest of arguments, while on the other hand they are seen to set great store in worthless propositions? (XII, 184; trans. by Drake 1957, 166).

In these last words there is perhaps a reference to Bellarmine and to that philosophical basis of his anti-Copernican conviction which the Cardinal had expounded in his letter to Foscarini.

At any rate Galileo, even if he despaired of ever being able to persuade those opponents who had imbibed the traditional philosophical ideas, did not stop from carrying out his program which for him was taking on ever more a character of extreme urgency. On the other hand he did not consider his *Letter to Castelli* to be adequate. It had provoked much criticism and he undoubtedly thought that he must respond in an indirect way to Bellarmine's comments to Foscarini.

4.   *Galileo's response. The* Letter to Christina *of Lorraine*

As we already know, Galileo had begun to compose a new, more ample letter addressed this time to Christina of Lorraine herself in which he proposed in a more systematic and deeper fashion the consideration contained in his letters to Castelli and Dini.[30]

After beginning by making reference to his discoveries Galileo emphasizes the reactions they had provoked among numerous philosophers "as if I by my own hand had placed such things in the sky in order to confuse nature and the sciences" (V, 309). These "professors" had composed against his discoveries "some writings full of vain discourses and, that which was even more serious, littered with testimonies from Sacred Scripture taken from passages not well understood by them and used in a way that had nothing to do with the case" (V, 309). As time went on, Galileo continued, the truth of his discoveries became known to everyone and those were convinced who had at first remained in doubt because of the "unexpected newness and because they had not had the opportunity to have a sense experience of them" (V, 310). But there remained the group who were by set purpose opposed.

> They know that as to the arrangement of the parts of the universe, I hold the sun to be situated motionless in the center of the revolution of the celestial orbs while the earth rotates on its axis and revolves about the sun.[31] They know also that I support this position not only by refuting the arguments of Ptolemy and Aristotle, but by producing

many counter arguments; in particular, some which relate
to physical effects whose causes can perhaps be assigned
in no other way.[32] In addition there are astronomical
arguments derived from many things in my new celestial
discoveries that plainly confute the Ptolemaic system while
admirably agreeing with and confirming the contrary
hypothesis. Possibly because they are disturbed by the
known truth of other propositions of mine which differ
from those commonly held,[33] and therefore mistrusting
their defense so long as they confine themselves to the
field of philosophy, these men have resolved to fabricate a
shield for their fallacies out of the mantle of pretended
religion and the authority of the Bible. These they apply
with little judgement, to the refutation of arguments they
do not understand and have not even listened to (V, 311;
trans. by Drake 1957, 177).

Galileo remembers, therefore, the attacks that were also
made against him from the pulpit, and not only against him
personally but against mathematicians in general in an attempt
to sway public opinion towards seeing that the new astronomical
ideas were heretical. In so doing, Galileo adds, his opponents
showed how ignorant they were in thinking that the ideas
expressed by him were in any way new. In fact, Copernicus was
their author and he in turn had taken them up again from
ancient Greece. And, Galileo continues, Copernicus had published
his theories in response to the request of and with the support
of many prelates and he had dedicated his book to Pope Paul
III, without there having been "the slightest indication of a
scruple on the part of the Church about his doctrine". How in
the world, Galileo asks, could it be that this Copernican theory
should be condemned right at this time when "we are
discovering how well founded it is based on manifest experience
and necessary demonstrations" (V, 312)? In fact, continues
Galileo, there is a simple explanation. The opponents have never
read Copernicus's book and they condemn the "new ideas" for
reasons that are quite far from being scientific; in fact, they are
based on a literal interpretation of those Biblical passages where
it is said that the Sun moves and the Earth stands still. Now
according to them:

. . . since the Scripture can never lie or err, it follows as a necessary consequence that the opinion of those who want to assert the sun to be motionless and the earth moving is erroneous and damnable (V, 315; trans. by Finocchiaro 1989, 92).

Of course, Galileo admits, the Bible can never err, but one must understand the true sense of what it says. And because many times it is not the literal sense, he who would insist on this sense would run the risk of making

. . . the Scripture appear to be not only full of contradictions and false propositions but also of serious heresies and blasphemies; for one would have to attribute to God feet, hands, eyes, and bodily sensations, as well as human feelings like anger, contrition, and hatred, and such conditions as the forgetfulness of things past and the ignorance of future ones. Since these propositions dictated by the Holy Spirit were expressed by the sacred writers in such a way as to accommodate the capacities of the very unrefined and undisciplined masses, for those who deserve to rise above the common people it is therefore necessary that wise interpreters formulate the true meaning and indicate the specific reasons why it is expressed by such words. This doctrine is so commonplace and so definite among all theologians that it would be superfluous to present any testimony for it (V, 315-316; trans. by Finocchiaro 1989, 92).

Therefore, concludes Galileo, one can admit without difficulty that with respect to the statements about natural phenomena the sacred writers have adhered to the same principle. It follows "that in disputes about natural phenomena one must begin not with the authority of Scriptural passages but with sensory experience and necessary demonstrations" (V, 316; trans. by Finocchiaro 1989, 93). These latter, in fact, make clear the inexorability of natural events which leave no doubt once it is established that one is dealing with facts and secure conclusions. And, because the truth is one, there can be no contradiction between the certain conclusions from this research into nature and the true meaning of Scripture. To summarize, it is a question of explaining that which is obscure (that is, the meaning of certain Biblical statements) by employing that which is clear (natural phenomena made evident by "sensory experiences" and by "necessary demonstrations") and not the opposite direction as the opponents claim to do. By employing this method, rather than contradicting Scripture, the secure conclusions of the natural sciences are most helpful "to the correct interpretation of Scripture and to the investigation of the truths they must contain, for they are most true and agree with demonstrated truths" (V, 317; trans. by Finocchiaro 1989, 93).

As we see, Galileo here formulates (he will develop it in the following parts of the Letter) that principle of the autonomy of the study of nature which will become one of the hinges of modern scientific research. But, at the same time, he does not see this autonomy as opposed to the content of the Christian faith or without any relationship to it. On the contrary, it is precisely autonomous scientific research which will allow a better understanding of the obscure meaning of certain Biblical passages concerning nature.

As a confirmation that Scripture has no intention of entering into statements of a scientific character, Galileo notes how rare it is that the Bible makes astronomical references:

> . . . one does not find there even the names of the planets, except for the sun, the moon, and only once or twice Venus, under the name of the Morning Star (V, 318; trans. by Finocchiaro 1989, 94).

In fact, such limited references could not be explained if one wanted to claim that the Scriptures intend to teach something about the motions of the heavens. This is also, continues Galileo, the opinion of St. Augustine. And he quotes the passage from the *De Genesi ad Litteram* (LII, 9) which I have already cited in the Introduction.[34] After having quoted an analogous passage from chapter 19 of the same work of St. Augustine, Galileo concludes with the following:

> Let us now come down from these matters to our particular point. We have seen that the Holy Spirit did not want to teach us whether heaven moves or stands still, nor

whether its shape is spherical or like a discus or extended along a plane, nor whether the earth is located at its center or on one side. So it follows as a necessary consequence that the Holy Spirit also did not intend to teach us about other questions of the same kind and connected to those just mentioned in such a way that without knowing the truth about the former one cannot decide the latter, such as the question of the motion or rest of the earth or the sun (V, 319; trans. Finocchiaro 1989, 95).

Galileo states that this conclusion coincides with "what I heard from an ecclesiastical person in a very eminent position [Cardinal Baronio], namely that the intention of the Holy Spirit is to teach us how one goes to heaven and not how heaven goes" (V, 319; trans. by Finocchiaro 1989, 96).[35] Galileo then concludes:

Because of this and because, as we said above, two truths cannot contradict one another,[36] the task of a wise interpreter is to strive to fathom the true meaning of the sacred texts; this will undoubtedly agree with those physical conclusions of which we are already certain and sure through clear observations or necessary demonstrations. Indeed, besides saying, as we have, that in many places Scripture is open to interpretations far removed from the literal meaning of the words, we should add that we cannot assert with certainty that all interpreters speak with divine inspiration since if this were so then there would be no disagreement among them about the meaning of the same passages; therefore, I should think it would be very prudent not to allow anyone to commit and in a way to oblige Scriptural passages to have to maintain the truth of any physical conclusions whose contrary could ever be proved to us by the senses and demonstrative and necessary reasons (V, 320; trans. by Finocchiaro 1989, 96).

As we see, in this passage, which is one of the most important in the *Letter*, Galileo states the priority of scientific considerations over exegetical ones in cases where Biblical passages deal with questions about nature and he distinguishes two cases. The first is where science has already come to secure conclusions. In this case it is up to the exegetes to discover the true sense of Holy Scripture which agrees with those conclusions. The second case is where there exists the *possibility* of a certain scientific conclusion in the future. Here exegetes should be very prudent and should avoid holding as true certain Biblical interpretations which could be denied by the possible scientific conclusions.

Having set up a foundation with these claims, Galileo goes on then to the counterattack. It is not he who is to be accused of wishing to interpret Scripture according to his own whim and fancy, but on the contrary the accusation goes to many of his opponents who use the *Bible* to condemn his discoveries. Galileo then gives concrete examples of attacks that have come from totally incompetent persons.

There remained the more delicate case of the theologians to which Galileo states:

> Among such lay writers should not be numbered some theologians whom I regard as men of profound learning and of the holiest life style and whom I therefore hold in high esteem and reverence. However, I cannot deny having some qualms, which I consequently wish could be removed; for, in disputes about natural phenomena they seem to claim the right to force others by means of authority of Scripture to follow the opinion they think is most in accordance with its statements, and at the same time they believe they are not obliged to answer observations and reasons to the contrary (V, 323-324; trans. by Finocchiaro 1989, 99).

The reason for this posture of theirs, claims Galileo, is that they think that theology, since it is the highest science, should never lower itself by adjusting itself to the statements of the inferior sciences, but on the contrary those sciences should recognize the eminent position held by theological knowledge "and change and revise their conclusions in accordance with theological rules and decrees" (V, 234; trans. by Finocchiaro 1989, 99). Even here Galileo twists the argument around. It is precisely because theology is the highest science (in the sense,

Galileo specifies, that its object is the highest possible and that its conclusions are founded on the teaching of divine revelation) that "it does not come down to the lower and humbler speculations of the inferior sciences, but rather, as stated above, it does not bother with them, inasmuch as they are irrelevant to salvation" (V, 325; trans. by Finocchiaro 1989, 100). Therefore, he concludes: "If this is so, then officials and experts of theology should not arrogate to themselves the authority to issue decrees in the professions they neither exercise nor study" (V, 325; trans. by Finocchiaro 1989, 100).

What then should be the attitude that a wise theologian would take? For his answer, Galileo turns back to a text of St. Augustine:

> There should be no doubt about the following; whenever the experts of this world can truly demonstrate something about natural phenomena , we should show it not to be contrary to our Scripture; but whenever in their books they teach something contrary to the Holy Writ, we should without any doubt hold it to be most false and also show this by any means we can; and in this way we should keep the faith of our Lord . . . in order not to be seduced by the verbosity of false philosophy or frightened by the superstition of fake religion (*De Genesi ad Litteram*, 1.1, Chapter 21; trans. from Finocchiaro 1989, 101).

In view of the criticisms of this text of St. Augustine by various Galileian scholars and the interpretation which Galileo himself gives to it (see below), it seems necessary in the first place to try to understand the meaning of St. Augustine's words. They are written at the end of a long discussion on the meaning of the "firmament" created on the "second day" according to the book of *Genesis*.

The Latin quotation of these words, which Galileo certainly took from the Jesuit Pereyra's commentary on *Genesis* (see Note 34), contains significant variations with respect to the text of the *De Genesi ad Litteram* published in the *Patrologia Latina* of Migne, which is certainly a more reliable text.[37] In particular, instead of the words "*sapientes huius mundi*" (the wise ones of this world) Migne's text has "*qui calumniari Libris nostrae salutis affectant*" (those who pretend to calumniate the Books of our salvation, i.e., Sacred Scripture). It seems to me that the reading "*sapientes huius mundi*" could have led Galileo to consider (erroneously, in my opinion) that the entire text of Augustine was referring to the Greek "men of science": "natural philosophers" and astronomers. As we will see right away, at least in the second case contemplated by St. Augustine, he does not seem to allude any more to these latter, even though the reading: "*sapientes huius mundi*" is kept. However that might be, it is the text given by Galileo to which we will continue to refer while at the same time taking account of the preceding comments as regards the interpretation of Augustine's thought.

As I have already emphasized in the Introduction, St. Augustine is not personally interested in "natural philosophy" nor in Greek astronomy. But he knows them well enough to admit that "the wise ones of this world" are able to provide clear demonstrations as regards "questions about nature" which are not connected with the Christian faith and remain, therefore, free to be discussed, as, in fact, the question of the physical structure of the "firmament". In such a case there can be no contradiction with the true meaning of Scripture, but rather such demonstrations help us to understand that meaning. As testified by many other texts of Augustine (see, for example, the two texts quoted in this letter by Galileo himself; V, 311), even in cases were such clear demonstrations do not yet exist, Augustine invites Christian exegetes not to pose as definitive personal interpretations which run the risk of being denied by possible future "scientific" demonstrations.

The second case contemplated by Augustine ("all of that, on the other hand, which they teach in their books contrary to Sacred Scripture") is that in which statements of the "wise ones of this world" about nature go against statements of Sacred Scripture *which pertain to the patrimony of the Christian faith* (as is evident from the following words) and which, therefore, are no longer free to be accepted. In such a case there is no longer a problem with the "proofs" of what they "teach". Since one is dealing with truths of the faith, the possibility of "scientific" demonstrations contrary to them is excluded *a priori*, even for the future. St. Augustine can, therefore, state that, in this case, whatever "the wise ones of this world" "teach" should be considered as "completely false and, as far as possible, shown to be such so as to keep solid the faith of Our Lord".

It appears to me, however, that here "the wise ones of this world" are no longer the "scientists" whose conclusions would only be taught but not proven. This seems to be confirmed by the final words of Augustine's quotation: "loquaciousness of a false philosophy", "superstition of a simulated religious posture", which do not seem to apply in their severity to natural philosophers and to Greek astronomers. In my opinion, in this second part of the passage St. Augustine most probably alludes instead to philosophers in general. Even though in his writings he recognizes the results attained by Greek-Hellenistic philosophical thought, he does not hesitate to point out the limitations and the errors involved in it. Precisely because it has no guaranty of certainty, all that is claimed by these philosophers is to be considered very cautiously. And whenever they make statements in direct contradiction to Biblical statements which are fundamental to the Christian faith (such as, for example, the statements about the creation of the world in *Genesis*) they should be considered to be false and, as far as possible, should be proven to be so.[38] And this interpretation seems, furthermore, to be confirmed if we remember that in this whole passage the presumed "*sapientes huius mundi*" (wise ones of this world) are in fact "*qui calumniari Libris nostrae salutis affectant*" (those who pretend to calumniate the Books of our salvation).

To conclude, contrary to what has been stated by various commentators of the *Letter*, this passage from St. Augustine does not seem to me to put the case where there are true demonstrations in matters of nature in opposition to the case where they are lacking. The opposition, in my opinion, is between questions in natural philosophy which are open to discussion (because not connected with the Christian faith) and those which are not (precisely because they are related to the faith). In the first case true "scientific" demonstrations are possible and the opposition with the Bible (in particular, with the *Genesis* account) is seen to be only apparent. In the end it is the scientific truth which prevails over the interpretations by

the exegetes of Biblical passages. In the second case the
teachings (those of the philosophers, more than those of the
scientists), which are opposed to the truths of the faith contained
in Sacred Scripture, are by that very fact certainly false and are
in every way to be demonstrated as such "in so far as possible".
In this case it is the truth obtained by the light of faith which
prevails over the error of human opinions.

Taking up this quotation almost letter for letter Galileo
comments in the following way:

> These words imply I think the following doctrine: in the
> learned books of worldly authors are contained some
> propositions about nature which are truly demonstrated
> and others which are simply taught; in regard to the
> former, the task of the wise theologians is to show that
> they are not contrary to Holy Scripture; as for the latter
> (which are taught but not demonstrated with necessity), if
> they contain anything contrary to the Holy Writ, then they
> must be considered indubitably false and must be
> demonstrated such by every possible means. So physical
> conclusions which have been truly demonstrated should not
> be given a lower place than Scriptural passages, but rather
> one should clarify how such passages do not contradict
> those conclusions; therefore, before condemning a physical
> proposition, one must show that it is not conclusively
> demonstrated. Furthermore it is much more reasonable and
> natural that this be done not by those who hold it to be
> true, but by those who regard it as false; . . . (V, 327;
> trans. Finocchiaro 1989, 101-102).

Various Galileian scholars have seen in this interpretation
(according to them correct) by Galileo of Augustine's text a
patent contradiction of the fundamental thesis of the *Letter*, the
autonomy of "scientific" research in matters to do with nature.
In fact, in the case of "matters of nature" "taught but not
necessarily demonstrated" he appears to give, without further
ado, the final word to the theologians and to forget what he has
already stated and which he will continue to emphasize many
times in the remainder of the *Letter*, namely, that a "scientific"
demonstration not yet certain today may become so tomorrow.

But I do not think that such a contradiction, in fact, exists. First, I take as basic the fundamental principle of hermeneutics whereby obscure passages of an author should be interpreted in the light of the clear passages. Now, this passage of the *Letter* is the only one where this contradiction seems to exist. (Other passages, adopted by these same scholars to confirm the supposed contradiction, do not turn out, if considered carefully, to support their theses.[39]) Is it possible that Galileo was so easily prepared to come to a meeting of minds with his adversaries and thus compromise everything that he had already stated, as well as all that he will continue to uphold in the following parts of the *Letter*? On the other hand, if he had truly seen a contradiction between this passage of Augustine and his thesis, he would simply have omitted it. Was anyone forcing him to quote it?

Secondly, even if Galileo appears to consider, contrary to what I think is more probable, that in both cases contemplated by St. Augustine the "wise ones of the world" were the scientists, he is certainly aware that in the second case it is a matter of Biblical passages strictly connected with the Christian faith.

Consistent, therefore, with this basic principle that a truth from Scripture cannot contradict a truth from our knowledge of nature, he is able in this case to exclude *a priori* the validity of any such contrary scientific proof without it being necessary to allude to the possibility of finding valid proofs in the future (this is simply not conceivable given the certainty of the Scriptural truth). Thus it is legitimate to state:

> . . . as for the latter (which are taught but not demonstrated with necessity), *if they contain anything contrary to the Holy Writ, then they must be considered indubitably false and must be demonstrated such by every possible means.* (V, 327; trans. by Finocchiaro 1989, 102; italics are by Fantoli).

The last words in italics are the translation of the text of Augustine which Galileo makes his own. But one must note that he emphasizes the hypothetical character of the case in question. While St. Augustine had written: "all that which", Galileo translates this to: "if there should be anything which". In other words, *admitting that the case is certain* and that it is a matter of a Biblical truth of faith, and, therefore, no longer free to be accepted or not, for Galileo there is no difficulty in following St. Augustine in his conclusion. In fact, that does not imply any contradiction with the principle of the autonomy of scientific research, which is applicable only in the case of questions which are open to discussion.

But there still remained the case of questions "which are to do purely with nature and which are not *de fide* [of the faith]" (V, 326). It is precisely this case to which reference is made with Galileo's concluding words regarding this quotation of Augustine: "and so it is required before condemning a proposition about nature, that it not be necessarily demonstrated". At least here, it appears that Galileo admits that, lacking necessary, i.e. certain, demonstration, theologians are authorized to condemn a proposition about nature, and in the present case, Copernicanism. And such is, as a matter of fact, the interpretation which the scholars mentioned above give to this conclusion of Galileo. At least here, he would be in obvious contradiction with the fundamental thesis of the *Letter*. It seems to me, however, that even here such a contradiction does not exist. From all the following reasoning (see V, 327-328) it becomes, in fact, clear that the authorization given by Galileo is clearly conditional. Theologians and their followers are invited to prudence and, at the same time, to intellectual honesty. Before condemning "a proposition about nature" they must show that it is inconclusive and this requires first of all that they study it and that they understand it.

Galileo has no doubt (as can be surmised from the passage which follows immediately) that such prudence and honesty will produce positive results. At any rate, even though he does not say it, he is persuaded that new arguments in favor of Copernicanism in the future will force the theologians to new examinations and, therefore, to a further suspension of their judgments and one day (Galileo is convinced of it) to change them.

Galileo does not, therefore, give to theologians the authority to condemn outright a proposition about nature which does not turn out at the moment to be demonstrated. In inviting them to a prudent and honest examination of the reasons for and against such propositions he certainly implies that he is convinced that, although not proven today, they may be proven tomorrow. If one reflects carefully upon it, therefore, this much discussed passage of the *Letter* by no means contradicts the principles previously formulated. And that appears to be confirmed by what Galileo states with respect to the interpretation of Scripture by the Fathers of the Church:

> From this and from other places [of St. Augustine, cited by Galileo previously] it seems to me, if I am not mistaken, the intention of the Holy Fathers is that in questions about natural phenomena which do not involve articles of faith one must first consider whether they are demonstrated with certainty or known by sensory experience, or *whether it is possible to have such knowledge and demonstration.* When one is in possession of this, since it too is a gift from God, one must apply it to the investigation of the true meanings of the Holy Writ at those places which seem to read differently. (V, 322; trans. by Finocchiaro 1989, 105; italics by the author).

The discussion is now shifted to the problem of the unanimous consent of the Church Fathers. As we have seen, Bellarmine, following the Council of Trent, had very much emphasized the necessity of keeping to this traditional interpretation in all cases where the Fathers would have been in agreement. Such agreement according to the Council of Trent constituted, in fact, a rule of faith. And the cardinal was, as a matter of fact, persuaded that the Fathers were in agreement in stating the immobility of the Earth and the motion of the Sun. Galileo comments that the common testimony of the Church Fathers can be validly applied

> . . . only to those conclusions which the Fathers discussed and inspected with great diligence and debated on both sides of the issue and for which they then all agreed to reject one side and to hold the other. However, the earth's motion and sun's rest are not of this sort, given that in

those times this opinion was totally forgotten as far from
academic dispute and was not examined, let alone followed,
by anyone; thus one may believe that the Fathers did not
even think of discussing it . . . Therefore, it is not enough
to say that all the Fathers accept the earth's rest, etc., and
so it is an article of faith to hold it; rather one would have
to prove that they condemned the contrary opinion. For I
can always say that their failure to reflect upon it and
discuss it made them leave it stand as the current opinion,
but not as something resolved and established (V, 335-336;
trans. by Finocchiaro 1989, 168).

On the other hand, continues Galileo, the fact that the
hypothesis of the Earth's motion is not erroneous from the point
of view of the Christian faith has been shown by some
theologian, who has begun to examine it, such as Diego de
Zuñiga in his commentary on the *Book of Job* (c. 9, 6), in which
he "concludes the mobility of the Earth is not against the
Scripture". He proceeds to deepen his argument by adding:

Furthermore, I would have doubts about the truth of this
prescription, namely whether it is true that the Church
obliges one to hold as articles of faith such conclusions
about natural phenomena, which are characterized only by
the unanimous interpretation of all the Fathers. I believe
it may be that those who think in this manner may want
to amplify the decrees of the Councils in favor of their own
opinion.[40] For I do not see that in this regard they prohibit
anything but tampering, in ways contrary to the
interpretation of the Holy Church or the collective
consensus of the Fathers, with those propositions which are
articles of faith or involve morals and pertain to edification
according to Christian doctrine; so speaks the Fourth
Session of the Council of Trent (V, 336-337; trans. by
Finocchiaro 1989, 108-109).

But, comments Galileo, the mobility or stability of the
Earth or of the Sun are not questions of faith or of morals, and
as to those who uphold the mobility of the Earth none of them
has ever wished to abuse the sacred texts by making use of
them to bolster his own opinion. And the opinion of the Council,

Galileo adds, is in agreement with the attitude of the Fathers who considered it useless to try to solve the problems of nature, as seems so in the case of St. Augustine who, when confronted with the question as to whether the heavens are fixed or move, answered (*De Genesi ad Litteram*, L.2, c.10):

> To them I answer that these things should be examined with very subtle and demanding arguments to determine truly whether or not it is so; but I do not have the time to undertake and pursue these investigations, nor should such time be available to those whom we desire to instruct for their salvation and for the needs and benefit of the Holy Church (V, 337; trans. by Finocchiaro 1989, 109).

Galileo then shows by quoting various other texts of Augustine, taken always from the *De Genesi ad Litteram* (see V, 339-341), "with what circumspection this most holy man walks before bringing himself to state resolutely any interpretation of Scripture as certain and so secure that one would have no fear of encountering some difficulty which would bring on some disturbance" (V, 339). At the end Galileo confronts the question of the authority which the Church has to take decisions with respect to questions having to do with nature which are related to Sacred Scripture. He emphasizes that "it belongs to no one other than the Supreme Pontiff or the Holy Councils to declare a proposition erroneous" (V, 342). Certainly, as Galileo had already emphasized previously (see V, 312), no Pope nor Council had ever prohibited the Copernican theory and this confirmed for him that geocentrism was not, at least directly, *of the faith*. But it is just as certain that the Pope has the authority to take a decision now on Copernicanism and eventually even to condemn it. It is precisely this which caused Galileo the deepest worries and which constituted the final motive for this *Letter to Christina of Lorraine*. Therefore, the words which Galileo writes on this matter constitute altogether the most important conclusion of this writing of his and an indirect but firm warning directed to Pope Paul V himself:

> For in regard to these [Copernican] and other similar propositions which do not directly involve the faith, no one

can doubt that the Supreme Pontiff always has the absolute power of permitting or condemning them; however, no creature has the power of making them be true or false, contrary to what they happen to be by nature and de facto. So it seems more advisable to first become sure about the necessary and immutable truth of the matter, over which no one has control, than to condemn one side when such certainty is lacking; this would imply a loss of freedom of decision and choice insofar as it would give necessity to things which are presently indifferent, free, and dependent on the will of supreme authority. In short, if it is inconceivable that a proposition should be declared heretical when one thinks it may be true, it should be futile for someone to try to bring about the condemnation of the earth's motion and the sun's rest unless he first shows it to be impossible and false. (V, 343; trans. by Finocchiaro 1989, 114).

The strictly doctrinal part of the *Letter* ends here. As we have seen, Galileo had tried in it to have recourse to the best doctrinal traditions of the Church in order to show that the Copernican theory was not to be condemned hurriedly on the pretext that it was opposed to Sacred Scripture. Galileo's fundamental thesis, which he had supported, as we have seen, in an implicit argument with Bellarmine by using numerous Patristic texts, especially those of Augustine, is that the choice between geocentrism and geokeneticism is not related at all to the religious message of the Bible, that is, it is not concerned with the truths of faith or of Christian morals. Nor could the choice be considered already made in favor of geocentrism on the basis of an alleged agreement of the Church Fathers which, in fact, does not exist and which, in any case, could not be considered to be the result of a conscious and reasoned assumption of a position. On the basis of the Council of Trent (quoted by Bellarmine himself in his reply to Foscarini) the theologians could leave the burden of choice to the astronomers and to those who cultivated "natural philosophy". "With experience, with long observations and with necessary demonstrations" they can go beyond the level of a "probable opinion and likely conjecture" to arrive at the level of "certain and demonstrated science". (V, 330). Despite the assertions of various scholars[41] Galileo is aware that such scientific certainty in favor of Copernicanism does not yet exist. But the least that one can say is that it remains possible in the future. Therefore, the choice between Ptolemaic view and that of Copernicus is to be left open in expectation of future "proofs". Theologians and the highest authorities of the Church are respectfully, but firmly, invited to be prudent.

For sure, the call to return to theological traditions and in particular to St. Augustine is taking place in an epistemic context profoundly changed. In reality, when Galileo states that there exists a "book of nature" which can be read with the new method of modern science just being born and which can thus become a source of certain knowledge alongside that knowledge which can be obtained from reading the sacred book, he is going well beyond the problematic of a St. Augustine or a St. Thomas Aquinas. Galileo, perhaps, was even aware of this. But for him it was enough to show that there existed in them, as in other authoritative representatives of traditional Christian thought, an openness of mind which at the same time provided a clear invitation to avoid precipitous decisions which did not yet seem to be mature.

The final part of the *Letter* contains an exegesis of the passage from Joshua 10, 12-14 which presents a reworking of what Galileo had already placed at the end of the *Letter to Castelli*.

Galileo reasons that the miracle whereby the Sun stood still "could not in any way have occurred, should the heavenly motions be determined by the Ptolemaic system", whereas with the "Copernican system one can call upon the most literal and easiest interpretation" (V, 346).

To understand Galileo's "demonstration" one must remember that in the Ptolemaic system the *diurnal* motion (from east to west) of all heavenly bodies, including that of the Sun, depends on the motion of the sphere of the *primum mobile*, while the motion proper to each planet (and also, therefore, the annual motion of the Sun from west to east through the signs of the zodiac) depends not on the *primum mobile* but on the autonomous motion of the spheres which regulate the motions proper to each planet. Using this distinction Galileo in substance states that in the Ptolemaic system it is impossible to save the *literal sense* of Joshua's command. In fact, if we wish to interpret the words of Scripture "in their pure and most proper sense", that is, as a command addressed *directly* to the Sun to stop the *motion proper to it which is in the opposite sense to its diurnal motion* and to leave, instead, this latter motion unchanged, then such a command would not have slowed down the occurrence of sunset but would rather have speeded it up. To have the Sun remain motionless at the position it had at the moment of the miracle, Joshua would have had to command the Sun not to stop but rather to accelerate enormously the motion proper to it so as to compensate exactly for the diurnal motion occurring in the opposite direction. That obviously goes against the letter of the Biblical account and furthermore implies a complete disruption of the normal heavenly motions. A much simpler interpretation, states Galileo, is that the sacred author made use of a manner of speaking adapted to the common way of thinking (which knew only that the Sun moved from east to west) and with his words was alluding to the arrest of the diurnal motion of all heavenly bodies (and, therefore, also the Sun's motion). From the astronomical point of view this means that the command was addressed not to the Sun directly but to the *primum mobile*. And this interpretation of the miracle, notes Galileo, is the one commonly given by the Fathers and by theologians. But even this second interpretation implies taking a distance from the literal meaning (the *primum mobile* is substituted for the Sun).

Galileo concludes that to adhere to the Ptolemaic system necessarily implies, therefore, taking a distance from the literal meaning of the passage from Joshua. But to do that appears to be neither prudent nor necessary, where there exists an explanation which allows one to save the literal meaning. Galileo claims, as a matter of fact, that such an explanation, which does not imply disrupting the motions of the heavenly bodies, is possible in the Copernican system, if one takes account of the rotational motion of the Sun on its own axis, "demonstrated" by him "in the *Letter on Sunspots*" and if one introduces an hypothesis (based on the former discovery) of what causes the rotation of the Earth on its own axis. Galileo introduces this hypothesis in this way:

> . . . the Sun may be regarded as a noble body . . . and it is the source of light . . . ; having conclusively demonstrated this, I do not think it would be far from correct philosophizing to say that, insofar as it is the greatest minister of nature and, in a way, the heart and soul of the world, it transmits to the surrounding bodies not only light but also, by turning on itself, motion; thus, just as the motion of an animal's limbs would cease if the motion of its heart were to cease, in the same way if the sun's rotation stopped then all planetary revolutions would also stop. (V, 345; trans. by Finocchiaro 1989, 116).

After having quoted, in support of this hypothesis, a text of "Blessed Dionysius the Areopagite" (see V, 345-346), Galileo concludes:

> Therefore, given that the sun is both the source of light and the origin of motion, and given that God wanted the whole world system to remain motionless for several hours as a result of Joshua's order, it was sufficient to stop the sun, and then its immobility stopped all the other turnings, so that the earth as well as the moon and the sun, and all the other planets, remained in the same arrangement; and during that whole time the night did not approach, and the day miraculously got longer. In this manner, by stopping the sun, and without changing or upsetting at all the way the other stars appear or their mutual arrangement, the day on the earth could have been lengthened in perfect accord with the literal meaning of the sacred text. (V, 346; trans. by Finocchiaro 1989, 117).

This attempt at a literal interpretation of the Bible using Copernicanism has been severely criticized by many scholars as an open contradiction of the fundamental thesis of the *Letter*, namely, that the Scriptures were not written to teach us "how the heavens go".

Although not wishing in any way to defend the contents of this "concordist" attempt, I think it is important to try to understand the significance of it, that of an argument *ad hominem*. The Biblical passage in question, perhaps more than any other, had been quoted in support of the Sun's motion and, therefore, of Ptolemaic geocentrism. Galileo puts himself on this same "concordist" plane of his adversaries to show that, even if one persists in a literal interpretation of the passage, this is practically impossible in the Ptolemaic hypothesis, while it becomes possible and simple in the Copernican hypothesis. As any *ad hominem* argument, this is also only a tactical argument for the sake of controversy, and not heuristic or directed to knowledge.[42]

What influence did this *Letter to Christina of Lorraine* have in subsequent developments of the dispute about Copernicanism? It is difficult to say. However, it seems to me that the immediate influence was probably none, since the *Letter* remained for the time being only in manuscript form and it was not put into circulation except among Galileo's most trusted friends.[43] As to its printing, this will happen only after Galileo's condemnation at Strasbourg in 1636. On the other hand, even had the *Letter* become known at the time that it was composed, it would have done nothing but increase the tensions to the point of the decisions which the Roman Church authorities will come to in the next year.

While Galileo was writing this *Letter to the Grand Duchess Christina*, new developments were happening in Rome in the way of activity against Galileo. On the one hand, it is true that the activity of Lorini did not develop as the latter had hoped. After much delay Galileo had finally returned the *Letter to Castelli* to the latter, but with explicit condition that he would not deliver it to the Archbishop of Pisa as the latter had requested, but that he would only read it to him.[44] And that is what Castelli did as he wrote to Galileo on 9 April. At the same time Castelli had shown Foscarini's letter to the Archbishop and, although the Archbishop had before shown himself to be opposed to Copernicanism and had exhorted Castelli not to let himself be pulled along by those opinions (XII, 154), he now had a change of heart and "he now begins to say that Copernicus was truly a great man and a great genius" (XII, 165).[45]

5. *The Dominican, Caccini, accuses Galileo before the Holy
    Office*

In the meantime the Holy Office had to busy itself with
another accusation against Galileo and the "Galileisti", this one
brought on by Tommaso Caccini. As we already know the latter
had arrived in Rome in March both to obtain a coveted office at
the Dominican monastery of the Minerva and to bring to
completion the attack which Lorini had begun. To that end he
had a meeting with Cardinal Agostino Galamini who was also a
Dominican and a member of the Holy Office. And the latter in
the weekly meeting of 19 March 1615 informed the members
that Caccini, convinced of Galileo's errors, wished to make a
deposition concerning them "for conscience' sake" (XIX, 276). The
request was accepted and the following day Caccini gave his
deposition in the presence of the Commissary General of the
Inquisition, the Dominican Michelangelo Segizzi. After having
recalled his sermon and the displeasure that this "charitable
admonition" of his had caused "to certain disciples of Galileo",
Caccini stated that Father Ferdinando Cimenes of the Church of
Santa Maria Novella had heard from some of them "scandalous
propositions about God and the saints". Caccini then went on to
a direct attack on Galileo and stated that Father Lorini had
shown him a copy of the *Letter to Castelli* "in which it seems to
me there is contained with respect to theological matters
doctrine which is not good". But he did not find it necessary to
add anything on that matter, since he knew that a copy of it
had been sent to Cardinal Sfondrati. And he concluded:

> Thus I declare to this Holy Office that it is a widespread
> opinion that the above-mentioned Galilei holds these two
> propositions: the earth moves as a whole as well as with
> diurnal motion; the sun is motionless. These are
> propositions which, according to my conscience and
> understanding, are repugnant to the divine Scripture
> expounded by the Holy Fathers and consequently to the
> faith, which teaches that we must believe as true what is
> contained in Scripture. And for now I have nothing else to
> say. (XIX, 308-309; trans. by Finocchiaro 1989, 138).[46]

During the questioning period which followed his deposition Caccini declared about Galileo:

> By many he is regarded as a good Catholic. By others he is regarded with suspicion in matters of faith because they say he is very close to Fra Paolo [Sarpi], of the Servite order, so famous in Venice for his impieties; and they say that letters are exchanged between them even now. (XIX, 309-310; trans. by Finocchiaro 1989, 139).[47]

Caccini then asserted that both Father Lorini and Father Cimenes held that Galileo was to be "suspected in matters of Faith" because of his opinions on the stability of the Sun and the mobility of the Earth and for his pretension at interpreting Scripture against the common opinion of the Fathers and he added:

> This man, together with others, belonged to an Academy - I do not know whether they organized it themselves - which has the title of Lincean. And they correspond with others in Germany, at least Galileo does, as one sees from that book of his on the sunspots. (XIX, 310; trans. by Finocchiaro 1989, 140).[48]

The investigation by the Holy Office to ascertain the truth of Caccini's statements was drawn out over a long period of time. On 13 November the inquisitor in Florence sent a report of the questioning of Father Cimenes and of a certain Attavanti (whom Caccini had given as a witness of the scandalous statements about God and the saints). While Cimenes had substantially confirmed Caccini's deposition, Attavanti had proven that the statements claimed about God and the saints were due to an equivocation by Caccini. Attavanti furthermore had given assurance that he had never heard Galileo speak against the Scriptures or the Catholic Faith. On the other hand he confirmed that he had heard Galileo speak in favor of Copernicanism and in this respect he quoted "some letters of his circulated in Rome under the title of The Sunspots to which I wish to refer as a confirmation of what I have said". (XIX, 318).

At the end, the Holy Office became convinced that the only objective point in Caccini's accusations was the one about Galileo's Copernican convictions. But it was a sufficiently important point, the more so since Foscarini's letter had in the meantime created a real turmoil among the conservatives, and the confusion that it ran the risk of provoking among educated people could not help but cause the Roman authorities to worry.

Since Galileo's work, *Sunspot Letters*, had been repeatedly mentioned, on 25 November (after the report of the inquisitor in Florence had been read) the Congregation of the Holy Office ordered that that work of Galileo be examined (XIX, 278).

As to this examination the opinion given by the censor has not been preserved, but it must not have been adverse to Galileo since this work of his was not included on the list of those which, as we shall see, will be placed the following year on the Index of forbidden books. In fact, the expressions favorable to the Copernican system in the *Sunspot Letters* were restricted, as we already know, to a few passages, more or less clear, but written *en passant*, and not in the way of a peremptory affirmation. But the lack of a condemnation of the book in 1616 was due more to the fact that, as a result of the censor's intervention at the time of publication, it did not contain references to Sacred Scripture, than to Galileo's caution in his statements about Copernicanism. Nevertheless, even leaving aside the *Sunspot Letters*, the fact remained there was too much evidence with respect to Galileo's Copernican convictions to permit any further doubt about them.

6. *Galileo goes to Rome to defend Copernicanism*

But let us get back to Galileo. Even though, since the proceedings of the Holy Office were surrounded by an extreme secrecy, he, as well as his Roman friends, had been left in the dark as to the content of the actions taken by Lorini and Caccini, he was worried about the possibility that there could be an official condemnation of Copernicanism and this grew as the months passed by. In an attempt to ward off the danger and at the same time answer to the opponents' attacks, Galileo carried on his activities on two levels. The first was that of a written defense. As he had already done in the *Letter to Castelli,* he also directed the two letters sent to Dini and especially the *Letter to Christina of Lorraine* towards persuading those who were still doubtful about or even contrary to Copernicanism, but not purposely.

But there were still the dye-in-the-wool opponents and especially the Aristotelians. By now Galileo had lost all hope of being able to convince them. But they had mounted a systematic campaign of tearing him down and this ran the risk of making a continuously growing impression upon Church authorities. To prevent the worst Galileo judged that activity at a different level, that of oral defense, would be required. In his letter to Dini of May 1615 he had already indicated the proposal to come to Rome as soon as his health, not good at that time, would so permit

> . . . in the hope of at least showing my affection for the Holy Church. My urgent desire on this point is that no decision be made which is not entirely good. Such it would be to declare under the prodding of an army of malign men who understand nothing of the subject, that Copernicus did not hold the motion of the earth to be a fact of nature, but as an astronomer merely took it to be a convenient hypothesis for explaining the appearances. Thus to admit it to use but prohibit it from being considered true would be to declare that Copernicus's book had not even been read, as I have explained more widely in my other writing. (XII, 184).[49]

Despite the contrary opinion of his Roman friends, who rather counselled him (as did Dini himself)

> . . . to be quiet and to strengthen his position with good and well founded reasons both from Scripture and from mathematics and at the right time to put them forth with greater satisfaction (XII, 181),

Galileo in the autumn took the decision to carry out the trip he had planned. The trip was announced on 18 November 1615 by the Grand Duke Cosimo II to the Tuscan ambassador in Rome,

Pietro Guicciardini, and he explained to him the reasons for the same. A like explanation is found in the letter of recommendation for Galileo which was sent on the same day by the Grand Duke to Cardinal del Monte (XII, 203-204).

Galileo's departure for Rome took place during the first days of December and he must have already arrived there about the eleventh. The Ambassador Guicciardini was far from showing enthusiasm at this initiative of Galileo. His cold realism shows through clearly in the words which he wrote about the matter to the Secretary of State of the Grand Duke, Picchena: " . . . and this is no fit place to argue about the Moon or, especially in these times, to try and bring in new ideas" (XII, 207; trans. by de Santillana 1955, 110).

As to Galileo, judging by the first conversations he had after his arrival, he had written to Picchena himself a letter of a completely different tenor (XII, 209). Later on, however, he himself became aware of the "very vigorous impressions" made by his opponents on many authoritative persons and of the necessity of taking an action in depth to neutralize them.

Galileo began, therefore, to carry out a program of feverish activity which is described in the following way by Antonio Querengo in a letter of 20 January 1616 to Cardinal d'Este:

> . . . he talks frequently with fifteen or twenty guests who argue with him now in one house, now in another. But he is also so well fortified that he laughs them off; and although people are left unpersuaded because of the novelty of his opinion, still he shows up as worthless the majority of the arguments with which his opponents try to defeat him. Monday, in particular, in the home of Federico Ghislieri, he was especially effective. What I enjoyed most was that before he would answer the arguments of his opponents, he would amplify them and strengthen them with new grounds which made them appear invincible, so that, when he proceeded to demolish them, he made his opponents look all the more ridiculous (XII, 226-227; trans. from Langford 1966, 80).

It is easy to imagine how much this feverish activity and this ridiculing of his opponents must have contributed to exacerbating the opposition. Having been silenced on the plane of science, his opponents took revenge by spreading malicious rumors and calumnies about Galileo, who saw himself forced to stay in Rome to destroy them.

As time went on the situation, instead of clearing up, became ever more confused and tense. By now even Galileo's friends had to employ thousands of precautions in dealing with him so as not to raise suspicions and criticisms.[50]

But despite everything Galileo remained fundamentally optimistic and that indicates how much he deluded himself about the effects of his actions. Such optimism is revealed by the report he gave to Picchena of a meeting he had on 6 February with Caccini at the latter's request. Before all else Caccini had excused himself for the words used in his sermon and offered to give to Galileo whatever satisfaction he might desire. Then he had tried to make him believe that he was not responsible for the rumors that had spread about Rome concerning Galileo. When other visitors joined them the conversation shifted to the Copernican controversy and as the discussion proceeded Caccini

> . . . showed himself to be very far from understanding what would be required in these matters and he gave little satisfaction to those present who left after a three hour meeting; and he reexamined and even went back to his first reasoning and sought to dissuade me from that which I know for certain. (XII, 231).

At the beginning of February Galileo had asked the Grand Duke permission to go to Naples, undoubtedly so that he could meet with Father Foscarini (who for some time had promised to enlarge his letter).[51] The intent was to specify with the Carmelite a decisive effort in the Copernican campaign, so much the more so since Galileo was by this time convinced that he had an important proof in support of the Copernican system. It concerned the one derived from the phenomenon of the tides. As we know the first idea of this had already flashed into his mind about ten years earlier. It was put in the form of a letter with the title: *Discourse on the ebb and flow of the tides* and it had been sent as early as 8 January 1616 to the very young

Cardinal Alessandro Orsini, an admirer of Galileo and one on whose help Galileo had clearly placed great hopes. Galileo himself admits this in a letter to Picchena of 6 February in which he asked for a special recommendation of the Grand Duke to the Cardinal (XII, 231).[52] As to Orsini, he, in fact, took to heart Galileo's problem but, as we will see, with quite a different result than the one that Galileo had hoped for.

7.   *The intervention of the Holy Office. The* De Revolutionibus *is placed on the Index.*

Just as Galileo was thinking upon this final effort to support the Copernican theory, the situation was, without his realizing it, proceeding to evolve in the opposite direction to what he had hoped. Even though the doubts about Galileo's orthodoxy had by now been cleared up to the satisfaction of the Church authorities in Rome, his intense activity to support Copernicanism, especially after his arrival in Rome, together with the position taken by a theologian such as Foscarini, had created too much confusion for the Church to be able to hesitate any longer to take a clear position with respect to the affair.

In fact, on 19 February, two propositions which summed up the principal declarations of the Copernican system were submitted to the examination of the qualificators of the Holy Office.[53] They were formulated thus:

I.   The Sun is the center of the world and hence immovable of local motion.

II.   The Earth is not the center of the world, nor immovable, but moves according to the whole of itself, also with a diurnal motion (XIX, 320; trans. by de Santillana 1955, 121).[54]

Although the theologians assigned to examine the propositions were competent in their own field,[55] they certainly were not so in the field of science. And yet they had no fear about giving an answer and they did so in the short period of time granted to them by the Holy Office (less than four days).

Obviously, in the unshakable certainty of their philosophical and theological convictions the qualificators did not consider it necessary that they have more time in order to pass judgment on an opinion which was so obviously absurd. And, as for that, after months in Rome of heated arguments about the case, they must have already had their minds clearly made up on what opinion they held.[56] Without a doubt that opinion was agreed upon in the meeting of 23 February (see XIX, 320).

On the following day (Wednesday, 24 February) in the next plenary session of the qualificators and the consultors of the Holy Office they agreed upon the following qualifications to be assigned to the two propositions.

On the first:

> All said that this proposition is foolish and absurd in philosophy, and formally heretical since it explicitly contradicts in many places the sense of Holy Scripture, according to the literal meaning of the words and according to the common interpretation and understanding of the Holy Fathers and the doctors of theology. (XIX, 321; trans. by Finocchiaro 1989, 146).

On the second:

> All said that this proposition receives the same censure [qualification] in philosophy and that in regard to theological truth it is at least erroneous in faith. (XIX, 321).[57]

On the same day of this meeting of the Holy Office during a consistory of cardinals Cardinal Orsini had pleaded Galileo's cause to the Pope. It could not have been a less propitious moment. According to the report sent eight days later by the Ambassador Guicciardini to Picchena:

> The Pope told him it would be well if he persuaded him [Galileo] to give up that opinion. Thereupon Orsini replied something, urging the cause, and the Pope cut him short and told him he would refer the business to the Holy

Office. As soon as Orsini had left, his Holiness summoned Bellarmine; and after discussing the matter, they decided that the opinion was erroneous and heretical; the day before yesterday, I hear, they had a Congregation on the matter to have it declared such. (XII, 242).[58]

We do not know from whom Guicciardini would have had this information. Orsini's intervention during the consistory of cardinals was public knowledge as was the Pope's response and, therefore, they had come easily to the ambassador's knowledge. The same holds true for Paul V's summons to Bellarmine. But, as to the rest, Guicciardini could do nothing but make conjectures, since the strictest secrecy surrounded the procedures of the Holy Office.[59] And from the Holy Office's documents with which we are already familiar we know that the activity of the Holy Office had begun before Orsini's intervention.[60]

On the following day, Thursday, 25 February, the usual weekly meeting of the cardinals of the Holy Office took place. The original copy of the minutes of that meeting has recently been found.[61] I reproduce here the Latin text of this important document together with an English translation:

> Illustrissimus Dominus cardinalis Millinus, notificavit quod relata censura Patrum Theologorum ad propositiones Galilei mathematici, quod sol sit centrum mundi et immobilis motu locali, et terra moveatur etiam motu diurno, Sanctissimus ordinavit illustrissimo Domino cardinali Bellarmino ut vocet coram se dictum Galileum moneat ad deserendas dictas propositiones, et si recusaverit parere, Pater commissarius coram Notario et testibus faciat illi praeceptum ut omnino abstineat hujusmodi doctrinam et opinionem docere aut defendere, seu de ea tractare; si vero non acquieverit, carceretur.
>
> (The Most Illustrious Cardinal Millini notified . . . that, after the reporting of the judgment by the Father Theologians against the propositions of the mathematician Galileo, to the effect that the sun stands still at the center of the world and the earth moves even with the diurnal motion, His Holiness ordered the Most Illustrious Cardinal Bellarmine to call Galileo before himself and warn him to abandon these opinions; and if he should refuse to obey,

the Father Commissary, in the presence of notary and witnesses, is to issue him an injunction to abstain completely from teaching or defending this doctrine and opinion or from discussing it; and further, if he should not acquiesce, he is to be imprisoned.) (XI, 321; trans. by Finocchiaro 1989, 146).

These original minutes were later on transcribed into the acts of the Holy Office and that transcription, together with that of the other acts and decrees of that Congregation regarding Galileo were collected in a booklet[62] which is now conserved in the Vatican Archives.[63]

Upon comparing the original with the transcription known up to the present, after the word "notificavit" at the beginning the transcription adds: "RR.PP.DD. Assessori et Commissario S.cti Officii" (the Reverend Fathers Lord Assessor and Lord Commissary of the Holy Office). It seems to me that this additional phrase unduly restricts the importance of the notification, which according to the original seems to be made to all of those present and not only, therefore, to the Assessor and the Commissary but also, and in first place, to the cardinals. Perhaps it is not completely unlikely to suppose that at the moment of the transcription the Commissary of the Holy Office had wanted to have added the words reported above which would put in a particularly clear light the role which had been entrusted (even if in a second hypothetical moment) to the Commissary himself. Is this a symptom of the action that the Commissary in his heart intended *in any case* to carry through to the end?

Whatever we make of the additional phrase, it is clear from both documents that the Pope did *not* take part in the session, contrary to what is generally stated.[64] Cardinal Millini, Secretary (Prefect) of the Holy Office, limited himself during the session to reporting[65] what the Holy Father had already decided in all probability the day before at the moment of his meeting with Bellarmine about which the Ambassador Guicciardini speaks in the letter I have cited above. It seems to me perfectly clear from the English translation of the document cited above that the words: "after the reporting of the judgment by the Father

Theologians . . . His Holiness ordered the Most Illustrious Lord Cardinal Bellarmine . . .", indicate that it was as a matter of fact Bellarmine who at that time informed the Pope of the "censures" given the day before by the qualificators and perhaps also of the ratification which took place on that same day at the time of the plenary session at the Holy Office of the qualificators and the consultors.[66] In the light of such censures Galileo's doctrines were clearly "erroneous in faith" and, as to the immobility of the Sun, outright heretical. But how was one to proceed with respect to the author? By now Galileo was famous throughout Europe and "the principal mathematician and philosopher" of the Grand Duke of Tuscany. And it was not possible, despite his astronomical ideas, to doubt the sincerity of his faith.[67] It was probably Bellarmine himself who proposed to Paul V the procedure of a private warning to be carried out in the way we have just seen. And this would explain the fact that the task to present such a warning was given by the Pope precisely to Bellarmine on the occasion of their meeting. With this expedient Galileo would be silenced once for all but without wounding his reputation (the eventuality that Galileo would dare to refuse to submit to be silent with the consequence of his imprisonment seemed to be extremely remote) and, therefore, without offending the Grand Duke. As to Copernicanism and the "theologians" who supported it, the Congregation of the Index (Bellarmine was a member) would see to neutralizing both of them in a convenient way.[68]

That Bellarmine carried out, in fact, the task assigned to him is verified by two documents contained in the same booklet of the "Trial" of Galileo, as also by a note added to the same page of the original minutes of which I have spoken above.

Let us begin with the two documents well known for some time. The first in time comes immediately after that of the session of 25 February. Here is an English translation:

Friday, the twenty-sixth. At the palace, the usual residence of the Lord Cardinal Bellarmine, the said Galileo, having been summoned and being present before the said Lord Cardinal, was, in the presence of the Most Reverend Michelangelo Segizzi of Lodi, of the Order of Preachers,

Commissary-General of the Holy Office, by the said
Cardinal, warned of the error of the aforesaid opinion and
admonished to abandon it; and immediately thereafter,
before me and before witnesses, the Lord Cardinal being
still present, the said Galileo was by the said Commissary
commanded and enjoined, in the name of His Holiness the
Pope and the whole Congregation of the Holy Office, to
relinquish altogether the said opinion that the Sun is the
center of the world and immovable and that the Earth
moves; nor further to hold, teach, or defend it in any way
whatsoever, verbally or in writing; otherwise proceedings
would be taken against him by the Holy Office; which
injunction the said Galileo acquiesced in and promised to
obey (trans. by de Santillana 1955, 126).[69]

The second document was published later. In fact, it is the
transcription of the minutes of the session of the Holy Office of
3 March following (in which notice was taken of the Decree of
the Congregation of the Index against the Copernican writings
of which I will speak shortly). In the first part of those minutes
one reads:

The Most Illustrious Lord Cardinal Bellarmine having
given the report that the mathematician Galileo Galilei had
acquiesced when warned of the order of the Holy
Congregation to abandon the opinion which he held till
then, to the effect that the sun stands still at the center of
the spheres but the earth is in motion . . . (XIX, 278;
trans. by Finocchiaro 1989, 148).

The difference between these two documents is obvious.
The second is in perfect agreement with the papal decision of
which notice was given to the Holy Office on 25 February.
Galileo was summoned and he was subjected to the admonition
of Cardinal Bellarmine. It would seem, therefore, that there was
no need for an intervention of the Commissary of the Holy Office
(since, as we know, such an eventual intervention was based on
the condition that Galileo would refuse to subject himself to
Bellarmine's admonition) and there is no mention of such an
intervention. Instead, in the first document we have a patent
contradiction with the established procedures. In fact, right after

Bellarmine's admonition we have the intervention of Commissary Segizzi in a menacing manner. But there is no statement that such an intervention had been motivated, as prescribed, by a refusal of Galileo to accept the admonition. Besides these contradictions internal to this document, there is also the fact that it lacks the signatures of Bellarmine, of Segizzi, of the notary who prepared it and of the two witnesses (Bellarmine's domestics) who are named in the document.

From the second half of the 19th century (from the time, that is, when these secret documents began to be known) all of this has brought about a series of contradictory interpretations, especially as regards the first document. It has come to the point of even holding that this document is a fraud, made up during the investigatory phase of Galileo's trial in 1632 in order to be able to bring accusations against him.[70] But an accurate examination of the *dossier* of the Holy Office has shown that without a doubt this document goes back to 1616. Another hypothesis, first proposed by von Gebler and then by de Santillana,[71] holds that the Commissary Segizzi, disillusioned by the too moderate manner in which Bellarmine had delivered the injunction and by the prompt assent of Galileo, decided to omit the official report despite the instructions which he had received. Then, as de Santillana reports, "On going back to his office, he [Segizzi] told his assistant to arrange a more helpful minute of the proceedings".[72]

However, all of this discussion is by now dated after the original minutes of the meeting of 25 February were found. On the same small sheet of paper we read, in fact, on the bottom line the following annotation:

> On the 26 of said [i.e., of said month] *the Most Illustrious Lord Cardinal Bellarmine warned Galileo of the error of the above mentioned opinion etc.* and afterwards the precept as above was enjoined on him by the Father Commissary etc. (italics indicate the part of the original in Latin; non italics the part in Italian).[73]

This annotation in agreement with the first document mentioned above definitely excludes the hypothesis of von Gebler and de Santillana. Segizzi's intervention took place, in fact, immediately after Bellarmine's admonition, even though there remains the mystery as to why the phrase which refers to this intervention was written in Italian, while the beginning of the annotation is in Latin.[74]

There still remains, however, the question of the reason for this intervention and the explanation of why it was not mentioned in the document of 3 March. Among the many attempts to offer an explanation the most plausible appears to be that proposed by G. Morpurgo-Tagliabue.[75]

According to this author, Galileo, after hearing Bellarmine's injunction, would have hesitated to answer (or might have made some objection). At this Commissary Segizzi, who was perhaps already piqued by the moderate tone of Bellarmine in his admonition,[76] decided to intervene and added without hesitation an express order of the most severe form. Faced with such an order Galileo did not hesitate to submit. But this uncalled for intervention of Segizzi must have displeased Bellarmine who did not consider that he had completed the part of the task assigned to him. And so, because he could not agree in conscience, the Cardinal refused to sign the document prepared at Segizzi's wish by the notary. And, after Segizzi had left, he must have reassured Galileo that Segizzi's intervention had been impulsive and not in accord with the instructions they had been given and Galileo, therefore, should not worry about it.[77] But Segizzi, although he was not able to have Bellarmine's signature affixed to the document, did not hesitate to have it inserted in the dossier as a transcript of what had in fact happened.

As we know already, on 3 March on the occasion of the weekly meeting of the Cardinals of the Holy Office, this time with the Holy Father present, Bellarmine let it be known that he had carried out the task assigned to him and that Galileo had assented. On the other hand, Bellarmine considered Segizzi's intervention to have been inopportune and contrary to the instructions given, so he did not mention it. And this explains the content of the document concerning the meeting and the contrast between it and the ones dated 26 February.

In the same meeting notice was given of the decision of the Congregation of the Index concerning the writings of Copernicus. The document refers to the incident as follows:

> . . . and the decree of the Congregation of the Index having been presented, prohibiting and suspending, respectively, the writings of Nicolaus Copernicus, of Diego de Zuñiga *On Job*, and of Paolo Antonio Foscarini, Carmelite Friar - His Holiness ordered this edict of prohibition and suspension, respectively, to be published by the Master of the Palace. (trans. by Finocchiaro 1989, 149).[78]

In fact the decree of the Congregation of the Index was published two days later (5 March 1616). After having announced the prohibition of various other works, the decree added:

> . . . And whereas it has also come to the knowledge of the said Congregation that the Pythagorean doctrine - which is false and altogether opposed to Holy Scripture[79] - of the motion of the Earth and the immobility of the Sun, which is also taught by Nicolaus Copernicus in *De revolutionibus orbium coelestium*, and by Diego de Zuñiga [in his book] on Job, is now being spread abroad and accepted by many - as may be seen from a certain letter of a Carmelite Father, entitled *Letter of the Rev. Father Paolo Antonio Foscarini, Carmelite, on the Opinion of the Pythagoreans and of Copernicus concerning the Motion of the Earth, and the Stability of the Sun, and the New Pythagorean System of the World, at Naples, Printed by Lazzaro Scorriggio, 1615*; wherein the said Father attempts to show that the aforesaid doctrine of the immobility of the Sun in the center of the world, and of the Earth's motion, is consonant with truth and is not opposed to Holy Scripture. Therefore, in order that this opinion may not insinuate itself any further to the prejudice of the Catholic truth, the Holy Congregation has decreed that the said Nicolaus Copernicus, *De revolutionibus orbium*, and Diego de Zuñiga, *On Job*, be suspended until they be corrected; but that the book of the Carmelite Father, Paolo Antonio Foscarini, be altogether prohibited and condemned, and that all other works likewise, in which the same is taught,

be prohibited, as by this present decree it prohibits, condemns, and suspends them all respectively. (XIX, 323; trans. by de Santillana 1955, 123).[80]

This Decree brings to an end that which is often called the first trial of Galileo. In fact, even though at the beginning there were denunciations against him and his writings, the conclusion of the affair prescinded from the person of Galileo (at least in the document which was made public, the Decree of the Congregation of the Index) and restricted itself to silencing Galileo with a precept of a wholly private character.[81] As I have said already, in this way one planned to avoid a clash with the Grand Duke Cosimo II, whose esteem for Galileo, "his primary mathematician and philosopher", was well known, as well as with Galileo himself, whose sincere allegiance to his Catholic faith was recognized (at least among the higher levels of the Church hierarchy).

The ambassador from Tuscany to Rome, Guicciardini, who right from the beginning was against Galileo's coming to the City, could now show the Grand Duke that he had been right. He had, as a matter of fact, already done so on the day before the publication of the Decree of the Index in the letter of 4 March to which I have already referred. In that letter he made the following observation:

> Galileo has relied more on his own counsel than on that of his friends. The Lord Cardinal del Monte and myself, and also several cardinals from the Holy Office, had tried to persuade him to be quiet and not to go irritating this issue. If he wanted to hold this Copernican opinion, he was told, let him hold it quietly and not spend so much effort in trying to have others share it. Everyone fears that his coming here may be very prejudicial and that, instead of justifying himself and succeeding, he may end up with an affront. (XII, 241-242; trans. by de Santillana 1955, 119)

And a little later he added:

> He [Galileo] is all afire on his opinions, and puts great passion in them, and not enough strength and prudence in

controlling it; so that the Roman climate is getting very dangerous for him, and especially in this century; for the present Pope, who abhors the liberal arts and this kind of mind, cannot stand these novelties and subtleties; and everyone here tries to adjust his mind and his nature to that of the ruler. . . . Galileo has monks and others who hate him and persecute him, and, as I said, he is not at all in a good position for a place like this, and he might get himself and others into serious trouble. (XII, 242; trans. by de Santillana, 1955, 116).[82]

Obviously Guicciardini wanted to persuade the Grand Duke to recall Galileo to Florence as soon as possible. But Galileo was not the kind of man who quits easily. The Decree of the Congregation of the Index had not mentioned him nor any of his writings. And he must have taken great care to avoid reporting exactly to Guicciardini (or to whomever else) all that had occurred in Bellarmine's residence, especially the intervention and injunction of Segizzi.[83] Therefore, it was not really the propitious moment to withdraw precipitously from Rome and thus give the impression of a personal defeat. Nor, obviously, did he agree with Guicciardini's version of the facts. In fact he wrote to Picchena on 6 March and said:

As one can see from the very nature of the business, I have no interest whatsoever in it, nor would I have gotten involved in it if, as I said, my enemies had not dragged me into it. What I have done on the matter can always be seen from my writings pertaining to it, which I save in order to be able to shut the mouth of malicious gossipers at any time, and because I can show that my behavior in this affair has been such that a saint would not have handled it either with greater reverence or with greater zeal towards the Holy Church. This perhaps has not been done by my enemies, who have not refrained from any machination, calumny and diabolic suggestion, as their Most Serene Highnesses and also Your Lordship will hear at length in due course. (XII, 244).

Obviously with the Secretary of the Grand Duke Galileo tended to make his behavior at Rome appear to be the most moderate and circumspect possible. And he also sought to minimize the importance of the Decree of the Index. In the same letter, after having observed that in that decree the Copernican theory had not been condemned as heretical but that only those books had been prohibited which sought *ex professo* to prove that such a theory was not contrary to Scripture, Galileo added:

> As for the book of Copernicus himself, ten lines will be removed from the preface to Paul III, where he mentions that he does not think such a doctrine is repugnant to Scripture; as I understand it, they could remove a word here and there, where two or three times he calls the earth a star. The correction of these two books[84] has been assigned to Lord Cardinal Caetani. There is no mention of other authors. (XII, 244; trans. by Finocchiaro 1989, 150).

Guicciardini was certainly not the only one to attribute the position taken by the Church to a lack of tact on Galileo's part. Even Kepler, whose work, *Epitome Astronomiae Copernicanae*, and, to be more exact, the first part of it, *Doctrina Sphaerica*, published at Linz in 1618, was prohibited as Copernican by the Congregation of the Index one year later (Decree of 10 May 1619), attributed that prohibition to the "inappropriateness of some who have treated of astronomical truths in places where they should not be treated and with improper methods".[85]

The audience granted to Galileo by Paul V just one week after the Decree of the Index shows that the Church wished to treat him in a special way. According to the report of the audience which Galileo gave to Picchena on the same day, 12 March, the Pope stayed with him at length ("three quarters of an hour"). The Pope showed himself quite benevolent and assured Galileo that he was convinced of his intellectual integrity and sincerity. And Galileo continued:

> Finally, since I appeared somewhat insecure because of the thought that I would be always persecuted by their implacable malice, he consoled me by saying that I could live with my mind at peace, for I was so regarded by His Holiness and the whole Congregation that they would not

easily listen to the slanderers, and that I could feel safe as long as he lived. Before I left he told me many times that he was very ready at every occasion to show me also with actions his strong inclination to favor me. (XII, 248; trans. by Finocchiaro 1989, 152)

The Grand Duke, under the influence of the Ambassador Guicciardini, wished that Galileo in the end be calm, and that, content with the testimony of kindness on the part of Paul V, he would become persuaded to return to Florence. But Galileo was not in a hurry. A few days before the decision of the Holy Office, the Grand Duke, ignorant of what was about to happen, had asked Galileo to await in Rome the arrival of Cardinal Carlo de' Medici so that he could appear at his side and with his conversation make the banquets of the Cardinal with the various Roman personalities more interesting (XII, 237). Galileo, therefore, had a good excuse for staying in Rome. His appearance beside the Cardinal would have constituted a proof in public that he enjoyed, no less now than he had previously, the favor of the Grand Duke and of personalities in the Church.[86]

8.   *Rumors of an abjuration by Galileo. Bellarmine's testimony for Galileo. Some final remarks*

It was not just self-love that dictated this posture to Galileo. By remaining in Rome he wanted undoubtedly to hear what would leak out about the affair in which he was involved, so that he might be able to parry the blows which his adversaries would try to direct with regard to the affair.

In fact, rumors began to spread right away that Galileo had been called by the Inquisition to give an account of his convictions about Copernicanism, that he had abjured these convictions, and that afterwards severe penances had been imposed on him by Cardinal Bellarmine.[87]

Since there was no indication that these rumors were going to die out, Galileo decided to have recourse to Bellarmine himself. On 26 May, the latter released to him the following declaration:

We, Robert Cardinal Bellarmine, have heard that Mr.
Galileo Galilei is being slandered or alleged to have
abjured in our hands and also to have been given salutary
penances for this. Having been sought about the truth of
the matter, we say that the above-mentioned Galileo has
not abjured in our hands, or in the hands of others here in
Rome, or anywhere else that we know, any opinion or
doctrine of his; nor has he received any penances, salutary
or otherwise. On the contrary he has only[88] been notified
of the declaration made by the Holy Father and published
by the Sacred Congregation of the Index, whose content is
that the doctrine attributed to Copernicus (that the earth
moves around the sun and the sun stands at the center of
the world without moving east to west) is contrary to Holy
Scripture and therefore cannot be defended or held. In
witness whereof we have written and signed this with our
own hands, on this 26th day of May 1616. (XIX, 348; trans.
by Finocchiaro 1989, 153).[89]

Guicciardini grew increasingly more exasperated with
Galileo's behavior. If we rely at any rate on the ambassador's
report to Picchena, far from appearing to be weakened by the
long battle and saddened by its epilogue, Galileo had not lost a
bit of his combativeness and of his capacity to enjoy life (XII,
259).

By now those in Florence were also tired of this affair
which was too drawn out and they were worried about its
possible further developments. On 23 May Picchena sent to
Galileo a courteous but clear invitation to return to Florence as
soon as possible (XII, 261) and Galileo began his return trip
during the first days of June. On the vigil of his departure,
however, he was furnished with a testimony of Cardinals Monte
and Orsini who emphasized that, as Galileo left Rome, he kept
intact his reputation and the esteem of all of those who had
dealt with him and they gave assurance that it was clear to
everyone how wrong it was that he had been calumniated by his
enemies (XII, 263-264). These testimonies were important for
Galileo who felt the pressure to avoid, at whatever cost, losing
the esteem and support of the Grand Duke, all the more so since
he was aware of the hostility from the ambassador Guicciardini

whom he feared would undoubtedly have given an account of the happenings not at all in his favor. We already know how well founded these apprehensions were.

And so ends an episode which Galileo and his friends tried to make appear as if it were in no way harmful to his reputation. But deep down inside they (and especially Galileo) must have felt a deep bitterness. The plan conceived by Galileo, to silence the opposition by convincing the Church authorities that they must not hastily judge Copernicanism, had failed.

But, despite all of that, Galileo was not the kind to resign himself to defeat. He was doubtlessly convinced that, as time went on with the possibility of finding decisive proofs in favor of Copernicanism, the posture of the Church would change. Meanwhile, it was necessary to assume an attitude of prudent reserve, working quietly to perfect the arguments in favor of heliocentrism. As to Galileo's adversaries, they must not have been totally satisfied with the conclusion of the affair. The real adversary was not Copernicus, by now dead for 70 years, but Galileo, who was alive (and very much so!) and who remained officially uncensured. Of course, something had come out of his having been called before Bellarmine and that had given rise to the gossip to which I have already alluded. But they were only rumors. Without a doubt to silence him definitively an open condemnation of the mathematician of the Grand Duke would have been preferable. At the same time, many of Galileo's admirers, sensing a contrary wind, drew back quickly to more secure positions.[90]

What was the attitude of the Jesuits in this whole affair? They have often been severely criticized by biographers of Galileo for not having taken a supporting role in Galileo's activities in promoting Copernicanism.[91] On the other hand, other biographers tend to highlight the fact that the reserve of the Jesuits is to be attributed to scientific reasons (at least for the most part). Convinced by now (as was Clavius at the end of his life) that the Aristotelian-Ptolemaic system could not be upheld, they would have provisionally adopted the cosmological views of Tycho Brahe, which avoided problems with Scripture. And it is stated that they were not prepared to give up this make-shift position until truly conclusive proofs in favor of

Copernicanism at the level of science were forthcoming. On the other hand, Galileo was not prepared to give such proofs (neither in 1615-1616 nor later on). The Jesuits, therefore, like true scientists, would have felt it necessary to stay silent.[92]

It is first of all, I believe, necessary to rethink the power to influence events which is customarily attributed to the Jesuits. In fact, I believe that some of the biographers of Galileo tend to attribute to the members of the Society of Jesus in general and to the astronomers of the Roman College in particular, an ability to influence the decisions of the Church of that time which is quite exaggerated.

Certainly there is no doubt that this religious order had had right from its beginning an important role in the Counter-Reformation and enjoyed particular favors from many Popes. This was due to the special characteristics impressed upon it by its founder, Ignatius of Loyola, with a view to its being of prompt and efficacious service to the Catholic Church, and also to the selection and preparation of its most choice members (the so-called "professed"), a process much stricter than that used by the other religious orders of that time. Its role continued to increase in depth and in breadth thanks especially to its activity in the field of education with schools (or "colleges") at all levels where the social and intellectual elite of the Catholic Europe of that time received their formation.

But alongside the Jesuits there also existed other older religious orders, the first among them being the Dominicans, who boasted of a very rich theological tradition, from St. Albert the Great and St. Thomas Aquinas onwards. And in theology the Dominicans, indeed, did not feel that they were less competent than the Jesuits, nor were they disposed to concede to the Jesuits the defense of Catholic orthodoxy. The proof of this was the long, clamorous, and bitter controversy, *De Auxiliis*, which concerned the reconciliation of divine grace with human free will. This controversy began in 1599 and went on until 1607 with the most renowned Dominican and Jesuit theologians as protagonists, and it came to an end without victor or vanquished when a decision was taken by Paul V (at the suggestion of Bellarmine), who ordered the two sides in the argument to put an end to the discussions and attacks going back and forth in expectation of a decision by the Pope on the questions in dispute (a decision which was never made).[93]

As we have seen, the beginning of the campaign against the thesis of Galileo on the theological level had come from some Dominicans, even though we must not forget that important members of this Order had immediately distanced themselves from such activity and, in fact, had severely criticized it. Also the majority of the qualificators and consultors of the Holy Office were Dominicans.

Having learned from the experience of the controversy, De Auxiliis, and the authoritarian way in which Paul V had put an end to it, the Jesuits, even if they had wanted to carry out activity in Galileo's favor, would have had to reflect more than once on the limitations of their influence.

But there was more to it than that. The mathematicians of the Roman College made up only a small minority with respect to the majority of their fellow religious, teachers of philosophy and theology. Now, the philosophy teachers, although they were not narrow-minded Aristotelians,[94] did not have available to them for the teaching of philosophy (not only natural philosophy, but also metaphysics and moral) anything other than the great Aristotelian synthesis, "Christianized" as we have seen in the Middle Ages. For sure, during recent decades deep cracks were continuing to open in the edifice of the natural philosophy of Aristotle, and Galileo's discoveries had further widened them, creating a crisis for the fundamental points of Aristotelian cosmology. But, I repeat once more, there did not yet exist a new natural philosophy (not to speak of a comprehensive philosophical synthesis).[95] In such a situation of uncertainty and disorientation it was inevitable that the philosophy professors of the Roman College (as for that of all the European universities of that epoch) would continue to teach Aristotelianism. Furthermore for the Jesuits, there was, as we know, the explicit recommendation by their Father General Acquaviva to do so.

As to the theology professors, the reconciliation of Copernicanism with Scripture weighed more heavily upon them than the problem of Aristotelianism. Even though they were at times more open than their colleagues in philosophy, the Jesuit theologians were certainly not capable of following in the wake of Father Foscarini. In the intellectual atmosphere in Rome which had by then become so tense, with many Dominicans (especially the consultors of the Holy Office) notoriously persuaded that the thesis of the immobility of the Sun was heretical, and with all the reserve (not to say more) shown by Bellarmine, how could the theology professors of the Roman College take up the defense of Copernicanism (even if they had wanted to do so)? And, if the recommendation of their Father General to follow Aristotle did not directly weigh upon them, the one concerning "uniformity of doctrine" did.

If one takes all of this into consideration, it is much easier to understand the attitude of Grienberger and the other mathematicians of the Roman College. By now there was among them, as we have seen already, those who were in their own hearts Copernican. Others (as Grienberger himself) were at least strongly inclined towards heliocentrism. But there were always some doubts. And as a further restraint to any activity by them in favor of Galileo there was the obedience which bound them (lacking evidence to the contrary) to the prescriptions of their Father General. With those conditions how would they have been able to take up favoring Galileo? And what possibility was there of succeeding, even if they had wanted to do so? There was nothing left but to hope (and even perhaps pray) that Galileo or others would finally succeed in providing convincing and irrefutable proofs for Copernicanism. In that case no one, not even their Father General or Paul V, would have been able any longer to force them to a "blind obedience" in favor of Aristotelianism.[96]

Therefore, these Jesuits were neither "pure scientists" nor for sure intellectual heroes. But neither were they frightened beings, nor like automatons in the hands of their superiors who forced them to sacrifice their intelligences *tout-court*. The human reality of their behavior, as always happens, cannot be explained by prefabricated clichés. If their conduct is not such as to arouse our admiration nor, perhaps, even our sympathy, it might at least be treated with understanding.

Special treatment must be given to the most famous Jesuit of that epoch, Cardinal Bellarmine. The statement of de Santillana that the responsibility in history for the decision of

1616 falls exclusively on the shoulders of Bellarmine[97] appears to be exaggerated. Surely, Bellarmine was the most authoritative Catholic theologian then living and his influence was profound. I have already had the opportunity to show his intellectual stance in the whole Copernican controversy, especially with respect to the letter of Foscarini, which contributed a great deal to the subsequent precipitous development of the situation.

From the whole complex of the documented information which has been examined up to the present, it seems that we can draw the conclusion that Bellarmine was one of the principal personages, but certainly not the only one, responsible for the decision of 1616. The antagonisms, at times full of partisan animosities, were too deep and too wide-spread, and the intellectual climate then existent in the responsible spheres of the Church were still too linked to the traditional world-view and besieged by the preoccupation to defend orthodox Catholicism against the "heresies" of those times to be able to allow hope for a peaceful solution to the affair, even leaving aside the influential intervention of Bellarmine.[98]

That Galileo's responsibility for the prohibition of the Copernican system was also an important one has been maintained since the time of Kepler to our own day, especially in "apologetic" writings by Catholics. According to these authors it was, as a matter of fact, Galileo's imprudence and his misplaced zeal in insisting on the Church's acceptance of Copernicanism, but without his supplying sufficient proofs for it, together with his intrusion into the field of Biblical exegesis that caused the Church to take an abrupt position which, otherwise, it would have been able to avoid.

As to the accusation of imprudence, I think I have succeeded in showing that on more than one occasion Galileo showed considerably more prudence that did his friends. Certainly his trip to Rome in 1605-1616, in this case against the advice of his Roman friends, proved in the end to be a tactical error, but it still remains true that it was motivated by his ever increasing worry that his adversaries would, as a matter of fact, end by provoking in a short time a decision contrary to Copernicanism. Given their temperament and the means which they employed, such a worry was surely not without a basis in fact.

As to the accusation that he had the pretence to have extracted from the Roman authorities with all available means a decision favorable to heliocentrism, this does not seem to correspond to the facts. As can be clearly established from his two letters to Dini, from his "reflections on the Copernican question", from the *Letter to Castelli* and, above all, from the *Letter to Christina of Lorraine*, Galileo was completely aware of the prudence required in order that the Church might come to a conclusion about Copernicanism.[99] In fact, what he sought by all means to bring about in 1615-1616 was that the Roman Church authorities would not make a hasty decision against Copernicanism, but that they would rather leave it as an open question which could be freely discussed.

As to Galileo's intrusion into Scriptural matters, he was surely not the first to venture into that area. As we have seen, it was, on the contrary, his adversaries who, more and more at a loss as to how to battle Galileo on the field of the natural sciences, retreated to the area of Scripture, using it as a weapon against Copernicanism. What should Galileo have done? Should he remain quiet and strengthen his case with scientific arguments as Grienberger had counselled him? But, as Galileo saw it, to remain silent would have meant that the arguments from Scripture were in themselves adequate to nullify a question which for him should remain open. Was Galileo guilty of imprudence and a lack of political savoir-faire? Perhaps. But to those factors we owe his declaration of the freedom of scientific research based on the separation of the fields of competence of scientists and of theologians. Galileo was one of the first, with a truly modern mentality, to proclaim such freedom in this context. The *Letter to Christina of Lorraine* is a splendid example of this very important turn in Western thought. It is precisely for that reason that I have chosen to give special attention to it in this chapter.

On the other hand the question still remains as to whether, had Galileo not intervened in the field of Scripture, the Church would have at that time been blocked from taking an official position. Foscarini had intervened. He being a theologian, the accusation of unwarranted intrusion in a field not of his competence, could not be sustained. But precisely because he was a theologian his attempt to reconcile Copernicanism with Scripture created, as we know, a special worry for Church of Rome. Ciampoli, quite a bit more perspicacious than Cesi, had foreseen that the *Letter to Christina* would be condemned much before Galileo's trip to Rome where he would find himself ever more involved in discussions about Scripture with his adversaries. And that condemnation could not have come about without having been motivated by the opposition between Copernicanism and Sacred Scripture, i.e., without a stance having been taken like the one which came about with the decree of the Index in 1616.

And as for the fact, repeated very often by Catholic "apologists", that Galileo had not brought forth decisive proofs for Copernicanism, it seems necessary to emphasize that from the totality of the indisputable data obtained from his observations, as well as from those of others including the Jesuits themselves, the system of Aristotle-Ptolemy had been irremediably put in crisis. There was, it is true, the geocentrism of Tycho Brahe, but it was promoted only by a small circle of "specialists". At any rate, the minimum that could be said was that Copernicanism appeared by now to be a real possibility. And that was sufficient authorization for Galileo to recommend to the Church that it not jump precipitously into a negative decision with respect to Copernicanism.

None of this, unfortunately, was taken into consideration by the qualificators of the Holy Office. As we have seen, they did not at all pose to themselves the problem of whether or not scientific proofs existed to support Copernicanism, since they were otherwise convinced that they had other much more solid and conclusive reasons for excluding *a priori* the possibility of finding any such proofs. The qualificators, in addition to being theologians, were also philosophers. And their philosophy was perfectly sufficient to exclude Copernicanism at the level of rational knowledge (which included, therefore, also that of scientific knowledge). "That the sun is the center of the world and hence immovable of local motion: is a proposition *foolish and absurd in philosophy*". If philosophy so declared, what need was there to enter into the field of astronomical considerations (which, for that, are never other than hypothetical considerations

- so were the qualificators persuaded)? Is truth not *one*, as Galileo himself had stated? If one is in possession of a philosophical truth, then one is certain *a priori* that one cannot have a scientific proof which contradicts it. It was precisely this which Bellarmine himself had implicitly said to Foscarini towards the end of his letter to him. *Philosophia locuta est, causa finita* (Philosophy has spoken, the case is closed). And so there is no doubt. The true sense of Scripture is the literal one, very much in agreement with the philosophy of common sense of the qualificators. They were, therefore, able to conclude without the shadow of a doubt and without fear of being proven wrong in the future: "[...] and formally heretical since it explicitly contradicts in many places the sense of Holy Scripture".[100]

One can, therefore, conclude that at the basis of the sureness with which in 1616 the Church rejected Copernicanism (with the intention that it be definitive) was not only the theology of the epoch, but also, and first of all, the philosophy[101] that was so closely linked to the theology as to constitute for a large part of the contemporaries of Galileo an inseparable whole.

Surely the enormous psychological difficulty of making theology independent of a world-view based on the obdurate convictions of common sense may provide extenuating circumstances for the erroneous decision of 1616. Another attenuating circumstance may be seen in the concern that serious danger to the unity of the Catholic faith, together with the challenge to the teaching authority of the Church, might be brought on by the new ideas being spread about by Galileo and by his attempt to reconcile them with Sacred Scripture, an attempt with which even a theologian like Foscarini had associated himself.

But, even granting these attenuating circumstances, there is still the grave objective error of having wished to resolve authoritatively and definitively a question which should have been left open and to have sought to silence in the same definitive manner those who promoted the new ideas. As we shall see, this "abuse of power", both doctrinal and disciplinary, will have its inevitable sequel in the trial and condemnation of

Galileo in 1633 and will continue for centuries to weigh heavily upon the relationship of the Church to modern culture.

NOTES

[1] For a biography of this daughter of Galileo see Favaro 1935.

[2] This is the thesis of L. Geymonat 1965, 58.

[3] On the other hand we should not forget that his studies on motion and the discoveries made during his time in Padua and the period immediately after that stay had opened Galileo's way of thinking to unlimited horizons. In view of that, a long period of reflection became necessary. Such reflection was not dismissed by Galileo, despite his activity in the field of Copernican polemics. Indeed, are not *The Assayer* and the *Dialogue* of 1632 two important stages in this reflection which he continues to deepen? I do not, therefore, find myself in complete agreement with Geymonat as to the Galileo's program of "cultural politics" and with his conclusion:

> It was only after his second and definitive defeat in 1633 that Galileo had to give up the struggle for his program and resume the purely scientific work in mechanics which he had begun during the Paduan period. (Geymonat 1965, 63).

It seems to me that, since Galileo was never a "pure scientist", he will never completely abandon research to enter into the arena of "cultural propaganda". For him research and popularization of that research (in the sense, as a matter of fact, of "cultural propaganda") constituted a single effort, in the same way as do theory and practice (with respect to this see de Santillana 1955, 19-24). And so he undoubtedly was convinced that he should continue his cultural politics even after the events of 1633, although in a more quiet way. In fact, the *Discourses* of 1638, by providing the basis for the modern science of motion and thereby preparing the future synthesis of Newton, will show the mature outcome both of Galileo's cultural activity and, at the same time, of his research.

[4] As a matter of fact Galileo had written:

> And so as for those very expert in astronomical science it was sufficient to have understood what Copernicus wrote in his Revolutions [*De revolutionibus orbium celestium*] to

ascertain the revolution of Venus about the sun and the truth of the rest of his system . . . (V, 195).

[5] It was not a question of a sermon, as de Santillana 1955, 27 maintained. Galileo himself speaks of "privati colloqui" (private talks; V, 291).

[6] Christina of Lorraine was a woman of strict piety and the Scriptural argument was of particular importance for her.

[7] In this interpretation of his Galileo did not choose the simplest route (and the one more in harmony with the general considerations of the first part of the letter) which would have consisted of observing that the stopping of the Sun was a manner of speaking and that one should not remain at this literal sense. Instead he tried straight out to turn the situation around by maintaining that this Scriptural citation showed the "falsity and impossibility of the system of Aristotle and Ptolemy, and on the contrary that it was excellently suited to that of Copernicus". For a comment on this see de Santillana 1955, 41-42.

[8] The theme of Caccini's sermon was from Chapter X of the *Book of Joshua* which contained the passage in whose regard Christina of Lorraine had questioned Castelli and which Galileo had treated at the end of his *Letter to Castelli*. It dealt with an argument which everybody was talking about in Florence. Caccini, forty years old at that time, had very close ties with the League of the *"Colombi"* (the Pigeons). As we know (see Note 46 to the Introduction) Caccini had read Tolosani's manuscript and the severe criticism of Copernicus contained therein. Later on (in 1635) he will give public lectures on such writings (see Bucciantini 1995, 37, Note 32). Added to his aversion for Copernicanism there was, of course, his enmity for Galileo against whom he may have already preached in Bologna as early as 1611 (see XII, 127). The reactions which the sermon provoked would provide sufficient grounds that its content was as rumors had it. XII, 123, 127, 129, 145, 156.

[9] Westfall considers these statements of Cesi to be very important as a proof that, contrary to what is commonly asserted, Galileo's difficulties with the Church did not begin in Florence with the activity of Lorini, Boscaglia and Caccini. According to Westfall, even before their activity and independent from it, Bellarmine

> had decided that Copernican astronomy was opposed to Scriptural truth and would have to be suppressed. With its repeated warnings to Galileo, the letter [of Cesi] also implies that Bellarmino had expressed some reservations about him as well. This puts the whole of the trial in a new perspective. (Westfall 1989, 13).

I do not completely agree with these statements. That Copernicanism was contrary to Scripture was a common conviction which had been held for a long time in responsible ecclesiastical circles. So Bellarmine did not have to "decide it" on his own initiative as Westfall states. As I have shown when I spoke of the reactions in Catholic circles to the publication of the *De Revolutionibus*, this book ran the risk of being condemned (not put on the Index since the Congregation of the Index did not yet exist) a little after the author's death. The fact that there was no condemnation at that time was due above all to the fact that the Copernican theory remained a mere hypothesis without any physical proof. For the Church the problem with Copernicanism began precisely when, after the astronomical discoveries of Galileo, that theory began to appear as a real threat to the traditional Christian view of the world. And we have already seen that the Roman ecclesiastical authorities (at the level of the Holy Office) had begun, as a matter of fact, to express their concern about the case on the occasion of Galileo's visit to Rome in 1611. Thus, the roots of the conflict between the Church and Copernicanism already existed before the accusations brought by Lorini and Caccini. On that point Westfall is correct. But, I repeat, they were quite a bit older and were independent of any presumed unilateral "decision" by Bellarmine. On the other hand, it also remains true that the actions of the League of the "Colombi" (Pigeons) exacerbated the situation and brought Galileo into the area of Scripture. As to the statements of Bellarmine to Cesi, they should be put in the balance with those he made to Dini about six months later. See the main text which follows and Note 18.

[10] With respect to the interpretation of Holy Scripture the Council of Trent had decreed in Session IV (8 April 1546), Decree 786:

> Furthermore, to control petulant spirits, the Council decrees that, in matters of faith and morals pertaining to the edification of Christian doctrine, no one, relying on his own judgment and distorting the Sacred Scriptures according to his own conceptions, shall dare to interpret them contrary to that sense which Holy Mother Church, to whom it belongs to judge of their true sense and meaning, has held and does hold, or even contrary to the unanimous agreement of the Fathers . . (Trans. by Blackwell 1991, 11-12).

As we see, the Council had limited these norms to questions of faith and morals. For Galileo the problem of the motion of the Earth was not a problem of faith (see the *Letter to Castelli* and then the *Letter to*

Christina of Lorraine). But for his opponents it was, or at least it was intimately connected with the truths of the faith. The crux of the theological problem, which will result in the listing of *De Revolutionibus* on the Index and later on to the condemnation of Galileo himself, is right here. On the IV Session of the Council of Trent see Blackwell 1991, 1-22.

[11] The Congregation of the Index had been established by Pius V in 1571 with the purpose of preventing the distribution of printed material containing ideas contrary to Catholic faith and morals. It was suppressed by Pope Benedict XV in 1917. From that time on the censorship of books was entrusted to the Holy Office. The whole practice of the censorship of books was completely changed after Vatican Council II. As for the Congregation of the Holy Office it is now called the Congregation for the Doctrine of the Faith.

[12] This letter of Lorini is contained in XIX, 293-421. In the same volume before this series of documents on the "Inquisition Proceedings" there is a series on the "Decrees" (XIX, 275-292). All of the preceding documents, in addition to some found more recently, have been published by Pagano 1984. At the beginning of this publication there is an important introduction which gives a description of the volume, Misc. Arm. X, 204, of the Vatican Secret Archives which contains the collection of the investigative proceedings concerning Galileo, those precisely published by Favaro. I will have the opportunity in the final chapter of this book to speak of the vicissitudes suffered by this collection during and after the time of Napoleon.

[13] For a review of the various existing manuscripts of the *Letter to Castelli* and for a history of the various editions, see *Avvertimento* (V, 263-270). The manuscript which Favaro selects as the closest to Galileo's original letter is manuscript G, which is kept with numerous others in the National Library in Florence (Mss. Galileiani, Part IV, T.1, car. 8r-10r). The copy sent by Lorini, wherein he underlined the passages which he considered to be theologically suspect, is found in XIX, 299-305.

[14] See Pesce 1992, 394-417. In an appendix to his article Pesce compares the variants in Lorini's copy with respect to the rest of the textual tradition and in particular with respect to manuscript G.

[15] As Pesce 1992, 409-410 notes, it would not be just, because he sent a revised copy, but one defined as authentic, to accuse Galileo of a disloyal falsification of his ideas. In fact, the new version presents no substantial modifications in Galileo's thought, but only the retouching of some expressions which could be misunderstood theologically (and which, in fact, the censor had declared not to appear at first sight to sound correct, even though they could be interpreted in a good sense).

Galileo left statements of a much greater importance, such as those on the irrelevancy of the Bible to scientific questions, as they were.

[16] Giovanni Ciampoli was born in Florence about 1590. After his philosophical and theological studies at Pisa he became a priest in 1614. Thanks to his great literary talents and his unusual intelligence he made rapid progress in his ecclesiastical career and was appointed Secretary of the Briefs by Pope Urban VIII. As a friend of Galileo, whom he knew in Florence in 1608, he made every effort to see that the *Dialogue* would be printed. As we shall see, Urban VIII considered that Ciampoli had betrayed him and he banished him from Rome and relegated him to secondary assignments. He died at Iesi in 1643.

[17] De Santillana 1960, 140 comments that Bellarmine, since he had received an authentic copy of the *Letter to Castelli*, would have been able to use it, while in the archives of the Holy Office there remained the copy falsified by Lorini "even though it was suspect to the Sacred Congregation". And he comments: "And this is one of the mysteries of the affair". Here de Santillana commits the error of supposing that Bellarmine was able of his own initiative to have the "authentic copy" we are dealing with deposited in the archives of the Holy Office, even presuming (which is probable but not certain) that it had been sent to him by Dini. As we know, the Holy Office had made a request for the original to the Archbishop of Pisa and they would certainly not have been satisfied with a copy sent by the very culprit and declared "authentic" by him. It rather appears to me that the Holy Office, convinced of Galileo's "orthodoxy" (even after the negative results of the investigation provoked by the accusations of Caccini, of whom I will speak shortly), terminated its work by putting aside the search for the original text in question. But the copy sent by Lorini remained as part of the Acts and, as we shall see, it will be resurrected and used at the end of Galileo's trial in 1633.

[18] These substantially moderate statements of Bellarmine reported by Dini are in contrast with the rather more harsh ones which Cesi refers to in the letter of the previous 12th of January which I have already quoted (XII, 129). Is it possible that Bellarmine, when he spoke first to Cesi and then only six months later to Dini, would have expressed such different opinions? Bellarmine was accustomed to weigh his words and he was certainly not one to give into the impulse of the moment, especially on a matter of such great importance. Must we then consider that either Cesi or Dini had not reported their conversations in a completely objective way? One might be able to put forth the hypothesis that, when he spoke with Cesi, Bellarmine had mentioned the opinion commonly held in responsible ecclesiastical circles without necessarily making it his own. To Dini he would have entrusted his

own point of view. That Bellarmine was not *personally* too certain with respect to the "heretical" character of Copernicanism seems to be borne out by the formulation (see later on in this chapter) of the Decree which placed the *De Revolutionibus* on the Index and which does not contain the qualification "heretical". If, as Westfall asserts, Bellarmine had truly "decided" that the Copernican theory was heretical, it would surely not have been easy to obtain his consent (he was a member with great authority of the Congregation of the Index) for the more moderate formulation of the Decree.

[19] Galileo proposed the following interpretation:

> I say, that the passage in Psalm 18 may have this sense, that is, that "God placed in the sun his tabernacle" as in the noblest seat in the whole universe; and then where it says "The sun proceedeth as a bridegroom from his chamber and exults as a giant in running his course," I would understand this to be said of the radiant sun, that is of the light and of the above-mentioned calorific spirit fertilizing all corporeal substances, which, leaving from the solar body, is swiftly diffused throughout the entire world, to which meaning all the words are punctually fitted. (V, 303; trans. by Drake 1978, 247-248).

On this Galilean idea of light and heat as a universal life-giving force see de Santillana 1955, 53-54 and 1960, 144. We have already seen that Copernicus had used a similar idea as a "speculative" justification for the heliocentric view, most probably under the influence of the thinking of the Renaissance.

[20] Paolo Antonio Foscarini (1580?-1616) from Calabria entered the Order of Carmelites and twice held the office of provincial. He also taught theology. He went to Rome in 1615 a little before Galileo's arrival there. A meeting of the two of them, planned to be held in Naples, never materialized as a result of the Decree of the Index of 1616. Foscarini died a few months after the Decree.

[21] Unfortunately Favaro has not included this *Letter* in the National Edition, although it was included in the Florentine Edition (1842-1856), Vol. IV, 73 ff. For an English translation, together with a critique by an unidentified theologian and a reply by Foscarini himself, see Blackwell 1991, 217-263.

[22] Here Foscarini also mentioned Clavius and his statement that it was necessary to find a better system than that of Ptolemy and he commented: "but what better one could be found than that of Copernicus?". This is quoted in Paschini 1965, 305.

[23] See Paschini 1965, 306-307. Blackwell 1991, 87-110 gives a detailed and interesting analysis of both the *Letter* and the reply to the theologian who had criticized it. As Pesce 1991, 70-71 comments, the Biblical hermeneutics of Foscarini had nothing to do with those of Galileo. They were, in fact, concordist "inasmuch as they tended to show how the Bible agreed with the Copernican system. The fundamental epistemological distinction [of Galileo] between nature and Scripture was no where to be found [in Foscarini]". And consequently, we might add, the distinction was no where to be found between the fields of competence of those who studied nature and those who interpreted Scripture.

[24] This is the thesis of Duhem 1908 who said: "Logic was on the side of Osiander and Bellarmine, and not on that of Kepler and Galileo; the former had grasped the exact significance of the experimental method, while the latter had been mistaken. . . " (quoted in de Santillana 1955, 107).

[25] In 1571, when he was just 29 years old and a professor at Louvain, Bellarmine had commented on the text of St. Thomas Aquinas about the stars (*Praelectiones Lovanienses: tertium dubium in I p. Thomae, q. 69, de opere tertiae diei*):

> . . . I say it is not the task of the theologians to analyze this order of phenomena . . . some attribute these phenomena to the movement of the earth . . . others have recourse to the hypothesis of epicycles and eccentrics; others to the autonomous motion of the heavenly bodies. Thus it is possible for us to select among them the one which best corresponds to the Sacred Scriptures. If one ascertained with evidence that the motions of the heavenly bodies are not autonomous, but they follow those of the heavens, one would have to consider a way of interpreting the Scriptures which would put them in agreement with the ascertained truth: for it is certain that the true meaning of Scripture cannot be in contrast with any other truth, philosophical or astrological [astronomical]. (trans. by Baldini and Coyne 1984, 20).

This has been quoted by Soccorsi who notes:

> This principle [of Scriptural interpretation], although applied by Bellarmine to a different question than that of Copernicanism, is, nevertheless, a general one and can also be referred to the Copernican question. (Soccorsi 1963, 38).

As we see, more than forty years earlier Bellarmine had been closer to the intellectual openness of St. Thomas Aquinas and had used a kind of reasoning like that of Galileo himself and of Foscarini with respect to the impossibility of there being a contradiction between an astronomical truth (truly proven as such) and the truth of Scripture. In fact, this idea still remains in theory at the basis of Foscarini's response. But it is completely overshadowed by a conviction in the opposite sense, as I shall explain shortly. The *Praelectiones Lovanienses* of Bellarmine have been published recently by Baldini and Coyne 1984. See also the article by Coyne and Baldini 1984, 103-110 as well as Baldini 1992, 285-344 for a more complete treatment of Bellarmine's letter and its philosophical and theological presuppositions.

[26] As we have seen in the Introduction, Bellarmine had taken part fifteen years earlier in the final phase of the trail which brought about the condemnation of Giordano Bruno to the stake. Even though Bruno's Copernican convictions do not seem to have been among the principal reasons for his condemnation, they were undoubtedly judged as contrary to Sacred Scripture and, therefore "heretical", at least in the broad sense of the term (see Note 61 of the Introduction). And the fact that Bruno had made use of Copernican heliocentrism to specify his vision of an eternal world, containing an infinity of inhabited worlds, with even "rational" creatures, must have contributed to making the Copernican idea appear even more dangerous in the eyes of the Roman inquisitors. Bruno's problem must undoubtedly have still been alive in Bellarmine's memory and it must have contributed to making him feel ever more sharply the imminent danger of putting under discussion the traditional world system which was by now so profoundly tied up with Catholic theological views.

[27] Blackwell 1991 has rightly emphasized this (undue) widening of the object of the assent *of faith* to everything that is said in Scripture as it was employed by Bellarmine in his response to Foscarini. See the comment by the same author on Bellarmine's response (Blackwell 1991, 104-107). Langford 1966, 62-68 also points out the debatable issues, from a theological point of view, of this response of Bellarmine and he shows, at the same time, the backward step of the Cardinal's position with respect to the best Catholic theological traditions. The fact that Foscarini's letter had deeply concerned not only Bellarmine but also in general the Church authorities is confirmed by a letter of Ciampoli to Galileo of March 1615 (XII, 160) in which he informs Galileo of the appearance of the publication of the Carmelite Father and foresees

that, because it enters . . . into the Scriptures, the book
runs a great risk of being suspended in the first
Congregation of the Holy Office which will be a month
from now. (XII, 160).

The reason for the concern caused by the letter of Foscarini was
certainly the fact that it had been written by a theologian from whom
the Roman authorities would have obviously liked to have had much
greater prudence. As for the attitude of the Church authorities towards
a scientist like Galileo here is how it is traced out by Ciampoli in the
same letter:

This morning with Monsignor Dini I was to see Cardinal
Dal Monte, who esteems you in a special way and shows
extraordinary affection for you. His Most Illustrious
Lordship said that he had had a long discussion with
Cardinal Bellarmine: and the conclusion was that when
you treat of the Copernican system and of its
demonstrations without entering into the Scriptures, the
interpretation of which they wish to be reserved to the
theology professors approved by public authority, there
should not be anything to the contrary; but that otherwise
it would be difficult to admit Scriptural declarations, even
though ingenious, when they would dissent much from the
common opinion of the Church Fathers. (XII, 160).

As we see, we are dealing here with an answer quite similar to the one
given a little before by Cardinal Maffeo Barberini to Ciampoli himself,
as the latter made known to Galileo.
[28] At the beginning of his letter Foscarini had written:

To anyone who has just encountered this opinion, it will
without doubt appear to be one of the oddest and most
monstrous paradoxes he has yet heard. This is caused
completely by old habits, strengthened over many
centuries. Once a habit is established and men are
hardened into opinions which are trite and plausible, and
which are part of everyone's common sense, then both the
educated and the uneducated embrace them and are hardly
able to be dislodged from them. The force of habit is so
great that it is said to be another nature. (Blackwell 1991,
218).

That which Foscarini considered to be a conviction founded only on ingrained custom, Bellarmine instead thought to be an objective certainty founded on experience which could not be doubted. Now, when a *philosophical* position of this kind comes into play, it is clear that any positive dialogue between the disputants becomes practically impossible.

[29] With respect to the second point of Bellarmine's letter, in which he had stated that it was against the Council of Trent "to expound Scripture against the common consent of the Fathers" (which in this case, according to Bellarmine, was in favor of geocentrism), Galileo noted:

> One is not asking that in case of doubt the interpretation of the Fathers should be abandoned, but only that an attempt be made to gain certainty regarding what is in doubt, and that therefore no one disparage what attracts and has attracted very great philosophers and astronomers. Then, after all necessary care has been taken, the decision may be made. (V, 369; trans. by Finocchiaro 1989, 85, No. 8).

Galileo also responded to Bellarmine's claim that every saying of Scripture was to be considered an object of faith.

[30] The *Letter*, probably completed in June 1615, circulated in manuscript form, as had the previous one to Castelli. The first printed edition appeared quite a bit later in 1636 at Strasbourg. It is found in V, 309-386. For an analysis of it see Langford 1966, 70-78; McMullin 1967, 33-35; Fabris 1986, 29-33; Finocchiaro 1986, 259-270; Pesce 1987, 239-284; Blackwell 1991, 75-82. For a comparison of Galileo's position with that of the exegetes of his time see Martini 1966, 115-124.

[31] This is even a more explicit profession of Copernicanism on Galileo's part than the one contained in the third of the *Sunspot Letters*.

[32] It is most likely that reference is being made here to the theory of the tides about which, as we know, Galileo had had an initial idea even from the first years he spent in Padua and which undoubtedly he continued to develop after his telescopic discoveries had definitively convinced him of the truth of the Copernican theory. As we will see, Galileo will, at the request of Cardinal Alessandro Orsini, put this theory in writing in January 1616 and entitle it the *Discourse on the Ebb and Flow of the Sea*. This *Discourse* will then be taken up in large part, sometimes letter for letter, in the Fourth Day of the *Dialogue on the Two Chief World Systems*.

[33] This probably refers to the floating bodies where Galileo had taken a position contrary to the Aristotelians, among whom was

Ludovico delle Colombe. As we know, delle Colombe had already before had recourse to Scriptural arguments against the Copernican statements.

[34] While in the *Letter to Castelli* quotations from the Church Fathers and from other sacred authors were completely absent, they are quite numerous (27) in this *Letter to Christina of Lorraine*. Many of them (15) are taken from St. Augustine and of these all except one are from the *De Genesi ad Litteram*. Obviously Galileo with these quotations wanted to beat back the thesis (repeated by Bellarmine in the letter to Foscarini) of the unanimous consent of the Church Fathers on the immobility of the Earth. In particular, he wanted to show that the rules for Scriptural interpretation given by one of the greatest of the Fathers, Augustine to the point, constituted a warning to theologians not to come to a precipitous decision against Copernicanism which was not justified and which might be shown to be wrong in the future. Galileo took many of these texts of Augustine from the work of the Jesuit Benito Pereyra (1535-1610), *Prior Tomus Commentariorum et Disputationum in Genesim* (1589) which he cites in the *Letter* (V, 320). On Pereyra (who besides Biblical exegesis also taught natural philosophy and theology) and Galileo's dependence on him see Fabris 1986, 29-33; Blackwell 1991, 29; Mayaud 1994, 84, Note 25. Galileo could have had other texts of Augustine, as well as those of St. Jerome, Tertullian and Dionysius the Areopagite, through Castelli, who wrote to him on 6 January 1615:

> I am close to the Barnabite Preacher, who is most attached to Your Lordship's teaching and has promised me certain passages from St. Augustine and from other Doctors which confirm Your Lordship's interpretation of Joshua. (XII, 126-127).

The Barnabite Preacher referred to was in all probability Pomponio Tartaglia (1581-1655) who was at that time superior of the College of Saint Frediano in Pisa. As Boffito 1933, III, 2-3 testifies we, in fact, read in an excerpt from the Acts of the College of the Barnabites: "1615. On 8 November the Father Superior preached in the cathedral". And it is noted there that the Superior (the eighth of the series) was Father Pomponio Tartaglia. It is very likely that Castelli is referring to this sermon when he calls Tartaglia the "preacher". As a Barnabite he must have acquired his propensity for Copernicanism during his philosophy studies at the College of Saint Barnaba in Milan, where Copernicanism was upheld, among other Barnabites, by the young philosophy professor, Angelo Confalonieri (1585-1617). To be remembered among his Barnabite students is Redento Baranzano

(1590-1622) who also supported Copernicanism as can be seen from his work *Uranoscopia seu de Coelo* which was published in 1617 at Annecy in Savoy. Obviously in the dark about the decisions taken by the Church in 1616 against Copernicanism (we will speak of this later on this chapter) Baranzano had defended heliocentrism against the difficulties arising both from Scripture and from Aristotelian philosophy, of which he was an open critic. His work ran the risk of creating a fuss and Baranzano was forced to retract. He did this the following year with a short composition in dialogue form. Still the *Uranoscopia* and other philosophical works of his made him known in Europe and Francis Bacon wrote him a letter from London in response to the one which Barazano had sent to him in the same year (1622) as his premature death. Bacon exhorted him to continue his studies of natural philosophy with the same spirit of independence from Aristotelianism which he had shown up until then. (See Colombo 1878, 34 ff. where Bacon's letter is found on pp. 58-61; Premoli 1922, 73-77; Boffito 1933, III, 73-80. I am grateful to the Barnabite Father Domenico Frigerio for the information in this paragraph.)

[35] Galileo himself adds in a note: "Cardinal Baronio". Baronio (1538-1607) had visited Padua together with Bellarmine in 1598. Galileo probably met him on that occasion at Pinelli's house. If this meeting occurred, this phrase of Baronio might indicate a preoccupation of Galileo beginning then with respect to objections from Scripture (already made or only foreseen) against the Earth's motion. This preoccupation may have driven him to question Baronio and to receive his reassuring (at least for Galileo) answer.

[36] This principle, which Galileo writes of quite often, had already been sanctioned by the Fifth Lateran Council. In Session VIII (19 December 1513) the Council stated against the theory of a double truth: "*Cumque verum vero minime contradicat, omnem assertionem veritati illuminatae fidei contrariam, omnino falsam esse definimus . . .*" (And because truth can in no way contradict truth, we define every statement contrary to the truth of the splendid faith to be completely false). See Denziger and Schönmetzer 1967, 1441; the First Vatican Council made these same words its own (Denziger and Schönmetzer 1967, 3017). And this principle was frequently used by theologians. For example, it was used by the famous Jesuit exegete, Benito Pereyra (1535-1610). He was quoted by Galileo himself (with his Latinized name *Pereirus*) in the passage preceding the one I am citing here. The passage in question, excerpted from the *Commentaria et Disputationes in Genesim*, declared:

It is also necessary to take care diligently to avoid at whatever cost that, in treating the doctrine of Moses, it does not happen that one thinks and says categorically things that do not agree with manifest experience and with the arguments from philosophy and from other disciplines: in fact, since truth always agrees with truth, the truth of the Sacred Scriptures cannot be contrary to the true arguments and experiments of human doctrines.

We have seen that Bellarmine himself had used it in his *Praelectiones Lovanienses*. See Note 25 above.

[37] See Migne, *Patrologia Latina*, Vol. 34, 262.

[38] The relationship to the truth of the faith is explicit in the text from the *Patrologia Latina* of Migne: "Quidquid autem de quibuslibet suis voluminibus his nostris Litteris, id est catholicae fidei, contrarium protulerint . . ." (Whatever they put forth in whichsoever of their volumes contrary to these [sacred] Letters of ours, that is, to the Catholic faith . . .) The invitation from Augustine to prove in every way possible the falsity of statements against the Christian faith by the "sapientes huius mundi" seems to confirm that the reference here is no longer to the "scientists". Augustine was not the type to invite Christians to spend precious time in a scientific dispute!

[39] A first passage (see Langford 1966, 72; McMullin 1967, 33; Blackwell, 1991, 78) is the following one:

Yet even in those propositions which are not matters of faith, this authority ought to be preferred over that of all human writings *which are supported only by bare assertions or probable arguments, and not set forth in a demonstrative way* (V, 317; trans by Drake 1957, 183; italics by the author).

Basing their discussion on this translation by Drake, the authors mentioned above see in this passage two contrasting cases: the one in which we have "human writings" of a scientific character, but supported only "by bare assertions or probable arguments"; and the other in which they are "set forth in a demonstrative way". They think that in the first case Galileo gives the *last word* to Sacred Scripture, clearly contradicting his principle of the autonomy of scientific research. But even if we admit the two contrasting cases, I do not think that one can deduce from them a sudden renunciation (even if only tactical or rhetorical) by Galileo of that principle, one, please note, that he had clearly formulated in the passage preceding the one under discussion

(V, 316, line 22 and ff.) and which he will repeat immediately
afterwards (V, 317, line 27 and ff.). In fact, Galileo states only that, in
the absence of true demonstrations, the authority of Holy Scripture
"ought to be preferred" (a better translation would be "should have
priority") over that of all human writings". But he does not at all say
that this prudent respect implies a *definitive assent* to the literal
meaning of Scripture and so a *renunciation of any further scientific
research*. Such research, as is clear from the whole context, remains
open (and must remain so) and possible future proofs will allow one to
discover the true meaning of the words of Sacred Scripture. Moreover,
it seems to me that the terminology and the sentence structure in the
original text of Galileo might suggest different contrasting cases than
those emphasized by the authors mentioned above who based
themselves on Drake's translation. Drake translates Galileo's "con
metodo dimostrativo" as "demonstrative way" and his "con probabili
ragioni" as "probable arguments". Drake also inverts the order of
Galileo's sentence, thereby favoring, as a matter of fact, the impression
of a contrast between "probable arguments" and "demonstrative way".
Galileo's original seems, in fact, to contrast two altogether different
kinds of "human writings": those written by a demonstrative method
("con metodo dimostrativo"), that is, those based on a rigorous scientific
method, as compared to those written in a purely narrative way or
with probable arguments ("con probabili ragioni"). The priority (or
higher authority) attributed by Galileo to Sacred Scripture over this
second kind of writing (to repeat, this is outside of the rigorous
scientific method) obviously eliminates at its foundation any
contradiction of his principle of the autonomy of science. On the other
hand "writings not by a demonstrative method" is not equivalent at all
to "writings without clear demonstrations". For Galileo the aim of the
demonstrative method is surely to have a "certain demonstration". But
this may not yet exist today. Galileo never tires of repeating this in the
Letter. See, for example, the long passage in V, 320-321. A second text
quoted by Blackwell 1991, 78-79 as being in contrast to the
fundamental thesis of Galileo is the following one:

> Here it should be noticed, first, that some physical
> propositions are of a type such that by any human
> speculation and reasoning one can only attain a *probable
> opinion and a verisimilar conjecture* about them, rather
> than a certain and demonstrated science; an example is
> whether the stars are animate. Others are of a type such
> that either one has, or one may firmly believe that it is
> possible to have, complete certainty on the basis of

experiments, long observations, and necessary demonstrations; examples are whether or not the earth and the sun move and whether or not the earth is spherical. As for the first type I have no doubt at all that, where human reason cannot reach, and where consequently one cannot have a science, but only opinion and faith, it is appropriate piously to conform absolutely to the literal meaning of Scripture. In regard to the second type of propositions, however, I should think, as stated above, that it would be proper to ascertain the facts first, so that they could guide us in finding the true meaning of Scripture; this would be found to agree absolutely with demonstrated facts, even though prima facie the words would sound otherwise, since two truths can never contradict each other. (V, 330; trans. by Finocchiaro 1989, 104; italics by the author).

I must confess that I cannot see how this text can be proposed as a proof of the stated Galileian contradiction. Here, in fact, Galileo contrasts the case in which human knowledge cannot go beyond conjectures to the one in which it can obtain a true scientific demonstration. The example of the first case is absolutely clear: "whether the stars are animate". Here to proceed from "a probable opinion and verisimilar conjecture" to a certain demonstration is absolutely excluded, *even in the future*, because we are dealing with problem which goes beyond the capacity of human comprehension. Galileo is, therefore, perfectly self-consistent in recognizing that in such a case it is necessary to adhere to the "literal meaning of Scripture" (assuming that Scripture is dealing with the problem). On the other hand in the case in which one has, *or might have*, a scientific demonstration (the examples given by Galileo are: "whether or not the earth and the sun move and whether or not the earth is spherical"), one must hold to this demonstration, once obtained, and not to the apparent meaning of Sacred Scripture. I insist on the fact that here Galileo distinguishes explicitly the case in which "one has" the demonstration from the case in which "one may firmly believe that it is possible to have it". While waiting for this possibility to actualize, the question remains open without any demand in the meantime to "conform absolutely to the literal meaning of Scripture". Langford 1966, 72-73 adds another passage which is the continuation of the preceding:

At one point he [St. Augustine] discusses the shape of heaven and what one should believe it to be, given that what astronomers affirm seems to be contrary to Scripture, since the former consider it round while the latter calls it stretched out like a hide. He decides one should not have the slightest worry that Scripture may contradict astronomers: one should accept its authority if what they say *is false and based only on conjecture typical of human weakness*; however, if what they say is proved with indubitable reasons, this Holy Father does not say that astronomers themselves be ordered to refute their demonstrations and declare their conclusion false, but he says one must show that what Scripture asserts about the hide is not contrary to those true demonstrations. (V, 331; trans. by Finocchiaro 1989, 104; italics by the author).

In the English quotation of this text Langford has involuntarily omitted the words: "is false", which appear on the other hand in Drake's translation which he uses (see Drake 1957, 198). And this makes even less plausible his claim that there is a contradiction in Galileo, a contradiction which in my opinion is sufficiently shown to be non-existent even if we take only the words: "based only on conjecture typical of human weakness". For a pertinent answer to these criticisms see also Finocchiaro 1986, 261 ff.

[40] Probably an allusion to Bellarmine.

[41] On the statement that Galileo was convinced, even at the time of the composition of the *Letter to Christina of Lorraine*, that he had a certain proof of the Copernican system (the one, that is, from the tides) see especially McMullin 1967, 33-34. According to McMullin it was precisely this erroneous conviction which led Galileo to concede to his adversaries *pro bono pacis* that where certain demonstrations were lacking one should give preference to the literal meaning of the Bible. (This contradicted his own thesis of the independence of scientific considerations from the Bible). It appears to me that neither at that time nor at the time of the composition of the *Dialogue* did Galileo have the conviction of possessing incontrovertible proofs in favor of the Copernican system. On the other hand the interpretation I have presented of the passages which have been taken as a proof of the alleged contradiction in Galileo (see Note 39) appears to show that such a contradiction does not exist. Galileo was far from showing himself in secure possession of certain proofs for Copernicanism; at the same time he was far from conceding that the Bible should have the last world in the field of science. He repeatedly insists on the fact that such proofs might be obtained in the future and so recommends prudence and that one refrain from hasty decisions in favor of the literal meaning of

Sacred Scripture. For a more detailed response to McMullin's thesis see Finocchiaro 1986, 241-272.

[42] See Pesce 1987, 258-261. The interpretation given by Pesce to the meaning of Galileo's exegesis of this Biblical passage seems to me to be very pertinent.

[43] As we shall see, it will only be on the vigil of the Galileo's trial in 1632 that, in a completely personal way, it will have become known to some members of the Church hierarchy, for example, Cardinal Capponi in Florence and Riccardi, the Master of the Sacred Palace in Rome. But in Rome at that time the *Letter* was already in the hands of number of people according to the declarations of the Jesuit Inchofer at the moment of the trial (XIX, 349-350). And a copy of this letter was found in 1994 by Pagano in the archives of the Holy Office. But, unlike the *Letter to Castelli*, it will not be mentioned in the document "Against Galileo" composed at the end of the trial of 1633. While awaiting the outcome of the study of the Holy Office's copy, one might hazard the opinion that this copy is the same one given by Magalotti to Riccardi (XIV, 381) and that the latter after the end of the trial would have deposited it in the Holy Office.

[44] Following the instructions of the Holy Office the Archbishop had taken great care not to make known to Castelli the reason that the *Letter* was requested. As to the recommendation of Galileo to Castelli not to deliver that manuscript to the archbishop, this might betray Galileo's concern that the Holy Office, once in possession of it, could accurately compare that manuscript with the copy sent by Lorini and thus verify that this latter copy was, in fact, a "true" copy and that instead the copy which Galileo had had sent to Cardinal Bellarmine was not authentic, but that he had retouched it. All of this might confirm the thesis of Pesce 1992, mentioned at the beginning of this chapter.

[45] It is strange that the Archbishop was satisfied to hear a reading of the *Letter* given by Castelli without having it handed over to him as the Holy Office had requested. Perhaps it was difficult for him to do so on that occasion without raising suspicions and he decided to put the affair off until later. To his relief later on the Holy Office no longer insisted on having the *Letter*. See Note 17.

[46] This deposition is found in XIX, 307-311.

[47] As we know, Paolo Sarpi had defended the rights of the Venetian Republic in the dispute between the Republic and the Pope and he was, therefore, a quite unpopular person in Rome. Caccini intentionally emphasizes this friendly relationship between Sarpi and Galileo so as to damage the latter before the Roman Inquisition.

[48] Germany was the homeland of Protestantism. This correspondence of Galileo with Germany was, therefore, also emphasized by Caccini in order to further discredit Galileo before the Roman authorities.

[49] The "other writing" of which Galileo speaks is the *Letter to Christina of Lorraine* which he was at that time bringing to completion. These words seem to be aimed especially at Bellarmine, who had, as a matter of fact, maintained in his answer to Foscarini that Copernicus had only wanted to put forth a mathematical hypothesis. Since he knew that the opinion of this Jesuit Cardinal at the highest levels of the Church hierarchy carried great weight, Galileo must have been truly worried about Bellarmine's erroneous interpretation on a point of such importance.

[50] Galileo himself states this very thing in a letter to Picchena of 23 January (XII, 227). In that same letter Galileo said that he was at times obliged to put in writing some arguments and have them sent to the interested parties

> since in many places I find much easier a concession to dead writings than to the living word, because the writings allow that others can, without embarrassment, admit and contradict and finally give in to the reasons, while we have no other witnesses except ourselves and our discourses; we do not do this very easily when it befits us to change an opinion publicly. (XII, 228).

According to Favaro (see V, 277, *Avvertimento*) the written "arguments" distributed in this way by Galileo are the very ones which Favaro himself had published under the title: "Considerations on the Copernican opinion". Bucciantini 1995, 84 ff. gives special importance to the role played by Francesco Ingoli (1578-1649) in opposing Galileo in the cultured circles in Rome. Ingoli had studied jurisprudence at the University of Padua, where he had probably known Galileo (see V, 509). He later became a priest and, thanks to his relations with Cardinal Bonifacio Caetani, an influential member of the Congregation of the Index, whom he served at that time, he had by now become an important personage in the Roman court circles. Two of his unedited manuscripts - *De Stella anni 1604* (On the Star of 1604) and *De Cometa anni 1607* (On the Comet of 1607) - testify to his interest in astronomy as well as in astrology, interests which he shared with Cardinal Caetani. He always took an active part in theological, philosophical and scientific arguments and he even had one such discussion with Galileo in the house of Lorenzo Magalotti, a cardinal-to-be. He then put in writing directed to Galileo the defense of his anti-

Copernican position under the title, *Disputatio de situ et quiete Terrae* (Disputation on the location and stability of the Earth) (V, 403-412). See Bucciantini 1995, 88-97 for an analysis of the content of this disputation. Bucciantini notes that it was "the first organic and comprehensive answer to the Copernican teaching upheld by Galileo" since it added philosophical and astronomical arguments to the theological ones. As such it must without a doubt have made Ingoli appear as one of the most authoritative supporters of philosophical-scientific, as well as theological, "orthodoxy" in the face of the danger arising from the Copernican ideas being championed by Galileo. We will see further on in this chapter how the "merits" so gained by Ingoli will find official recognition in his appointment as consultor of the Congregation of the Holy Office on 10 March 1616. Following this Ingoli will extend his anti-Copernican activity by seeing that in June 1617 a copy of the *Disputatio* gets into the hands of Kepler with a request for his comments and objections. Kepler will respond in the beginning of 1618 with his *Responsio ad Ingoli Disputationem de systemate* (Response to Ingoli's disputation on the world system). See Bucciantini 1995, 106-114 for a description of the contents. Ingoli in turn will reply in October 1618 with a long writing, *Replicationes Francisci Ingoli Ravennatis de situ et motu Terrae contra Copernicum ad Joannis Kepleri Caesarei mathematici impugnationes* (Answers of Francis Ingoli of Ravenna on the place and motion of the Earth against Copernicanism in reply to the arguments of the Caesarean mathematician Johannes Kepler), which has been published in the appendix of Bucciantini 1995.

[51] On 20 June Cesi had informed Galileo of this new treatise of Foscarini, quite a bit more detailed and in Latin with a view, obviously, to having it distributed throughout Europe (XII, 190). But this treatise was never published nor have any notes been found concerning it. See Blackwell 1991, 109.

[52] By this time Galileo was convinced that he did not have to fear personally but that the danger lay in a hurried decision of the Church authorities against the Copernican system. And it was precisely to avert such a danger that he was busying himself with every possible means. The same concern also shows through from the letter to Picchena of 13 February in which, after alluding to "unthinkable stories made up by three most powerful story-makers, from ignorance, envy and disrespect", he continued:

> And although my enemies realize that as to being able to offend me they have reached the end and there is nothing more they can do, still they never cease to try, with every

kind of machination and evil stratagem, to vent themselves
at least against the works of others, who have never taken
into consideration their ignorance nor given a thought to
them, and they seek not only to blacken the reputation of
these others but to annihilate their works and studies, so
noble and useful for the world. But I hope in the divine
goodness that not even in this effort will they succeed.
(XII, 234).

As we see, Galileo still kept up his hopes only two weeks before the
consultors of the Holy Office took their position. I will be speaking
about this right away.

[53] At the time of Galileo the Congregation of the Holy Office was
composed of a certain number of cardinals who had religious or secular
clerics as consultors. In turn these latter were assisted by
"qualificators" whose task it was to designate (qualify) the theological
censure which was to be attached to a given proposition being
examined. Langford 1966, 88 clarifies the fact that in the case of
Galileo: "We are certain that at least six of those who censured the two
propositions were consultors of the Holy Office".

[54] It is interesting to note that the formulation of the two
propositions is taken more or less word for word from Caccini's
synthesis of Galileo's ideas about Copernicanism in the deposition
Caccini made against Galileo the year before (XIX, 307-308). Obviously
this deposition had not been forgotten, even after it had been filed
away. And the qualificators certainly knew very well that the
propositions submitted for their examination were upheld by Galileo.
They are explicitly attributed to him in the document of 25 February
(XIX, 321). I will have the opportunity to speak about this. On the
other hand, the statement contained in the act of accusation against
Galileo, which was presented to the cardinals of the Holy Office on 16
June 1633 and according to which the two propositions had been seen
"in the book of the sunspots" (XIX, 294), is completely without
foundation. In no place in any of the three letters of Galileo to Welser
is there found any trace of those propositions.

[55] Langford 1966, 90 notes that the greater part of the
theologians were eminent Dominicans. The names are listed in XIX,
321. Among them there figures one Jesuit, Benedetto Giustiniani.

[56] Even more so, if we are to believe what Guicciardini says about
Galileo's enemies among the Dominicans of the Holy Office (and, in
addition to the influential Cardinal Galamini, there were, as a matter
of fact, six Dominicans among the theologians consulted), their opinion
on the propositions under accusation was already set for some time,

even before Galileo arrived in Rome. On the role of Galamini ("Cardinal Aracoeli") in orchestrating Caccini's accusation against Galileo see Bucciantini 1995, 38 ff.

[57] This meeting of 24 February was only for the qualificators and the consultors, not the cardinals. The cardinals met the following day, as we will see right away. As to the censures agreed upon in that meeting, that of "formally heretical" means in theological language that the proposition is directly contrary to a doctrine of the faith (it is the most serious theological censure possible). According, therefore, to the qualificators and the consultors the statements of the Scriptures and the Fathers on the motion of the sun were a doctrine of faith. On the other hand, the qualification given to the second proposition is somewhat less grave: "erroneous in the faith". This means that the qualificators and consultors recognized that the immobility of the Earth is not stated in a totally clear manner in Scripture and its negation (that is, the affirmation of the Earth's motion), therefore, is not directly contrary to Scripture. However, since one had to accept on faith the motion of the Sun about the Earth, there was only one *theological* conclusion possible: that is, that the Earth did not move. This is, as a matter of fact, the significance of the censure, "erroneous in faith".

[58] With the words "The day before yesterday" Guicciardini refers to the meeting of the Holy Office of 3 March. That he was completely in the dark (given the secrecy of the Holy Office) as to the content of that meeting is shown by his statement that in the meeting the Copernican opinion would have been declared "heretical". Drake 1978, 252 gives the following interpretation of Guicciardini's account:

> On 23 February Orsini spoke to the pope on Galileo's behalf but was told instead to dissuade Galileo, since Paul V now felt he should have turned the matter over to the Inquisition. When Orsini left, the pope called in Bellarmine, on whose advice a papal commission was appointed to determine whether Copernicanism was erroneous and heretical.

It does not appear to me that these statements can be sustained. First of all, Orsini's intervention happened on Wednesday, as Guicciardini himself makes clear, and that was (as Favaro himself notes) the 24th and not the 23rd. Secondly, there was no need for advice from Bellarmine to call a "papal commission" (?). The propositions under accusation had, as we know, already as of the 19th been distributed to the qualificators and their answer had been accepted by the consultors as their own on the very day of the consistory of cardinals. According to Drake the "papal commission", or as Drake specifies later on, "a technically independent panel of theologians", would have given their answer on the following day, the 24th. Putting aside the qualification "technically independent", attributed to this "panel of theologians", which I do not understand, Drake supposes here that these theologians would have had only a day to decide on the question! It was, therefore, little more than a farce. Despite the reservations we might harbor for the procedures of the Holy Office at the time of Galileo, the qualificators had, in fact, about four days available to them. That is always too few, but it is better than one. (It is even reduced to zero by the error which Drake commits in the date.)

[59] On this secrecy of the Holy Office see Redondi 1987, 151.

[60] Drake 1978, 254 states correctly that Guicciardini (at whose residence Galileo was staying) could not have helped but know of Bellarmine's summons of Galileo (see later on) and he adds that Galileo probably told him only that he had been informed of a coming decree and that he had promised to obey it; thus Guicciardini was able to write as he did to Florence on 4 March, even before the decree was formally adopted. There remains, however, the fact that Guicciardini had stated in the same letter that the Pope and Bellarmine had concluded that the opinion of Galileo "was erroneous and heretical". And Guicciardini had surely not known this from Galileo, given the tenor of the declaration made by Bellarmine to Galileo, in which the opinion on the stability of the Sun had not at all been qualified as "heretical" (and it is not in the Decree of the Index). From whom, therefore, did he come to know this? In our opinion, he had been able to do nothing else but speak of rumors that were circulating among the circles of the Papal Curia. I think that Bellarmine, called by Paul V, had had the time to speak to the Pope of the response of the qualificators (and perhaps even of the consultors' decision of that same day) in which the immobility of the Sun (not directly the "opinion of Galileo") was qualified as heretical. Therefore, it is not that Paul V and Bellarmine "put a stop" to (that is, decided) the matter in this sense on their own initiative. They took note of the response and they decided how Galileo was to be dealt with as one who spread support for Copernicanism. See the comment at the end of Note 79.

[61] See Pagano 1984, 222-223.

[62] For the history of this booklet see Pagano 1984, 1 and ff. I will have the opportunity to return to the vicissitudes of this booklet in the last chapter of this book.

[63] The booklet is catalogued: Misc. Arm. X, 204. See Note 12.

[64] See, for example, Drake 1978, 253. In the original Latin text the words, *"relata censura"*, are grammatically an ablative absolute and

"Sanctissimus" is the subject of a subordinate proposition introduced by *"quod"*. Therefore, the only correct translation is that given in the text and from which it is clear, I repeat, that Paul V did *not* take part in the meeting (otherwise there would have been no sense to the use of the word *"notificavit"*). Had the Pope been present, the text should have been: *relata a cardinale Millino censura Patrum Theologorum ad propositiones . . . quod sol sit . . . Sanctissimus ordinavit . . .*

[55] Obviously this report was made to all of those present and in the first place to the cardinals. And so, the added precision in the copy in the files is unduly restrictive.

[66] As we know, the meeting of the qualificators alone had already taken place on the day before, Tuesday, 23 February (XIX, 320) and the qualifications which among themselves they had agreed upon on that occasion had certainly become immediately known to Bellarmine. Bellarmine would, therefore, have been able to communicate them to the Pope at the time of the consistory even if the plenary session (of the qualificators and the consultors) had not yet occurred. Undoubtedly, in such a case Bellarmine had to be certain that the plenary session would have done nothing other than give the official seal to the response of the qualificators, as in fact happened.

[67] Drake 1978, 253 writes:

> In view of all the documents I believe that though the Pope probably wanted the Holy Office to proceed against Galileo personally, Cardinal Bellarmine counseled a less personal procedure.

But it appears to me that this presumed severity on the part of Paul V is given the lie by the audience granted by the Pope to Galileo, as we shall see, a little after the appearance of the Decree of the Index. The repeated statements made on that occasion by Paul V, that he was convinced of Galileo's sincere faith and that he was prepared to help him, seem to reflect a personal conviction of the Pope. On the other hand, it is certainly true that neither was Bellarmine personally ill-disposed towards Galileo and that it was probably he who suggested the solution which was taken up without difficulty by the Pope. The severe attitude taken by Paul V and by Bellarmine was not, therefore, with respect to Galileo but with the Copernican theory, which both (the former perhaps more than the latter) considered heretical. But even this severity was moderated by the resistance of some cardinals, among them Maffeo Barberini. See the Notes 78 and 79 to follow.

[68] We now know that this task too was entrusted to Bellarmine. See Note 78 below.

[69] The Latin original is found in XIX, 321-322. The words of Segizzi's injunction ("*nec eam ... quovis modo teneat, doceat aut defendat*") implied not only that Galileo could not hold the Copernican theory, that is, accept it as true (this was in agreement with Bellarmine's command), but that he could not treat of it in any way whatsoever nor defend it even as only a hypothesis (this latter part was not mentioned in Bellarmine's command). As we shall see, at the time of the trial which followed the publication of the *Dialogue*, this injunction of Segizzi will be central to the first interrogation. Its existence, in fact, repudiated at its roots the licitness of the permission to print the *Dialogue*. For that reason Galileo will try to defend himself by stating that he had forgotten the precise content of the injunction, and he will instead have recourse to the admonition of Bellarmine.

[70] For example, this is the opinion of Wohlwill 1910 and 1926.

[71] See von Gebler 1876 and de Santillana 1955, 266. In a subsequent Italian edition de Santillana 1960, 504-505 has somewhat softened his statements.

[72] De Santillana 1955, 266; 1960, 505.

[73] Father Pagano kindly furnished me a photographic copy of the original of the minutes containing the annotation in question. This allowed me to verify that the two documents are in the same handwriting, including the last phrase in Italian: "ed in appresso dal Padre Commissario gli fu ingiunto il precetto come sopra etc." (and afterwards the precept as above was enjoined on him by the Father Commissary etc.).

[74] Is this anomaly to be interpreted as a further indication of the illegality of Segizzi's intervention and, at the same time, of the care he took to make sure that everything that happened was filed away? I would be tempted to give the following interpretation. The secretary-copyist who had taken part in the session of 25 February while editing the original minutes (later transcribed into the *dossier* of the Holy Office with the addition of which we have spoken) received on the following day (from Bellarmine himself?) the message that Bellarmine had carried out the admonition and he, therefore, added on the same little page the annotation about this. The Commissary Segizzi, after reading it a little later, told the copyist excitedly (obviously in Italian) that he Segizzi had "enjoined the command as above" and the copyist, perhaps intimidated, docilely added the words forgetting to put them into Latin.

[75] See Morpurgo-Tagliabue 1963, 14-25. Drake 1978, 253-254 proposes a reconstruction of the events which, although substantially close to that of Morpurgo-Tagliabue, is extremely subjective and, therefore, debatable in its details. Specifically, I do not agree with

Drake's supposition that the presence of Commissary Segizzi at the summons to Galileo was against the rules. According to Drake the eventual injunction of the Commissary would, following the instructions given, have taken place at the Holy Office, subsequent to and distinct from Bellarmine's admonition. But this is not in any way implied in the notification given by Cardinal Millini. On the other hand, how, in the absence of a notary and witnesses, could one prove that Galileo in the end refused to accept Bellarmine's admonition? It was more straightforward (and simple) in view of whatever might happen to have everyone present right from the beginning in Bellarmine's residence.

[76] Bellarmine was an extremely courteous person as de Santillana 1960, 189 himself agrees.

[77] This appears to be confirmed by the ease with which shortly thereafter (as we shall see) Galileo requested from the aging Cardinal a written declaration of what had taken place on that day of 26 February.

[78] The Latin original is found in XIX, 278. Even the printer of Foscarini's book incurred the wrath of the Inquisition in Naples and was imprisoned by Cardinal Carafa of Naples who was lauded for it by the Holy Office (XIX, 324). This indicates how great the resentment of the Roman authorities was at the appearance of Foscarini's book. Some important documents, found in the archives of the Holy Office and which throw light on what was happening behind the scenes of this decree of the Index, have been made known (but only in a summary fashion) by Brandmüller on the occasion of the Italian translation (*Galileo e la Chiesa ossia il diritto ad errare*) of his book: *Galileo und der Kirche - oder das Recht auf Irrtum* (Brandmüller 1992, 79-81). Subsequently, the documents have been published in their entirety (Brandmüller and Greipl 1992, 145-151). On the basis of the first of these documents (Document A, Brandmüller and Greipl 1992, 145-146) we now know that it was once again Bellarmine who received from the Pope the task of placing before the cardinals of the Congregation of the Index the problem as to what measures should be taken with respect to the works of Copernicus, de Zuñiga and Foscarini. On 1 March the meeting on this matter was held at Cardinal Bellarmine's residence. I have personally examined the text at the Archives of the Holy Office. At the top of the page there appears: 1616, and immediately below this: *Die pa. [prima] Martii.* The date (*Die 21 Martii*) which appears at the beginning of this Document A in Brandmüller and Greipl 1992 is obviously erroneous (this is all the more evident since the decree of the Index - which this meeting was to prepare - followed on 5 March). Equally in error is the affirmation of the same author, already presented in the previous volume and repeated several times in the

second one, that the Master of the Sacred Palace (present at this meeting as he had been at the others) was none other than Nicolò Riccardi! As is known Riccardi became Master of the Sacred Palace only in 1629. Among others at the meeting there were Cardinals Maffeo Barberini and Bonifazio Caetani, since they were members of the same Congregation. The discussion must have been a protracted and heated one to judge from the minutes: . . . et "mature" prius inter dictos Ill.mos [cardinales] discusso hoc negotio, "tandem" decreverunt (. . . and after a "mature" discussion among the above mentioned Very Illustrious Cardinals on this matter, "finally" they decided . . . ; quotation marks inserted by Fantoli). As a result of the discussion it was decided that Foscarini's work should be prohibited, while those of Copernicus and de Zuñiga were to be "suspended until they were corrected". A second document (Document B, Brandmüller and Greipl 1992, 146) records the Pope's approval of this decision together with his desire that the suspension and prohibition of these works would not be published separately but together with those of other books, and this is what in fact occurred. Brandmüller comments correctly that this probably reflects the desire to avoid in this way giving too much importance to the provision, taking into account, I might add, the opinion of some Cardinals (such as Bellarmine and Caetani). As to this, see the following note.

[79] We must note that in the decree of the Congregation of the Index the word "heretical" does not appear although it was used by the consultors with reference to the thesis of the immobility of the Sun. According to a statement found in the diary of Gianfrancesco Buonamici for the date 2 May 1633, while Buonamici was in Rome at the time of Galileo's trial, this is to be attributed to an intervention by Cardinals Caetani and Barberini.

> In the time of Paul V this opinion was opposed as erroneous and contrary to many passages of Sacred Scripture; therefore, Paul V was of the opinion to declare it contrary to the Faith; but through the opposition of the Lord Cardinals Bonifatio Gaetano and Maffeo Barberini, today Urban VIII, the Pope was stopped right at the beginning on account of the good reasons taken by their Eminences and the learned writing of the said Mr. Galileo on this matter addressed to the Lady Christina of Tuscany about the year 1614. (XV, 11).

Putting aside this last reason adopted - a completely unlikely one - the intervention of Maffeo Barberini seems to be confirmed by the statements made by the latter, by this time Pope, to Tommaso Campanella in 1630:

> It was never our intention [to prohibit Copernicus]; and if he had been left to us, that decree [of the Congregation of the Index] would not have been made. (XIV, 88).

We now know by means of the document of the Holy Office made known by Brandmüller and Greipl 1992 (see the previous note) that in reality both Caetani and Bellarmine participated in the meeting held at Bellarmine's residence where the formulation of the decree of the Congregation of the Index regarding the *De Revolutionibus* and the books which supported Copernicus was discussed. It is, therefore, likely that their action was carried out right in those circumstances. If they were not successful in doing away with the idea of the decree of the Index, they were at least able to have removed the note of "heretical" with respect to the Copernican teaching. In these circumstances it was perhaps Caetani who took the initiative of defending the scientific value of the *De Revolutionibus* and of proposing, in lieu of an unconditional condemnation, its suspension *donec corrigatur*. Caetani, as I will show in detail in note 98, had wanted to study up on Copernicanism and so had requested the opinion of Tommaso Campanella and perhaps had already read the manuscript entitled: *Apologeticus pro Galileo*, sent to him by the latter as a study help. Caetani's defense would explain the fact that the task of making the correction came in fact to rest in his lap. As to Bellarmine, at the end he accepted the point of view of Cardinals Barberini and Caetani. This seems to confirm the fact that, as we have already seen, he too was not totally certain of the note "heretical" given by the qualificators-consultors. As for that, in his admonition to Galileo to abandon Copernicanism, Bellarmine had not labelled it as "heresy". Probably he, as well as Paul V, had decided to await the verdict of the Congregation of the Index.

[80] The different attitude towards the books of Copernicus and De Zuñiga on the one hand and of Foscarini on the other comes from the fact that, after applying certain changes and deletions, the first two could still be read without problems and, in fact, with profit (specifically, the *De Revolutionibus* was in this way reduced to a pure mathematical hypothesis, right in line with the preface of Osiander, while in the *Commentary* of De Zuñiga it was sufficient to eliminate the passage in which the compatibility of Copernicanism with Scripture was upheld). But the book of Foscarini, which was totally dedicated to proving such compatibility, was to be condemned in its entirety. No mention was made of the writings of Galileo. This is not surprising in the case of those writings still in manuscript form (such as the *Letter*

to Castelli and the *Letter to Christina of Lorraine*). But it is surprising in the case of a printed work such as the *Sunspot Letters*, even more so since this work had been examined by the Holy Office in November 1615. But, as I have already mentioned, it was not the intention of this book to prove the compatibility of Copernicanism with Scripture and, furthermore, the Copernican statements were limited to a few phrases, written almost in passing. It was just for this reason that it was not incriminated by the qualificator of the Holy Office. As to the corrections to be made to the *De Revolutionibus*, it happens that, from further documents cited by Brandmüller and Greipl (1992, 148-151), the task to study the situation fell to the lot of Francesco Ingoli (see Note 50 above). Immediately after the listing of the *De Revolutionibus* on the Index Ingoli was appointed in the session of 10 March 1616 a consultor of the Congregation of the Index. After the death of Cardinal Caetani in June 1617 Ingoli had taken up the task of inserting the corrections into the *De Revolutionibus*. Although an adversary of Copernicus, Ingoli was personally convinced of the great usefulness of the *De Revolutionibus* at the level of mathematics. So at the meeting of the Congregation of the Index held on 2 April 1618, once more at Bellarmine's residence, he presented the proposals for the corrections to be made (Document F, Brandmüller and Greipl 1992, 148). So as to be more sure of themselves, the cardinals decided to place these proposals before the mathematicians of the Roman College as experts in the subject (Document G, Brandmüller and Greipl 1992, 148). Bellarmine assumed the job and entrusted the examination of the question to Fathers Grienberger and Grassi. Their totally positive opinion was made known to the meeting of the Congregation of the Index on the following 3rd of July (Document H, Brandmüller and Greipl 1992, 148-149) and so Ingoli's plan for corrections was approved. However, it would still take two years before the decision (taken at the meeting of 16 March 1620) would be reached that the *De Revolutionibus* ("in which many very useful things are found") could be published with Ingoli's corrections which were reported in the minutes (Document N, Brandmüller and Greipl 1992, 149-151). The decree in this respect was published two months later (15 May 1620) and it is the one already known for some time (XIX, 400-401). As happened as a matter of fact, such a corrected edition never saw the light of day and Copernicus' work remained, as we shall see, on the Index of forbidden books up until 1835. In the meantime, one had to be happy with adding the corrections prescribed with a pen to the texts kept in the libraries and , as with all other books on the Index, scholars could obtain special permission to consult these. As to the parallel action carried on by Ingoli against Kepler (see Note 50 above), that had come to an end a year before with the decree of a complete prohibition of the *Epitome Astronomiae Copernicanae*. The decree was based on the opinion presented by Ingoli himself at the session of the Congregation of the Index of 28 February 1619 (see Brandmüller and Greipl 1992, 149). With the formulation of these two decrees of the Congregation of the Index Ingoli must have been convinced that his anti-Copernican "mission" was finished, so much so that Galileo, silenced by Bellarmine's precept, had made no reply to the *Disputation*. This silence was interpreted in Roman circles as a victory for Ingoli's arguments. On the other hand, in 1622 Ingoli will be appointed secretary of the Congregation of the Propagation of the Faith which had just been established and this assignment will from that time on absorb all of his energies.

[81] Bucciantini 1995, 70 ff. maintains that when Galileo came to Rome in December 1615, it was not by dint of his own choice but that he was summoned by the Holy Office, where he would subsequently have to respond to series of interrogators. In other words, it would have come down to an outright trial. But there exists no trace of these interrogators among the archival documents on Galileo in the Holy Office.

[82] It is hardly necessary to emphasize here how much this letter (as the others of Guicciardini) shows the little sympathy, even hostility, there was on the part of the ambassador of the Grand Duke with respect to Galileo. Among other things the latter is called (here as well as in the other letters of Guicciardini): "the Galileo". And yet, Guicciardini, like any good diplomat, knew how to use, when he wished to do so, the grandiose titles of courtesy of that epoch.

[83] As I have already said (see note 60), Galileo must have given to Guicciardini the least compromising version possible of the facts. He was surely aware of the feelings of Guicciardini in his regard and, indeed, did not wish to risk a report on the ambassador's part which would not be in his favor in the eyes of the Grand Duke.

[84] In addition to the *De Revolutionibus*, the *Commentary* of De Zuñiga.

[85] The text is quoted in the *Edizione Fiorentina* of the *Opere di Galileo* (1842-1856), Vol. V, Part II, 633. English translation by Coyne from Paschini 1965, 354.

[86] It goes without saying that Guicciardini was dismayed to learn that Galileo should have appeared at the Cardinal's side and he revealed all of his apprehension to Picchena in the letter of 4 March which I have already quoted. The latter, therefore, wrote to Galileo on 30 April to counsel that: "when you are seated at the table of the Lord Cardinal, where it is most likely that there will be other cultured

persons, Your Lordship should not begin to debate about those subjects which have aroused persecution by the monks". (XVIII, 422).

[87] See the letter of Sagredo to Galileo of 11 March (XII, 246). Sagredo probably relied on information sent to Rome at the end of February by Simone Contarini, an orator of the Venetian Republic (XX, 570). See also the subsequent letter (23 April) of the same Sagredo and the one of Castelli (20 April; XII, 254). Also the brother of Father Caccini, Tommaso, when he wrote on 11 June from Rome, spoke of an abjuration by Galileo (XII, 265).

[88] From the original of this certified document, which is found in the Vatican archives (Galileo, as we shall see, will deliver it to the Holy Office at the time of his trial in 1633) one sees that Bellarmine had originally written "although", but that then he canceled this expression and in its place put the clearer expression: "but only". See de Santillana 1960, 638, note 6. The original draft of the document, with many more corrections, kept in the Jesuit Roman Archives, was published recently by Baldini and Coyne 1984 together with the *Lectiones Lovanienses* of Bellarmine. See Note 25.

[89] It is interesting to note that Bellarmine does not speak of the acquiescence by Galileo. This was the last time that Galileo and the aging Cardinal met. Bellarmine died five years later in 1621.

[90] A case in point is that of Canon Querengo, whose rather enthusiastic comment on Galileo's activity in Rome before the Decree of 1616 we already know. Soon after the publication of the Decree, he precipitously scrambled backwards and wrote:

> The disputes of Signor Galileo have dissolved into alchemical smoke, since the Holy Office has declared that to maintain this opinion is to dissent manifestly from the infallible dogmas of the Church. So here we are at last, safely back on a solid Earth, and we do not have to fly with it as so many ants crawling around a balloon . . . (XII, 243; trans. by de Santillana 1955, 124).

Also Luça Valerio, a professor at the *Archiginnasio Romano*, had wanted to present his resignation from the *Accademia dei Lincei* since he considered it to have been discredited by the Copernican thinking of its most influential member, Galileo. See Paschini 1965, 344-345. For an up to date biography of this mathematician, who had been a Jesuit from 1570 to 1590 and who had deservedly enjoyed a high esteem from Galileo, see Baldini and Napolitani 1992.

[91] Thus, for example, writes Geymonat:

The chief cause of Galileo's defeat may perhaps be sought in the action of the Jesuits. At first they seemed disposed to support Galileo; in fact, on the sixteenth of May, Monsignor Dini had written to his friend: "I hear that many Jesuits are secretly of the same opinion, though they remain silent." But they preferred to stand apart, concerned lest the triumph of the Copernican system bring excessive discredit on Aristotelian philosophy. Probably this indirect responsibility on their part did not escape Galileo, which would explain the sharpening of his antagonism toward them after 1616. (Geymonat 1965, 85).

De Santillana is even more critical of the posture of the Jesuits. See de Santillana 1955, 142-143.

[92] Such, for example, is the opinion of Langford 1966, 81.

[93] On this famous controversy see Blackwell 1991, 48 ff.

[94] As we have already seen, in the lectures of the Jesuit philosophy professors of the Roman College, which Galileo made wide use of for his courses at Pisa, one does not notice a slavish following of Aristotle. As a matter of fact, the insistence of Father General Acquaviva that it was necessary to keep to Aristotelian doctrine, shows that the Jesuits were not doing so enough.

[95] René Descartes (1596-1650), who is often called the "father of modern philosophy", had just about two years earlier, in 1614, completed his studies at the famous college of the Jesuits, La Flèche. As to Francis Bacon (1561-1626), he was just then putting together the various drafts of his *Novum Organum* (finished much later) in which were laid the foundations for a new scientific method to replace that of Aristotle. As I said, modern philosophy was still in its gestation period. And Galileo himself, who was the one moving most consciously in the direction of a new natural philosophy, was far from being able to offer a unified view of that which would one day come to birth.

[96] This was what Grienberger had recommended to Galileo through Dini who had written to Galileo on 7 March 1615:

. . . he [Grienberger] would have liked you to first carry out your demonstrations, and then get involved in discussing the Scripture . . . (XII, 151; trans. by Finocchiaro 1989, 59).

[97] On this matter de Santillana writes:

Bellarmine, in his double role as minister and chief theologian, decided that it was nothing other than a matter of "petulance". He did not even pose the question, one might say, to his experts in astronomy; if he posed it, they did not dare to tell him anything other than what he was thinking. They would perhaps have wished to say "more, if they had been able to"; but that was not possible because they were like him subject to blind obedience. He summoned the Qualificators, and from them he again did not have other than the echo of his own thoughts. On the 25 he had the decree of the index prepared, he submitted it for the Pope's signature, and he entrusted the execution of it to the Holy Office. The historical responsibility for the outcome falls upon Bellarmine and on him alone. (de Santillana 1960, 292).

This excerpt shows the aprioristic tendency which de Santillana shows here as elsewhere in his interpretation of the facts. First of all, Bellarmine was not "minister", nor was he "chief theologian" (these two offices did not exist in the Church at those times). He was one of the seven cardinals who were members of the Holy Office. At the same time he was a member of the Congregation of the Index. As to "his experts in astronomy" they were Jesuits whom he consulted, as we have seen, right from the time of the preceding trip of Galileo to Rome (1611) and who gave him at that time very frank answers (which supported Galileo). Bellarmine again consulted them (at least Grienberger: XII, 151) in 1615. Grienberger (and other colleagues of his) had certainly responded that, as to decisive proofs in favor of Copernicanism, Galileo had not yet provided any. This was the simple truth and "blind obedience" had nothing to do with the case; nor did it have anything to do with Bellarmine. Once he had become a cardinal, he was no longer subject in obedience to his general superior. (On the other hand, if in his case the obligation of blind obedience still held, the final responsibility would not have been Bellarmine's, but Father General Acquaviva's! Or even of the Pope if de Santillana wished with his words "blind obedience" to allude to an obedience due to the Roman Pontiff). As to the summons to the "Qualificators" that was not done by Bellarmine, but by Millini, the prefect of the Holy Office. Among the qualificators there was a Jesuit, but at least six of them were Dominicans. And among these latter, as we know, Galileo had sworn enemies. On the other hand, it is hardly necessary to emphasize yet again that the Dominicans, just a few years removed from the very bitter controversy with the Jesuits in the field of theology, would, for sure, not have been inclined to accept lying down impositions from the Jesuits in the person of Bellarmine. The response of the qualificator was, therefore, in no way an "echo" of Bellarmine's thinking. It was, surely, in tune with Bellarmine's thought but only because it was the philosophical and theological opinion current at that time. Furthermore, if Bellarmine had really had the super-power which de Santillana attributes to him and had orchestrated the whole unfolding of the procedures against Galileo, why would he have kept Galileo from receiving a public censure? And why, at least if the qualificator had not expressed other than "the echo of his thoughts" and Bellarmine had really "had the Decree of the Index prepared", why, I repeat, did the Decree not carry the severe censure of "heretical" and "erroneous in the Faith" which had been given by the qualificators themselves?

[98] On the other hand it would be equally unjust to make the Dominicans the principal orchestrators of the listing of the *De Revolutionibus* on the Index. We have already seen that influential personages were not lacking among them, such as Maraffi, favorable to Galileo. And we must remember that it was a Dominican, Tommaso Campanella, who wrote from prison an apology for Galileo which, according to Langford 1966, 86, represents "the best evaluation of the state of affairs yet formulated". At the beginning of February 1616 (if not before) Cardinal Caetani had written to Campanella to ask his opinion on the problem of Copernicanism and Galileo, obviously in order to prepare himself with documents. And the Dominican had responded with a brief tract entitled: *Apologeticus pro Galileo Mathematico Florentino*, which was sent to the Cardinal at the end of February or the beginning of March. (See Campanella 1971, 27). In this tract Campanella did not consider the scientific proofs offered by Galileo, but he dealt only with the problem as to whether Galileo was free or not to propose his world-view or whether instead this was to be condemned on the basis of Scripture and the traditional interpretation of the Fathers. As to himself Campanella did not embrace Copernicanism. But he had at heart the intellectual freedom of Catholic thinkers and on that account he came to the conclusion that it was not allowed to hinder the research of Galileo nor to withdraw his writings from circulation. We do not know whether Cardinal Caetani was able to read this *Apologeticus* before the Decree of 1616. But we are already familiar with a testimony whereby he and Cardinal Maffeo Barberini had opposed the condemnation of the Copernican theory as heretical and they succeeded in their intent. See Note 79. In any case, just the fact that he wished to be informed counts in favor of the intellectual honesty of Caetani. As to the *Apologeticus*, it was printed at Frankfurt, Germany in 1622 with the title, *Apologia per Galileo*, and it was subsequently included on the Index of forbidden books. For a detailed analysis of the contents of this work see Bonansea 1986, 205-239.

[99] In response to Bellarmine's comments to Foscarini Galileo had noted:

> Not to believe that a proof of the earth's motion exists until one has been shown is very prudent, nor do we demand that anyone believe such a thing without proof. Indeed, we seek, for the good of the Holy Church, that everything the followers of this doctrine can set forth be examined with the greatest rigor, and that nothing be admitted unless it far outweighs the rival arguments. (V, 368-369; trans. by Drake 1957, 169).

[100] The problem as to how the qualificators of the Holy Office could pass a sentence also on philosophical topics, without having been asked to do so, shows up also in the case of one of Galileo's contemporaries who writes:

> We do not know the reasons which moved the Sacred Congregation to condemn the opinion of the motion of the earth and the fixity of the sun as absurd and false in philosophy. But if we are permitted to guess them, they may have been because physically, and not by capricious philosophizing on mathematical and metaphysical possibilities, it is necessary to base the conclusions on the natural motion and fixity of bodies on the evidence of the sensations; now through universal and continuous experience of the senses the whole human race is in a position to affirm that the sun moves and that the earth stands still. (*Argomento fisicomatematico*, page 33; quoted by Paschini 1965, 339).

[101] We are in our interpretation in agreement with Viganò 1969, 116-119. This author concludes his analysis with the following words:

> Therefore, we must conclude that the philosophical censure establishes the psychological certainty with which they pronounced the theological censure, which was the only one, of course, which interested the judges of the Holy Office and which determined their later decisions.

CHAPTER 4

THE CONTROVERSY ABOUT COMETS
AND *THE ASSAYER*
MAFFEO BARBERINI IS ELECTED POPE

1.   *The three comets of 1618 and the* Disputatio Astronomica
     of Grassi

Upon his return to Florence Galileo became convinced that
for the present there was nothing left to do except to wait in
silence until times changed. After all, the position taken by the
Church could be changed. Had it not happened many times that
a Pope had seen works put on the Index which later on were
held to be beyond censure by a later Pope?[1] Rome might be
eternal but, fortunately, the cardinals of the Holy Office were
not, nor was the Pope himself. Both Paul V and Bellarmine were
by now advanced in age. One could always hope that when they,
as well as other principals in the 1616 decision, passed away,
the official position of the Church could change. And for all that,
strictly speaking the Church had not condemned Copernicanism.
It had rather limited itself to the requirement that
Copernicanism be proposed as a mere hypothesis.[2]
Galileo was an optimist by temperament and he would not
let himself be beaten down despite all of the bitterness that he
must have felt because of the turn of events. Making use of the
peace and the free time that was once more his, he dedicated
himself to the revision of his longstanding studies on motion by
selecting and reordering the material from his time at Padua,
probably with the intention of preparing a publication. But it
was a slow undertaking, broken up by periods of sickness which
recurred repeatedly in subsequent years and which pushed him
to move to the villa of Bellosguardo in the environs of Florence
where he resided from 1617 to 1631.
When his health permitted him to do so, Galileo once again
would also dedicate his time to astronomical observations. Thus
he was able (probably in August 1616) to observe the change in

the forms of the "satellites" of Saturn. He discovered them, as we know, at the end of his stay in Padua and then they apparently disappeared. Now they reappeared but no more as two little globules, but in the form of two semi-ellipses touching the body of Saturn.[3]

But his observations of the satellites of Jupiter were much more numerous. Not long after their discovery, Galileo came up with the idea of using the phenomenon of their eclipses, due to their rotation about the planet, for the exact determination of longitude on the earth. That determination constituted a very important problem for navigation, but in Galileo's time it was still very far from being solved in a satisfactory way.

In order to apply Galileo's method it was essential to construct tables containing the times of eclipses of each of the satellites throughout the year. A first part of such tables had been published in the appendix to the *Discourse on Floating Bodies* (1612) and in September of that same year the Grand Duke of Tuscany had sent information to the Spanish King about Galileo's method. And so negotiations began as to its use by the Spanish, and Galileo hoped that it would succeed in bringing him bountiful remunerations. The negotiations were exceedingly drawn out and then they were definitively broken off in 1632.[4]

As I have already said, Galileo's silence on questions to do with Copernicanism was a matter of prudence which did not at all mean that he was definitely renouncing his ideas or his program. This is seen clearly in the response Galileo sent in May 1618 to Archduke Leopold of Austria (brother of the Grand Duchess Christina) who had written to ask him "something about his person". Galileo's letter accompanied a gift to the Archduke of two telescopes and a copy of the *Sunspot Letters*, in addition to a manuscript of the *Discourse on the ebb and flow of the sea* which he had already presented, as we have seen, to Cardinal Orsini. In the letter Galileo wrote:

> With this I send you a treatise on the causes of the tides which I wrote at a time when the theologians were thinking of prohibiting Copernicus' book and the doctrine announced therein, which I then held to be true, until it

pleased those gentlemen to prohibit the work and to declare the opinion to be false and contrary to Scripture. Now, knowing as I do that it behooves us to obey the decisions of the authorities and to believe them, since they are guided by a higher insight than any to which my humble mind can of itself attain, I consider this treatise which I send to you to be merely a poetical conceit, or a dream, and desire that your Highness may take it as such, inasmuch as it is based on the double motion of the Earth and, indeed, contains one of the arguments which I brought in confirmation of it.

But even poets sometimes attach a value to one or other of their fantasies, and I likewise attach a value to this fancy of mine. . . I have also let a few exalted personages have copies, in order that in case anyone not belonging to the Church should try to appropriate my curious fancy, as has happened to me with many of my discoveries, these personages, being above all suspicion, may be able to bear witness that it was I who first dreamed of this chimera. What I now send is but a fugitive performance; it was written in haste and in the expectation that the work of Copernicus would not be condemned as erroneous eighty years after its publication. . . . But a voice from heaven aroused me and dissolved all my confused and tangled fantasies in mist. May therefore your Highness graciously accept it, arranged as it is. And if divine mercy ever grants that I may be in a position to exert myself a little, your Highness may expect something more solid and real from me. (XII, 390-391; trans. by de Santillana 1955, 151).[5]

While Galileo was thus awaiting the opportunity to "be able to tire himself a little bit" about the problem which he had never for a moment stopped thinking about, the adversaries of Copernicanism, strengthened by the Church's decision, did not hesitate to write in support of geocentrism, even though they had to face the embarrassment of explaining the phenomena which had come to light in recent years.[6]

Despite his good intentions Galileo's silence was not to last very long. Right towards the end of that same year of 1618 three comets appeared one after the other over a short period of time. The third one, because of its magnitude[7] did not fail to arouse the deep impression which usually accompanies the appearance of heavenly phenomena which are interpreted as a forewarning of cataclysms and of wars. And, in fact, the apparition of these comets coincided with the beginning of the long war which subsequently became known in history as the Thirty Years War, a fact which seemed to confirm such popular beliefs.

Among astronomers and philosophers the discussions became extremely heated. Some maintained the opinion of Aristotle whereby, as we know, the comets were sublunar phenomena, that is, exhalations of the Earth which, as they rose to the highest zone of the sphere of fire, became heated and they were made to rotate in a circle because of the motion of the sphere of the moon immediately above it. According to this explanation, the disappearance of the comets coincided with the total extinction of their combustible material. Others instead subscribed more or less faithfully to the opinion of Tycho Brahe (based on his observations of the parallax of the comet of 1577). This opinion held that the comets were located quite a distance beyond the Moon close to the orbit of Venus and moved with irregular motion about the Sun in an orbit which was probably not circular but oval, thus explaining their varying distance from the Earth. Their appearance and disappearance showed that one was dealing with a transitory celestial phenomenon, in a certain sense similar to that of the *novae* but, in contrast to the latter, taking place in the region of the planets.

Galileo was prevented from observing these comets because of a sickness which forced him to stay in bed during the entire period of their apparition, as he himself will recall later on in *The Assayer* (VI, 225). On the other hand he at first did not feel that he could make responsible statements and so he limited himself to the expression of doubts about the explanations which were being proposed on these matters. In addition to a respect for prudence, the conviction (which he will harbor right to the last years of his life) that the phenomenon of the comets was very difficult to understand had an influence on Galileo's reticence.

In contrast the Jesuit, Orazio Grassi, seemed to have nourished fewer doubts on the subject. At that time he held the chair of mathematics at the Roman College in the place of

Grienberger.[8] He held a public conference there which was published in 1619 with the title: "An Astronomical Discussion (*Disputatio*) on the Three Comets of 1618" (VI, 21-35; I shall refer to this as the *Disputatio*), but without the author's name. (As in the case of Scheiner, this anonymity and use of fictitious names was in response to the desire of Jesuit superiors that the Society of Jesus avoid being directly involved in controversies because of the writings of its members.)

Grassi held that the comets (and in particular the third one, which was much more spectacular) were located quite beyond the Moon, probably between the Moon and the Sun.[9] On this point he showed himself to be in agreement with Tycho Brahe and he explicitly distanced himself from Aristotle. But with respect to the orbit of the comets, Grassi seems to have considered the Earth and not the Sun as their center. It was an attempt to salvage what was salvageable of Aristotelian cosmology, which, as we know, put the Earth at the center of all celestial motions. And yet the Jesuits of the Roman College had all by now accepted the idea of the satellites of Jupiter.

Galileo had received information on the comets together with requests for his opinion from some of his correspondents among whom the very youthful Cesarini.[10] Later on at the beginning of March 1619 he received from another Roman correspondent, Giovanni Battista Rinuccini the news of the printing of the *Disputatio* of Grassi:

> The Jesuits presented publicly a Problem [on the distance of the comet] which has been printed, and they hold firmly that it is in the sky [that is, beyond the moon], and some others besides [others than] the Jesuits have spread it around that this thing overthrows the Copernican system, against which there is no surer argument than this. (XII, 443; trans. by Drake 1978, 265).

And Rinuccini insisted that Galileo enter into the debate and present his opinion.

2.   *The response of Galileo: the* Discourse on the Comets

Rinuccini's hint of the phenomena of the comets having been used against Copernicanism had been vague. Very recent studies, based on unpublished documents, allow us to see in a better light the group of Roman intellectuals "besides the Jesuits" who had drawn those triumphant conclusions. In fact, the discussions on the comets going on in Rome were not limited to the circle of Jesuits at the Roman College. From an unpublished writing of Francesco Ingoli, *Treatise on the comet of 1618*, we have come, in fact, to know that the subject of the comet was at the center of meetings of the intellectuals who gravitated about Cardinal Scipione Cobelluzzi (also called Cardinal of Santa Susanna). Among them were Giovanni Remo, medical doctor and mathematician of the Archduke Leopold of Austria, Giovanbattista Agucchi and Ingoli himself. In his treatise, in answer to the question of the cardinal: "an ex motu huius cometae aliquo modo Copernicus Terrae motus confundi possit" (whether from the motion of this comet one could in any way draw an argument against the Copernican motion of the Earth), Ingoli stated:

> We answer that from the motion of the comet it seems possible not only to refute the Copernican theory, but also to draw forth arguments, whose efficacy is not to be disdained, in favor of the stability of the Earth.[11]

We do not know whether Galileo had any more precise information on these discussions in the Roman circles. But just the hint from Rinuccini was enough to give him serious concerns. On the other hand, once he had reviewed the content of Grassi's public lecture he undoubtedly noticed that the latter had, notwithstanding the contradictions already noted, based his arguments mostly on Tycho Brahe's theory of comets. Now, Galileo must have known that Tycho Brahe had put forth this theory precisely because of the difficulties, for Brahe insurmountable, which the phenomena of comets presented for Copernicanism. Grassi's statements, therefore, even if not explicitly so, were, in fact, anti-Copernican. So Galileo decided to intervene. But he preferred not to involve himself directly and so he had an old pupil of his, Mario Guiducci,[12] speak in his place. The latter presented a paper on the comets at the Florentine Academy and it was published at the end of June 1619 with a dedication to the Archduke Leopold of Austria (who had also sought Galileo's opinion on this celestial phenomenon). The title was: *Discourse on the comets by Mario Guiducci* (VI, 39-105). The manuscript of the *Discourse*, which has been preserved, shows that, in fact, Guiducci was author of only the beginning and that Galileo composed the remainder in addition to having corrected parts of the beginning section. Galileo, therefore, not only inspired the work but he was the true author of the major part of it.[13]

In it Guiducci began with the affirmation that, after having expounded the theories of the ancient philosophers and of modern astronomers on the comets, he planned, since he had doubts about them, to refer to the conjectures of Galileo as merely probable.

Among the doctrines of the ancient philosophers the one of Aristotle, which I have recalled above, was to be dismantled, thus showing the absurdity of the physics implied there. In particular this meant the circular motion which was supposed to have been communicated to the exhalations of the earth by the movement of the contiguous sphere of the moon, thereby setting it on fire. But Guiducci was not even content with the modern theories, that is, the one of Tycho Brahe, taken up by the Jesuit author of the *Disputatio* (Guiducci never mentions the name of Grassi). According to Guiducci the argument from parallax could not be applied to the comets unless one had first proven that they were true material bodies. For example, Guiducci noted, in the case of phenomena due to the reflection of light by vapors (such as the rainbow and the northern lights) the parallax method is not valid.[14] Even less (at any rate) could one invoke the argument from the lack of magnification in telescope observations to prove the enormous distance of the comets. Guiducci severely criticized this opinion of the Jesuit author and defined it as "most vain and false".[15]

In like manner Guiducci criticized the opinion of Tycho Brahe of a motion (perhaps not even circular) of the comets

about the Sun or - in the case of the mathematician of the
Roman College - of their circular motion about the Earth.[16]

After this critical review of the opinions, Guiducci put forth
Galileo's opinion in the manner of a more likely hypothesis, but
without pretending to give a *solution to the problem*. According
to this opinion the comets could be optical phenomena caused by
the reflection of sunlight by the exhalations or vapors rising
vertically from the Earth and extending to the regions beyond
the Moon. Even though Galileo seemed thus to be recalling the
opinion of Aristotle as to the origin of the "material" of the
comets, he distanced himself radically from that opinion for
three reasons: 1) the light of the comets did not come from a
"fire" of such exhalations; 2) their motion was not circular; 3)
above all else, the "exhalations" of the Earth were capable of
rising from the terrestrial region of the four elements right up
to the celestial region above the Moon (a contradiction to the
Aristotelian dogma of the radical distinction between the earthly
and heavenly bodies and their inability to penetrate one
another).[17]

Having once risen up to that height, those exhalations were
illuminated by sunlight and in that way they became visible and
thus they later on disappeared (due to the continuous movement
away always in a straight line). That it was a matter of "vapors"
and not of real true heavenly bodies, seemed confirmed,
according to Guiducci, by the fact that it was possible to observe
stars through the comets, even through their most brilliant
"tail".[18]

Guiducci admitted that there remained a serious problem
in this theory:

> I shall not pretend to ignore that if the material in which
> the comet takes form had only a straight motion
> perpendicular to the surface of the earth [that is, from the
> center to the sky] the comet should have seemed to be
> directed precisely toward the zenith, whereas, in fact, it did
> not appear so, but declined toward the north. This compels
> us either to alter what was stated, even though it
> corresponds to the appearances in so many cases, or else
> to retain what has been said adding some other cause for
> this apparent deviation. I would not be able to do the one,

nor should I venture to do the other. Seneca was aware and he wrote how important it was to have a sure determination of these things, to have a solid and unshakable knowledge of the order, of the disposition, and of the states and movements of the parts of the universe, a knowledge which is lacking to our century: however, we should be content with that little bit that we can conjecture amidst the shadows, until we are told the true constitution of the parts of the world, because what Tycho had promised remained imperfect. (VI, 98-99).[19]

With these words Guiducci made clear the difficulty of explaining the phenomenon of the comets in an age like his which lacked a credible "cosmology" within which to set such a phenomenon. Aristotelian cosmology was false; there remained no possible doubt of that. That of Tycho Brahe had remained "imperfect" (Guiducci here had used a moderate expression, but the whole complex of the *Discourse* led to a more severe conclusion, at least as to the theory of the comets by Tycho). Copernican cosmology was left (which for Guiducci was certainly the only true one) but one could not speak about it; the only course left, therefore, was to try to thus "conjecture amidst the shadows".

In substance, Galileo - through Guiducci - had wished, rather than to give a theory of the comets, to show the insufficiency, even the incorrectness (in light of the observations themselves) of the position of Tycho Brahe and of all of those who more or less followed him and, in particular, the Jesuits of the Roman College. Of course, it was a question of a criticism on only a single point of the system of Tycho, but that was enough, at least for Galileo, as a response *ad hominem* to whomever had claimed to see, in declaring to have confirmed Tycho Brahe's vision on this point, a proof of the validity of the system in general (and thus the falsity of Copernicanism).[20] Furthermore, there was no lack here and there of stinging words with respect to "the mathematician of the Roman College".[21] And the whole context of the *Discourse* was a criticism not only of the theory of Brahe but also of the scientific posture of the Roman Jesuits. It was unavoidable that this would be felt as an offense to the latter and to Father Grassi in particular. It was that which

Ciampoli correctly feared; in a letter to Galileo in July 1619 he let him know how worried he was about the consequences of this foreseeable estrangement of the Jesuits of the Roman College from Galileo (XII, 466).[22]

The comets continued to be the order of the day and discussion and writings about them rapidly proliferated. The Aristotelians disputed with the followers of Tycho Brahe and thus also with the views of Father Grassi. But they did not seem to have it in for Galileo, at least for the moment, perhaps because of the apparent Aristotelianism of his position and even more so because of his criticism of Tycho's theory of the comets.

At any rate, everyone had understood that the true author of the *Discourse* was Galileo. On 23 July 1619 Giovanni Remo (mathematician of the Archduke Leopold of Austria) notified Kepler of the *Discourse on the comets* and he stated that it was the work of Galileo.[23] Later on the same Remo thanked Galileo in the name of the Archduke for the dedication of the *Discourse* to the latter and he added that Leopold of Austria had immediately sent a copy to Father Scheiner since Scheiner had been mentioned in the document. Quite rightfully the Jesuit resented this mention of himself; it did not at all do him honors and, according to what Remo wrote, he promised to respond to Galileo and repay him "with the same money" (XII, 489).[24]

3.   *Grassi's response: the* Libra Astronomica

There was no waiting for Grassi's response to Galileo. In fact, it appeared in the autumn of that same year 1619 at Perugia under the title, *Libra astronomica ac philosophica* (The Astronomical and Philosophical Scale), a work in Latin in the name of "Lothario Sarsi Singensano" which was the anagram of "Horatio Sarsi Saloniensi" (VI, 109-180). In it Sarsi, who presented himself as a disciple of Grassi, stated that he wanted to revenge the reputation of his master which had been injured by Galileo's attack.[25]

At first Galileo did not want to believe the information furnished to him by Ciampoli that Grassi was the true author of the *Libra*. In fact Galileo, through Guiducci, had not attacked the Jesuit by name and the major part of his criticisms had been directed rather to Tycho Brahe. But, as we have seen, he had also made some rather stinging comment on the scientific value of the statements of the mathematicians of the Roman College (not to speak of the assertions with respect to Scheiner, gratuitously offensive) and he should not, therefore, have been so surprised to receive a response "to the point". However, it is also true that in "evaluating" Galileo's reasons, Grassi had not spared his darts which were at times impregnated with insidious irony.

On 6 December Ciampoli himself, however, confirmed to Galileo that Grassi was the author of the *Libra*:

> . . . I see that you cannot bring yourself to believe that Father Grassi is the author of "Libra Astronomica"; but I return to assure you once again that His Reverence and the Jesuit Fathers want you to know that it is their work and they are so far from the judgement that you make about it that they glory in it as a triumph. Father Grassi deals with Your Reverence with much more reserve than do many other Fathers to whom the word to annihilate has become very familiar; but the truth is that from Father Grassi I have never heard such a word uttered; on the contrary, he behaves so modestly in his speech that I am surprised all the more that he has produced such a vainglorious writing and with so many biting jokes. (XII, 498-499).[26]

The purpose of the present work does not allow me to take up a detailed examination of the contents of the *Libra*. From a scientific point of view Grassi showed in this work that he was well informed even with respect to the most recent publications, such as those of Kepler. In particular, his answers in the field of optics were often pertinent and had the upper hand over the statements on such matters in the *Discourse* of Guiducci.[27] No less justified was the criticism of the contradiction, already noted by me, into which Guiducci had fallen as to the parallax. On the one hand he accepted its use to state that the comet was located well beyond the Moon. On the other hand, he doubted that it was legitimate to make use of it by suggesting the possibility that the comet was only an optical phenomenon.

At the same time, however, Grassi shows (in strident contrast with personal comments of an experimental character and certainly of value) a strange trust in the opinions of ancient authors (such as that of the eggs which the Babylonians are said to have caused to cook by rotating them rapidly in slings) or of others who claimed that cannonballs melted during their trajectory because of the heat developed by air friction.[28] Furthermore, he at times presented Galileo's statements in a non objective way, if not outright distorting them, at the same time saying that he wished to "evaluate" them impartially.[29] This fact together with the "biting jokes" which were not lacking certainly did not contribute to keeping the discussion on a level of equanimity.[30]

Among such biting jokes the most insidious was without a doubt the comment which Sarsi made as to the words already quoted of "Guiducci" on "some other reason" for the apparent deviation towards the north of the straight-line motion of the comet, an explanation which nonetheless (Guiducci had added) "I would not venture to do". Sarsi, who in his quotation had substituted "some other reason" with the words "*motus alius*" (another motion), commented:

> What is this sudden fear in an open and not timid spirit which prevents him from uttering the word that he has in mind? I cannot guess it. Is this other motion which could explain everything and which he does not dare to discuss - is it of the comet or of something else? It cannot be the motion of the circles, since for Galileo there are no Ptolemaic circles. I fancy I hear a small voice whispering discretely in my ear: the motion of the Earth. Get thee behind me thou evil word, offensive to truth and to pious ears! It was surely prudence to speak it with bated breath. For, if it were really thus, there would be nothing left of an opinion which can rest on no other ground except this false one. . . . But then certainly Galileo had no such idea, for I have never known him otherwise than pious and religious. (VI, 145-146; trans. by de Santillana 1955, 154-155).[31]

Galileo was certainly not the kind of individual to consider himself easily "annihilated" as his Jesuit critics claimed. But at the same time he sensed how dangerous it was to alienate himself definitively from the influential astronomers and mathematicians of the Roman College.[32] He, therefore, sought the advice of his Roman friends as to what he should do. They showed themselves to be in agreement as to the necessity of responding to the publication of Grassi. But the majority of them thought that it would be better if Galileo did not respond directly, not only because Grassi had also preferred to have one of his disciples as a fictitious author of the *Libra* and, therefore, it was not fitting that a master like Galileo should lower himself to debate with a disciple, but also and especially so as not to exacerbate his conflict with the Jesuits.[33] In the end it was decided that Galileo would direct his response to Cesarini.

As to Guiducci, given that his *Discourse on the Comets* had been pronounced by himself and subsequently published under his own name, he felt it to be necessary to give to the press his response also in the form of a letter addressed to Father Tarquinio Galluzzi, who had been his professor at the Roman College. Guiducci first declared that, if Sarsi had not attacked him so sharply, he would have abstained from responding (as Galluzzi himself had counseled him), but that he was forced to respond because of the inconsiderate applause that Sarsi was receiving from his supporters "without perhaps having read my writings". Then he maintained that he was the author of the *Discourse*, although he had reproduced the opinion of Galileo "to which he was inclined more than to any other". At the same time he declared that he had absolutely not wanted to offend Father Grassi and the Jesuits of the Roman College. But he claimed for himself the freedom to hold a scientific opinion different from that of the "Reverend Mathematician of the Roman College".[34]

4. The Assayer *is born. Maffeo Barberini is elected Pope.*

But Galileo, it seems, was in no hurry to compose the projected work. And this caused an increasing preoccupation for his friends who judged this silence to be harmful to his reputation and they urged him repeatedly not to put off the project any longer, even though they unanimously recommended that he avoid polemical tones for obvious reasons of prudence.[35]

Even without the counsel of his friends, Galileo was well aware of the need to be very cautious. It is true that Paul V had died in January 1621, followed by Bellarmine in September of the same year. But more importantly on 28 February of that same year his protector and faithful admirer, the Grand Duke Cosimo II, had unexpectedly passed away. While they awaited the coming of age of his son Ferdinando, who was only eleven at that time, the regency of the Grand Duchy was taken up by the Grand Duchess Christina and by Ferdinando's own mother, Maria Magdalena of Austria. These two ladies of a rigid piety could be influenced for religious reasons by the adversaries of Galileo. And one of the most ruthless among them, Caccini, had returned just a short while before to Florence and surely he did not cease to "keep a check on" Galileo.

Finally in the summer of 1621 Galileo took up the task of preparing a response and he completed the bulk of the work as that same year came to an end.[36] But almost another whole year would have to go by before he would finally in October 1622 announce to Cesi that he had sent the manuscript to Cesarini. It was entitled *The Assayer* (XIII, 98).[37] In fact, it arrived right after that to Cesarini, who looked through it and sent it on to Cesi. And the latter wrote to Galileo at the end of December and stated that he was reading *The Assayer* "with very great consolation". He repeated his promise to give it back as soon as possible to Cesarini so that it could be printed (XIII, 103). For his part Cesarini, who had had various copies of the manuscript made and distributed to various members of the *Accademia dei Lincei* and to Ciampoli, was awaiting their comments on it so that he could send them to Galileo. The common opinion was that the work should be printed in Rome. With respect to this Cesarini wrote to Galileo in January 1623:

> . . . I tell you that we certainly wish to publish the work, and that we wish to do it in Rome, despite the power of the adversaries, against whom we will arm ourselves with the shield of truth, and also [avail ourselves] of the favor

of our masters.[38] There is no doubt that we will be contradicted; but I have firm hope that we will overcome them. Already the news of this apology [*The Assayer*] has arrived to Sarsi and to the Roman College, notice having been given by the Fathers from here that it had arrived in Rome; and furthermore, upon my reading it to some here, they have fathomed everything. But it has not arrived in their hands, nor will they see it except in print. They are eager and anxious and they even dared to ask me for it; but I have refused them it because they would have been able more effectively to obstruct its publication. (XIII, 106).[39]

Cesarini also took up the task of obtaining permission for the printing. The examination of the work was entrusted to the Dominican Niccolò Riccardi. On 2 February 1623 he declared that not only had he not found anything erroneous in Galileo's work but that, on the contrary, he had

noted many fine considerations which have to do with natural philosophy . . . thanks to the subtle and solid speculation of the author in whose days I consider myself happy to have been born, when, no longer with the steelyard and roughly, but with such delicate assayers the gold of truth is weighed. (VI, 200).[40]

So as not to lose time Cesarini put into the text the modifications proposed by Cesi and by other members of the *Accademia dei Lincei*, modifications which had no importance, as he himself informed Galileo (XIII, 111), and he saw to it that the printing began immediately. But the process was slower than foreseen. While the printing was in progress, Pope Gregory XV was taken sick and died on 8 July 1623, after only two years of his pontificate. One month later the new Pope was elected. It was Cardinal Maffeo Barberini and he took the name of Urban VIII.

This election was greeted with enthusiasm by progressive Catholics throughout Europe. A man of noteworthy intelligence and culture and an able diplomat,[41] he seemed, at 53 years of age, the ideal person to lead the Church in such difficult times as those through which Europe was passing. The difficulties were most serious on the political plane (the Thirty Years War had begun five years earlier) but, as to the cultural aspects, they were also profound. As we have already seen, Urban VIII had shown as a cardinal a notable moderation with respect to the problem of Copernicanism. To be sure, he had not taken a position in favor of Copernicanism. Maffeo Barberini was convinced - and so he will always remain - that no astronomical theory could lay claims to being other than a mere hypothesis, given the incapacity of the human mind to penetrate the mystery of the creative will of God. But he had not failed to show his personal sympathy and admiration for Galileo. The latter, in turn, aware of the importance of such relationships with the influential cardinal, had not hesitated to make him gifts of his books.

Even at the moment of the decision of the Holy Office in 1616, as we know, it seems that Maffeo Barberini had intervened together with Cardinal Caetani to prevent the Copernican opinion from being declared heretical. Nor had he cut off the bridges with Galileo after 1616. Rather, he had sent him on 20 August 1620 a Latin ode, *Adulatio perniciosa*, in which he showed his admiration for the discoveries on Jupiter and Saturn and of the sunspots. In the letter which accompanied the ode Maffeo Barberini requested Galileo to accept it as a "small sign of the great good will that I have toward you" (XIII, 49). And only one month and a half before his election to the papacy in another letter in which he thanked Galileo for the congratulations which Galileo had sent on the occasion of the doctorate obtained by his nephew Francesco, the Cardinal had added:

> I remain much obliged to Your Lordship for your continued affection towards me and mine and I wish to have the opportunity to do likewise to you assuring you that you will find in me a very ready disposition to serve you out of respect for what you so merit and for the gratitude I owe you. (XIII, 119).

One can, therefore, well imagine what Galileo must have felt at the news that Maffeo Barberini was now at the head of the Church. And the news which continued to come to him from

Rome in those first months was such as to encourage the greatest hope. Thus the academician Francesco Stelluti announced to him in August that Urban VIII had appointed Virginio Cesarini as Master of the Chambers and that he had confirmed Ciampoli as Secretary of the Briefs to the Princes and had furthermore appointed him as Privy Chamberlain. Stelluti concluded: "In the meantime let us pray to the Lord God that he keep this Pope for a long time, because there is hope here of an excellent government" (XIII, 121).

Galileo's feelings are shown clearly in the letter of congratulations sent by him to the Pope's brother, Carlo Barberini, and to his nephew Francesco (destined to become a cardinal). To the latter he wrote in September:

> . . . to make it clear to you how inexplicably happy I am that His Beatitude has ascended to the most sublime throne it will be a congruent argument to say to you how delightful it is for me to have whatever remains of my life, and how much less heavier than usual will death be at whatever moment it overtakes me: I will live most happy, the hope, up to now altogether buried, being revived to see the most unusual studies recalled from their long exile; and I will die content, having been alive at the most glorious success of the most loved and revered master that I had in the world, so that I would not be able to hope for nor desire other equal happiness. (XIII, 130-131).

In the meantime the printing of *The Assayer* had been taken up again with new vigor. Stelluti informed Galileo in September 1623 that it had been decided to dedicate it to the Pope in the name of the *Accademia dei Lincei* (XIII, 129). Finally, after Cesarini had composed the letter of dedication, the work could be issued.[42]

At the beginning of this work Galileo briefly recalls all of the opposition which his previous works had met and he dwelt especially on the claim of Simon Mayr to have discovered the satellites of Jupiter.[43] Convinced that so many attacks and so much envy were coming from an

. . . ill feeling and stubborn opposition that existed against
my works, I considered remaining perfectly silent in order
to save myself any occasion for being the unhappy target
of such sharpshooting, and to remove from others any
material capable of exciting these reprehensible talents.
(VI, 218; trans. by Drake 1957, 232).[44]

But even this proposal, Galileo continued, had remained
without effect because of the attack directed at him by "Lottario
(sic) Sarsi, a completely unknown person", who had claimed to
see in him the author of the *Discourse on the Comets* by
Guiducci. Galileo had, therefore, decided to speak. And he
promised to do so not like the person who had made use of that
Lotario Sarsi as a mask but rather openly. On the other hand,
he added, he would respect the anonymity of his interlocutor so
that he might face him more frankly.

I realize that often those who go about in masks are low
persons who attempt by disguise to gain esteem among
gentlemen and scholars, utilizing the dignity that attends
nobility for some purpose of their own. But sometimes they
are gentlemen who, thus unknown, forgo the respectful
decorum attending their rank and assume as is the custom
in many Italian cities the liberty of speaking freely about
any subject with anyone, taking at the same time as much
pleasure in the fact that anyone whosoever he may be can
rally and struggle with them without respect. I believe that
it must be one of the latter who is hidden behind the mask
"Lothario Sarsi," for if he were one of the former it would
indeed be poor taste for him to impose upon the public in
this manner. Also I think that just as he has permitted
himself incognito to say some things that he might perhaps
repress to my face, so it ought not be taken amiss if I,
availing myself of the privilege accorded against
masqueraders, shall deal with him quite frankly. Let
neither Sarsi nor others imagine me to be weighing every
word when I deal with him more freely than he may like.
(VI, 219-220).

The irony is evident but the tone is still mannerly. But
soon things change and the irony becomes a whip. In

commenting on the title of Sarsi's work (*Libra Astronomica e Filosofica*) and Sarsi's own remark that the title had been suggested by the fact that the great comet of 1618 had appeared in the constellation of *Libra* (Scales), Galileo observes that, in fact, it had appeared in the constellation of *Scorpione* (Scorpion). He concludes thus:

> Therefore, much more proportionally and also more truthfully, if we look at his writing itself, he would have been able to entitle it the "ASTRONOMICO E FILOSOFICO SCORPIONE" (THE ASTRONOMICAL AND PHILOSOPHICAL SCORPION), a constellation called by our sovereign poet Dante the figure of the cold animal "which strikes people with the tail"; and truly stings are not lacking against me, and much more serious than those of the scorpions, since these, as friends of man, do not injure if they are not first offended and provoked, and that one bites me although I have not troubled him, not even in thought. But it is my good fortune that I know the antidote and the remedies at hand for such stings! I will, therefore, break and rub that very scorpion on the wounds, where the poison reabsorbed by its own body will leave me free and healthy. (VI, 221).

These initial quotations may give an idea of the style of the work which is correctly considered to be "a stupendous masterpiece of polemical literature".[45] And, in fact, the problem of the comets, rather than being the fundamental theme of *The Assayer*, really makes up only the point of departure. If, therefore, we were to stop only at the answer given to Sarsi on the nature of the comets, that is, if we were to limit ourselves to an evaluation of the purely astronomical value of *The Assayer*, even without coming to judge it to be "a mistaken book",[46] one could at least consider it to be unjust with respect to the scientific value of the ideas of Tycho Brahe (at the center of Galileo's criticisms as in the previous *Discourse on the Comets*) and of Grassi. But that would mean losing sight of that which is more outstanding and more fertile in *The Assayer*, namely,

. . . its wealth of problems, its innumerable special investigations in which Galileo's exceptional acumen as an observer shines forth, and in its biting polemical arguments, which are often transformed into ingenious indications of new themes for scientific research.[47]

We cannot enter here into a description, even a summary one, of the very rich content of this work which Galileo had initially conceived as a simple letter, but which he had seen grow in his hands until it took on a much more noticeable bulk.[48] Even if, because of the polemical character of the work (which leads Galileo to comment point for point the *Libra* of Sarsi and to follow, therefore, the order of questions established by his adversary), Galileo does not put forth a systematic treatise on scientific methodology or on the philosophy of science, still the new methodological and philosophical posture at the basis of his arguments is seen clearly in its essential features.

At the beginning of *The Assayer* in criticizing the display of quotations from famous authors which Sarsi lined up as a justification for his own theories, Galileo wrote:

> In Sarsi I seem to discern the firm belief that in philosophizing one must support oneself upon the opinion of some celebrated author, as if our minds ought to remain completely sterile and barren unless wedded to the reasoning of some other person. Possibly he thinks that philosophy is a book of fiction by some writer, like the *Iliad* or *Orlando Furioso*, productions in which the least important thing is whether what is written there is true. Well, Sarsi, that is not how matters stand. Philosophy is written in this grand book, the universe, which stands continually open to our gaze. But the book cannot be understood unless one first learns to comprehend the language and read the letters in which it is composed. It is written in the language of mathematics, and its characters are triangles, circles, and other geometric figures without which it is humanly impossible to understand a single word of it; without these, one wanders about in a dark labyrinth. (VI, 232; trans. by Drake 1957, 237-238).

This passage, justly famous, has been often cited as a confirmation of the so-called "Platonism" of Galileo. But, more than treating ex professo of the problem of the mathematical nature of reality, Galileo here rather wishes to contrast the subjectivism of the principle of authority (in which so much can be left to fantasy as in poetic books) to the objectivity of the study of nature which has at its base a rigorous mathematical method.[49]

What Galileo really thought about the relationship between mathematics and physical reality, that is, what was the new natural philosophy championed by him, comes out clearly from the considerations developed by him towards the end of The Assayer on the problem of heat. Aristotle had stated that "motion was the cause of heat"[50] and "Guiducci" had denied it, thus rejecting the Aristotelian explanation for the origin of the comets in the highest regions of the terrestrial atmosphere. In the Libra Sarsi had wanted instead to prove that the Aristotelian principle was correct, but without thus implying that he was making his own the Aristotelian theory on comets.[51]

Before explaining in what sense this Aristotelian principle might be true Galileo wanted first to make clear the concept of "hot", and so he commented on it:

> . . . I suspect that people in general have a concept of this which is very remote from the truth. For they believe that heat is a real phenomenon, or property, or quality, which actually resides in the material by which we feel ourselves warmed. Now I say that whenever I conceive any material of corporeal substance, I immediately feel the need to think of it as bounded, and as having this or that shape; as being large or small in relation to other things, and in some specific place at any given time; as being in motion or at rest; as touching or not touching some other body; and as being one in number, or few, or many. From these conditions I cannot separate such a substance by any stretch of my imagination. But that it must be white or red, bitter or sweet, noisy or silent, and of sweet or foul odor, my mind does not feel compelled to bring in as necessary accompaniments. Without the senses as our guides, reason or unaided imagination would probably never arrive at qualities like these. Hence I think that

tastes, odors, colors, and so on are no more than mere
names so far as the object in which we place them is
concerned, and that they reside only in the consciousness
[sensitive body]. Hence if the living creature were removed,
all these qualities would be wiped away and annihilated.
(VI, 347-348; trans. by Drake 1957, 274).

And a little further on Galileo makes this concept more
precise:

> To excite in us tastes, odors and sounds I believe that
> nothing is required in external bodies except shapes,
> numbers, and slow or rapid movements. I think that if
> ears, tongues and noses were removed, shapes and
> numbers and motions would remain, but not odors or
> tastes or sounds. The latter, I believe, are nothing more
> than names when separated from living beings. (VII, 350;
> trans. by Drake 1957, 276-277).

We have here in a concise form, but already very explicit
and clear, that distinction between two types of properties (those
which truly reside in a body: "figures, numbers, and motions"
and those which reside only in the sentient subject: "taste,
smells, colors, etc.") which will one day be systematized by John
Locke with his distinction between "primary" and "secondary"
properties.[52]

As Geymonat (1965, 105) observes: "the clarity and
importance of these Galilean pages must be evident, because
they indubitably opened the way which has since been travelled
by modern science".[53] In fact, it is only through translation into
quantitative terms (and, therefore, rigorously measurable) that
it is possible to establish optics, acoustics, etc., as sciences.

But it seems to me that this passage also has a
philosophical import. Surely, it is a philosophy which remains
(and will always remain) more under an implicit than an explicit
form. And it is formulated in a fragmentary way according as
the occasion offers possibilities. But even if Galileo did not have
the opportunity (and probably not even the purely speculative
interest) required to come to a systematization of his
philosophical ideas on the reality of the physical world, his

thinking is sufficiently clear. For him physical reality is no longer   what it was conceived to be within the ambient of the hylomorphism of Aristotle and the Scholastics. Just as "prime matter" and "substantial form", so also the qualitative properties of bodies (or their "accidental forms") are nothing else than "pure names". In the place of the traditional natural philosophy and metaphysics with their proper predominant interest in these qualitative aspects of bodies (as the only way to know their essence) Galileo introduces the new philosophy of their figures, numbers, and local motion. Certainly, this philosophy is not a regress to Platonism. The value which Galileo gives to sense knowledge and to experiments, the incontestable certainty of being able to construct a new philosophy as a *secure* knowledge of the material world, are all elements which indicate a position quite different from that of traditional Platonism. After Plato came Aristotle and Archimedes and Galileo certainly did not forget that sequence. At the same time he had inherited the new movement which had begun to show its presence already in the late Middle Ages and later in the Renaissance and as such Galileo conceived philosophy ever more as a "mechanistic" natural philosophy: physical reality, the world system is seen as an enormous mechanism whose macroscopic components (visible bodies endowed with quantitative properties and with motion) come about through aggregations of innumerable microscopic components, the "atoms" of Democritus and Lucretius.[54]

In *The Assayer* Galileo shows an extremely cautious attitude towards Copernicanism. Even if Paul V and Bellarmine were dead, the Decree of the Congregation of the Index always remained in force and his adversaries were on the alert, ready to collect the least indication that Copernican convictions still kept hold of him. A proof of this was the dangerous allusion made in this respect by Grassi in the *Libra*.

Galileo, therefore, never fails to profess repeatedly his submission to the decision of the Church on Copernicanism. But he nonetheless insists that one must prove also with "natural reason, when one can, the falseness of those propositions which are declared to be against Holy Scripture" (VI, 240).

Taking courage in the fact that the Church had not prohibited Copernicanism as a mathematical hypothesis, Galileo does not fail to emphasize - in his dispute with Sarsi - the fact that it is superior (as an hypothesis, even if one must then put it aside "for superior reasons") to all other theories proposed.

> If the movement attributed to the Earth, which I, as a pious and Catholic person, consider most false and null, is suitable for explaining so many and such diverse appearances which are observed in the heavenly bodies, I am not sure that it so false, could not deceitfully respond to the appearance of the comets, if Sarsi does not descend to considerations more distinct than those which he has produced up until now. (VI, 311).[55]

Galileo showed even more caution as to Scriptural arguments. Past experience had taught him quite enough in this regard. Thus he now refuses to follow Sarsi down the path of quotes from Scripture to confirm ones own points of view.

At the end of *The Assayer*, not without a subtle irony, he writes in this regard:

> And since I could greatly fool myself in penetrating the true meaning of matters which by too great a margin go beyond the weakness of my brain, while leaving such determinations to the prudence of the masters of divinity, I will simply go on discussing these lower doctrines, declaring myself to be always prepared for every decree of superiors, despite whatever demonstration and experiment which would appear to be contrary. (VI, 366).

The prudence shown by Galileo on questions of Copernicanism and of Scripture, together with his vivacious style full of polemical irony, which spared nothing of the simple-mindedness of Sarsi, must have given much pleasure to Urban VIII. In fact, we know from Cesarini's letter to Galileo, written at the time of the first consignment of a copy of *The Assayer*, that this book had "so arisen in the esteem of His Holiness that he has it read at table" (XIII, 141).

And a little later Ciampoli also, upon informing Galileo that some pages of *The Assayer* which he had read to Urban VIII pleased him very much, added these words which must have further increased the great hopes which Galileo already harbored:

> Here is greatly desired something else new from your talent; whence if you should resolve to have printed those concepts which up until now remain in your mind, I am sure that they would be received most gratefully by Our Lord [the Pope], who does not cease to admire your eminence in all matters and to retain intact for you that affection which he has had for you in times gone by. (XIII, 146-147).

Father Grassi's reaction was obviously quite different. This is how Stelluti described it when he wrote to Galileo from Rome. After having said that the first copy of *The Assayer* had been displayed at the *Libreria del Sole* (Bookshop of the Sun), he adds:

> . . . and immediately Sarsi ran there, the real one, however, since the fictitious one is only a name: He requested the said book and upon reading the frontispiece he changed color and said that Your Lordship had made him wait anxiously three years for this response, but perhaps upon reading it it will appear to him to be too hasty. He immediately put the book under his arm and went off, nor since then did I hear anything except that a father of the College, who read it entirely, said that the book is magnificent, and that Your Lordship has behaved too modestly, and that Sarsi will have much to do if he wishes to respond. In brief, the Fathers consider themselves well treated by Your Lordship. (XIII, 147-148).

As had happened other times, Galileo's friends showed themselves to be too optimistic. In fact, when he targeted Sarsi-Grassi, Galileo undoubtedly had also struck out at other Jesuits. As to Father Grassi, he immediately put himself to work to respond to *The Assayer*. At the same time, however, he tried to avoid a definitive break with his adversary and, as a matter of fact, he showed a desire to meet with him personally.[56] And Guiducci wrote from Rome that during the visits he had made

to Grassi while he was sick he had admitted that with respect
to the motion of the Earth

> when a demonstration of the said motion should be found
> it would be necessary to interpret Sacred Scripture
> differently that had been done in the passages where it
> speaks of the stability of the earth and the motion of the
> heaven, and this according to the judgement of Cardinal
> Bellarmine. (XIII, 205).[57]

5.   *A new response of Grassi. The* Ratio Ponderum Librae et
      Simbellae

Grassi's response was soon ready, but its publication was
delayed due to problems with the printing. They were not due,
as Guiducci thought,[58] to obstacles placed by the Father General
of the Jesuits to the publication, but to the fact that the book
was being printed in Paris and Father Grassi received the page
proofs with a long delay and he could not personally goad the
editor.[59] And that Paris was chosen as the place for the printing
was surely due to motives of prudence. Grassi (and more so his
superiors) wanted to avoid creating problems by attacking a book
which had been dedicated to the new Pope and esteemed by him
in a way that was notoriously favorable to the author. Paris was
far off and a book printed there with different censors than the
ones in Rome would have been less obvious.

Galileo, for his part, was not in a hurry to put out his
hand to Grassi. Undoubtedly he was waiting the appearance of
the reply before he could conclude whether it was indicated or
not for him to accept the offers of peace and friendship.

Finally in 1626 Grassi's answer appeared in Paris still
under the pseudonym of Sarsi and with the title: *Ratio
ponderum Librae et Simbellae* (Comparison of the weights [of
the arguments] of the *Libra* and *The Assayer;* hereafter referred
to as the *Ratio).* Galileo read this work and annotated it with
no less steely irony than that which he had already employed
with the *Libra*.[60] But he did not think that it was worth the
trouble to respond any further since "he judged this answer [of
Grassi's] to be too frivolous and that it would be just a waste of
time, it being open knowledge that the author was resolved,

regardless of the means required, to have the last word" (XIII, 371).

The tone of the *Ratio* was to all appearances well mannered but its content was still polemical. And it did not lack insinuations, the most serious of which concerning the theological implications of the atomistic explanation of sense experience given by Galileo in *The Assayer*. As we have seen, Galileo had stated that the sense qualities as color, odor, and taste were subjective. Now, according to Grassi that contradicted the Catholic doctrine of the Eucharist in which the substance of bread and wine is transformed into the body and blood of Christ, but the "species", namely color, odor and taste of bread and wine are miraculously preserved. The miracle was completely useless if it is simply a matter of preserving "pure names" (VI, 486-487). Grassi had stated beforehand that he had felt the need to make known in this way "a scruple which bothered him".[61] In his annotation to this passage Galileo wrote:

> This scruple is left completely to you, because *The Assayer* is printed in Rome with the permission of superiors and it is dedicated to the supreme head of the Church; it has been reviewed by those who are responsible for protecting the faith incorrupt (*excubant incorruptae fidei tutelae*) and they, having approved, will have also considered how one might get rid of that scruple. (VI, 486 [149]).

Despite these words Galileo was, nonetheless, worried by this accusation of Grassi and he asked Castelli to speak about it to Father Riccardi (XIII, 389, 391). Through Castelli the latter reassured Galileo by stating that his opinions "were not otherwise against the Faith, since they were simply philosophical" and he offered to help him should there be the need (XIII, 393-394).[62]

The Assayer had no other responses, besides Grassi's. But Kepler treated of it in an appendix to his work against Chiaramonti, who had attacked the system of Tycho Brahe and defended the system of Ptolemy.[63] In it Kepler corrected a statement[64] by Galileo and above all he defended the character of a true third alternative between the system of Ptolemy and that of Copernicus, the character, that is, of Tycho Brahe's system. This opinion, as we know, was contrary to that of Galileo who had always considered Tycho's system to be void of physical meaning.

Galileo was stricken by these comments made against him by Kepler and he considered that appendix to be a "most weak piece" and he added:

> It is true that I understand very little of the appendix, I do not know whether thanks to my little capacity or rather to the extravagant style of the author of whom I think that, since he was not able to defend his Tycho from my imputations, he has put himself to writing what others cannot understand, perhaps not even he himself. (XIII, 310-302).[65]

As we see, Galileo, who had never entertained a great sympathy for Kepler and even less so for his style, by this time was distancing himself from the great German astronomer, even though Kepler had supported him with a disinterested sincerity in the most delicate moments at the time of his astronomical discoveries. Without a doubt here, as in other cases, Galileo's self esteem, as well as his fiery temperament, prevented him from showing equanimity.[66]

NOTES

[1] Bellarmine himself in August 1590 had seen the first volume of his very famous work the *De Controversiis* put on the Index by Pope Sixtus V who found his theory on the temporal power of the Popes to be insufficiently positive. (Bellarmine had maintained that the Pope did not have temporal sovereignty over the whole world and that the temporal authority of individual sovereigns came from God not through the Popes but through the consent of the governed [*De controversiis*, I, III, 5]). Fortunately for Bellarmine Sixtus V died before the completion of the new edition of the Index of prohibited books. His successor, Urban VII, had sufficient time, even in his very short pontificate of twelve days, to have the publication suspended and to remove the prohibition of Bellarmine's work. See Blackwell 1991, 30.

[2] It was the opinion of many of Galileo's contemporaries that the theory of Copernicus had not been condemned, nor that it was

condemnable as a mathematical theory. Such, for example, was the opinion of the Theatine Father from Naples, Placido Mirto, about whom Castelli speaks to Galileo in a letter of May 1617 (XII, 316).

[3] With respect to this see Drake 1978, 259-260.

[4] For an explanation of the problem given by Galileo himself see V, 419-425: "A Proposal on Longitude". According to Favaro it would have been sent to the Spanish government in 1613 at the time of the first proposal; but Drake 1978, 257 thinks that it goes back to a time after that, i.e., to 1616. Peiresc had also had since September 1611 the idea of using the satellites of Jupiter for the same purpose. But instead of the eclipses, he based his method on the relative configuration of the satellites at a given moment. It was too imprecise, however, and his attempt failed. See Humbert 1948, 383-384, which is quoted by Paschini 1965, 381, note 39. Galileo, in fact, proposed a method in which account was taken both of the relative configurations and of the eclipses and promised a precision of the order of "half a minute of an hour" in the determination of the position of a ship (equivalent, as he himself explained, to an error of four miles in the ship's position). See the *Relazione Generale*, sent by Galileo to Spain at the end of 1616 (V, 423-425). Galileo had also sought to assure precise observation on shipboard. But this always remained as one of the principal problems.

[5] Drake thinks that Galileo probably was hoping that the Archduke would take the initiative of an anonymous publication of that writing of Galileo's, as Welser had done with Scheiner's letters on the sunspots, and for that reason he would at the same time have sent to Leopold of Austria a copy of his *Sunspot Letters*. See Drake 1978, 262.

[6] Even scholars who had before sympathized with Copernicus, saw themselves obliged to retreat to the traditional positions, in so far as it was possible after the astronomical discoveries of the last years. Paschini 1965, 356-366. Among these scholars Paschini cites Giuseppe Biancani (1566-1624). But Biancani's case must be completely reexamined in the light of new documents from the Jesuit Roman Archives, *Fondo Gesuitico*, recently published by Baldini 1984 and 1992. See also Blackwell 1991, 148-153. Based upon these documents, Biancani does not appear as an adversary of Galileo (though at times he criticized some of his calculations), but rather as an admirer. And if after the Decree of 1616 he was obliged (in his work *Sphaera mundi, seu cosmographia*, Bologna 1620) to deny Copernicanism, he did so reluctantly as is shown by these words:

> But that this opinion [heliocentrism] is false and should be rejected (*even though it is established by better proofs and arguments*) has nevertheless become much more certain in

our day when it has been condemned by the authority of
the Church as contrary to Sacred Scripture. (Book IV,
Chapter 2, 37; trans. by Blackwell 1991, 153; italics by
Fantoli).

This dilemma and the intellectual tension of the Jesuit scientists when
faced with the instructions to follow Aristotelianism and above all with
the Decree of 1616 is clearly reflected also in Grienberger's judgement
on the work of Biancani:

It appears to me that he has not employed his talents
sufficiently in writing the *Cosmographia*. But I can
willingly excuse him on this point because his hands like
ours have thus far been tied. So he has treated many
points in an inappropriate way since he is not allowed to
say freely what the matter requires. (Baldini 1992, 236).

[7] This third comet, observed for the first time on 27 November,
had become visible in all of its exceptional grandeur (about 30 degrees
in length) towards the middle of December and it disappeared in the
following January 1619. It was the object of many writings, among
which was that of a disciple of Scheiner, J. B. Cysat. Paschini 1965,
395, Note 1.

[8] Grassi was born at Savona in 1583 and at the age of 18 entered
the Society of Jesus. Later on he went to Rome, where he held the
chair of mathematics at the Roman College (in the place of
Grienberger) between 1617 and 1624 (that is, precisely at the time of
his controversy with Galileo) and then again from the end of 1626 to
1628 or to 1632 (precise data are lacking for this last period). In the
intervening two year period (1624-1626), he was Rector of the College
in Siena. Grassi is also known as the designer of the great *Chiesa di
Sant'Ignazio* (Church of Saint Ignatius), which was erected within the
perimeter of the Roman College. He died in Rome in 1654. On the
basis of documents found recently in the archives of the old Holy Office
we know that Grassi had in 1616, together with Grienberger, given a
favorable opinion as to the publication, provided some corrections were
made, of the *De Revolutionibus*. Note 80 of Chapter 3.

[9] Grassi based his argument on the small parallax for the comets
relative to the lunar parallax and on the "confirmation" deduced from
an assertion that they were, compared to the Moon, less magnified by
a telescope. In that regard he had added:

I know that this argument is of little significance to some, but perhaps they have given little consideration to the principles of optics, from which one deduces the very great power of that argument for convincing us about the matter we are dealing with. (VI, 333).

As we shall see, Galileo was rather taken back by this phrase which he took as an insinuation that he was ignorant in optics. Later on Grassi stated that he had not alluded to Galileo but only to those who refused to give credit to the results obtained with the telescope which they considered to be the result of pure optical illusions. And there is no reason to doubt his sincerity.

[10] The Duke Virginio Cesarini, the nephew of Federico Cesi, was born at Rome in 1596. He had come to know Galileo during the latter's stay in Rome in 1615-1616 and had been elected a member of the *Accademia dei Lincei* in 1618 when he was only 22. He died before his 30th birthday in 1624. For some interesting particulars on his intellectual training see Redondi 1987, 90 ff. In a letter to Galileo of December 1618 Cesarini spoke of the appearance of the third comet which he himself had observed. And he added:

I noted that which I sent to Your Lordship, written on the enclosed paper and (not trusting in my little experience) I today have conferred with the mathematicians of the Jesuit Fathers who have done me the favor to be here with me and I send you the said writing confirmed by their opinion. (XII, 422-423).

This writing, which has been lost, is certainly by Cesarini as proven by the words quoted here, and it is not, therefore, a manuscript copy of the *Disputatio* of Grassi, as Drake 1978, 264 is inclined to believe.

[11] See also Bucciantini 1995, 151-153. After the unpublished text quoted by Bucciantini, which corresponds to Chapter X of the *Treatise*, Ingoli furnishes the "proof" of his statements. He bases this on Brahe's objections to the Copernican system drawn from the absence of a variation in the parallax of the comet (a variation which should have been visible if the Earth were moving about the Sun).

[12] Mario Guiducci was born at Florence in 1585. After having been a student of the Jesuits at the Roman College, he received his law degree at the University of Pisa. In 1618, before the appearance of the *Discourse on the Comets*, he had worked together with Nicola Arrighetti as an assistant of Galileo's and transcribed the notes edited by Galileo during his time at Padua. This seems to imply that Guiducci

lacked neither interest nor a certain knowledge of the scientific issues. Otherwise Galileo would not have considered entrusting to him the responsibility of being his spokesman.

[13] This is confirmed by the letter whereby Galileo informed the secretary of state Picchena that the *Discourse* was in print and that he would send him a copy and one to the Grand Duke (letter of May 1619: XII, 457). Galileo does not even mention Guiducci and takes upon himself the role of author. Copies were also sent by Galileo to many friends and influential persons among whom Cardinals Orsini and Maffeo Barberini. In my review of the contents of the *Discourse* I will use the name of Guiducci, but it should almost always be taken as "Galileo".

[14] A serious contradiction remains in Guiducci's arguments on parallax. If it was true that parallax could not be applied to show that the comets were a *sopralunar* phenomenon, unless one had first proven that the comets were true material bodies, how could Guiducci then propose his hypothesis (further on in the text) whereby on the one hand one denied such a nature of material body for the comets, but it was taken for granted that their optical appearance happened *beyond the moon* as proven (against the Aristotelian theory of the comets as "sublunar fires") "*from the smallness of the parallax observed with utmost care by so many excellent astronomers*" (VI, 63, italics by Fantoli). It is truly strange that Galileo was not aware of this contradiction which Grassi naturally did not fail to make evident in his reply (the *Libra*) which I will discuss later on (VI, 118). An objection of this kind came also from his old disciple from Padua, Giovanni Remo (XII, 485).

[15] With respect to the argument based on the lack of magnification Guiducci said:

> . . . I truly had no intention to say anything since it appeared to me most vain and false and I did not think that it would have found assent except among people of such little authority that it mattered little to take it into consideration. But having most recently seen, at the discourse held at the Roman College on this subject, how such great esteem is given to these reasonings by those mathematicians, that not only do they applaud them but they blame whoever disdains those reasonings as being of little expertise in the principles of perspective and of the effects understood and observed by them in the telescope through long experiences and excellent demonstrations; it has made me somewhat pensive and wavering over those

considerations through which I was persuaded by our Academician [Galileo] of the weakness of such a foundation; that Academician of ours, I say, who, if not the only one, was at least the one who more resolutely and publicly than any other has contradicted that discourse and has considered it to be of no value, much before the above named work was seen. (VI, 73-74).

The phrase, "they blame whoever disdains those reasonings as being of little expertise in the principles of perspective", indicates that Galileo had interpreted the words of Grassi quoted in Note 9 as directed at him. And his resentment had driven him to use for the Jesuits of the Roman College expressions which could not help but hurt them deeply for they sensed that they were being implicated as a group in the affair and were practically being accused of incompetency in the matters discussed. There is no doubt that in this case Galileo's excessive susceptibility not only made him see an allusion where there was none but caused him to forget, together with his equanimity, also his prudence. The responsibility for having begun this dispute with the Jesuits is, therefore, entirely his doing and that of his friends.

[16] VI, 51-52. Even though in this section at the beginning of the *Discourse* Guiducci criticizes the planetary explanation of the comets according to the "Pythagoreans and the Stoics", the criticism is also directed (even especially so) towards the theory of Tycho Brahe and of Grassi who had also favored the opinion that the comets had a planetary character. The point of departure for Guiducci's argument is the fact that the last of the three comets (the one better observed because it was the brightest) was already bright at its first apparition with very little increase occurring in the first phase of the observations and afterwards it had rapidly diminished in brightness until it finally disappeared. How was it possible, Guiducci asked himself, to explain such changes of the comet in such a short period of "forty days" and also take account "of the space covered, in that short time, in our hemisphere" as well as explain the fact that the circular orbit implied its periodic return? There were only two possible answers. The first was to attribute to the comet a circular orbit of immense dimensions and so accommodate the supposition that the comet had appeared antecedently in 1577 (no other comet of equal magnitude had been observed in the intervening time). But that implied two absurdities: 1) the circular orbit of the comet had to be immense; 2) relative to such a length for the total orbit, the piece covered in "forty days" of observations was minimal. How was one to explain then the enormous

variation of the dimensions of the comet in such a short time? As to the second possible answer, Guiducci wrote:

> And if to avoid such an absurdity somebody else would want to say that during these days it has gone through enough degrees of its orbit as are sufficient for its apparent change with respect to the firmament, you will run into another difficulty which would be that its return should in this case occur after a few months; and that does not happen. (VI, 52).

Against such arguments there was only one way out: that of supposing that the comet was a transitory celestial phenomenon. Such, indeed, had been the idea of Tycho Brahe; and Grassi had followed him in this (*Disputatio Astronomica*: VI, 32, line 22; VI, 33, lines 16 and 17). Later on Guiducci came back to this point and commented:

> To say with Tycho that [comets] are imperfect stars and almost jokes of nature and playthings of the true stars, but that, short-lived as they may be, they possess, nonetheless, a certain kind of celestial character and habits and that such an almost divine condition is sufficient [to explain their appearances]; this [explanation] has much more of poetic pleasantry than of philosophical solidity and seriousness, so that it does not merit any consideration, because nature does not delight in poems. (VI, 87-88).

It seems to me that all of these arguments of Galileo against the thesis of the planetary nature of the comets *according to Tycho Brahe and Grassi* are relevant. As always happens, it is naturally easier to criticize a thesis of an adversary than to put forth a more convincing one. And that holds also for the proposal which is generally considered the "thesis" of Galileo. But, in fact, Galileo will always protest that he wished only in a hesitant manner to put forth an hypothesis. And without a doubt his only intent was to show that the explanation of Tycho Brahe and that of Grassi could not be upheld, a fact which is confirmed (it is hardly necessary to mention it) by modern theories on the comets.

[17] Despite the fact that the *Discourse* shows most lucidly that the position of Galileo on the origin of the comets cannot be assimilated in any way to that of Aristotle, many Galilean scholars continue to assert the contrary. Thus, for example, does Shea: "The position he maintained - in the name of progress - was that of decadent Aristotelianism" (Shea 1972, 85). "His refusal to consider comets as real bodies cast him in the role of a conservative Aristotelian" (Shea 1972,

87). Shea had asserted in a previous passage from the same book that in our times one "witnesses the demythologizing of the heroes of the scientific revolution" (Shea 1972, 76) and the whole treatment in Chapter 4 of his work is clearly directed to making a contribution in that sense. I have no objection with respect to an *objective* plan to demythologize. But it does not seem that such objectivity is always present in the treatment (otherwise detailed and interesting) by Shea, as shown by the case in point, namely, the Aristotelian pretensions of the "theory" on the comets of Galileo. And it seems difficult - although I do not wish at all to take away from the scientific value of various statements of Grassi - to follow Shea when he states that "Grassi's writings prove him to be Galileo's superior in scholarship" (Shea 1972, 88). This kind of statement - without the necessary qualifications - runs the risk of giving the impression (certainly not intended by Shea) of replacing the myth of Galileo with the myth of Grassi. A totally different position, and it seems at times excessively critical as to the scientific value of Grassi's writings, is the one of Drake 1978, 268-270, 276-278.

[18] Based on our modern knowledge comets are made up of a *nucleus* with a diameter varying from some tens of meters to several tens of kilometers and they contain meteoritic material and ice (made up for the most part of water, methane, ammonia, and carbon dioxide). These "nuclei" go about the sun in hyperbolic or parabolic orbits (in the case of non-periodic comets) and elliptical orbits (in the case of periodic comets). However, even in this latter case, we are dealing with extremely elongated orbits. When these "nuclei" arrive at some hundreds of millions of kilometers from the Sun, the ice begins to sublimate due to the heat and the molecules, thus sublimated and ionized, absorb the solar radiation and in their turn become luminous, thus giving origin to the so-called "coma" (which can acquire a diameter up to 100,000 kilometers). Another part of these ions, due to the "solar wind" formed from high velocity protons and electrons, produce the so-called "tail" of the comet (in the opposite direction to the Sun) which can reach a length equal to the Earth-Sun distance. From what we have said it is obvious that the comet would be completely invisible if it were not for the phenomenon of the "coma" and of the "tail". *In this sense (and naturally only in this sense)* Galileo's hypothesis that the comets were due to the reflection of sunlight by the "vapors" located quite beyond the Moon was perhaps closer to the truth than the "poetic" imaginings of Tycho Brahe and, in his wake, those of Father Grassi. Since it is impossible to observe a comet when it is too close to the Sun, the observations of Galileo's time were limited to the final phases of approach to the Sun and above all to that phase when,

having completed their turn about the Sun, the comets progressively
get further and further from it along an almost straight-line trajectory
since the orbit has such large eccentricity. Of course, this last fact was
not known at that time. Grassi, who upheld the idea that the comet
moved on a great circle with the Earth at its center, had explained the
apparent rectilinearity of the cometary orbit as the result of the
projection, when observed from the Earth, of a motion along a great
circle (VI, 32-33). Galileo - who as we have seen, had demonstrated the
contradiction in this position - sensed encouragement to speak of a *true*
rectilinear motion of the comet constantly going away from the Earth.
It is to be noted that the attribution of this rectilinear motion to the
comet by Galileo was a confirmation that for him the comet could not
be assimilated to a true and proper "heavenly body". In fact, even for
Galileo, a heavenly body had to have a circular motion.

[19] It is interesting to note that this quotation of Seneca is the
same one which Galileo had transcribed into his notes in the
preparation of his three public lectures on the *nova* of 1604. Even the
idea of "straight motion" in the comets movement away from the Earth
was similar to the one aired for the *nova* (Chapter 1).

[20] There was also the fact (certainly known also to Galileo) that
Tycho Brahe had been led to reject Copernicanism also because the
comets did not seem to show the phenomena of "being stationary" and
of "retrograde motion", as the planets did. Tycho did not know that
that was due to the fact that the comets were observed only in the
sections of their orbits which were nearer to the Sun and the Earth
where "stationary points" and "retrogressions" do not appear any longer
(Bortle 1981). Of course, Galileo did not know this either. And so to
deny, as he did, that the comets were true heavenly bodies, similar in
some way to the planets, eliminated at its roots the difficulty of Tycho
Brahe against the Copernican system.

[21] In Note 15 we have already seen a most obvious example of
such words (dictated, as I have already pointed out, by an unjustified
resentment). See also VI, 93, at the beginning of the page.

[22] Ciampoli had written:

> As you ask for my frank opinion, I willingly tell you
> something which has not resulted in pleasing anyone here,
> namely that you have wanted to have at it with the
> Roman College where they have publicly professed to honor
> Your Lordship so much. The Jesuits consider themselves
> much offended and are preparing a reply; and though on
> this matter I know and recognize the soundness of your
> conclusions, still I am sorry that among them [the Jesuits]

the benevolence and applause they used to have for your
name have been so greatly diminished. (XII, 466).

A witness to the state of mind of the Jesuits of the Roman College
after the *Discourse* is given in the draft of a letter (not dated but of
July 1619) written by Father Grienberger to a certain Ricardo de Burgo
in Florence and preserved in the Archives of the Pontifical Gregorian
University (Codex 530, II, folio 48r). De Burgo had submitted to
Grienberger an objection he had from geometry to a demonstration
given by Galileo in his *Discourse on Floating Objects* (the one which is
found in IV, 76). Before proposing an answer Grienberger wrote:

> As to the affairs of Galileo, I would prefer not to get mixed
> up in them after he has behaved so badly with the
> mathematicians of the Roman College [Grienberger writes
> in his Latin text: "the Mathematics of the Roman College"]
> by whom he was treated, in fact, more than once not less
> well than with sincerity. If even one mention of him had
> been made in the *Disputatio Romana* or if he had been
> refuted in any way, I would be less resentful towards him
> (*minus ei succenserem*). But since no thought at all was
> given to him and the whole question turned on the fact
> that the comets were found much higher than common
> opinion maintained and use was made here of an
> hypothesis which up to now it had been licit to admit, I
> cannot marvel enough at how it could have leapt into
> Galileo's mind (*quid in mentem venerit Galileo*) to consider
> himself under attack, and how he has preferred to suspect
> temerariously, rather than excuse if perhaps some
> statement less in conformity or even contrary to his
> opinions had been made. It has, therefore, been enough for
> me to give a reading to his academic discourse. And it has
> been enough for me to know once for all that which he
> feels in our regard. As to a reply, I have not even begun
> thus far to think upon it, especially since I know that
> there are very few to whom this attempt (*conatus*) of
> Galileo does not appear unsatisfactory. Here many think
> that a response is required and they are already intent
> upon doing it. I do not oppose their ideas, as long as they
> let me follow mine.

As we see, this old friend and admirer of Galileo, who had remained
such even after 1616 (XII, 285) was now disturbed and resentful. But
he did not have the polemical temperament of Grassi and was more

impartial than him; so he preferred to keep quiet and disassociate himself from the initiatives of some of his Jesuit confreres. The Latin text of this letter of Grienberger to de Burgo has been published with explanatory notes in Baldini 1992, 194-195 and 208-209. I refer the reader to this very valuable study for other particulars on this correspondence, as also for an attempt to identify the individual who was involved in this correspondence with Grienberger (Baldini 1992, 186-188).

[23] See XII, 469. From the summary which Remo made for him of the *Discourse*, Kepler came to know that Galileo refuted the Aristotelians with new arguments and that he also criticized the "fictitious Apelle". Later on, however, Kepler judged that Galileo was going against his own theory on the origin of the comets. In fact, according to Kepler the comets originated in local occasional condensations, in the form of clouds, from the "ethereal" breeze which filled the heavenly world. These clouds of ethereal air, opaque to sunlight, receive an impulse from sunrays which illuminate them and cause them to move with a rectilinear motion according to their own direction, thus giving birth to the typical form of the comets. But this same impulse tends to disperse the material of the comet and, therefore, it little by little disappears.

[24] Guiducci spoke in the *Discourse*

> of the attempt at usurping praise made by those, who desired to make themselves inventors of his [Galileo's] other ideas and feigned that they were Apelle, when with badly colored and worse lined designs they have given clearly to understand that in painting they are not comparable to even the masters of mediocre value. (VI, 47-48).

The autograph copy in Galileo's handwriting was no less severe (VI, 47). Indeed, it is not surprising that Scheiner was resentful! Thus Galileo put himself at the same time in bad relationships with two Jesuits. Scheiner, much more so than Grassi, will be his bitter enemy from this moment on. Drake even puts forth the hypothesis that Scheiner had perhaps prepared a first response to Galileo (in expectation of the more massive *Rosa Ursina*, which will be published in 1630) and that Grassi would have been forced to insert it unwillingly in the *Libra* that which would explain the sharpness of many passages in this book. But it does not seem that Grassi with his punctilious and independent temperament would have easily accepted pressures in that sense from Scheiner or other Jesuits. Neither Scheiner nor others would have been able to strengthen their case with respect to Father

Grassi by relying upon Father General Vitelleschi (successor to Acquaviva), who on the contrary had recommended on that occasion - in case Grassi would intend to respond - that such a response would be "well considered and well founded and that it be characterized by religious modesty". (Letter of Vitelleschi to the Rector at Florence, where Grassi was at that moment, 9 August 1619; Roman Archives of the Society of Jesus). One might ask how much Grassi had heeded this recommendation, at least as far as "religious modesty" is concerned.

[25] Thus Grassi declared clearly that the true author of the *Discourse* was Galileo and he based his declaration on the statements of the latter to his Roman friends (whom Grassi had obviously come to know) and on the very words of Guiducci in the *Discourse*, which Grassi did not quote correctly, giving them the sense of a dependence "almost under dictation" (VI, 114).

[26] According to Drake these words could be a confirmation that the "biting jokes" of the *Libra* were not the workmanship of Grassi but of Scheiner.

[27] Shea 1972, 79-81 states that, even if Galileo in the *Discourse* had had the upper hand in refuting the statement of Grassi that the telescope magnifies nearby objects more than distant ones, his refutation (whereby Galileo maintained that the telescope allows one to measure the angular size of the stars) does not imply that he had "a clear understanding of the properties of lenses" (Shea 1972, 80). Without a doubt in the field of optics Kepler (Grassi shows that he had read him attentively) had already formulated an exact theory of lenses and of vision in his book, *Ad Vitellionem Paralipomena* (1604) to which he makes reference in his *Dissertatio cum Sidereo Nuncio*. Later on in the *Epitome Astronomiae Copernicanae* (1618), published a little before the beginning of the debate on the comets, he relies upon experience to deny that the telescope would detect a real angular size of the stars. He wrote:

> The expert artisans deny that with the telescope it is possible to note [in the stars] any extension at all in the form of round bodies. Rather, the more perfect the instrument, so much more do the fixed stars appear as mere points, from which there emerge luminous rays which spread out like a mane.

See Casanovas 1985, especially 69-71. However, Galileo had not been able to read the *Epitome* before the *Discourse* came out. Kepler had not spontaneously sent him a copy. Because the *Epitome* could not be found in Florence due to its prohibition by the Congregation of the Index (28 February 1619), Galileo had requested a copy from the Archduke

Leopold of Austria and, using Giovanni Remo as an intermediary (Remo's letter to Kepler of July 1619, cited in Note 23 above), Leopold had passed on the request to Kepler. Kepler sent the requested copy to Remo (Kepler's letter to Remo cited in Bucciantini 1995, 139, Note 66) and a few weeks later Remo assured Kepler that he would sent it as soon as possible to Galileo (XII, 481). Even assuming that the delivery of the book came to a happy conclusion, Galileo did not receive it until more than a year after the publication of the *Discourse*.

[28] See the ostentatious show of quotations of ancient and modern authors in the *Libra* (*Examen Tertium, Secunda Propositio*: VI, 160-169) with the respective comments of Galileo. In particular for the Babylonians and the eggs, VI, 165; for the cannon balls and gunshot, VI, 166. Galileo will take up again and expand upon his comment on the heated eggs with the sling in a famous passage of *The Assayer* (VI, 340).

[29] For some examples of such distortions of Galileo's thought, Drake 1978, 277-278. Drake's judgement on the *Libra* is very severe. Instead, that of Shea, as I have noted, is completely the opposite (Shea 1972, 83 ff.).

[30] In the *Discourse* Guiducci had accused Sarsi of slavishly following Tycho Brahe. In the *Libra* Sarsi stated that he had followed him only with respect to the measures of parallax. And he added:

> Let it be granted that my master followed Tycho. Is this such a crime? Whom instead should he follow? Ptolemy? whose followers' throats are threatened by the out-thrust sword of Mars now made closer. Copernicus? But he who is pious will rather call everyone away from him and will spurn and reject his recently condemned hypothesis. Therefore, Tycho remains as the only one whom we may approve of as our leader among the unknown courses of the stars (VI, 116; trans. by Shea 1972, 84).

Shea himself could not keep from noting in this respect:

> This is a good example of how the Decree of 1616 proscribing the heliocentric theory inhibited and vitiated scientific discussion. It was too convenient a tool not to be used, especially against an adversary who had taken it upon himself to launch an unwarranted attack. Grassi's reference to the condemnation of Copernicus set an unfortunate precedent that was only too willingly followed by lesser minds. It is particularly regrettable in view of the

fact that his criticism of Galileo is on the whole penetrating and to the point. (Shea 1972, 84).

On the sense of the remark of Grassi on Ptolemy and Mars, See once again Shea 1972, 106, Note 16.

[31] The National Edition gives, together with the text of Grassi, also the annotations of Galileo on the copy of this work which he possessed. By means of these one sees how Galileo passed little by little from a good-natured irony to open anger, giving to Grassi titles like: "oxen", "lousy buffalo" and "elephantine".

[32] Doubtlessly the silence of the Jesuits at the moment of the Copernican controversy of 1615-1616 deeply displeased Galileo who was not able to evaluate objectively the causes. His friends, among whom there were not lacking impassioned adversaries of the Jesuits, such as Sagredo and Cingoli, had contributed further to ill disposing Galileo towards those whom he had so much esteemed in the past. But it does not seem that at the time of the *Discourse* Galileo had (as he faced the attempt at compromise represented by the *Disputatio* of Grassi) decided to "open a sharp and general polemic against the kind of scientific reasoning used by the professors of the Collegio Romano" (Geymonat 1965, 99). Despite his growing aversion for the way of thinking of those professors, which comes out here and there in the *Discourse,* it does not appear that Galileo then had the intention of beginning an open battle against the Jesuits. His surprise at the resentful and biting answer of Grassi and his hesitation as to what to do, are the most evident proof of this.

[33] In particular this was the opinion of Stelluti (XIII, 20-21). But Ciampoli, Cesarini and Cesi also thought the same. Cesi had even had the idea of directing Galileo's response to Father Grienberger (a sign that Grienberger, despite his first reaction of shock and resentment upon reading the *Discourse,* had remained substantially objective and, in so far as it was possible, independent as to the initiatives of the other Jesuits). But this idea of Cesi was immediately put aside by the other Roman friends (as Ciampoli wrote to Galileo in July) "so as not to put that poor Father in difficulties, as we surely know from example will come about" (XIII, 44). What was Ciampoli alluding to here? Perhaps to the removal of Father Guldin from Rome which happened in 1617. Among the Jesuits Guldin had been one of the most fervent admirers of Galileo and, even more than Grienberger, he had remained so even after the decree of 1616 (XII, 285). It appears that this had created problems between him and other Jesuits of the Roman College so that *pro bono pacis* he was advised (by Grienberger himself) to stay at least for the moment far from Rome. This is clear from a letter of

November 1617 addressed by Guldin from Graz to Grienberger and preserved in the Archives of the Pontifical Gregorian University (Codex 534, folio 45r).

[34] This letter of Guiducci is found in VI, 181-196. Guiducci himself says that the "Reverend Mathematician of the Roman College" was Grassi and he notes that Grassi "was at that time the only professor of Mathematics in the said College, and that only he among the fathers wrote on the comets" (VI, 187). As we know there were other Jesuit mathematicians at the Roman College at the time of the *Disputatio*, among them Grienberger. But at that time Grassi was the only titular professor of mathematics or "first mathematician" [*primo matematico*]. It appears that Galileo had no part in the drafting of that letter, except for some experiments which are described therein. But Guiducci certainly must have consulted him before writing it and publishing it.

[35] In that period Galileo had repeated sicknesses and he was taken up, at least in part, by other tasks even literary ones (as, for example, the compilation of notes for a comparison of Ludovico Ariosto and Torquato Tasso, which went all in favor of the former).

[36] See Cesi's letter of 2 December 1621 in which he congratulates Galileo on having completed his work (XIII, 80).

[37] Galileo, in responding to the *Libra* (a normal scale or "steelyard") of Sarsi, had entitled his work *The Assayer* (a precision scale used by goldsmiths), and he explained the meaning of this title right at the beginning:

> This [work] I have wanted to entitle with the name ASSAYER, thus keeping myself within the same metaphor taken up by Sarsi. But because it seemed to me that, in weighing the opinions of Mr. Guiducci, he has made use of a steelyard which is a little too large, I have desired to make use of an assayer's scale, which is so exact that it responds to less than a sixtieth of a grain; and employing every possible diligence with this, not neglecting any proposition produced by that one, I will produce the assays of all of them. (VI,220).

[38] Cesarini had been appointed in March 1621 as the Privy Chamberlain of the new Pope Gregory XV and Ciampoli the Secretary of the Briefs to the Princes. And this position of power at the service of the "masters" (*padroni*) led Cesarini to be very optimistic.

[39] In the same letter Cesarini informed Galileo that at Rome the sale and distribution of the *Apologia pro Galileo* was prohibited. This

had been composed, as I have already said, by Tommaso Campanella in 1616 (probably a little before the decision of the Holy Office) and it was printed in 1622 at Frankfurt. It had just arrived in Rome. Cesarini also added that in the inaugural lectures of the new academic year, held at the Roman College, the Jesuit professors had spoken against

> the finders of novelties in the sciences and with long orations they sought to convince the students that there was no truth outside of Aristotle, not without blame and derision from anyone who dared to rise up against the servile yoke of authority. (XIII, 107).

[40] It is Cesarini who refers this testimony to Galileo and also tells him that Father Riccardi had expressed the desire to make Galileo's acquaintance personally (XIII, 109). Thus this Dominican entered into the life of Galileo. As we shall see, he will have an important role to play some ten years later in the printing of the *Dialogue*. Redondi (1987, 46) speaks of the "ecclesiastical authorization" given by Riccardi. That is not an exact statement. Authorization (the final *Imprimatur*) could only be given by the Master of the Sacred Palace, who at that time was the Dominican Nicolò Ridolfi (Redondi 1987, 101) or his associate (which is what happened, in fact, in this case: VI, 200). Riccardi only spoke his theological opinion, that is, a conditional *Imprimatur* (*imprimatur si videbitur Reverendissimo P. Magistro Sacri Palatii Apostolici*; let it be printed if it seems opportune to the Most Reverend Father Master of the Sacred Palace). And that allowed Riccardi to add his quite positive and personal comments, without there be anything special about it.

[41] Maffeo Barberini was born in Florence in 1568. After completing his higher studies in Rome at the Roman College he obtained his laurea in jurisprudence at Pisa in 1588. He took up a career in the Church and he very soon was assigned to important posts, culminating in that of Nuncio to Paris (1604). He was named cardinal in 1606 by Paul V.

[42] The original text of *The Assayer* is found in Volume VI of the National Edition, 199-372. A partial English translation is given by Drake 1957, 229-286.

[43] Simon Mayr (1570-1624), of whom I have spoken in Chapter 1, had been at Prague to study astronomy with Tycho Brahe, but Brahe died soon afterward (1601). Then he had enrolled in the faculty of medicine at Padua. In his work, *Mundus Jovialis* (1614), he had argued with Galileo about the priority of the discovery of the satellites of Jupiter, which he had rebaptized with the name, *Sidera Brandenburgier*, in honor of the Margrave of Ausbach-Brandenburg, at

whose court Mayr was mathematician. But it seems that this assertion of Mayr, made four years after the publication of the *Starry Message*, contains little truth. See Drake 1978, 154 and 236.

[44] Galileo, of course, does not say a word about the admonition of Bellarmine who was, as we know, the real reason for his silence.

[45] The expression is from Geymonat 1965, 101.

[46] So states Geymonat 1965, 101. Of course, Geymonat evaluates quite differently the value of the book on the level of the philosophy of science. But it still seems to me that his judgment, even on the plane of astronomy alone, is too severe. Obviously Galileo did not have today's knowledge of the nature and motion of the comets and so he spoke of "exhalations" and "vapors". By putting forth the hypothesis of a terrestrial origin for them he wished to emphasize that one could very well use notions from terrestrial physics to explain "heavenly" phenomena and he denied that there was any distinction between terrestrial and heavenly material (a distinction which remained in the theories of Tycho Brahe, of Grassi, and even of Kepler). On the other hand, the idea that the brilliance of the comets was due to an interaction between those "vapors" and sunlight was, I repeat once again, in a certain sense a more modern explanation than the one proposed by Tycho Brahe and by Grassi. In addition see de Santillana 1960, 306.

[47] Geymonat 1965, 101.

[48] Galileo himself states this (VI, 220).

[49] Geymonat writes:

> He [Galileo] does indeed declare decidedly that only mathematics can guarantee correct logical form in our reasoning, but he does not appear to be concerned in any way with the metaphysical hypothesis here assumed. In the end, his appeal to mathematics rests upon a methodological rule; the philosophical defense of this rule does not interest him, but is left in the distant depths of the debate. The desire to read more than this into *The Assayer* - to see there a retrogression to mathematical Platonism - may hide from us the living heart of the work. (Geymonat 1965, 110).

It seems, however, to me that Geymonat underestimates too much the philosophical element present in *The Assayer*. I judge that there is in this work an *implicit philosophy* (which is not Platonic): a natural philosophy (or better, the philosophy *ut sic* championed by Galileo). One must not forget, I repeat, that Galileo always wished to be considered first a philosopher and then a mathematician.

[50] Aristotle, *De Coelo*, II, 7.

[51] With this claim for the correctness of the Aristotelian principle Grassi (who as we know followed Tycho Brahe and not Aristotle as to the location of the comets) had wanted to "prove" only that Galileo's criticism of Aristotle was in error on this point. Of course, this "proven" error of Galileo's was intended already by itself to discredit the whole explanation given by Galileo on the origin of the comets.

[52] Galileo is certainly not the author of this distinction. See comments on these matters by Drake 1978, 285.

[53] Geymonat 1965, 105.

[54] On Galileo's mechanistic and atomistic view of the world see Dijksterhuis 1961, 333-359 and Shea 1972, 103-106. Redondi 1987, 9-27 treats at length the atomism of Galileo with a view to the central thesis of his book, which I will have the opportunity to speak about later on.

[55] As we know Grassi had made his own, at least in general, the thesis of Tycho Brahe, as he admitted that it was the only one left to him since, Ptolemy's system (Grassi was not able to name Aristotle) could not be upheld and that of Copernicus, after the Decree of 1616, was unacceptable (note 30 above). In *The Assayer* Galileo answers him:

> I do not see for what reason Tycho is chosen and placed before Ptolemy and Nicolò Copernico from the two of whom we have the systems of the world complete and constructed with the most excellent craftsmanship and brought to an end; something which I do not see that Tycho has done, if already it is not enough for Sarsi to have denied the other two and promised another but then never carried out. Not having convinced the other two of falsity, I would like someone to recognize it in Tycho's case . . . As to the Copernican hypothesis if for the benefit of us Catholics by the most sovereign wisdom we were not delivered from error and our blindness illuminated, I do not believe that such a favor and benefit could be obtained from the reasons and the experiments provided by Tycho. Since, therefore, the two systems are certainly false and that of Tycho null, Sarsi should not have it out with me if with Seneca I wish the true constitution of the universe. (VI, 232-233).

From this passage the fundamental motive why Galileo had entered with the *Discourse* into the debate on the comets becomes clear. It was a matter of "destroying" the attempt to use the system of Tycho as a way out of the *impasse* created by denying the other two systems. With all of his severity, at times unjust, with respect to Tycho Brahe, Galileo was substantially correct: the system of Tycho was a compromise solution, a hybrid system that was completely unsatisfactory from the point of view of a *physical* explanation of the world. But it was this physical explanation which had to be put forward and not a new purely mathematical theory. If, on the other hand, Grassi distanced himself from Tycho, as to the center of motion of the comets, he was invited to give *his* system of the world, a thing which the Jesuit had been very careful not to do.

[56] See the letters to Galileo of T. Rinuccini in December 1623 (XIII, 154) and of Guiducci two weeks later (XIII, 161). According to Rinuccini, Grassi had praised Galileo "saying that in his writing [*The Assayer*] there was much that was good, but that, considering everything, he wanted to reply".

[57] It seems to me that it would be incorrect to see for sure in these statements of Grassi a two-faced attitude. Grassi was not a crafty and insincere person as certain biographies of Galileo have attempted to depict him. In the Historical Archives of the Society of Jesus in Rome (Med. 50, folio 132) there is preserved a judgement on him (perhaps by the superior of the college at Savona, where Grassi was at that time, 1632-1633). It is quite positive. Grassi is considered "*aptus ad gubernandum*" (fit to be a superior). And there is the additional remark: "great progress in areas of speculation, especially in mathematics; a rather melancholy temperament (*complexio valde melancholica*)". This melancholy, which is the only negative note in the general evaluation of him, must have made Grassi insecure and at the same time rather sensitive (from a whole other series of documents we know that he suffered from ill health during most of his life). That may have favored certain contradictions that are noticed in his attitudes. These contradictions were exacerbated by the difficult psychological position in which the Jesuit mathematicians found themselves at that time, since they were forced to steer a middle course between the results of their studies and the proscriptions of their General Superior and - higher up the ladder - of the Church.

[58] On 4 January 1625 Guiducci wrote to Galileo with respect to the delay in Grassi's response: "If I am not mistaken it seems that Sarsi has some difficulty from his own people as to printing the response to *The Assayer*" (XIII, 247). And seven days later he clarified: "The work of Sarsi seems to be frozen and I begin to wonder about some hitch or obstacle by the General" (XIII, 249).

[59] This is confirmed by a letter sent by the Father General Vitelleschi to Father Grassi, who was at that time in Siena, as rector of the Jesuit college (1625-1626). The letter is dated 26 July 1626 (The

Historical Archives of the Society of Jesus in Rome, Rom. 19, f. 247).
Vitelleschi said:

> I would have hoped that your Reverence had had complete
> satisfaction as to the printing of your *apologia*, which is
> also being looked after by Father Arnulfo [a French Jesuit
> in Paris], and I am extremely unhappy that it has come
> out badly, as Your Reverence reports. I believe that it is
> not due to lack of diligence on the part of the Fathers, but
> to the Printers to whom the author's presence usually
> creates a sense of application, etc. With all that we will not
> omit sending our advice. But I am afraid that it will be in
> vain, since I fear that the advice will arrive when the
> printing is finished and it will be necessary to seek
> patiently a remedy elsewhere.

As we can see, far from blocking the printing of Grassi's book, the
Father General Vitelleschi sought to bring it about that the job would
be done without too much delay.

[60] This work of Grassi with Galileo's annotations is found in VI,
375-500. The *Ratio* was dedicated to Cardinal Francesco Boncompagni.
In the dedication Grassi had expressed the wish that "*litibus rite
compositis, inutilium altercationum fax omnis, nisi per alios steterit,
restinguatur*" ("once, as should be, the disputes are quieted, may every
fire of useless arguments be quenched, unless others are intent on
keeping them alive") and he concluded "*Discordes animos compone,
hasque opprime flammas*" ("put to rest the feelings of discord and put
out these flames"). Galileo added to this two lines of comment: "Signs
of peace are seen on one's face, but on the inside one's heart seeks
revenge and looks for nothing else" (VI, 377). These and other
annotations by Galileo indicate how deep a chasm had grown by now
between him and his old friends and admirers of the Roman College.

[61] Shea, whom we know to be in general quite well disposed to
Grassi, observes here: "This argument was unfair, not only because it
set up a philosophical interpretation as a doctrine of faith, but because
it carried the debate on grounds Galileo was not allowed to tread"
(Shea 1972, 103).

[62] Redondi (1987) in his book, *Galileo Heretic*, already quoted by
me and of which I will speak later on, makes this passage the point of
departure for the thesis he upholds there. Costabel 1987 has made this
thesis of Redondi's his own.

[63] This work of Kepler is entitled: *Hyperaspistes adversus
Scipionis Claramontis Antitychonem* and the appendix: *Spicilegium ex
trutinatore Galilaei.*

[64] Galileo had stated that the variation in the magnitude of Mars and Venus was a proof of their movement about the Sun. Kepler denied this, asserting that the true proof of Venus' motion about the Sun was found in the phenomenon of the phases.

[65] These words are contained in a letter of 17 January 1626 to Cesare Marsili. In a subsequent letter to Marsili Galileo indicated his intention to write to Kepler "both for his own and my reputation, although the answers are so easy that anyone moderately versed in these studies can see that he is completely wrong" (XIII, 315). But the answer will come only a long time afterwards in the *Dialogue* when Kepler had already been dead for two years.

[66] It would, however, be unjust to attribute to Galileo the full responsibility for this chilling of his relationship to Kepler. Ever since 1618 Kepler had already shown himself to be unjust towards Galileo by his statement (in the *Epitome Astronomiae Copernicanae*) that Simon Mayr was the first to determine the period of the satellites of Jupiter. But the figures which he showed in this regard were the same ones published by Galileo in his book, *Discourse on Floating Objects*. And Kepler never mentioned the predictions of the motions of the satellites contained in the *Sunspot Letters* (a copy of which Galileo had sent to him). Drake 1978, 275.

CHAPTER 5

THE RESUMPTION OF THE COPERNICAN PROGRAM

THE *DIALOGUE* IS PUBLISHED

1. *A new trip of Galileo to Rome and conversations with Urban VIII*

In the previous chapter I have already noted what hopes were aroused in Galileo's heart by the election to the papacy of his friend and admirer, Maffeo Barberini. And the fact that Urban VIII had given positions of trust to three of the members of the *Accademia dei Lincei*, among them two great friends of Galileo, Cesarini and Ciampoli, was another auspicious sign. It is not, therefore, strange that Galileo got the idea of travelling to Rome with the pretext of paying homage to the new Pontiff, but especially, in fact, to see whether it were not possible for him to obtain a change in the Church's attitude towards Copernicanism. This idea already appears in the letter sent by Galileo to Cesi on 9 October 1623:

> I have great need of Your Excellency's advice (in which more than in any other I trust) about carrying out my desire, and even, maybe, my obligation to come to kiss the feet of His Holiness. But I would like to do it at the correct moment and I will await from you the indication of when that might be. I am turning over in my mind things of considerable importance for the learned world which, if they are not carried out in this marvelous combination of circumstances, it will be impossible, as least as far as I can foresee, to hope to find ever again anything similar. (XIII, 135).

Cesi's response was not long in coming and it was such as to remove any doubt that might have remained in Galileo's mind:

> Your coming here is necessary and it will very much please
> His Holiness who asked me if and when Your Lordship
> was coming; and I answered him that I was thinking that
> to you one hour seemed a thousand years, and I added
> that which seemed necessary with respect to the devotion
> of Your Lordship to him, and that I would soon bring him
> your book: in a word he showed that he loved you and
> esteemed you more than ever. (XIII, 140).

The book to which Cesi alludes here is *The Assayer* which,
as we have seen, had been dedicated to the Pope and for which
later on Urban VIII expressed his great pleasure and enjoyment.

Because of ill health Galileo had to put off his departure
for Rome until the beginning of the following April (1624).
During the trip he stopped at Acquasparta, where Cesi was at
that time. The latter had invited him in order that he could
bring him up to date on the situation in Rome, so that Galileo
would arrive there "not in the dark but well informed as to what
might be necessary" (XIII, 141). While he was still there word
arrived of the sudden death of Virginio Cesarini and so Galileo
was deprived of a valuable support during his stay in Rome.

Galileo arrived in Rome on 23 April and just a day later he
was received in audience by Urban VIII. Galileo wrote about it
to Curzio Picchena and he showed that he was quite satisfied:

> I was kept for an hour of time by His Holiness with
> various discussions and to my most singular delight. On
> the following day for the same interval of time I was with
> the Most Illustrious Cardinal Barberino [Francesco
> Barberini] and with just as much satisfaction. (XIII, 175).

Later on Galileo returned five times to the Pope's presence.
Undoubtedly he was satisfied with the first meeting, where the
discussion would have been about matters in general, but, as
concrete matters slowly emerged, this must have changed into
a feeling of increasing uneasiness. Urban VIII had not responded
in the way Galileo had hoped he would to his prudent soundings
with respect to the issue of Copernicanism. After three weeks
Galileo wrote to Cesi that he was convinced that "time, coolness
and patience" would be required (XIII, 179). And without a

doubt, despite his desire to see a prompt realization of his intentions, he preferred to persist in his prudence. He compensated by using his free time for various visits and conversations which would serve to prepare the ground for his future undertakings. During two such encounters with Cardinal Zollern, Bishop of Osnabruck in Germany, Galileo had assured himself that this prelate would provide him authoritative support before the Pope.[1]

In fact, the Cardinal spoke with Urban VIII before his return to Germany, as Galileo informed Cesi on 8 June:

> Zollern left yesterday for Germany, and he told me that he had spoken with His Holiness on the matter of Copernicus, and how the heretics are all of his opinion and hold it as most certain, and that, therefore, one must go very circumspectly in coming to any determination: to which His Holiness responded that the Holy Church had not condemned it nor was she [the Church] about to condemn it now as heretical, but only as temerarious, though it was not to be feared that there would ever be anyone to demonstrate it as necessarily true. (XIII, 182).

These last words merit particular attention because they show clearly what was, and will always remain, the personal conviction of Urban VIII on these matters. He was open and intelligent, but he was convinced (despite all of his admiration for Galileo) that the astronomical systems already considered and those which might be thought up in the future would never be able to decipher the mystery of heavenly motions, a mystery known only to God. It was a matter of a theologically-based skepticism as to the ability of human science to explain the secrets of the universe. His skepticism contrasted in the sharpest way possible with the conviction, on which all of Galileo's scientific research was founded, that the human mind is capable of deciphering the book of nature with certainty.[2]

Without a doubt, Galileo himself had heard directly from the Pope this statement, which, on the other hand, he already knew from the time when Maffeo Barberini was a cardinal. In fact, we know from Agostino Oregio, Barberini's great friend who later became his Papal theologian, of a conversation which took place (we do not know precisely when) between Barberini himself and Galileo. According to Oregio's testimony, Barberini

> conceding him all that he had thought out, asked him at the end whether God could not have the power and wisdom to dispose and move in another way the orbs and the stars and all that is seen in the sky and all that is said of the motions, order, location, distance and disposition of the stars . . . Because if God knew how and had the power to dispose all of this in another way than that which has been thought: in such wise as to save all that has been said: we cannot limit the divine power and wisdom to this way. Having heard this, that most learned man remained silent.[3]

Galileo had to resign himself to no visible spectacular change in the situation, disillusioned perhaps by what he had expected before having talked to Urban VIII. However, there still remained one positive point. The new Pope was not an obscurantist. Even if Galileo could not harbor hopes, at least for the moment, that the decree of the Index of 1616 would be suppressed, he felt free to take up in public his discussion of the issue of Copernicanism.[4] He was not to speak of the Copernican system except in a hypothetical way (Urban VIII must have been very clear on this point). But he would have always been able to demonstrate that, as a hypothesis, it was by far superior to the others. There remained the theological objection of Urban VIII noted above. Since the Pope could not be moved on this point, Galileo was prepared to concede. He would put the thesis of his august adversary at the end of all of the arguments. After all, it was up to the reader to judge and there was no doubt as to how an intelligent reader, without theological prejudices as to the thesis presented, would have reacted. To put it succinctly, the strategy was to crush the opposition to Copernicanism definitively on the level of science. Little by little the resistance on the level of philosophy and theology would collapse by itself.

2.   *The* Letter to Ingoli

But previous experience had taught Galileo that the greatest danger came from people like Caccini and delle Colombe. They would not have hesitated to create an uproar against Galileo should he have tried to realize his plans right away. It was more than ever necessary to be prudent.

It was, therefore, decided among Galileo and his friends that it would be better to proceed gradually. Galileo would begin with some essay, not too engaging, in which the issue of Copernicanism would be dealt with in a rather indirect manner. Later on, after the reactions had been weighed, they would see whether it was indicated that they should carry on in a more decisive way.

By now Galileo was anxious to leave Rome so that he could get to work. This fourth stay in the "Eternal City" had made him quite aware of how much time would be required to reach more tangible results. And by now Galileo felt the weight of his sixty years. His frequent illnesses during the previous years had led him to fear that not many years were left to him. It was, therefore, urgent that he not lose precious time.[5]

On 7 June Galileo took leave of the Pope. Yet again, he received a proof that Urban VIII was benevolent and generous with his favors, except on that point which most concerned Galileo.[6] The following day a Brief (composed by Ciampoli) was delivered to him. In it the Pope recommended Galileo to the benevolence of the Grand Duke.

Despite his delusion as to the results of his trip, Galileo's return this time to Florence was undoubtedly by a long shot better than the previous one. Above all, Galileo thought that he could pick up the trail he had interrupted. And his innate optimism must have caused a light from the far future to shine upon the still obscure present.

Upon his return to Florence Galileo immediately went to work. The inspiration for his new writing was offered to him by the dissertation which, as we know, Francesco Ingoli[7] had published eight years earlier with the title: *De situ et quiete terrae contra Copernici systema disputatio ad doctissimum mathematicum D. [Dominum] Galilaeum Galilaeum*

(A disputation on the location and stability of the earth against the system of Copernicus to the most learned mathematician Galileo Galilei; V, 403-412) in which he impugned the theory of Copernicus with arguments from mathematics, physics and theology.

Galileo had been prevented from responding to him because of the events immediately following 1616.[8] But when he returned to Rome after eight years, he became aware of how much the failure to respond to Ingoli had damaged him. In fact, many had believed that Galileo's silence depended upon the fact that he had been convinced by the arguments of his adversary. So there was all the more reason to respond now, even though with so much delay.

Galileo's answer in the form of a letter addressed to Ingoli, had already been completed towards the end of September 1624.[9] Putting aside theological arguments, Galileo took up only the scientific aspect of the question and he stated right from the beginning of the letter that he had decided to write not

> . . . with the thought or aim of supporting as true a proposition which has already been declared suspect and repugnant to a doctrine higher than physical and astronomical discipline in dignity and authority. Instead I do it to show that earlier, when I was entangled with astronomers and philosophers, I was not so blind and stupid that, because I had not seen or understood your objections, I was thereby led to think the Copernican hypothesis could and should be true and the common Ptolemaic one false. (VI, 510-511).

Taking up the argument used by Cardinal Zollern with Urban VIII, Galileo added that he wished to show to the Protestants that the exclusion of the Copernican system (which by now was followed by "those with greater reputations" among the Protestants themselves) did not originate, on the part of Catholics, from ignorance of natural reasons, but

> . . . because of the reverence we have toward the writings of our Fathers and because of our zeal in religion and faith. Thus, when they see that we understand very well

all their astronomical and physical reasons, and indeed also others much more powerful than those advanced till now, at most they will blame us as men who are steadfast in our beliefs, but not as blind to and ignorant of the human disciplines; and this is something which in the final analysis should not concern a true Catholic Christian - I mean that a heretic laughs at him because he gives priority to the reverence and trust which is due to the sacred authors over all the arguments and observations of astronomers and philosophers put together. (VI, 511; trans. by Finocchiaro 1989, 156).

In fact, in the long letter the "reasons, experiences, observations and demonstrations" in favor of Copernicanism are piled up with an increasing force. Galileo could well tell him:

. . . Mr. Ingoli, if your philosophical sincerity and my old regard for you will allow me to say so, you should in all honesty have known that Nicolaus Copernicus had spent more years on these very difficult studies than you had spent days on them; so you should have been more careful and not let yourself be lightly persuaded that you could knock down such a man, especially with the sort of weapons you use, which are among the most common and trite objections advanced in this subject. (VI, 152; trans. by Finocchiaro 1989, 156-157).[10]

Undoubtedly, Galileo had played a dangerous game. Would his statement of not being Copernican "for higher motives" be accepted in good faith in Rome? And how would his old adversaries and Ingoli himself have reacted? That Galileo was far from at peace in these matters we see from his recommendation of prudence to Cesare Marsili to whom, through Father Castelli, he had on 17 December sent a copy of this *Letter* for his comments.[11]

Such prudence was all the more necessary since the anti-Copernicans were unceasing in their agitation. As Galileo informed Marsili in December 1624 (XIII, 235), Scipione Chiaramonti had just published at that time a new work, this time against the motion of the Earth and against Galileo's discourse on the tides (even though this discourse had not been printed, as Galileo himself noted). Certainly he must by now have been aware (after the equivocation into which he had fallen in *The Assayer* with respect to the *Antitycho* of Chiaramonti) that the "scientific" activity of this convinced Aristotelian was not at all to be feared. But such activity was a symptom of the hostilities that were brooding against the new ideas and which were, on the contrary, quite to be feared, as Galileo had learned from past experience.

Another symptom, which caused even greater worries, came to light with the inaugural lecture held toward the end of September 1624 by a professor of philosophy of the Roman College, Fabio Spinola. Guiducci gave word of it to Galileo and described it as "very vehement and violent against the followers of the new opinions which were contrary to those of the peripatetics" (XIII, 226-227). Galileo's first reaction was to respond to this professor, but then he thought it better not to bother about him, at least for the moment (XIII, 260).[12]

The *Letter to Ingoli* arrived in Rome in October. Guiducci had a copy of it and showed it to Ciampoli (XIII, 224), who thought of making some corrections to it to prevent dangerous misunderstandings (XIII, 226). So Guiducci counselled Galileo to wait until this revised copy was sent back to him before sending the letter to Ingoli. But Ciampoli was rather busy and had not yet at the end of November sent back the corrected copy (XIII, 229). Ingoli, who had come to know of Galileo's response, asked Guiducci to let him see it, but the latter refused to do so (XIII, 230).

Since towards the end of December Ciampoli had not yet made the corrections, Guiducci advised Galileo to make them himself (XIII, 242). But it appears that Galileo did not do so.

The situation was drawn out. Towards the end of March of the following year (1625), Ciampoli had still not given the copy back to Guiducci, who again promised that, when he finally had it, he would see to a new transcription with the corrections and would himself deliver it to Ingoli (XIII, 261). Finally on 18 April he wrote to Galileo to tell him that he had, with Cesi's advice, put off delivering the corrected copy to Ingoli. Guiducci added that he promised to leave it with Filippo Magalotti, before his own return to Florence, with instructions not to deliver it unless Galileo himself so ordered (XIII, 265-266).[13]

3.   The Assayer *denounced by a "pious person" to the Holy Office*

The reason why Cesi had given the above-mentioned advice to Guiducci was that some months before "a pious person" had proposed to the Holy Office that *The Assayer* be prohibited or at least corrected since that book praised the teaching of Copernicus on the motion of the Earth. Indeed, it is true, added Guiducci, that the person, Giovanni Guevara, assigned by a cardinal (not identified) to examine *The Assayer* had given approval to the book. Furthermore, Guiducci gave assurances, that Guevara had also

> . . . put in writing some defenses to the effect that, even if that doctrine of motion were held, it did not seem to him to deserve condemnation; so the matter quieted down for the time being (XIII, 265; trans. by Finocchiaro 1989, 205).[14]

But Guevara, Guiducci added, had gone off to France to accompany Cardinal Francesco Barberini. And so, since these two persons who were favorable to Galileo were absent, it was better not to run risks

> . . . for in the letter to Ingoli Copernicus's opinion is explicitly defended, and though it is clearly stated that this opinion is found false by means of a superior light, nevertheless those who are not too sincere will not believe that and will be up in arms again (XIII, 265; trans. by Finocchiaro 1989, 205).

There was also the fact, Guiducci once more said, that "we are opposed here by another powerful man, who once was one of your chief defenders".[15] To whom was Guiducci referring? It is probable that he meant Cardinal Orsini, of whom Guiducci himself speaks in a postscript to this letter: "The Lord Cardinal remains very affectionate toward you, but Apelle has a great influence on His Most Illustrious Lordship" (XIII, 266; trans. by Finocchiaro 1989, 206). Actually Alessandro Orsini had some years before joined the Jesuit order. The fact that Scheiner (who had returned to Rome and stayed there until 1633) and Orsini were now fellow religious explains how the cardinal could have become "contrary in this part" (that is, opposed to Copernicanism), whereas, as we know, he "at one time" (in 1616) "took the lead in defending you".

In this rather worrisome framework there was, it is true, the positive fact that Ciampoli had used the copy given to him by Guiducci to present an ample reading of the *Letter to Ingoli* to the Pope (already in December of the previous year), and he had informed Galileo right away that Urban VIII had particularly liked some passages of it (XIII, 295). But it is probable that Ciampoli chose with dexterity those passages where there was no risk of offending the susceptibility of the Pope and, therefore, one could not deduce too much from such a favorable reaction by the Pope.

4.   *A return to the* Discourse on the ebb and flow of the sea

In the meantime Galileo took up again the work which was dearest to him, namely, the *Discourse on the ebb and flow of the sea*, in which phenomenon, as we know, Galileo had been convinced for many years that he had found the most important argument in favor of the Earth's motion.[16] He had already written about it to Cesi in September 1624:

> Now I have returned to the ebb and flow [of the sea], and I have come to this proposition: if the earth is immobile it is impossible that the ebb and flow occur; if it moves with the motions already assigned to it, it is necessary that they occur, with all of the characteristics that are observed in them. (XIII, 209).

He again spoke about it in a letter to Marsili of December of that same year:

> In the meantime I am making headway with my Dialogue[17] on the ebb and flow [of the sea], which as a consequence

supports the Copernican system, and, by the grace of God, my health is good enough that I can employ some hours in this service. (XIII, 236).

The following year we have another reference to it in the letter written on 20 October 1625 to Elia Diodati[18] in Paris.:

Then, in so far as it is granted to me by my age, which is much, and by my health, which is scanty, I go on employing my time in writing some dialogues on the ebb and flow of the sea, where, moreover, there will be a copious treatment of the systems of Ptolemy and Copernicus, and you can expect that the cause of that phenomenon is referred by me to motions attributed to the earth, etc. (XIII, 282).

Little by little Galileo was beginning to make more concrete his plan for "a book on the system of the world" which he had already spoken about in the *Starry Message* (III, Part I, 73) and which will become seven years later the *Dialogue Concerning the Two Chief World Systems*.

It appears that at the beginning Galileo had hoped that he would be able to complete this work of his quickly.[19] But he took sick in March 1625 and was forced to interrupt the composition of the work, which he carried forward at a rather slow pace during the next three years. Beside his state of health, the situation was influenced by various other works and long-standing interests and research areas which were revivified in Galileo's mind as the *Dialogue* slowly went on developing.[20] And it was probably the massiveness of this project, the many points to be clarified and deepened and arguments which would have to be refined which delayed Galileo.[21] But, it seems, there was above all else the need to collect more data on the phenomenon of the tides, since difficulties had been raised contrary to his arguments. Galileo found himself facing "almost inexplicable" difficulties, as he will say later on, once he was convinced that he had overcome them.[22]

5.   *The* Rosa Ursina *of Scheiner and the completion of the*
     Dialogue

While Galileo was struggling with these difficulties, a
personage whom we already know returned to the scene, the
Jesuit Scheiner. As I have already said, the latter had arrived
in Rome toward the end of 1624. Guiducci informed Galileo the
following January and he also passed on to him the knowledge
which he received from a friend who had spoken with Scheiner,
that the Jesuit "wanted now to print a book where he would
demonstrate the making of a new telescope with new inventions
and uses of it" (XIII, 249).
    A year later Francesco Stelluti confirmed the news:

> There is here the Jesuit Father Scheiner who I believe is
> printing his observations of the sunspots; and some days
> ago he said to our Mr. Fabri [Faber] that Your Lordship
> was printing something again; to which he responded that
> he did not know that; and he [Scheiner] answered that he
> had understood that you were printing the ebb and flow of
> the sea, and that he wished to see it and that he agrees
> with Your Lordship's opinion about the world system.
> (XIII, 300).[23]

Scheiner's book also had a long incubation period,
especially as to the printing. Three years later (February 1629)
it was Castelli's turn to inform Galileo that rumors were going
around in Rome that Scheiner had finished printing his book *De
Maculis Solis* (On Sunspots). (XIV, 22).[24] But it still required a
year before the volume was finally published (1630). It contained
784 double-columned pages and was entitled *Rosa Ursina* as a
sign of deference toward his protector, Prince Paolo Orsini,[25]
whose press took care of the printing of the book and to whom
the book was dedicated.
    Right from the beginning of the work Scheiner took an
adversarial position with respect to Galileo. As we know, in the
Discourse on Comets of Guiducci Galileo had made a sharp
attack on "Apelle" accusing him of plagiarism. And Scheiner had
also interpreted similar expressions contained in *The Assayer* as
directed at him. Even sharper and more implacable was

Scheiner's response to his "censor" (in the *Rosa Ursina* Galileo's name is reserved for references which were not offensive or, on rare occasions, laudatory) as well as to "his Angel" (Angelo de Filiis, the author of the Preface to the *Letters on the Sunspots*). This was a response which took up the whole of Book I, a total of 66 pages, and it was taken up time and time again in the rest of the book. Having decided to "repay Galileo in kind" as he had promised (see XII, 489), Scheiner claimed not only that his own discovery was independent from that of Galileo but also that he had the priority in the scientific study of the spots. In this he certainly held a good hand since, as we know, his first letters to Welser had preceded by several months those of Galileo. On the other hand he was completely unfair in his accusation (very frequently repeated in the *Rosa Ursina*) that Galileo had maintained that the spot trajectories were rectilinear and parallel to the plane of the ecliptic. Scheiner had stated the same thing (albeit at the beginning with some doubt which appeared to disappear) at the time of the composition of the letters to Welser (see V, 49 and 61). And Galileo's statements in this regard, which were criticized so severely by his antagonist, go back to this same period. Undoubtedly, Galileo was at a disadvantage at not having continued the study of the sunspots in the systematic and extremely meticulous manner with which Scheiner on the other hand had carried on and deepened his studies over many years. And now he used his position of strength to "destroy" his adversary by accusing him of crass ignorance of the most fundamental astronomical notions (see the *Rosa Ursina*, 35) and of complete incompetence. Even Galileo's statements about the Suns's rotation on its own axis and that the spots were surface features of the Sun drew his criticism as not being based on scientific reasons or even as being due to "chance" (see the *Rosa Ursina*, 51).

The heavy and implacable polemic against Galileo with which this work of Scheiner is impregnated was undoubtedly the source of the comments made about it with a severity no less excessive and unjust by Galileo's friends[26] who probably did not read beyond Book I. In fact, beginning with Book II and continuing through most of Book IV Scheiner presented the results of his innumerable observations of sunspots carried out over a period of eighteen years and the results which he was able to draw from them. He thus presented the most complete and most valuable treatise on solar physics of that epoch. By this time he was fully convinced of the Sun's rotation on its own axis and that the spots were surface features on the Sun. He had furthermore determined that their trajectories were curved and he even presented the dates of the maxima and minima of the curvature with a truly noteworthy precision, given the instruments of that time.[27] His observations of the bright areas (called by him "faculae"), which were visible next to the dark spots on the solar surface, were also important. Galileo had also noted them but he did not take time to study them in detail.

The final part of the book was dedicated to the criticism of the fundamental presuppositions of Aristotelian cosmology, such as the incorruptibility of the heavens, which contrasted with Scheiner's conclusion that the spots were phenomena on the Sun, and the solidity of the celestial spheres on which, according to Aristotle, the motion of the heavenly bodies depended. By citing a massive array of texts from Scripture and from the Fathers Scheiner upheld the thesis of the "liquidity" (or "fluidity") of the heavens. This allowed bodies to move in the heavens with their own motion. This thesis was also put forth by Bellarmine and shared by Prince Cesi, as is shown by their correspondence which Scheiner reprints at the end of his book. In this way Scheiner had undoubtedly sought to free the scientific research of the Jesuits from the heavy bonds imposed on it by the obligations of fidelity to Aristotle. This constitutes without a doubt a further merit of the *Rosa Ursina*.

It appears that Galileo was in a position to have a copy of Scheiner's book only toward the end of 1631[28] and that he had immediately written a protest letter to Prince Paolo Orsini, from whose press at Bracciano the *Rosa Ursina* had been published. There is still the response of Orsini sent on 30 December (XIV, 322). The Prince was obviously embarrassed and excused himself stating that he was unaware of what Scheiner had written.[29] But he added that he was not surprised at the Jesuit's lack of discretion, since he had behaved badly towards the Prince himself, thus breaking off their relationship. And he ended by restating his esteem for Galileo.

Galileo followed the advice of his friends[30] and did not respond to the *Rosa Ursina,* but he rested content with what he had written in the *Dialogue* on the priority of the discovery of the sunspots.[31]

Let us turn now to the composition of the *Dialogue.* Toward the end of September 1629 Galileo had finally succeeded in overcoming the great difficulty by which he had been blocked during the last three years. He himself informed his friend, Diodati, in Paris of this:

> . . . you must know that a month ago I took up again my *Dialogue* about the tides, put aside three years on end, and by the grace of God have got on the right path, so that if I can keep on this winter I hope to bring the work to an end and immediately publish it. In this, besides the material on the tides, there will be inserted many other problems and a most ample confirmation of the Copernican system by showing the nullity of all that had been brought by Tycho and others to the contrary. The work will be quite large and full of many novelties, which by reason of the freedom of dialogue [form] I shall have scope to introduce without drudgery or affectation (XIV, 49; trans. by Drake 1978, 310).

In these words we not only have delineated the plan of the *Dialogue,* but also its true intention. To the Protestant Diodati Galileo could write without subterfuge: it was a question of a "most ample confirmation of the Copernican system". The last remaining obstacle, since the Aristotelian-Ptolemaic system was by now admitted to be untenable, was Tycho Brahe's conception of the universe. And so, Galileo mentioned here in particular the need to demonstrate the "nullity" of it.

Even Galileo himself, in a letter sent one month later to Giovanfrancesco Buonamici in Madrid, made it clear that in the *Dialogue,* which was by now taking a definitive form, the new vision of the world was based upon the phenomenon of the tides as the strongest argument. He wrote:

> . . . Your Lordship should know that I am about to finish some dialogues in which I treat of the constitution of the universe, and among the principal problems I write of the

ebb and flow of the sea, and I believe I have found the
true reason for it, very far from the those to which up to
now that effect has been attributed. I estimate it to be true
and so do all of those with whom I have conferred about it.
(XIV, 54).

However, the expressions used by Galileo ("I believe I have
found" and "I estimate it to be true") seem to denote, despite
everything else, that there remained a bit of uncertainty deep
inside him. This seems to be confirmed by the desire (expressed
in the same letter) to have further confirmation of an
"experimental" character of his theory by those who had
travelled the distant seas.[32]

At the end of 1629 the work was more or less completed.
Galileo gave word of this to Cesi on 24 December:

> . . . having as of two months ago taken up the pen again,
> I have almost completed my Dialogues, and I have
> unfolded more clearly those obscure points which I had
> always held as almost inexplicable. Very little remains of
> those things which concern doctrine, and that little bit is
> of things already assimilated and easy to explain . . . I am
> perplexed about the printing of them [the Dialogues] as to
> whether it would be good for me to move in due time there
> so as not to trouble others with the correction; and I
> rejoice in the desire to see again my very dear masters and
> friends before losing my sight, which because of my
> advanced age is on its way to darkness. (XIV, 60).[33]

Galileo's friends were also in agreement about having the
printing done in Rome and they began looking for a way to have
this done. Once again the events seemed to favor Galileo. As of
June 1629 the new Master of the Sacred Palace had been
appointed. This was that same Father Riccardi who had given
such a favorable judgment on The Assayer and who was by now
for some time among those who were Galileo's friends. Father
Castelli, who was in Rome, had already spoken with him about
the Dialogue and had assured Galileo "that for his part he
was certain that things will be going well" (XIV, 78). Ciampoli
also showed a certain confidence, but his optimism was more

cautious than that of Castelli, as the latter recognized in the following part of his letter. He wrote:

> In short, he [Ciampoli] hopes well for this business although he cannot promise anything for certain: but he nevertheless holds as solid that, with your coming here, with your way of managing things, with your discourse, with your manners, with the work itself in hand, you will overcome whatever difficulty you might meet. (XIV, 78).[34]

6.   *Galileo in Rome. The events surrounding the permission to print the* Dialogue

His friends were, therefore, waiting impatiently for Galileo in Rome and they exhorted him to come before the summer heat set in. But, due to his bad health, Galileo had to put off his departure (XIV, 85). He made use of the time by working on the final additions to and on a revision of the text of the *Dialogue.* He applied himself so much that Suor Maria Celeste, as always close to her father with her affection and care, became worried about the situation.[35]

Finally, with an improvement in his health, Galileo left Florence on 1 May 1630 and arrived on the evening of 3 May in Rome where he was the guest of the Ambassador of Tuscany, Francesco Niccolini[36] at the Villa Medici. Niccolini, who had succeeded in 1621 to Guicciardini, received him with a warmth which was in clear contrast with the ill-concealed antipathy of his predecessor (XIV, 103, 105, 106). And undoubtedly the hospitality was made even more cordial by the solicitude of Niccolini's wife, Caterina Riccardi, a relative of the Master of the Sacred Palace, Father Riccardi, who now had the responsibility to grant permission for the printing of the *Dialogue.*

Everything, therefore, seemed to promise a happy outcome to this fifth trip to Rome, which Galileo was anticipating would provide the crowning of his struggles, his efforts, and his hopes.[37] As usual he did not lose time. On 18 May he was received by Urban VIII who, by Galileo's report, was very kind to him (XIV, 105). On the basis of what Urban VIII himself stated two years later we may argue that Galileo spoke on that occasion of the book he wanted to print and that the Pope had been quite explicit in repeating his own position with respect to the problem of Copernicanism. Still, from Urban VIII's attitude Galileo must have concluded that he was not opposed in principle to the publication of the *Dialogue*.[38]

While Galileo was in Rome an event occurred which could have had the direst of consequences for him. During the first half of May news spread through the city of a horoscope which foretold among other things the approaching death of Urban VIII and of his nephew, Taddeo Barberini. The horoscope was attributed to the Vallombrosian Father Orazio Morandi, abbot of St. Praxedes in Rome. Someone among Galileo's enemies tried also to implicate him, as a friend of Morandi; and there were some who even went so far as to make Galileo the author of the horoscope, as can be deduced from a "Notice" written on 18 May by Antonio Badelli:[39]

> . . . Here we have Galileo, who is a famous mathematician and astrologer, and he is trying to print a book in which he impugns many opinions held by the Jesuits. He has let it be known that Lady Anna [wife of Taddeo Barberini, nephew of Urban VIII] will give birth to a male son, that at the end of June we will have peace in Italy, and that a little afterwards Sir Taddeo and the Pope will die. The last point is supported by Caracioli Neapolitan, by Father Campanella, and by many written discourses, which treat of the election of a new Pontiff, as if the See were vacant. (XIV, 103).

Urban VIII, who was very superstitious,[40] had Morandi imprisoned shortly after Galileo's departure from Rome. And at the end of the year the unfortunate priest died in prison still awaiting trial.

Even before Morandi's arrest Galileo was undoubtedly very worried because of rumors about him and he probably beseeched Michelangelo Buonarroti,[41] who was to have met Cardinal Francesco Barberini, to deny that he had played any part at all in that affair. As verified by a note sent on 3 June by Buonarroti to Galileo after the meeting, the Cardinal had assured Buonarroti that "Galileo had no better friend than him and the Pope himself, and that he knew who he was and he knew that he did not have these kinds of matters in his head" (XIV, 111).

Obviously Galileo breathed a sigh of relief. But the incident showed how strong and tenacious was the hatred harbored against him by his enemies. They were certainly not ignorant of the great esteem which Urban VIII had for him. And it was precisely this esteem which they had sought to ruin by arming themselves with calumnies to increase the susceptibility and impressionability of the Pope.[42]

Without a doubt Father Riccardi, whose responsibility it was, as we have seen, to grant the *imprimatur* of the *Dialogue* at Rome, was up to date on Urban VIII's ideas with respect to Copernicanism. By this time the Pope was in the eighth year of his Pontificate and the euphoria with which he begun it had given place to constantly increasing worries. The Thirty Years War which had begun twelve years earlier was increasing more than ever in its violence in alternating phases and certainly did not allow much in the way of optimism. Relations with France were in a delicate phase, given the personality of Cardinal Richelieu who was not at all inclined to surrender to Rome. Urban VIII had had the bitter experience of failure (and he was to experience it yet again in the future). All of that had brought him to become ever more suspicious and irritable and to take a rigid stand whereby he required obedience without hesitation, nor would he at all tolerate contradictions from those who, according to him, were obliged to show him obedience.

Riccardi knew, therefore, that he had to be prudent despite the signs of esteem which the Pope continued to show to Galileo. The reading, therefore, of the manuscript which Galileo had delivered to Riccardi must have brought him more than one moment of apprehension. Despite his promises, Galileo had written a book which was decidedly favorable to Copernicanism (even though the final conclusion was ostensibly left open). Thus Riccardi decided that the book should be revised by supplying it with an introduction and a conclusion in which it would be made sufficiently clear that one was dealing with hypotheses. The rest of the book was also to be adapted "in such wise as to show that the Holy Congregation [of the Index] in reproving Copernicus had acted in an entirely reasonable way".[43]

The job of reviewing the manuscript was given to another Dominican, Raffaele Visconti, a professor of mathematics and friend of the Master of the Sacred Palace. Visconti made various corrections, but for the rest he approved the book and declared that he was ready to give a testimonial in its favor.

But this did not bring an end to Riccardi's worries and scruples[44] and he decided on his own account to reexamine the whole book. But

> . . . since the author complained about the unusual practice of a second revision and about the delay, to facilitate the process it was decided that before sending it to press the Master [Riccardi] would see it page by page. In the meantime, to enable the author to negotiate with printers he was given the *imprimatur* for Rome and the book's beginning was sketched. (XIX, 325-326).

Finally on 16 June Father Visconti was able to give Galileo the much looked for news:

> The Father Master [Riccardi] . . . says that he likes the work and that tomorrow morning he will speak with the Pope for the frontispiece to the work and, for the rest, after arranging a few little things, like those which we settled together, he will give him the book. (XIV, 120).

We can be certain that the result of Riccardi's audience with the Pope was favorable. It was, perhaps, on that occasion that Urban VIII manifested the desire that the title of the work be changed from the original one, "On the ebb and flow of the sea", to that of "Dialogue on the Chief Systems" or something similar. Obviously Urban VIII did not want it to be seen right from the title that the book was principally based on the "Copernican" explanation of the phenomenon of the tides.

On 26 June Galileo left Rome, convinced that he had accomplished the purpose of his trip. Even his leave-taking of the Pope had been of the most cordial kind and Galileo had been invited to dinner by Cardinal Francesco Barberini. Three days later Ambassador Niccolini wrote in this respect to the Secretary of State, Andrea Cioli in Florence:

. . . Signor Galileo left here last Wednesday completely satisfied and with complete success in that most pleasant business of his, thanks to his valor and his most gentle manners. The Pope was glad to see him, he gave him many caresses, as did His Lord Cardinal [Francesco] Barberini, who also had him to dinner; and he was esteemed and honored by the whole Court as was his due. (XIV, 121).

Obviously this warm and benevolent attitude of the Pope and of the Papal court was to be attributed to the fact that no one (except Riccardi and Visconti) was aware of the true content of the book.

Upon his return to Florence Galileo had the intention of completing the few points that were still missing[45] and then of sending the manuscript immediately to Rome to Prince Cesi who had decided to print the *Dialogue* under the auspices of the *Accademia dei Lincei*. But right at that crucial moment an event took place which had a profound negative influence on the whole further development of the affair: the death of Cesi himself which took place on 1 August 1630. With his death Galileo lost one of his most genuine and, at the same time, valuable friends.

Cesi had left no will and in the confused situation in which the *Accademia dei Lincei* now came to find itself[46] Galileo understood that he would now have to think of printing the *Dialogue* in some place other than Rome. This was exactly what Castelli himself had suggested to him on 24 August:

> . . . for many most weighty reasons which I do not wish to commit to paper at this time, in addition to the fact that Prince Cesi has passed away, I would think it best that Your Most Illustrious Lordship would have your book printed there in Florence and that you do this as soon as possible. I have dealt with Father Visconti to see if there would be any difficulty with this; he has replied that there is no difficulty whatsoever and that he is very desirous that this work be published. (XIV, 135).[47]

Although he had thought for a moment of having the *Dialogue* printed in Genoa,[48] Galileo must have decided at the end in favor of Florence, even though he was worried about the insufficiency of the printing equipment which was available there. But now it was necessary to obtain permission to have the printing done in that city, since Riccardi's authority, as Master of the Sacred Palace, to grant an *imprimatur* was limited to Rome. Riccardi, when consulted by Castelli on the matter, put down the condition that he must have a copy of the book "in order to correct with Monsignor Ciampoli what was necessary". Once these changes ("some small matters in the introduction and in the work itself") had been made Galileo would have had permission to have the work printed wherever he most desired to do so (see XIV, 150).

But just then the plague was rampant in Italy so that not only travel but even the shipment of large packages was extremely difficult because of the rigorous quarantine measures taken by the Papal States. So Galileo requested permission to do the final revision of the book in Florence, leaving only the preface and the final part to be sent to Rome for the corrections which Riccardi wanted done.

Thanks to the intervention of the ambassador's wife, Caterina Riccardi, with her relative, Riccardi finally accepted the proposal (XIV, 156-157) under the condition, however, that the review of the text be done at Florence by a Dominican Father and that Galileo would still send him the introduction and the conclusion of the *Dialogue*. Galileo was granted his request that the review be entrusted to Father Jacinto Stefani, a consultor of the Inquisition in Florence.

But Riccardi, who in the meantime must have received the introduction and the conclusion of the book (XIV, 168 and 216), showed no hurry to send the corrected versions back along with the instructions which he had promised for Father Stefani.[49]

In the end Galileo lost his patience and in March 1631 wrote a long letter to the Secretary of State of the Grand Duke, Cioli. After having described the situation that had come about, he added:

> Some months ago Father Benedetto Castelli wrote to me that he had met the Most Reverend Father Master several times and heard from him that he was about to return the above-mentioned preface and ending, revised to his

complete satisfaction; but this has never happened, and I no longer hear even a simple mention of the matter. In the meantime the work stays in a corner, and my life is wasted as I continue living in constant ill health. (XIV, 217).

Informed by Cioli the Grand Duke decided to intervene through Ambassador Niccolini. But Father Riccardi would not let himself be budged and he showed little trust in Father Stefani. As time went on the atmosphere in Rome tended to become more tense. Most likely the ill-intentioned persons had again taken up their actions against Galileo (as already demonstrated on the occasion of Morandi's horoscope). And so Riccardi, better informed about the situation than Galileo, must have feared the consequences of even the smallest imprudence.

Finally, Niccolini's insistence, and that of his wife, seemed to have the upper hand over the fears of the Dominican. Niccolini, in fact, announced in a letter of 19 April to Cioli that Riccardi had finally given his consent to the printing, but under specific conditions that he himself would put in writing so that the ambassador would be able to forward them as they were without the fear of misunderstandings.[50] As we know from a letter written a few days later by Riccardi himself to Niccolini among these conditions was the one that the preface and conclusion of the book should be sent in their final form to the Master of the Sacred Palace.[51] Riccardi, it should be understood, would have preferred to have the whole book. But if this were not possible, he would himself have written a letter to the inquisitor in Florence in order to explain to him which were the points to examine before giving permission for the printing (XIV, 254).

Upon coming to know of this letter Galileo saw nothing in it except vague promises with nothing concrete.

> . . . there is neither an order to print, nor any declarations, nor anything else, but rather new delays based upon certain claims and questions of his; but it is months and months since I have satisfied all of these . . . (XIV, 259; trans. by Finocchiaro 1989, 210).

Despairing by now that he could in any other way put an end to the situation, Galileo proposed that a meeting be held with the presence of the Grand Duke, Cioli, Count Orso d'Elci (member of the Grand Duke's council), the Inquisitor of Florence and Father Stefani. Galileo would have brought along

> . . . the work with all the censures and emendations made by the Father Master of the Sacred Palace himself, by his associate Father Visconti, and by Father Stefani; then from seeing them the Father Inquisitor could understand how minor are the things that had been noted and that have been emended. Furthermore, he and all those present could see with how much submission and reverence I agree to give the label of dreams, chimeras, misunderstandings, paralogisms, and conceits to all those reasons and arguments which the authorities regard as favoring opinions they hold to be untrue; they would also understand how true is my claim that on this topic I have never had any opinion or intention but that held by the holiest and most venerable Fathers and Doctors of the Holy Church. (XIV, 259; trans. by Finocchiaro 1989, 211).

At any rate Galileo sent to Rome the last version of the preface and of the conclusion of the book. On 27 May Niccolini assured Cioli that he would have delivered those pages to Riccardi and have requested him to grant finally the permission so long awaited (XIV, 261).

In fact, Riccardi in the end decided to send the instructions to the inquisitor in Florence, the Dominican Clemente Egidi, to whom he gave the faculty to determine for himself whether or not to give the *imprimatur*.[52]

Thus the long-desired permission had virtually arrived and Galileo was finally ready to see to the beginning of the printing.[53] On 15 July he was able to inform Marsili in Bologna that the first six of a total of more than fifty folios in all had already been printed.[54]

On 19 July Riccardi decided to send to the inquisitor in Florence (by way of Niccolini) also the

> . . . beginning or preface to be placed on the first page; the author is free to change or embellish its verbal expressions,

as long as he keeps the substance of the content. The ending should be on the same theme. (XIX, 330; trans. by Finocchiaro 1989, 213).[55]

Riccardi's hesitations were justified by Niccolini to Galileo in this way:

> The Father Master of the Sacred Palace indeed deserves to be pitied, for exactly during these days when I was spurring and bothering him, he has suffered embarrassment and very great displeasure in regard to some works recently published as he must have done at other times too; he barely complied with our request, and only because of the reverence he feels for the Most Serene name of His Highness our Master [the Grand Duke] and for his Most Serene House. (XIV, 284; trans. by Finocchiaro 1989, 214).

On 16 August Galileo informed Diodati that a third of the work had already been printed and that he was hoping that it would be published in about three months (XIV, 289).[56]

Galileo's friends, such as Castelli (always exuberant and rather simplistic in his enthusiasm), were impatient to see the work finally published. But there was always the less optimistic one who showed serious worries about the reactions which the book might provoke.[57]

The printing took longer than foreseen. Finally on 21 February 1632 the printer Landini was able to announce to Marsili that on that very day the work was completed and that they would begin immediately to ship the copies requested (XIV, 331).

7. *The* Dialogue Concerning the Two Chief World Systems

The *Dialogue* carried the ecclesiastical printing permission of the Vicegerent of Rome, of the Master of the Sacred Palace, of the Vicar General of Florence, and of the Florentine inquisitor, in addition to that of the government of the Grand Duke,[58] and 1632 was placed as the year of publication.

The title had been composed according to the wish of
Urban VIII:

Dialogue
of
Galileo Galilei, Lincean
Special mathematician of the University of Pisa
And Philosopher and Chief Mathematician
of the Most Serene
Grand Duke of Tuscany.
Where, in the meetings of four days, there is discussion
concerning the two
Chief Systems of the World,
Ptolemaic and Copernican,
Propounding inconclusively the philosophical and physical
reasons
as much for one side as for the other.
With copyright
in Florence, by G.B. Landini, 1632.
Licensed by the authorities.[59]

After the dedicatory letter to the Grand Duke of Tuscany
there followed the preface ("To the Discerning Reader") which,
as we have seen, was one of the points of major concern for
Riccardi and which he had reviewed meticulously.

Galileo began his preface by alluding to the decree of the
Index of 1616:

> There were those who impudently asserted that this decree
> had its origin not in judicious inquiry, but in passion none
> too well informed. Complaints were to be heard that
> advisors who were totally unskilled at astronomical
> observations ought not to clip the wings of reflective
> intellects by means of rash prohibitions.
>
> Upon hearing such carping insolence, my zeal could not
> be contained. Being thoroughly informed about that
> prudent determination, I decided to appear openly in the
> theater of the world as a witness of the sober truth. I was
> at that time in Rome; I was not only received by the most
> eminent prelates of that Court, but had their applause ;

indeed, this decree was not published without some previous notice of it having been given to me. (VII, 29; trans. by Drake 1967, 5).

For those of us who know how the events of 1615-1616 turned out these words of Galileo ring with an irony that has a hint of mockery. This is especially true of the last phrase:"this decree was not published without some previous notice of it having been given to me". For a person who had had that "previous notice" in the form of an admonition from Bellarmine that was certainly a fine way to report the facts! But Galileo, who had a long time ago learned the rules which held for whoever wanted to appear "in the theater of the world", had made the decision to play his role right to the end. His intention was surely not to mock but to establish the truth. If to be a "witness of the sober truth" it was necessary to put on a mask and at times present a farce, it was not his fault but the fault of his adversaries with their "passion none too well informed". They were the ones who had the effrontery "to clip the wings of reflective intellects".[60]

Galileo had, perhaps, spoken in this manner because he thought that the only ones who were knowledgeable of what had happened in his regard in 1616 were all dead. In fact, this was not true.[61] And in any case he was not aware that there existed in the Holy Office a document which reported what had taken place in Bellarmine's residence. This will provide material for a very serious accusation at the time of his trial one year later.

Galileo added:

Therefore I propose in the present work to show to foreign nations that as much is understood of this matter in Italy, and particularly in Rome, as transalpine diligence can ever have imagined. Collecting all the reflections that properly concern the Copernican system, I shall make it known that everything was brought before the attention of the Roman censorship,[62] and that there proceed from this clime not only dogmas for the welfare of the soul, but ingenious discoveries for the delight of the mind as well.

To this end I have taken the Copernican side in the discourse, proceeding as with a pure mathematical hypothesis and striving by every artifice to represent it as superior to supposing the earth motionless - not, indeed, absolutely, but as against the arguments of some professed Peripatetics. These men indeed deserve not even that name, for they do not walk about;[63] they are content to adore the shadows, philosophizing not with due circumspection but merely from having memorized a few ill-understood principles. (VII, 29-30; trans. by Drake 1967, 5-6).

Galileo then went on to spell out the plan of the *Dialogue*:

Three principal headings are treated. First, I shall try to show that all experiments practicable upon the earth are insufficient measures for proving its mobility, since they are indifferently adaptable to an earth in motion or at rest. I hope in so doing to reveal many observations unknown to the ancients. Secondly, the celestial phenomena will be examined, strengthening the Copernican hypothesis until it might seem that this must triumph absolutely. Here new reflections are adjoined which might be used in order to simplify astronomy, though not because of any necessity imposed by nature. In the third place, I shall propose an ingenious speculation. It happens that long ago I said that the unsolved problem of the ocean tides might receive some light from assuming the motion of the earth. This assertion of mine, passing by word of mouth, found loving fathers who adopted it as a child of their own ingenuity. Now, so that no stranger may ever appear who, arming himself with our weapons, shall charge us with want of attention to such an important matter, I have thought it good to reveal those probabilities which might render this plausible, given that the earth moves.

I hope that from these considerations the world will come to know that if other nations have navigated more, we have not theorized less. It is not from failing to take count of what others have thought that we have yielded to asserting that the earth is motionless, and holding the contrary to be a mere mathematical caprice, but (if for nothing else) for those reasons that are supplied by piety, religion, the knowledge of Divine Omnipotence, and a consciousness of the limitations of the human mind. (VII, 30; trans. by Drake 1967, 6).

As we see, Galileo in these last lines took up again, with the semblance of making it his own, the reasoning of Urban VIII on the incapacity of the human intellect to penetrate the creative omnipotence of God and, therefore, to arrive at secure conclusions in the field of astronomy.

As is apparent in this long quote, the formulation is measured and careful, so that at the end the introduction of the Pope's argument seems, as it were, natural. But it will be otherwise in the course of the *Dialogue* wherein we witness a crescendo in a Copernican key, which reaches a climax with the "proof" from the tides. Of course, Galileo had stated that he wished to "take the Copernican side in the discourse, proceeding as with a pure mathematical hypothesis". But could a "physical" argument, and specifically the very proof from the tides, be considered "a pure mathematical hypothesis"? As we will see, the opinion of the "experts" who will be consulted on this matter by the Holy Office will be quite different.

As the title states, and as Galileo himself will explain in the following part of the preface, the reasonings are carried out

> . . . in the form of dialogues, which, not being restricted to the rigorous observance of mathematical laws, make room also for digressions which are sometimes no less interesting than the principal argument. (VII, 30; trans. by Drake 1967, 6).

Two of the protagonists in this *Dialogue* impersonate two of Galileo's close friends, by now deceased, Salviati and Sagredo. Salviati is the defender of the Copernican point of view and so he takes up and defends the arguments of Galileo.[64] It is precisely for this reason that Galileo feels the need to have him make the following declaration in the second Day:

> Before going further I must tell Sagredo that I act the part of Copernicus in our arguments and wear his mask. As to the internal effects upon me of the arguments which I produce in his favor, I want you to be guided not by what I say when we are in the heat of acting out our play, but after I have put off the costume, for perhaps then you shall

find me different from what you saw of me on the stage.
(VII, 157-158; trans. by Drake 1967, 131).

This is another declaration which will surely not convince
Galileo's adversaries nor even the examiners of the *Dialogue*.

At the side of Salviati the role of Sagredo is described as:

> that of an educated layman between the two experts,
> Salviati and Simplicius: he is favorably disposed to the new
> doctrines and he puts no limits to his enthusiasm when he
> is convinced of something; often he summarizes the more
> difficult arguments, already adduced, and he expounds
> them again in a simpler form; he also adds his own
> reasons; above all in his mouth are put those ideas for
> which the author does not want to take full responsibility,
> but which he still thinks should be fittingly introduced into
> the discussion.[65]

The third protagonist is Simplicius. As Galileo himself
explains, the name is that of the famous commentator of
Aristotle.[66] He represents the predominant science and
philosophy in the universities of Galileo's time. They were
conservative "science" and philosophy, based on the writings of
Aristotle and of other "classical" authors, and thus they did not
permit the possibility of calling into discussion the opinions of
such venerable authors. In the *Dialogue* Simplicius presents all
of the arguments which the Aristotelian contemporaries of
Galileo brought forth against the Copernican system. Simplicius,
therefore, is an educated person in the manner of the dominant
university culture of those times. But his arguments, one after
the other, fall to pieces before the concise critique of Salviati, so
that, putting it altogether, Simplicius gives the idea of being a
"simpleton" who believes blindly in a physical science no longer
supportable.[67]

The *Dialogue* takes place imaginatively on an
undetermined date in Venice at the Sagredo Palace on the
Grand Canal and it is divided into four "Days".

The **first Day** is dedicated to the consideration of the
fundamental concepts on which the two chief world systems are

founded. Galileo knew very well that the opposition to the ideas of Copernicus had its deepest roots in the worldview contained in the natural philosophy of Aristotle. In order to come to an acceptance of the view of the Earth as a simple planet it was first of all necessary to show that the distinction between the terrestrial (sublunar) and heavenly world could not be upheld either on the theoretical plane or from experience.[68]

Galileo's reasoning on the theoretical plane develops by beginning with a denial of the two types of distinct "natural motion", rectilinear for terrestrial bodies and circular for celestial bodies. Contrary to Aristotle, Galileo asserts that the only natural motions in an ordered universe are circular ones.[69] If some part of the universe does not move in a circular motion and yet is ordered, then it must be in a state of rest. And such a part of the universe is not the Earth. Addressing himself to Simplicius and to the Peripatetics, Salviati states:

> I might add that neither Aristotle nor you can ever prove that the earth is *de facto* the center of the universe; if any center may be assigned to the universe,[70] we shall rather find the sun to be placed here, as we will understand in due course. (VII, 58; trans. by Drake 1967, 33).

The affirmation of circular motion as the *unique* natural motion nullifies not only the Aristotelian "proof" for geocentrism, but also the distinction between "ungenerated" and "incorruptible" heavenly bodies and the "generated" and "corruptible" terrestrial ones. Galileo states that all bodies in the universe are equally subject to change. Simplicius can no longer contain himself and he protests:

> This way of philosophizing tends to subvert all natural philosophy, and to disorder and set in confusion heaven and earth and the whole universe. However, I believe the fundamental principles of the Peripatetics to be such that there is no danger of new sciences being erected upon their ruins. (VII, 62; trans. by Drake 1967, 37).

The courteously ironical response of Salviati is in keeping with the one already sketched out by Galileo in the *Starry Message*:

> Do not worry yourself about heaven and earth, nor fear either their subversion or the ruin of philosophy. As to heaven, it is in vain that you fear for that which you yourself hold to be inalterable and invariant. As for the earth, we seek rather to ennoble and perfect it when we strive to make it like the celestial bodies, and, as it were, place it in heaven, from which your philosophers have banished it. (VII, 62; trans. by Drake 1967, 37).

Gradually the discussion moves onto the experimental plane. Simplicius claims to show that the Aristotelian theory of immutability of the heavenly bodies is confirmed by "sensible experiments", that is, by the fact that no change has ever been noted in them. Salviati responds by bringing to bear the heap of new facts which have come to light from the recent telescopic discoveries. And he concludes:

> I declare that we do have in our age new events and observations such that if Aristotle were now alive, I have no doubt he would change his opinion. (VII, 75; trans. by Drake 1967, 50).[71]

The central thesis of the **second Day** is the one about the daily motion of the heavenly bodies. This motion could be explained, Salviati notes, either by the rotational motion of the Earth or by the motion of the rest of the world, excluding the Earth. Against this last opinion (which is the one of Aristotle and Ptolemy) Salviati shows with various reasons how the opinion of Copernicus of the motion of the Earth alone is more probable. This refutation of the Aristotelian-Ptolemaic system is one of the strongest points of the *Dialogue* and provides the occasion for Galileo to expound on the principles of kinematics which, as we have seen, he had gone on formulating during the previous long years of study and which will be taken up again in a more rigorous and comprehensive manner in the *Discourse and Demonstrations* of 1638.[72]

Of particular importance is the refutation of the "classic" argument against the motion of the Earth, deduced from the fact that, if the Earth really did move, then the effect of this should be seen in the fall of a mass from the top of a tower. It would, that is, not fall vertically but, if we suppose that the Earth rotates from west to east, would deviate to the west, and experience contradicts this. According to the Aristotelians this is exactly what happens in the case of a weight which is let fall from the top of a ship's mast. If the ship is stationary, the weight will fall perpendicularly; but if it is moving, the weight will fall with a displacement towards the stern.

Salviati responds that, both when the ship is moving and when it is stationary, the weight falls at the base of the mast with no displacement. The phenomenon, that is, of a falling mass follows the same law both when the reference system is at rest and when it is moving.[73] And so Salviati could conclude:

> Therefore, the same cause holding good on the earth as on the ship, nothing can be inferred about the earth's motion or rest from the stone falling always perpendicularly to the foot of the tower. (VII, 170; trans. by Drake 1967, 144-145).[74]

In the **third Day** the debate moves on to the question of the motion of revolution of the Earth about the Sun.[75] The discussion's beginning offers the opportunity to Salviati to go right to the bottom of his criticism of the 1628 book of Scipione Chiaramonti, *De Novis Stellis* (On the New Stars), a criticism already initiated (together with that of his other book, *Antitycho*) in the previous Days. It is obvious that Galileo had sensed the need to retract in this way his incautious reference to Chiaramonti in *The Assayer*.[76] And the data of Tycho Brahe on the *nova* of 1572 are widely used here to refute the statement of Chiaramonti (taken up by Simplicius) that this star had, in fact, been a sublunar phenomenon (in agreement with Aristotelian theory). In the rest of the debate Salviati considers the two most serious objections from the "scientific" point of view against the revolution of the Earth: the invariability during the year both of the apparent brightness of the fixed stars and of

their   position.[77]   Following   Copernicus   he   answers   these
objections by stating that, given the enormous distances of the
fixed stars from the Earth, such phenomena are not observable.[78]
On   the   other   hand,   retorts   Salviati,   there   are   enormous
difficulties against the Ptolemaic system and the most important
thing is that the solution to them is found precisely by accepting
the Copernican system. "The illnesses are in Ptolemy, and the
cures for them in Copernicus" (VII, 369; trans. by Drake 1967,
341). The   principal   difficulty   for   Ptolemy   consisted   in   the
explanation of the irregular motion of the planets:

> And what are we to say of the apparent movement of a
> planet, so uneven that it not only goes fast at one time and
> slow at another, but sometimes stops entirely and even
> goes backward a long way after doing so? To save these
> appearances, Ptolemy introduces vast epicycles, adapting
> them one by one to each planet, with certain rules about
> incongruous motions - all of which can be done away with
> by one very simple motion of the earth. (VII, 370; trans. by
> Drake 1967, 342).[79]

And Salviati shows how this comes about whenever one
adopts a motion of the Earth about the Sun (VII, 370-372).[80]

Together with these mathematical considerations, which are
developed very carefully beginning with the observational data
(as, for example, that on the nova of 1572),   we find ample
mention of the observations carried out with the telescope. These
observations,   comments   Salviati,   if   they   do   not   prove
Copernicanism, "they absolutely favor it and greatly" (VII, 363;
trans. by Drake 1967, 335) or at least they serve to weaken
numerous difficulties brought against it by the adversaries. One
such difficulty, states Salviati, comes from the fact that in the
Copernican system one had to admit that the Earth was a
unique exception since, while all the other planets moved alone
about the Sun, the Earth moved together with the Moon which
behaved as a satellite. But now, after the discovery that Jupiter
is "like another earth, going around the sun in twelve years
accompanied not by one but by four moons", such an "apparent
absurdity" has been eliminated (VII, 367-368; trans. by Drake
1967, 340).[81]

Further on Salviati mentions the discovery of the sunspots about which he states: "The original discoverer and observer of the solar spots (as indeed of all other novelties in the skies) was our Lincean Academician" (VII, 372; trans. by Drake 1967, 345). The polemical nature of these words becomes clear from the report which Salviati gives of the controversies "with a certain fictitious Apelle" and from his comment that with three letters to "Velsero" the same Lincean Academician had shown "how vain and foolish were the ideas of Apelle" (VII, 373; trans. by Drake 1967, 346) with respect to the sunspots.

Salviati emphasizes not only the value to be drawn from the phenomenon of the spots, considered as part of the Sun's surface, as a proof against the incorruptibility of heavenly bodies (in this case the Sun) but also their importance for deducing the motion of the Earth about the Sun. On this point Salviati cites the phenomenon of the curvature of the trajectories described by the spots and of the variation (in a period of one year) of the form and inclination of the curvature. As we have seen, this phenomenon had been accurately observed by Scheiner and described in the *Rosa Ursina*.[82] But Galileo differs from Scheiner by giving an explanation according to the Copernican system. After an accurate description of the phenomenon of the periodic variation of the trajectories and of its geometric implications (VII, 375-379) Galileo concludes that, if we admit the daily and annual motion of the Earth, then one more motion, that of a rotation (in less than a month) of the sun on its axis, which is inclined with respect to the ecliptic, is enough to explain the sunspot trajectories. But in the case of a geostatic theory one would have to attribute up to four motions to the Sun. The first and the second are those postulated by the geostatic theory of Ptolemy, that is, the movement of the annual rotation of the Sun along the ecliptic and that one (common to all heavenly bodies) of a daily rotation about the axis of the "*equinoziale*" or celestial equator. The third is a movement of rotation (of the length of about a month) about an axis inclined with respect to the axis of the ecliptic. The fourth, finally, comes from the fact that this axis of a monthly rotation does not keep a fixed direction, but describes in its turn a cone of rotation about yet another axis, distinct from that of the ecliptic and of the "*equinoziale*". (VII, 380-382).

Salviati's conclusion is that the explanation of the sunspot trajectories on the Copernican hypothesis is simple, whereas on the geocentric hypothesis it is complex and moreover has the disadvantage of having to postulate solar axial movements which are incongruous.[83]

The **fourth Day** represents the climactic point of the *Dialogue* and is completely focussed on the phenomenon of the ebb and flow of the tides, which, as we know, was for Galileo the strongest argument in favor of the Copernican system.

Before all else Salviati recognizes that, on the basis of the principle already explained in the **second Day**, terrestrial phenomenon are not capable of confirming whether the Earth is at rest or moving. But he adds:

> . . . it is only in the element of water (as something which is very vast and is not joined and linked with the terrestrial globe as are all its solid parts, but is rather, because of its fluidity, free and separate and a law unto itself) that we may recognize some trace or indication of the earth's behavior in regard to motion and rest. (VII, 442-443; trans. by Drake 1967, 417).

Right after this Salviati offers what were the fruits of lengthy reflections:

> After having many times examined for myself the effects and the events, partly seen and partly heard from other people, which are observed in the movements of the water; after, moreover, having read and listened to the great follies which many people have put forth as causes for these events, I have arrived at two conclusions which were not lightly to be drawn and granted. Certain necessary assumptions having been made, these are that if the terrestrial globe were immovable, the ebb and flow of the oceans could not occur naturally; and that when we confer upon the globe the movements just assigned to it, the seas are necessarily subjected to an ebb and flow agreeing in all respects with what is to be observed in them. (VII, 443; trans. by Drake 1967, 417).

As is evident from this quotation, Galileo was not ignorant of the fact that the traditional explanations, as well as recent, even very recent, ones, attributed the phenomenon of the tides to other causes, especially to the influence of the moon. And it was precisely this objection, enunciated by Simplicius, which must above all be considered and done away with.

Salviati, as well as Sagredo (but more peacefully), puts aside these opinions, qualifying them as "poetical". Nor is he any kinder in his judgement on Kepler, the most authoritative supporter of the lunar explanation of the tides.

> But among all the great men who have philosophized about this remarkable effect, I am more astonished at Kepler than at any other. Despite his open and acute mind, and though he has at his fingertips the motions attributed to the earth, he has nevertheless lent his ear and his assent to the moon's dominion over the waters, to occult properties, and to such puerilities. (VII, 486; trans. by Drake 1967, 462).

These words raise the legitimate doubt as to whether Galileo had ever read the Preface of the *Astronomia Nova* where Kepler gave his theory of the tides. The great German astronomer had begun with the brilliant supposition of an "attractive force" between the Earth and the Moon. This force would have acted in such wise that, if the two heavenly bodies had been capable of approaching one another, they would have come to collide after having travelled according to the inverse proportion of their proper sizes. This movement, Kepler had added, existed, in fact, in the case of the sea since it had a fluid nature which made it less strictly bound to the Earth.[84] And that explained the phenomenon of the tides. Seen against this general picture of a germinal concept of gravity, Kepler's theory of the tides went well beyond the traditional explanations based on the Moon's "dominion" of the waters and other occult properties. Driven by his instinctive repugnance to admit such "occult properties" and their affinity to the attempted explanation given by Aristotle's followers to so many natural phenomenon whose cause was unknown, Galileo undoubtedly was lacking in objectivity (in this as in other cases to do with Kepler) and he treated Kepler's theory as one of those traditional "fantasies".[85] And this led him to exclude the lunar explanation for the tides.

On the other hand the idea that a purely terrestrial (in the sense specified above) interpretation of the phenomenon of the tides was possible, once it became fixed in his head, fascinated him and no longer allowed him that intellectual freedom which was required for a completely objective evaluation of the phenomenon.

The majority of the authors who deal with this "proof" of Galileo's emphasize that it was completely erroneous.[86] In fact, there exists an effect on the tides of the Earth's rotation and in this sense Galileo's intuition was substantially correct at least from a qualitative point of view. But his error is in the quantitative treatment: the size of this effect is, in fact, very small and is, therefore, completely masked by the principal cause of the tides, namely the Moon's attraction.

On the other hand, even if the effect of the Earth's motion had been more important than it is in fact, it would have shown itself in the opposite sense to that of the actual motion of the tides. And that is the "drama" of this "proof" of Galileo's. In his effort to give an explanation of facts known since time immemorial (specifically the two-day, the monthly and the annual periods of the tides) Galileo was driven to use extraordinary subtleness and ingenuity, but without ever succeeding in giving an account of the real facts.[87]

By now the *Dialogue* is winding towards its end and as usual Sagredo is given the job of summarizing the fruit of the long discussions of the four Days.

> In the conversations of these four days we have, then, strong evidences in favor of the Copernican system, among which three have been shown to be very convincing - those taken from the stoppings and retrograde motions of the planets, and their approaches toward and recessions from the earth; second, from the revolution of the sun upon itself, and from what is to be observed in the sunspots; and third, from the ebbing and flowing of the ocean tides. (VII, 487; trans. by Drake 1967, 462).[88]

But Salviati must keep the promise which he made at the beginning of the *Dialogue* to remove the mask of Copernicanism. And he finally does it with these words:

> Now, since it is time to put an end to our discourses, it remains for me to beg you that if later, in going over the things that I have brought out, you should meet with any difficulty or any question not completely resolved, you will excuse my deficiency because of the novelty of the concept and the limitations of my abilities; then because of the magnitude of the subject; and finally because I do not claim and have not claimed from others that assent which I myself do not give to this invention, which may very easily turn out to be a most foolish hallucination and a majestic paradox.
>
> To you, Sagredo, though during my arguments you have shown yourself satisfied with some of my ideas and have approved them highly, I say that I take this to have arisen partly from their novelty rather than from their certainty, and even more from your courteous wish to afford me by your assent that pleasure which one naturally feels at the approbation and praise of what is one's own. (VII, 487-488; trans. by Drake 1967, 463).

After such long and varied discussions carried out with such rigor and with such weighty arguments in favor of the Copernican system how could Salviati now with such ease put down the mask and speak of "fantasies", of "a most foolish hallucination" and of "a majestic paradox"? At least for once it is Simplicius to whom we look to give the explanation of this psychological portent.

> As to the discourses we have held, and especially this last one concerning the reasons for the ebbing and flowing of the ocean, I am really not entirely convinced; but from such feeble ideas of the matter as I have formed, I admit that your thoughts seem to me more ingenious than many others I have heard. I do not therefore consider them true and conclusive; indeed, keeping always before my mind's eye a most solid doctrine that I once heard from a most eminent and learned person, and before which one must fall silent, I know that if I asked whether God in His

infinite power and wisdom could have conferred upon the watery element its observed reciprocating motion using some other means than moving its containing vessels, both of you would reply that He could have, and that He would have known how to do this in many ways which are unthinkable to our minds. From this I forthwith conclude that, this being so, it would be excessive boldness for anyone to limit and restrict the Divine power and wisdom to some particular fancy of his own. (VII, 488; trans. by Drake 1967, 464).

It is the argument of Urban VIII. But placed here, and in the mouth of the one who throughout the *Dialogue* has been the partisan of the most backward and insupportable ideas, gives it the semblance of a ridiculous and illusory *deus ex macchina*. We shall see how, in all probability, Galileo's adversaries will not fail to make this known to the person concerned.

For once Salviati finds himself in agreement with Simplicius.

An admirable and angelic doctrine, and well in accord with another one, also Divine, which, while it grants to us the right to argue about the constitution of the universe (perhaps in order that the working of the human mind shall not be curtailed or made lazy) adds that we cannot discover the work of His hands. Let us, then, exercise these activities permitted to us and ordained by God, that we may recognize and thereby so much the more admire His greatness, however much less fit we may find ourselves to penetrate the profound depths of His infinite wisdom. (VII, 489; trans. by Drake 1967, 464).

With these words the *Dialogue* practically comes to an end. It is a work which is not, nor was it intended to be, a dry treatise in astronomy and natural philosophy. It is rather a polemical writing and, at the same time, a didactic one in support of Copernicanism. In writing it Galileo remembered quite distinctly the long years of battles with the Aristotelians, their unshakable opposition to new ideas and to new discoveries. It was a matter of an entire worldview, the one based on the *Physica* (Physics) and on the *De Coelo* (On the heavens) of

Aristotle, which had to be demolished so as to prepare the way for a recognition of heliocentrism by educated persons (including ecclesiastics) in Italy and all of Europe. But in order to get to that point it was necessary to add to the rigor of argumentation on the plane of the new natural philosophy, of which Galileo made himself a flag bearer, all the rich variety of considerations and digressions required to convince the vast public whom Galileo was addressing.

It is, therefore, a work of patient pedagogy with which Galileo seeks to lead the reader mentally and at the same time psychologically along the lengthy and tiring stretch of road that leads from the old to the new view of the world.

But it would be wrong, it seems, to see in this a work rather of "cultural propaganda" than of true scientific content. Although Galileo has not given a rigorously valid and "decisive" proof of the motion of the Earth nor does he claim to have done so,[89] he has still with perfect scientific rigor removed the obstacles which had been set up against accepting Copernicanism, including those deriving from the convictions of "common sense" which had had such significance in the thinking of Aristotle, Ptolemy and, as we have seen, in that of Bellarmine. This scientific rigor of Galileo's was based on results already obtained in the field of astronomical observations, as well as in that of the new "natural philosophy", whose foundations he had been laying since his years in Padua and which was now for the first time being presented to the educated public in expectation of a more systematic and comprehensive formulation in the *Discourses* of 1638. In this way Galileo has without a doubt made a decisive contribution to the triumph of Copernicanism.[90]

Finally, the *Dialogue* is a profoundly human work. It is full of the richness of Galileo's personality, not less than of the echoes of the drama of his life. It is an interior drama, before it opens out into the exterior one, which we must consider in the following pages. There are the repeated protests of uncertainty, of doubt precisely at the moment when the conclusion of Copernicus seems to be most convincing; there are the words such as "hallucination", "fantasy", "paradox" which suddenly come forth upon a tighly-knit rigorous reasoning; there is especially the claim of Salviati that his Copernicanism is no more than a "mask" and that his true conviction is shown at the end of the *Dialogue* with his unconditioned assent to the comment of Simplicius. All of this has scandalized many biographers of Galileo so that they have accused him of being two-faced, of playing around disloyally and of being afraid. To us those judgements seem to be profoundly unjust. If Galileo had wished to be disloyal, to play at being two-faced, to seek protection, he should have covered his hand better. In fact, the very evidence from Galileo's "game" is, it seems, the indication of a temperament too sincere to be able to successfully play games.

Sixteen years earlier Galileo himself had written in the *Letter to Christina of Lorraine*:

> . . . to command that the very professors of astronomy themselves see to the refutation of their own observations and proofs as mere fallacies and sophisms is to enjoin something that lies beyond any possibility of accomplishment. (V, 325; trans. by Drake 1957, 193).

The *Dialogue* is the clearest proof of that impossibility.

NOTES

[1] In the letter to Cesi of 15 May, cited above, Galileo wrote as regards this German cardinal:

> . . . although his knowledge of our studies is not very deep, he nonetheless shows a good understanding of the point and of what is required in these matters, and he told me that he wished to deal with His Holiness about them before he left (XIII, 179).

[2] On this matter see the beautiful pages written by Galileo in the *Dialogue* (VII, 126-131) where he especially makes evident the certainty attainable by the human being about mathematical propositions:

> . . . the human understanding can be taken in two modes, the *intensive* or the *extensive. Extensively*, that is, with regard to the multitude of intelligibles, which are infinite,

THE *DIALOGUE* IS PUBLISHED   361

the human understanding is as nothing even if it
understands a thousand propositions; for a thousand in
relation to infinity is zero. But taking man's understanding
intensively, in so far as this term denotes understanding
some proposition perfectly, I say that the human intellect
does understand some of them perfectly, and thus in these
it has as much absolute certainty as Nature itself has. Of
such are the mathematical sciences alone; that is, geometry
and arithmetic, in which the Divine intellect indeed knows
infinitely more propositions, since it knows all. But with
regard to those few which the human intellect does
understand, I believe that its knowledge equals the Divine
in objective certainty, for here it succeeds in understanding
necessity, beyond which there can be no greater sureness.
(VII, 128-129; trans. by Drake 1967, 103).

But, as we know, for Galileo mathematics is at the foundation of the
"necessary demonstrations" which are obtained by beginning with
"sense experience". Therefore, these necessary demonstrations may also
partake (although not with the same immediacy as mathematical
propositions) of the certainty of these latter.

[3] See de Santillana 1955, 127, Note 2 and 165, Note 7. Agostino
Oreggi (or Oregio from the Latin *Oregius*, 1577-1635) had studied at
the Roman College thanks to the help of Cardinal Bellarmine. He
became a priest and entered the court of Cardinal Maffeo Barberini
who, when he became Pope, appointed him as pontifical theologian and
in November 1633 he will make him a cardinal.

[4] Naturally, Galileo had not said a word, when he spoke with
Urban VIII, of Bellarmine's admonition and less so of the injunction
given him immediately thereafter in February 1616 by the Commissary
of the Holy Office, Segizzi. Drake comments in regard to the injunction
that, although Galileo was doubtlessly led to keep silent, relying upon
the declaration given him by Bellarmine, "in the end that omission on
his part turned out to be a fatal error" (Drake 1978, 291). But Galileo
surely had no suspicion that there existed a report which Segizzi had
had inserted in the archives of the Holy Office and, therefore, as I see
it, he must not have even thought of the problem. His error, instead,
was to keep quiet about Bellarmine's admonition. As we shall see, at
the time of the trial of 1633, the testimony which Bellarmine gave to
him, and which was presented by him on that occasion, was not
considered at all to be an attenuating circumstance, but rather an
aggravating one, as the condemnation sentence itself makes quite clear.

[5] In this regard see the words written by Galileo to Cesi in June (XIII, 183). Galileo's state of mind is expressed even more clearly in a letter to Picchena, who had encouraged him to stay and await patiently an improvement in the situation:

> The rest of the time I go on spending on various visits which in the final analysis make me sense, like touching it with my hand, that I am old, and that courting is the business of the young for they, because of their physical robustness and the allurement of their hopes, are strong in tolerating such toils; thus I, because of lack of these [robustness and allurement], wish to return to my peace and I will do so as soon as I can. (XIII, 175).

[6] For a brilliant attempt to reconstruct this meeting of Galileo with Urban VIII see de Santillana 1960, 321-323. But de Santillana is wrong when he writes:

> The Pope will have said, for sure, that there were misunderstandings about Copernicus, misunderstandings which he had given the job to dissipate already in the meeting of the Congregation of 25 February 1616. (de Santillana 1960, 321).

Maffeo Barberini was not among the Cardinals who were members of the Holy Office in 1616 and, therefore, did not make an intervention (nor did Cardinal Caetani, who was also not a member) at that session, but he did so in another place and on another occasion, mostly likely at the time of the meeting of the Congregation of the Index (of which he and Caetani, indeed, were members) in Bellarmine's residence a few days later. See Notes 78 and 79 of Chapter 3. On the other hand, had Maffeo Barberini participated at that session, he would have been informed of the precept to be imposed on Galileo and he would certainly have remembered that precept at the time of his conversations with Galileo in 1624. In that case his indignation with Galileo in 1632 for having kept quiet about that precept would be inexplicable.

[7] On Ingoli see Chapter 3, notes 50 and 80. As we know, in 1622 he had become secretary of the Congregation of the Propagation of the Faith to which the control of the missionary activity of the Church had been assigned.

[8] As we have already seen (see Chapter 3, Note 50), Kepler had instead answered Ingoli and had obtained another reply from him. Campanella had also come to know of the work while he was still in prison in Naples and he had written to Galileo (3 November 1616),

stating that he was ready to confute Ingoli if Galileo wanted him to (XII, 287). But Galileo was very wary of accepting a proposal like that, as he will be with others that will come later on from the Dominican thinker. Besides the obvious need to be prudent, there was and always will be Galileo's instinctive reserve deriving from a temperament and an intellectual posture totally different from those of Campanella. For the preparation of his reply, Galileo had requested and obtained from his Roman friends copies of Ingoli's *Disputation* and of his *Answers* to Kepler.

⁹ See the letter of Galileo to Cesi of 23 September 1624 (XIII, 209). The *Lettera a Francesco Ingoli* is found in VI, 509-561.

¹⁰ Despite the severity of these words, this *Letter to Ingoli* "had nothing of the sharp polemic character of *The Assayer*, but appeared to be sincerely devoted to persuasion, to the elimination one by one of all the doubts raised by the opponent, and to the exploration with him of every difficulty" (Geymonat 1965, 117). For a more thorough treatment of this letter, see Geymonat 1965, 114-121 and more recently Drake 1978, 291-295 and Bucciantini 1995, 158-168.

¹¹ See XIII, 240. Cesare Marsili from Bologna had met Galileo during his last stay in Rome. And Galileo had had such a fine impression of his intellectual gifts as to consider him to be "a worthy successor and heir of Mr. Filippo Salviati" (letter of Galileo to Cesi of May 1624: XIII, 179). Galileo will keep up his correspondence with Marsili right up to the latter's death in 1633.

¹² On this inaugural lecture see Redondi 1987, 132-134. Redondi gives particular importance to the expressions used by Father Spinola, especially the one, "seeds of heresy" being spread around by the new doctrines. According to Redondi these would give an indication of the reactions of the Jesuits of the Roman College (particularly of Father Grassi) to certain statements of Galileo in *The Assayer* and especially to his atomistic ideas (see Note 62, Chapter 4). Furthermore, according to Redondi, Grassi, since he considered such ideas in sharp contrast with the Catholic dogma of the Eucharist, would later on have made an accusation about it to the Holy Office and this was the real (even though secret) cause of Galileo's condemnation. I will have the opportunity to return to this thesis of Redondi (see the following note 14), presented in a brilliant and enticing way, but, in my opinion, completely lacking in objective foundations.

¹³ Another person whom Galileo had decided, despite his intentions at the beginning, not to allow to read the copy of the *Letter to Ingoli* was Father Grassi, who was at that time preparing his response to *The Assayer* and who, by Guiducci's words, was courting

the latter and showing himself to be well disposed to Galileo (as I have noted before).

[14] Guiducci told Galileo that Guevara was "a General of a kind of Theatines, who I believe are called the *Minimi*", but he was wrong. Guevara was General of the Clerks Regular Minor, a religious congregation founded in Naples at the end of the XVI century. Redondi 1987, 166-175 has furnished detailed information on Guevara. According to Redondi the word given by Guiducci to Galileo on the accusation presented to the Holy Office about *The Assayer* was the result of an equivocation (by Guiducci himself or by Cesi from whom Guiducci had received it). In fact, the accusation was not about the Copernicanism of *The Assayer*, but once again about Galileo's atomism with respect to the phenomenon of heat. According to the author of the accusation this was in opposition to the doctrine of the Eucharist sanctioned by the Council of Trent. Redondi 1987, 149 ff. claims to have discovered the original text of this accusation in a document found by him in the archives of the Holy Office. To support his interpretation Redondi emphasizes the fact that in *The Assayer* Galileo is extremely cautious about making declarations on Copernicanism, so that an accusation of Copernicanism, based upon this book, would not have had any serious foundation. See the comment by Drake 1978, 300 as regards this accusation: "The complaint that Galileo had praised Copernicanism in the book was simply false". Moreover, it would seem unlikely that Guevara would have put in writing any kind of defense of Copernicanism or even more unlikely that with this response of his things would have quieted down. The decree of 1616 still carried its full force and it would have been truly strange if Guevara had shown himself to be so little concerned while Galileo showed great caution. But it seems that the opinion given by Ferrone and Firpo 1985a against the hypothesis of Redondi of an equivocation by Guiducci (or by Cesi) merits consideration. As these authors emphasize:

> . . . there are at least about fifteen references to Copernicus in *The Assayer* . . . , and, although all of them are accompanied by a dutiful act of submission to the 'salutary edict' of 1616, they always leave the impression of a subtle strategy of proposing over again the heliocentric theory, as Grassi also had no difficulty pointing out right away in his *Ratio* (Ferrone and Firpo 1985a, 205, note 45).

On the other hand, still according to Ferrone and Firpo, Guevara would have easily been able to write in defense of Copernicanism, on the condition that he spoke of it from the point of view of a mere mathematical hypothesis (Ferrone and Firpo 1985a, 205-206). The remarks of Bucciantini 1995, 171-172, Note 72, seem also to be quite to the point both as to the exactness of Guiducci's statements and as to the meaning which Guevara's "defense" of Copernicanism might have, since the theory was not condemned as heretical. At any rate it seems that Redondi surely goes too far in his reconstruction of the facts, when he puts forth another hypothesis (central to his book), namely, that Grassi was the author of the accusation. For sure the latter in his response to *The Assayer*, which was published a little more than a year after this accusation, puts forth serious difficulties (dealing still with the Catholic doctrine of the Eucharist) against the theory of Democritus which, according to Grassi, Galileo had made his own. Nonetheless, I find it impossible to follow Redondi in his declaration that Grassi is the author of the accusation. Besides the fact that the comparison of the handwriting of the text of the accusation with that of a letter of Grassi (see Figures 7 and 8 in Redondi 1987) is far from convincing nor does it even suggest that the authors are the same (although Redondi affirms the opposite), all of Redondi's reasoning "by exclusion" to prove that the only possible author of the accusation was Grassi seems, indeed, too simplistic. And, as far as I know, this appears to be the opinion of the best specialists on Galileo, who have all together refused to follow Redondi's conclusions. Again, for a critique that is detailed and to the point consult the full article of Ferrone and Firpo 1985a, 177-238. Redondi 1985, 934-968 has responded to their article in the same review and there was a further response to Redondi by Ferrone and Firpo 1985b, 957-968. It appears to me that the response of Westfall 1989, 84-99 to Redondi is also important, as is the one of Mayaud 1992a.

[15] Drake 1978, 300 states that Father Scheiner could have been the "pious person" who denounced *The Assayer* to the Holy Office. But this is also a pure supposition. And it collapses completely (together with the thesis of Redondi) if one accepts what has been put in evidence by Pagano 1984, 46-47, namely, that the watermark of the paper on which the anonymous document is penned shows "the escutcheon of an ecclesiastic, no doubt an archbishop or cardinal".

[16] As we know, the first idea of this "proof" in favor of Copernicanism had come to Galileo during his time in Padua. In 1615-1616 (if not even before that) the idea had taken a more precise form and he had communicated it in a manuscript to Cardinal Orsini and later to the Archduke Leopold of Austria. (This manuscript was published by Favaro in V, 377-395. For an English translation see Finocchiaro 1989, 119-133). But it appears that Galileo had continued, although by fits and starts, to dedicate time to it.

[17] As we see, Galileo had by now decided to put his treatise in the form of a dialogue.

[18] Elia Diodati (1576-1661) was the son of parents from Lucca but they had taken refuge in Geneva because they were Calvinists. Later Diodati moved to France and became a lawyer at the Paris Parliament. His acquaintance with Galileo probably went back to the time of his first trip to Italy (1620). Galileo had one of his best portraits painted for Diodati by the painter Giusto Sustermans. Diodati, in addition to Galileo, had been in communication with many of the most eminent politicians and scientists of his day.

[19] He must have said this to Ciampoli, who in his reply of 28 December 1624 (XIII, 295) rejoiced with Galileo for having almost completed his work.

[20] Undoubtedly family problems continued to occupy a great deal of his time. In August 1627 his brother, Michelangelo, returned to Florence from Munich with all of his numerous family, which he then entrusted to Galileo (for more than a year) when he departed anew for Germany. Even after the death of Michelangelo, which occurred three years later, Galileo continued to take an interest in his nephews.

[21] Here is an opinion of de Santillana:

> He [Galileo] was no Bruno or Campanella, to rush into print with generous certainties and uncertain reasons. The "immense design" was proving even more appalling as he faced it at long last, and more difficult to encompass. As the physicist's thought was grappling with its difficulties, it had to mature at the same time the foundations of that theory of motion which was to be the subject of his later *Discourses on the Two New Sciences*. They were taking shape in his own mind even as he labored at his cosmological exposition. All could not but go together (de Santillana 1955, 173).

[22] That the fundamental reason for the interruption was to be found in the work itself seems to be confirmed by the words which Galileo wrote to Cesi on 24 December 1629:

> . . . having two months ago taken up the pen again I have brought close to port my Dialogues, and I have explained very clearly those obscurities which I had almost always held as inexplicable. (XIV, 60).

Also in a letter written a little before that to Diodati Galileo said:

> I have taken up again work on the Dialogue of the Ebb and Flow of the Sea, which was left aside for three years,

and with God's grace I have found the right line, which ought to allow me to terminate it within the winter; it will provide, I trust, a most ample confirmation of the Copernican system (XIV, 49; trans. by de Santillana 1955, 173).

Westfall 1989, 59 ff. sees other reasons for this long delay in the composition of the *Dialogue*, and, above all, in the fact that Galileo feared the reactions of his enemies who were always active in Rome and Florence (with the danger that the latter would be able to influence the regent Christina of Lorraine and thus compromise his position as mathematician of the Grand Duke). It is possible that such fears played a part, but it seems to me that they did not play a determining role in delaying the composition of the book.

[23] Perhaps with these words Stelluti intended only to say that Scheiner had subscribed to Galileo's theory of the sunspots (as was so); however, see Note 26 to follow.

[24] A not very kind comment of Galileo to this news is found in a letter of his to Marsili of 19 April 1629:

I hear . . . that the fictitious Apelle is printing in Bracciano a long treatise on sunspots; and the fact that it is long makes me very doubtful as to whether it is not full of blunders, which, being as they were infinite, can soil many pages, where there is little place for the truth; and I am certain that, if he will say anything other than what I have already said in my sunspot letters, he will be speaking only vanities and lies. (XIV, 36).

As we see, here as so many times elsewhere, when dealing with his adversaries, Galileo lost his equanimity, not to speak of his modesty!

[25] Prince Paolo Orsini (1591-1656) was the older brother of Cardinal Alessandro Orsini, whom we have already met.

[26] Particularly harsh was Castelli's comment in his letter to Galileo of 26 September 1631 (XIV, 297). Likewise harsh was the judgment on this work of Scheiner by the Galileian "hagiography" of the last century, especially in Italy. See the remarks made in this regard by Baldini 1992, 98 ff. As Baldini has emphasized it has only been from the end of the last century (and mostly outside of Italy) that there has occurred a reevaluation of Scheiner's work (see Baldini 1992, 115-116, Note 107 for a bibliography in this respect). Baldini 1992, 100-101 reports the "censures" placed on the Rosa Ursina by Jesuit mathematicians, among them Grassi. In the rather positive judgment given by all of these "censors", Baldini sees a confirmation of the fact

that among Jesuits this work was seen as a just claim for the freedom of scientific research when faced with the bonds of Aristotelianism. On the contribution given to the decline of Aristotelianism in the XVII century see MacColley 1942.

[27] As we shall see, Galileo in the *Dialogue* will use the phenomenon of the curvature of the trajectories described by the sunspots as an argument in favor of the rotation of the Earth about the Sun. Later on Scheiner with very harsh words will accuse Galileo of having made up this argument by making use of the data contained in the *Rosa Ursina* without mentioning the source (see the letter to Pietro Gassendi of 16 July 1633: XV, 183). Also, various Galilean scholars have maintained that Galileo, having come to know of the data of Scheiner, exploited them by introducing at the last moment (in the third "Day") his Copernican argument based on those characteristics of the trajectories of the sunspots. It appears, however, that the contrary arguments brought forward by Drake 1970b, 177-199 and 1978, 333-335 are very strong. At any rate, the merit still goes to Galileo for at least having seen the importance of such a phenomenon for the Copernican system and for having given the correct interpretation to it. Scheiner, on the other hand, since he was not able to do likewise, was driven in the *Rosa Ursina* to a veritable *tour de force* in order to explain the phenomenon within the picture of a stationary Earth. And, according to some historians, it was just this dissatisfaction with his attempt that had brought Scheiner to subscribe in secret to Copernicanism. See again Drake 1978, 498, Note 5. Should this be true, Stelluti's statement, which I have cited above in the text, would be true.

[28] See Drake 1978, 332-334.

[29] Orsini had travelled to Naples before the issue of the *Rosa Ursina* and it is, in fact, possible that he had not yet seen the volume. But even if he had had it in his hands, the massiveness of it would have discouraged him. Still, it would have been enough to read the first pages to become aware of how bitter the tone was that Scheiner used in Galileo's regard. Surely Galileo had a great deal to do with the deterioration in the relationships with the Jesuit, but the latter had, indeed, wanted to get back at him "tit for tat".

[30] See Castelli's letter to Galileo of 20 February 1632 (XIV, 330) which reports the advice of Ciampoli from Rome not to waste "a single word on the German". Ciampoli probably thought that a further aggravation of the situation between Galileo and Scheiner, and with the Jesuits in general, was absolutely to be avoided. But his formulation of the sentence would seem to indicate a concrete worry about eventual reactions from "the German". We do not know what was in the air and

we will probably never know it with any certainty. But, as we shall see, there will not be lacking those who, after the trial and condemnation of Galileo, will, as a matter of fact, attribute the primary responsibility for it to Scheiner.

[31] According to Drake 1978, 333 the only addition made at the last moment to the *Dialogue* was the reference to the first observations of the sunspots which Galileo stated he had made while he was still at Padua, a year before the documented observations which he made while he was in Rome in April 1616. Drake, however, comments that in the *Sunspot Letters* there is no mention at all of these previous observations, despite the fact that the debate was already going on about the priority between Galileo and Scheiner. And this seems to incline Drake to doubt the reality of the observations in Padua. Still according to Drake, the addition made by Galileo was suggested to him by a letter received at the end of 1631 by Micanzio who recalled that he had participated, together with Sarpi who was by now deceased, at the first observations of the sunspots a little before Galileo's departure for Florence (XIV, 299). But it seems to me that to prove that Galileo's addition does not correspond to the true facts, it would be necessary to explain why in the world Micanzio ought to have recounted (with such abundant vivid detail) the "story" of the observations at Padua. Was it a "little white lie" to help his friend Galileo in the argument with Scheiner? It does not seem that Micanzio was a person who would lie in that way or even that all alone he would have dreamt up an event which never happened. As to the fact, moreover, that Galileo had kept quiet about those observations in the *Sunspot Letters*, it might be answered that the question of priority had not yet degenerated into an open dispute and, on the other hand, Galileo had perhaps not wanted to draw into play the witness of two men, such as Sarpi and Micanzio, who were so unpopular, especially the first, in the view of the Roman religious authorities. We should not forget that the *Sunspot Letters* were to be printed in Rome with the approval of the Roman Church authorities. And we should remember that in the deposition against Galileo, made three years later to the Holy Office by Caccini, one of the charges against Galileo was his friendship with Sarpi (XIX, 310). This should be enough to see how well founded would have been the prudence of Galileo (which, for that matter, is also visible in the *Dialogue* where Sarpi and Micanzio are not mentioned, but it is only said: "I spoke about it with several of whom some are still alive" [VII, 372]). To conclude, it could be quite true, as Drake thinks, that the words about the observations in Padua were an addition made at the last moment influenced by Micanzio's letter. But my opinion is that this letter reported a true fact, that Galileo had certainly not forgotten,

but that he omitted making a report in the *Sunspot Letters* for the reasons of prudence already mentioned. On the other hand, a vague mention without names, such as the one in the *Dialogue*, was certainly not enough to lay claims to rights of priority. And so, in the *Sunspot Letters* Galileo had decided to keep completely quiet about the former observations in Padua (which, in fact, remained in a state of uncertainty, not yet clarified, as we can see from the very letter of Micanzio).

[32] See XIV, 73-76, 93, 278. Galileo will never overcome his uncertainty about the "proof from the tides". To me this seems to be confirmed by the fact that towards the end of his life he put this "proof" aside and accepted the traditional interpretation of the "lunar" origin of the tides. When he wrote to Micanzio in November 1637 to tell him of the discovery of the three-fold libration of the moon with three different periods of a day, a month, and a year, he added the comment:

> Now what would Your Most Reverend Paternity say in face of these three lunar periods with the three periods of a day, a month and a year for the movement of the sea *of which, by the common consent of all, the moon is the referee and the superintendent?* (XVII, 215; italics by Fantoli).

[33] Here we have one of the first hints from Galileo of the poor conditions of his sight. The situation will get worse in the coming years and he will finally end up completely blind.

[34] Castelli himself had seen that caution was always necessary. While he was speaking with Cardinal Francesco Barberini on Galileo's argument from the ebb and flow of the sea, another person present was heard to object that in that argument Galileo presupposed the motion of the Earth. Castelli had to beat a quick retreat by saying that Galileo

> was not asserting that as true but only that it showed that should the motion of the earth be true, there would necessarily follow the ebb and flow [of the sea]: and although the Lord Cardinal showed himself to be quite adverse to the principle, still he received me for a long time alone in his chamber, and substantially he told me that it was his opinion that, given the motion of the earth, it would be necessary that it be a star, and this seemed to be too contrary to theological truths. To this I responded that Your Lordship would have many demonstrations to the contrary, and that you would have proved that the

earth was not a star . . . and so he told me that Your Lordship must prove this, and that for the rest things could be let go. (XIV, 78)

In his response, Castelli had probably played on the difference between *star* and *planet*. But the Cardinal certainly did not pay attention to this subtlety and, when the *Dialogue* appeared he had to persuade himself that, contrary to what Castelli had stated, Galileo had, as a matter of fact, made the Earth a *star*.

[35] See XIV, 90.

[36] He was the son of the Ambassador Niccolini who had hosted Galileo at the time of his first trip to Rome in 1611.

[37] Besides the support of his friends such as Cesi (who had taken up the task of editing the *Dialogue* in the name of the *Accademia dei Lincei*) and Ciampoli, Galileo now also had in Rome his friend and most faithful disciple, Castelli, who had been appointed by Urban VIII as lecturer in mathematics at the "Sapienza" and at the same time tutor to his nephew, Taddeo Barberini. Ciampoli, therefore, had every right to state that now was the most opportune moment to obtain permission to publish the work, an opportunity which perhaps would never again present itself (see XIV, 82).

[38] In that same audience Urban VIII promised Galileo the grant of an ecclesiastical pension, which was, in fact, given to him together with another one which he received in 1631.

[39] In the biographical information to do with Antonio Badelli Favaro states that "from 1628 to 1644 he belonged to that 'noble assembly of novelists' who gathered in Rome at the Church of the Minerva or in that of S. Andrea della Valle to assemble information from around the world which was then distributed through the so-called handwritten *Notices*" (XX, 378).

[40] However, Urban VIII's severity was not dictated only by superstition. Since the horoscope foresaw the imminent death of the Pope, it risked nourishing a psychological situation of a "political vacuum" which was totally to Urban VIII's disadvantage, since he was at that time confronted with particularly urgent and difficult decisions, so that the full possession of pontifical authority was a necessity for him.

[41] He was the son of Lionardo, brother of the great Michelangelo, and he was born in 1568. He held various public offices and he was a member of the Florentine Academy and of the Academy of the *Crusca* (*crusca* literally means chaff; this was the name of the Florentine Academy of Letters). He died in 1646.

[42] In addition to reporting the rumor that Galileo was the author of the horoscope the "Notice" also spoke (as we have seen) of the book which he was trying to get printed "in which he impugns many opinions that are held by the Jesuits". Where did this information come from? Perhaps from some slip of the tongue by Father Riccardi? At any rate it must also have contributed to keeping Galileo's adversaries on the alert.

[43] See the report written by Riccardi at the time of Galileo's trial (XIX, 325).

[44] While Father Visconti had taken a positive stand with respect to the *Dialogue*, Urban VIII had, on the other hand, shown "annoyance" at the fact that Galileo claimed to show that the ebb and flow of the sea depended on the motion of the Earth. See the letter of Orso d'Elci to Galileo of 3 June 1630 (XIV, 113). Riccardi was doubtlessly aware of this annoyance of Urban VIII and it must have worried him. In the same letter d'Elci seems to say that Visconti hoped to persuade the Pope. But this attempt must never have occurred, since a little later Visconti (who was a friend of Orazio Morandi and who, like him, had an interest in astrology and had written an "Astrological Discourse" on the life of Urban VIII) became involved in Morandi's trial. Even though Visconti, unlike Morandi, succeeded in freeing himself from any blame, he was exiled from Rome. Thus, Riccardi could no longer count on his support. Nor could Galileo.

[45] In the letter sent much later to Andrea Cioli (7 March 1631) Galileo mentioned as elements still to be added "the table (index), the dedication and other circumstantial matters" (XIV, 216). He does not speak of any changes to be made. In fact, based on Visconti's words quoted above, it appears that Father Riccardi was to have taken care of the "some few little things". Probably Riccardi did not have time to do it before Galileo's departure and so at the end he gave the manuscript as it was back to Galileo who by now was impatient to return to Florence.

[46] After Cesi's death the *Accademia dei Lincei* was left without "a prince" or president, at the wish perhaps of Cardinal Francesco Barberini who was its protector, but definitely at the wish of Urban VIII who did not accept very well its attitude of independence. In all likelihood the condemnation of Galileo, who was its most famous member, contributed to the decline and to the gradual snuffing out of this Academy.

[47] As before Visconti was an optimist. But Castelli, for once at least, showed a sudden preoccupation but without any explanation of what was the matter. It is likely that Galileo's enemies who, as we know, were already aware of the imminent publication of his new book,

continued to cause trouble in Rome by seeking out new ways to damage him after the failure of their insinuations of his authorship of the horoscope. It is important to take account of this movement against Galileo which existed even before the publication of the *Dialogue*, in order to be able to understand the orchestrated "furor" at the time it appeared in Rome. Undoubtedly there were many who carried forth this action against Galileo, although, considering the actual state of the documentation, it is not possible to point with certainty to a particular group (Jesuit or Dominican), and even less so to particular individuals (such as Grassi or Scheiner).

[48] See Galileo's letter to Baliani of 6 August 1630 (XIV, 130) and Baliani's answer of 24 October (XIV, 160).

[49] Father Stefani had put himself right to the task and, except for a few word changes, had given a clear positive judgement according to what Galileo wrote to Cioli on 7 March 1631 (XIV, 217).

[50] XIV, 251. Niccolini justified all of this prudence with the words: "But the truth is that these opinions are not received well here, especially by superiors".

[51] As we see the preface and the conclusion of the book were the parts to which Riccardi gave most importance. As we have seen, Galileo had already sent these two parts of the book to Riccardi. But it seems that Riccardi never sent them back corrected. So the new request by the Master of the Sacred Palace to have them sent could only refer to the text which Galileo now wished to have printed.

[52] These instructions are found in XIX, 327. In them among other matters Riccardi said:

> Your Very Reverend Paternity can avail yourself of your authority and dispatch or not dispatch the book without depending in any way on my review. However, I want to remind you that Our Master [the Pope] thinks that the title and subject should not focus on the ebb and flow but absolutely on the mathematical examination of the Copernican position on the earth's motion, with the aim of proving that, if we remove divine revelation and sacred doctrine, the appearances could be saved with this supposition; one would thus be answering all the contrary indications which may be put forth by experience and by Peripatetic philosophy, so that one would never be admitting the absolute truth of this opinion, but only its hypothetical truth without the benefit of Scripture. It must also be shown that this work is written only to show that we do not know all the arguments that can be advanced

for this side, and that it was not for lack of knowledge that
the decree was issued in Rome; this should be the gist of
the book's beginning and ending, which I will send from
here properly revised. With this provision the book will
encounter no obstacle here in Rome. (trans. by Finocchiaro
1989, 212).

As we see, Riccardi returned to the argument with which Galileo had
justified, in his *Letter to Ingoli*, taking up again the consideration of
the Copernican system despite the decree of the Index of 1616. Father
Egidi promised to keep himself to this prescript and he emphasized
that Galileo was prepared to introduce the changes which had been
requested of him (XIX, 328).

[53] The inquisitor in Florence and Father Stefani (the consultor of
the Holy Office in that city) had already been for some time before
favorable to the publication and they must have readily provided their
approval. Thus the printing could begin almost immediately after the
receipt in Florence of Father Riccardi's instructions.

[54] The printing went slowly because of the large number (1000)
of copies which the editor was having printed.

[55] The text sent by Father Riccardi is found in XIX, 328-330 and
has been inserted in the *Dialogue* just as it is. As we have seen, it had
been written by Galileo and then sent to Father Riccardi, who does not
appear to have made any important changes in it. As to the conclusion
Riccardi had written nothing, limiting himself to the request:

> . . . at the end the peroration has to be made . . in
> accordance with this preface, and Galilei should add [in it]
> the reasons of the divine omnipotence spoken to him by
> Our Lord [the Pope] and these should put the mind at
> peace, even if there is no way of getting away from those
> arguments. (XIX, 330).

Since Galileo had already sent to Riccardi the conclusion of his book
along with the preface (XIV, 216), it is difficult to make sense of these
instructions of Riccardi, unless we suppose that the famous final
argument by the mouth of Simplicius had been added at the last
moment with the express purpose of respecting this request. Riccardi,
of course, had certainly not suggested that Simplicius himself would be
the exponent of the "theological" argument of Urban VIII!

[56] In the same letter Galileo expressed his regret that he had not
been able to put the original title which he had chosen ("On the ebb
and flow of the sea"), even though this was the principal argument of
the work. But he was thus consoled:

. . . but well is it granted that I propose the two chief systems of Ptolemy and Copernicus, with the statement that both be examined, and that I produce for one and the other all that can be said, leaving the judgement on them pending. (XIV, 289).

[57] So Francesco Duodo, a former student of Galileo's at Padua, wrote to him on 27 December with the proposal that he have the book printed in Venice and he even suggested that he come back to teach at Padua (XIV, 321). Galileo had himself considered momentarily having the *Dialogue* printed in the Republic of Venice (XIV, 130), but he later put the idea aside.

[58] As we see, Galileo was more than generous in his listing of these approbations, the first two of which were not called for, since the book had no longer been printed in Rome. And this will be one of the points on which he will be accused.

[59] VII, 25 (trans. by Drake 1986, 158). This volume contains the *Dialogue* up until page 520. From page 521 to page 526 there are included fragments related to it. For a thorough analysis of its content, see Finocchiaro 1980. Drake 1986 states that the abbreviated form, *Dialogue Concerning the Two Chief World Systems*, in use since the 1744 edition, "has ever since masqueraded as" the original title, thus allowing scholars to imagine that:

. . Galileo promised a book about planetary astronomies, though he certainly did not present one . . . The title page of the *Dialogue* promised no astronomic reasoning whatever, but only philosophical and "natural" - which is to say, metaphysical and physical - arguments, presented without positive determination. Scholars knew that Galileo's original title for the book had been deleted by censors before the *Dialogue* went to press, but they did not attach great importance to that. In the context, the phrase taken from the subtitle had originally made *reasonings*, not astronomical *systems*, the subject of discussion. (Drake 1986, 158-159)

I agree with Drake that the consideration of the two chief world systems, promised by the *Dialogue*, was not one of planetary astronomy (if by this term is to be understood a purely mathematical treatment of the pros and cons for Ptolemaic and Copernican astronomy) but a philosophical and "natural" consideration (as is evident from the fact that the word *Ptolemaic* is an abbreviation of *Aristotelian-Ptolemaic*).

But I do not share in his statement that Galileo had not promised any kind of astronomical reasoning and that such reasonings are, in fact, almost non-existent in this work of Galileo. Such a statement seems to be contradicted both by the preface to the *Dialogue* (VII, 30, line 10 ff.) and by the content of the second and third Days. Nor can I agree with Drake's use (here as well as elsewhere) of the word "metaphysical" with respect to the considerations of the first Day, which concern the *principles of the new natural philosophy* which Galileo is advocating, and not the *ultimate principles* of philosophy, which are, as a matter of fact, what is implied by the term "metaphysical". But above all I fail to see how the abbreviation of the title (used by Drake himself in 1967 for his English translation of the *Dialogue*) could lead (almost inevitably, it appears!) to the ambiguity suggested, while the full title would not. I, likewise, fail to understand the sense of his last phrase, whereby the object of discussion (found still in the original title) would be "one reasons". "Reasonings" without content? Galileo certainly wanted to reason about the chief *world systems* in the full meaning of that term (which is different than that of pure *astronomical systems*). And this seems to be implied in the abbreviated title no less than in the original one. If there were ambiguities as to the meaning of the *Dialogue*, they depended on the failure to understand its *content*, not its *title*.

[60] Drake 1990 has taken up again the theme of a "reexamination" of the *Dialogue*, a theme already treated in his contribution mentioned in the previous note. Although I intend to return to this argument at the end of the present chapter, I wish here only to note that according to Drake the apparent "sarcasm" of Galileo's words would disappear if we allow that the original order of the preface (which ought to have opened according to Drake with the mention of the tides) had been changed by Riccardi after Urban VIII had requested that the title, "Dialogue on the ebb and flow of the sea", should be changed to the one with which we are familiar. I have myself already emphasized that Riccardi had meticulously reviewed this preface. But it does not seem to me to be at all proven, or even provable, that the Master of the Sacred Palace had gone so far as to put the mention of the tides in the third, instead of the first, place. In fact, Galileo will introduce the treatment of the argument about the tides only in the fourth Day. And that he would, as a matter of fact, follow this order in his preface, thus describing the contents of his book, seems, therefore, only natural. Then as to Drakes's affirmation that the mention of the edict of 1616 right at the beginning of the preface comes in "so abruptly", whereas that would not be the case if there had been a preliminary mention of the phenomenon of the tides, this seems to me to be quite unconvincing. As

I see it, since the whole of the *Dialogue*, and not only the part on the ebb and flow of the sea, puts forth once again publicly the discussion of Copernicanism, it was altogether necessary for Galileo to make it clear from his first words that he was quite familiar with the edict of 1616 and that he was of the firm decision to respect it. At any rate, I fail to see how a simple change in the order of the phrases could cancel from Galileo's words that "sarcastic" tone which the words themselves seem to have in the actual structure of the preface.

[61] In addition to Paul V and Bellarmine, both of whom died in 1621, there was also Segizzi who had died in 1625 as bishop of Lodi. Urban VIII was not a member of the Holy Office in 1616 and, therefore, knew nothing, as I have already noted, of the admonition to Galileo by Bellarmine. But three of the cardinals who were members of the Holy Office in 1616 (Galamini, Zapata and Centini) were still alive, even though at that moment they were far away from Rome. However, as we shall see, Centini will be present in the final phase of Galileo's trial. (See Chapter 6, Note 55).

[62] This passage was added by Galileo in order to respect the instructions given by Riccardi to Egidi. See Note 52.

[63] Galileo is playing here on the original meaning of the Greek word, *peripatos* (a stroll), which gave birth to the designation of "Peripatetic" for the school of Aristotle, because instruction took place along the covered walkways of the *Lykaeion* at Athens.

[64] Only when reference is made to his discoveries or to his person is Galileo alluded to in the *Dialogue* with such expressions as: "the Lincean academician", "our common friend", etc.

[65] Favaro, Avvertimento (VII, 9).

[66] Simplicius lived in the VI century of the Christian era and was a famous commentator of the works of Aristotle, such as the *Categories*, the *Physics*, the *De Coelo* (Of the Heavens), and the *De Anima* (Of the Soul).

[67] In choosing the name, Simplicius, Galileo certainly played with the assonance between that name and the adjective, "simple", in the sense of "simpleton".

[68] For the beginning of this theoretical consideration see VII, 42.

[69] Galileo states:

Rectilinear motions (by necessity accelerated) are only momentarily possible, i.e., when there is a disordered situation, and occur in order to bring bodies back to order, i.e., to rest or to circular motion. And this is true for all bodies in the world (VII, 43 ff.).

This idea of Galileo's that circular motion, uniquely uniform and infinitely repeatable, is true natural motion and that rectilinear motion (which cannot be uniform) is by necessity a violent motion is already found in Copernicus (*De Revolutionibus*, I, chap. 8). Still according to Drake 1970b, 270   these preliminary considerations on circular motion would have been dictated by a pedagogical purpose, namely, to begin with the notions which a reader would more easily understand and then, when it was time to be more precise, to teach instead the more elaborate notion of tangential motion. Drake 1990, 195 has recently returned to this argument: "The first of the four "days" of discussion . . . is, in a way, severed from the rest of the book." The reason for this statement (if I have correctly understood the author's thought) is that the considerations which I have very briefly summarized in the text would have a "metaphysical" character and Galileo would have put them at the beginning of the book because they were "the kind of thing most likely to attract the readers of his time, not because he intended to deduce his physics from it" (Drake 1990, 197). I agree with Drake that Galileo did not intend to deduce his physics from the considerations presented in the first "Day". But I do not think that Galileo wrote these first pages *only* to satisfy the fashion of that epoch and not even *only* for a pedagogical purpose (as Drake had stated previously). I rather think that those considerations held a great importance for Galileo as a general approach to the criticism of the natural philosophy of Aristotle and, to be more precise, the criticism of the foundation of that philosophy which consisted in the absolute distinction between natural terrestrial motions and the heavenly ones. Of course, this criticism will be carried forth in much more detail in the subsequent "Days" of the *Dialogue*, but Galileo had sensed the need to show right from the very beginning that the new natural philosophy which he was promoting was based on a unification, on a cosmic scale, of all natural phenomena. In other words, there are not two natural sciences but only one, applicable to all bodies whether earthly or heavenly.

[70] This comment is interesting because it appears to allude to the possibility of an infinite universe, in which there would be no center. The question of the finiteness or infinity of the universe will be treated later on more explicitly. See Note 78.

[71] Above all Salviati alleges two phenomena against the changelessness of the heavens: that of the *novae* (of 1572 and of 1604) and that of the sunspots. Towards the end of the third "Day" the discussion centers on the discoveries about the Moon which show unequivocally its likeness to the Earth. Further on (VII, 83-85) Salviati again takes up the argument and develops the idea that the mobility

of the Earth comes about precisely from the innumerable changes that take place on it and without which the Earth would be reduced to

> a useless lump in the universe, devoid of activity and, in a word, superfluous and essentially nonexistent. This is exactly the difference between a living animal and a dead one; and I say the same of the moon, of Jupiter, and of all other world globes" (VII, 83; trans. by Drake 1967, 58-59).

As we see, for Galileo the perfection of worldly bodies does not consist in their immutability but in their mutability because the latter is a sign of activity and of life. Therefore, to put the heavens together with the Earth in the category of "corruptible" bodies does not mean to degrade the heavens but rather to give them life.

[72] In this exposition Galileo takes up more comprehensively the considerations already presented in the *Letter to Ingoli*.

[73] This law is formulated in this way by Salviati later on in the second "Day":

> First of all it is necessary to reflect that the movement of the descending bodies is not uniform, but that starting from rest they are continually accelerated. This fact is known and observed by all . . . But this general knowledge is of no value unless one knows the ratio according to which the increase in speed takes place, something which has been unknown to all philosophers down to our time. It was first discovered by our friend the Academician, who, in some of his yet unpublished writings, shown in confidence to me and to some other friends of his, proves the following.
> The acceleration of straight motion in heavy bodies proceeds according to odd numbers beginning with from one . . . In sum, this is the same as to say that the spaces passed over by the body starting from rest have to each other the ratios of the squares of the times in which the spaces were traversed. Or we may say that the spaces passed over are to each other as the squares of the times. (VII, 248; trans. by Drake 1967, 221-222).

In fact, however, supposing the Earth to move, the composite motion of the heavy body is not, according to Galileo, rectilinear but circular (VII, 191). This (together with other similar expressions of Galileo in the *Dialogue*) has led Alexandre Koyré (1940 and 1966) to conclude

that Galileo, blinded by his "fixed idea" of circular motions, was led to
formulate a general principle of circular inertia: a body in motion, if let
to fall without the influence of any external forces, will not continue to
move along a straight line but in a curve. This interpretation of the
well known French historian of scientific thought has been taken up by
other historians of science, but has been later on denied with good
arguments by Drake 1970b, 246 ff. and 260 ff.

[74] We have here the formulation of the principle which rightly
today is called "the principle of Galilean relativity. This states that on
the basis of a mechanical experiments performed within a system, it is
impossible to decide whether that system is at rest or in uniform
rectilinear motion" (Geymonat 1965, 119).

[75] At the beginning of this "Day" there is a long discussion,
supported by an abundant supply of calculations, intended to
demonstrate that the *novae* (especially that of 1604) are not sublunar
phenomena, but belong to the "highest celestial regions" (VII, 301-343).

[76] When he was composing *The Assayer* Galileo had received
notice of the appearance of the book of Chiaramonti, *Antitycho*, in
which this Aristotelian philosopher (who was later on appointed to a
chair of philosophy at Pisa) attacked the system of Tycho Brahe.
Galileo had obviously read only the title and had made a reference to
it which sounded positive (VI, 231 and 683). Later on, when he became
aware of the content of *Antitycho*, he had to reappraise the situation
and now the *Dialogue* offered him the chance to put things straight.

[77] In fact, if we suppose that the Earth moves, it would be located
at opposite seasons (Spring and Autumn, for instance) respectively,
closer and more distant from certain fixed stars whose apparent
magnitude would, therefore, vary. As to the shift in the position of the
fixed stars on the celestial sphere, that is what we call the
phenomenon of the "parallax", to which we have already alluded (see
Introduction). This part of the *Dialogue* constitutes an answer to the
Disquisitiones mathematicae of Scheiner, published, as we have seen,
in 1614 under the name of one of Scheiner's disciples.

[78] See Copernicus, *De Revolutionibus*, Book I, Chap. VI. Galileo
was aware of the difficulties proposed by Tycho Brahe against this idea
of the enormous expanse of the universe and he gave an answer based
substantially on the evidence given, thanks to his use of the telescope,
that the estimate of the angular size of the fixed stars was erroneous
(very much too large). Galileo estimated that the measurement of the
angular size for a sixth magnitude star required that it be located
(supposing that it was as intrinsically as bright as the Sun) at a
distance from the Earth so as to make it practically impossible to
detect a parallax. See VII, 385-387. On this passage of the *Dialogue* see

the article by Casanovas 1985, 68 ff. With respect to the enormous dimensions of the universe Salviati had already made a more extensive and explicit comment than the one considered in Note 70. When speaking of the center of the universe, he had, in fact, stated:

> I might very reasonably dispute whether there is in nature such a center, seeing that neither you nor anyone else has so far proved whether the universe is finite and has a shape, or whether it is infinite and unbounded. Still, conceding to you for the moment that it is finite and of bounded spherical shape, and therefore has its center, it remains to be seen how credible it is that the earth rather than some other body is to be found at the center. (VII, 347; trans. by Drake 1967, 319-320).

These words bring to mind Cusanus, but they come not from a vague consideration based on mathematical concepts, as they did for the German thinker, but from the realization that the confines of the universe had been enormously increased with the use of the telescope. From such observations it is a small step to the question as to whether the universe is finite or infinite. Even if Galileo does not take a definite stand, we can see in him (as before in Copernicus) a tendency which will become more explicit in Descartes and in the following development of scientific thought. As we know, Giordano Bruno explicitly affirmed the infinity of the universe and that the stars were other Suns, but Galileo was quite careful (here as elsewhere) to avoid referring to Bruno's thinking. Still we find an expression which sounds like Bruno's:

> . . . and how the stars, *which are so many suns,* agree with our sun in enjoying eternal rest. (VII, 354; trans. by Drake 1967, 327; italics by Fantoli).

[79] As we know already, by accepting the Copernican view the epicycles, introduced by Ptolemy to explain the irregular motion of the planets, are automatically eliminated. But, there are still many other epicycles which are needed to correct the difference between the observations and the theoretical calculations. It would be possible to do away with these epicycles only by accepting Kepler's theory of elliptical orbits. As we have already mentioned, Galileo will always stick to the idea of circular orbits, as did Copernicus. But in such a case, the vaunted simplification, although true in theory, was in fact on the practical plane less than Galileo here admits.

⁸⁰ In this whole discussion Simplicius stays on the defensive and
only alludes to a book which he has and which he intends to use to
beat back Salviati's arguments. This book is none other than the
Disquisitiones Mathematicae, cited in Note 77. Salviati has fine fun in
pointing out its fallacies and at times its gross errors. The unnamed
author is also criticized for having

> . . . mixed passages from the ever venerable and mighty
> Holy Scriptures among these apish puerilities, and his
> having tried to utilize sacred things for wounding anybody
> who might, without either affirming or denying anything,
> philosophize jokingly and in sport, and having made certain
> assumptions argues about them familiarly. (VII, 384).

As we see Galileo wishes absolutely to avoid getting drawn into the
area of Scripture and he criticizes Scheiner for not having stayed on
the plane of "natural and human discourse" and "of natural reason"
(VII, 385). This critique of Scheiner, which includes also that of Tycho
Brahe on whom the former based his arguments, follows point by point
the objections contained in the *Disquisitiones* against the motion of the
Earth and it is very severe. Many years had by now gone by since the
Sunspot Letters and the discussion which was still polite at that time
becomes here more polemical and full of biting irony. Campanella will
have good reason, having once read the *Dialogue*, to comment: "Apelle
will be very disturbed by this book" (XIV, 367).

⁸¹ This caused Sagredo, always ready to show enthusiasm, to
exclaim: "O Nicholas Copernicus, what a pleasure it would have been
for you to see this part of your system confirmed by so clear an
experiment!" (VII, 367; trans. by Drake 1967, 339). But Salviati takes
the opportunity to emphasize the greatness of Copernicus' genius since,
even though the "sensate experiences" were against him, he continued
to sustain his ideas with the strong "reasons" he had found. (VII, 367).

⁸² As we know (see Chapter 2, Note 79) the first news that
Galileo had of the curvature of the sunspot trajectories was that from
his great friend, the Dominican Morandi, who had in turn received the
news from Francesco Sizzi. But it does not appear that Galileo had at
that time given any particular importance to this news, perhaps
because he was absorbed with other interests, which took him away
from solar observations. According to his statement in the *Dialogue*
(VII, 374) Galileo would have become aware of the phenomenon of the
curvature "after some years" on the occasion of a series of solar
observations which he carried out while he was at the "Villa delle
Selve". And on that occasion he would have intuited the importance of
that discovery for the Copernican system. But it is strange, if this

"discovery" is true, that he did not speak about it even to his most intimate friends. At any rate it is certain that his interest in the phenomenon was awakened (or reawakened?) when Galileo was composing the *Dialogue* and was looking for every possible proof or lead in favor of Copernicanism.

[83] For an exposition of this "proof" from the sunspots with an emphasis upon the philosophical value of the "principle of simplicity" in Galilean thought see Clavelin 1968, 409 ff. Clavelin's point of view has been criticized by Finocchiaro 1986, 247.

[84] It is interesting to note that Galileo in the *Dialogue* uses, as we have seen, the same observation of the fluidity of the element of water and consequently its freedom of motion as the point of departure for his theory of the tides based on the Earth's motion. Is this an indication that, after all, he had read the *Astronomia Nova*?

[85] Drake 1970b, 209 ff. states, nonetheless, that Kepler had not made the least effort to make his theory square with the observational data and that, therefore, Galileo would not have had any reason to adopt it in preference to his own theory. In fact, fifty-five more years will be required to reach, with the *Principia* of Newton, the law of universal gravity and, therefore, the complete scientific formulation of the Moon's attraction as the principal cause of the tides. And we know that Newton himself will only reluctantly use the word "attraction" without claiming to give it a final justification.

[86] Geymonat himself writes:

> Actually it was entirely wrong, and Galileo should have been the first to see this if he had correctly applied to the earth the laws of composition of motion that he himself had discovered. But even the greatest scientists fall sometimes into gross errors. (Geymonat 1965, 131).

Geymonat adds that Galileo would have been able to draw a really conclusive proof of the Earth's rotation from one of the comments he made in the second Day. He writes:

> This is the fact that because of the earth's rotation, a ball falling freely from a sufficient height must strike somewhat forward of the vertical point, rather than behind it as the adversaries of Copernicus assumed. (Geymonat 1965, 132).

Galileo's comment is found in VII, 259-260. Even if Galileo did not succeed in evaluating the full importance of this comment, Geymonat concludes:

. . . the simple fact of his having glimpsed such an
apparently paradoxical consequence of the earth's motion
constituted a scientific achievement of the highest order.
(Geymonat 1965, 132).

[87] Zagar states in this regard:

Galileo did not have enough quantitative data to judge the
nature of the actions which he examined; for example, the
one to three ratio which he assumed for the equatorial to
the orbital velocity, no less than twenty times larger than
the actual ratio, was quite apt for leading the conclusions
astray. But to wish to see in his conclusions inaccuracies
of a dynamic character or even to claim that the Galilean-
Copernican edifice collapses into nothing because of those
conclusions would be an unjustified exaggeration. (Zagar
1964, 64).

For a detailed treatment of this argument from the tides and for a
response to the criticism (repeated time and time again, but it seems
without justification) whereby in Galileo's theory of the tides there is
room only for one maximum and one minimum per day see Drake
1970b, 200-213. As Drake states, Galileo's treatment of the tides is not
at all limited to considering the effect of the double movement of the
Earth. Galileo was well aware of the complexity of the causes which
were contributing to this phenomenon and he had tried in his
explanation to account for them with observations of considerable
scientific value. A reevaluation, at least partial, of Galileo's argument
from the tides as a proof of the Earth's motion is given in an important
article by Burstyn 1962 who notes:

Galileo was not primarily concerned with explaining the
tides. His theory was developed to prove that the earth
moves. Did it accomplish its creator's aim? To our modern
view, Galileo's proof is a partial success. Though the
primary cause of the tides is not what Galileo thought it
to be, his theory demands that the earth rotate on its axis
and revolve in orbit around the sun, and these are the
conditions demanded by a correct theory of the tides.
Hence Galileo offered good evidence for the motion of the
earth around the sun, the point which he had to establish
beyond doubt to prove the Copernican hypothesis. (Burstyn
1962, 181-182)

Further on Burstyn says:

> Galileo's theory of the tides is an imperfect theory of a
> "tide of reaction". The tide called for by Galileo's theory is
> thus the same as the Newtonian equilibrium tide on the
> side of the earth opposite the disturbing body, and
> whatever insight into the tidal motion Galileo provided was
> incorporated into Newton's theory of the tides. (Burstyn
> 1962, 182).

[88] Galileo adds:

> To these there may perhaps be added a fourth, and maybe
> even a fifth. The fourth, I mean, may come from the fixed
> stars, since by extremely accurate observations of these
> there may be discovered those minimal changes that
> Copernicus took to be imperceptible. (VII, 487; trans. by
> Drake 1967, 462-463).

Galileo alludes here to the parallax effect, which had become at least
in theory observable, with the use of the telescope. But two centuries
would have to pass before these "extremely accurate observations" could
be made. As to the fifth proof, it had been suggested by Cesare Marsili
who "has observed a continual change, though a very slow one, in the
meridian line" (VII, 487; trans. by Drake 1967, 463). But Galileo makes
only a remark about it in expectation of more precise data. And, in
fact, it was impossible to obtain such data with the instruments then
available. See Drake (1967, 491) for a note on Cesare Marsili.

[89] Rivers of ink have been spilled out on the question as to
whether or not Galileo has claimed in the *Dialogue* to have in hand a
decisive proof. Drake has, as a matter of fact, claimed that Galileo
limited himself to presenting his arguments in favor of Copernicanism
in the form of "hypothetical demonstrations" and that:

> . . . the entire *Dialogue* was intended to show that absolute
> proof of the Copernican system lay beyond the power of
> science, which could do no more than reason about it *ex
> suppositione*. Undeniable first principles from which
> Copernicanism could be derived simply did not exist. In
> Galileo's conception of science the uncertainty of the
> Copernican assumptions, and his own assumptions in
> physics, would be indefinitely reduced with the passage of
> time, but that would still not be irrefutable proof of them.
> (Drake 1986, 169-170).

I, however, do not feel inclined to subscribe to these statements which appear to project modern concepts about science's validity into a context which is profoundly different. Specifically, Drake's use of the expression, *ex suppositione*, does not seem to be the same as Galileo's. See Wallace 1986, 22 ff. and Blackwell 1991, 80, Note 50. If we put together all of Galileo's writings, including his letters, it appears that he would be the first to refute this interpretation. On this question of Galileo's intentions Drake seems to see but two possibilities: that of painting him to be a "Copernican zealot" (Drake 1986, 164) who claims to give definitive (even "absolute"!) proofs which, in fact, he does not have or that of presenting him rather as a Popper or a Kuhn of the XVII century. It seems to me that, taking together all of the facts and the writings presented in the current study, we may conclude with adequate certainty that Galileo arrived progressively at the conviction that the Copernican system was the only true explanation of the world and that he undoubtedly tried to use his own talents to have it accepted (or at least not condemned) in the educated circles of his time, both lay and ecclesiastical. But I have also made quite an effort to show that Galileo by temperament never let himself be dragged along like an "ardent enthusiast" or even a "zealot" by his convictions. He was quite aware of the limitations of the arguments he possessed in favor of Copernicanism, including the one from the tides. And this, it seems, appears clearly even in the *Dialogue*. He had, therefore, no illusion of already having in his possession "definitive proofs" or even "absolute(?)" ones. But that certainly does not mean that he halted at a merely hypothetical or even only probable position. Innumerable statements of his in the *Dialogue*, as well as in previous works (especially in the *Letter to Christina of Lorraine*), prove his conviction that the scientist can reach the truth and that, as to the case in point, the truth stood towards the side of Copernicanism. The *Dialogue* constitutes an attempt to realize the methodological program traced out in the *Letter to Christina of Lorraine*. As we have seen by examining that *Letter*, even though in a summary way, the totality of the arguments taken up by Galileo, even if for sure they do not constitute a "decisive proof", were sufficient to tip the balance from a position of equal probability for the two systems, Aristotelian-Ptolemaic and Copernican, to a position clearly favoring the latter. As we shall see, that view did not escape Galileo's judges who will not rest content with such expressions as "hypothetical" and "purely probable" with which Galileo was forced (in order to satisfy Urban VIII's command) to soften the weight of his arguments. It seems strange to me that neither

Drake 1986 nor Finocchiaro 1986 have given enough attention to this
fact in their analyses of Galileo's intentions in the *Dialogue*.

[90] It has often been stated (and at times it still continues to be
stated), especially by Catholic "apologists", that Galileo did not succeed,
despite his contrary claims, in giving "decisive" proofs in favor of
Copernicanism; and they give special emphasis, of course, to the failure
of the "proof" from the tides. Thus an attempt has been made to justify,
or at least to excuse, the position taken by the Church in 1633, as well
as already in 1616. Most recently this thesis has been championed in
the book of Brandmüller 1992. But, first of all, the totality of the
arguments presented in the *Dialogue* were entirely probative against
the natural philosophy of Aristotle and the Ptolemaic system. And
Galileo was surely correct, as I have emphasized many times, in
refusing to give a "physical" sense to the system of Tycho Brahe (and,
therefore, to attribute to it the value of a "third cosmological
hypothesis"). In this regard see the comments by Finocchiaro 1986, 255-
256. In this respect Galileo was much more a "modern physicist" than
was Kepler. Therefore, only the Copernican hypothesis was left. See
what Salviati has to say towards the end of the **third Day** with respect
to the arguments in favor of Copernicanism that had been reviewed
thus far:

> I do not give these arguments the status of either
> conclusiveness or inconclusiveness, since (as I have said
> before) my intention has not been to solve anything about
> this momentous question, but merely to set forth those
> physical and astronomical reasons which the two sides can
> give me to set forth. I leave to others the decision, *which
> ultimately should not be ambiguous, since one of the
> arguments must be true and the other false. Hence it is
> not possible within the bounds of human learning that the
> reasons adopted by the right side should be anything but
> clearly conclusive, and those opposed to them, vain and
> ineffective.* (VII, 383; trans. by Drake 1967, 356; italics by
> Fantoli).

Galileo is speaking here of the arguments derived from the retrograde
motions of the planets and from the phenomenon of the trajectory of
the sunspots. But his reasoning is obviously valid, even more so, for the
totality of the considerations in the *Dialogue*. The one true objection
that could be made to this reasoning of Galileo is that it will not, in
fact, be the Copernican system *as conceived by the great Polish
astronomer which will come to be the one true alternative to the
Aristotelian-Ptolemaic system but rather the Copernican system*

perfected by the planetary laws of Kepler. (We will have the opportunity to see in the final chapter of this book how this will come to be adopted by the Commissary of the Holy Office, Olivieri, in 1820 as the justification for the decree of 1616 and the condemnation of the *Dialogue* in 1633). But if the laws of Kepler finally allowed us to obtain the much desired coincidence between the mathematical theory of the planetary motions and the observations, they substantially confirmed the heliocentric concept of Copernicus and they certainly did not require the founding of a *third system* of the world. As to the Church's attitude, there was no consideration in 1616, even less so in 1633, as to whether Galileo's proofs were conclusive or not. As we know in 1616 the qualificators-consultors of the Holy Office did not even take such proofs under examination, because for them the matter was already decided from the beginning on the plane of the natural philosophy of Aristotle (i.e., it was "absurd in philosophy"), not to speak of the theological plane. Then in 1632-1633 the whole discussion was centered, as we shall see, on the question as to whether Galileo had violated or not the injunction given to him by Bellarmine and Segizzi in 1616. On that occasion the question of the scientific (or "philosophical") value of the *Dialogue* was not even touched upon.

CHAPTER 6

THE STORM BREAKS LOOSE

THE TRIAL AND CONDEMNATION OF GALILEO

1.   *The* Dialogue *arrives in Rome. The reactions against it begin*

As soon as it came off the press the *Dialogue* began to spread about in Italy and in Europe, thanks also to the numerous copies which Galileo had sent to friends and influential people.[1] Father Riccardi also received a copy, the one, that is, that was sent by the inquisitor of Florence to the Holy Office in Rome and then redirected to Riccardi. This was the usual procedure and in the letter of 6 March 1632 to the Florentine inquisitor, in which Riccardi acknowledged receipt of the copy, there is nothing out of the ordinary.[2]

The book's reception by Galileo's friends and admirers was, as usual, enthusiastic, although frank reservations on the argument from the tides were not lacking.[3] Of course, among the most enthusiastic was Castelli, who had been able to read one of the first few copies which had arrived in the meantime in Rome.[4] He wrote as follows to Galileo:

> As to Your Lordship's book, you should know how two of them have arrived here at Rome, one of which was given to His Most Eminent Lord Cardinal Francesco Barberini, and I had the favor of His Eminence to see it, and I still have it by me, having read it from cover to cover to my infinite amazement and delight; and I read parts of it to friends of good taste[5] to their marvel and always more to my delight, more to my amazement, and with always more profit to myself. (XIV, 357; except for first four lines the trans. is from Drake 1978, 336).

In a marginal note to this letter of 29 May 1632 Castelli states:

> Monsignor Ciampoli continues to carry out his assignment, and there is no more news other than the previous; and

> Monsignor carries on splendidly with due esteem for the
> masters, and laughing to himself at the things of this
> world as they deserve (XIV, 358).

The reason for this marginal note was a question addressed
to him by Galileo, as to rumors which were going about in
Florence that Ciampoli had fallen out of favor with Urban VIII
(XIV, 352). As usual Castelli was too much the optimist.
Ciampoli had really lost the Popes's confidence ever since the
month of April, not, as has been often stated, because of Galileo
and the printing of the *Dialogue*, but for various other reasons,
one of the most important of which is perhaps that he had
aligned himself with the group of Spanish-leaning cardinals at
a political moment extremely difficult for the Pope.[6] Right from
the beginning of his Pontificate Urban VIII had supported
France with the aim of counterbalancing the danger of a
Hapsburg hegemony, the fruit of an understanding between
Spain and the German Empire. By following this strategy he
now found himself, in one of the most dramatic phases of the
Thirty Years War, in favor of an agreement between the King of
France (Louis XIII), the Duke of Bavaria (representing the
neutral Catholic League of Germany) and the Protestant
Gustavus Adolphus, the King of Sweden, at that time at the
apex of his military successes against the German Empire. By
acting in this way Urban VIII had exposed himself to ever
sharper criticism from the partisans of Spain and of the Empire,
in whose eyes the Papal strategy appeared to be a betrayal of
the Catholic cause in Europe.

It was, as a matter of fact, in March 1632 that the tension
between the Pope and the Hapsburg party showed itself in a
most clamorous way. During a consistory Cardinal Gaspare
Borgia, who carried out the functions of Ambassador to Spain,
openly and violently attacked the Pope with accusations of
favoring the cause of the heretics and with an invitation to show
that same "apostolic zeal" which had characterized his "more
pious and more glorious" predecessors.[7]

The situation had been made even more thorny for the
Pope because of accusations of nepotism and earthly ambitions,
which had a wide-spread resonance among the population of

Rome. Urban VIII sensed that he would have to salvage the situation before it was too late. And that led to a hardening of his position, a susceptibility born of exasperation and suspicion, and to a continuous tension in this period of his Pontificate. Ciampoli was one of the first victims of this new posture of the Pope. We will see right away how this state of mind of Urban VIII will have a negative influence also on Galileo's affairs.[8]

If the *Dialogue* had moved Galileo's friends to praise and admiration, it had also certainly begun to awaken reactions from his opponents. In this respect many recent biographers of Galileo cite the letter of Castelli to Galileo of 9 June in which he wrote:

> Father Scheiner, while he was in a bookshop where there was also a certain Olivetan father [Vincenzo Renieri] who had come from Siena during the past days, heard the Olivetan father give merited praise to the Dialogues celebrating them as the greatest book that had ever been published and he was completely shaken up, his face changing color and with a huge trembling of his waist and his hands, so much so that the book dealer, who recounted the story to me, marvelled at it; and furthermore told me that the said Father Scheiner had stated that he would have paid ten gold *scudi* for one of those books so as to be able to respond right away. (XIV, 360).

And these words of Castelli are taken as an argument to confirm the thesis, which, as we shall see, will circulate beginning with the period immediately following Galileo's condemnation, according to which Scheiner would have been, as a matter of fact, one of those who brought about the condemnation. I will have an opportunity to return to this argument. Here I will limit myself only to noting that Scheiner was certainly not the one who began the reaction against the *Dialogue*. Since there were very few copies of the *Dialogue* which had arrived in Rome in that period, it seems that, despite all of his impatience, the Jesuit had not yet during the first days of August been able to read the book. Tommaso Campanella, who had spoken with Scheiner, wrote, in fact, on 5 August from Rome to Galileo:

Apelle will complain a lot about this book, and he guessed, speaking with me, that Your Lordship was attacking him [in the *Dialogue*] because at any rate he would wish to be the author of the Spots, and he sends me many letters of that time in his favor. At the beginning he gave me his book [the *Rosa Ursina*] but since his writing is tedious I cannot say that I have given it a good reading etc. (XIV, 367).

And Campanella continued:

I defend against everyone how this book is in favor of the decree *contra motum telluris* (against the movement of the Earth) etc., so that some quack writer would not disturb the course of this teaching: but my disciples know the mystery.[9] (XIV, 367).

As we see, Campanella distinguishes in this letter of his the *possible* reaction of Scheiner, based on the question of the priority of the solar discoveries and not on the Copernican thesis of the *Dialogue*, from that of "some quack writer", based instead on this latter thesis.

While Scheiner was still waiting to read the *Dialogue*, the reaction against this book had gone on growing well beyond and much higher up than Campanella could have imagined. Obviously Galileo's enemies had not had to work too hard to decipher the "mystery" of the *Dialogue*, even without having to become followers of the Calabrian philosopher, and they had not failed to begin a new anti-Galilean campaign.

2.   *Urban VIII becomes aware of the contents of the*
      Dialogue. *The first dispositions are taken against the book.*

Had the opposition already succeeded in having their voice heard even by Urban VIII? It is likely, even though it cannot be strictly proven. What we know for sure is that Urban VIII had become aware of the contents of the *Dialogue* between the end of June and the middle of July and that he had been disturbed by it.[10] On 25 July, in fact, we have the first indication that something serious was maturing. On that day Father Riccardi wrote to the Florentine inquisitor, Clemente Egidi:

> There has arrived here the book of Mr. Galileo and there are many things that are not acceptable and the Masters wish at any rate that it be revised. Meanwhile it is the order of Our Lord (but no more than my name is to be mentioned) that the book be withheld and that it not be sent here without there having been sent from here that which is to be corrected, nor should it be sent to other places. Please have an understanding about it, Your most Reverend Paternity, with the Illustrious Monsignor Nuncio; and working in a pleasant way, see that everything succeeds efficaciously. (XX, 571-572).

After the signature there follows an interesting *post scriptum*:

> Would Your most Reverend Paternity advise me as soon as possible whether the seal with the three fish is the printer's or from Mr. Galileo and would you see to writing to me with dexterity what it means. (XX, 571-572).

As we see the tone is still rather peaceful and Father Riccardi, in the apparent bureaucratic style with which he deals with the matter, does not seem (or at least does not wish) to show any excessive worry. The Pope had probably given a quick look here and there at the book (granted that he had already had it in his hands at that date) and he was not happy with it. And his unhappiness would have taken on a rather more precise form, if, as seems to me probable, such a reading had taken place as a response to indications from persons hostile to Galileo, perhaps even in their presence, or at least from persons who were very surprised and scandalized that one could write, with such visible approval of Church authorities, a work so openly favorable to the Copernican system. And, with or without their help, Urban VIII would have easily seen how his arguments (in the course of his lengthy conversations with Galileo years before) against the possibility of a proof of any "world system", already thought out or thinkable by human reason, had been reduced to one argument only, presented very briefly and, to top that off, in the mouth of Simplicius. And then a doubt had pestered him (perhaps also cleverly insinuated to him by others?) concerning the three dolphins which were designed on the frontispiece of the book. Could it be an allusion to his nephews, protected by him with a partiality which was the object of criticism and of popular disdain? The fact that this suspicion could have flashed into the Pope's mind (or have taken hold of him) was a sign of the tense atmosphere in which he was living at that time. The times of euphoria and of self confidence belonged by now to the past. If even the cardinals dared to criticize him openly, if even a Ciampoli, despite all of the favors received from him, was taking the side of the faction adverse to him and if now Galileo was allowing himself to give such little importance to his formal requests and, who knows, was even coming to the point of making insinuations about his nepotism, then it was necessary to take serious measures. It would be necessary to make it clear to the one time favorites that one could not play around with equivocations. Something had burned out in Urban VIII's heart: the admiration he had had for Galileo, which had one time (how long ago by this time it must have seemed to him) led him to write the *Adulatio perniciosa* (Pernicious Adulation). In place of that admiration, a resentment was being born and it would get deeper as time went on.

From the moment of this first letter of Riccardi to the Florentine inquisitor we will assist at a continuous "crescendo" in the development of the events contrary to Galileo. On 7 August in a letter from Rome to Mario Guiducci (who was at that time in Florence) Filippo Magalotti alluded to rumors, to which he had not attributed importance, that "some reflection" was taking place about the said book (the *Dialogue*) so as to correct it or delay it or perhaps prohibit it (XIV, 368). Magalotti then spoke of a meeting with Father Riccardi, who had asked him to turn in all of the copies of the *Dialogue* which he had brought from Florence with the promise that he would have given them back to him within at the most ten days. Magalotti had replied that the copies had by now been distributed by him and that, therefore, it would not be possible for him to respect the request. Riccardi had also confessed to Magalotti that there "had occurred a great deal of reflection on the undertaking . . .

and there are here three dolphins and one has in its mouth the other's tail". Magalotti with a laugh had explained that it was the seal of the printer Landini.

> On hearing this, he [Riccardi] appeared greatly relieved and told me that, if indeed I could assure him that such was the case (now see what trifles rule our actions in this world), the result would be most happy for the author. (XIV, 369; trans. by de Santillana 1955, 189).

Magalotti went on to give the reasons for Father Riccardi's steps:

> So the matter stands. Any other motive for censure I do not think there is, except that already mentioned by the Master of the Sacred Palace; namely, that the book has not been printed precisely according to the original manuscript and that, among other things, two or three arguments have been omitted at the end which were invented by our Lord's Holiness himself and with which, he says, he convinced Signor Galileo of the falsity of the Copernican theory. The book having fallen into His Holiness's hands, and these arguments having been found wanting, it was necessary to remedy the oversight. (XIV, 370; trans. by de Santillana 1955, 190).

But, according to Magalotti, there was more to it. At the basis of all the uproar there was the activity of the Jesuits.

> This is the pretext; but the real fact is that the Jesuit Fathers are working most valiantly in an underhanded way to get the work prohibited. The reverend Father's own words to me were: 'The Jesuits will persecute him most bitterly.' This good Father, being mixed up in the matter himself, fears every stumbling block and wishes naturally to avoid bringing trouble on himself for having given the license. Besides which, we cannot deny that our Lord's Holiness holds an opinion directly contrary to this [of Galileo's]. (XIV, 370; trans. by de Santillana 1955, 190).[11]

Riccardi's preoccupation to get back the books which had arrived in Rome was indubitably a response to a more general order given by Urban VIII: it was necessary to retrace and to get back all of the copies which had already started circulating. In fact, we see Father Riccardi writing again to Florence, the same day on which Magalotti sent his letter, to advise the Inquisitor Egidi that information on the number of copies printed and on their destinations must be "diligently" gathered "so that one could be careful to see that they were had back". However, the tone is still moderate. At the end Riccardi added: " . . . reassure the author to be of good heart" (XX, 572).

But how could Galileo be of good heart in the face of such steps of the Roman authorities? After further distribution of the *Dialogue* had been blocked, he had written to Micanzio (that same 7 August) with a tone about which Micanzio himself in his response commented: "I have read the 7 [August] letter of Your most Illustrious and Excellent Lord with disdain and anger, but not with surprise" (XIV, 371).[12]

Undoubtedly Galileo decided to have recourse to the Grand Duke and the latter would have to have a letter sent to the ambassador Niccolini requesting him to protest to Father Riccardi the disposition of having put the hold on a book which had been issued with all the required authorizations. In fact, Niccolini wrote on 15 August to the Secretary of State Cioli:

> . . . I have not been able to see the Master of the Sacred Palace in regard to the question of Mr. Galilei. However, because I hear that there has been set up a Commission of persons versed in his profession, all unfriendly to Galileo, responsible to the Lord Cardinal Barberini,[13] I have decided to speak about it to His Eminence himself at the earliest opportunity. Furthermore, because they are thinking of calling a mathematician from Pisa, named Mr. Chiaramonti and rather unfriendly to Mr. Galileo's opinions, it will be necessary that His Highness have someone talk to him, to make sure he pursues the cause of truth here, rather than his emotional feelings . . . (XIV, 372; trans. by Finocchiaro 1989, 227).

Cioli wrote another time four days later from Florence: "In the affair of Mr. Galileo, His Highness [the Grand Duke] will take it badly if persecution of his works by those who are envious of his learning continues" (XIV, 373). Unfortunately these "envious" persons now became stronger with the changed attitude of the Pope. And against the Pope, and one of the temperament of Urban VIII,[14] very little was to be gained by protests, at least the protests of a Grand Duke who was still very young and of a temperament quite less decisive than his father. Niccolini himself would come to realize this quite soon.

In the meantime the correspondence, both official and private, between Rome and Florence intensified. On 22 August Niccolini informed Cioli that he had insisted with Cardinal Francesco Barberini that the distribution of the *Dialogue* be permitted

> . . . since it is already in print with the required licenses, has been reviewed and examined here and in Florence, and has had the beginning and the ending revised as the authorities wanted. Furthermore, I have petitioned that some neutral persons be appointed to the Commission which has been set up on the matter since the present members are opponents of the same Mr. Galilei. (XIV, 374-375; trans. by Finocchiaro 1989, 227-228).

The Cardinal, according to Niccolini's information, did not compromise himself and promised only that he would refer the matter to the Pope, even though he added that what was involved were the interests "of a subject, a friend of His Holiness by whom he is loved and esteemed" and towards whom he himself nourished "good will". Niccolini concluded: "I hear then from some friend that the thought is not to prohibit it but to see to it that some words be modified" (XIV, 375).

Despite all of his "good will" Francesco Barberini did not want to commit himself further when Niccolini again visited him with a very detailed letter, written by Cioli in the name of the Grand Duke.[15]

3. *The charges against the* Dialogue *are specified.*

In a second, quite long letter of Magalotti to Guiducci of 4 September we have more detailed information on the charges with respect to the *Dialogue*. Magalotti had obtained them during the course of a conversation with Father Riccardi. Substantially it was a matter of the preface, separated from the body of the book and, furthermore, printed in different typeset (which thus gave the impression of extraneous material), and especially of the fact that the arguments of Urban VIII were reduced to one only, and to top it off put in the mouth of Simplicius "a personage very little esteemed in the whole treatment, in fact, rather treated with derision and mockery".[16] In this respect Magalotti had made the . comment that that argument

> could not be put in the mouths of the other two [Salviati and Sagredo] because he did not wish to make those two different than they are and that the conclusion that Salviati made with that passage from the Holy Scripture made it convincingly clear that the said Salviati had given it the required appreciation and was at peace with it. (XIV, 379).

Substantially Magalotti was an optimist:

> . . . it appeared to me to understand that the business was somewhat sweetened, because where before I had had some misgivings of a somewhat immature resolution, I see now that he is inclined to see that matters are taken in stride. And if his words do not speak differently than his heart does, I hope that with some small thing that is removed or added on for greater caution, according to the claims that they make, the book will remain free. (XIV, 379-380).[17]

At any rate Magalotti recommended great prudence and patience and counselled absolutely against trying to force the course of events with inopportune interventions, especially with Urban VIII. Instead, unfortunately, right on that very day the ambassador Niccolini, even though not on his own initiative,[18] had spoken of Galileo with the Pope with results which were exactly what Magalotti had feared. Niccolini gave this account of his attempt:

> While we were discussing those delicate subjects of the Holy Office, His Holiness exploded into great anger, and

suddenly he told me that even our Galilei had dared entering where he should not have, into the most serious and dangerous subjects which could be stirred up at this time. (XIV, 383; trans. by Finocchiaro 1989, 229).

Before such words, which betrayed all of the tension existing in Urban VIII's spirit in that difficult moment of his pontificate, Niccolini would have been better off to have kept quiet. Unfortunately, the instructions from the Grand Duke forced him to insist. And there was also his friendship for Galileo to make him forget diplomatic prudence. Therefore, he went ahead:

> I replied that Mr. Galilei had not published without the approval of these ministers of his [the Pope's] and that for that purpose I myself had obtained and sent the prefaces from here. (XIV, 383).

Niccolini had touched the wrong key: the "ministers" (Ciampoli and Riccardi, especially the former) were by now a long way from having kept the trust of Urban VIII.

> He answered, with the same outburst of rage, that he had been deceived by Galileo and Ciampoli, that in particular Ciampoli had dared tell him that Mr. Galilei was ready to do all His Holiness ordered and that everything was fine, and that this was what he had been told, without having ever seen or read the work; he also complained about the Master of the Sacred Palace, though he said that the latter himself had been deceived by having his written endorsement of the book pulled out of his hands with beautiful words, by the book being then printed in Florence on the basis of other endorsements but without complying with the form given to the inquisitor, and by having his name printed in the book's list of imprimaturs even though he has no jurisdiction over publications in other cities. (XIV, 383-384; trans. by Finocchiaro 1989, 229).

Perceiving the danger, Niccolini tried to at least obtain from the Pope that Galileo would be granted the right to justify

himself before the Congregation or Commission summoned by
Urban VIII.

> Then His Holiness answered that in these matters of the
> Holy Office the procedure was simply to arrive at a
> censure and then call the defendant to recant. I replied:
> Does it thus not seem to Your Holiness that Galileo should
> know in advance the difficulties and the objections or the
> censures which are being raised against his work, and
> what the Holy Office is worried about? (XIV, 384; trans. by
> Finocchiaro 1989, 229-230).

For sure Niccolini had forgotten who was facing him.

> He [the Pope] answered violently: I say to Your Lordship
> that the Holy Office does not do these things and does not
> proceed this way, that these things are never given in
> advance to anyone, that such is not the custom; besides, he
> knows very well where the difficulties lie, if he wants to
> know them, since we have discussed them with him and he
> has heard them from ourselves. (XIV, 384; trans. by
> Finocchiaro 1989, 230).

Even the comment made by Niccolini, that they were
dealing with a book dedicated to the Grand Duke and that he
was, therefore, hoping that consideration would be had for his
personage, met the most biting answer:

> He said that he had prohibited works which had his
> pontifical name in front and were dedicated to himself, and
> that in such matters, involving great harm to religion
> (indeed the worst ever conceived), His Highness too should
> contribute to preventing it, being a Christian prince. (XIV,
> 384; trans. by Finocchiaro 1989, 230).

Niccolini insisted once again with the statement:

> . . . that I did not believe that His Holiness would bring
> about the prohibition of the already approved book without
> at least hearing Mr. Galilei first. His Holiness answered
> that this was the least ill that could be done to him and
> that he should take care not to be summoned by the Holy

Office; that he has appointed a Commission of theologians and other persons versed in various sciences, serious and of holy mind, who are weighing every minutia, word for word, since one is dealing with the most perverse subject one could ever come across; and again that his complaint was to have been deceived by Galileo and Ciampoli. (XIV, 384; trans. by Finocchiaro 1989, 230).

At the end Urban VIII made the additional remark:

. . . he [the Pope] has used every civility with Mr. Galilei since he explained to the latter what he knows, since he has not sent the case to the Congregation of the Holy Inquisition, as is the norm, but rather to a special Commission newly created, which is something, and since he has used better manners with Galileo than the latter has used with His Holiness, who was deceived. (XIV, 384; trans. by Finocchiaro 1989, 230-231).

In the face of such a total failure of his mission Niccolini could only conclude:

Thus I had an unpleasant meeting, and I feel the Pope could not have a worse disposition toward our poor Mr. Galilei. Your Most Illustrious Lordship can imagine in what condition I returned home yesterday morning. (XIV, 384; trans. by Finocchiaro 1989, 231).[19]

For Niccolini the experience had been a bitter one. And so, when he was faced with new instructions which had come to him from Florence to intervene on Galileo's behalf,[20] he preferred to hear once again the opinion of Father Riccardi. The latter counselled in the most absolute fashion against any other interventions, at least for the moment, "so as not to end up by ruining Mr. Galilei and by breaking off with His Holiness". After having reported the words of Riccardi on the points which had provoked the reactions of the Pope, Niccolini added:

In the meantime His Most Reverend Paternity [Riccardi] is reviewing the work and is trying to fix it in certain places so that it is acceptable; when this is completed he intends to bring it to the Pope and tell him that he is sure it can be allowed to circulate and that His Holiness now has the opportunity of using his customary mercy with Mr. Galileo. (XIV, 389; trans. by Finocchiaro 1989, 233).

As to the question to request, as Campanella himself had proposed,[21] to have Campanella and Castelli included among the members of the commission to which the examination of the *Dialogue* had been assigned, Riccardi was convinced that, not only was this against the practice of the Holy Office, but that it would also have been counterproductive, since both of them were looked upon with suspicion in Rome.[22]

Riccardi had, however, sought to reassure Niccolini with respect to the members of that commission. One of them was he himself, Riccardi, who had every reason to defend Galileo (so much the more so since he had "endorsed the book"); another member was the Pope's theologian (Agostino Oreggi) of whom Riccardi said: "he truly has good will"; a third, proposed by Riccardi, was in all probability the Jesuit Melchiorre Inchofer, who, according to Riccardi, was "his [Riccardi's] confidant" and was moved "by correct intentions" (XIV, 389).[23]

4.   *The discovery of the injunction of Segizzi to Galileo and the answer of the commission appointed to examine the Dialogue*

But together with this "reassuring" news (at least in Riccardi's intentions) there was some news of a quite different tenor. In complete secrecy Riccardi had confided to Niccolini that

> . . . there had been found in the books of the Holy Office that, twelve years ago, it having been heard that Galileo entertained this opinion and spread it in Florence, he had been summoned to Rome and forbidden by Cardinal Bellarmine in the name of the Pope and the Holy Office to hold this opinion, and that this alone is enough to ruin him utterly. (XIV, 389; trans. de Santillana 1955, 209).

Even supposing that Niccolini was mistaken in reporting the date (twelve instead of sixteen years ago), Riccardi had not made an exact reference either to the surrounding circumstances or to the content of the document recovered from the archives of the Holy Office.[24] As evidenced by the acts of the Trial (XIX, 325 and 327) we are dealing with the document in which, after the admonition of Bellarmine, there was placed the formal injunction of the Commissary Segizzi (XIX, 294). In fact, the existence of this injunction (whose authenticity was not doubted by the Roman authorities, as it is no longer by now doubted by us) enormously aggravated Galileo's conduct, in the case that it would be proven that he had defended the Copernican theory. And the common opinion was that Galileo had done precisely this.[25]

The response of the commission summoned by Urban VIII only confirmed this. After having held five meetings its judgement was that it was absolutely impossible to avoid having a diligent examination of the *Dialogue* by the Holy Office.[26] Upon being informed of this answer of the commission Urban VIII on 15 September sent one of his secretaries to the ambassador Niccolini so that the latter would give notice of it to the Grand Duke. Three days later Niccolini made a last attempt with the Pope with the purpose of persuading him to desist from the measures being taken. But, despite the fact that this time Urban VIII showed himself more relaxed and even inclined to joking, he was immovable in his decision. After having made it known that in the whole procedure he had had a particular regard for the Grand Duke "and that Mr. Galileo was still his friend" he had insisted that

> . . . these opinions were condemned about sixteen years ago and Galileo had gotten himself into a fix which he could have avoided; for these subjects are troublesome and dangerous, this work of his is indeed pernicious, and the matter is more serious than His Highness thinks. (XIV, 392; trans. by Finocchiaro 1989, 236).

As to the possibility of correcting the *Dialogue* and then allowing it to be printed, Urban VIII showed that he did not believe it possible, even though his answer, in a benign and almost joking tone, left Niccolini with some hope.

5.   *Galileo is summoned to Rome by the Holy Office.*

By now the Holy Office's machine had started rolling and it would not have been easy for anyone to stop it, not even Urban VIII. On 23 September there was a meeting of this Congregation with the Holy Father and eight cardinals present (XIX, 279). During the meeting a report was read on the facts concerning the printing of the *Dialogue* which at the end, in a synthetic form, contained the responses of the commission which had examined Galileo's work.[27] And there was joined to it that which will become the most serious charge:

> . . . he has further been deceitfully silent about the command laid upon him by the Holy Office, in the year 1616, which was as follows: *ut supradictam opinionem, quod sol sit centrum mundi et terra moveatur, omnino relinquat, nec eam de caetero, quovis modo, teneat, doceat aut defendat, verbo aut scriptis; alias, contra ipsum procedetur in Sancto Officio. Cui praecepto acquievit et parere promisit* (To relinquish altogether the said opinion that the sun is the center of the world and immovable and that the Earth moves; nor henceforth to hold, teach, or defend it in any way whatsoever, verbally or in writing, otherwise proceedings would be taken against him by the Holy Office, which injunction the said Galileo acquiesced in and promised to obey). (XIX, 279; trans. by de Santillana 1955, 210).[28]

According to the practice of the Holy Office the minutes of the meeting in question do not report discussions or opinions which emerged. Nevertheless, in a letter sent by Campanella to Galileo two days later (XIV, 397) there is word of an intervention in Galileo's favor by one of the cardinals present, who was opposed to beginning the procedure of the Holy Office in Galileo's regard.[29]

> At the conclusion of the meeting Urban VIII ordered that a letter be sent to the inquisitor of Florence so that he would tell the same Galileo, in the name of the Sacred Congregation, to appear within the month of the coming

October in Rome, before the Commissary general of the
Holy Office, and that he receive from him the promise to
obey that command, the promise to be made in the
presence of witnesses who - if necessary - will be able to
testify in case he does not wish to accept this command
and does not promise to obey. (XIX, 279-280).[30]

On the first of October Galileo was, in fact, called by the
Florentine inquisitor who delivered the precepts to him according
to the instructions he had received. Galileo declared that he
willingly accepted the command received (XIX, 331-332). In
reality, this order took him completely by surprise and deeply
disturbed him.[31] What to do? On the one hand, he knew very
well that it was not possible to play around with the Holy Office
and that it was best for him to show that he was "most obedient
and most zealous for the Holy Church". On the other hand, he
nourished a profound apprehension with respect to the
"persecutions from unjust suggestions which, without my having
merited it, lined up against me the thinking, indeed most holy
thinking, of my superiors" (XIV, 403). In the end he chose the
route of putting the matter off and sought with every pretext
possible to avoid going to Rome.
    Thus, while the Holy Office continued to issue new
dispositions in expectation of the trial,[32] Galileo put himself to
work with his friends and persons in authority who could help
him in his plans. The most important step he took was with
Cardinal Francesco Barberini, who in the past had shown
himself favorable to him.[33] On 13 October he sent a long letter
to this nephew of Urban VIII. After having said that he had
foreseen the opposition which the *Dialogue* had met, given the
opposition which had been raised against his previous works, but
that he had been taken by surprise by the influence which his
opponents' hatred had had on "the most holy minds of
superiors", and that the prohibition to continue the printing of
the book had been for him "a most grievous notification", he
went on to speak of the order from the Holy Office to appear in
Rome.

I cannot deny - he confessed - that (this) is a great
affliction for me; while I go on pondering to myself the

fruits of all of my studies and labors over so many years, studies which for a long time have brought my name to the ears of lettered persons with a fame not totally obscure, and now those fruits are turned into serious accusations against my reputation by encouraging my enemies to rise up against my friends and sealing their voices not only as to praising me but also as to excusing me, with the allegation that I have finally merited to be cited by the Tribunal of the Holy Office, an action which is not taken except in the case of those who are seriously delinquent. (XIV, 407).

Given this state of mind which caused him continuous insomnia, in addition to the weight of his seventy years and other indispositions, Galileo sought recourse in the intercession of the Cardinal, so that he might obtain from the Holy Office some assistance in making easier the way whereby he was to explain his actions. And he proposed, in fact, two possible ways to do this. The first was that of sending a detailed account of all that he had written and done right from beginning of the opposition shown against the Copernican opinion.[34] Galileo said that he trusted that this report would be adequate to persuade the fathers of the Holy Office of his innocence. And if they then would have wished not to accept this justification in writing, Galileo suggested another way of giving an account of his behavior: " . . . here are the inquisitor, the Nuncio, the Archbishop and other ministers of the Holy Church, to whom at every request I am completely prepared to present myself". And he concluded:

> And finally to conclude, when neither my advanced age nor my many bodily ills, nor my troubled mind, nor the length of a journey made most painful by the current suspicions, are judged by this sacred and high Court to be sufficient excuses for seeking some dispensation or postponement, I will take up the journey, preferring obedience to life itself (XIV, 410).[35]

In the meantime Galileo's friends had also become involved in trying to avert the storm that was brewing against him. In particular, Castelli had taken steps with Father Riccardi and with the Commissary of the Holy Office, Vincenzo Maculano (also called Fiorenzuola). He himself informed Galileo about this with his letter of 2 October. After having stated that he had found "an apparently quite good attitude" on Father Riccardi's part, he reported about a long conversation with the Father Commissary. Castelli had offered to explain to the latter that part of the *Dialogue* which dealt with the motion of the Earth. Encouraged by these favorable inclinations shown by the Commissary, Castelli had frankly admitted that the fundamental thesis of the *Dialogue* was, as a matter of fact, the proof of the Earth's motion. As to Maculano's reaction Castelli wrote:

> The Father I have spoken of answered me that as for him he was of the same opinion, that the question should not be concluded with the authority of the Sacred Letters; and he even told me that he wanted to write about it, and that he would have made it known to me . . . (XIV, 402).

There is no justification for us to surmise that Father Maculano's attitude was insincere. Even during the trial we will see that he shows himself not to be hostile to Galileo. Therefore, his words to Castelli seem to be an indication of the disparity of views that existed among the Church authorities themselves on the Copernican question.

Even the Grand Duke of Tuscany through his secretary Cioli tried to support Galileo's requests by assigning the ambassador Niccolini to do "everything that might ever be possible to help him, taking notice of that which he writes" (XIV, 413).[36] But Niccolini, to whom the task had been entrusted of delivering Galileo's letter to Barberini, became worried about the unfavorable reactions it might provoke and he waited so as to be able to consult Castelli on the matter. Castelli was at that time absent from Rome. In regard to this he wrote to Galileo:

> And if I am allowed to speak freely I think that the letter is more likely to sharpen than ease the situation; because while you indicate that you are able to defend and justify that which you have written, all the more will the intention grow stronger to condemn the work thoroughly (XIV, 417).

The only request that would have probably been accepted, continued Niccolini, was a postponement of the departure for Rome. For the rest, Niccolini counselled Galileo:

> . . . do not take on the defense of those matters which the Congregation does not approve, but defer them to it [the Congregation] and retract in the way that its Cardinals will desire; otherwise you will encounter extreme difficulties in the solution of your cause. (XIV, 418).

And he added frankly his forecast:

> In this manner you would be able to find an easier solution to your cause; but I do not believe that this will happen without a trial and, consequently, without some restrictions on you personally.

Nonetheless, after having finally consulted with Castelli, Niccolini decided to deliver the letter to Cardinal Barberini.[37] At the same time he applied himself to contacting Church authorities in Rome so as to bring it about that they would renounce having Galileo come there. Not content with that, he spoke on 13 November with Urban VIII himself trying to get leverage from Galileo's advanced age, his poor health and the problem of the quarantine because of the pestilence still in force. As Niccolini wrote on that very day to Galileo (XIV, 427), Urban VIII could not be dissuaded from the point that Galileo must come to Rome, even though he granted to Galileo that he "take advantage of all possible conveniences", and he assured him that he would take care that the quarantine would be shortened for him. Niccolini added that Cardinal Barberini had also excused himself with the ambassador for not being able to take a position contrary to that of the Pope, but he had given assurance that he would take steps to see that as far as possible the quarantine was eased.

This report of Niccolini to Galileo was, however, partial. In fact, the ambassador of the Grand Duke had, so as not to cause further discouragement to Galileo, kept quiet about some particulars of the audience with Urban VIII to which he did, on

the other hand, make reference on that same day in a letter to
Cioli. The Pope had said that

> . . . it was necessary to examine him [Galileo] personally,
> and that God would hopefully forgive his error of having
> gotten involved in an intrigue like this after His Holiness
> himself [when he was cardinal] had delivered him from it.
> (XIV, 428; trans. by Finocchiaro 1989, 239)

Niccolini, who had again insisted on the fact that the book
had been approved, added:

> . . . However, I was interrupted by being told that
> Ciampoli and the Master of the Sacred Palace had behaved
> badly and that subordinates who do not do what their
> masters want are the worst possible servants; for, when
> asking Ciampoli many times what was happening with
> Galilei, His Holiness had never been told anything but
> good and had never been given the news that the book was
> being printed, even when he was beginning to smell
> something. Finally, he reiterated that one is dealing with
> a very bad doctrine. (XIV, 428-429; trans. by Finocchiaro
> 1989, 239).

These words of the Pope about Ciampoli show that Urban
VIII was more than ever convinced that he had been tricked by
his men of trust in the entire question of the *Dialogue*.[38] This
conviction had been the death blow with respect to Ciampoli
who, as we know, had already compromised himself by having
lined up against the Pope with the Spanish-leaning faction. In
fact, this man who at one time had enjoyed the trust of the Pope
and who was spoken about as a future cardinal, had to leave
Rome on 23 November to go as governor in a small town of the
Marches, Montalto, under prohibition of coming back to Rome.[39]
The intransigent attitude of Urban VIII towards Galileo's
coming to Rome was the consequence of a decision which he had
taken during the meeting of the Holy Office of 11 November.
During the course of that meeting consideration had been given
to the request of the Grand Duke of Tuscany that Galileo,
because of his advanced age, would be permitted not to come to
Rome. "His Most Holy Person had not wished to make any

concession, but he ordered to write that he obey and [to write] the inquisitor so that he would force him to come to Rome" (XIX, 280).

The Florentine inquisitor responded on 20 November to Cardinal Antonio Barberini (who had informed him of this Papal decision) assuring him that he had carried out the assigned task. Galileo, although stating that he was most prepared to go, had once again put forth his age and his state of health. But the inquisitor had, in the presence of a notary and two witnesses, predetermined for him a period of one month. And the same inquisitor concluded: " . . . and he again showed himself ready to come: but then I do not know whether he will carry it out" (XIX, 333).

On 9 December the Holy Office again met and, after having noted the postponement of a month granted to Galileo by the Florentine inquisitor, commanded the latter to oblige Galileo absolutely to come to Rome, once the postponement had expired, by way of the route through Siena, despite whatever else to the contrary might occur. (XIX, 281 and 334).

In spite of the resoluteness of the Holy Office and the pressure exerted on him by friends like Niccolini and Castelli, increasingly worried that Galileo's enemies would make use of his failure to come to Rome to accuse him of showing himself to be "rebellious and contumacious",[40] Galileo continued to procrastinate. But there is no doubt that the excuses about his health were not just a pretext.[41]

As a last attempt Galileo had sent to Rome a declaration of his bad health, prepared by three doctors on 17 December (XIX, 334-335). This testimony was examined in the meeting of the Holy Office of 30 December. By now Urban VIII had very definitely lost his patience. That is very obvious in the formulation of the decision taken in this regard:

> Sanctissimus [the Pope] has commanded that we write to the inquisitor that His Holiness and the Sacred Congregation cannot and absolutely must not tolerate subterfuges of this sort; and for the purpose of verifying if he [Galileo] really is in such a condition that he cannot come to the City [Rome] without danger to his life, His Holiness and the Sacred Congregation will send a

commissary there together with doctors who will visit him and make a specific and clear report on his state of health; and if he is in such a state as to be able to come, they should send him imprisoned and in chains; if on the other hand, because of his health and the danger to his life it will be necessary to put off the move, as soon as he will have recovered and the danger has ceased, he should be transported imprisoned and in chains. Furthermore, the Commissary and the doctors should be sent at his expense, because he is the one who has reduced himself to this state of affairs and has not taken care to come and to obey at the appropriate time. (XIX, 281-282; 335).

As we see the tone is most severe. The obvious desire was to scare Galileo, bringing him finally to set forth on his own initiative, before the draconian measures alluded to would be taken. In fact, the letter which Cardinal Antonio Barberini wrote at the Pope's order to the Florentine inquisitor on 1 January 1633 severely criticized, it is true, Galileo:

This Congregation of the Holy Office has taken it quite badly that Galileo Galilei has not promptly obeyed the command given to him to come to Rome: and he should not excuse his disobedience because of sickness, since it is through his own fault that he is reduced to these conditions; and it is very bad for him to seek an excuse by making out he is sick, for the fact is that His Holiness and these my Most Eminent Lords do not wish in any way to tolerate these fictions, and it is also bad for him to dissimulate his coming here. (XX, 575).

But he added: " . . . Your Lordship should however tell him that if *he does not obey right away* a Commissary will be sent there . . ." (XX, 575-576; italics by the author).

The injunction was read to Galileo by the Inquisitor Egidi, who reported as follows to Cardinal Antonio Barberini on 8 January:

I have read the letter of Your Most Eminent Lord to Galileo Galilei, because I found him in a state to be able to do it; and in brief he has resolved to wish as soon as

possible to come to this city [Rome] and he says that he is
most ready to obey, and he will make known also by
doctors there in Rome his poor health, and that he did not
wish to dissemble in any way. (XIX, 335).

After the meeting with Egidi Galileo hastened to write to
Cioli who was with the Grand Duke in Pisa. Was he perhaps
still hoping in the possibility that an intervention of the Grand
Duke would bring it about that he would not have to leave? At
any rate, Cioli's response of 11 January, although full of
sympathy, was clear:

> Also His Highness [the Grand Duke] to whom I made
> known the letter of Your Lord sympathizes with it; but
> since it is proper in the end to obey the higher tribunals it
> displeases His Highness that he cannot bring it about that
> you would not go. But perhaps your readiness to obey and
> the uprightness of your intention, with your presence, will
> reconcile to your favor those minds which appear to be
> stirred up against you. Thus does His Highness desire out
> of the love and the esteem he has for you. (XV, 21).

Obviously, in view of the Pope's state of mind, the Grand
Duke and Cioli had judged that it was useless, even
counterproductive, to try any more to put things off. But to
sweeten the bitter pill, the Grand Duke provided one of his
litters for Galileo and arranged that he would be hosted in Rome
in the house of Ambassador Niccolini.[42]

Finally Galileo realized that there was nothing left to do
but set out for Rome. Before leaving Florence he left a will
naming his son Vincenzio as heir (XIX, 520-522). That same day
(15 January) he wrote to Elia Diodati in Paris informing him of
his departure for Rome.

> . . . at the moment I am about to go to Rome, summoned
> by the Holy Office, which has already suspended my
> *Dialogue*. From reliable sources I hear the Jesuit Fathers
> have managed to convince some very important persons
> that my book is execrable and more harmful to the Holy
> Church than the writings of Luther and Calvin. Thus I am
> sure it will be prohibited, despite the fact that to obtain

the license I went personally to Rome and delivered it into the hands of the Master of the Sacred Palace . . . (XV, 25-26; trans. by Finocchiaro 1989, 225).

Where was the basis for this statement of Galileo about the presumed pressures exerted by the Jesuits on the Roman authorities? Perhaps in the letter already mentioned which Magalotti had written from Rome to Guiducci on 27 August 1632? In fact, in all of the collected papers of that period there is nothing other than this report of Magalotti, based on a sentence of Riccardi, who in turn was expressing only a forecast and not a matter of fact.[43] On the other hand what appears as obvious is the personal position taken by Urban VIII, attested to by Niccolini, as we have seen. But Galileo could not believe that his friend and one time admirer had so radically changed his attitude without outside influences. A justification was needed for such a sudden and complete change, and Galileo had to look for it elsewhere.

On 20 January 1633 Galileo finally set out on his trip to Rome. The Florentine inquisitor made the announcement of this at the Holy Office and he must obviously have drawn a sigh of relief.[44] Perhaps Cioli also felt relieved, at least from a political point of view. But the letter whereby he informed Niccolini of Galileo's departure showed also a sincere compassion:

Poor Mr. Galileo has finally set off on his journey there; and if Your Lord could send him as he goes along some ray of consolation, by telling him at least to come along happily, that he will not be put in prison, it would diminish our fear about his health, because it must be true that he departed plagued by sickness; and His Highness [the Grand Duke] has had provided for him a good carriage of the Most Serene Household and has given orders to Your Excellency to receive him and take care of him. (XV, 29).

Because of the plague Galileo had to spend a quarantine period in Ponte a Centina near Acquapendente on the border between the Grand Duchy of Tuscany and the Papal States. The lodging which he had to make use of proved to be very uncomfortable and the stop much longer than foreseen.[45] On Cioli's invitation Niccolini wrote him an encouraging letter: "May Your Lordship keep a peaceful spirit and take good care of yourself, because we await you here with the wish to serve you in this house, and for the rest the blessed God will help your right intention".(XV, 35). As we see, Niccolini did not want to tip the scales by going so far as to assure Galileo that he would not have been put in prison.

Finally the quarantine passed and Galileo was able to take up his trip once more. He arrived the evening of 13 February in Rome where he took up lodging at the Tuscan embassy at Villa Medici. After all of the anxiety and the profound uncertainty which had tormented him during his painful trip, there was now at least a little light and heat and the friendship and good feelings which he felt around him from the ambassador and his wife, Caterina Riccardi. And indubitably this friendship must have helped Galileo feel in himself a rebirth of the old warrior spirit. After all he would now find himself facing the real situation with precise questions to which he would be able to respond. What tired and exhausted him was not the clash with those real difficulties but the need to try to identify and battle adversaries who appeared, like shadows and phantasms, to be always escaping his grasp.

The day after his arrival in Rome Galileo made haste to present himself to Monsignor Boccabella, who had just left the office of Assessor of the Holy Office and who had shown himself well disposed to Galileo. Obviously Galileo wanted to seek advice and possibly obtain some information about what was maturing. Upon Boccabella's advice Galileo went immediately to visit the new Assessor, Francesco Albizzi, and then to the Commissary of the Holy Office, Vincenzo Maculano, whom, however, he did not find.[46]

But after this first day's activity there followed a long period during which Galileo did not leave his house. Niccolini explained to Cioli the reason for this on 16 February:

> The Lord Cardinal Barberini has warned him not to socialize and not to bother talking with everyone who comes to visit him since for various reasons this could

cause harm and prejudice; thus he stays home in seclusion, waiting to be told something. (XV, 41; trans. by Finocchiaro 1989, 242-243).[47]

A little afterwards the same thing was made known to him by the Commissary of the Holy Office himself who said that it was not a question of an order but of "friendly advice".[48] Galileo understood right away what this "friendly advice" meant and he scrupulously observed it, even though it was hard for him, who was used to moving about, not to leave home.

Even though the Holy Office did not provide any information to Galileo, he continued little by little to regain courage and hope. In fact, he was left in the house of the ambassador of Tuscany who treated him "with an undescribable kindness". Even the notices which had been given to him and the two visits which Monsignor Lodovico Serristori, consultor of the Holy Office,[49] had made to him had been marked by a kindness which allowed one to hope for the best. Galileo said as much to Cioli in a letter of 19 February in which he noted, among other things, that: " . . . this seems to be a beginning of a procedure which is very gentle and kind, and completely unlike the threatened ropes, chains and prisons, etc." (XV, 44).

For his part Niccolini had continued to take action. He had gone to visit Cardinals Scaglia and Bentivoglio to recommend Galileo to them and he had found them very well disposed.[50] From these conversations, as well as from others which he and also Castelli had had, it emerged that

> . . . the greatest difficulty seems to lie in the claim by these Lords that in the year 1616 Mr. Galilei received an injunction not to dispute about or discuss this opinion. However, he says that the order does not have this form, but rather that he should not hold or defend it; he thinks he can justify himself . . . (XV, 55; trans. by Finocchiaro 1989, 244).[51]

Finally on 26 February Niccolini spoke with Urban VIII himself. As he wrote the day after to Cioli, the ambassador had informed the Pope of the arrival of Galileo in Rome and had emphasized the attitude of complete submission with which he

had come. For his part Urban VIII had underlined the fact that
Galileo had been accorded an altogether exceptional treatment
by allowing him to live in the Tuscan Embassy rather than at
the Holy Office, and this had been done only out of respect for
the Grand Duke. As to how long the procedure would last the
Pope had declared:

> . . . the activities of the Holy Office ordinarily proceeded
> slowly, and he did not really know whether one could hope
> for such a quick conclusion, since they were in the process
> of preparing for the formal proceedings and had not yet
> finished with that. (XV, 56; trans. by Finocchiaro 1989,
> 245).

And he added:

> . . . that, in short, Mr. Galilei had been ill-advised to
> publish these opinions of his, and it was the sort of thing
> for which Ciampoli was responsible; for although he claims
> to want to discuss the earth's motion hypothetically,
> nevertheless when he presents the arguments for it he
> mentions and discusses it assertively and conclusively;
> furthermore, he had also violated the order given him in
> 1616 by the Lord Cardinal Bellarmine in the name of the
> Congregation of the Index. (XV, 56; trans. by Finocchiaro
> 1989, 245).

Niccolini had sought to respond in Galileo's defense:

> . . . but as the subject is delicate and troublesome, and as
> Your Holiness gives the impression that Mr. Galileo's
> doctrine is bad and that he even believes it, the task is not
> easy. Furthermore, even if they should be satisfied with his
> answers, they will not want to give the appearance of
> having made a blunder, after everybody knows they
> summoned him to Rome. (XV, 56; trans. by Finocchiaro
> 1989, 245).

Encouraged by Urban VIII's attitude, which seemed to be
less severe than before, Niccolini had also recommended Galileo
to Cardinal Francesco Barberini who

. . . replied that he felt warmly toward Mr. Galilei and regarded him as an exceptional man, but this subject is very delicate for it involves the possibility of introducing some imaginary dogma into the world, particularly into Florence where (as I know) the intellects are very subtle and curious, and especially by his reporting much more validly what favors the side of the earth's motion than what can be adduced for the other side. (XV, 56; trans. by Finocchiaro 1989, 246).

Meanwhile time went on and Galileo received no communication from the Holy Office. He sought to console himself by considering that this delay would have contributed to bringing about the nullification of many charges against him.[52] But he was wrong. He did not take due notice of what Niccolini, as a consummate diplomat and knowledgeable in Roman affairs, had written to Cioli: the Holy Office could not allow the trial to fade into nothing, even if Galileo would have been able to bring forth in his defense proofs which were satisfactory. And above all he was not taking into account the depth of the hatreds and jealousies that were nesting against him. Others were able to take note of these better than he was. For example, Luca Holste,[53] who, after having informed Nicolas Fabri de Peiresc that Galileo had come to Rome, added:

It would take a long time to report the cause of the hatred harbored against the very fine old man [Galileo] but one thing cannot be seen without irritation, that is, that persons completely incapable have been given the task of examining the book of Galileo and the whole Pythagorean and Copernican system, while it is above all a matter of the authority of the Church which will suffer widely from a less correct judgment. Galileo suffers from the envy of those who see in him the only obstacle to their having the reputation of the highest mathematicians. Because this whole storm was raised by the personal hatred of a monk whom Galileo does not wish to recognize as the first among mathematicians; at the moment he is commissary of the Holy Office. (XV, 62).[54]

Still Galileo and his friends sought to gain the support of influential persons, especially among the members of the Holy Office and to this end they requested other letters of recommendation from the Grand Duke.[55]

For his part Niccolini had gone back to Urban VIII on 13 March with the pretext of thanking him in the name of the Grand Duke for the privilege granted to Galileo to stay at the Tuscan embassy. In the report of that audience, sent on the same day to Cioli, Niccolini stated that he had again insisted that there be a prompt solution of the affair. But Urban VIII had replied that he did not think it would be possible to avoid having Galileo called to the Holy Office on the occasion of his interrogation. Such, in fact, was that Congregation's practice and there was no substitute for it. Niccolini had insisted expressing the hope that the Pope would wish to dispense Galileo from such an obligation in consideration also of his age, of his poor health and of the fact that he was prepared to accept any censure whatsoever. But Urban VIII showed himself to be immovable:

> . . . but he again said he does not think there is any way out, and may God forgive Mr. Galilei for having meddled with these subjects. He added that one is dealing with new doctrines and Holy Scripture, that the best course is to follow the common opinion, and that may God also help Ciampoli with these new opinions since he too is attracted to them and is a friend of the new philosophy; further, Mr. Galileo had been his friend, they had conversed and dined several times together familiarly, and he was very sorry to have to displease him, but one was dealing with the interests of the faith and religion. I think I went on to add that if he is heard, he will easily give every satisfaction, though with the proper reverence which is due the Holy Office. He replied that Mr. Galilei will be examined in due course, but there is an argument which no one has ever been able to answer: that is, God is omnipotent and can do anything; but if He is omnipotent, why do we want to bind him? (XV, 68; trans. by Finocchiaro 1989, 247).

As we see, Urban VIII returned to his favorite argument. It was a delicate point and Niccolini would have done better to have stopped there. But, perhaps encouraged by Urban VIII's moderate tone, he desired to add something:

> I said that I was not competent to discuss these subjects but I had heard Mr. Galilei himself say that first he did not hold the opinion of the earth's motion as true and then that since God could make the world in innumerable ways, one could not deny that He might have made it this way. However, he got upset and told me that one must not impose necessity on the blessed God; seeing that he was losing his temper, I did not want to continue discussing what I did not understand, and thus displease him, to the detriment of Mr. Galilei. (XV, 68; trans. by Finocchiaro 1989, 247).[56]

And so Niccolini switched the discussion, even though he came back to it later on, seeing that Urban VIII had calmed down, to ask if it would not be possible to allow Galileo to remain in the embassy. Urban VIII promised that "he would see to it that certain rooms, which are the best and the most comfortable in this place, were assigned to him" (XV, 68).

Upon his return home Niccolini gave Galileo a summary account of the conversation without, however, indicating to him that they were thinking of calling him to the Holy Office, "because I was sure that it would cause him great anxiety and would make him live in an agitated state until the time came, especially since it is not possible at present to know how long they really want him [to remain there]." (XV, 68).

6.   *Beginning of the trial and Galileo's defense*

Finally the two-month long uncertainty came to an end. Niccolini was summoned by Cardinal Francesco Barberini, who informed him that by order of the Pope and of the Congregation of the Holy Office Galileo should be summoned to that same Holy Office. He also let him know that, as a special gesture of respect to the Grand Duke, since a few hours of interrogation would not be enough, it would perhaps be necessary to retain him at the Holy Office. Once more Niccolini tried to make clear the state of health of Galileo, who, as he wrote three days later to Cioli, "for two nights running here had groaned and complained continuously of his arthritic pains, of his age and of the suffering he would experience from all of this" (XV, 85) and he asked the cardinal if it would not be possible to allow him to return each evening to the embassy. But the cardinal did not want to make any promises, even though he gave assurances that Galileo "would be kept there not as if in a prison nor in secret, as was usually done with others, but that he would be provided with good rooms which would perhaps even be left open" (XV, 85).

On 9 April Niccolini went to thank the Pope for the special respect shown towards the Grand Duke, but he found him more than ever fixed in the positions taken: "His Holiness complained that he [Galileo] has entered into that matter which for him [the Pope] it is still a most serious matter and one that has great consequences for religion" (XV, 85).

Niccolini was worried about such rigidity on Urban VIII's part and, as he informed Galileo of the imminent summons to the Holy Office, he recommended that he not try to defend his positions but "that he submit to what he might see they would want him to believe and hold in that particular about the mobility of the earth". And Niccolini added: "He is extremely afflicted by this; and judging by how much I have seen him go down since yesterday, I have very serious worries about his life" (XV, 85).

On 12 April Galileo appeared before the Commissary of the Holy Office who, as Niccolini wrote to Cioli four days later,

> . . . received him in a friendly manner and had him lodged in the chambers of the prosecutor of that Tribunal, rather than in the cells usually given to criminals; thus, not only does he reside among the officials, but he is free to go out into the courtyard of that house. (XV, 94; trans. by Finocchiaro, 250).

Niccolini added that they allowed his domestic to serve him and stay with him and that the servants of the embassy would bring him his food in the morning and the evening.[57] "These unusual and pleasing ways" made Niccolini hope for a quick and benign solution to the matter. The ambassador again promised to continue to work towards such an end, even though they were dealing with a very delicate task because, as he wrote, "in that Tribunal one deals with men who do not speak, nor do they answer, either vocally or by letter, thus it is even more difficult to deal with them or to penetrate what they are thinking" (XV, 95).

Through the acts of Galileo's trial we are able to know the details of the first interrogation which was held on the same day.[58] After some preliminary questions, the Commissary began to interrogate Galileo about the events of 1616. Obviously they wanted to clarify his responsibility in transgressing the orders received from Bellarmine, for this constituted, as we know, the principal charge against him.

After having stated that he had come on his own to Rome on that occasion because he had heard that doubts were being raised about the Copernican opinion and in order to make sure that "he hold only holy and catholic opinions", Galileo admitted that he had treated of the Copernican doctrines with some cardinals of the Holy Office who were desirous of having explanations of Copernicus' book, because it was so difficult to understand for those who were not mathematicians or astronomers.

At this point Father Maculano asked Galileo to tell him what had been decided on that occasion about the problem of Copernicanism. Galileo answered:

> Respecting the controversy which had arisen on the aforesaid opinion that the Sun is stationary and that the Earth moves, it was decided by the Holy Congregation of the Index that such an opinion, considered as an established fact, contradicted Holy Scripture and was only admissible as a conjecture [ex suppositione], as it was held by Copernicus [sic]. (XIX, 338; trans. by de Santillana 1955, 238).

The Commissary insisted: "Were you notified of the aforesaid decision of the Congregation of the Index, and by whom?" Galileo answered: "I was notified of the aforesaid decision of the Congregation of the Index, and I was notified by the Lord Cardinal Bellarmine". And immediately afterwards, upon being further questioned by Maculano, he specified:

> The Lord Cardinal Bellarmine signified to me that the aforesaid opinion of Copernicus might be held as a conjecture, as it had been held by Copernicus, and His Eminence was aware that, like Copernicus, I only held that opinion as a conjecture, which is evident from an answer of the same Lord Cardinal to a letter of Father Paolo Antonio Foscarini, provincial of the Carmelites, of which I have a copy, and in which these words occur: "It appears to me that Your Reverence and Signor Galileo act wisely in contenting yourselves with speaking ex *suppositione* and not with certainty." This letter of the Cardinal is dated April 12, 1615. It means, in other words, that that opinion, taken absolutely, must not be either held or defended. (XIX, 339; trans. by de Santillana 1955, 238-239).

Indubitably this answer of Galileo must have appeared to be completely insufficient to the Commissary who knew of the document found in the archives of the Holy Office. So he made the question more specific: "What would he say had been decided and notified to him at that time, that is in the month of February 1616"? And Galileo answered:

> In the month of February, 1616, the Lord Cardinal Bellarmine told me that, as the opinion of Copernicus, if adopted absolutely, was contrary to Holy Scripture, it must neither be held nor defended but that it could be taken and used hypothetically. In accordance with this I possess a certificate of Cardinal Bellarmine, given on May 26, 1616, in which he says that the Copernican opinion may neither be held nor defended, as it is opposed to Holy Scripture, of which certificate I herewith submit a copy. (XIX, 339; trans. by de Santillana 1955, 239).[59]

The difference between the content of the document signed by Bellarmine, presently before his eyes, and the one from the archives could not escape the Commissary. The latter document, as we know, spoke of the intervention of Maculano's predecessor right after the communication given by Bellarmine to Galileo.

The Commissary, therefore, put another question to Galileo: "When the above communication was made to him, were any other persons present, and who?" Galileo admitted that: "When the Lord Cardinal made known to me what I have reported about the Copernican views, some Dominican Fathers were present, but I did not know them and have never seen them since." Finally Maculano could put to him the most important question: "Was any other command [*praeceptum*] communicated to him on this subject, in the presence of those Fathers, by them or anyone else, and what?" Galileo answered:

> I remember that the transaction took place as follows: The Lord Cardinal Bellarmine sent for me one morning and told me certain particulars which I had rather reserve for the ear of His Holiness before I communicate them to others.[60] But the end of it was that he told me that the Copernican opinion, being contradictory to Holy Scripture, must not be held or defended. It has escaped my memory whether those Dominican Fathers were present before or whether they came afterward; neither do I remember whether they were present when the Lord Cardinal told me the said opinion was not to be held. It may be that a command [*precetto*] was issued to me that I should not hold or defend the opinion in question, but I do not remember it, for it is several years ago. (XIX, 339-340, trans. by de Santillana 1955, 239-240).

As if to recall to Galileo's memory a fact which he had forgotten, Maculano said that that command given to him in the presence of witnesses contained the words: " . . . that he must neither hold, defend, nor teach [*nec docere*] that opinion in any way whatsoever [*quovis modo*]" and he asked Galileo whether he now remembered how and from whom that command had been enjoined on him. Galileo repeated what he had already declared:

> I do not remember that the command was intimated to me by anybody but by Cardinal Bellarmine verbally; and I remember that the command was "not to hold or defend." It may be that "and not to teach" was also there. I do not remember it, neither the clause "in any way whatsoever" [*quovis modo*], but it may be that it was; for I thought no

more about it or took any pains to impress the words on my memory, as a few months later I received the certificate now produced, of the said Lord Cardinal Bellarmine, of May 26, in which the order [*ordine*] given me, *not to hold or defend* that opinion, is expressly found. The two other clauses of the said command which have just been made known to me, namely, *not to teach* and *in any way*, I have not retained in my memory, I suppose because they are not mentioned in the said certificate, on which I have relied, and which I have kept as a reminder. (XIX, 340; trans. by de Santillana 1955, 240-241).

Galileo's response was clever. He knew he held a precious document, that of Bellarmine, and he had made use of it to his own advantage. But the fact still stood that Galileo had admitted having received a command from Bellarmine not to hold or to defend the Copernican opinion. And this was enough for Maculano, even leaving aside the document of the Holy Office archives which was even more precise and stronger.[61] And so the Commissary insisted: "How in the world, therefore, despite that command, had Galileo written and published the *Dialogue*? Had he received a special permission allowing him to do it?".

Therein stood the crux of the question and Galileo knew it. But by now he had decided upon his line of defense. And so he responded:

After the command mentioned above I have received no permission to write the aforementioned book . . . because I do not claim by writing said book, to have at all gone against the command given to me not to hold nor defend nor teach the opinion in question, but to refute it. (XIX, 340).

To refute it! This statement of Galileo must have caused the Commissary to give a start, since he knew well what the commission had thought of this "refutation", the commission to whom the previous September there had been passed along the examination of the *Dialogue*. At any rate, the affair would have been examined by a new commission and so it was of no use to start arguing now with Galileo.[62]

There remained the more delicate question, the one to do with the permission to print. Maculano put the question to Galileo in these terms:

> When asking permission to print the book, did he tell the Master of the Palace about the *precetto* which had been issued to him? (XIX, 341; trans. by de Santillana 1955, 241).

Galileo's reply was in line with the previous one:

> I did not happen to discuss that command with the Master of the Palace when I asked for the imprimatur, for I did not think it necessary to say anything, because I had no doubts about it; for I have neither maintained nor defended in that book the opinion that the Earth moves and that the Sun is stationary but have rather demonstrated the opposite of the Copernican opinion and shown that the arguments of Copernicus are weak and not conclusive. (XIX, 341; trans. by de Santillana 1955, 241).[63]

And so the first interrogation was completed. Galileo signed the minutes[64] and he took the oath to observe secrecy. He was then told to stop in at the Holy Office, at the Prosecutor's apartment. Galileo had undoubtedly hoped to be able to return to Villa Medici that same day. But the courteous attitude of the Commissary and the special respect shown to him must have made his disillusionment less bitter. And he perhaps had some consolation in the fact that it would only be a matter of a few days.

In fact, that is not the way it was. On 23 April he was still at the Holy Office. He wrote on that same day to Geri Bocchineri from his bed where he was suffering from a leg pain and among other matters he said:

> A little while ago the Commissary and the Prosecutor, who are the ones who examine me, came to pay a visit; and they gave me their word and the firm intention to dispatch matters for me as soon as I had gotten out of bed, answering me many times that I be of happy and of good spirit. I give more importance to this promise than to any

of the hopes that have been given me in the past, hopes which experience has shown to have been founded more on conjectures than on real knowledge. I have always hoped that my innocence and my sincerity would come to be known, and now my hope is greater than ever. (XV, 101).

Even Niccolini seemed fundamentally optimistic. When he wrote that same day to Cioli, among other things he told him:

As to Mr. Galileo, he is still in the same place, with the same comfortable arrangements. He writes to me every day, and I answer him and I freely tell him my intentions, without giving a second thought to it, and I go on wondering whether this matter [questa festa] is not destined to finish on some one else's shoulders. He has been examined once only, and I think that they will free him as soon as His Holiness returns from Castel Gandolfo, which will be for the Ascension.[65] Up to now there is no talk of the material of the book and the only pressure is to find out why the Father Master of the Sacred Palace has given permission for it, while His Holiness says that he never knew anything and that he had not ordered that permission be granted. (XV, 103-104).[66]

In fact during the rest of the trial the permission to print will not be dealt with anymore. Indubitably it was concluded that the permission had been given on the initiative of Ciampoli, who had probably adduced an order of the Pope which, in fact, had never been given. Still the question of Galileo's personal responsibility in the request for permission to print will not be put aside. As we will see, he will, in fact, be faulted in the sentence of condemnation with having "warmly and cunningly" extorted that permission.

7.   The extra-judicial attempt by the Commissary Maculano

What had happened at the Holy Office after the first interrogation of Galileo? Since he had stated that he had not wished to defend the Copernican doctrine in the Dialogue, the latter was again put to the examination of three theologians: Oreggi (the Pope's theologian), the Jesuit Inchofer and the

Theatine Pasqualigo. The first two, and probably also Pasqualigo, had already been part of the commission which, as we have seen, had examined the book the previous September at the Pope's orders (but independently of the Holy Office). But now these three theologians were to reexamine it in an official form, that is, under assignment from the Holy Office, with a precise question to which they had to give an answer: had Galileo transgressed the command not to hold, teach or defend in any way, by word or in writing, the opinion of the Earth's motion and the immobility of the Sun? On 17 April they gave their response individually and they all stated that Galileo, by writing the *Dialogue* and defending the Copernican system, had in effect transgressed the command of the Holy Office. More specifically, he had certainly *taught and defended* the opinion of the Earth's motion and the Sun's immobility and was vehemently suspected of having personally *held* it as true.[67] This was an important confirmation for the Holy Office itself of the insincere attitude of Galileo and it constituted an aggravation which would have required a greater severity in his regard. Such was, in fact, the opinion of the cardinal members of the Holy Office in their meeting of 27 April, as Maculano wrote on the following day to Cardinal Francesco Barberini, who was at Castel Gandolfo with Urban VIII.

> In compliance with the commands of His Holiness, I yesterday informed the Most Eminent Lords of the Holy Congregation of Galileo's case, the position of which I briefly reported. Their Eminences approved of what has been done thus far and took into consideration, on the other hand, various difficulties with regard to the manner of pursuing the case and of bringing it to an end. More especially since Galileo has in his examination denied what is plainly evident from the book written by him, as a consequence of this denial there would result the necessity for greater rigor of procedure and less regard to the other considerations belonging to this business. Finally, I suggested a course, namely, that the Holy Congregation should grant me permission to treat extrajudicially with Galileo, in order to render him sensible of his error and bring him, if he recognizes it, to the confession of the

same. This proposal appeared at first sight too bold, not much hope being entertained of accomplishing this object by merely adopting the method of argument with him; but, upon my indicating the grounds upon which I had made the suggestion, permission was granted me. That no time might be lost, I entered into discourse with Galileo yesterday afternoon, and after many and many arguments and rejoinders had passed between us, by God's grace, I attained my object, for I brought him to a full sense of his error, so that he clearly recognized that he had erred and had gone too far in his book. And to all this he gave expression in words of much feeling, like one who experienced great consolation in the recognition of his error, and he was also willing to confess it judicially. He requested, however, a little time in order to consider the form in which he might most fittingly make the confession, which, as far as its substance is concerned, will, I hope, follow in the manner indicated.

I have thought it my duty at once to acquaint your Eminence with this matter, having communicated it to no one else; for I trust that His Holiness and your Eminence will be satisfied that in this way the affair is being brought to such a point that it may soon be settled without difficulty. The court will maintain its reputation; it will be possible to deal leniently with the culprit; and, whatever the decision arrived at, he will recognize the favor shown him, with all the other consequences of satisfaction herein desired. Today I think of examining him in order to obtain the said confession; and having, as I hope, received it, it will only remain to further question him with regard to his intention [*sopra l'intentione*] and to receive his defense plea; that done, he might have [his] house assigned to him as a prison, as hinted to me by your Eminence. (XV, 106-107; trans. by de Santillana 1955, 252-253).

How are we to interpret the contents of this letter? It undoubtedly reflects an attempt to overcome the impasse in the trial by using a "benign" procedure. On the one hand, as we have already noted, Galileo had clearly appeared insincere in his claim that he had not wanted to defend Copernicanism in the *Dialogue*. And that would have justified, in order to get a first confession out of Galileo, a "greater rigor in rendering justice", which in the practice of the Inquisition of that time meant a rigorous examination "*super intentionem*" (on his intention) with the accompanying torture. But Galileo was as always the "first Philosopher and Mathematician" of the Grand Duke of Tuscany and was being solicitously helped by him through the ambassador Niccolini. Furthermore, he was one of the most famous and respected men in the Europe of his day. All of this made up those "considerations" to which the Holy Office had thus far given its "attention". Despite everything, it was an attention which could not be easily dismissed.

I think that Maculano's proposal was aimed at avoiding that which was euphemistically called "the way to convince him with reasons" (that is, the way of the rigorous examination and torture[68]), by using persuasive tactics which, as such, were foreign to the tasks of a trial judge, such as Maculano, and which, therefore, would become an extrajudicial initiative.

Was such an initiative taken by Maculano on his own? The "foundation" of which he made mention and which was enough to overcome the doubts expressed on the matter by members of the Holy Office, must have carried significant weight. More than the weight of a cardinal such as Francesco Barberini (who did not have any special authority with respect to the other cardinals of the Holy Office) I think it might have been the weighty influence of Urban VIII himself, who had probably made known to Maculano through his cardinal nephew[69] his preference for a "benign" proceeding which excluded torture. Thus Maculano would have felt that in making the proposal his flanks were protected.

According to the letter Galileo's reaction had been positive and gave all the appearances of a sincere admission of his own errors. Maculano had in mind to go ahead on that same day, taking up again the role of trial judge, to an examination in order to obtain a confession in the juridical forum.

It is the end of the letter which creates the greatest problems of interpretation. After the confession, states Maculano, "there was nothing to do but interrogate him on his intentions and to give him the opportunity to defend himself". That agrees with the practice of the Inquisition of those times, whereby the guilty party, having confessed, was also obliged to express his intentions, that is, the reasons why he had committed his error. Even the granting of a written defense was part of the procedure of the Inquisition[70]. But what does the final statement mean, the one, that is, that "he might have [his] house assigned to him as a prison", as it had been referred to by Cardinal Francesco Barberini? Was Maculano alluding here to the conclusion of the trial in a benign form with no formal sentence and with no abjuration, but only with house arrest and the condemnation of the *Dialogue*, which was inevitable?

I think that such an interpretation is to be excluded. A few lines before Maculano had shown that he did not know what the "Tribunal", that is, the Holy Office, would in the concrete decide. That indicates that Cardinal Bellarmine had only alluded to the dispatch of Galileo to the Tuscan Embassy after the procedures referred to above had terminated. And he would have remained there "in prison" (that is, without being able to go out freely) to await the definitive decision which had to be the responsibility of the Holy Office. In fact, it seems unthinkable that Francesco Barberini and Urban VIII could have had the intention to leap frog that Tribunal, where the Cardinal was a member and the Pope presided. The events which follow upon this letter totally confirm, I think, this interpretation.

The second interrogation of the trial, which Maculano hoped would finally have brought Galileo to the point of making a full confession, took place on 30 April. Galileo stated that he had during those days reflected continuously, especially with respect to the injunction given him in 1616 by order of the Holy Office "not to hold, defend or teach in any way the opinion by then condemned of the mobility of the earth and the stability of the sun". And having reread the *Dialogue,* which he had not looked at for three years, so that he might examine whether he had really failed to follow the command, he confessed that his writing

> . . . in several places seemed to me set forth in such a form that a reader ignorant of my real purpose might have had reason to suppose that the arguments brought on the false side, and which it was my intention to confute, were so expressed as to be calculated rather to compel conviction

by their cogency than to be easy of solution: two arguments
there are in particular - the one taken from the solar
spots, the other from the ebb and flow of the tide - which
in truth come to the ear of the reader with far greater
show of force and power than ought to have been imparted
to them by one who regarded them as inconclusive and
who intended to refute them, as indeed I truly and
sincerely held and do hold them to be inconclusive and
admitting of refutation. (XIX, 342 -343).

As an excuse for this attitude of his Galileo adduced

. . . the natural complacency which every man feels with
regard to his own subtleties and in showing himself more
skilful than the generality of men in devising, even in
favor of false propositions, ingenious and plausible
arguments. With all this, although with Cicero "avidior sim
gloriae quam sat est," [I am more desirous of glory than is
merited] if I had now to set forth the same reasonings,
without doubt I should so weaken them that they should
not be able to make an apparent show of that force of
which they are really and essentially devoid. My error,
then, has been - and I confess it - one of vainglorious
ambition and of pure ignorance and inadvertence. (XIX,
343; trans. by de Santillana 1955, 255-256).

After having released this declaration Galileo returned to
his rooms. But, as the minutes report,

. . . he came back after a moment (*post paullulum*),
asking to be allowed to make a supplementary
statement: "And in confirmation of my assertion that I
have not held and do not hold as true the opinion
which has been condemned, of the motion of the Earth
and stability of the Sun - if there shall be granted to
me, as I desire, means and time to make a clearer
demonstration thereof, I am ready to do so; and there
is a most favorable opportunity for this, seeing that in
the work already published the interlocutors agree to
meet again after a certain time to discuss several
distinct problems of Nature not connected with the
matter discoursed of at their meetings. As this affords

me the opportunity of adding one or two other 'days', I
promise to resume the arguments already brought in
favor of the said opinion, which is false and has been
condemned, and to confute them in such most effectual
manner as by the blessing of God may be supplied to
me. I pray, therefore, this holy Tribunal to aid me in
this good resolution and to enable me to put it in
effect." (XIX, 344; trans. by de Santillana 1955, 256).

This deposition of his and especially the final addition have
been the object of criticisms, at times very severe, with respect
to Galileo.[71] Undoubtedly these statements of Galileo were
influenced by the state of tension of the last months and
especially of the last weeks. But it seems exaggerated to
consider them to be the fruit of a state of bewilderment, even of
panic, in the face of an imprecise, pressing danger. After all, the
conversation with Maculano had been friendly and Galileo's
deposition had even occurred in an atmosphere without special
tension. It is, therefore, probable that Galileo was still
sufficiently *compos sui* to take a reasoned decision. With that
proposal - for us absurd and even degrading - to write against
Copernicanism he had perhaps deluded himself that he would be
able to salvage something of his case. He was hoping, in other
words, that his yielding (well beyond that which his judges
themselves expected in this regard) would not only have avoided
his condemnation, but also and above all, the unconditional
prohibition of the *Dialogue*. This latter might have been
suspended, until it had been corrected with the elimination of
those parts which through the excessive "subtlety and vanity" of
the author had given the impression that they constituted a
confirmation of Copernicanism. And the final doubts in this
matter would have fallen away with the appendage of one or two
additional Days, which would have made absolutely clear that
the intention of the *Dialogue* was not only not Copernican but,
as a matter of fact, anti-Copernican. After all this was in line
with the position taken by Galileo right from the first
interrogation.
    What would be the thoughts of those who one day would
read a *Dialogue* thus emasculated and supplied with (or followed
by) such an unbelievable addition? Galileo probably trusted that

at least the more intelligent among them would have been able to decipher the "mystery".

Was the declaration made by Galileo, apart from his later proposal, in line with what Maculano expected? It is difficult to think so. On the other hand as the author of and the one responsible for the plan, Maculano probably did not want to admit before the Holy Office and Urban VIII himself that it had failed. Did he perhaps hope that, although unsatisfactory, this admission of an error (the first made by Galileo during the trial) could be accepted as a good one by the members of the Holy Office, who were not ill-disposed to Galileo, and perhaps even by Urban VIII himself? To all appearances Maculano himself accepted it as good. On that same day of 30 April, in fact, the Commissary of the Holy Office, "having considered the bad health and the advanced age of the above mentioned Galileo Galilei" and having obtained the Pope's permission,[72] granted that Galileo could return to the Tuscan Embassy, which would have been for him *loco carceris* (a substitute prison), with the order to deal with no one except with those who dwelt there, to present himself at every request of the Holy Office and to keep silent under oath. (XIX, 344).

Niccolini gave notice of this on 1 May:

> Signor Galileo was sent back to my house yesterday when I was not expecting it at all, since his examination has not been completed and this came about through the offices of Father Commissary together with Cardinal Barberini who on his own, without the Congregation, had him freed so that he could recover from the discomforts and ill health which plagued him continuously. Father Commissary himself also manifests the intention of wishing to arrange it that this cause be dropped and that silence be imposed on it; and if this is achieved, it will shorten everything and will free many from troubles and dangers. (XV, 109-110).

Niccolini was obviously well informed almost certainly by Father Maculano himself. As we know from the letter we have already quoted of Maculano to Cardinal Barberini, the permission to send Galileo off to the Embassy after the interrogation had been given beforehand by Francesco Barberini to the Commissary, undoubtedly with the permission of Urban VIII. As to Maculano's intention to arrange it that the case would be annulled and no more said about it, this was an intention which, if true, was probably born from a personal wish of his, perhaps agreed to by Francesco Barberini, but which at any rate remained subordinate to the final decision of the Holy Office. And that decision, as we shall see, will be very different.

The following letter of 3 May was also full of optimism. Galileo was in better health and the Commissary seemed to have the intention of coming to visit him in order to bring the trial to as rapid a conclusion as possible "by continuing the business of being as nice to him as possible and of showing himself most well inclined towards this Most Serene House" (XV, 112).[73]

But the visit of the Commissary did not come to pass. Was this a first warning of the coming change in the situation? It is hard to say. On 10 May Galileo was recalled to the Holy Office. From the records of the trial (XIX, 345) we know that the Commissary "assigned him a period of eight days to put together his defense, if he would have had the intention to do so". But Galileo had already prepared this defense and so he delivered it immediately, together with the original document given to him by Bellarmine (as we have seen, he had presented only a copy of this at the first interrogation). After having signed the minutes, Galileo was allowed to return to the Embassy. Thus far everything seemed to go on as foreseen. And the fact that Galileo had his defense already prepared is an indication of this.

In his defense Galileo explained the reason why, at the time he requested permission to print the *Dialogue*, he had not informed Father Riccardi of the command which, according to the Holy Offices version, had enjoined him not "to hold, defend or teach in any way" the Copernican opinion. To this end Galileo attached the original declaration given him by Bellarmine (and he explained the circumstances in which he had requested this from him). It ensued from this declaration that he had been told only that the doctrine attributed to Copernicus could not be held or defended. This was the tenor itself of the Decree of the Congregation of the Index, known to everyone and which involved everyone. Galileo emphasized the fact that, relying upon this one document of Bellarmine, it was not possible to deduce that any specific command had been given him 16 years ago and, therefore, that he was "quite reasonably excused" for not having thought it necessary to notify Father Riccardi of the command which the latter was familiar with (that is, the general command of the Congregation of the Index). But what then was to be said about the *personal* command with the words *vel quovis modo docere* (or in any way to teach) which, according to the version of the Holy Office, had been enjoined him at the time of his summons to Bellarmine? As he had done during the course of his first interrogation, Galileo did not deny the possibility that the order had been imposed on him, but he excused himself saying that he had forgotten, in the long intervening time, its exact formulation, so much so that the attestation of Bellarmine had freed him from any worry about other details.

Galileo, therefore, showed the strong hope that his judges would remain convinced that he had not "knowingly and willingly transgressed the commands" which had been given him. But he admitted again that he had been excessive in the arguments proposed in his book "because of vain ambition and the pleasure of appearing more clever than the common run of popular writers", and he said that he was prepared to correct the incriminating passages. And he ended by putting himself at the mercy of the judges to whom he made known

> . . . my pitiable state of bodily indisposition, to which, at the age of seventy years, I have been reduced by ten months of constant mental anxiety and the fatigue of a long and toilsome journey at the most inclement season - together with the loss of the greater part of the years to which from my previous condition of health, I had the prospect. (XIX, 347; trans. by de Santillana 1955, 259-260).

After this final act Galileo must have thought that he was by now close to a benign solution to the trial. And in fact during the two following weeks this possibility seemed to be there. Niccolini was received by Urban VIII on 21 May and he had come to know from him and from Cardinal Francesco Barberini

that the trial would most probably be concluded with the
meeting of the Holy Office set for eight days later. But Niccolini
was not optimistic about the fate of the *Dialogue*. In fact he
wrote to Cioli on the following day:

> I very much fear that the book will be prohibited, unless
> it is averted by Galileo's being charged, as I proposed (to
> His Holiness), to write an apology. Some salutary penance
> will also be imposed on him, as they maintain that he has
> transgressed the command issued to him by Bellarmine in
> 1616. I have not yet told him all this, because I want to
> prepare him for it by degrees in order not to distress him.
> (XV, 132; trans. by de Santillana 1955, 276).

The prohibition of the *Dialogue* and the salutary penances
which Urban VIII had mentioned to Niccolini do not as such
indicate an evolution in the situation in Galileo's disfavor.[74] Both
provisions were, in fact, the minimum to be expected as a
conclusion of the trial and for some time they were already
taken for granted.

And to all appearances things continued to be encouraging.
And so the request made by Niccolini towards the end of May to
obtain permission for Galileo "to be able to go out of the house
once in a while to get a bit of air and to walk" was granted and
Galileo was even able to go "in a half-covered carriage" through
the gardens of Rome and surrounding areas, even as far as
Castel Gandolfo (about 25 kilometers from Rome).

8.   *The condemnation and abjuration of Galileo*

The days went by and nothing seemed to happen. In reality
the storm was thickening. In fact a decision was maturing which
was much more rigorous than what could have been hoped for
from the information received by Ambassador Niccolini.
According to various biographers of Galileo that would have been
due to a change in the equilibrium existing up until that time
within the Holy Office between a more benign tendency toward
Galileo and a more rigorous one, which in the end prevailed.[75]
The "rigorists" would only have reluctantly and for the moment
accepted the proposal of Maculano. Once they had viewed

together the statements made by Galileo in the course of the extrajudicial proceedings and the defense document which he presented subsequently, they would have expressed their own strong dissatisfaction, not to say their indignation.

Furthermore, according to these biographers of Galileo, the action of the "rigorists" within the Holy Office could be detected in the first part of the document "Contro Galileo Galilei" which summarized the charges against Galileo, the events surrounding the permission to print the *Dialogue* and the content of the interrogations (including the defense presented by Galileo). This document was submitted to the meeting of the Holy Office of 16 June. At the beginning of it there was placed the denouncement of the *Letter to Castelli* made by Lorini in February 1615 and the incriminating passages from it were reproduced according to the text sent by Lorini himself, but without mentioning the non-adverse censure which the work had received.

Then there was placed the interrogation of Caccini of 20 March 1615.

> Examination was made of Father Caccini, who testified, in addition to the above, that he had heard other erroneous opinions uttered by Galileo: That God is an accident, that He laughs, weeps, etc., and that the miracles said to be made by the Saints are not true miracles. (XIX, 293; trans. by de Santillana 1955, 279).

But in reality not even Caccini himself had stated that such opinions had been expressed by Galileo. It is true that immediately afterwards the report specified that from an examination of the witnesses "it is deduced that such propositions were not assertive on the part of Galileo and his pupils, but only disputative" (XIX, 293). But even this is false. In the deposition of Attavanti (XIX, 319) these propositions are, in fact, not attributed in any way, not even in a disputative form, to Galileo.

Undoubtedly this part of the document seems to have been composed with the intention of putting Galileo in a bad light. Such an intention is also clear at times in the followings parts of the document. Thus, for example, it reports with respect to the book on the sunspots:

> Then, having seen in the book on the sunspots printed in Rome by this same Galileo the two propositions: *Sol est centrum mundi, et omnino immobilis motu locali; Terra non est centrum mundi, et secundum se tota movetur etiam motu diurno* [the Sun is the center of the world, and is completely immobile as to local motion; the Earth is not the center of the world, and as a whole it moves also with a diurnal motion]: they were qualified as absurd in philosophy: ... [italics in original text]. (XIX, 294).

Now, as we have already remarked those propositions are not at all found in that work of Galileo, but they are taken from the deposition of Caccini (see XIX, 307-308). Thus also the mention of the precept of Bellarmine is grossly inexact:

> Therefore on February 25, 1616, His Holiness ordered Cardinal Bellarmine to summon before him Galileo and to command him [*facesse precetto*] to abandon and not discuss in any manner said opinion of the immobility of the Sun and the stability [*sic*] of the Earth. (XIX, 294; trans. by de Santillana 1955, 280).

This is also inexact. The Pope's order, as we know, had foreseen two possible phases of the injunction. The compiler of the document must have known this, since he had available to him the complete *dossier* on Galileo, and he must have known (also through the archive documentation) that, in fact, the rigorous injunction had not been given by Bellarmine but, immediately afterwards, by the Commissary Segizzi. The following statement is still more inexact and as always to Galileo's disadvantage:

> On that 26th day [of February] the aforementioned precept was given to him by that same Cardinal in the presence of the Father Commissary of the Holy Office, a notary and witnesses and he promised to obey it. The tenor of it [the precept] is that *omnino desereret dictam opinionem, nec etiam de caetero illam quovis modo teneret, doceret et*

defenderet, alias contra ipsum in S. Officio procedetur ...
[he must give up the aforementioned opinion, nor should he
hold, teach or defend it in any way whatsoever, otherwise
procedures will begin against him in the Holy Office ...]
(XIX, 294).

As we know, the precept in the words given in the
quotation above, was not given by Bellarmine but by Segizzi.
And the original declaration of Bellarmine, given to Galileo, was
the confirmation of this. The report could not avoid citing this
declaration. But it limited itself to doing it quite briefly: "He
confessed the command, but based on the above mentioned
declaration [that of Bellarmine], in which there are not recorded
the words not to teach in any way, says that he has no memory
of this" (XIX, 295).

This document undoubtedly distorts many facts and always
in Galileo's disfavor. As such, it could, in fact, reflect a hostile
tendency towards Galileo within the Holy Office. But it seems to
me that, even prescinding from the existence of a rigorist group,
it would have been difficult for the trial to have come to a
conclusion different than the actual one. Galileo had, without a
doubt, violated a precept of the Holy Office (even considering
only the one given to him by Bellarmine in a "benign" form) and
had upheld, at least as probable, a doctrine declared to be
contrary to Holy Scripture (Decree of the Index of 1616). As
such, he had from the viewpoint of his judges incurred a "serious
suspicion of heresy" from which he could not be absolved except
by a public abjuration. It was likewise inevitable that, as
expiation for his crime, he be condemned to the prison of the
Holy Office.

On this important point we will speak in more detail later
on in this chapter. Here I think it is necessary to point out that
a condemnation to an abjuration and to prison would have been
inevitable even if Galileo had frankly admitted his true
intentions in writing the *Dialogue*. Such an admission would, in
fact, have only confirmed the violation of the precept and the
serious suspicion of heresy. What a sincere confession would
have surely avoided would have been the recourse to a "rigorous
examination" (which, as we have already noted, implied torture)

in order to obtain the truth. In my opinion, I repeat, it was precisely the preoccupation to avoid the recourse to such a "rigorous examination" which established the motivation for Maculano's initiative.

To conclude, I think that the final decision taken in the Holy Office's session of 16 June was already in the cards without necessarily implying a shift of balanced positions at the last moment in favor of the "rigorist" current. In fact, as we will see, Urban VIII will declare later to the ambassador Niccolini that such a decision was unanimous.[76] Here is the text of the acts of the session:

> *Sanctissimus* [the Pope] *decrevit* [decreed] that said Galileo is to be interrogated on his intention, even with the threat of torture, and, *si sustinuerit*,[77] he is to abjure *de vehementi* [under vehement suspicion of heresy] in a plenary assembly of the Congregation of the Holy Office, then is to be condemned to imprisonment at the pleasure of the Holy Congregation, and ordered not to treat further, in whatever manner, either in words or in writing, on the mobility of the Earth and the stability of the Sun; otherwise he will incur the penalties of relapse. The book entitled *Dialogue of Galileo Galilei the Lincean* is to be prohibited. (XIX, 283; trans. by de Santillana 1955, 292-293).

Furthermore, disposition was given to send copies of the sentence of condemnation to all of the nuncios and inquisitors of the Faith, and in particular to the inquisitor in Florence so that he would read it in a plenary session of the Florentine Inquisition, in the presence of as many professors of mathematics as it was possible to invite.

As we see from this document, the only "new" element in the rigorist sense is contained in the first lines and consists in the Pope's decision that Galileo be subjected to the rigorous examination, including the threat of torture, concerning his intentions. But even here, in fact, we are dealing only with the logical consequences of the previous events. As we have already emphasized, the extra-judicial attempt of Maculano was aimed precisely at avoiding that rigorous examination and the torture connected to it by obtaining a sincere confession from Galileo. But the confession which Galileo made was not considered adequate (how could it have been?), neither by the members of the Holy Office nor by Urban VIII. Therefore, in order to ascertain Galileo's true intention, there was nothing left but "the way of convincing him with reasons", that is, to be exact, the rigorous examination. But even in this rigorous decision there still remains after all something of the "benign": torture will only be threatened, not actually applied.

When Niccolini presented himself three days later in an audience with Urban VIII, he was received by him with "an infinity of most kind demonstrations". Encouraged, Niccolini begged yet once again that Galileo's cause be resolved with dispatch. The Pope responded that it had already been concluded and that Galileo would have been called to the Holy Office to hear the sentence some morning of the following week. And when Niccolini pleaded that its rigor be mitigated as a gesture of benevolence towards the Grand Duke, Urban VIII replied that he had

> . . . willingly done every favor to Mr. Galileo out of the warmth he feels toward the Most Serene Patron. However, he said that in regard to the issue, there is no way of avoiding prohibiting that opinion, since it is erroneous and contrary to the Holy Scripture dictated by the mouth of God; and in regard to the person, as ordinarily and usually done, he would have to remain imprisoned here for some time because he disobeyed the orders he received in the year 1616; but as soon as the sentence is published, His Holiness will see me again and will discuss with me what can be done to cause the least pain and the least affliction to him, for there is no way of avoiding some personal punishment. (XV, 160; trans. by Finocchiaro 1989, 359).

At Niccolini's insistence, as he came back to his plea for clemency "toward the advanced age of seventy years of this good old man and also toward his sincerity", the Pope repeated that it would not have been possible not to take some measure of confinement against Galileo, since the Congregation "all of it united and with no one dissenting [*et nemine discrepante*]^{78} was inclined in this direction about penalizing him" (XV, 160).

As usual Niccolini limited himself to reporting to Galileo only the part of the conversation less difficult to bear by informing him of the proximate conclusion of the trial and of the prohibition of the book, without mentioning the punishment to be provided against his person.

Galileo was not, therefore, prepared except partially for that which awaited him when he was requested to present himself to the Holy Office on the morning of Tuesday, 21 June. The interrogation began, according to set plans, with the question put to him by the Commissary Maculano "*super intentione*" with the purpose of clarifying once for all the real intention which Galileo had had in writing the *Dialogue*. To the question as to "whether he holds or has held, and how long ago, that the Sun is the center of the world and that the Earth is not the center of the world and moves, and also with a diurnal motion", he answered:

> A long time ago, i.e., before the decision of the Holy Congregation of the Index, and before the injunction was intimated to me, I was indifferent and regarded both opinions, namely, that of Ptolemy and that of Copernicus, as open to discussion, in as much as either one or the other might be true in Nature; but after the said decision, assured of the wisdom of the authorities, I ceased to have any doubt; and I held, as I still hold, as most true and indisputable, the opinion of Ptolemy, that is to say, the stability of the Earth and the motion of the Sun. Being told that from the manner and connection in which the said opinion is discussed in the book printed by him subsequently to the time mentioned - nay, from the very fact of his having written and printed the said book - he is presumed to have held this opinion after the time specified, and being called upon to state the truth freely as to whether he holds or has held the same, he answered: As regards the writing of the published dialogue, my motive in so doing was not because I held the Copernican doctrine to be true, but simply, thinking to confer a common benefit, I have set forth the proofs from Nature and astronomy which may be brought on either side; my object

being to make it clear that neither the one set of arguments nor the other has the force of conclusive demonstration in favor of this opinion or of that; and that therefore, in order to proceed with certainty, we must have recourse to the decisions of higher teaching, as may be clearly seen from a large number of passages in the dialogue in question. I affirm, therefore, on my conscience, that I do not now hold the condemned opinion and have not held it since the decision of the authorities. (XIX, 361-362; trans. by de Santillana 1955, 302-303).[79]

At this point the examiner repeated that

. . . from the book itself and from the arguments brought on the affirmative side, it is presumed that he holds the opinion of Copernicus, or at least that he held it at that time; and that, therefore, unless he make up his mind to confess the truth, recourse will be had against him to the appropriate remedies [remedia juris et facti opportuna].

Galileo replied:

I do not hold and have not held this opinion of Copernicus since the command was intimated to me that I must abandon it; for the rest, I am here in your hands - do with me what you please. (XIX, 361-362; trans. by de Santillana 1955, 303).

Father Maculano exhorted him once more to tell the truth, because "they will otherwise have recourse to torture". But Galileo had no fear, nor did he change his tone.[80] "I am here to submit (far l'obbedienza); and I have not held this opinion after the determination was made, as I have said".

The minutes end with the comment: "not being able to obtain anything else towards the execution of the decree (of 16 June), having obtained his signature, he was sent back in locum suum (that is, to his dwelling in the Holy Office)" (XIX, 362).

Galileo was kept at the Holy Office until the following day. We can well imagine what must have been the state of mind with which he passed those long hours. This was the failure of

all of his Copernican efforts, a failure which was by now passing
through his mind as inevitable. And, in contrast to 1616, this
time his book and he himself would be at the center of the
Church's decision. As to the *Dialogue* Galileo knew already that
it would have been prohibited. But what precisely was in wait
for him? The last illusions which he had still been able to
entertain were completely extinguished when he was forced to
put on the penitential garb,[81] and was led to the Dominican
convent of S. Maria sopra Minerva at the center of Rome, where
the cardinals and other officials of the Holy Office had gathered
together "in plenary session".[82]

Galileo was ordered to kneel down and the reading of the
sentence of condemnation began:

> We say, pronounce, sentence, and declare that you, the
> said Galileo, by reason of the matters adduced in trial, and
> by you confessed as above, have rendered yourself in the
> judgement of this Holy Office vehemently suspected of
> heresy, namely of having believed and held the doctrine
> which is false and contrary to the sacred and divine
> Scriptures - that the Sun is the center of the world and
> does not move from east to west and that the Earth moves
> and is not the center of the world; and that an opinion
> may be held and defended as probable after it has been
> declared and defined to be contrary to the Holy Scripture;
> and that consequently you have incurred all the censures
> and penalties imposed and promulgated in the sacred
> canons and other constitutions, general and particular,
> against such delinquents. From which we are content that
> you be absolved, provided that first, with a sincere heart
> and unfeigned faith, you abjure, curse, and detest before us
> the aforesaid errors and heresies and every other error and
> heresy contrary to the Catholic and Apostolic Roman
> Church in the form prescribed by us for you.
>   And, in order that this your grave and pernicious error
> and transgression may not remain altogether unpunished
> and that you may be more cautious in the future and an
> example to others that they may abstain from similar
> delinquencies, we ordain that the book of the "Dialogue of
> Galileo Galilei" be prohibited by public edict.

We condemn you to the formal prison of this Holy Office during our pleasure, and by way of salutary penance we enjoin that for three years to come you repeat once a week the seven penitential Psalms. Reserving to ourselves liberty to moderate, commute, or take off, in whole or in part the aforesaid penalties and penance. (XIX, 402-406; trans. by de Santillana 1955, 310).[83]

After the reading of the sentence, for Galileo there was nothing more except to obey. Still kneeling down he read the formula of abjuration which had been presented to him:

I, Galileo, son of the late Vincenzio Galileo, Florentine, aged seventy years, arraigned personally before this tribunal and kneeling before you Most Eminent and Reverend Lord Cardinals Inquisitors-General against heretical pravity throughout the entire Christian commonwealth, having before my eyes and touching with my hands the Holy Gospels, swear that I have always believed, do believe, and by God's help will in the future believe all that is held, preached, and taught by the Holy Catholic and Apostolic Church. But, whereas - after an injunction had been judicially intimated to me by this Holy Office to the effect that I must altogether abandon the false opinion that the Sun is the center of the world and immovable and that the Earth is not the center of the world and moves and that I must not hold, defend, or teach in any way whatsoever, verbally or in writing, the said false doctrine,[84] and after it had been notified to me that the said doctrine was contrary to Holy Scripture[85] - I wrote and printed a book in which I discuss this new doctrine already condemned and adduce arguments of great cogency in its favor[86] without presenting any solution of these,[87] I have been pronounced by the Holy Office to be vehemently suspected of heresy, that is to say, of having held and believed that the Sun is the center of the world and immovable and that the Earth is not the center and moves:
Therefore, desiring to remove from the minds of your Eminences, and of all faithful Christians, this vehement suspicion justly conceived against me, with sincere heart and unfeigned faith I abjure, curse, detest the aforesaid

errors and heresies and generally every other error, heresy, and sect whatsoever contrary to the Holy Church, and I swear that in future I will never again say or assert, verbally or in writing, anything that might furnish occasion for a similar suspicion regarding me; but, should I know any heretic or person suspected of heresy, I will denounce him to this Holy Office or to the inquisitor or Ordinary of the place where I may be . . .

I, the said Galileo Galilei, have abjured, sworn, and promised, and bound myself as above; and in witness of the truth thereof I have with my own hand subscribed the present document of my abjuration and recited it word for word at Rome, in the convent of the Minerva, this twenty-second day of June, 1633.

I, Galileo Galilei, have abjured as above with my own hand. (XIX, 406-407; trans. by de Santillana 1955, 312-313).[88]

9.   Some final considerations on the condemnation of Galileo

And so the trial came to an end. From the legal point of view the trial had been conducted in a sufficiently objective manner and with altogether exceptional consideration paid to Galileo, considering the practice of that epoch. The only "black spot", but an important one, is constituted by the summary report "Against Galileo Galilei" which betrays, as we have seen, the intention to present Galileo in a completely unfavorable light and which was placed in a synthetic manner at the beginning of the sentence of condemnation (XIX, 403, 15-27). But what follows in the sentence, although it is severe, does not betray a grudge or an intent to distort the facts.

The serious problem for us arises from the ending of the trial with the condemnation for being vehemently suspected of heresy and especially with the imposition of the abjuration. Undoubtedly today these appear to us to be the outcome of an abuse of power both on the doctrinal plane and with respect to Galileo's personal conscience. But in what sense can we speak of an abuse *by Galileo's judges*?

In attempting to give a balanced response to such a question it seems to me that one must first of all avoid

projecting *sic et simpliciter* (without qualification) our modern
ideal of freedom of thought back to an age of increasing
"absolutism", as was Galileo's time, where the principle of
authority (both in civil and ecclesiastical affairs and no less in
the Protestant than in the Catholic camps) was considered
superior to the principle of individual intellectual freedom.

It was precisely this principle of authority which the
appearance of the *Dialogue* had put under scrutiny. Convinced
that the "marvelous conjuncture" of the election to the papacy of
his patron and admirer, Maffeo Barberini, would not happen
again and overestimating the Pope's esteem for him, Galileo had
in substance decided to play his cards, having been encouraged,
as we have seen, by Urban VIII's apparent positive reaction to
the *Letter to Ingoli*. But it was a card game which ended in
disaster. Despite the rhetorical expedients which Galileo devised
to maintain the purely hypothetical character of his principal
conclusions in the *Dialogue*, it was, in fact, too obviously pro-
Copernican to escape becoming a challenge to ecclesiastical
authority and specifically to the authority of Urban VIII. And
the challenge was all the more "scandalous" given the reputation
of Galileo throughout Europe. It is precisely this which Urban
VIII will emphasize when he comes to accuse Galileo of having
"given such universal scandal to Christianity". If one takes into
account the difficult situation existing at that time both within
and outside the Church, a severe reaction by ecclesiastical
authorities to that challenge was not only inevitable but also
justified.

Furthermore, I think it is necessary to take account of the
different juridical position in which Galileo had come to find
himself in 1633 as compared to the one in 1615-16. As we have
seen, the Church had not taken an official position with respect
to Copernicanism, except at the end of what is frequently
referred to as "the first trial of Galileo", when the Congregation
of the Index issued the decree of 5 March 1616. Precisely
because there was no previous official decision with respect to
this matter, Galileo (and, for that matter, Foscarini himself) was
not *personally* condemned. In Galileo's case recourse was had to
the order of Cardinal Bellarmine, strengthened by the one in a
much more severe and general form imposed on him by the

Commissary Segizzi. The existence of the decree of the Index and of those orders are new facts, compared to the first "trial" of Galileo, and they place the trial of 1633 on a completely different juridical plane and give it a much more serious character.

An obvious proof of this comes from a careful reading of the condemnation of Galileo. In fact, he is condemned both for having contravened the decree of the Index (in which the doctrine of Copernicanism is "declared false and altogether contrary to the divine Scripture") and for having "cunningly and purposely extorted" permission to print the *Dialogue* without making known to the responsible Church authorities the existence of the precept.

As to the first infraction, the sentence comments that the claim of Galileo to have left the question of Copernicanism "undecided and expressly probable" "is a most serious error since an opinion declared and defined to be contrary to the Divine Scripture could in no way be probable".

As to the second infraction, the sentence notes that, even granting that Galileo at the time he asked permission to print the *Dialogue* no longer remembered the strict precept of Segizzi (which forbade him even to treat of Copernicanism), but only the one "benignly" communicated by Bellarmine in witness of which there was the declaration given by him to Galileo, the existence of this declaration did not constitute an attenuating circumstance. On the contrary it constituted an aggravating circumstance for the accused since, "while in it [the declaration of Bellarmine] that opinion is said to be contrary to Holy Scripture" he had "nonetheless dared to treat of it, to defend it, and to persuade others that it was probable".

As we have seen, Galileo had always, in the course of the trial, as well as at the time of the examination *sopra l'intentione* (concerning his intentions), denied that he had wanted to defend the Copernican system or even that he had wanted to propose it as probable. But the statements to the contrary which appear in the sentence appear to us, as they did to Galileo's judges, to be sufficiently objective. They could not, therefore, do otherwise than issue a sentence of condemnation.

As to the theological motivation of the sentence, that is "for being vehemently suspected of heresy" various studies[89] have shown that in Galileo's time the term "heresy" had a double meaning: the traditional narrower one referring to the denial of a truth of the faith which was expressly declared to be such by the Pope or by an ecumenical council, or the considerably wider one ("inquisitorial heresy") which not only included any statement contrary to Holy Scripture but also the infraction of a precept of the Inquisition. By writing the *Dialogue* Galileo had upheld (even if only as probable) a theory which had been "defined and declared" (by the Congregation of the Index) as contrary to Holy Scripture and had furthermore violated a precept of the Inquisition (the one, in fact, of Bellarmine and Segizzi). That was sufficient to motivate a condemnation for being "vehemently suspected of heresy" without it being implied that Copernicanism was defined as "heretical" in the stricter meaning of the term. By taking into account this distinction, the decree condemning Galileo does not represent a step backward, as a more rigorous doctrinal statement, when compared to the decree of the Index. In fact, in the part of the sentence of condemnation penned explicitly in reference to Galileo the Copernican doctrine is declared "false" and "completely contrary to Holy Scripture" but not "heretical". The qualification of "heretical" given in 1616 by the qualificators to the Copernican statement on the immobility of the Sun is, indeed, quoted in the sentence as part of the antecedent facts of the trial but without any necessary implication that the trial takes it as a reason for the condemnation. Galileo's behavior is also defined as a "serious and pernicious error and transgression" but not "heresy". The expression "errors and heresies" which appears in the final part of the sentence, as well as in Galileo's abjuration, comes from the fact that both the sentence and the act of abjuration were put together by using (for the generic part) the formulary in use at that time (in which, indeed, those expressions occur) and thus in Galileo's case they imply nothing more than the "inquisitorial" meaning of the term "heresy"[90].

Once the fact of being vehemently suspected of heresy, even if only in the broader inquisitorial sense, had been verified the only way for the accused to "purge himself" of such suspicion was the abjuration. To refuse to abjure would change the suspicion of heresy into "proven" heresy and in such a case the inevitable punishment was burning at the stake. That explains why the abjuration constituted, in the regular procedures of the Inquisition at that time, the normal (and happy!) ending of a trial at whose conclusion the accused (in the course of the examination *sopra l'intentione* [on his intentions]) had responded, as had Galileo, in a "Catholic way", that is, he had shown himself disposed to renounce his own errors. The abjuration was the juridical "proof" of the renouncement.

But, together with its character of purging from being suspected of "heresy", the abjuration also established a very serious precedent should a subsequent "relapse" occur. In such a case there was nothing left for the "*relapsus*" (even in the case of only an inquisitorial heresy) but condemnation to burning at the stake.[91] Thus Galileo's judges could be sure that he, with the condemnation for being vehemently suspected of heresy and with the abjuration, would have remained quiet forever. And that is what happened.

If then we consider *only the juridical position* of Galileo in 1633, his condemnation and abjuration can be viewed as fully justified according to the regular practice of the Inquisition at that time, on the basis of the doctrinal and disciplinary decisions of 1616. And, as we have already noted, the existence of these decisions with the consequent vehement suspicion of heresy precluded, in fact, any possibility of a less severe decision. Galileo's attitude during the trial had only, in the judges' eyes, given further reason for such severity.

Thus the question of an abuse of power by the Church in condemning Galileo, comes down, in its juridical aspects, to the doctrinal and disciplinary basis of that condemnation, that is, to the provisions established in 1616. We have already had the opportunity to show how such provisions, and particularly the Decree of the Index, were, objectively considered, the outcome of an authoritarianism in doctrine which was excessively worried about preserving the *status quo* of the traditional Christian view of the world and which was incapable of grasping the importance of the new problematic created by the Copernican view and by Galileo's discoveries. To declare that the Copernican teaching was "false and completely contrary to Holy Scripture" meant that one wanted to cut off the problem definitively, and so preclude also any position of prudent waiting in view of possible future proofs. As we have already noted, such a possibility was excluded (for the present and the future), in the first place at the level of "natural philosophy", by the qualification of "absurd in philosophy" given by the definers of the Holy Office with respect to the Copernican thesis. This was a qualification which set up the basis for their certainty in responding theologically. For that reason neither in 1616 nor in 1633 was any consideration given to the question as to whether Galileo had decisive proofs or not for heliocentrism. Any proof whatsoever was, I repeat, excluded *a priori*.[92]

It is this myopic authoritarianism, from which flowed an undue doctrinal and disciplinary closure to a question which should have been left open (and this was the judgment of those more attentive spirits, even within the Church[93]), which can be considered, in fact must be considered, the original abuse of power. From it there came about, as an inevitable conclusion, the condemnation of Galileo.

But in turn this very inevitability, and the kind of results it brought about (the condemnation of Galileo to prison, the prohibition of the *Dialogue*, the abjuration), came about because of the existence of a doctrinal and disciplinary power exercised by an institution, namely the Holy Inquisition, whose central organism was the Holy Office. The fact that from the Middle Ages until well beyond Galileo's time there had developed in the Church a system which controlled "Catholic" thought and activity and which was, in fact, despite the attribution of "holy", based on coercion and, when necessary, on physical or psychological violence, constitutes an institutionalized abuse of power which can never be sufficiently deprecated.[94]

Galileo, with his tactical errors and with his behavior at the time of the trial, must undoubtedly bear a weighty part of the responsibility for the *fact* of the condemnation. But the responsibility for the *way* in which the condemnation occurred, and especially for the abjuration[95] falls without a doubt on the shoulders of the Church of those times and specifically on the

organisms and on the methods which were used in the exercise
of her authority.

Thus, even though correct and justifiable in the immediate
juridical context, the condemnation and abjuration of Galileo are
the final and most clamorous manifestation of that
institutionalized abuse of power. As such, therefore, they cannot
but be subject to the severe judgment which such abuse imposes
today.

Any balanced historical judgment must certainly, I repeat,
be derived from a clarification of the internal logic and the
motivation of the actions, whether of individuals or of
institutions, as they occurred against the background of the
culture of a specific period of history. It is precisely this which
I have endeavored to do in the presentation of the happenings
and of the ideas which led to the condemnation of Galileo. But
it is also true that, however much one strives to found a
historical judgement primarily on an objective reconstruction of
what happened, it is not possible in the end to avoid judging the
value and the consequences of those actions in light of
humanity's subsequent journey.[96] And it appears undeniable
that, although not accepting those many interpretations which
can be branded as illuministic, positivistic and anticlerical, the
consequences of the condemnation and abjuration of Galileo have
been in the history of Western thought clearly and profoundly
negative. As the "tribunal" of human actions, history cannot but
take account of it.

Galileo's judges surely did not have this presentiment as
they returned to their homes after the Congregation's session.
On the contrary they must have thought with relief that finally
that thorny question had been brought to an end and that from
that time on there would be no more talk of Copernicus, and not
even of Galileo, at least among Catholics. Those who were more
benevolent towards Galileo must have felt, of course, sorry for
that poor old man, but in conscience they felt at peace. In the
end that which had happened was the fault of Galileo alone, of
his imprudence, obstinacy and lack of sincerity.[97] And there was
no doubt that the Church had been magnanimous with him. All
knew that imprisonment was a formality on which there would
be no insistence. For sure the abjuration must have been

difficult for Galileo. But it was a lesson which in the end would save him from worse evils.

And so for the cardinals and officials of the Holy Office the "Galileo affair" was by now a closed chapter. They had no suspicion that the true "Galileo affair" was instead beginning right on that very day 22 June 1633 and that their names, together with those of their predecessors of 1616, would pass to posterity not only as judges of the tribunal of the Holy Office but also and above all as the accused, destined to be called innumerable times in the centuries to come before the much more severe tribunal of history.

I do not think it would be correct to unload their responsibilities onto Galileo's enemies, who had begun to take action against the *Dialogue* by influencing Urban VIII and continuing their activity through the faction adverse to Galileo within the Holy Office.

Let us begin with those who are mainly accused in this plot to ruin Galileo, that is, the Jesuits. Undoubtedly Galileo himself was convinced that they had been at the origin of his misadventures. We have already seen a first proof of this conviction of his in the letter written to Diodati on the vigil of his departure for Rome. As I have already commented, that was probably based on the letter sent by Magalotti to Guiducci in August of the previous year. And the statement of Magalotti ("The Jesuit Fathers must be working underhandedly and valiantly to see that the work is prohibited") depended in turn explicitly on what Father Riccardi had told him: "The Jesuits will persecute him in a most bitter way". This is a matter, I repeat it yet again, of a prediction and not of an accomplished fact.

Even a year after his condemnation, upon writing again to his friend Diodati in Paris, Galileo showed himself convinced of the responsibility of the Jesuits in the whole drama. After having stated that the anger of his "most powerful persecutors", far from quieting down, was continuously increasing, he added:

> These persons [his persecutors] have finally wanted to reveal themselves to me, seeing that a dear friend of mine while he was in Rome about two months ago conversing

with   Father   Christopher   Grienberger,   Jesuit,
Mathematician of that College, my affairs having come up
for discussion, the Jesuit spoke these formal words to that
friend: "If Galileo had known how to keep the affection of
the Fathers of this College, he would live gloriously in this
world and none of his bad times would have come to pass
and he would have been able to write as he wished about
everything, even, I say, about the motion of the earth,
etc.": thus Your Lord sees that it is not this or that opinion
which has caused and does cause war for me but the fact
that I am in the disfavor of the Jesuits. (XVI, 116-117).

It seems to me difficult to give to these statements of
Galileo, based in their turn on those of a "dear friend" of his, the
probative value attributed to them by many biographers.[98] First
of all, from Galileo's words it is clear that he himself, before he
received the message from his friend, did not have any *certain*
evidence of an action carried out against him by the Jesuits. As
to the interpretation which Galileo gives to the words of
Grienberger (granted that they were indeed faithfully reported),
it is quite debatable. For sure, the support of the Jesuits was
not there for Galileo at the conclusive moment of the affair, just
as it was lacking at the time of the ecclesiastical decision of
1616. Besides the reasons, already known to us, for this latter,
reasons which will continue to be operative in 1633, there was
undoubtedly that further reason represented by the fact that for
some time by now the relations between Galileo and the Jesuits
had been irremediably ruined. Grienberger put all of the
responsibility for this on Galileo and that was not correct. But
in the eyes of the Jesuits the beginning of the arguments (both
in the case of Scheiner and, above all, in the case of Grassi) had
come from Galileo and from his friends and in this sense
Grienberger was substantially correct. However that might be,
all that the by now elderly mathematician of the Roman College
had stated was that Galileo with his attitude had lost the
support of the Jesuits. Not that the latter were out to persecute
him. Nevertheless, it seems to me rather debatable that
Grienberger really had made those declarations in the terms
referred to by Galileo. If we believe these latter then
Grienberger would have wanted to have his correspondent

understand that the mighty power of the Jesuits would have permitted Galileo (if he had remained their friend) to maintain whatever theory, even the one on the motion of the Earth. This statement, in sharp contrast with the temperament and the posture always shown by Grienberger,[99] was absurd. Yes, the Jesuits were powerful and influential. But they were certainly not omnipotent, especially with a Pope like Urban VIII.[100]

Galileo (followed by many of his biographers) wanted to attribute to this asserted and unbelievable *boutade* of Grienberger a much more determined and serious meaning than that which it truly involved, that is the admission by the Jesuits that his condemnation was their responsibility.

That there was among those who attacked the *Dialogue* also some Jesuit, specifically Scheiner,[101] I cannot nor do I wish to deny. The break by now complete between the Jesuits and Galileo and the fiery polemical climate, which had already existed before the publication of the *Dialogue* and which the latter had only heated up more, could have led to hostile initiatives by one or other Jesuit, with the possibility that they had travelled even to Urban VIII. But it does not seem to me that there is any foundation (beyond "street rumors") to assert the existence of a *collective* action of the Jesuits directed towards getting Galileo condemned.

Still under the trauma of the epilogue to the trial, Galileo was not able to resign himself to the idea that Urban VIII had been able to change so radically his attitude towards him. Convinced that he had not been excessive in his publication of the *Dialogue* and that, therefore, the reason for the Pope's sudden harshness had to be sought elsewhere, Galileo found it finally in the Jesuits, who thus became the "scapegoat" for his whole drama. This was true for him and, after him, for many others right up to the present.[102]

In the group who opposed Galileo there was a confluence, it seems to me, of persons of diverse backgrounds and ideas (right up to the rigorist current within the Holy Office): members of various religious orders, representatives of the regular clergy, as well as intransigent lay persons or those who were jealous of Galileo`s celebrity.

But granted all of that, the fact remains that if Urban VIII had not been *personally convinced* that Galileo had betrayed his expectations and had contravened the promises made, helped by men who had been the Pope's confidants and by whom the Pope had felt himself "tricked", he would never have yielded to outside pressures, no matter how strong.[103] To me that which Galileo always refused to believe seems unquestionable, namely, the fact that at the basis of his misadventure there was, as a matter of fact, the personal reaction of the Pope to the contents of the *Dialogue*. For sure, Galileo's adversaries were able to *hasten on* or *facilitate* this reaction. But it did not grow to assume the dimensions we are aware of except when Urban VIII became aware *on his own* of how different the *Dialogue* was from the book which he had recommended Galileo to write. And it is certain that, even without any real or presumed "machination" of Jesuits or Dominicans or have what you will, once he understood this,[104] Urban VIII would have reacted more or less in the same way.

NOTES

[1] Among those to whom it was sent there was also Pierre Gassendi at Lyons. His answer to Galileo is found in XIV, 422. In it he says that Mersenne had also "read the *Dialogue* avidly". For a partial inventory of the copies of the *Dialogue* (as well as the Latin translation published in 1635) existing at this time in public and private collections see Westmann 1984.

[2] "The process [i.e. the inquisitorial dossier] has arrived, I mean the book of Mr. Galilei and I have already received it some days ago from the officials of the Holy Office" (Cioni 1908; quoted by Paschini 1965, 501). Six months later when Riccardi, by order of Urban VIII, drafted a memorandum on how the events which had led up to the printing of the *Dialogue* had unfolded (XIX, 324-326 and 294), he will state:

> . . . the book having been printed and published without any knowledge on his [Riccardi's] part, seeing the first copies of it, he kept it in customs, seeing that orders had not been followed.

As we see, this version of the facts is quite different from what is drawn from the letter of acknowledgement to the Florentine inquisitor quoted above. If Riccardi had been truly surprised at the printing of the *Dialogue* without his knowledge, and above all if he had read it, finding "that orders had not been followed", he should have expressed his complaints to Father Egidi, upon whom in the end fell the responsibility of having allowed the printing. He did not do that either on 6 March, or later on (otherwise he would have made sure to enclose a copy of the indicated letter, as a document in his favor, with the memorandum itself, as, on the other hand, he did for other documents). Even the statement of having kept "the first copies" in customs does not correspond to the truth. Riccardi kept in customs the copies which arrived much later, when "the scandal" of the publication by Galileo of a shameless apology for Copernicanism had already broken out in Rome and Urban VIII had perhaps already given the orders to confiscate all the copies in circulation. Obviously with this version of the facts twisted in his favor, Riccardi was trying to save face before the Pope. And he was all the more free to do so since Ciampoli, by this time far from Rome, could no longer intervene to deny his version.

[3] Of particular importance, in this regard, is the letter of G. Battista Baliani to Galileo of 23 April 1632 (XIV, 342). On Baliani's critique of Galileo's theory of the tides see Costantini 1969, 41 and 45-51.

[4] Since the plague epidemic was still going on, it was possible to send only a limited number of copies (XIV, 351) through highly placed persons who were going to Rome, and thus avoid the severe quarantine measures of which the Ambassador Niccolini speaks in a letter to Cioli of 28 March (XIV, 339).

[5] Among these friends to whom Castelli read the *Dialogue* there was also Evangelista Torricelli, who will be at Galileo's side in the last period of his life and who, together with Cavalieri, will be the most illustrious Italian scientist of the period immediately after Galileo. See also XIV, 359-360.

[6] For particulars in this regard see Paschini 1965, 506-507 and, more recently, Redondi 1987, 227-232 and Biagioli 1993, 335-336. A different explanation of Ciampoli's fall into disgrace was given by the ambassador Niccolini in a dispatch of 25 April 1632 (see State Archives, Florence, *Mediceo* 3351). Urban VIII had personally composed a pastoral letter in Latin and had it distributed for a first review to the cardinals and the diplomatic corp. Ciampoli had shown that he did not appreciate the Pontiff's Latin style and he composed a more elegant version of the letter which he showed to various persons. This deeply

hurt Urban VIII. See Favaro 1983 cited together with other
documentation on Ciampoli by Westfall 1989, 82, Note 68 and 95-96.
See also Biagioli 1993, 333-335. This false step of Ciampoli was
probably a further factor in Urban VIII's loss of faith in him, a loss
which already existed as a consequence of Ciampoli's well-known links
to the Spanish-leaning cardinals, Aldobrandini and Ludovisi, who were
involved in the conclave scandal which I have spoken of in the text.

[7] See Gregorovius 1879, 46-59 and for the diplomatic reports of
that time which refer to this incident 139-151. See also von Pastor
1938, 287-294. In addition see Redondi 1987, 228-232 for an interesting
and brilliant synthesis of the events and of the new rigorous
intellectual climate that followed upon the liberal one of the first years
of the Pontificate of Urban VIII and that took place at the conclusion
of the bitter conflict between Urban and the Spanish leaning current.
With respect to this Redondi writes:

> When the political crisis is at its peak, under the
> threatening pressure of Hapsburg intimidation, the Pope is
> forced to yield and furnish ample guarantees and
> satisfaction to the Spanish party. The official measure of
> the political and ideological turn which took place in the
> Curia are the diplomatic instructions sent to the Nuncios
> by the cardinal-nephew. On May 1, the Pope bitterly
> complained of: "very false suspicions and conjectures
> without foundation . . . a thousand judgments of distrust,
> calumnies, and erroneous judgments - many of which with
> time and truth have been clarified. And the same can and
> must be believed and said about the others; that is, that
> they will always be found to be mendacious and without
> any substance." Against those "contrary or malign or
> ignorant persuasions", the pope was obliged to promise
> from now on a greater rigor and clarity about his real
> intentions ("the counsels and sentiments of hearts")
> regarding the protection of orthodoxy. (Redondi 1987, 231).

There is no doubt that this new direction of a rigorous "protection of
orthodoxy" will have a decisive influence on the attitude of Urban VIII
with respect to the *Dialogue*.

[8] As Shea 1984, 286 comments the *Dialogue* began to be known
in Rome some weeks after the clash between Urban VIII and the
Spanish-leaning party. The timing could not have been less felicitous,
all the more so since Ciampoli was by now in a compromising position.
In fact (and it is perhaps useful to be precise here), one of the first

copies of the *Dialogue* (the one sent to Riccardi) had arrived two days before the famous session of the consistory. It is probable that Riccardi was very cautious for the moment of speaking to the Pope about the fact that the printing of the *Dialogue* had occurred. And even if he did so (one would expect with some reassuring word about the contents) Urban VIII clearly had other matters to think about before he could and would desire at that moment to explore in more detail the matter of the *Dialogue*. Another copy of the *Dialogue*, as we know, had been sent by Galileo himself to Cardinal Francesco Barberini. The latter, because of the very difficult situation of the Pope, his uncle, was also too preoccupied to have the will to read this massive volume, which he instead handed over to Castelli, perhaps with the request that he read it and give him a judgement on it. Obviously, Castelli could not, at any rate, give anything but the best possible judgement. The consequence of this situation was that when, towards the end of June and the first half of July, Urban VIII received the first information on the contents of the *Dialogue* it came to him probably not from persons well disposed towards Galileo but from others hostile to him or at least stupefied and alarmed because of the clearly Copernican thesis of the book. In that climate in which there was such open and severe criticism of the Pope's lack of Catholic zeal, the *Dialogue* could constitute a further and serious reason for accusing him, and Urban VIII could not but take a clear position. With a copy of the book in hand, he was able to ascertain personally the unsatisfactory way in which Galileo had presented his famous "theological" argument against the claim of scientists to arrive at secure conclusions on the constitution of the world. Profoundly dissatisfied and wounded in his pride, Urban VIII wished to have an answer also with respect to the accusations of Copernicanism attributed to the *Dialogue*. And to that end he decided, as we will see, to have recourse to a commission of theologians constituted by himself. Here lies the starting point for the progressive, dramatic estrangement of the Pope from his one time friend.

[9] Campanella concluded his letter with the famous and prophetic words: "These truths of ancient novelties, of new worlds, new stars,, new systems etc. . . . are the beginning of a new age" (XIV, 367; trans. by Langford 1966, 132). Despite his very positive judgment on the *Dialogue*, Campanella with his usual frankness had in the same letter expressed his reservations with respect to the argument from the tides: " . . . as to the motion of the tides I am for the present not altogether in accord with Your Lordship, although it is much better written than had been made known to me by friends who did not know how to answer the arguments, and in due time I will advise Your Lordship about this" (XIV, 367).

[10] See Note 8 above.

[11] These last words of Magalotti are very important. After having spoken of the "persecutions" of Galileo by the Jesuits, Magalotti admits that Urban VIII himself is absolutely contrary to the *Dialogue*. I will have the opportunity to return to this point at the end of the present chapter so as to reassess the role (real or presumed) played by the Jesuits and by others in the condemnation of Galileo. As I have already said, ever since the time of Galileo the one among the Jesuits who takes the blame is Scheiner. Among many others that thesis is taken up again by Drake (1978, 467): "He [Scheiner] remained at Rome through the trial of Galileo, which he was instrumental in bringing about". See also D'Addio 1985, 76-77, Note 51. As to Grassi's responsibility, as we have seen many times, this is the principal thesis of Redondi 1987, a thesis, however, which, I repeat, appears altogether unconvincing.

[12] In the course of the letter Micanzio tried to give encouragement to Galileo. Alluding to the reactions of the critics of the *Dialogue*, he wrote:

> May that not disturb Your Lord nor distract you from going ahead. The blow has been made: you have produced one of the most singular works that have been published by philosophical genius. To forbid its circulation will not diminish the glory of the author: it will be read despite the evil jealousy, and Your Lord will see that it will be translated into other languages. (XIV, 372).

[13] Campanella had also heard this "Congregation" spoken of, that is, a commission which should examine the *Dialogue*. He wrote of it in a letter of 21 August to Galileo:

> I have heard (with great disgust) that they are having a commission of irate theologians to prohibit your *Dialogue*; and there is no one on it who understands mathematics or recondite things . . . I fear the violence of people who do not know. The Father Monster [Riccardi] makes fearful noises against it; and, says he, *ex ore Pontificis*. But His Holiness is not informed, nor can he think this way. My advice is, have the Grand Duke write that, as they have put Dominicans, Jesuits, Theatines, and secular priests on this commission, they should admit also Father Castelli and myself. (XIV, 373; trans. by de Santillana 1955, 191).

[14] The well known Church historian L. von Pastor describes Urban VIII in this way:

> One had the impression of being in the presence of a self possessed and keenly observant man who brooked no contradiction. . . . Renier Zeno, the Venetian envoy, admired Urban VIII's thorough acquaintance with political conditions which he had acquired during his Paris nunciature. The deep insight which he had obtained made him cautious and distrustful. He never relied on mere words but always insisted on written agreements. He was slow to make up his mind and easily roused though also quickly calmed down. His self-reliance was such that he disdained other people's opinions and would not even listen to them. (von Pastor 1938, 35-36).

We will have the occasion to see a complete confirmation of this description of the personality of Urban VIII in the reports of the conversations which the ambassador Niccolini had with him.

[15] The letter was of 24 August (XIV, 375-376). In it the Grand Duke put forth his wish to have "that which in all other causes and in all of the courts is granted to the accused, that is, defenses against the accusers, and that those accusations and censures which are raised against this book and because of which it is suppressed, should be put down on paper and sent here so that they may be seen and evaluated by the author of that book" (XIV, 376). In this whole question it is a marvel to see the frequency and the rapidity of the diplomatic correspondence between Rome and Florence. Without a doubt Cioli, and especially Niccolini, were driven by the best of intentions in Galileo's regard and they were proving it with the facts.

[16] We will again find this accusation in the document attached to the proceedings of the Trial of Galileo (XIX, 326, n. 6: "Corpo di delitto" [Body of the crime], 2).

[17] Later on in the conversation with Riccardi Magalotti had mentioned the *Letter to Christina of Lorraine*. Riccardi had shown an interest in seeing it and, after having consulted Castelli, Magalotti had him read it and afterwards he left him a copy of it. At any rate, Father Riccardi was strongly inclined to the opinion of Tycho Brahe. "As to this, Magalotti commented, it is of little consequence, as long as they do not make any extravagant resolution against the *Dialogue*". At any rate, he added, if Galileo had persevered in his good disposition to obey, "they would have gone along with him in the most pleasant manner and in a way that he would be pleased" (XIV, 381). Magalotti

showed an analogous optimism the day after when he wrote directly to
Galileo (XIV, 382).

[18] Niccolini had gone to Urban VIII for matters concerning the
relationship between the Holy See and the Grand Duchy. Quite
probably they had dealt with the problem of the Tuscan subject
Mariano Alidosi, under accusation at the Holy Office, but whom the
Grand Duke refused to have judged, as had been requested, at Rome.
See D'Addio 1985, 79 and 83. The discussion about Galileo was brought
up not by Niccolini but by the Pope, as Niccolini himself states.

[19] In the last part of the letter Niccolini said that he had spoken
(beforehand on 30 August) with Father Riccardi, who had shown
optimism and thought that it would not come to a prohibition of the
book but that it would be corrected and changed in some points. As a
final remark Niccolini counselled, as did Magalotti, that things be
taken with a certain sweetness and that a direct confrontation with the
Pope be avoided, "because when His Holiness becomes obstinate, it is
a lost cause, especially so if one has intentions of opposing or
threatening or asserting oneself, because under those conditions he is
hard to deal with and shows respect for no one" (XIV, 385). Drake
1978, 339-340 states that the severity shown all of a sudden by the
Pope as regards Galileo provides a strong reason to suppose that Urban
VIII had in the meantime come to know of the document kept in the
archives of the Holy Office in which, as we have seen, there was talk
of a formal injunction given to Galileo, at the time when he was called
to meet Bellarmine, not to deal in any way with the Copernican
question. In respect to this Drake writes:

> No other explanation of the Pope's sudden and implacable
> anger seems adequate. Galileo, when asking for permission
> to publish a book on the system of the world in 1624, had
> not told Urban about the incident in 1616; hence the Pope,
> whose only information about the events of that year came
> from the unsigned notarial memorandum, believed himself
> to have been deliberately deceived by a trusted friend.
> There is no way he could have known what Cardinal
> Bellarmine had told Galileo about the commissary's
> intervention and precept. (Drake 1978, 339-340).

It seems, however, to me that Urban VIII would have been able to
have other information about the events of 1616 by means of the
minutes of the meetings of the Holy Office, respectively on the
assignment given to Bellarmine with the exact instructions implied
therein (XIX, 321) and on the fulfillment of that assignment (XIX, 278).
But perhaps the person who had free access to the archives (and there

were very few such) and pulled out the document with the injunction of Segizzi, preferred not to draw attention also to other documents which were much less compromising for Galileo. (On this point see further discussion in Note 27.) And, as far as I can judge, no one else had the possibility to do so or cared to do so in the course of the trial.

[20] These instructions had come to him the day after his conversation with the Pope, as Niccolini himself states at the end of the letter quoted above, and he dates them 30 August. Since there is no trace at all of instructions with that date, they would, according to Favaro, be those contained in the letter of Cioli of 24 August, which would, in fact, have been sent only on 30 August (XIV, 385, Note 1). These last instructions were based on a note prepared by Galileo himself (XIV, 375-376).

[21] See Note 13 above. We see that Galileo, at least for once, had followed the suggestion of Campanella and had brought the latter's proposal to the attention of the Grand Duke who, through Cioli, had assigned Niccolini to speak of it to Riccardi.

[22] Riccardi had said textually with respect to Campanella: "because he has produced an almost similar work, which was prohibited, nor would he be able to defend it, while he is guilty". With all probability the reference is to the *Apologia pro Galileo* (Apology for Galileo), composed as we know in 1616 but printed in Germany in 1622 and which had come with much delay to the attention of the Roman authorities.

[23] Was there also a fourth member of the Commission whom Riccardi had not mentioned? Campanella, in the letter already quoted in Note 13 above, had spoken also of "Theatines". Redondi (1987, 249-255) draws the conclusion that the Theatine Zaccaria Pasqualigo, who will be part of the second Commission which was established in the final phase of Galileo's trial, was also called, together with Oreggi and Inchofer, into this first Commission. Redondi attributes a special importance to the presence of Pasqualigo, a specialist in matters of the Eucharist. And this, still according to Redondi, would be a further proof that the true cause of the incrimination of Galileo was not Copernicanism but, as a matter of fact, the doctrine of the Eucharist, which, as we have already seen, he would have been accused of having indirectly denied with his atomistic theory of the sense qualities. As to Inchofer, Riccardi had shown himself to be decidedly too optimistic. In fact, the Jesuit was a strict adherent of the geocentric theory, in whose defense he would have the following year published a book entitled: *Tractatus syllepticus*. On this book and more in general on Inchofer see once again Redondi 1987, 253-255 as well as Shea 1984, 283 ff. In his article Shea emphasizes how Inchofer was not indeed competent in the

field of astronomy and physics, despite his claim to make pronouncements on the Copernican question, and that he undoubtedly depended upon Scheiner. Also in the judgment which Inchofer will give on this occasion, as in the following year, his polemic ardor will lead him to go beyond the limits of a simple response to the questions which had been submitted to him and to formulate accusations against Galileo, at times severe and insidious ones, which are not present in the responses of the other members of the Commission. See, for example, XIX, 352, No. 1; 353, No. 7. Riccardi, who was Inchofer's friend, must certainly have known how hostile the latter was to Copernicanism. And he could have very well foreseen that precisely his "good intentions" would have led him to a thorough criticism of Galileo. How in the world could Riccardi himself,. therefore, have been the one to propose Inchofer as a member of the Commission? Shea thinks that, since at that moment Inchofer himself was in a difficult position before the Holy Office because of the publication of a book in which he vindicated the historical truth of a letter said to have been written by the Virgin Mary to the people of Messina (a book which the following year will be placed on the Index), Riccardi must have thought that the Jesuit, aware of his difficult position with respect to the Holy Office, would have limited himself to giving the most innocuous opinion possible. Shea, of course, realizes that Riccardi was mistaken and that Inchofer wanted, on the contrary, to show, in his own interests also, that he was an ardent champion of the official position of the Church in the matter at hand. Even if one admits this interpretation of the choice made by the Master of the Sacred Palace, it seems to me that by this time Riccardi, desperately looking for a way out, was more or less consciously playing a double game. With Galileo's friends he tried to uphold that the Commission was not against Galileo and that he personally, having given permission for the *Dialogue*, could not help but defend it. But, in fact, together with Oreggi he will give a version of the facts and a judgment on the *Dialogue* (see the memorandum on this in Note 2 above) not for sure "in defense" of Galileo, even if the possibility was left open for an emendation of the book. Perhaps Riccardi could rest in peace with his conscience with the thought that, after all was said and done, this latter was the only possibility of "defense" that remained.

[24] This seems to confirm that the document of the Holy Office had not been recovered by the commission. Otherwise, in fact, Riccardi, as one of its members, would have been more exactly informed.

[25] In his first letter to Galileo (11 September 1632: XIV, 387-388) Evangelista Torricelli sent along the following interesting information:

Father Grienberger, who is a very good friend of mine, confesses that the book of Your Lord has given him very great pleasure, and that there are many fine things, but that the opinion does not please him, and even if it bodes well, he does not hold it as true. When I spoke of it to Father Scheiner, he praised it shaking his head; he also says that it tires one to read it because of the many digressions. I recalled to him the very same excuses and defenses which Your Lord in many places goes on weaving. Finally he says that Your Lord has behaved badly towards him and he does not want to speak of it. (XIV, 387).

As he himself states in this letter (in which he makes his own presentation of himself to Galileo), Torricelli had been a student of the Jesuits for two years and he was very much a friend of Grienberger. His words, therefore, appear credible. From this letter we learn that the *Dialogue* had finally come into the possession of the Jesuits. And it seems that Scheiner was still reading it, a fact which would exclude that he had already become a promoter of anti-Galilean action. This seems confirmed by the tone of his comments, which would have been quite different in the contrary case.

[26] See the letter of Cardinal Francesco Barberini to the Nuncio in Florence, G. Bolognetti (XIV, 398).

[27] This report, prepared as we have already mentioned by Riccardi and Oreggi under orders from Urban VIII, is found in XIX, 324-327, first in a more concise form (324-325) and then in a more extensive one (325-327). On the basis of the minutes of the meeting (*Relata serie totius facti circa impressionem libri a Galileo de Galileis Florentiae factam, nec non precepto eidem ab hoc S. Officio anno 1616 facto* . . . (After having read the report on the sequence of all that happened concerning the printing of the book done in Florence by Galileo Galilei, as well as on the precept made to the same by this Holy Office in the year 1616. . .) it seems that the document of the Holy Office was read immediately after the reading of the report. This seems to indicate that the document was not included in the report itself. And that would be logical since the report concerned only "the sequence of all that happened concerning the printing of the book done in Florence by Galileo Galilei" (see the beginning of the report itself). Shea 1984, 287 maintains that the Commission appointed by Urban VIII would have had access at the Holy Office to the documents concerning Galileo and would thus itself have discovered the document in question. That, however, is completely unlikely, since the Commission had been created by the Pope in a first procedural stage

independent of the Holy Office and with the sole purpose of examining the contents of the *Dialogue*. Furthermore, access to the secret archives of the Holy Office was precluded to anyone who was not a member. See also Note 24 above (together with the text to which it refers) for a further probable confirmation of the opinion expressed here. The discovery of the document of 1616 must, therefore, have been made independently. Perhaps it .was made by some member of the Holy Office hostile to Galileo who, worried and unhappy that the question of the *Dialogue* could be resolved outside of the Holy Office, had perhaps wanted to look again, "just to be sure", at the documents of sixteen years earlier, assisted, one might expect, by some archivist who knew that among those documents there were several concerning Galileo. After all, the rumor that Galileo had at that time abjured into the hands of Bellarmine had been, as we know, widespread in Rome and someone could have very well remembered it. All the more reason to check it out.

[28] In the more concise report (see Note 27) right after the series of facts and a very brief synthesis of the judgement on the *Dialogue* there is placed the document of the Holy Office of 1616, preceded by the accusatory words: "and furthermore that he fraudulently kept quiet about a precept given to him by the Holy Office of the year 1616, which is of this tenor . . ." And it concludes: "Now it is necessary to decide on the way to proceed both as to the person and as to the book already printed (*tam circa personam quam circam librum iam impressum*)". In the more extensive report, which comes immediately thereafter and begins with the words: "In fact . . .", the criticisms of the *Dialogue* are quite a bit more detailed and grouped into eight points. After these there come the words: "All of these things could be corrected, if it is decided that the book to which such favor should be shown is of any value" (trans. by de Santillana 1955, 211). And finally, in a separate paragraph the precept of 1616 is repeated with the simple words: "The author had the precept of 1616 from the Holy Office . . . " without the aggravating statement, "of which he had furthermore fraudulently kept quiet", of the abbreviated version. From this comparison it seems one can argue that the report written by Riccardi and Oreggi is the second more extensive one and that it limits itself to reporting the facts and also the criticisms against the *Dialogue*, but without showing hostility, but rather leaving the door open to a possible emendation of the *Dialogue* itself. The more concise report, on the other hand, must have been put together by some official of the Holy Office, in preparation for the meeting of that Congregation and it used the Riccardi-Oreggi report, but with the final part quite less "malleable" with respect to Galileo and his *Dialogue*. And this seems

to be confirmed by the mention of the name of Father Raffaello Visconti who is placed correctly in the more extended version but is erroneously transcribed as "Raffaele Visconte" in the more concise one.

[29] According to D'Addio 1985, 85 Campanella's statement seems to be confirmed by what is reported by the canon Niccolò Gherardini, who came in contact with Galileo on the occasion of the trial. Gherardini speaks of a "most high prelate" who had tried to get Galileo off from the condemnation "in order to counteract at least partially the malign intention of another personage who held great authority in that Court" (XIX, 634). Still following D'Addio 1985, 87 the "most high prelate" could be Cardinal Zacchia, who was one of the two cardinals to whom the Grand Duke had written to recommend Galileo before the beginning of the trial (XV, 46) and who will not sign the decree of condemnation. But it could have as well been Cardinal Bentivoglio or Cardinal Francesco Barberini.

[30] However, in the instructions sent by the cardinal of Saint Onofrio (Antonio Barberini) to the inquisitor in Florence two days after the meeting of the Holy Office (XX, 573) there was the explanation that Galileo was not to be given a "formal command", that is, they were not to speak to him of a notary and witnesses, even though they should be present and sign. Only if Galileo should refuse to obey should a command with all the formalities be intimated to him. As we see, there was still some consideration for him, in contrast with the severe form with which the decision was formulated at the time of the meeting of the Holy Office. But in that meeting, in which Cardinal Gaspare Borgia had also taken part, Urban VIII had probably felt it necessary to make visible his intransigence in the field of doctrine. When speaking confidentially after the meeting with his brother, Antonio Barberini, the Pope had probably assigned him to sweeten the instructions in the manner I have referred to above.

[31] Three days later Galileo wrote to Cioli (who was then with the Grand Duke at Siena): "I am in a state of great confusion because of a summons which was made to me three days ago by the Father Inquisitor on order from the Sacred Congregation of the Holy Office in Rome" (XIV, 402-403). Galileo also alluded to his desire to go to Siena to consult with the Grand Duke on what to do. But it appears that this plan could not be realized (see XIV, 405-406).

[32] On 18 September Father Riccardi commanded the inquisitor in Florence to send to the Holy Office "the original penned text of Mr. Galileo, together with the approval of the . . . examiner . . . to add it to those [documents] we have here" (XX, 572). On 7 October he again wrote to him and gave him the task of trying to get back the copies of

the *Dialogue* which had been spread around or sent off (Cioni 1908, 26, No. XX; quoted by Paschini 1965, 520, Note 119).

[33] In the letter of Filippo Magalotti to Mario Guiducci of 7 August 1632, which I have quoted, Magalotti had already suggested having recourse in support of the *Dialogue* to this cardinal:

> . . . whom I judge to have a most benign attitude to the author and has a great esteem for the work [the *Dialogue*], nor is he inclined by nature to hurry into any precipitous resolution, except when he realizes that there is no other way out, and in order not to displease. (XIV, 370).

[34] I have with me all of the writings which for that occasion I did here and in Rome from which writings . . each and everyone will understand that I did not get myself involved in this undertaking except out of zeal for the Holy Church, and in order to submit to its ministers the information which my long studies had rendered me, and some part of which might be needed by someone, since it deals with matters which are obscure and a long way from the more usual doctrines. (XIV, 408).

[35] With the same purpose in mind Michelangelo Buonarroti had also written the day before, 12 October, to Barberini (XIX, 332-333).

[36] With the same letter Cioli had sent a copy of the letter of Galileo to Cardinal Barberini.

[37] See the letter of Castelli to Galileo of 30 October (XIV, 419-420). See also the letter of the same date of Niccolini to Galileo (XIV, 421). Niccolini confirmed on 6 November that he had delivered the letter to Cardinal Barberini, who, although showing himself extremely cautious as to what would be decided, had appeared very well disposed towards Galileo (XIV, 424-425). From Niccolini himself (see his letter to Cioli of 13 November: XIV, 428) we know that Cardinal Barberini had had the letter read by Urban VIII. In fact, the latter wrote in his own hand on the outside of the letter:

> This affair was dealt with in the last Congregation of the Holy Office: no other reply is required; it is only necessary to know from the Assessor if the orders of that Congregation have been carried out (XIV, 410).

These words were obviously written for Cardinal Barberini, to whom the letter was returned. The session of the Holy Office to which Urban VIII alludes is that of 11 November (XIX, 280; see XX, 574).

[38] Urban VIII will come back to repeat this to Niccolini a month later (see XIV, 439).

[39] Serving always as governor Ciampoli in sequence went from Montalto to Norcia, then to Fabriano and finally to Jesi, where he will die in 1643. The news that Ciampoli had been sent off was given to Galileo by Castelli, who added that "he truly loves you and he esteems your value and your worth as you merit, and he kisses your hands" (XIV, 430-431). However, Ciampoli's removal was not due exclusively, not even principally, to the problem of the *Dialogue*. In fact, in the same letter Castelli wrote: " . . . nor up to the present is it known from whence they come nor what are the complaints against him [Ciampoli], since nothing has been said to him". It is true that there is a report, written by Giovanfrancesco Buonamici, which attributes the cause of Ciampoli's misfortune to the publication of the *Dialogue*:

> They direct the persecution against the Father Monster [Riccardi] who excuses himself: first, by stating that he had orders to approve the book from His Holiness himself; but because the Pope denies this and gets irritated, Father Monster says that the secretary Ciampoli on orders from the Pope had commissioned him to do it; the Pope replies that simple words cannot be trusted; finally Father Monster pulls out a note from Ciampoli, whereby it is stated that His Holiness (in whose presence Ciampoli asserts he is writing) commanded him to approve the book" (XIX, 410).

However, this report presents many debatable points and should, therefore, be taken with a certain amount of caution. One might perhaps say that the problem of the *Dialogue* gave the final blow to a situation which had been getting continually worse from the time when, as I have said, Ciampoli had shown that he was capable of taking positions independent of Urban VIII, even on very delicate and important points in the political arena. On the other hand, Urban VIII could not give this reason for his removal, given the strength of the Spanish-leaning party. And so the printing of the *Dialogue* was able to provide him the official pretext to carry out his political revenge. All of this is valid, even more so, if one considers as the decisive cause for Ciampoli's fall into disgrace the affront he brought to the literary pride of Urban VIII (see Note 6 above).

[40] See the letter of Castelli to Galileo of 25 December (XIV, 442). Niccolini had already written for his part to Cioli on 11 December (XIV, 438-439), recommending that he would persuade Galileo to set

out; and the day after he wrote to Galileo with the same message. In this latter letter he said:

> And in any case, from that which I gather, the biggest issue is that to His Holiness it has seemed that you have aspired to fool him; and of this I am sure Your Lordship will not fail, on your part, to find a way to justify your behavior: nor is there any doubt, if what I hear is credible, that Your Lordship would be worse off by not presenting yourself [here] than by coming. (XIV, 439).

[41] On 16 December Cioli wrote to Niccolini: "Poor Mr. Galileo has put himself to bed, and he runs the risk of passing to the other world rather than remaining in this one" (XIV, 440). Probably there was a bit of exaggeration, but Galileo's bad health was certainly real (see XIV, 440: letter of Galileo to Cosimo del Sera of 17 December).

[42] As Geri Bocchineri explained, when he wrote to Galileo from Pisa on 12 January (XV, 22), the fact that the latter would arrive in Rome with the litter of the Grand Duke and would be lodged at his expense in the embassy at Rome, must have made it clear to all that Galileo enjoyed the complete esteem of the Grand Duke himself.

[43] We will come back to this argument later on in this chapter.

[44] XIX, 336. A report of this letter was given at the session of the Holy Office of 3 February (XIX, 282).

[45] From a letter of Bocchineri to Galileo of 5 February (XV, 37) we know that during that period Galileo had to eat only "bread, wine and eggs".

[46] Letter of Niccolini to Cioli of 14 February (XV, 40-41).

[47] In the same letter Niccolini gave notice that the Commissary had promised to emphasize with Urban VIII and the Roman authorities that the readiness in obeying shown by Galileo "appears to be a very important point". Also Cardinal Francesco Barberini, by the fact that he went on 16 February to the Wednesday session of the Congregation of the Holy Office, which was held at the convent of Santa Maria sopra Minerva and to which he did not customarily go, seemed to have wished to testify to the special interest he had for the Galileo's cause. All in all Niccolini was optimistic: " . . . considering the little light that one has about such things, it seems that they ought not to be so bad" (XV, 41).

[48] See the letter of Niccolini to Cioli of 19 February (XV, 45). Galileo too gave the same information to Cioli (XIV, 44).

[49] As Niccolini explained to Cioli, Serristori had come to Galileo: " . . . to hear what Mr. Galilei says, what his attitude is, and how he defends himself, so that they can then decide what to do and how to

proceed" (XV, 45; trans. by Finocchiaro 1989, 244). It seems that this visit of Serristori had been decided in the meeting of the Holy Office of 16 February and it appears to indicate that "despite the discussions that had already taken place during the last months of 1632, obviously no agreement had yet been reached on the tack to follow in judging the case and the viewpoints must have still been discordant" (D'Addio 1985, 97).

[50] XV, 45. Cardinal Desiderio Scaglia (1569-1639), a Dominican, and Cardinal Guido Bentivoglio (1577-1644), who had sat under Galileo as a lecturer in Padua, were members of the Holy Office.

[51] Galileo had alluded to the same thing in his letter to Geri Bocchineri of 25 February (XV, 50) and showed that he was convinced that "from this [charge] only I will not have difficulty in freeing myself, when they will have heard my justifications".

[52] See the letter to Geri Bocchineri of 5 March (XV, 58).

[53] Luca Holste (Holstein, 1596-1661), a German, had been recommended by Peiresc to Cardinal Francesco Barberini during the latter's stay in Paris in 1625. Upon being invited to Rome, he became a member of the cardinal's court and was appointed as librarian in 1636.

[54] Letter of 7 March (XV, 62). Even Gherardini in his life of Galileo written in 1654 makes mention of the "malign intention [against Galileo] of another personage who claimed great authority in that tribunal [Holy Office]" (XIX, 634). But nothing is known precisely about this personage. Drake 1978, 499, Note 11 states that Holstein's words reflect opinions shared by Cardinal Francesco Barberini who was well informed. But the fact remains that the attribution of the initiative for the persecution against Galileo to the Commissary of the Holy Office, that is, to Father Maculano, is in strident contrast with the posture shown by this latter with respect to Galileo throughout the trial, a posture which is not at all hostile. I put aside the fact that Maculano had never claimed (as far as we know) to be "first among the mathematicians", as Drake himself recognizes.

[55] See the letter of Galileo to Cioli of 19 March (XV, 69-70) and that of the same date of Niccolini to the same Secretary of the Grand Duke (XV, 73-74). In this letter Niccolini gave the list of the cardinals who were members of the Holy Office: besides Bentivoglio and Scaglia, S. Onofrio (Antonio Barberini), Barberino (Francesco Barberini), Borgia (Gaspare), Gessi (Berlingero), Ginnetti (Marzio Ginetti), S. Sisto (Laudivio Zacchia), Verospi (Fabrizio). Niccolini had supplied the list of the cardinal inquisitors who were in residence in Rome. In addition to them there were three other non residents: Galamini, Zapata and Centini, all of whom were already members of the Holy Office in 1616.

But Galamini, who since 1613 was bishop of Loreto, will not come back to Rome from 1626 until his death 1639 (Mayaud 1992b, 270). Zapata, a Spaniard, had already definitively gone back to Spain as Grand Inquisitor (Mayaud 1992b, 277). As for Centini (also named d'Ascoli), who became a bishop in 1611, he was at that time absent from Rome and would not return until the end of April. So he participated in the meetings of the Holy Office from 4 May on (Mayaud 1992b, 270) and was, therefore, present only for the final phases of Galileo's trial. But the fact that he was the only one of the present members of the Holy Office who was directly knowledgeable of the happenings of 1615-1616 might have brought it about that he would have played a significant role in the decisions which culminated with the condemnation and abjuration of Galileo. As to the letters of recommendation to the cardinals who resided in Rome, they were, in fact, written (see the letter of Geri Bocchineri to Galileo of 20 March, XV, 74-76), but they have been lost. Niccolini promised Cioli to deliver them to the addressees (XV, 85), as in fact he did (XV, 95). According to the ambassador's statement some of the cardinals had hesitated to accept the letter "because of the risk of being censured" (XV, 95). As to Cardinal Scaglia, he had put himself to read the *Dialogue* with Father Castelli's help and from this he had formed "a concept which, if not completely opposite, is at least very different and far removed from the one that he had formed before" (XV, 71). For his part Cardinal Capponi at Florence had read the *Letter to Christina of Lorraine* and after that had gone on to the *Dialogue* and showed himself "to be most satisfied that the opinion of Copernicus was not erroneous" (Letter of Mario Guiducci to Galileo of 19 March; XV, 71).

[56] According to D'Addio 1985, 96-97 this irritation of Urban VIII reveals the fact that discussions were still going on within the Holy Office with respect to the *Dialogue* and perhaps not all of the cardinals shared Urban VIII's idea that it was not possible to give a true demonstration of the Copernican system.

[57] Even Galileo, writing on that same day to Geri Bocchineri, after having informed him of his "business", added: " . . . for the continuation of which it has been arranged for me to remain in retreat, but with unusual largesse and comfort, in 3 rooms which are a part of those where the Lord Prosecutor of the Holy Office lives, and with free and ample permission to take walks in wide spaces. As to my health I am well, thanks to God and to the exquisite government of the most courteous house of the Lord Ambassador and of Her Ladyship, who are most careful about providing all comforts even beyond the most abundant for me". (XV, 88).

[58] XIX, 336-342. In addition to Father Maculano, who functioned as examining judge, his assistant, Father Carlo Sincero, who as fiscal procurator of the Holy Office fulfilled the role of public prosecutor, and a secretary, who transcribed the minutes, were also present.

[59] The original declaration will be delivered by Galileo on 10 May.

[60] D'Addio writes in this regard:

> The Commissary was very careful not to insist. To what are we to attribute that "particular"? Was it to the fact that Maffeo Barberini had intervened on behalf of Galileo in 1616 by maintaining that the Copernican opinion should not be declared heretical, not even formally so, and that this was the understanding to which the majority of the Cardinals of the Congregation of the Inquisition had arrived, and that, with reference to this precedent, the Pope had agreed to the publication of the *Dialogue*? Galileo kept this particular to himself and he did not speak of it any more in the following depositions, nor was he asked to clarify it, to specify why he had to speak of it first directly to the Pope and why he could not speak of it to the Commissary and the members of the Congregation: in this case the true intentions of the accused were not sought out, it was agreed that he should keep his "secret", most probably with appreciation for Galileo's reserve. (D'Addio 1985, 99).

While I consider D'Addio's interpretation to be plausible, I would like to note that "formally heretical" is not an attenuation of the qualification "heretical" (as the expression "not even formally heretical" used by him seems to suggest) but, on the contrary, it gives it a more explicit and stronger meaning. Furthermore, in 1616 Maffeo Barberini was not a member of the Holy Office but of the Congregation of the Index. Given the extreme secrecy which bound the deliberations of the Holy Office, he was not at all, therefore, in a position to know anything about "an understanding to which the majority of the Cardinals of the Congregation of the Inquisition had arrived". Rather, as we know (see Chapter 3, Note 79), it is most probable that it was within the Congregation of the Index that he successfully opposed the qualification of the Copernican thesis as "heretical".

[61] On the implication of Segizzi's precept see Chapter 3, Note 69. On the other hand, even if we limit ourselves to the content of Bellarmine's testimony, it spoke of the communication given to Galileo that the Copernican theory could not "be either held or defended". Even though this was not a personal command in Galileo's regard, it was the

communication of a command which bound every Catholic and, therefore, Galileo himself. It is precisely that which Maculano himself will later on make Galileo notice (and it will be emphasized in the final sentence of the condemnation). Galileo was surely aware of the problem. Indubitably it was for that reason that he will claim immediately thereafter that he had not wanted to defend Copernicanism but that, on the contrary, he had wished to prove that it was false.

[62] On the other hand, during this interrogation, as well as following it, the Commissary did not show hostility towards Galileo. He interrogated him because of the obligations of his office but without showing a grudge or an argumentative punctiliousness.

[63] Geymonat (1965, 149) comments: "This absurd pretense [i.e. to have wanted to show that Copernicus' reasons were invalid and not conclusive] was in fact the downfall of Galileo's position; it impaired the value of all his subsequent replies". D'Addio 1985, 101 also speaks of "an excessive defense" on Galileo's part and he adds:

> Surely Maculano thought to make Galileo remember this statement of his which he could no longer deny: if this had been his intention, he must recognize that the arguments developed in the *Dialogue* did not correspond to it, because they always concluded in favor of the Copernican thesis.

It appears to me, nevertheless, that terms like "absurd pretense" and "excessive defense" are a projection of our reaction (correct as it might be) upon the scene which unfolded more than 350 years ago in that chamber of the Holy Office, and they do not take into account that Maculano did not necessarily have to have had the same type of reaction. Far from showing himself "scandalized" by Galileo's statements, the Commissary (undoubtedly acting on instructions received from Cardinal Francesco Barberini, with the assent of Urban VIII) will try in fact, in the phase immediately following this first interrogation, to save Galileo with an extra-judiciary procedure, about which I will speak immediately. This is a further proof of the good dispositions of the Commissary towards Galileo, even after the first interrogation.

[64] In XIX, 342 the confirmation in Galileo's hand placed on the minutes is reproduced: "I Galileo Galilei have born witness as above". Comparing this attestation with that of the second interrogation held on 30 April, the writing on the former appears to be much more nervous, a sign of the tension with which Galileo had presented himself at the first interrogation. We will find a similar, even greater, tension in Galileo's writing after the interrogation of 21 June.

[65] That year the feast of the Ascension fell on Thursday, 5 May.

[66] The last words of Niccolini seem to confirm, as we have already seen, the version of the facts given by Buonamici (XIX, 410).

[67] See XIX, 340-360. The response of Inchofer is an especially long one (XIX, 348-356). Later on Inchofer had to leave Rome because of one of his writings against castration (a practice which assured the supply of "white voices" to the choir of the Sistine Chapel). He will die in Milan in 1648. As we know the prohibition against *teaching, defending or holding* (in any way whatsoever) the teaching of Copernicus was contained in Segizzi's precept, which had been imposed on Galileo immediately after the admonition of Bellarmine. I have already made clear (see Note 69 of Chapter 3) how the first two prohibitions implied that it was forbidden to treat of Copernicanism and to defend it, even if only as a hypothesis, as being superior to geocentrism. Therefore, the answer given by the theologians with respect to these two prohibitions was equivalent to a proof that Galileo had already violated Segizzi's precept by the very fact of having written the *Dialogue* in which he defended Copernicanism. The answer with respect to the third prohibition was, however, even more serious. Despite Galileo's statements to the contrary, from the whole content of the *Dialogue* one deduced that he could be *vehemently suspected* of having, at the moment of writing it, held Copernicanism as true or at least as more probable than geocentrism. In this way Galileo had not only violated Segizzi's third precept (and this time also that of Bellarmine) but, by upholding a doctrine defined as contrary to Holy Scripture by the Congregation of the Index, he had taken a position against the doctrinal basis of those precepts, namely the Decree of the Index. As we will see, in the practice of the Inquisition of those times, being vehemently suspected of holding a doctrine contrary to Sacred Scripture became *ipso facto* a suspicion of heresy. This will be confirmed as the trial continues to develop.

[68] On the term "rigorous examination" (different than "simple examination") and the torture connected with it see Mereu 1990, 208 ff. He shows that in the terminology of the Inquisition of that time the term "rigorous examination" was *sic et simpliciter* synonymous with "torture".

[69] The fact that Maculano, in writing to the Cardinal, was able to limit himself to a simple allusion to the "foundation" seems to confirm that Francesco Barberini had been the intermediary through whom Urban VIII had made known his wish to Maculano. It is also quite probable that the Pope was in agreement with sending Galileo off to Villa Medici as soon as the second interrogation was ended.

[70] Here Maculano seems, contrary to the Inquisition's practice, to put the interrogation on his intention before granting Galileo his defense. The Inquisition's practice foresaw the written self-defense of the accused first and then, if that were judged not to be convincing, the examination on intention. In the case of a grave suspicion of heresy, the latter was a "rigorous examination" implying torture (see Note 68 and Mereu 1990, 210). In fact, it is just this order which will also be followed in Galileo's case with a "rigorous examination" which will imply, as we shall see, the threat of torture, although not its execution. But in this letter Maculano seems to reduce the examination to a mere juridical formality without any mention of torture. That was probably part of the plan for a "benign" solution to the trial, put together by himself and Cardinal Barberini with the consent of Urban VIII himself (see Note 69). As we shall see, it will be precisely the inadequate response of Galileo which will change this examination into a rigorous examination.

[71] Koestler, as usual bitter and unjust with respect to Galileo, tries to find the psychological motives for these statements of his in

... the unavoidable reaction of one who thought himself capable of outwitting all and making a fool of the Pope himself, on suddenly discovering that he has been found out. His belief in himself as a superman was shattered, his self esteem punctured and deflated. (Koestler 1968, 496).

[72] This provision of Maculano, taken at the Holy Office in the presence of two witnesses and probably at the very moment at which Galileo was sent off to the Tuscan embassy, is said to have been brought about by the Commissary "*facto prius verbo cum Sanct.mo*" (that is, after having spoken with the Pope). But, as we know, the Pope was at Castel Gandolfo. It seems very difficult for Maculano to have succeeded on that very day of 30 April, after having written to Cardinal Barberini the letter already quoted, to have then proceeded to the second interrogation of Galileo, to have dispatched to the Pope immediately afterwards the request for permission to send Galileo off to Villa Medici and finally, with the consent of Urban VIII, to have proceeded to the "freeing" of Galileo. It is much more probable that Maculano based these actions on a previous consent of Urban VIII which had been communicated to him by Francesco Barberini (see Note 69).

[73] Galileo too had given signs of being optimistic in the letters he wrote to his family and friends right after his return to the

Embassy. This optimism was based not only on the permission received to return to Embassy but also on the favorable reactions of Maculano with respect to his "confession". Had things been different, the Commissary would not have failed to show his displeasure (seeing the failure of his attempt at compromise) and Galileo would certainly have been aware of this.

[74] Also the fact that Cardinal Francesco Barberini had confirmed to Niccolini that the trial could have been terminated a few days afterwards, seems to indicate that the situation had not changed substantially. Later on, as we shall see, the name of Francesco Barberini disappears from the correspondence of Niccolini and from the documents of the final session of the trial. Is this a sign that he had not approved the rigorous solution later adopted and that he had wanted to remove himself from taking part in the final decision against Galileo?

[75] Niccolò Gherardini, in his *Vita* [of Galileo] speaks of the "malign intention [against Galileo] of a . . . personage who held a high position of authority in that Tribunal [of the Holy Office]" (XIX, 634). And this "personage" has been often identified, as a matter of fact, with Ginetti who would have been against Galileo from the very beginning. Other "rigorists" are often identified by biographers of Galileo with Cardinals Gessi, Verospi and possibly including the Assessor Pietro Paolo Febei (by office he was the superior of Father Maculano). It remains possible (see Note 55) that an adversarial role was played by Cardinal Centini, the only one of the cardinals present at the Holy Office in the final stage of Galileo's trial who had direct knowledge of the decisions taken in Galileo's regard in 1616. It would also be possible that the dusting off of the accusations of Caccini (we will speak of this right away in the text) had been done on indications from Centini. But we do not know and we will probably never know precisely what happened.

[76] From the acts of the meeting of 16 June we verify that the Commissary Maculano was also present. So he thus gave, at the end, a vote in agreement with that of the other members.

[77] The term "*si sustinuerit*" is ambiguous and is open to contradictory interpretations: from one like "if he has given satisfaction" to "if he has remained firm in maintaining the previous statements". Whatever interpretation is chosen, the fact remains that the Decree would seem to prescribe the provisions to be taken "in the case that . . . ", without indicating what should be done *in the opposite case*, in resounding contrast with the precision with which the various possible cases had been foreseen in 1616, and the respective measures to be taken at the time of Galileo's summons by Bellarmine. Nonetheless, I

think that this apparently strange juridical position is easily avoided
if we translate the expression "*si sustinuerit*" by "once having
undergone [this examination of intention]". It would certainly have
been more correct to write: "*postquam sustinuerit [hanc
interrogationem]*" (once having undergone [this interrogation]). But
the Latin of the Holy Office documents for this period is far from being
Ciceronian. If we accept this translation, all is clear. Urban VIII,
having taken account of the vote against Galileo by the cardinals
present at the meeting, had decided the condemnation and the
abjuration for suspicion of heresy. But in the case of suspicion of heresy
an examination *super intentione*, including the threat of torture, was
prescribed by the rules of the Inquisition. And so this examination
(which had been foreseen, we must not forget, also after the procedure
suggested by Maculano and for the same reason) was put as a
preliminary step, before the condemnation and the abjuration.

   [78] It is interesting to note that in the meeting of the Holy Office
of 16 June Cardinal Francesco Barberini was not present. Instead there
were Cardinals Bentivoglio and Scaglia, who had previously shown
themselves favorable to Galileo.

   [79] As we see, Galileo established his claim not to hold the
Copernican thesis on higher motives. That is, not on motives of the
natural sciences and astronomy (at whose level it was not possible to
come to a certain proof, neither for nor against), but on those of "more
sublime doctrine". This was Urban VIII's thesis which Galileo sought
once more to make pass as his own. But the judges did not allow
themselves to be convinced, as is shown by the persistence of the
following questions. It is also to be noted how, at the time of this last
interrogation, Galileo had let fall as completely absurd his previous
statement of having wished in the *Dialogue* to prove, as a matter of
fact, the falsity of Copernicanism. By now he knew from Niccolini that
his book would be condemned and he therefore accepted the fact that
his attempt *in extremis* to save it (with that unmaintainable claim,
coupled with the unbelievable proposal of that appendix) had failed.
And, probably, in the days of relative calm which had followed upon his
return to the embassy, he had himself become aware of the absurdity
of his statement and of his proposal and he repented of it.

   [80] Almost all scholars today agree on the fact that the threat of
torture, in the case of a man of Galileo's age, was nothing other than
a pure legal formality. For that matter recourse to torture at Rome
rarely occurred. In Galileo's case it was limited to *territio verbalis*, that
is to the purely verbal threat of torture. In other cases it was possible
to come right to the *territio realis*, that is right to the point of
displaying the instruments of torture. De Santillana himself, generally

not by any means benevolent towards the Holy Office, states: "At least in the central organs of government we know that the procedure was meticulous and the judgement correct. The apparatus of severity was shown for the purpose of inciting a holy fear but it was not used casually or brutally" (de Santillana 1960, 549). A different opinion in this regard has been maintained by Drake 1978, 500. He states that up to the present time no regulation has been found which would prohibit in Galileo's day the torture of an elderly person. According to Drake, the exemption from torture would have been due to a personal intervention of Cardinal Francesco Barberini. But there is no evidence that would validate such a hypothesis. For a detailed treatment of the question see D'Addio 1985, 107-108, Note 106. If our interpretation of the expression *si sustinuerit* is accepted (see Note 77 above), this whole interrogation *super intentione* (and therefore also the threat of torture) appears as a mere juridical formality. The true intention of Galileo was already fully known to the Holy Office. He had clearly defended Copernicanism and he was, therefore, (as the sentence of condemnation will say) "vehemently suspected of heresy". Therefore, he was already condemned to an abjuration without it being necessary to await the outcome of the interrogation. But this latter had at least served to make clear the disposition of Galileo to "be obedient" and to allow the conclusion (as the sentence of condemnation itself will recognize) that he had responded "in a Catholic way". Thus the Holy Office could be certain that he would not have refused to abjure on the following day.

[81] According to de Santillana 1960, 559 Galileo "was led (to the Minerva) on the mule of the Inquisition, dressed in the white gown of the penitents". For sure G. Giacomo Bouchard wrote from Rome to Micanzio on 29 June: "Our good old friend has finally been oppressed. Kept again for two days at the Holy Office, he was led on Wednesday as a guilty person in the penitential garb to the Minerva before the cardinals and the others of the Congregation" (XIV, 166).

[82] Of the ten cardinals members of the Holy Office then resident in Rome, only seven were present. Among those absent there was Francesco Barberini. It is true that he had rarely taken part in the previous sessions, but on this particularly solemn occasion his absence seems to carry a special meaning, that is that he was opposed to a procedure which he had sought to avoid but which had come to prevail at the last moment. Another of those absent (also habitually so) was Cardinal Gaspare Borgia. On the basis of what we know of his doctrinal attitude, it seems difficult to think that he too had been contrary to the provision for condemnation. Had he perhaps wanted an even harder and more radical condemnation? But for a completely different interpretation see Drake 1978, 351. The third one absent was

Cardinal Zacchia. D'Addio 1985, 110-111 discusses at length the meaning of these absences. But the whole question of the significance of these absences must be reexamined in light of the results of Mayaud's (1992b) careful study. On the basis of the statistics of the presence of the cardinals at the meetings of the Holy Office between 1611 and 1642, one can conclude that the presence of seven out of ten was completely satisfactory, so that Urban VIII had not exaggerated by speaking of the meeting as "plenary".

[83] While the sentence of condemnation carries at the beginning the list of names of the ten cardinal members of the Holy Office, in whose name it is released, the final signatures are only from seven cardinals.

[84] As we see, the Holy Office attributed full juridical validity to the intimation made to Galileo by Segizzi and it is here quoted in first place.

[85] These words have to do with the notification given by Bellarmine to Galileo. This one alone was sufficient to bind Galileo.

[86] This was the unanimous response of the Commission, twice appointed to examine the *Dialogue*.

[87] These words certainly do not mean: "without providing any proof" (that is any completely probative argument in favor of Copernicanism), as has been maintained, but: "without having brought solutions to these reasonings", that is "without having brought forth sufficiently positive arguments against them" (in such wise that these reasonings would definitely wind up having no value). It would, in fact, be absurd to think that Galileo's judges (persuaded as they were of the irreducible opposition of Copernicanism to Scripture) would have wished to criticize Galileo for not having succeeded in providing irrefutable proofs of heliocentrism.

[88] These last words, followed by Galileo's signature, are the only ones written by him at the end of the document of abjuration.

[89] The first of such studies is the one published by Garzend 1912. Largely based on this work is the contribution by Giacchi 1942. For a thorough examination of the Inquisition's practices in the 16th and 17th centuries see Mereu 1990 (especially 292-326, for the trial of Galileo).

[90] The formulary under discussion is one of those which is found added on to one of the most widespread manuals used by the Inquisition at the time of Galileo, *Arsenale ovvero pratica della Santa Inquisizione* (see Masini 1621). The comparison (given by Mereu 1990, 379-381) of the text for an abjuration in this formulary with the one for Galileo's abjuration proves clearly how this formulary was also used, apart some variants, on this occasion.

[91] Should the "recidivist" have shown himself repentant for his relapse, he would get the "favorable treatment" of being first hung or decapitated and then burned. In the other case in which the "recidivist" was impenitent right to the end he was burned alive. See Mereu 1990, 289.

[92] As we know, Bellarmine in his response to Foscarini had faced the possibility, although with a considerable and basic skepticism, that a proof for Copernicanism might be given. But by signing, as he did, the ecclesiastical decisions of February-March 1616, he had himself by now come to preclude completely that possibility, however tenuous it might be. And, I repeat, the other Churchmen were also precluding it. Therefore, to hold that the provisions of 1616 were only intended to break the untimely zeal of Galileo for Copernicanism without blocking further careful scientific research on the matter appears to me to be completely untenable. On the contrary, in the following chapter we will see how the blocking of Copernicanism, sanctioned by the Decree of the Index, and the very existence of this decree, weighed heavily on the Church throughout the 18th and right up to the beginning of the 19th century. As to the negative influence which this cutting off of Copernicanism had upon the progress of astronomy in Italy, it seems to be undeniable (although it was probably not the only one negative factor) considering the fact that after Galileo astronomical studies with a Copernican orientation almost completely disappear for the remainder of the 17th century. The problem arising from the concomitant stagnation of scientific research in Italy is much more complex and still in need of further study.

[93] Alongside the intellectual "openness" shown in various degrees by Castelli, Dini, Micanzio, Campanella, Mersenne, Gassendi, the mathematicians of the Roman College and by many other Churchmen, contemporaries of Galileo, we must also remember that shown by Cardinal Maffeo Barberini himself. As we have seen, after he had already become Pope, he stated that, had it depended upon him, the Decree of 1616 would never have come to be. And it seems probable that this was also the opinion of Cardinal Caetani. To this group of "illuminated" Churchmen one must then add that still more numerous group of scientists and of lay intellectuals interested in Copernicanism without necessarily being supporters of it. From the collected correspondence contained in the National Edition of the Works of Galileo it is sufficiently evident how all of these, no less than ourselves today, saw the doctrinal closure decreed by the Church in 1616 as unwise or even as an abuse of power. Of course, they were not free, for obvious reasons, to express their dissent publicly. I think it is important to emphasize all of this in order to rebut certain attempts

to present the intellectual world at the time of Galileo, both lay and ecclesiastical, as monolithically aligned with the Aristotelian-Ptolemaic positions and, therefore, substantially in solid support of the decisions of 1616, as well as later with those of 1633.

[94] In a confidential letter sent to 141 cardinals in preparation for the consistory of June 1994, which later became of public knowledge, John Paul II wrote:

> How can we then remain quiet about the many forms of violence perpetrated even in the name of the Faith? Religious wars, the tribunals of the Inquisition and other forms of the violation of human rights ... In light of what has been said by the Second Vatican Council the Church must also of its own initiative reexamine the obscure aspects of its history and evaluate them in the light of the principles of the Gospel. (L'Unità Due, 1 May 1994, p. 3).

These explicit and courageous statements were then taken up again, although in a more generic and notably softened form, in the Apostolic Letter, "*Tertio Millennio Adveniente*" (Awaiting the Third Millennium) published on 14 November 1994 in preparation for the Jubilee Year 2000. At number 35 of the document we read:

> Another painful chapter [besides the breakup of Christian unity] to which the sons and daughters of the Church must return with a spirit of repentance is that of the acquiescence given, especially in certain centuries, to intolerance and even the use of violence in the service of the truth. (John Paul II 1994, N. 35, p. 45).

On the concrete forms whereby coercion and violence became manifest in the institutions of the Inquisition down through the centuries up to Galileo one should consult all of the documentation contained in Mereu 1990.

[95] It is not for us to ask with what feelings in his heart and with what interior assent Galileo was able to bring himself to read that act of abjuration which denied, at least publicly, everything which up to then he had labored and battled for and which he certainly continued to consider as being closer to the truth. But it is undoubtedly a question for the Church of his time and, in its repercussions, also for today's Church.

[96] This, I think, is the meaning of the dictum: *Historia magistra vitae* (History is life's teacher). History, that is, teaches us to live

better by avoiding past errors, those which history itself, as a matter of fact, witnesses to by reconstructing past happenings and placing a judgement on their value.

[97] One of the cardinals present at the abjuration, Guido Bentivoglio, wrote in his *Remembrances*:

> God knows how I suffered to see him [Galileo] come out an Archimedes so unhappy through his own fault in having wanted to publish printed works of his new opinions about the motion of the earth against the true common sense of the Church. Those opinions caused him to appear here in the Holy Office of Rome, where I at that time carried out the office of Supreme Inquisitor General and where I sought to help his cause in so far as I could. (Cited by Paschini 1965, 548).

[98] See for example de Santillana 1960, 537-538.

[99] The statements attributed to Grienberger on this occasion are in fact in profound contrast with his temperament and his posture, as appears clearly from the correspondence published in Favaro 1968 and in the much more abundant correspondence now published in Baldini and Napolitani 1992. A reserved temperament, prudent even to being scrupulous, with moderate attitudes, even when around him other Jesuits showed a much greater animosity towards Galileo - that was Grienberger. Let it be enough to remember the letter quoted in Note 22 of Chapter 4, written by Grienberger at the beginning of the argument between Galileo and Grassi on the comets, as well as the comment, quite other than hostile, expressed by the at this time elderly Jesuit mathematician with respect to the *Dialogue*. That Grienberger could make a statement, such as that attributed to him by Galileo's "friend", so full of boasting about the power of the Jesuits, appears to me truly incredible. It is much more likely that this friend of Galileo's had added his own to the original statement of the Jesuit.

[100] Seven years earlier, the "Santarelli affair" (see Redondi 1987, 103-106) had threatened to damage seriously the relationship between Urban VIII and the France of Cardinal Richelieu. The crisis was overcome, but it had created a serious blow to the prestige of the Jesuits (to whose Order Father Santarelli belonged) and brought a nasty public rebuke by the Pope to the Father General Vitelleschi. Grienberger, who was in Rome, was certainly not in the dark about what had happened. And now, seven years later, everyone in Rome knew that the Jesuits would have to be prudent so as not to give an

impression to the most suspicious Urban VIII that they were secretly backing the Spanish-leaning faction in the Roman Curia.

[101] In favor of this thesis there is the testimony contained in the letter of Peiresc to Gassendi of 6-10 September 1633:

> I have been a little shocked to see how he [Scheiner] cannot abstain from attacking this poor old man [Galileo] after having brought him to the dirt before his feet and having had him condemned not only to recant but also to perpetual imprisonment. (XV, 244).

We are dealing, as one can see, with a quite precise and serious testimony with respect to Scheiner. But it seems to me that it is always quoted without a sufficient critical reconstruction of the sources for it. Peiresc, despite his sincere admiration for Galileo and his displeasure for his condemnation (which is clear from the words reported above, as from other letters of his at that time) was also in good relationships with the German Jesuit and this excludes the wish to calumniate him gratuitously, and thus, at least at a first look, this weighs in favor of the credibility of his statements. Furthermore, his friendship with Cardinal Francesco Barberini enabled him to have first-hand information. On the other hand, Peiresc was writing not from Rome but from Aix en Provence. His information on Scheiner's attitude had not come to him either directly from the latter nor from Rome but by means of two letters of Scheiner sent to two correspondents of Peiresc, Gassendi and Athanasius Kircher and sent on by them to him for his information. As to Gassendi, Scheiner had written to him on 16 July (less than a month after Galileo's condemnation) saying, among other matters, that:

> I defend myself [in the new work, the *Prodromus*, at that time just completed] for the second time [that is, after the *Rosa Ursina*] against Galileo, a usurper of my discoveries. I marvel at the impudence with which this man has wanted to obtain for himself such great dishonor. You will see one day and you too will be amazed, when you read my defense. (XV, 183).

With good reason Peiresc was saddened by the tone of these words, as is clear from the beginning of his letter in response to Gassendi cited above: "I have been a little shocked to see how he [Scheiner] cannot abstain from attacking this poor old man [Galileo]". But as to what he added on immediately thereafter Peiresc based himself on a second letter which Scheiner had sent (the same day as the previous one, 16 July) to his fellow Jesuit, Athanasius Kircher, and which the latter had transcribed and sent to Peiresc (see XV, 219). After having announced to Kircher the completion of his new work against Galileo (the *Prodromus*) "in favor of the mobility of the sun and of the stability of the earth" written "upon the exhortation of the Pontiff, of our General, of the Assistants and of all those who follow a better path" he added:

> A few days ago Galileo, guilty . . . of a vehement suspicion of heresy, has abjured and condemned his opinion on the stability of the sun and the mobility of the earth, before the inquisitor and in the presence of 20 witnesses. His book will be prohibited. (XV, 219).

The satisfaction of Galileo's adversary that the abjuration and the condemnation had occurred is clear between the lines. On the other hand, the allusion (it is difficult to judge how credible) to the composition of his *Prodromus* "upon the exhortation of the Pontiff, of the General . . ." gave the impression that Scheiner had, as it were, received an official investiture for the battle against Galileo's ideas. Linking these statements of Scheiner with the victorious tone with which the Jesuit spoke immediately afterwards of the abjuration and condemnation of Galileo, Peiresc must have concluded that a personage so influential could have very well been, in fact must have been, the author of Galileo's condemnation. Therefore, he added (still in the passage cited at the beginning of this note): ". . . after having brought him to the dirt before his feet and having had him condemned not only to recant but also to perpetual imprisonment". The unlikelihood of this last assertion seems to me to justify a legitimate doubt about the value of all of Peiresc's statements. As I have said Peiresc, as a friend of Cardinal Francesco Barberini, had an active correspondence with members of the cardinal's court and received from them in that period lots of information on the progress of the trial and then on the condemnation of Galileo. But in none of them did the name of Scheiner appear. Yet again we must remember that the very strict secrecy which bound all of those in the Holy Office who had taken part in the Galileo affair (and among them Cardinal Francesco Barberini himself) made it impossible to have an objective picture of the events and their protagonists, and so the only thing left to do was to hypothesize. This caution with respect to the statements of Peiresc appears to me to be necessary also with respect to other statements on the responsibility of the Jesuits and specifically of Scheiner, such as those made by Buonamici (XIX, 410), by the Frenchmen Gabriel Naudé (XV, 87-88, 164-165) and Jacques Gaffarel (this latter was, however, more prudent by saying: "Father Scheiner, a Jesuit, has played this trick on him, as it is believed" XV, 141), as well as the Austrian Mathias Bernegger

(XVII, 365). For a response by a Jesuit author to these statements see Soccorsi 1963, 82-84.

[102] For example, de Santillana 1955, 286 ff. proposes a reconstruction of the facts as brilliant as it is debatable. On the other hand he admits later on: "But the final decision was taken by the Pope at Castel Gandolfo and it carries his imprint" (de Santillana 1955, 301).

[103] The example of what had happened on the occasion of the "Morandi case" (see Chapter 5) is instructive. Despite the fact that Galileo's adversaries had wanted to involve him, the Pope on that occasion kept intact his esteem and trust in Galileo.

[104] It is absurd to think that Urban VIII would have been able to ignore for very much longer or even for always the contents of the *Dialogue* without the activity of Galileo's enemies. We know how much time he had dedicated to conversations with Galileo concerning the plans for the book. And we know that he had repeatedly requested Ciampoli and Riccardi for information about what was going on with the book itself. Indeed, it is very possible (for me rather probable) that Urban VIII had come to know of the actual publication of the *Dialogue* from some person hostile to Galileo, or at least someone alarmed and scandalized because the tendency of the book was clearly in favor of Copernicus, before he was informed by Ciampoli or Riccardi. And such persons would, who knows, have brought to the Pope's attention the fact that his "theological" argument had been put in the mouth of the "stupid" Simplicius. All of that could have, I repeat, hastened the reaction of Urban VIII. But in any case he would have known of the publication of the *Dialogue*, and he would have certainly wanted to check on his own, or at least have others check for him, whether Galileo had observed their agreement and specifically how he had expounded and given evidence for the argument, or rather the arguments, which according to the Pope were decisive for nullifying any attempt whatever to explain the system of the world which was based on human reason alone.

CHAPTER 7

THE "GALILEO AFFAIR"

FROM THE TRIAL'S END UNTIL TODAY

1. *Galileo returns to Florence. The* Two New Sciences
    published in Holland

The purpose of this book has not been to give a complete
biography of Galileo, but rather to reconstruct through the
events of his life the origins, the development and the conclusion
of his drama as a scientist and a believer. The eight and one
half years between the end of the trial and the death of Galileo
will, therefore, receive only a brief treatment. This certainly does
not mean that I give less value to that period from either a
human or a scientific point of view. In fact, Galileo was never as
great as he was in those final years, which saw him wrestling
with incredible courage and tenacity against so much physical
and moral suffering, so as to leave his most lasting scientific
testament, the *Discourses*.

The day after his condemnation and abjuration the
"imprisonment" of Galileo in the Holy Office was commuted to
one in the gardens of the Tuscan Embassy. And the following
week he was granted permission to move to Siena under house
arrest in the residence of his old friend, Archbishop Piccolomini.

After another six months, thanks to the intercession of the
Grand Duke, Urban VIII allowed Galileo

> . . . to return to his villa [at Arcetri near Florence] to live
> there in solitude, without summoning anyone, or without
> receiving for a conversation those who might come, and
> that for a period of time to be decided by His Holiness.
> (XIX, 389).

Even though in February 1638 Galileo, by now almost
completely blind and sick, will be allowed to move into a house
on his own property in Florence in order to cure himself, the
condition of house arrest will not be sweetened except to allow

him to go to Mass in a nearby Church.[1] And right up to his death the aged Galileo will have to experience how severe would remain the control under which he was held by the Holy Office.

We have already referred to the moral and physical suffering of Galileo in this final period of his life. Without a doubt the prohibition of the *Dialogue*, and especially the abjuration, had been for him one of his greatest sorrows. There awaited him after his return to Arcetri a still greater suffering of a different kind, the death of his daughter, Sister Maria Celeste. During his trial and the subsequent stay in Siena this young religious had been close to her father in a special way with letters from which there comes forth from this favorite daughter of Galileo's the full richness of heart, the profound intelligence and sensitivity, together with a religious conviction which was not at all ostentatious or forced. We can, therefore, well understand the increasingly important place that she had proceeded to occupy in her father's heart and thoughts and, consequently, the deep sorrow into which Galileo was thrown in April 1634 by her short illness and death.[2]

As to his physical sufferings, the cruelest was surely the one caused by his loss of eyesight. The topic of the worsening condition of his sight and then of his blindness comes back time and time again in Galileo's letters between 1637 and 1639, a moving human documentation of the hardest trial he had to undergo.[3] But Galileo was not the kind of person to give in to discouragement. In this twilight of his life we see him react to many misadventures and sufferings with a strength which appears prodigious.

Since it was by now no longer possible for him to carry on his explicitly Copernican program, Galileo had decided to put together in a definite systematic way his studies in dynamics, well aware that they had a "Copernican" importance even greater than that of his previous works. It was a long-term program and he certainly had no illusions that he could bring it to completion by himself. But the results accomplished by him in so many years of research constituted the basis for the new "natural philosophy" which, upon further development by others, would have led to a definitive replacement of Aristotelianism. Once this new "natural philosophy" had been set up, geocentrism would have been seen as a lost cause without any shadow of a doubt and the Church would have had to change her mind.

Spurred on by his friends and disciples, old and new, who had remained faithful to him even after the condemnation,[4] Galileo succeeded in carrying ahead his work, to which he gave the title: *Discourses and Mathematical Demonstrations about two new sciences belonging to Mechanics and local motions* (following Drake 1978 I refer to this as the *Two New Sciences*). It was printed in 1638 in Leiden, Holland by the famous Elzevier.[5]

Upon its publication this new work quickly became widely distributed, especially in France and Germany, where it awakened great interest.[6] Numerous copies quickly arrived also in Rome as Castelli informed Galileo in January 1639. This old faithful friend of Galileo's also informed him that permission had been given for its sale, so that he himself had requested a copy as had Cardinal Francesco Barberini (VIII, 14-15). In a few weeks the fifty copies which had arrived were all sold and many had not been able to get one (XVIII, 23). Obviously the ecclesiastical authorities had decided not to raise any problem for the printing of the *Two New Sciences*, and what is more in a Protestant country, once it was clear that there was no mention of Copernicanism in this work. And perhaps it had not displeased them that in this book, also composed in the dialogue form with the same interlocutors as the *Dialogue*, the figure of Simplicius had lost that pedantic and at times ridiculous character which had been its previous hallmark.[7]

There was a long delay before Galileo had the book in his hands, but unfortunately he could not see it since he was by now completely blind. Nevertheless, he must have felt a great joy at having thus brought to a completion his scientific testament.

2. *Galileo's last years and his death. The plan for a mausoleum in his honor is put aside.*

But neither this accomplishment nor his blindness signalled the end of Galileo's activities. Thanks to the help of friends, among whom Father Settimi of the Clerks Regular of the Pious

Schools,[8] and especially of his last and youngest disciple, Vincenzo Viviani (who remained at his side from October 1639 until his death), Galileo continued his scientific activity right up to the last weeks of his life with a truly extraordinary strength of spirit.[9]

Towards the end of 1641 the conditions of Galileo's health had continued to worsen as he himself informed his relative Alessandra Bocchineri Buonamici in the letter which is believed to be the last written by Galileo (XVIII, 374). He continued little by little to weaken and get worse and the end was not far off. According to what was written later on by Viviani, who witnessed Galileo's death together with his son, Vincenzio, and Evangelista Torricelli:

> On Wednesday, 8 January 1641 [1642] from the Incarnation at four o'clock in the night[10] at the age of seventy-seven years, ten months and twenty days, with philosophical and Christian constancy he [Galileo] rendered his soul to his Creator, sending it forth, as far as we can believe, to enjoy and admire more closely those eternal and immutable marvels, which that soul, by means of weak devices with such eagerness and impatience, had sought to bring near to the eyes of us mortals. (XIX, 623).

The news of Galileo's death was given four days later to Cardinal Francesco Barberini by the Nuncio in Florence, Giorgio Bolognetti.

> Galileo [il Galileo] died on Thursday the 9th, on the following day his body was privately placed in Santa Croce [Church of the Holy Cross in Florence]. The word is around that the Grand Duke wishes to provide a sumptuous tomb for him comparable to and facing that of Michelangelo Buonarroti and he is of a mind to give the modelling of the tomb to the Academy of the Crusca. Out of my respect for you I thought that Your Eminence should know this. (XVIII, 378).

"Il Galileo" (The Galileo), that was how the old ambassador to Rome, Guicciardini, used to designate him. With the same lack of respect as the ambassador, but without his spite and his preoccupation, the Nuncio could announce that "The Galileo" was finally dead and that, therefore, he had stopped once and for all causing trouble, at least in person, because there still remained the problem of the "sumptuous tomb" which the Grand Duke was considering. And the Nuncio, well educated by experience, had wanted to protect himself and so he informed the responsible party about it, "out of my respect for you".[11]

It is not known how Francesco Barberini reacted to the news. Certainly he informed the Pope and the latter spoke of it to Niccolini who was still ambassador in Rome. On that same day Niccolini gave a report to Florence on the contents of the conversation.

> This morning I found His Holiness seated in the usual place, but however on a portable chair; he appeared to me to be quite exhausted, and his head was so lowered that his shoulders were almost level with it. After some familiar exchanges, we came to speak of the new Cardinal Fiorenzuola, His Holiness praising him as a person of great talent and genius. . . And because on such an occasion His Holiness remembered that he had been Commissary of the Holy Office when the then Galileo Galilei was being examined on his book about the motion of the earth, he told me that he wanted me to share with him in confidence a particular and only for the simple purpose of conversation and really not that I should be obliged to write anything about it: it was that His Holiness had heard that the Most Serene Master [the Grand Duke of Tuscany] may have had plans to have a tomb for him erected there in Santa Croce, and he asked me if I knew anything about it. In truth I have heard it talked about for many days now, nonetheless I answered that I did not know anything about it. The reply from His Holiness was that he had heard some news, but did not yet know whether it was true or false; at any rate he nonetheless wished to tell me that it would not be at all a good example to the world that His Highness would do this thing, since he [Galileo] had been here before the Holy Office because of a very false and very erroneous opinion, with which he had impressed many others around here,

and had given such universal scandal with a doctrine that
was condemned. (XVIII, 378-379).

So we see that Urban VIII had not at all softened his
position with respect to his old "friend". It was almost nine years
since Galileo's condemnation and the Pope was still speaking of
a "very false and very erroneous opinion" and of "universal
scandal" given to Christianity. But certainly Urban VIII wanted
also to justify before Niccolini the intransigent severity of his
position with respect to Galileo. Still the fact that neither he nor
Francesco Barberini nor the Nuncio in Florence were capable of
a single word of human feeling with respect to the deceased is
something which cannot fail to strike us today. It probably also
struck Niccolini. But his long years of contacts with the Pope
must have taught him a great deal, including the wisdom of
"putting off to another time" the thought of a monument to
Galileo, as he counselled in the following part of the letter.[12]
This reaction of the ecclesiastical authorities to the news
of Galileo's death is in striking contrast with that of his friends
and admirers. On 18 January Luca Holste wrote the following:

> Today news has also come of the loss of Signor Galilei,
> which touches not just Florence, but the whole world and
> our whole century that from this divine man has received
> more splendor than from almost all the other ordinary
> philosophers. Now, envy ceasing, the sublimity of that
> intellect, will begin to be known which will serve all
> posterity as a guide in the search for truth. (XVIII, 378;
> trans. by Drake 1978, 436).

Holste was too optimistic in thinking that envy would cease
because of Galileo's death. Even though at Rome they did not
want to take a strong position, for the weak Ferdinand II the
advice of Niccolini, and perhaps also the words placed "skillfully"
in his ear by the Florentine inquisitor, were more than enough.
The Body of Galileo remained *for the moment* ". . . in a room
behind the sacristy" (XIX, 596) of the Church of the Holy Cross.

3.   *The mausoleum is finally built. The Holy Office allows a
conditional reprinting of the* Dialogue.

That *for the moment* had to go one for almost one hundred
years. It was, in fact, only in 1734 that the Holy Office gave
permission for the construction of a mausoleum, on the
condition, however, that they would be informed of the
inscription that was planned to be placed there (XIX, 399). On
13 March 1736 Galileo's remains were moved inside the church,
not far from the tombs of Michelangelo and Machiavelli. And the
following year the mausoleum was finally constructed with
money left for that purpose by Viviani.[13]

The fact that this time the Holy Office had not opposed the
construction of the monument nor the inscription which was
placed there[14] is indubitably an indication of the evolution in the
last scores of years of the attitude of the Roman ecclesiastical
authorities with respect to the Copernican theory. The new
"natural philosophy", the foundations of which had been
established by Galileo's *Two New Sciences,* had by now evolved
and been brought to completion by Isaac Newton in his great
work: *Philosophiae Naturalis Principia Mathematica* (1687). And
its knowledge and influence were by now spread throughout the
learned world of Europe and so superseded in a definitive way
the old Aristotelian "physics".

The new Newtonian physics had already given the true
theoretical justification for Copernicus' assignment of the Sun's
central position (with the modifications coming from Kepler's
three laws) and had thus conclusively demolished any geocentric
conception, including that of Tycho Brahe. And then in 1728 the
English astronomer, James Bradley, by discovering the
phenomenon of the aberration of starlight, had furnished the
first observational proof of the Earth's movement about the Sun.
And the Italian translation of the fifth volume of the
Philosophical Transactions, where it had been reported, made
this discovery known also in Italian scientific circles as of the
year 1734.[15]

And so we have that which Bellarmine himself had
admitted, that is, the necessity to reexamine the interpretation
of Scriptural passages regarding the motion of the Sun and the

stability of the Earth in the face of incontestable proofs to the contrary coming from "natural philosophy" and from astronomy. That necessity came to weigh more and more heavily on the Roman authorities and they could no longer ignore it.

On the other hand there was still the Decree of the Index of 1616 and the one of the condemnation of Galileo by the Holy Office of 1633. As we have seen, this latter had been the unavoidable juridical outcome of the excess of authority by which the Church had determined in 1616 that Copernicanism was opposed to Holy Scripture, thus pretending to close once and for all the question. Such an excess of authority had been implicitly recognized by various Catholic writers beginning with the period immediately following Galileo's condemnation.[16]

But in order that this excess of authority would be officially recognized by the Church, drastic changes would be required and they will only mature through a laborious process lasting for centuries. It is to this process that I would like to dedicate the following pages which necessarily present only a summary.

Let us go back, then, to the situation at the time of the construction of the mausoleum to Galileo. At a little more than 100 years from the trial the atmosphere was far from being ripe for a courageous examination of conscience by the Church. It was preferable, therefore, not to act head on, but "behind the scenes", with the hope that the embarrassing situation created by the existence of two anti-Copernican decrees in an age when there were no longer any reasonable doubts about the movement of the Earth,[17] could be overcome without fuss, without "scandalizing" the faithful and, to be precise, especially without compromising the prestige of the Church.

The permission finally granted for the construction of the mausoleum had been a first, quiet step in this direction. Seven years later in 1741 another step forward was accomplished by the Holy Office with the authorization of the first almost complete edition in four volumes of the works of Galileo (including the *Dialogue* but excluding the *Letter to Christina of Lorraine*), carried out through the initiative of the Abbot Giuseppe Toaldo and printed at the press of the Seminary of Padua in 1744.[18] The authorization of the Holy Office had been given in response to a letter of the inquisitor of Padua, who, on behalf of the printers of the Seminary of Padua, had communicated the request for permission to "reprint all of the works of Galileo Galilei, Florentine, with the obligation to print also all of the declarations to be prescribed by this Congregation [of the Holy Office] and with the other conditions expressed in said letter". The Holy Office decreed that the inquisitor would be permitted "the printing of the works referred to, observing, however, the conditions listed in the aforementioned letter" (XIX, 292). Unfortunately this letter of the inquisitor is not known, but one can deduce, it seems to me, the tenor of the conditions which it contained from the formulation of the preface placed at the beginning by Toaldo. In it he stated:

> This very famous dialogue, printed clandestinely [*alla macchia*] so many times, is finally published for free public use with the required permissions. Indeed, it merited this because of the unusual and exquisite doctrines which it contains and because of the supreme facility with which they are explained. As to the principal question of the motion of the Earth, we also are in conformity with the treatment and the declaration of the Author by stating in the most sublime way that it may not be nor must it be admitted to be other than a pure mathematical hypothesis, which is useful for explaining more easily certain phenomena. For that reason we have removed or reduced to a hypothetical format the marginal annotations, which were not or did not appear to be indeterminate; and for the same reason we have added the Dissertation of Father Calmet, where an explanation is given of the meaning of the passages in Sacred Scripture pertaining to this material as by common Catholic belief. For the rest the *Dialogue* appears in its integrity, except for some places where, in order to illustrate his point better, some additions have been made by the Author himself who has left this written in on the printed copy which is kept in this Library of the Seminary. These additions have been printed in different typeset in order to respect the good faith with which we are pursuing this work. Regarding these additions we again repeat the declaration written above, since we do not wish in the slightest matter to

depart from the venerated prescriptions of the Holy Roman Church.[19]

As we see, this preface contains a whole series of statements full of contradictions. At the beginning Toaldo justified the printing of the *Dialogue* "because of the unusual and exquisite doctrines which it contains". But when it came to the question of the motion of the Earth, these doctrines were qualified as not "other than a pure mathematical hypothesis" in conformity with "the treatment and the declaration of the Author". A "declaration" which, as we know, had been rejected as "a deceit" by the Holy Office in 1633. And the elimination of the marginal annotations carried out by Toaldo and the motivation for so acting were also in obvious contradiction with the qualification of "pure mathematical hypothesis". Moreover this statement was completely contradicted by the inclusion with the *Dialogue* of the sentence of condemnation and the abjuration of Galileo. The contradiction even deepened with the addition of the dissertation of Father Calmet on the meaning of the Scriptural passages "pertaining to this material", an addition which was completely superfluous if it was truly a question of a "pure mathematical hypothesis". All of these jarring contradictions seem to me very difficult to explain unless we suppose that Toaldo had been forced to write this preface in obedience to prescriptions from the inquisitor of Padua which were approved by the Holy Office.

I have dwelt on this example of Toaldo, because it seems to me to give a clear indication of how hesitant and ambiguous the readjustment to the new situation remained. The Roman authorities were trying to bring it about by slow steps and without creating any fuss.[20]

4.   *The Decree of 1616 is omitted from the new edition of the* Index *of prohibited books. The* Settele *case*

A subsequent confirmation of this attitude is found in the provision finally taken a few years later in 1757 by the Congregation of the Index to omit, in the new edition of the

Index of forbidden books (published the following year 1758), "the decree [of 1616] which prohibits all books which teach the immobility of the sun and the mobility of the earth" (XIX, 419). One might have expected that the omission of this decree would have brought with it the omission in the same edition of the books of Copernicus, Diego de Zuñiga, Foscarini, Kepler and Galileo. But such was not the case. Obviously, the omission of the decree of 1616 (which did not imply its formal and official revocation) was a fact which would have been noticed almost only by the experts, while the disappearance from the Index of the Copernican works would have created a great deal more fuss in the educated circles of Europe.

And so, precisely because of this concern to avoid "scandal to pious souls" and, even more so, out of fear at having finally to take a clear position with respect to the behavior of the Church, the books mentioned above remained on the Index of forbidden books right up to and including the edition of 1819.[21] There is no need to stress how much this delaying tactic went on at the expense of the real "decorum" and "good name" of the Church by leaving to the following generations the ungrateful task of seeking a definitive and unambiguous solution of the problem.

In fact, this inherited task presented itself in 1820 on the occasion of an almost unbelievable affair whose protagonists were the canon Giuseppe Settele (1770-1841), professor of astronomy at the University of Rome, "La Sapienza", and the Master of the Sacred Palace, the Dominican Filippo Anfossi. In 1818 Settele had published the first volume, dedicated to optics, of the *Elements of Optics and Astronomy* and now he wished to publish the second volume, dedicated to astronomy. This volume would teach the Copernican system as a thesis and not just a hypothesis. The Master of the Sacred Palace, Anfossi, denied permission for the printing, alleging a "disposition of 1606 [certainly an error for 1616] in which, when the question arose in Rome of printing a book which stated this motion [of the Earth], upon reviewing the book, it was decided that this assertion was erroneous and heretical.[22]

Thanks to an intervention in Settele's favor by the Commissary of the Holy Office, the Dominican Olivieri, and by the Assessor, Monsignor Turiozzi, Settele obtained that the examination of the question would be passed on to the Holy Office itself. After a thorough study of the problem on the basis of the documents available at that time,[23] on 16 August 1820 the cardinals of the Holy Office

> . . . decreed according to the opinion of the Father Consultor [Antonio Maria Grandi] who had written: "There is nothing contrary to the fact that one might defend the opinion of Copernicus on the motion of the earth in the manner in which today it is usually defended by Catholic authors; and as to the meaning [of this decision]: it means that it be suggested to the Most Reverend Master of the Sacred Apostolic Palace that he not prevent the printing of the Elements of the canon Giuseppe Settele; and then that it be suggested to Settele to insert in the said work some things whereby he shows that the Copernican opinion, as it is presently defended, is no longer subject to those difficulties to which it was liable in times gone by, before the observations which were subsequently completed". (XIX, 420)[24]

Despite the "suggestion" made to the Master of the Sacred Palace not to oppose any longer the printing of the Elements, he did not give in[25] and he persisted in his opposition. That made it necessary to have another decree of the Holy Office. Released on 11 September 1822 it said:

> The most excellent [cardinals] have decreed that there must be no denial, by the present or by future Masters of the Sacred Apostolic Palace, of permission to print and to publish works which treat of the mobility of the earth and of the immobility of the sun, according to the common opinion of modern astronomers, as long as there are no other contrary indications, on the basis of the decrees of the Sacred Congregation of the Index of 1757 and of this Supreme [Holy Office] of 1820; and that those who would show themselves to be reluctant or would disobey, should be forced under punishments at the choice of [this] Sacred Congregation, with derogation of [their] claimed privileges, where necessary. (XIX, 421).

This decree was approved two weeks later by Pope Pius VII.[26]

With this decree of the Holy Office the official *dossier* regarding the Copernican question is closed. Through an "irony of chance" (*ironia della sorte*)[27], which I would prefer to call "an irony of history", that same Holy Office, which in 1616 had imposed on Galileo the promise not to defend any more the Copernican opinion and which in 1633 had condemned him for having transgressed that promise with the publication of the *Dialogue*, was now seeing itself forced to threaten "punishments at its choice" against the ecclesiastics responsible for the printing of the book in Rome (the Masters of the Sacred Palace), should they further oppose permission for the Copernican books!

Thirteen years later in 1835, on the occasion of the new edition of the Index of forbidden books, the Copernican books, which had been condemned *nominatim* (and, therefore, the *De revolutionibus* as well as Galileo's *Dialogue*), were finally removed from the list. It was by then one hundred and fifty years after the publication of Newton's *Principia* and one hundred years after the first scientific confirmation of the Earth's motion of revolution about the Sun!

5. *The Galilean dispute in the XIX century and the "opening" of the Vatican archives to scholars*

But if the Holy Office (and the Church in general) was hoping to have thus resolved once for all the Copernican problem and, therefore, at least indirectly, that of Galileo, the following decades of the last century saw instead a development, in all its clarity and often virulence, of the question of the responsibility of the Roman authorities in the prohibition of Copernicanism and above all in the condemnation of Galileo. Without a doubt that was due to the dramatic spread and highlighting of that profound evolution of ideas which had had its beginning a century before with Illuminism and had reached an "explosive" phase with the French Revolution.[28] Even if, after the fall of Napoleon, the policy of the "Restoration" had sought to bring Europe back to the pre-revolution *status quo* and in a certain sense even the pre-Illuminism one, this effort had only hampered and slowed down momentarily that movement which subsequently came back and strengthened its thrust. As they confronted and opposed a Church always less able to maintain the ability to exert a doctrinal influence in Catholic countries, more and more substantial parts of the Church's old "faithful" were going on to swell the ranks of "laicism". This latter, in its most pugnacious form of protest represented by the "free thinkers", turned into "anti-clericalism", that is a movement of open warfare against what it considered as the oppression exercised for centuries by the Church in intellectual and spiritual matters.

As to the Catholics who continued instead to recognize the rights and the authority of the Church, they were often aligned in defensive positions, but not for that reason less "militant" than the positions of their adversaries. They thus became known as the "clericals".

In this situation of polemics, very often sharp and prejudiced, Galileo became, for his "lay" biographers, an emblematic figure, the symbol, that is, of the man "above all prejudices",[29] who becomes the martyr of intellectual and spiritual obscurantism. Instead, in the view of his Catholic biographers he was frequently the one ultimately responsible for his misadventures with his impetuous temperament, his scornful irony, the untimeliness of his actions directed towards making the Catholic Church recognize the Copernican vision of the world (despite the lack of conclusive proofs), and above all with his lack of sincerity which he displayed during the whole course of the trial.

For an objective reappraisal of the Galilean question it became ever more urgent for the Church to put at the disposition of scholars the documents concerning Galileo, kept in the pontifical archives. But towards the middle of the XIXth century the tensions and the antagonisms in intellectual matters, to which there were being added political considerations caused by the movement for the unification of Italy, were too strong to allow the Church a courageous stand on the issue. As usual, the pressures from outside were the factors which prepared and subsequently made it impossible to delay the change of attitude of ecclesiastical authorities.

The first of such pressures came about precisely on the occasion of the revolutionary movements which led in 1848-1849 to the constitution of the ephemeral *Roman Republic* and to the concomitant flight of Pius IX to the stronghold of Gaeta. That brief interregnum made possible in March 1849 the entrance of the Minister of Finances of the Republic, Giacomo Manzoni, into the Archives of the Holy Office with the intention of searching out the documents regarding the Galileo trial. Manzoni entered again later on in the company of his friend Silvestro Gherardi (who shortly thereafter became Minister of Public Education). On that occasion they hurriedly compiled copies of documents which interested them. Specifically, Gherardi transcribed from the registry of the *Decrees* those texts which he could find[30] and which he used later on for his publication: *The Trial of Galileo Reseen through Documents from a New Source*, which appeared in 1870 in Florence as an abstract of the *Rivista Europea*.[31]

Once pontifical sovereignty was restored in Rome, the fact that the Archives of the Holy Office had been violated could not but concern the ecclesiastical authorities. An attempt to fend off possible blows in advance (as, in fact, the one which would come from Gherardi twenty years later) was carried out by Marini, the Prefect of the Secret Vatican Archives with his work: *Galileo and the Inquisition. Critical-Historical Memories Directed to the Roman Academy of Archaeology* (1850).[32] Despite the fact that Marini was at that time one of the very few (even among ecclesiastics) who could freely consult the volume of Galileo's trial, which a little before by the desire of Pius IX had been placed in the Secret Vatican Archives, he was careful not to give an integral edition of it. On the contrary, Marini limited himself to sporadic citations of documents here and there in his book whose fundamental purpose was to offer an apology for the behavior of the Holy Office with respect to Galileo, by dissipating the suspicions of an inhuman rigor of the treatment of him during the trial of 1633.

The work of Marini was severely criticized by the Frenchman Henri de L'Epinois, who obtained from the successor of Marini, Agostino Theiner, permission to consult the volume of the trial of Galileo. But despite the intention of de L'Epinois to publish in its entirety the contents of that volume, the copies of the documents were transcribed too hurriedly and were not any further compared with the originals. So the book which L'Epinois published in Paris in 1867 with the title: *Galilée, son procès, sa comdamnation d'après des documents inédits*, did not correspond to expectations.

Not much better than the work of de L'Epinois was that of his severe critic, Domenico Berti. He also obtained permission to consult the volume of the trial and in turn he published in 1876 a book entitled: *Il processo di Galileo Galilei pubblicato per la prima volta* (The trial of Galileo Galilei published for the first time). This work spurred de L'Epinois to a new edition of the trial documents, carried out with a greater scientific rigor. It was published in 1877 in Paris with the title: *Les pièces du procès de Galilée précédées d'un avant-propos* and it turned out to have a value quite superior to that of Berti because of the care with which the text of Galileo's trial was reproduced with interesting historical and explanatory notes.

A still greater critical rigor and an even more scrupulous fidelity to the reproduction of the texts characterizes the work published in the same year (1877) at Stuttgart by the German scholar Karl von Gebler: *Die Acten des Galileischen Prozesses* (Proceedings of the Trials of Galileo). That work followed by a year the then highly praised biography of Galileo by the same author (von Gebler 1876): *Galileo Galilei und die Römische Kurie* (Galileo Galilei and the Roman Curia). As we see, the Roman authorities had by now set off in the direction of opening the Vatican Archives, but they limited access to very few scholars and under very rigorous conditions.[33]

A more effective liberalizing program began only in 1880-1881 with the opening of the Secret Vatican Archives decreed by the new Pope Leo XIII. The most conspicuous fruit of this program, as to Galilean studies, was the complete edition of all of the documents concerning Galileo's trial, which are contained in Volume XIX of the National Edition of the Works of Galileo, edited between 1890 and 1909 by Antonio Favaro.

The same Pope Leo XIII dealt later on in 1893 in his encyclical *Providentissimus Deus* with the problem of the relationship between Sacred Scripture and Science and he based his treatment on theological principles very similar to those used almost three centuries before by Galileo in his *Letter to Christina of Lorraine*. A reference, at least, to the Galilean problem, which was at the center of disputes in that epoch profoundly influenced by the spirit of laicism and positivism, would have been more than proper. Instead the Pope limited himself to an allusion, formulated in extremely cautious terms, to errors committed by individual Church Fathers and, in following epochs, by their interpreters in the interpretation of Biblical passages which were related to questions which today we consider scientific:

> From the fact that we must take a position of strenuously defending the Sacred Scriptures it does not follow that we should maintain equally all of the opinions expressed by individual Fathers and later by their interpreters in the act of declaring its meaning. In fact, in the case of the explanation of Scriptural passages which deal with physical questions, they held to the opinions of their time with the results that *they perhaps did not always judge truthfully and stated things which are no longer approved today.* (Denzinger and Schönmetzer 1967, No. 1948; italics by Fantoli).[34]

As we see, even in the time of an "open" Pope such as Leo XIII, the Church was still quite far from wishing to make even a single explicit mention of the Galilean problem. It seemed preferable instead to respond in an indirect manner to the attacks and the criticisms by encouraging the publication of works of an apologetic character by Catholic authors.[35]

6. *The Galileo of Pio Paschini and Vatican Council II*

A first attempt on the part of the Church to overcome this "apologetic position" occurred with the initiative taken in 1941 by the Pontifical Academy of Sciences[36] for the publication of a biography of Galileo on the occasion in 1942 of the 300th anniversary of his death. On the basis of the opinion of the commission set up specifically for that purpose, the President of the Academy, the Franciscan Agostino Gemelli, assigned the work to Monsignor Pio Paschini, professor of Church History and

Rector at the *Pontificio Ateneo Lateranense* (Pontifical Lateran University) in Rome.[37] A little later, on the occasion of the inauguration of the sixth academic year of the Academy of Sciences with Pope Pius XII present, Gemelli clarified the intent of the planned work by declaring:

> . . . Pio Paschini . . . will give us not just a life, but rather he will present us the figure of Galileo by situating his work in the historical framework of the knowledge of his time and by thus again putting . . . the figure of the great astronomer in its true light.

And Gemelli concluded:

> The planned volume will therefore be an effective demonstration that the Church did not persecute Galileo but it abundantly helped him in his studies. It will not however be a work of apologetics, because this is not the task of scientists, but of scientific and historical documentation.[38]

Even though a deadline had not been given to Paschini, the wish was clear that the work would be published not too long after the 300th anniversary being commemorated. This was a wish which cannot help but cause wonder, if one thinks of the nature of the planned work (of "scientific and historical documentation") and of the fact that the author was not an expert in scientific questions and had not up until then, even in the field of history, had the occasion to be involved with Galilean studies. Nevertheless, with great application Paschini dedicated all of his free time to the study of the documents and of the main biographies of Galileo,[39] and thus succeeded in bringing the work to its completion in only three years.

Nonetheless, the results of that scrupulous and honest research by Paschini did not please the Roman authorities who considered that it was not very opportune to publish that voluminous work which was judged to be an apology for Galileo.[40] As we see, even though the original intentions of the Pontifical Academy of Sciences had been to publish an objective and impartial study, the ecclesiastical atmosphere characteristic of the pontificate of Pius XII was still too impregnated with the concern of safeguarding the "decorum and good name" of the Church to allow the publication of the book. That did not become possible until twenty years later (two years after Paschini's death), under the Pontificate of Paul VI, and only then after a correction of the text which often arrived at the point of altering or changing the meaning of it even on points of great significance.[41]

The pontificate of Pope Paul VI saw, as is known, the conclusion of that great effort of the Second Vatican Council, begun by Pope John XXIII, to rethink the position and role of the Church in the modern world. Particularly important to that end was the Pastoral Constitution *Gaudium et Spes* whose theme was, as a matter of fact, that of the Church in the modern world. It was promulgated in December 1965 at the last session of the Council. Given that theme, it was not possible to ignore the consideration of the relationships between the vision of the Christian faith and that of modern science, which plays such a large part in today's world. During the preparatory phase of the document the proposal was put forth for a frank recognition of the errors committed by the Church with respect to Galileo,[42] and it became partially accepted by the "joint commission" which dedicated a new paragraph (No. 40) to the question of the autonomy of culture, where a brief mention was made of the error of the condemnation of Galileo.[43] But against the appropriateness of making such a mention there was, among others, the intervention of the co-president of the commission, Monsignor Pietro Parente. It is thus summarized in the proceedings:

> Galilei. Not appropriate to speak of it in this document - so as not to ask the Church to say: I have been wrong. [The Galilean question] should be judged on the basis of those times. In the work of Paschini everything is put in its true light.[44]

As a result of this opposition of the majority, the preference was to insert in the definitive text of *Gaudium et Spes* (at paragraph 36) the following words:

At this point may we be permitted to deplore certain mental attitudes, sometimes found too among Christians, which come from not having sufficiently understood the legitimate autonomy of science, and which, giving rise to misunderstandings and controversies, draw many spirits to a point where they hold that science and the faith are opposed to one another.

And to the text at this point was added the following note: "See Pio Paschini, *Vita e Opere di Galileo Galilei*, 2 vol., Pont. Academia Scientiarum, Vatican City State, 1964". As we see, Paschini's work, which only two years earlier had still been considered "not appropriate" by Monsignor Parente himself and which had finally been published just in time for this honorable citation by the Council, all of a sudden received the seal of an official document. With very few exceptions, such as most probably that of Monsignor Parente, none of the "Conciliar Fathers" was obviously knowledgeable of the fact that this extraordinary "rehabilitation" of Paschini's work had been made possible only by means of the changes already mentioned (see Note 41), especially those more important and drastic ones which concerned the original judgement of Paschini on the behavior of the Church in 1616 and in 1633.

It is truly regrettable to have to realize that the concern to save the "decorum of the Church" remained so strong and radical, even in the new climate of the Second Vatican Council, as to result in the citation by the same Council (and moreover in the very context of its solemn declaration on the freedom of "scientific research"!) of a work which, with its tortured history and with the "corrections" (see Note 41) with which it was published, did not indeed provide a proof of such freedom and which the author himself would have certainly refused to recognize as his own.

Given that almost all of the "Conciliar Fathers" were completely in the dark about the behind the scenes of that publication, it would be completely wrong to cast the responsibility for what happened upon the Council itself. But the fact that a solemn declaration was linked to such an episode only makes heavier the responsibility of those who originated the affair.

7.   *John Paul II and the frank recognition of the errors of the past*

Despite the persistence of this traditional attitude of the defense of the good name of the Church, which, as we have seen, operated with success right up to the final phases of the Second Vatican Council, the process of rethinking the identity of the Church, its finality and at the same time its concrete journey in the course of history, set forth by the Council itself, could not but provoke the collapse of many "taboos" and of many false senses of shame. And among these there were, as we have amply seen thus far, also those concerning the "Galileo case". To wish to ignore the responsibility of the Church in it had become by now completely anachronistic in the religious climate which was in rapid and at times dramatic evolution during the first ten postconciliar years. Thus we come to the discourse given on 10 November 1979 by the present Pope John Paul II to the Pontifical Academy of Sciences on the occasion of the 100th anniversary of the birth of Albert Einstein.[45]

In this discourse the Pope dealt at length with Galileo, taking his cue from the words of the President of the Academy who had stated that, like Einstein, Galileo had also characterized an epoch. Among other things Pope John Paul II said:

> The greatness of Galileo is known to everyone, like that of Einstein; but unlike the latter, whom we are honoring today before the College of Cardinals in the apostolic palace, the former had to suffer a great deal - we cannot conceal the fact - at the hands of men and organisms of the Church. The Vatican Council recognized and deplored certain unwarranted interventions . . . (Bucciarelli 1980, 79).

(At this point there followed the citation of the Constitution, *Gaudium et Spes*, which we have reported above together with the footnote). The Pope continued:

> To go beyond this stand taken by the Council, I hope that theologians, scholars and historians, animated by a spirit

of sincere collaboration, will study the Galileo case more
deeply and, in a loyal recognition of wrongs from whatever
side they come, will dispel the mistrust that still opposes,
in many minds, a fruitful concord between science and
faith, between the Church and the world. I give all my
support to this task, which will be able to honor the truth
of faith and of science and open the door to future
collaboration. (Bucciarelli 1980, 79).

As a concrete sequel to this proposal of Pope John Paul II
a Commission was constituted with various sections (exegetical,
cultural, scientific-epistemological and historical-juridical). In the
letter establishing the Commission, the wish was expressed that
"the work be carried out without delays and that it lead to
concrete results".

The first of such concrete results was the publication of
Galileo Galilei, 350 ans d'histoire 1633-1983, Tournai, 1983 (for
Italian and English editions see Poupard 1984), which was
intended to bring together the results obtained up until that
time in the study of the Galilean question.[46]

Without a doubt of greater importance was the publication
of *I documenti del processo di Galileo Galilei* (The Documents on
Galileo Galilei's Trial) edited by Pagano with the collaboration
of A.G. Luciani (1984), which appeared the following year.[47]
Based on an extensive consultation of the documents relative to
Galileo conserved in the Vatican Archives and in those of the
Holy Office, it has value not only in the sense of a verification
of the scrupulosity and scientific probity of the collection of the
documents inserted by Favaro in the National Edition of
Galileo's Works, but also in the sense that it confirmed that the
work of Favaro had already provided, with very few exceptions,[48]
the totality of the documents concerning Galileo's trial which
have been found up to the present time. But, although it has
offered an important contribution to Galilean historiography,
Pagano's publication cannot give assurance that there do not
exist other documents, in the archives mentioned above or in
those of other Roman Congregations, which could throw light on
the Galilean question.[49] Despite their great diligence it was not
possible for the editors of the collection of documents, who were
not experts in Galileo, to examine all of the enormous volume of

documents which could have some relationship with Galileo. For this it would be necessary to have a real and complete opening to scholars of all of the Roman ecclesiastical archives. Despite everything the consultation of those archives is still bound by special permissions.[50]

Besides these two publications, since 1983 until the present there has been published, under the sponsorship of the scientific-epistemological section of the Pontifical Commission, a series of *Studi Galileiani*, under the editorship of the Vatican Observatory (see the list of these publications in Westfall 1989). These are valuable publications which allow one to deepen one's knowledge of particular aspects of Galileo and of other protagonists of the Galileo affair, as well more generally of questions concerning the relationship between science and faith.

For his part Pope John Paul II has repeatedly gone back to treat of Galileo. In May 1983 the Pope declared before numerous scientists:

> To you who are preparing to commemorate the 350th anniversary of the publication of the great work of Galileo Galilei, *Dialogue Concerning the Two Chief World Systems*, I would like to say that the experience lived by the Church at the time of and following upon the Galileo case has permitted a maturing and a more correct understanding of the authority which is proper to the Church. . . Thus is it understood more clearly that divine Revelation, of which the Church is guarantor and witness, does not involve as such any scientific theory of the universe and the assistance of the Holy Spirit does not in any way come to guarantee explanations which we might wish to maintain on the physical constitution of reality. That the Church was able to go ahead with difficulty in a field so complex, should neither surprise nor scandalize. The Church, founded by Christ who has declared himself to be the Way, the Truth, and the Life, remains nonetheless composed of limited human beings who are an integral part of their cultural epoch.[51]

Six years later, Pope John Paul II has treated again of Galileo on the occasion of his visit to the city of Pisa and he stated:

. . . How could we not remember at least the name of that
Great Man who was born here and who from here took his
first steps towards an ever-lasting fame? *Galileo Galilei* I
speak of, whose scientific work opposed improvidently in its
beginnings, is now recognized by all as an essential stage
in the methodology of research and, in general, in the path
towards the knowledge of the natural world.[52]

Most recently John Paul II returned to the theme of
Galileo on 31 October 1992 in a discourse given to the Pontifical
Academy of Sciences.[53] After having traced out a picture of the
causes and of the responsibility of the "tragic reciprocal
misunderstanding" between Galileo and the new science on the
one hand and the theologians on the other, the Pope spoke of "a
sort of myth" in existence "beginning with the century of
Illuminism and down to our own days", because of which the
Galileo case has become "the symbol of the claimed refusal, on
the part of the Church, of scientific progress, or of a dogmatic
obscurantism opposed to free search for the truth". And he
added: "From the Galileo case one can draw a lesson which
applies to today, in view of analogous situations which come
forth today and which may come forth in the future".

Thus 350 years after the death of Galileo when the Pope
of that time, Urban VIII, had declared, as we have already seen,
that Galileo had made himself guilty of an "opinion very false
and very erroneous and which had given scandal to the whole
Christian world", his modern successor recognizes not only his
greatness on the scientific level but also the role which that
drama had played in the "more correct understanding of the
authority which is proper to the Church" and that drama's
function of "teaching" the Church. To be sure much water has
passed under the bridges of the Tiber in these 350 years of
history.[54]

From what has been presented above should we come to
the conclusion (as has happened in various sectors in the press
in their comments on the Papal discourse of 31 October 1992
cited above) that the "Galileo Affair" is closed? From the point
of view of historical research there is no doubt that the large
number of noteworthy studies which have appeared in the last
scores of years in an intellectual climate for the most part free

of the extremisms which characterized so many of the conclusions of past studies, has led to a considerable number of results which by this time can be considered definitive. But historical research (especially research so complex and so much still in need of clarification as that with respect to Galileo) is an undertaking which can never be considered "closed", nor obviously declared to be so.˙ My personal opinion is that this is true even from a "religious" point of view. Indubitably, the actual position of the Church with its frank recognition of past errors establishes an important and definitive achievement. But it seems to me erroneous, even from a religious point of view, to claim that by now the "Galileo Affair" is a thing of the past, a question closed forever. It remains, and should remain, "open", on the contrary, as a severe lesson of humility to the Church at all levels and as a warning, no less rigorous, not to wish to repeat in the present or in the future the errors of the past, even the most recent past.

NOTES

[1] For the permission granted to Galileo to move to Florence see XIX, 287. Urban VIII had agreed to that permission for health purposes but with the condition that Galileo would not leave his home and would not receive anyone at home so that he might treat "of that condemned opinion of the past about the motion of the earth". As to the permission to go to Mass on feast days, it was prescribed, as Francesco Barberini communicated to the inquisitor of Florence in the month of April, that Galileo would do this at convenient times and with little display and few accompanying persons. The one exception to these severe measures seems to have been the permission granted Galileo to meet on 16 October 1635 at Poggibonsi (about 50 kilometers south of Florence on the way to Siena) his old disciple from Padua, Francois de Noailles, who the year before had become the French Ambassador in Rome. (XVI, 500-501, 512). Three or four years later Galileo received (this time at Arcetri) a visit from John Milton. During his trip to Italy Milton stopped in Florence in August-September 1638 and then came back again in February 1639. It is more probable that he visited Galileo during his first and longer sojourn in Florence. On this visit and on its echoes in Milton's *Paradise Lost* see Paschini 1965, 609. See

also Guthke 1990, 127-131 for many more particulars on Milton's position with respect to Copernicanism.

[2] See Galileo's letter of 27 April 1634 to Geri Bocchineri (XVI, 84-85) and that of 15 July to Elia Diodati (XVI, 116).

[3] See XVII, 94, 126-127, 237. On 19 December 1637, the date of this last letter, Galileo had lost the sight of both eyes. On 2 January he wrote to his friend Diodati the by now famous words:

> . . . alas, my lord, your dear friend and servant Galileo has for the past month become irreparably blind. Now imagine, Your Lordship, how afflicted I am as I think about that sky, that world and that universe which I with my marvelous observations and clear demonstrations had opened up hundreds and thousands of times more than had been commonly seen by the sages of all bygone centuries; now for me it is diminished and limited so that it is not any greater than the space I occupy. The novelty of what has happened has not provided me time enough to adapt myself to be patient and tolerant with this misfortune, a condition to which at any rate as time goes by I must accustom myself. (XVII, 247).

[4] Beginning with Castelli and going on to Bonaventura Cavalieri and Evangelista Torricelli, who were indubitably the most gifted of his disciples.

[5] The decree of condemnation of Galileo by the Holy Office had not been published in France. For that reason in 1635 at Strasbourg the Latin translation of the *Dialogue* was printed by Mattia Bernegger who had been requested to do it by Elia Diodati (XVII, 364-365). This printing had been entrusted to the Dutch editor Elzevier who in the following year 1636 also edited the *Letter to Christina of Lorraine* together with a Latin translation. All of this encouraged Galileo to have recourse to the same editor for the *Two New Sciences* after plans to have it printed in Austria and then in Moravia had failed. Furthermore, since Holland was a Protestant country, worries about permission from ecclesiastical authorities were thus eliminated.

[6] Just one year later Mersenne, who had had the possibility of looking at Galileo's manuscript before the printing, was able to publish in Paris a reworking in French of the *Two New Sciences*, wherein he kept Galileo's dialogue form with the same interlocutors.

[7] The matter was also noticed by Castelli, who in his letter to Galileo of 12 February 1639 (XVIII, 26) showed his surprise and also a certain regret because the colorful nature of the previous figure of Simplicius had thus been lost.

[8] As a matter of fact, it was to Settimi that Galileo dictated an important letter of 12 February 1639 on the cycloid, addressed to Cavalieri (XVIII, 153), and various additions and corrections to the *Two New Sciences*.

[9] To his scientific activity on the theoretical plane there was added his practical research, especially in relation to the problem of the determination of longitude at sea. I have already spoken of this project of Galileo, taken up again by him right after his return to Arcetri and which he developed in lengthy dealings with the Dutch and Spanish governments. Even though they were definitively brought to a halt towards the end of 1639, Galileo continued to think of problems connected with that project and specifically of the problem of constructing more precise clocks than those then in use. As Viviani will write later on, Galileo would have had in 1641 the idea of applying the principle of the pendulum to clocks, but it is more probable that this idea had come to him even earlier. However that may be, because of his loss of sight Galileo was not able to make drawings nor construct models, and he was forced, therefore, to speak of the idea to his son Vincenzio. The latter did not have the time to construct the model until several years after his father's death in 1649 with the help of Viviani. But the premature death of Vincenzio that same year did not allow the project to go beyond the stage of modelling. Nevertheless it seems certain that the invention of the pendulum clock by Galileo had happened before that of Huygens.

[10] According to the usage of that epoch "four o'clock in the night" corresponds to our 10-11 p.m. The majority of the biographers of Galileo report with Favaro this date of 8 January indicated by Viviani. On the other hand the Nuncio to Florence (see the remainder of the main text) gives the date of 9 January. The death certificate and that of burial, reproduced in Favaro (XIX, 558) are not altogether in agreement.

[11] Another person who had hastened to give news of Galileo's death had been the Florentine inquisitor, Muzzarelli. We know this from the response sent to him on 25 January 1642 by Francesco Barberini in which the Cardinal wrote:

> . . . His Beatitude [the Pope], in agreement with my fellow Most Eminent Cardinals, has resolved that you, with your usual skill should see to it that it gets to the ear of the Grand Duke that it is not a good thing to construct mausoleums to the corpse of one who has been given a penance by the Tribunal of the Holy Inquisition, and who died while the penance was still in effect because good

people could be scandalized to the prejudice of His Highness's [the Grand Duke's] piety. But if indeed it will not be possible to turn aside this plan, you should give a warning that on the epitaph or inscription to be placed on the tomb one should not read words which could injure the reputation of this Tribunal. You should give the same warning to whoever will preach the funeral oration and take care to see it and consider it carefully before it is recited or printed. His Holiness places the solution to this business in the wise understanding of Your Reverence. (XVIII, 379-380).

[12] Also in a subsequent meeting with Urban VIII on 8 February 1642 Niccolini found the Pope to have the same severe attitude with respect to the deceased Galileo. (XVIII, 381-382).

[13] Viviani had organized a collection right after the death of his master, precisely for the construction of the mausoleum planned at that time. It seems that the sum collected by Viviani was left by the latter to Galileo's descendants. According to the Florentine Inquisitor Ambrogi's report of 8 June 1734 to the Holy Office, the money available at that time amounted to about 4000 scudi and had been left "since the year 1689 by a descendant of the named Galileo through a legal will to his heirs" (see Pagano 1984, 214-215).

[14] The mausoleum consists of the urn containing Galileo's remains on top of which is mounted his bust, and to each side there is a statue, one representing Astronomy and the other Geometry. There is no third statue to Philosophy to which Galileo, as we know, would have been even more attached than to the other two. It is probable that this omission was due to reasons of symmetry. At any rate this void is filled by the Latin inscription: «GALILAEUS GALILEIUS PATRIC. FLOR. ASTRONOMIAE GEOMETRIAE PHILOSOPHIAE MAXIMUS INSTAURATOR NULLI AETATIS SUAE COMPARANDUS HIC BENE QUIESCAT». (Galileo Galilei, Florentine Patrician, very great Innovator of Astronomy, of Geometry and of Philosophy. Incomparable to anyone of his time. May he here rest well).

[15] Pierre Costabel states:

If the discovery of stellar aberration, furnishing a geometrical argument for the movement of the earth around the sun, dates back to James Bradley a century earlier, these findings were not published until 1797-1805 [sic!]. They did not give rise to the important complementary work of Herschel and Bessel until publication dating ca. 1820, and these required several years for a wide and thorough circulation. On the other hand, it was Foucault's experiment of 1851 on the rotation of the plane of oscillation of a pendulum relative to the earth that marked the first crucial evidence of the earth's spin. It is also not without value to recall that the works of Copernicus were removed from the Index in 1757 [sic!], and those of Galileo in 1822 [sic!]. If it is true that scientific discoveries have had an influence in Vatican decisions, it can be pointed out that such decisions sometimes occurred when discussions in the scientific world had not been concluded by the appearance of definitive argumentation. And we can congratulate ourselves that the church did not wait for the progress of these discussions to lift condemnations that, at their time, caused much regret to many religious minds. (Costabel 1984, 197).

I have given this long quotation, because the statements of Costabel contained therein seem to be influenced in their inexactness by an "apologetic" preoccupation which one would have preferred not to find in a publication such as the one in which this article appeared and which had been planned with the intention of offering an impartial summary of the results of Galilean studies by now well established.

[16] For a summary review of the works published in Catholic countries on the Copernican question and on the theological interpretation to be given to the condemnation of Galileo see: Paschini 1965, 591-598; Viganò 1969, 227-242; D'Addio 1985, 113-116; Grant 1984; and Brandmüller and Greipl 1992, 21 and ff.

[17] At least no educated and well informed person could doubt it. There remained, of course, those not few in number who preferred to keep their eyes shut so they would not have to admit scientific progress and the by now unassailable conclusions. We will see right away how persons of this latter type will remain active in the Church hierarchy right up the first decades of the 19th century.

[18] Born in 1719, Toaldo was just a twenty-five year old at the time of the printing of the Works of Galileo. A supporter of mathematics and astronomy, he was the founder of the Astronomical Observatory of Padua. This explains his interest and his admiration for Galileo. For his edition of the *Dialogue* Toaldo was able to make use of a precious copy of the first edition, kept in the library of the Seminary of Padua, with marginal notes and autograph additions by Galileo himself (VIII, 10, *Avvertimento* by Favaro). See also Restiglian 1982, 235. How did it ever happen that that copy belonging to Galileo had wound up in Padua? Together with other writings of Galileo's it

was in the possession of his son Vincenzio and had passed to the latter's son Cosimo. This grandson of Galileo had for five years (1658-1663) been secretary of the bishop of Bergamo, Gregorio Barbarigo, who was himself interested in astronomy and mathematics, a great friend of Viviani and an admirer of Galileo. In fact, it seems that Cosimo had been recommended to Barbarigo by Viviani, if not by the Grand Duke of Tuscany himself. All of this explains why Cosimo would donate this precious volume of the *Dialogue* to Barbarigo before he left Bergamo to enter the Congregation of the Mission of Saint Vincent de' Paoli (he will die there as a member in 1672). As to Barbarigo, appointed in the meantime cardinal, he went on in 1664 to rule the diocese of Padua and he carried the volume of Galileo with him. He then left it, at his death, in the Seminary library of that city where it is still found. See Bellinati 1982, 221.

[19] Quoted by Favaro 1966-1968, Vol. II, 315. In the preceding pages (311-314) Favaro reviews the previous attempts that had been made to publish the works of Galileo. Upon the failure of the initial project (Galileo himself had thought of doing this and it was then taken up again by Viviani) to publish the Italian texts together with a translation into Latin (the language of the educated classes of Europe), partial editions of the works of Galileo and of his correspondence (the *Dialogue* and the *Letter to Christina of Lorraine* being excluded because of the 1633 condemnation) were completed at Bologna in 1655-1666 with the cooperation of Viviani himself and later on in 1718 in Florence. A secret edition, comprising indeed the Copernican writings of Galileo (the *Dialogue* and the *Letter to Christina of Lorraine*, together with the *Letter of Foscarini* and some passages taken from Kepler and from de Zuñiga), appeared in 1710 in Naples (even though, for security reasons, it was said to be published "in Florence"). It is undoubtedly this edition to which Toaldo refers in the preface to the *Dialogue* quoted in the text when he states that this text was "printed clandestinely many times". For full details on this first new edition of the *Dialogue* see Ferrone 1982, 136 ff. Brandmüller tends to present this fact, as well as the edition by Toaldo, as a proof of "the liberal way with which [by this time] the ecclesiastical and state censure were applied". It appears to me that such an interpretation is clearly contradicted by the binding conditions which were placed on the edition of Toaldo and which we have discussed in the text. As for the 1710 edition, the fact of the false indication of the city where it was printed seems to prove that it was published without ecclesiastical permission. And this seems to be confirmed by the remarks of Toaldo mentioned above about previous "clandestine" editions, as well as be the fact that

the *Letter to Christina of Lorraine*, which is included in the 1710 edition, was excluded from the edition of Toaldo.

[20] This attitude remained despite the more open climate begun by Pope Benedict XIV (1740-1758). Already, during the time he had been at Bologna as Archbishop, he had taken an interest in the sciences and he set up a professorship and a museum of anatomy there. When he became Pope he reformed the *Accademia dei Lincei* (the Lincean Academy), to which, as we know, Galileo belonged. This was subsequently called the *Accademia dei Nuovi Lincei* (the New Lincean Academy), and he instituted professorships of chemistry and of mathematics at the University of Rome, "La Sapienza". He kept up relationships and correspondence with numerous European scientists, such as Pierre de Maupertuis, a member of the French Academy of Sciences and the author of a 1732 treatise, *Discours sur la figure des astres* (Discourse on the shape of the celestial bodies), in which he followed the theory of Newton. Soon after his election to the Pontificate, Benedict XIV saw to the reform of the Congregation of the Index by prescribing that alongside the theologians there would also be experts on "profane" questions for the purpose of guaranteeing a greater balance in the examination of publications. For his moderation and openmindedness this Pope enjoyed the respect of numerous European intellectuals, including severe critics of the Church, such as Voltaire. The first edition of the *Encyclopédie* of Diderot and d'Alembert (Tome IV, 1754) contained in the article on Copernicus a long passage on Galileo in which the hope was expressed that, as had already happened in France, the error of condemning Galileo would also be recognized in Italy. The *Encyclopédie* added:

> Such a change would be truly worthy of the enlightened pontiff who governs the Church today [Benedict XIV]; it falls upon him, a friend of scientists and a man of science himself, to dictate rules to the inquisitors on this subject, as he has already done on other more important matters".
> (Quoted by Jacqueline 1984, 190).

I have made use of this article also for the previous information on Benedict XIV. Indubitably the provision of the Index of 1757 (on which see later in the text) was favored by this new climate created by the "enlightened pontiff". But, as amply proven by both the past and recent history of the Church, even the most open Pope has to deal with the "inertial forces" established by central Church organisms. And that inertial force saw to it that the works of Copernicus would remain, despite everything, included in the edition of the Index published in 1758 and, as we will see, well beyond that.

[21] The fact that the omission of the decree of 1616 in the new edition of the Index of forbidden books, which appeared in 1758, did not at all carry with it the cancellation of the Copernican works (and, therefore, the *Dialogue*) from the same Index has escaped many authors, even very recent ones. See, for example, Costabel 1984 where, as we already know, it is stated that "the elimination from the Index of the works of Copernicus took place in 1757 and of those of Galileo in 1822". As we will see, the works of Copernicus and of Galileo will be finally eliminated from the Index only on the occasion of the printing of the edition of 1835. Jacqueline 1984 speaks of "the explicit removal from this catalog [of forbidden books] of the books which taught the motion of the earth and the immobility of the sun (1757)". According to this author the provision of 1757 would even have led in that same year to the cancellation of the *Dialogue* from the Index! See also Jacqueline 1984, 192-193. Even D'Addio 1985, 117 seems to have fallen into a similar error:

> Once authorization had been granted for the printing of the *Dialogue*, it no longer made any sense to prohibit the books which supported the theory of the movement of the earth; in 1757 with the decree of the Congregation of the Index there were excluded, as a matter of fact, from the new Index all of the writings which supported the heliocentric theory.

We know under what conditions the authorization had been granted for the printing of the *Dialogue* in the Works of Galileo edited by Toaldo. It was not indeed a matter of recognizing the true contents of the work of Galileo! Nor do I feel, naturally, that I can share what the same D'Addio adds as a comment:

> . . . the implicit consequence was a substantial, even if indirect, declaration of nullity of the essential presupposition on which the sentence of 1633 was based: the motion of the earth was false in philosophy. In this way the judgement on Galileo's behavior and the condemnation to abjure no longer had any juridical justification: in the end the nullity of the presupposition struck the sentence as a whole.

May I be allowed to make the comment that the essential presupposition on which the sentence of 1633 was based was not that the motion of the Earth was *false in philosophy*, but that the immobility of the Sun was directly contrary to Holy Scripture. A simple *false in philosophy* would certainly not have justified the abjuration imposed on Galileo in so far as he was "vehemently suspected of heresy". The resolution of the Index in 1757 had no intention, not even indirect, to touch the abjuration of Galileo and even less to invalidate the juridical justification for it. So true is this that, as we have already said and will see better as we proceed, the *Dialogue* will remain on the Index together with the other Copernican works right up to 1835.

[22] See Settele's Diary for 3 January 1820 in Maffei 1987, 285 ff. In all probability the book to which Anfossi alludes is the *Letter to Father Foscarini*. Thus Anfossi committed three errors: the *Letter* had already been printed (in Naples) before the response of the qualificators and this concerned, as we know, not the *Letter* (at least directly) but the Copernican statements of Galileo, just as they were reported in Caccini's accusation. Finally, the subsequent decree of the Index had avoided qualifying the Copernican doctrine as heretical, defining it only as "false and altogether contrary to Divine Scripture". As for the meaning of the term heresy, which appears in the sentence condemning Galileo in 1633, I have already explained its wider "inquisitorial" meaning. Anfossi, however, will affirm its stricter "theological" meaning and later on, relying on it, will maintain that the motion of the Earth about the Sun was a theological heresy and that, therefore, the statement at the beginning of Settele's book ("The Earth moving about the Sun") was also strictly heretical. See *Scritto di Filippo Anfossi, da lui presentato al Papa [agosto 1820]* (A Writing of Filippo Anfossi Presented by Him to the Pope [August 1820]) in Brandmüller and Greipl 1992, 310 ff.

[23] Among the documents regarding the Copernican question the dossier of the trial of Galileo was missing, having been carried to France at the time of Napoleon I and brought back only in 1844. See Pagano 1984, 10 ff.

[24] D'Addio (1985, 119) comments thus on this decision of the Holy Office:

> The sentence of 1633 was thus substantially and definitively "annulled": the intention of Galileo, his profound conviction that there did not exist any opposition between the new science of nature and the Word, that one could demonstrate as true the Copernican theory without failing in the principles of the faith, was correct, Catholic, in agreement with the usual way in which it is now defended by Catholic authors (*modo quo nunc ab auctoribus catholicis defendi solet*): he was a Catholic author, because he had always been one. Furthermore, the accusation of heresy was recognized as unfounded: the trial *de vehementi*

haeresis suspicione, the condemnation to a solemn
abjuration, which caused him so much affliction, appeared
now as a true and proper "excess of power".

Once again I take the liberty of dissenting. The decision in question of
the Holy Office is certainly to be considered as an abrogation *de facto*
of the decree of the Index of 1616, even though as usual the cardinals
of the Holy Office avoid going on to an explicit abrogation, *de jure*.
That which concerned them at that time was not the question of the
truth of Copernicanism, by now generally recognized even in Catholic
countries, but the manner in which they could save the "*decentiam S.
Sedis*", that is, the good name of the Holy See. It is precisely this
which one reads in the passage immediately preceding the one reported
in the text:

> Concerning the request of the Professor Giacomo [sic]
> Settele . . . for permission to print his work on the doctrine
> of the mobility of the earth, denied to him by the Master
> of the Sacred Apostolic Palace . . . it is ordered that
> someone of the consultors write on the posture to be taken
> in this matter so as to safeguard the good name of the
> Holy See. (XIX, 420).

As we have seen in the text, the writing was in fact presented by the
Barnabite Father Grandi. Working in agreement with Olivieri and
basing himself on his argumentation, he had tried to realize the
objective of saving the good name of the Holy See, substantially by
emphasizing the fact that the Copernican system, by then recognized
even by Catholic authors, had been purified from errors and
inconsistencies which had made it unacceptable in its original form.
This was equivalent to maintaining that the Church had not erred in
1616 by putting on the Index a work at that time so defective at the
level of physics and that now the Church was legitimately authorized
to approve it after its errors were corrected. And it was, as a matter
of fact, this which "was suggested" to poor Settele to make skillfully
known in his work. As to the nullification of the condemnation of
Galileo, there is not a word about that. And even less on the injustice
or "excess of power", as D'Addio prefers to call it, of the abjuration
imposed on Galileo. The reasoning with respect to Copernicus was
certainly valid also in Galileo's case, although Olivieri-Grandi make no
mention of it. That is, the Church had been right in condemning *the
latter from a scientific point of view*, because Galileo had also upheld
heliocentrism in its unsatisfactory Copernican form and, moreover, he
had not been able to give convincing proofs of heliocentrism. There

remained the question of the abjuration, which was outside the scientific considerations, but not a word is said about it (as not connected, fortunately for the Roman authorities, with the problem of Settele's book). Any comment on this attempt at a solution of the problem created for the Church by having put Copernicus on the Index seems superfluous.

[25] See the document of Anfossi cited in Note 22.

[26] Maffei 1975 has discussed the affair of Canon Settele's book. In complete agreement with what I have stated in Note 24, he concludes that the Settele case led the Church to a *de facto* and definitive acceptance of the Copernican system but it did not go so far as to have a decision taken on the "Galileo Affair". Later on the Settele affair was reviewed, in addition to D'Addio 1985, also by Pagano 1984, 41, Note 89. It then became the central theme of Maffei's book (1987) in which the author has also published all parts of the Diary of Settele which have to do with the question. From this one concludes that Settele believed, too optimistically, that his action would have brought about a "rethinking" of the Church on the trial of Galileo. Even more recently Brandmüller 1992 has dedicated the last part of his book to the Settele affair. All of the documentation concerning the affair has been most recently published by Brandmüller and Greipl 1992. Brandmüller gives special importance to the part played in the whole affair by the Commissary of the Holy Office, Olivieri, who in his Reflections (Brandmüller and Greipl 1992, 184-287) had already formulated the principles which justified the permission to print the work of Settele. Brandmüller also shows how Olivieri in 1822 became the champion of the initiative to have cancelled from the Index the works of Copernicus, de Zuñiga, Foscarini and Galileo. The initiative came up against the resistance of the consultors of the Holy Office, who were, as usual, concerned about "the image that the Curia would have given", and so it was necessary to wait until the new edition of the Index in 1835 to see the efforts of Olivieri realized (Brandmüller and Greipl 1992 127-128 and 440-484). While I find important and meritorious the contribution made by Brandmüller with the publication of all of this documentation (as well as that already quoted in Chapter 3, Notes 78 and 80), I am not able to share in any way his final judgement, namely, that Olivieri had thus "found the definitive solution to the Galileo case" (Brandmüller 1992, 184), a judgement which is taken up again in Brandmüller and Greipl (1992, 129-130).

[27] The expression is from D'Addio 1985, 118.

[28] The fact that Napoleon, after his conquest of the Papal States, had had all of the Roman archives, including those of the Holy Office, carried to Paris is a meaningful indication of such an atmosphere. It

seems that the same Napoleon had conceived a project for an edition of the volume of the Archives of the Holy Office which contained the documents of Galileo's trial. For a detailed and interesting exposition of this whole affair, I recommend Pagano 1984, 10 ff. Napoleon's interest in the Galilean question had been undoubtedly nourished by the tendencies towards Illuminism with which France was impregnated both before and after his coming to power. In the *Bibliografia galileiana*, published by Favaro 1896, there are included 236 volumes dedicated to Galileo in the XVIII century (the "century of Illuminism"). To these must be added at least 18 others, inserted for the same period by G. Boffito in his *Supplemento alla Bibliografia galileiana* (1943).

[29] Thus had he been described by the French Encyclopedia.

[30] As I have already indicated (see Note 28 above) the Archives of the Holy Office had been transported in 1810, together with other pontifical archives, to Paris. After the fall of Napoleon, the part of the archives which were not destroyed or lost, returned to Rome between 1815 and 1817. But the volume on Galileo's trial (the one most requested by the Roman authorities) was not returned until 1843 after long vicissitudes. Gherardi, nonetheless, was not able to consult it because Pius IX, before he took refuge in Gaeta, delivered it to Monsignor Marini, Prefect of the Secret Vatican Archives. This was yet a further indication of the importance attributed to it by the Church and of the will of ecclesiastical authorities of that time to guard jealously those Galilean documents.

[31] Given the haste with which he had to copy the documents which he found during the brief interregnum of the *Roman Republic*, Gherardi was not able to check his copies against the originals. Thus the work came out full of errors, in addition to being vitiated by the anticlerical spirit of the epoch.

[32] More than 30 years earlier Marini had been assigned to the recovery in Paris of the Archives of the Holy See. On that occasion he became responsible for the "enormous historical archival damage" brought about by the sale of a large number of the acts of the trials of the Holy Office and of the Inquisition as paper for pulp to a Parisian paper dealer. See Pagano 1984, 21-22. Might I add that, despite this, Marini was made the Prefect of the Secret Vatican Archives!

[33] This was to the particular disadvantage of Italian scholars, given the political tension between Italy and the Holy See, following the occupation of Rome by the Italian government in 1870.

[34] One should note that Leo XIII had already, just two years earlier on the occasion of the refoundation of the Specola Vaticana (Vatican Observatory), entrusted to Church scientists, expressed with specific actions his intention to support science. And that intention was

repeated in the founding document (*motu proprio*), *Ut Mysticam*. See Maffeo 1991, 207-210. Even this document, however, shows how far one still was from the conditions for a true dialogue between the Church and science.

[35] Such, for example, were the works of two Jesuits: that of H. Grisar 1882 and that of A. Müller 1909. The same apologetic tendency is noted in the articles dedicated to Galileo in the *Dictionnaire apologétique de la Foi catholique*, 1911 and in the *Dictionnaire de la Théologie catholique*, 1920.

[36] This Academy was born in 1936 by the transformation of the *Pontificia Accademia dei Nuovi Lincei* (Pontifical Academy of the New Lincei). By giving it new statutes and a new name, Pius XI wished that its activity would be carried out in a way as to favor the meeting of the Christian faith with modern science. The members of this Academy are elected by reason of their particular competence in areas which are of scientific interest to this institution and with no criterion as to their religious confession.

[37] Pio Paschini (1878-1962) was born in Friuli, Northern Italy and had studied at the seminary of Udine, where, after his ordination to the priesthood, he became professor of Church History. He was distinguished for his openmindedness and this, in that period of "anti-modernist" reaction, gave birth to some suspicions about him. In 1913 he was called to Rome to teach the same subject at the then Lateran Seminary. He had been selected instead of Angelo Roncalli, the future Pope John XXIII. He became Rector in 1932 of the *Ateneo del Seminario Romano* (University of the Roman Seminary, which later became the Pontifical Lateran University) and he remained in that office until 1957. Two months before his death he was made a bishop by Pope John XXIII.

[38] See *L'Osservatore Romano*, 1-2 December 1941, pages 3-4. It is difficult to see how the, at least *de facto*, clearly apologetic intent traced out in the first of these two sentences could be reconciled with the required characteristics of the work which are emphasized in the second sentence. We will see immediately how this latent contradiction in the *desiderata* of the Pontifical Academy of Sciences and, in all probability, of the Roman Church authorities themselves, did not fail to produce its fruits. For his part Paschini, with the openmindedness and scrupulous honesty which were characteristic of him, sought to realize his assignment of "scientific and historical documentation" without worrying about "apologies".

[39] Paschini was able to work with the rich documentation of the Vatican Library and he obviously made abundant use of Favaro's original *Edizione Nazionale delle Opere di Galileo* and other studies of

this great Galilean expert. As we shall see, later on Paschini will be reproached for having become too subject to the severe judgements on the Jesuits contained in some of those studies of Favaro. And he will be criticized for having based himself predominantly on Italian publications for his documentation on Galileo. But given the urgency of his work Paschini obviously had to make choices. Putting all of the criticisms aside, the amount of work which he brought to a completion in less than three years is most noteworthy, the more so if one considers that his lack of an adequate preparation in the field of science made it necessary for him to make an effort at documentation which, by his own confession, was quite heavy. That in such conditions his book, alongside of its value with respect to the collection of bibliographical material, prevalently in Italian, and even more so with respect to the honest evaluation of that material, should clearly show its limits was inevitable and Paschini himself (who had tried from the beginning to decline the assignment) was well aware of this.

[40] For details of the misfortunes of this publication, see Bertolla 1980, Nonis 1980 and Maccarrone 1980. This last article has appeared in four other journals in 1963, 1969 and 1979 with numerous variations (see Simoncelli 1992, 16, Note 1). For a synthetic exposition of the same argument, based on the documentation furnished by Bertolla and Maccarrone, see Tramontin 1982, 159-167 and also Simoncelli 1988 (95-102), Scandaletti 1989 (241-246) and Brandmüller 1992 (19-20). Later on the question has been treated as the central theme in the work of Simoncelli 1992. While Maccarrone has used, for the reconstruction of the life of Paschini and of the affair regarding Paschini's book, *Vita e Opere di Galileo Galilei*, documents in his possession and various testimonies which he had collected, Bertolla has on the other hand drawn from a very extensive file, conserved in the Udine seminary library, of correspondence between Paschini and his friend Vale, an old colleague of Paschini at that seminary. Furthermore, when Bertolla compared Paschini's manuscript for the book on Galileo (the manuscript was donated to the Udine seminary library by Monsignor Maccarrone after the publication of the book had taken place in 1964) with the text given to the printers, he was the first to notice the changes which Paschini's original had undergone. Maccarrone had made no mention of these changes, at least in the article I have consulted. I will discuss these changes shortly. As to Simoncelli, his book presents all of the documentation put in the public domain by Bertolla and Maccarrone plus numerous other citations from the Paschini-Vale correspondence. Furthermore, Simoncelli has personally checked against the Paschini manuscript the modifications made to it after the author's death and he thus confirmed the

conclusions of Bertolla. As these studies show, the first negative reactions to the manuscript presented by Paschini towards the end of January 1945, came from within the Pontifical Academy of Sciences. The chancellor Salviucci and, thereafter, the academician Armellini, Director of the Astronomical Observatory of Rome (who had previously judged the sections of the book dealing with scientific matters to be sufficiently accurate), considered the work to be too favorable to Galileo, in particular as to what concerned the judgements on the Jesuits and, therefore, they thought that its publication would not be proper. The manuscript was sent, together with this negative judgement (backed in the meantime by Gemelli himself), to the Secretariat of State. Pope Pius XII (who had previously shown great interest in and encouragement for the work of Paschini) then decided to transmit it to the Holy Office for an opinion on the matter. The censors of the Holy Office extended the examination to other points, thus aggravating the negative judgement on the appropriateness of publication, which was thus definitively blocked. Neither the vibrant protests of Paschini to Gemelli nor the steps taken with Monsignor Montini, the then Deputy Secretary of State (Sostituto), who showed him much understanding and tried to help him, were able to disentangle the situation. Finally, Paschini was received by the then Assessor of the Holy Office, Monsignor Ottaviani, and he heard repeated some criticisms of his work which had been already orally transmitted to him by Montini: that he had done nothing else but an apology for Galileo, and that he had not given due importance to the fact that Galileo had not brought forth decisive proofs for his heliocentric system and that he had used phrases or expressions which were too drastic (see the letter of Paschini to Montini of 12 May 1946, quoted by Maccarrone 1980, 82-83, Note 112). Paschini on that occasion requested and obtained the return of the manuscript and he kept from then until his death the strictest silence on what had happened.

[41] According to what Maccarrone 1980 states (see Note 40) after the death of Paschini, who had left the manuscript of the book to him in his will, he felt the moral obligation to work towards having the work published. A first step taken in 1963 with Monsignor Dell'Acqua, the new Deputy Secretary of State (Sostituto) found "benevolence and encouragement". On his part the Jesuit V. Monachino, Dean of the Faculty of Church History at the Pontifical Gregorian University, upon being asked to examine the manuscript, gave an opinion in favor of its publication. Obviously one of the reasons for requesting this opinion, as Maccarrone recalls, was that "the first accusations had been provoked by the harshness of Paschini towards the Jesuits in the Galileo affair" and so it was important to have a judgement on the matter by a

Jesuit. A little later, the election of Pope Montini having occurred, Maccarrone carried his activity further ahead. When he had recourse to Salviucci, chancellor of the Pontifical Academy of Sciences, he found him favorable ("now, what a coincidence" comments ironically Simoncelli 1992) , the more so since the 400th anniversary of the birth of Galileo was approaching. But there remained doubts about the appropriateness of publishing the manuscript of Paschini as it was. After his first reading of it Father Edmond Lamalle of the Historical Archives of the Society of Jesus in Rome had pointed out its limits and things that were lacking. Also at the Holy Office, the Assessor Pietro Parente put forth reservations about the usefulness of the book since "it substantially added nothing new", and he too questioned the "appropriateness" of its publication. But the imminent conclusion of the Second Vatican Council put in a new light (see the following part of the main text) the usefulness of publishing Paschini's work and thus the Holy Office finally on 4 March 1964 gave its approval. As Maccarrone states, that approval did not imply any reservations and, therefore, there was no need to correct the work. But, as we know, there were still reservations on the part of the Pontifical Academy of Sciences with respect to the scientific value of the work, which had remained, for all that, more than twenty years without being brought up to date. The Academy President, the well known Belgian scientist Monsignor Lemaître, consented in the end to the project with the condition that Father Lamalle would review the text and would furnish it with an *Introductory Note* in which the reasons were to be explained for why the work was published as it was despite its limitations and the practical impossibility of bringing it up to date. In fact, Lamalle prepared the *Introductory Note* (two times, since the first draft had appeared too severe to Monsignor Maccarrone) and in it he stated that his interventions "both in the text and in the notes" had been "by his own choice most discrete, being limited to some   rectifications . . . which seemed indispensable and to a minimum of bibliographical updating". In reality, as made evident by Bertolla and confirmed by Simoncelli (and as I myself have been further able to verify from the notes) the interventions of Lamalle amount to about 100 in the text and at least about 60 in the notes. Indubitably Lamalle, as an expert in the history of the Galilean period, must have found himself in disagreement with Paschini's judgements which must have seemed to him not a few times to have been too "rude" and simplistic. Faced with the number and the importance of the modifications which he would have considered necessary ("It was not possible to pose the question of modifying the perspectives of the book: it would have been just as easy to write another one" he himself confessed in the *Introductory Note*), it was possible that Lamalle was in good faith when he defined his interventions as "by his own choice most discrete". However, precisely because he was an historian and a consummate archivist, Lamalle knew very well that one is not authorized to retouch even a simple word of a text which is published posthumously (and therefore with no possibility to obtain the consent of the author) without distinguishing the word thus changed from the original. That holds all the more for interventions on entire sentences and especially when the meaning of the statements are profoundly altered, as in this case the five or six drastic interventions with respect to Paschini's judgement on the events of 1616 and 1633, or at least three others concerning Father Scheiner. No one would have objected to the addition to Paschini's original of a critical apparatus, clearly distinct from the text, where it would have been perfectly right to suggest the changes which were judged necessary (and which in many cases appear in fact justified). It is difficult to imagine that Lamalle (whom I have known personally and whose qualities as a scrupulous researcher I have been able to appreciate) did not consider the problem. And if he did consider it, what prevented the publication of a critical edition? And why in the world did he not then protest when he saw his *Note*, entitled: *Nota Introduttiva all'Opera*, published by the Pontifical Academy of Sciences only in the *Miscellanea Galileiana* (*Pontificiae Academiae Scripta Varia 27, Ex Aedibus Academicis in Civitate Vaticana, MCMLXIV*) in three volumes, where the first two comprised Paschini's work, *Galileo*, and not in the other editions which contained only Paschini's work? These other editions include the one of the Pontifical Academy of Sciences itself, which was published almost simultaneously with the *Miscellanea* edition in the manner of a reprint of the first two volumes, and the one published a year later by Herder in a single volume through the initiative of Maccarrone. (This is the edition listed in my Bibliography under Paschini 1965). As to this latter edition (Paschini 1965) I have been able to ascertain that a certain number of copies were distributed for sale after the first bound pages were torn out and replaced with new pages glued in which contain a preface by Maccarrone. The most obvious interpretation of this fact is that the editor must have taken out the *Note* of Lamalle, which had not been authorized, and replaced it with the preface of Maccarrone. It is truly difficult to understand why it was not desirable to preface this edition with at least the most important part of Lamalle's *Note*, precisely that part which concerned Paschini's work. The reader would thus have found at least a mention of Lamalle's interventions, however much they were open to discussion and unspecified. There naturally also remains the question as to why Lamalle himself gave no reply whatsoever after Bertolla had made

clear the mass of his interventions and the manner in which they had
been made. Too many questions still remain unanswered to be able to
draw secure conclusions about the responsibility (most probably not
limited to Lamalle) of such a publication.

[42] The text of the proposal XIII, *De Ecclesia in mundo hujus
temporis* (The Church in the modern world), had been sent on 3 July
1964 to the Council Fathers together with a booklet of Additions. In
Chapter IV, No. 22 of this proposal: *De cultura rite promovenda* (On
the need for a just promotion of culture) with the Addition III: *De
culturae progressu rite promovendo* (On the need for the just promotion
of the progress of culture), there was recognized "the legitimate
autonomy of the sciences and of all of culture". The discussion of the
proposal began on 20 October and the problems of culture, as
Maccarrone notes, "had relatively little space, [being] discussed in the
congregations of 30 October and 4 November" (Maccarrone 1980, 90).
It was, as a matter of fact, during this latter congregation that the
auxiliary bishop of Strasbourg, Monsignor Arthur Elchinger, put forth
the proposal of a declaration on Galileo. In all probability this initiative
of Elchinger was taken in tune with a petition that had been
transmitted to Paul VI towards the end of March by the President of
the *PAX Romana* and which was signed by the Dominican, Father
Dominque Dubarle, an ecclesiastical counselor of the *Union des
Scientifiques Français*, and by numerous scientists and university
teachers, who requested "a solemn rehabilitation of Galileo" by the
Church. This petition was forwarded by the Secretariat of State to the
Holy Office on 15 April. The Holy Office considered it, as we will see
in Note 44 to follow, in its meeting of the following 15 May.

[43] The paragraph said:

> May we be permitted to deplore certain mental attitudes
> which are alien to healthy scientific research and which in
> centuries past showed themselves visible perhaps internal
> to the Church itself (*intra ipsam Ecclesiam fortasse videri
> sese manifestaverunt*). Giving birth as they did to disputes
> and controversies, these mental attitudes were the cause
> whereby many ended by opposing science to faith with
> most grave damage to both. On the other hand, these
> errors are easily understood, given those times, and they
> were not exclusive to Catholics, since similar attitudes
> were present in other religions [the writer of this
> paragraph probably wanted to say: other religious
> denominations such as Protestants]. Still it is necessary
> that we do our best, in so far as human frailty permits,
> that such errors, as for example the condemnation of

Galileo, are never repeated. (Maccarrone 1980, 91 gives the Latin original).

As we see, in this text, formulated in an extremely cautious way, the reference to Galileo was reduced to a very small insertion. Something quite different, therefore, than the frank confession suggested by Monsignor Elchinger. And yet even this reference was deemed, as we will see immediately, "inappropriate"!

[44] The intervention of Monsignor Parente took place in the meeting of 1 April 1965. See Maccarrone 1980, 91-92. Parente, as Assessor of the Holy Office, was completely knowledgeable about all that had been decided by the Holy Office since the year before. As we know (see Note 41 above) the Holy Office had on 4 March given a favorable vote to the publication of Paschini's *Galileo* and two days later that decision had been approved by Paul VI. An echo of that resolution is found in the response of the Holy Office to the request for a "rehabilitation of Galileo" which had been forwarded to it by the Secretariat of State (see Note 42 above). The memorandum sent to the cardinals of the Holy Office in preparation for the meeting of 15 May 1964 said:

> Such a rehabilitation of Galileo by the Church has already implicitly taken place a long time ago. Since 1757 there has been removed from the book of the Index the phrase: "all books which teach the mobility of the earth and the immobility of the sun"; this principle was again sanctioned by the Congregation of the Index in 1822. In the following edition of 1835 the Index of Forbidden Books no longer reports as listed on the Index itself the famous work of Galileo Galilei, "Il Dialogo sopra i due massimi sistemi del Mondo Tolemaico e Copernicano" [Dialogue of the Two Chief World Systems of Ptolemy and Copernicus]. *Recently the Pontifical Academy of Sciences is preparing the edition of the posthumous book of Monsignor Pio Paschini on Galileo* [italics by Fantoli]. On the occasion of that meeting the decision of the Cardinals was: "*Satis provisum per publicationem operis mons. Paschini; si autem ei placuerit S. Pontifex, data occasione, aliquid dicat de eadem quaestione*" (Enough care has already been taken of this subject through the publication of the work of Monsignor Paschini; if, nonetheless, it should please the Supreme Pontiff, he might, when the occasion offers itself, say something about the issue in point).

And the document ends with: "S.mus 17-VI-1964: Adprobavit" (His Holiness has approved on 17 June 1964, R.V. 1964.13.Prot.304/64). The suggestion of the Holy Office was taken up by Paul VI a year later but in an extremely indirect manner. Speaking at Pisa on 10 June 1965 on the occasion of the closing of the Eucharistic Congress, Paul VI said among other things:

> And then to the People of Tuscany, who today welcome us on our visit, we repeat the same words: Love, Sons of Tuscany, the Christian faith of this privileged and blessed land; the faith of your Saints, the faith of the great spirits, whose immortal memory has been celebrated yesterday and today, Galileo, Michelangelo and Dante; the faith of your fathers . . .

As we see, even though Galileo was included among "the great spirits" whose "immortal memory" was being celebrated and whose faith was being pointed to as an example for everyone, and even though his name was mentioned first (but in a discourse given at Pisa, his birthplace, that was only natural), there was not even the least mention of his condemnation by the Church. The same silence had been maintained antecedently, when the publication of Paschini's book occurred. A copy of the *Miscellanea* edition in three volumes (see Note 41 above) was offered to Paul VI shortly before the solemn audience granted to the Pontifical Academy of Sciences on 3 October 1964. On that occasion the Pope referred to those three volumes with the words:

> We have had before Our eyes the series of researches already published in the official collection of the "Commentarii" of the Pontifical Academy of Sciences, as well as the three volumes of the "Miscellanea Galileiana" which have been presented to Us in your name. (*L'Osservatore Romano*, 4 October 1964, page 1).

The Pope maintained an analogous silence when, in the course of a private audience on the following 3 November, Monsignor Maccarrone presented him with the reprinted edition of the two volumes of Paschini's Galileo. *L'Osservatore Romano* of 5 November 1964 in its column, *Nostre Informazioni*, gave the following report:

> In the same audience Monsignor Maccarrone offered to the August Pontiff the two volumes of the illustrious deceased Monsignor Pio Paschini "Vita e opere di Galileo Galilei" published by the Pontifical Academy of Sciences on the occasion of the Galilean centenary. His Holiness expressed

His fatherly pleasure at this double homage, noticing the
filial dedication and diligent care of all who had
participated therein [in this work]; and he imparted a
special Apostolic Benediction upon them.

Was Paul VI knowledgeable of what was implied in that "filial
dedication" and that "diligent care" of all those who had collaborated
in the publication? Even if we admit that he was informed of the
revisions which Lamalle had made (as I have said in Note 41 above,
Lamalle's *Note* was missing in the two volume edition offered to Paul
VI by Monsignor Maccarrone), in all probability he remained completely
in the dark as to the manner in which the revisions had been carried
out.

[45] For an English translation of this discourse see Bucciarelli
1980, 77-81.

[46] We have already had the occasion to cite articles contained in
this volume. To my regret I have to say that some of the contributions
seem to have been written in a hurry and with a degree of
impreciseness, at times serious, which noticeably hurt the overall value
of the work. One has the impression that the exhortation to carry out
the work "without delay" together with the necessity of having the
volume come out in time for the 350th anniversary of the trial and
condemnation of Galileo, have caused too much of a rush in carrying
out the project with serious prejudice, I repeat, for its scientific value.
And it would have been desirable to have had a more international
selection of the contributions and one less "confessional" (of the seven
authors five are French and five are ecclesiastics).

[47] We have already cited this important publication on numerous
occasions.

[48] On documents which are new with respect to those contained
in the Favaro edition see the Introduction of Pagano 1984, 42. The
most important are the originals of two decrees concerning the
proceedings of 1616 (XIX, 321) and of 1633 (XIX, 360-361). In Chapter
3 I have already had the opportunity to dwell on the first of these two
originals. Pagano 1984 also gives the document containing the request
for an opinion on *The Assayer*, found on the occasion of Redondi's
researches and used by him as the basis of the thesis of his book
(Redondi 1987).

[49] The discovery of the document used by Redondi seems to be
particularly instructive. Without the specific interest of a researcher
such as Redondi himself and a precise request formulated by him it is
probable that the by now famous "anonymous opinion on *The Assayer*
of Galileo" would not have been found, or, even if found, could not have

been evaluated in its true importance. I repeat that the research work of an archivist, even the most diligent and capable, has need, in this field of Galilean studies as in others, of assistance from the "clinical eye" of experts in the subject.

[50] Pagano himself has admitted that there could be documents not yet "discovered" when he wrote: "not much remains unexplored". Not much, perhaps, but there could be something interesting and that would justify an exhaustive search which I hope can be carried on further with cooperation between the Church archivists and the experts in Galileo. The discovery in the archives of the Holy Office of the documents cited first in summary by Brandmüller 1992 and now published in their entirety (Brandmüller and Greipl 1992), and used by me in notes 78 and 80 of Chapter 3, provide a confirmation that there was still something unexplored, and indeed of not little importance, after the publication of the documents by Pagano 1984.

[51] See John Paul II 1983.

[52] See John Paul II 1989.

[53] See John Paul II 1992.

[54] The new posture of the Catholic Church and the discourses of John Paul II have led certain sectors of the press to speak of a "rehabilitation of Galileo". I disagree absolutely with the use of this expression. Yes, Galileo had been judged "vehemently suspected of heresy" and for that condemned by the Church in 1633. But right from the time of the condemnation the more open minds of Catholic Europe considered the sentence unjust (even if they did not always have the courage, shown, for example, by the Archbishop of Siena, Piccolomini, to express their opinions frankly; see XIX, 393). And that judgement continually gained ground as time went on and as the ability of the Church to intervene against it weakened. On the basis of this "judgement of history" (which finally has now become proper to the Church itself) Galileo was never guilty nor such as to be condemned and in that sense he had no need of rehabilitation at that time, as, with even more reason, he has no need of it now.

BIBLIOGRAPHY

Baldini, Ugo 1984, "Additamenta Galilaeana I. Galileo, la nuova astronomia e la critica dell'aristotelismo nel dialogo epistolare tra Giuseppe Biancani e i Revisori romani della Compagnia di Gesù", in *Annali dell'Istituto e Museo di Storia della Scienza di Firenze*, IX, 2, 13-43.

_____ 1992, *Legem impone subactis, Studi su filosofia e scienza dei gesuiti in Italia 1540-1632* (Rome: Bulzoni Editore).

Baldini, Ugo and **Coyne**, George V. 1984, "The Louvain Lectures of Bellarmine and the Autograph Copy of His 1616 Declaration to Galileo", in *Studi Galileiani* (Vatican City State: Vatican Observatory Publications) Vol. I, No. 2.

Baldini, Ugo and **Napolitani**, Pier Daniele 1992 (eds.) *Christoph Clavius: Corrispondenza* (Pisa: Department of Mathematics of the University).

Banfi, Antonio 1962, *Vita di Galileo Galilei* (Milan: Feltrinelli).

Barone, Francesco 1983, "Diego de Zuñiga e Galileo Galilei. Astronomia eliostatica ed esegesi biblica", in *Critica Storica*, XIX, 3.

Bellinati, Claudio 1982, "Gregorio Barbarigo, Cosimo Galilei e il Dialogo sopra i due Massimi Sistemi nel Seminario di Padova (cod. 352)", in *Galileo Galilei e Padova* (Padua: Studia Patavina, Rivista di Scienze Religiose) 29, 3, 221-234.

_____ 1984, "Il Dialogo con postille autografe di Galileo", in *Novità Celesti e Crisi del Sapere*, ed.: P. Galluzzi, Annali dell'Istituto e Museo di Storia della Scienza (Florence: Giunti Barbèra) 127-128.

_____ 1991, "Galileo Galilei e lo Studio di Padova", *L'Osservatore Romano*, 2-3 September 1991, p.3.

Bertolla, Pietro **1980**, "Le vicende del *Galileo* di Paschini", in *Atti del convegno di studio su Pio Paschini nel centenario della nascita: 1878-1978* (Udine: Pubblicazioni della Deputazione di Storia Patria del Friuli: Tipografia Poliglotta Vaticana) 172-208.

Biagioli, Mario **1993**, *Galileo Courtier* (Chicago: University of Chicago Press).

Blackwell, Richard J. **1991**, *Galileo, Bellarmine and the Bible* (Notre Dame: University of Notre Dame Press).

Boffito,   Giuseppe **1933**, *Scrittori Barnabiti*, 3 Vols. (Florence: Leo S. Olschki).

_____ **1943**, "Bibliografia Galileiana 1896-1940. Supplemento alla Bibliografia Galileiana di Alarico Carli e Antonio Favaro", in *Indice Cataloghi del Ministero dell'Educazione Nazionale*, Vol. XVIII (Rome: Libreria dello Stato).

Bonansea,   Bernardino M. **1986**,   "Campanella's Defense of Galileo",   in   *Reinterpreting   Galileo*,   ed.:   W.A.   Wallace (Washington: Catholic University of America Press) 205-239.

Bortle, John B. **1981**, "Comets and How to Hunt Them", *Sky and Telescope*, 61, 123-125.

Brandmüller, Walter **1992**, *Galileo e la Chiesa ossia il diritto ad errare* (Vatican City State: Libreria Editrice Vaticana).

Brandmüller, Walter and **Greipl**, Egon J. **1992**, *Copernico Galilei e la Chiesa* (Florence: Leo S. Olschki).

Brodrick, James **1961**, *Robert Bellarmine, Saint and Scholar* (Westminster: Newman Press).

Bucciantini, Massimo **1995**, *Contro Galileo, Alle origini dell'Affaire* (Florence: Leo S. Olschki).

Bucciarelli, Brenno **1980**, "Speech of His Holiness John Paul II", in *Einstein Galileo* (Vatican City State: Libreria Editrice Vaticana) 77-81.

Bulferetti, Luigi **1964**, *Galileo Galilei nella società del suo tempo* (Taranto: Manduria).

Burstyn, Harold L. **1962**, "Galileo's Attempt to Prove that the Earth Moves", *Isis*, 53, 161-185.

Campanella, Tommaso **1971**, *Apologia per Galileo*, ed.: S. Femiano (Milan: Marzorati); translated by G. McColley as *The Defense of Galileo* (Smith College Studies in History, 1937); see also Campanella, Tommaso 1968, *Apologia di Galileo*, ed.: L. Firpo (Turin: Unione Tipografica Editrice Torinese).

Carugo, Adriano and **Crombie**, Alistair C. **1983**, "The Jesuits and Galileo's Ideas of Science and of Nature", in *Annali dell'Istituto e Museo di Storia della Scienza di Firenze*, Anno VIII, 2, 3-46.

Casanovas, Juan **1985**, "The Problem of Annual Parallax in Galileo's Time", in *The Galileo Affair: A Meeting of Faith and Science*, eds.: G.V. Coyne, S.J., M. Heller and J. Zycinski (Vatican City State: Vatican Observatory Publications, distributed by the Libreria Editrice Vaticana) 67-74.

Cioni, Michele, **1908**, *I documenti Galileiani del S. Uffizio di Firenze* (Florence: Libreria Editrice Fiorentina).

Clagett, Marshall **1971**, *Greek Science in Antiquity* (New York: Abelard-Schuman).

Clavelin, Maurice **1968**, *La philosophie naturelle de Galilée* (Paris: Armand Colin); translated by A.J. Pomerans as *The Natural Philosophy of Galileo* (Cambridge, Massachusetts: MIT Press, 1974).

Cohen, Morris and Drabkin, Israel E. 1975, *A Source Book in Greek Science* (Cambridge, Massachusetts: Harvard University Press).

Colombo, Giuseppe 1878, *Intorno alla Vita e alle Opere del P. Redento Barazano* (Turin: Vincenzo Bona).

Copleston, Frederick 1964, *A History of Philosophy*, 16 Volumes, Image Books Edition (Garden City, NY: Doubleday & Company).

Cornford, Francis M. 1971, *Plato's Cosmology. The Timaeus of Plato* (New York: Liberal Arts Press).

Costabel, Pierre 1984, "Galileo, Ieri e Oggi", in *Galileo Galilei, 350 Anni di Storia 1633-1983*, ed.: P. Poupard (Casale Monferrato, Italy: Edizioni Piemme) 196-209; see English translation listed under Poupard 1984.

_____ 1987, "L'atomisme, face cachée de la condamnation de Galilée", *Comptes-Rendus, série générale*, Tome 4, 39-365.

Costantini, Claudio 1969, *Baliani e i Gesuiti* (Florence: Giunti Barbèra).

Coyne, George V. and Baldini, Ugo 1984, "The Young Bellarmine's Thoughts on World Systems", in *The Galileo Affair: A Meeting of Faith and Science* (Vatican City State: Vatican Observatory Publications, distributed by the Libreria Editrice Vaticana) 103-110.

Coyne, George V., Heller, Michael and Zycinski, Joseph (eds.) 1985 , *The Galileo Affair: A Meeting of Faith and Science* (Vatican City State: Vatican Observatory Publications, distributed by the Libreria Editrice Vaticana).

Cozzi, Gaetano 1979, *Paolo Sarpi fra Venezia e L'Europa* (Turin: Einaudi).

Crombie, Alistair C. **1969**, *Augustine to Galileo*, 2 Vols. (London: Falcon Press).

D'Addio, Mario **1985**, "Considerazioni sui Processi a Galileo", *Quaderni della Rivista della Storia della Chiesa in Italia* (Rome: Herder) No. 8.

Dame, Bernard **1968**, "Galilée et les taches solaires", in *Galilée. Aspects de sa vie et de son oeuvre*, ed.: S. Delorme (Paris: Presses Universitaires de France).

Danjon, André and **Couder**, André **1935**, *Lunettes et Télescopes* (Paris: Editions de la Revue d'Optique Théorique et Instrumentale).

D'Elia, Pasquale M. **1960**, *Galileo in China: Relations through the Roman College between Galileo and the Jesuit Scientist-Missionaries (1610-1640)*, trans.: R. Suter and M. Sciascia (Cambridge, Massachusetts: Harvard University Press).

Delorme, Suzanne (ed.) **1968**, *Galilée. Aspects de sa vie et de son oeuvre* (Paris: Presses Universitaires de France).

Denzinger, Henricus and **Schönmetzer**, Adolfus, **1967**, *Enchiridion Symbolorum, definitionum, et declarationum de rebus fidei et morum*, 34th Edition (Freiburg im Breisgau: Herder).

Dijksterhuis, E.J. **1969**, *The Mechanization of the World*, trans.: C. Dikshoorn (Oxford: Oxford University Press).

Drake, Stillman **1957**, *Discoveries and Opinions of Galileo* (New York: Doubleday & Company).

_____ **1967**, *Dialogue Concerning the Two Chief World Systems* (Berkeley: University of California Press).

_____ 1968, "Galileo in English Literature of the Seventeenth Century", in *Galileo Man of Science*, ed.: E. McMullin (New York: Basic Books), 415-431.

_____ 1970a, "Renaissance Music and Experimental Science", *Journal of the History of Ideas*, XXXI, 483-500.

_____ 1970b, *Galileo Studies* (Ann Arbor: University of Michigan Press).

_____ 1978, *Galileo at Work: His Scientific Biography* (Chicago: The University of Chicago Press).

_____ 1986, "Reexamining Galileo's Dialogue", in *Reinterpreting Galileo*, ed.: W. A. Wallace (Washington: Catholic University of America Press) 155-175.

_____ 1987, "Galileo's Steps to Full Copernicanism and Back", *Studies in History and Philosophy of Science*, Vol. 18, 93-105.

_____ 1990, *Galileo: Pioneer Scientist* (Toronto: University of Toronto Press).

Drake, Stillman and **Drabkin**, Israel E. **1969**, *Mechanics in Sixteenth Century Italy* (Madison: The University of Wisconsin Press).

Dreyer, Johann L.E. **1953**, *A History of Astronomy from Thales to Kepler*, revised by: W.H. Stahl (New York: Dover Publications).

Duhem, Pierre **1908**, *Essai sur la notion de théorie physique de Platon à Galilée* (Paris: Hermann); translated by E. Doland and C. Maschler as *To Save the Phenomena: an Essay on the Idea of Physical Theory from Plato to Galileo* (Chicago: University of Chicago Press, 1969).

_____ 1913-1959, *Le Système du Monde* (Paris: Hermann) 10 volumes.

Ernst, Germana 1984, "Aspetti dell'astrologia e della profezia in Galileo e Campanella", in *Novità Celesti e Crisi del Sapere*, ed.: P. Galluzzi, Annali dell'Istituto e Museo di Storia della Scienza (Florence: Giunti Barbèra) 255-266.

Fabris, Rinaldo 1986, *Galileo Galilei e gli orientamenti esegetici del suo tempo* (Rome: Pontificia Academia Scientiarum).

Favaro, Antonio 1886a, *Carteggio inedito di Ticone Brahe, Giovanni Keplero e altri celebri astronomi e matematici dei secoli XVI e XVII con Giovanni Antonio Magini* (Bologna: Zanichelli).

_____ 1886b, "La Libreria di Galileo Galilei descritta ed illustrata", in *Bolletino di Bibliografia e Storia delle Scienze Matematiche e Fisiche*, XIX, May-June, 219-293.

_____ 1887, *Miscellanea Galileiana Inedita* (Venice: Carlo Ferrari) 35-89.

_____ 1896, *Bibliografia Galileiana. Indici e cataloghi*, Vol. XVI (Rome-Florence: Fratelli Bencini).

_____ 1919, *Oppositori di Galileo. Vol. III. Cristoforo Scheiner* (Venice: Carlo Ferrari).

_____ 1935, *Galileo Galilei e Suor Maria Celeste* (Florence: Giunti Barbèra).

_____ 1966-1968, *Galileo e lo Studio di Padova* (Padua: Antenore) 3 volumes.

_____ 1968, *Edizione Nazionale delle Opere di Galileo Galilei*, original edition 1890-1909, reprinted 1968 (Florence: Giunti Barbèra).

_____ 1983, "Giovanni Ciampoli", in *Amici e Corrispondenti di Galileo*, ed.: P. Galluzzi, 3 Vols. (Florence: Salimbeni) I, 164-168.

Ferrone, Vincenzo 1982, *Scienza, Natura, Religione* (Naples: Jovene).

Ferrone, Vincenzo and **Firpo**, Massimo 1985a, "Galileo fra inquisitori e microstorici", *Rivista Storica Italiana* 97, 177-238; see English translation as "From Inquisitors to Microhistorians: A Critique of Pietro Redondi's *Galileo Eretico*", in *Journal of Modern History* 58 (1986) 485-524.

_____ 1985b, "Replica", *Rivista Storica Italiana* 97, 957-968.

Field, Judith V. 1984, "Cosmology in the Work of Kepler and Galileo", in *Novità Celesti e Crisi del Sapere*, ed.: P. Galluzzi, Annali dell'Istituto e Museo di Storia della Scienza (Florence: Giunti Barbèra) 207-215.

Finocchiaro, Maurice A. 1980, *Galileo and the Art of Reasoning: Rhetorical Foundations of Logic and Scientific Method* (Dordrecht-Boston: D. Reidel Publishing Company).

_____ 1986, "The Methodological Background to Galileo's Trial", in *Reinterpreting Galileo*, ed.: W.A. Wallace (Washington: The Catholic University of America Press) 241-272.

_____ 1989, *The Galileo Affair, A Documentary History* (Berkeley: University of California Press).

Firpo, Luigi 1993, *Il Processo di Giordano Bruno* (Rome: Salerno Editor).

Fitzpatrick, Edward A. (ed.) 1933, *St. Ignatius and The "Ratio Studiorum"* (New York-London: McGraw-Hill Book Co.).

Flora, Ferdinando 1953, *Opere di Galileo Galilei* (Milan: Riccardo Ricciardi Editore).

Fredette, Raymond **1972**, "Galileo's De Motu Antiquiora", in *Physis* 14, 321-348.

Gabrieli, Giuseppe **1938-1942**, "Il carteggio linceo della vecchia Accademia di Federico Cesi (1603-1630)", in *Memorie della R. Accademia Nazionale dei Lincei.*

Ganss, George **1970**, (translator), *The Constitutions of the Society of Jesus* (St. Louis: Institute of Jesuit Sources).

Garin, Eugenio **1957**, *L'educazione in Europa (1400-1600)* (Bari: Laterza).

_____ **1965**, *Scienza e vita civile nel Rinascimento italiano* (Bari: Laterza).

_____ **1971**, "A proposito di Copernico", *Rivista di Storia della Filosofia*, 26, 79-96.

_____ **1973**, "Alle origini della polemica copernicana", *Studia Copernicana VI* (Wroclaw: Ossolineum) 31-42.

Garzend, Léon **1912**, *L'Inquisition et l'hérésie [Distintion de l'hérésie théologique et de l'hérésie inquisitoriale: à propos de l'affair Galilée]* (Paris: Desclée De Brouwer et Cie).

Gebler von, Carl **1876**, *Galileo Galilei und die römische Kurie* (Stuttgart); translated by Mrs. G. Sturge as *Galileo Galilei and the Roman Curia* (Merrick, NY: Richmond Publishing Company, 1977).

Geymonat, Ludovico **1965**, *Galileo Galilei: A Biography and Inquiry into His Philosophy of Science*, trans. by S. Drake (New York: McGraw-Hill Book Company).

Giacchi, Orio **1942**, "Considerazioni giuridiche sui due processi contro Galileo" in *Nel terzo centenario della morte di Galileo Galilei*, ed.: Università Cattolica del Sacro Cuore (Milan: Vita e Pensiero) 383-406.

Grant, Edward **1975**, *A Source Book in Medieval Science* (Cambridge, Massachusetts: Harvard University Press).

_____ **1978**, "Cosmology" in *Science in the Middle Ages*, ed.: David C. Lindberg (Chicago: The University of Chicago Press) 265-302.

_____ **1979**, *Physical Science in the Middle Ages* (Cambridge, Massachusetts: Harvard University Press).

_____ **1984**, *In Defense of the Earth's Centrality and Immobility: Scholastic Reaction to Copernicanism in the 17th Century* (Philadelphia).

Gregorovius, Ferdinand **1879**, *Urbano VIII e la sua opposizione alla Spagna e all'imperatore: Episodio della guerra dei trenta anni* (Rome: Bocca e C.).

Grisar, Hartmann **1882**, *Galileistudien* (Regensburg: Friedrich Pustet).

Guthke, Karl S. **1983**, *Der Mythos der Neuzeit* (Bern: A. Francke AG Verlag); English translation by H. Atkins as *The Last Frontier* (Ithaca, NY: Cornell University Press).

Guthrie, W.R.C. **1971-1981**, *A History of Greek Philosophy* (Cambridge: Cambridge Unversity Press) 6 volumes.

Heath, Thomas **1981**, *Aristarchus of Samos* (New York: Dover Publications).

Hooykaas, Reijer **1984**, "Rheticus' Lost Treatise on Holy Scripture and the Motion of the Earth", *Journal for the History of Astronomy*, 15, 77-80.

Humbert, P. **1948**, "Le problème des longitudes entre 1610 et 1666", *Archives Internationales d'histoire des sciences*, I, 383-384.

Jacobs, L. 1975, "Jewish Cosmology", in *Ancient Cosmologies*, eds.: M. Loewe and C. Blacker (London: George Allen & Unwin Ltd.) 69.

Jacqueline, Bernard 1984, "La Chiesa e Galileo nel Secolo dell'Illuminismo", in *Galileo Galilei, 300 Anni di Storia 1633-1983*, ed.: P. Poupard (Casale Monferrato, Italy: Edizioni Piemme) 181-195; see English translation listed under **Poupard** 1984.

John Paul II 1983, *Discourse to the Symposium, Galileian Studies Today, on the Occasion of the Commemoration of the 350th Anniversary of the Publication of the Dialogue on the Two Chief World Systems* (Vatican City State: L'Osservatore Romano) 9-10 May 1983, 1, 3.

_____ 1989, *Discourse to the City of Pisa* (Vatican City State: L'Osservatore Romano) 24 September 1989, 4.

_____ 1992, "Discourse on the Occasion of the Plenary Session of the Pontifical Academy of Sciences and the Conclusion of the Work of the Study Commission on the Ptolemaic-Copernican Controversy", in *Discorsi dei Papi alla Pontificia Accademia delle Scienze* (Vatican City State: Pontificia Academia Scientiarum) 271-280.

_____ 1994, *Apostolic Letter "Tertio Millenio Adveniente"* (Vatican City State: Libreria Editrice Vaticana)

Kepler, Johannes 1937-1993, *Gesammelte Werke*, eds.: M. Caspar and F. Hammer (Munich: C.H. Beck'sche Verlagsbuchhandlung).

Koestler, Arthur 1959, *The Sleepwalkers* (London: Hutchinson & Co. LTD).

Koyré, Alexandre 1940, *Etudes Galiléennes* (Paris: Hermann); English translation by J. Mepham as *Galileo Studies* (Atlantic Highlands, New Jersey: Humanities Press, 1978).

_____ 1957, *From the Closed World to the Infinite Universe* (Baltimore: Johns Hopkins University Press).

_____ 1966, *Etudes d'histoire de la pensée scientifique* (Paris: Hermann).

_____ 1974, *La révolution astronomique* (Paris: Hermann).

Kristeller, Paul Oskar **1965**, *Renaissance Thought II* (New York: Harper and Row).

Kuhn, Thomas **1971**, *The Copernican Revolution* (Cambridge, Massachusetts: Harvard University Press).

Langford, Jerome J. **1966**, *Galileo, Science and the Church* (Ann Arbor: University of Michigan Press).

Lattis, James M. **1994**, *Between Copernicus and Galileo* (Chicago: The University of Chicago Press).

Lear, John **1965**, *Kepler's Dream*, trans. by P.F. Kirkwood (Berkeley and Los Angeles: University of California Press).

Le Bachelet, Xavier Marie **1923**, "Bellarmin et G. Bruno", in *Gregorianum* IV, 193-210.

Lindberg, David C. (ed.) **1978**, *Science in the Middle Ages* (Chicago and London: University of Chicago Press).

Litt, A. **1963**, *Les corps célestes dans la philosophie de S. Thomas d'Aquin* (Louvain: Pubblications Universitaires).

Lloyd, Geoffrey E.R. **1973**, *Greek Science After Aristotle* (New York: Norton).

Maccarrone, Michele, **1980**, "Mons. Paschini e la Roma ecclesiastica", *Atti del convegno di studio su Pio Paschini nel centenario della nascita: 1878-1978* (Udine: Pubblicazioni della

Deputazione di Storia Patria del Friuli: Tipografia Poliglotta Vaticana) 49-93.

MacColley, Grant **1942**, "Ch. Scheiner and the Decline of Neo-Aristotelianism", *Isis*, 32, 63-69.

MacDonnell, Joseph, S.J. **1989**, *Jesuit Geometers* (Vatican City State: Vatican Observatory Publications; distributed by the Institute of Jesuit Sources: St. Louis).

Maffei, Paolo **1975**, "Il sistema copernicano dopo Galileo e l'ultimo conflitto per la sua affermazione", *Giornale di Astronomia*, 1, 5-12.

_____ **1987**, *Giuseppe Settele, il suo diario e la questione galileiana* (Foligno: Edizione dell'Arquata).

Maffeo, Sabino **1991**, *In the Service of Nine Popes, 100 Years of the Vatican Observatory* (Vatican City State: Vatican Observatory Publications, distributed by the University of Notre Dame Press).

Martini, Carlo M. **1966**, "Gli esegeti al tempo di Galileo", in *Nel Quarto Centenario della Nascita di Galileo Galilei* (Milan: Vita e Pensiero) 115-124.

Masini, Emilio **1621**, *Arsenale ovvero pratica della Santa Inquisizione* (Genoa).

Mayaud, Pierre-Noël **1992a**, "Une nouvelle affaire Galilée?", *Revue d'Histoire des Sciences*, XLV/2-3.

_____ **1992b**, "Les 'Fuit Congregatio Sancti Officii in ... coram ...' de 1611 à 1642: 32 ans de vie de la Congrégation du Saint Office", in *Archivum Historiae Pontificiae* (Romae: Pontificia Universitas Gregoriana) 30, 231-289.

_____ **1994**, "Deux textes au coeur du conflit: entre l'Astronomie Nouvelle et l'Ecriture Sainte: la lettre de Bellarmin à Foscarini et la lettre de Galilée à Christine de Lorraine", in *Après Galilée*, ed.: P. Poupard (Paris: Desclée de Brouwer).

McMullin, Ernan (ed.) **1967**, *Galileo, Man of Science* (New York: Basic Books).

_____ **1987**, "Bruno and Copernicus", *Isis*, 78, 55-74.

_____ **1988**, "Natural Science and Belief in a Creator: Historical Notes", in *Physics, Philosophy and Theology: A Common Quest for Understanding*, eds.: R.J. Russell, W.R. Stoeger and G.V. Coyne (Vatican City State: Vatican Observatory Publications, distributed by the University of Notre Dame Press) 49-79.

Mercati, Angelo **1942**, *Il sommario del processo di Giordano Bruno con appendice di documenti sull'eresia e l'inquisizione a Modena nel secolo XVI* (Vatican City State: Biblioteca Apostolica Vaticana).

Mereu, Italo **1990**, *Storia dell'Intolleranza in Europa* (Milan: Bompiani).

Michel, Paul-Henri **1965**, "Le Soleil, le Temps et l'Espace", in *Le Soleil à la Renaissance* (Brussels-Paris: Presses Universitaires de France) 397-414.

Migne, J.P. **1865**, (ed.) *Patrologiae Cursus Completus. Series Prima Latina* (Paris: MPL).

Morpurgo-Tagliabue, Guido **1963**, *I processi di Galileo e l'epistemologia* (Milan: Edizione di Comunità); also (Rome: Armando, 1981).

Müller Adolf **1909**, "Galileo Galilei und das Kopernikanische Weltsystem" and "Der Galilei Prozess", in *Stimmen Aus Maria Laach* (Freiburg in Breisgau: Herder), Nos. 101 and 102.

Neugebauer, Otto **1969**, *The Exact Sciences in Antiquity* (Providence: Brown University Press).

_____ **1975**, *A History of Ancient Mathematical Astronomy I-III* (Berlin-Heidelberg-New York: Springer-Verlag).

Nonis, Pietro **1980**, "L'ultima opera di Paschini, Galilei", in *Atti del convegno di studio su Pio Paschini nel centenario della nascita: 1878-1978* (Udine: Pubblicazioni della Deputazione di Storia Patria del Friuli: Tipografia Poliglotta Vaticana) 158-172.

Norlind, Wilhelm **1953**, "Copernicus and Luther. A Critical Study", *Isis*, XLIV, 273-276.

_____ **1954**, "A Hitherto Unpublished Letter from Tycho Brahe to Christopher Clavius", *The Observatory*, Vol. 74, 20-23.

_____ **1955**, "Thycho Brahe et ses rapports avec l'Italie", *Scientia*, February, 1-15.

_____ **1970**, *Tycho Brahe: A Biography* (Lund: C.W.K. Gleerup).

Orbaan, Johannes A.F. (ed.) **1920**, *Documenti sul Barocco a Roma* (Rome: Miscellanea della Regia Società Romana di Storia Patria).

Pagano, Sergio M. (ed.) **1984**, *I Documenti del Processo di Galileo Galilei* (Vatican City State: Pontifical Academy of Sciences and Vatican Archives).

Paschini, Pio **1965**, *Vita e Opere di Galileo Galilei* (Rome: Herder).

Pastor von, Ludwig **1938**, *History of the Popes from the Close of the Middle Ages*, Vol. XXVIII, trans.: E. Graf (London: Routledge & Kegan Paul).

Pedersen, Olaf **1978**, "Astronomy", in *Science in the Middle Ages*, ed.: D.C. Lindberg (Chicago and London: University of Chicago Press) 303-337.

_____ **1991**, "Galileo and the Council of Trent", in *Studi Galileiani* (Vatican City State: Vatican Observatory Publications, distributed by the Libreria Editrice Vaticana) Vol. I, No. 1.

_____ **1992**, *The Book of Nature* (Vatican City State: Vatican Observatory Publications, distributed by the University of Notre Dame Press).

Pedersen, Olaf and **Pihl**, Mogens **1974**, *Early Physics and Astronomy* (London); revised edition: Pedersen, Olaf, **1993** (Cambridge: Cambridge University Press).

Pesce, Mauro **1987**, "L'interpretazione della Bibbia nella Lettera di Galileo a Cristina di Lorena e la sua ricezione", in *Annali di Storia dell'Esegesi*, 4, 239-284.

_____ **1991**,"Momenti della ricezione dell'ermeneutica biblica galileiana e della Lettera a Cristina nel XVII secolo", in *Annali di Storia dell'Esegesi*, 8, 55-104.

_____ **1992**, "Le redazioni originali della Lettera Copernicana di G. Galilei a B. Castelli", in *Filologia e Critica*, XVII, 394-417.

Poppi, Antonino **1993**, *Cremonini, Galilei e gli inquisitori del Santo a Padova* (Padua: Centro Studi Antoniani).

Poupard, Paul (ed.) **1984**, *Galileo Galilei, 350 Anni di Storia 1633-1983* (Casale Monferrato: Edizioni Piemme); translated by I. Campbell as *Galileo Galilei: Toward a Resolution of 350 Years of Debate - 1633-1983* (Pittsburgh: Duquesne University Press, 1987).

Premoli, Orazio M. **1922**, *Storia dei Barnabiti nel Seicento* (Rome: Industria Tipografica Romana).

Redondi, Pietro **1985**, "Galileo eretico: Anatema", *Rivista Storica Italiana*, 97, 934-956.

_____ **1987**, *Galileo Heretic*, trans.: R. Rosenthal (Princeton: Princeton University Press).

Restiglian, Marco **1982**, "Nota su Giuseppe Toaldo e l'edizione toaldina del Dialogo di Galileo", in *Galileo Galilei e Padova* (Padua: Studia Patavina, Rivista di Scienze Religiose) 29, 3, 235-239.

Ronan, A. **1991**, "The origins of the reflecting telescope", *Journal of the British Astronomical Association*, 101, 335-342.

Ronchi, Vasco **1958**, *Il cannocchiale di Galileo e la scienza del seicento*, Second Edition (Turin: Einaudi - Boringhieri).

_____ **1968**, "Galilée et l'astronomie", in *Galilée, Aspects de sa vie et de son oeuvre* (Paris: Presses Universitaires de France).

_____ **1983**, *Storia della Luce. Da Euclide a Einstein* (Roma-Bari: Laterza).

Rosen, Edward **1971**, *Three Copernican Treatises* (New York: Dover Publications).

_____ **1975**, "Was Copernicus's *Revolutions* Approved by the Pope?", *Journal of the History of Ideas*, Vol. 36, 531-542.

_____ **1984**, *Copernicus and the Scientific Revolution* (Malabar, Florida: Krieger Publishing Co.).

Santillana de, Giorgio **1955**, *The Crime of Galileo* (Chicago: The University of Chicago Press).

_____ **1960**, *Processo a Galileo*, trans.: G. Cardona and A. Abetti (Milan: Arnoldo Mondadori).

Scandaletti, Paolo **1989**, *Galileo Privato* (Milan: Camunia Editrice).

Segre, Michael **1989**, "Galileo, Viviani and the Tower of Pisa", *Studies in History and Philosophy of Science*, 20, 435-451.

_____ **1991**, *In the Wake of Galileo* (New Brunswick: Rutgers University Press).

Shea, William R. **1972**, *Galileo's Intellectual Revolution: Middle Period, 1610-1632* (New York: Science History Publications).

_____ **1984**, "Melchior Inchofer *Tractatus Syllepticus*: A Consultor of the Holy Office Answers Galileo", in *Novità Celesti e Crisi di Sapere*, ed.: P. Galluzzi, Annali dell'Istituto e Museo di Storia della Scienza (Florence: Giunti Barbèra) 283-292.

Simoncelli, Paolo **1988**, "Inquisizione Romana e Riforma in Italia" in *Rivista Storica Italiana* 100, 5-125.

_____ **1992**, *Storia di una censura. "Vita di Galileo" e Concilio Vaticano II* (Milan: Franco Angeli).

Soccorsi, Filippo **1963**, *Il Processo di Galileo* (Rome: Edizioni "La Civiltà Cattolica").

Thomas, Aquinas **1947**, *Summa Theologica*, American Edition, 3 Vols. (New York, Boston, Cincinnati, Chicago, San Francisco: Benziger Brothers).

Tramontin, Silvio **1982**, "Galileo Galilei nella recente storiografia", in *Galileo Galilei e Padova* (Padua: Studia Patavina, Rivista di Scienze Religiose) 29, 3, 159-167.

Vernet, Juan **1972**, "Copernicus in Spain, Colloquia Copernicana I", in *Studia Copernicana* (Wroclaw) V, 271-291.

Viganò, Mario **1969**, *Il Mancato Dialogo fra Galileo e i Teologi* (Rome: Edizioni "La Civiltà Cattolica").

Villoslada, Riccardo **1954**, *Storia del Collegio Romano dal suo inizio (1551) alla soppressione della Compagnia di Gesù (1773)* (Rome: Gregorian University Press).

Waard de, Cornelius Jr. **1907**, *L'invention du télescope*, in Ciel et Terre, année 28, 81-88, 117-124 (Bruxelles: M. Weissenbruch).

Wallace, William A. **1977**, *Galileo's Early Notebooks: The Physical Questions* (Notre Dame: The University of Notre Dame Press).

_____ **1978a**, "Galileo Galilei and the Doctores Parisienses", in *New Perspectives on Galileo*, ed.: R.E. Butts and J.C. Pitt (Dordrecht: D. Reidel Publishing Company).

_____ **1978b**, "The Philosophical Setting of Medieval Science", in *Science in the Middle Ages*, ed.: D.C. Lindberg (Chicago and London: University of Chicago Press) 91-119.

_____ **1981**, *Prelude to Galileo: Essays on Medieval and Sixteenth-Century Sources of Galileo's Thought* (Dordrecht-Boston: D. Reidel Publishing Company).

_____ **1984a**, *Galileo and His Sources* (Princeton: Princeton University Press).

_____ **1984b**, "Galileo's Early Arguments for Geocentrism and His Later Rejection of Them", in *Novità Celesti e Crisi del Sapere*, ed.: P. Galluzzi, Annali dell'Istituto e Museo di Storia della Scienza (Florence: Giunti Barbèra) 31-40.

_____ (ed.) **1986** , *Reinterpreting Galileo* (Washington: The Catholic University of America Press).

Westfall, Richard S. **1989**, "Essays on the Trial of Galileo", in *Studi Galileiani* (Vatican City State: Vatican Observatory

Publications, distributed by the University of Notre Dame Press)
Vol. I, No. 5.

Westmann, Robert S. **1984**, "The Reception of Galileo's
Dialogue. A Partial World Census of Extant Copies", in *Novità
Celesti e Crisi del Sapere*, ed.: P. Galluzzi, Annali dell'Istituto e
Museo di Storia della Scienza (Florence: Giunti Barbèra) 329-
337.

Wisan, Winifred L. **1984**, "On the Chronology of Galileo's
Writings", in *Annali dell'Istituto e Museo della Scienza di
Firenze*, 9, 2, 85-88.

Wohlwill, Emil **1870**, *Der Inquisitionsprozess des Galileo
Galilei* (Berlin: R. Oppenheim).

_____ **1910**, **1926**, *Galilei und sein Kampf für die
kopernikanische Lehre*, 2 volumes (Leipzig); reprinted
(Wiesbaden: Martin Sändig, 1969).

Yates, Frances A. **1969**, *Giordano Bruno and the Hermetic
Tradition* (Chicago: University of Chicago Press); earlier edition
(London: Routledge and Kegan, 1964).

Zagar, Francesco **1964**, "Galileo Astronomo", in *Fortuna di
Galileo*, (Bari: Laterza).

INDEX OF NAMES

Academy of Florence, see
  Florentine
Academy of Sciences, see
  French
Academy of Sciences, see
  Pontifical
Academy of the New Lincei,
  517,523
Accademia dei Lincei, 131,
  139,145,159,164,170,210,
  266,284,285,287,301,319,
  339,371,372,541
Acquapendente, Gerolamo
  Fabrizio di, 66,413
Acquaviva, Claudio, 132,
  133,161,165,167,231,267,
  309
Agucchi, Giovanbattista,
  276
Aguilon, François D', 146
Albert the Great, Saint, 230
Albizzi, Francesco, 414
Aldobrandini, Pietro,
  Cardinal, 458
Alexander of Aphrodisias,
  41
Alhazen, see Ibn
Alighieri, see Dante
Ammannati, Giulia, 48
Anfossi, Filippo, 497,519,
  521
Apelle, see Scheiner
Apollonius of Perga, 6
Aquinas, Thomas, Saint,
  15-18,37,38,205,230,243,
  244,550

Archimedes, 10,50,51,89,
  135,293,483
Ariosto, Ludovico, 312
Aristarchus, 10,12,31,37,40,
  76,95,542
Aristotle, 1-6,9-11,15,16,18,
  19,23,28,31,33,36,37,41,
  49,50,56,57,59,61,62,67,
  69,71,79-81,92,97,98,101,
  111,112,120,122,123,132,
  135,142,156,160,161,166,
  167,189,231,232,235,238,
  267,274,275,277,278,291,
  293,304,313,315,332,348-
  350,359,377,378,387,388,
  544
Armellini, Giuseppe, 525
Arrighetti, Niccolò, 301
Atkins, Helen, 542
Attavanti, Giannozzo, 210,
  437
Augustine, Saint, 12,14,15,
  192,195-197,199-201,203-
  205,247,249,537
Averroes, 15,37
Avicenna, 15

Bacon, Francis, 248,267
Badelli, Antonio, 336,371
Badouère, Jaques, 108,150
Baldini, Ugo, xviii,93,98,
  158,159,161,162,243,244,
  266,299,300,308,367,483,
  533,536
Baliani, Giovanni Battista,
  373,457,536

Banfi, Antonio, 533
Baranzano, Giovanni
  Antonio (Redento),
  247,248
Barbarigo, Gregorio,
  Cardinal, 516,533
Barberini, Antonio,
  Cardinal, 410,411,
  467,471
Barberini, Carlo, Cardinal,
  287
Barberini, Francesco,
  Cardinal, 287,320,327,
  336,338,339,370,372,389,
  396,397,405,407,408,414,
  416,419,427,429,430,433-
  435,459,465,467,468,470,
  471,474-479,484,485,489-
  492,511,513,
Barberini, Maffeo, Cardinal
  (see also Urban VIII),
  130,136,141,179,245,259,
  262,263,269,271,283,285,
  286,302,313,319,321,322,
  361,362,447,473,481
Barberini, Taddeo, 336,371
Bardi, Giovanni, 88,166
Barone, Francsco, 42,533
Baronio, Cesare, Cardinal,
  105,248
Bartolucci, Giovanni, 87
Bartolucci, Marina, 87,88
Bellarmine, Robert, Saint,
  35,44,45,104,105,126-
  130,134,157,158,175,178,
  180-183,185-188,201,204,
  217-222,227-230,232,233,
  236,238,239,241-249,252-
  254,257-264,266-269,271,

284,293,296,298,314,332,
  345,359,361,377,388,402,
  403,416,421-424,430,434-
  436,438,439,447-449,462,
  466,475,477,480,481,493,
  533,534
Bellinati, Claudio, 90,104,
  105,516,533
Benedetti, Giovanni
  Battista, 29,59
Benedict XV, 240,517
Bentivoglio, Guido,
  Cardinal, 415,467,471,
  478,483
Bernegger, Mathias, 485,
  512
Berti, Domenico, 502
Bertolla, Pietro, 524-
  527,534
Bessel, Friedrich W., 514
Biagioli, Mario, 153,159,
  163,457,458,534
Biancani, Giuseppe, 146,
  299,300,533
Blackwell, Richard J., xviii,
  42,45,158,160,161,239,
  240,242-247,249,250,255,
  267,298-300,386,534
Boccabella, Alessandro, 414
Bocchineri, Geri, 425,470-
  472,512
Bocchineri Buonamici,
  Alessandra, 490
Boffito, Giuseppe, 247,248,
  522,534
Bolognetti, Giorgio, 465,490
Bonansea, Bernardino M.,
  269,534
Bonaparte, see Napoléon

Boncompagni, Francesco,
Cardinal, 317
Borgia, Gaspare, Cardinal,
390,467,471,479
Bortle, John B., 306,534
Boscaglia, Cosimo, 172,238
Bouchard, Gian Giacomo,
479
Bradley, James, 493,514
Brahe, Tycho (Tyge), 28-33,
42,43,60,61,73-76,91,98,
99,103,107,111,120,134,
135,142,151,160,229,235,
274-277,279-281,289,297,
303-306,310,313-316,333,
351,380,382,387,461,493,
539,547
Brandmüller, Walter, 45,
261-265,387,515,516,519,
521,524,532,534
Brodrick, James, 158,534
Bruno, Giordano, 29,34,35,
40,43-45,65,123,128,129,
157,163,244,366,381,540,
544,546,552
Bucciantini, Massimo, 149,
238,254,255,257,265,301,
310,363,365,534
Bucciarelli, Brenno, 507,
508,531,534
Bulferetti, Luigi, 96,535
Buonaiuti (Galilei), 47,88
Buonamici, Francesco, 56,
Buonamici,
Giovanfrancesco, 262,
333,469,475,485,490
Buonarroti, Lionardo, 371
Buonarroti, Michelangelo,
336,371,468,490,493,530

Buridan (Buridano), Jean,
38
Burgo, Ricardo de, 307,308
Burstyn, Harold L., 384,
385,535
Buseo, Teodoro, 164

Caccini, Tommaso, 42,175-
177,209-211,214,238,239,
241,253,254,256,266,284,
323,369,437,438,477
Caetani, Bonifazio,
Cardinal, 254,262-
264,269,286,362,481
Caetani, Enrico, Cardinal,
52,226
Callippus, 5,36
Calmet, Agostino, 495,496
Calvin, John, 412
Campanella, Tommaso, 122,
156,157,263,269,313,336,
362,363,366,382,391,392,
402,404,459,460,463,481,
535,539
Capella, Martianus 36
Capponi, Luigi, Cardinal,
253,472
Capra, Baldessar, 83,99,102
Caracioli, Napolitano, 336
Carbone, Ludovico, 92,93
Carugo, Adriano, 56,57,
92-94,535
Carusi, Enrico, 44
Casanovas, Juan, xvii,309,
381,535
Castelli, Benedetto, 86,115,
137,154,155,163,172,173,
175-177,179,180,189,205,
208,209,212,234,238-241,

246,247,253,264,266,297,
299,325,334,339,340,343,
370-372,389-391,402,406-
408,410,415,437,457,459-
461,468,469,481,489,512,
548
Cavalieri, Bonaventura,
457,512,513
Centini, Felice, Cardinal,
377,471,472,477
Cesalpino, Andrea, 49
Cesarini, Virginio, 275,
283-285,287,301,311-313,
319,320
Cesi,Federico, 131,139,143,
145,146,149,165,171,175,
176,182,235,238,239,241,
255,284,285,301,311,319-
321,327,328,332,334,339,
360,362-364,366,371,541
Chiaramonti, Scipione, 297,
325,326,351,380,396
Christina of Lorraine, xix,
14,87,172,173,182,189,
203,208,212,234,235,238,
240,247,252,254,262,264,
272,284,360,367,386,461,
472,494,503,512,516
Ciampoli, Giovanni, 179,
235,241,244,245,280,281,
284,287,294,306,311,312,
319,323,326,328,334,340,
366,368,371,389-391,394,
399,401,409,416,418,426,
457,458,469,486,540
Cicero, Marcus Tullius, 431
Cigoli, Ludovico Cardi di,
143,145,156,164,168

Cimenes, Ferdinando, 209,
210
Cioli, Andrea, balì, 338,
340-342,372,373,396,397,
407,409,412-415,417,418,
420,426,436,457,461,463,
467-472
Cioni, Michele, 456,467,
535
Clagett, Marshall, 535
Clavelin, Maurice, 383,535
Clavius, Christoph, xvii,30,
42,51-53,56-58,67,74,75,
85,90-93,95,97,98,120-
123,126,127,131-134,147,
155-157,229,242,533,547
Clement VII, 24,25
Cobelluzzi, Scipione,
Cardinal, 276
Cohen, Morris, 36,536
Colombe, Ludovico delle,
117,124,125,130,135,137,
154,157,247,323
Colombo, Giuseppe, 248,
536
Colpo, Mario, 91
Commandino, Federico, 51,
53
Confalonieri, Angelo, 247
Congregation of the
Propagation of the Faith,
265,362
Contarini, Simone, 266
Conti, Carlo, Cardinal, 141,
170
Copernicus (Copernik),
Mikołaj, 1,8,10,19,20,
22-29,31-34,36,38-42,,44,

58,60,61,68-71,81,91,95-
97,107,111,112,120,124,
128,132,134,151,156,161,
176,180-183,188,190,205,
208,212,222,223,226,228,
229,237,238,242,254,261-
264,273,276,297-299,310,
315,321,324,325,327,329,
337,347,349,350,352,359,
362,364,375,378,380-383,
385,388,421,422,425,434,
442,443,452,472,475,486,
497,498,515,517,518,520,
521,544,546,547,549,550

Copleston, Frederik, 536

Cornford, Francis M., 536

Corradino, Saverio, xvii

Costabel, Pierre, 317,514,
515,518,536

Costantini, Claudio, 457,
536

Couder, André, 150,537

Council of Trent, see Trent

Coyne, George V., xiv,
xvii-xx,243,244,265,266,
533,535,536,546

Cozzi, Gaetano, 104,536

Cremonini, Cesare, 65,66,
72,76,84,85,96,97,99,100,
102,123,128,129,154,158,
165,548

Crombie, Alistair C., 37,38,
56,57,92-94,535,537

Curzio, Matteo, 41

Cusanus (von Kues),
Nikolaus, 40, 381

Cysat, Johann Baptist, 139,
166,300

D'Addio, Mario, 460,462,
467,471-474,479,480,515,
518-521,537

Dame, Bernard, 163-165,
537

Danjon, André, 150,537

Dante, Alighieri, 91,289,
530

D'Elci, Orso, 342,372

D'Elia, Pasquale, 90,162,
537

Delorme, Suzanne, 150,
537

Denzinger, Henricus, 503,
537

Descartes, René, 267,381

Digges, Leonard, 149

Digges, Thomas, 29,149,
150

Dijksterhuis, E.J., 38,315,
537

Dini, Piero, xii, 177-182,
188,189,212,234,239,241,
245,267,481

Diodati, Elia, 333,343,366,
412,453,512

Dobrzycki, Jerzy, xviii

Dominis, Marcantonio de,
149

Drabkin, Israel E., 36,95,
536,538

Drake, Stillman, xx,60,62,
68,77,79,80,88,90,91,94-
100,102,103,108,114,141,
149-152,154,155,158,163,
164,167,168,171,174,182,
188,190,242,249,250,252,
257-261,270,275,288,290,
292,299,301,305,308-310,

313-315,318,333,345-358,
360,361,363-365,368,369,
375,376,378-387,389,460,
462,471,479,489,492,537,
538,541
Dreyer, Johann L.E., 33,
36,43,98,538
Dubarle, Dominique, 528
Duhem, Pierre, 243,538
Duodo, Francesco, 375

Egidi, Clemente, 342,374,
377,393,396,411,412,457
Einstein, Albert, 507,534,
549
Elchinger Arthur, 528,529
Encyclopédie, L', 517,522
Épinois, Henri de L', 501,
502
Ernst, Germana, 156,539
Estoile, Pierre de L', 150
Euclid, 49-52,55,67,89
Eudoxus, 5,36

Faber, Johannes, 139,165
Fabri, Nicole, see Peiresc
Fabricius, Johann, 138,
139,163,164
Fabris, Rinaldo, 246,247,
539
Fantoni, Filippo, 54,55,89
Favaro, Antonio, xiv,xx,55,
56,74,85,87,91,94-96,102-
105,152,162,163,168,177,
237,240,242,254,257,299,
365,371,377,458,463,483,
502,508,513,515,516,522,
524,531,534,539
Febei, Pietro Paolo, 477

Femiano, Salvatore, 535
Ferrone, Vincenzo, 364,
365,516,540
Field, Judith V., 149,540
Filiis, Angelo de, 145,146,
148,331
Filonardi, Marcello, 34
Finocchiaro, Maurice, xiv,
177-181,185,191-195,198,
199,201-204,207,209,210,
216,218,220,223,226-228,
246,251-253,267,325,327,
328,341-343,365,374,375,
383,386,387,396,397,399-
403,409,413,415-420,441,
471,540
Fiorenzuola, see Maculano
Firpo, Massimo, 44,45,364,
365,535,540
Fitzpatrick, Edward A.,
161,540
Flora, Ferdinando, 88,540
Florentine Academy, 91,
159,277,371,490
Foscarini, Paolo Antonio,
182,183,186-189,204,214,
215,223,232-234,236,242-
247,254,255,261,263,270,
422,447,481,497,516,519,
521,546
Fredette, Reynold, 56,92,
541
French Academy of
Sciences, 517
Frigerio, Domenico, 248

Gabrieli, Giuseppe, 159,
541
Gaffarel, Jacques, 485

Galamini, Agostino,
Cardinal, 209,256,257,
377,471,472
Galen, 49
Galilei, Cosimo, 516,533
Galilei, Livia I, 48
Galilei, Livia II, 87,169
Galilei, Michelangelo, 48,
366
Galilei, Vincenzio, 47,48,
49,51,63,88,90,445
Galilei, Vincenzio II ,87,
412,490,513,516
Galilei, Virginia I, 48
Galilei, Virginia II, see
Suor Maria Celeste
Galluzzi, Paolo, 533,539,
540,550,551,552
Galluzzi, Tarquinio, 283
Gamba, Marina, 87,88
Ganss, George, 160,541
Garin, Eugenio, 42,89,541
Garzend, L., 480,541
Gassendi, Pierre, 132,368,
456,481,484
Gebler, Karl von, 221,260,
502,541
Gemelli, Agostino, 503,504,
525
Genesis, Book of, 1,12,15,
184,195,197
Gessi, Berlingero, Cardinal,
471,477
Geymonat, Ludovico, 237,
266,267,292,311,314,315,
363,380,383,384,474,541
Gherardi, Silvestro, 501,
522
Gherardini, Niccolò, 89,94,

467,471,477
Ghislieri, Federico, 213
Giacchi, Orio, 480,541
Giese, Tiedemann, 25,27,
41
Gilbert, William, 29,83
Ginetti, Marzio, Cardinal,
471,477
Giustiniani, Benedetto, 256
Gonzaga, Ferdinando,
Cardinal, 136
Gonzaga, Vincenzo, 102
Grandi, Antonio Maria, 520
Grant, Edward, 38,515,542
Grassi, Orazio, 264,271,
274,275,277,279-283,285,
288-291,293-297,300-312,
314-317,363-365,367,373,
454,483
Gregorovius, Ferdinand,
458,542
Gregory XIII, 52,90
Gregory XV, 285,312
Greipl, Egon J., 45,261-265,
515,519,521,532,534
Grienberger, Christoph,
126,127,146,157,162,165-
167,178,180,181,188,232,
234,264,267,268,275,300,
307,308,311,312,454,455,
465,483
Grisar, Hartmann, 42,523,
542
Gualdo, Paolo, 85,120,123,
146,165,166
Guevara, Giovanni di, 327,
364
Guicciardini, Piero, 130,
159,213,216-218,224-228,

256-258,265,335,490
Guiducci, Mario, 148,159,
167,168,277-283,288,291,
295,296,301-304,308-310,
312,316,326-328,330,364,
394,397,413,453,468,472
Guldin, Paul, 311,312
Guthke, Karl, 511,542
Guthrie, W.R.C., 542

Harriot, Thomas, 109,163
Harvey, William, 97
Hasdale, Martin, 119,154
Heath, Thomas, 542
Heller, Michael, 535,536
Heraclides Ponticus, 10,36,
37
Herschel, William, Sir, 514
Hipparchus, 6
Holste (Holstein), Luca,
417,471,492
Holy Office (also Roman
Inquisition), xvii,34,35,
38,44,45,65,96,128,130,
153,175,179,209-211,215-
223,224,226,227,231,232,
235,239-241,245,253,255-
266,268,270,271,286,300,
313,327,345,347,361-365,
369,374,377,388,389,398,
400-422,424-427,429,430,
433-446,451-453,455,456,
462,464-468,470-474,476-
480,483,485,487,488,491,
493-499,501,508,512,514,
519-522,525,526,528-530,
532,550
Hooykaas, Reijer, 42,542
Horky, Martin, 116-119,

125,154
Humbert, P., 299,542
Huygens, Christian, 103,
161,513

Ibn al Aytam (Alhazen), 17,
18
Ignatius of Loyola, Saint,
132,158,161,162,230,300,
540
Inchofer, Melchior, 253,
402,426,463,464,475,550
Index, Congregation of the,
45,176,179,219,220,223-
226,228,239,240,242,254,
261-265,268,293,309,337,
362,416,421,434,435,442,
447,449,473,475,496,498,
517,518,529
Ingoli, Francesco, 254,255,
264,265,276,301,323-328,
362,363,374,379,447
Inquisition Roman, see
Holy Office

Jacobs, L., 13,543
Jacqueline, Bernard, 517,
518,543
Job, Book of, 27,42,124,202,
223
John Paul II, ii,xi,xiii,xiv,
482,507-510,532,534,543
John XXIII, 505,523
Joshua, Book of, 38,41,175,
184,205,206,238,247

Kepler, Johann, 22,29,30,
34,35,39,47,69-73,75,97,
98,103,104,107,115-119,

123,138,149,150,154-156,
158-160,163,226,233,243,
255,264,280,281,297,298,
308-310,314,317,318,355,
362,363,383,387,388,497,
516,538,540,543
Kircher, Athanasius, 132,
484,485
Kirkwood, P.F., 544
Kirwitzer, Wenceslaus, 162
Koestler, Arthur, 42,98,
476,543
Koyré, Alexandre, 40,379,
543
Kristeller, Paul Oskar, 96,
544
Kuhn, Thomas, 4,7,8,11,20,
21,39,89,386,544

Lamalle, Edmond, 526-528,
531
Landini, G.Benedetto, 343,
344,395
Langford, Jerome J., 171,
213,244,246,249,251,252,
256,267,269,459,544
Lattis, James M., 42,544
Lear, John, 150,544
Le Bachelet, Xavier Marie,
45,544
Lemaître, Georges, 526
Leo X, 24
Leo XIII, 502,503,522
Leopold of Austria, 272,
276,277,280,299,310,365
Lindberg, David C., 542,
544,548,551
Litt, Thomas, 37,38,544
Lloyd, Geoffrey E.R., 544

Locher Boius, Johannes
Franz, 146,147
Locke, John, 292
Lorenzini, Antonio, 76,100,
102
Lorini, Niccolò, 171,176,
177,179,208-211,238-241,
253,437
Loyola, see Ignatius
Luciani, Antonio G., 508
Ludovisi, Ludovico,
Cardinal, 458
Luther, Martin, 41,412,547
Lykaeion of Athens, 377

Maccagni, Carlo, xvii
Maccarrone, Michele, 524-
531,544
MacColley, Grant, 368,545
MacDonnell, Joseph, 90,
545
Maculano, Vincenzo, 407,
407,414,421-427,429,430,
432,433,436,440,442,443,
471,473-478,491
Maelcote, Odo Van, 98,126,
127,131-134,159,160
Maffei, Paolo, xviii,519,
521,545
Maffeo, Sabino, xiv,xvii,
xviii,xx,523,545
Magalotti, Filippo, 326,
394-398,413,453,460-
462,468
Magalotti, Lorenzo, 253,
254
Magini, Giovanni Antonio,
54,74,98,115-117,125,
134,146,147,154,539

Manetti, Antonio, 91
Manzoni, Giacomo, 501
Maraffi, Luigi, 175,179,269
Mariani, Innocenzo, xvii
Marini, Marino, 501,522
Marsili, Cesare, 318,325,
   328,342,343,363,367,385
Martina, Giacomo, xvii
Martini, Carlo Maria, 246,
   545
Marzimedici, Alessandro,
   137,163
Masini, Emilio, 480,545
Mästlin, Michael, 29,42
Mauri, Alimberto, 154
Mayaud, Pierre Noël, xix,
   247,365,472,545
Mayr, Simon, 83,99,287,
   313,314,318
Mazzoni, Jacopo, 69,71,96
McCarthy, Martin F., xiv,
   xviii
McMullin, Ernan, 45,246,
   249,252,537,546
Medici, Carlo de', Cardinal,
   227
Medici, Cosimo I de', 49,
   82,172
Medici, Cosimo II de', 82,
   86,87,110,112-114,136,
   150,151,162,212,224,284
Medici, Christina, see
   Christina of Lorraine
Medici, Ferdinando I de',
   284
Medici, Ferdinando II de',
   284
Medici, Giovanni de', 137
Medici, Giuliano de', 155

Medici, Leopoldo de', 62
Medici, Lorenzo de', 41
Melanchthon (Schwarzerd,
   Philipp), 41
Mercati, Angelo, 43,44,546
Mercuriale, Girolamo, 78,
   101
Mereu, Italo, 475,476,
   480-482,546
Mersenne, Marin, 456,481,
   512
Micanzio, Fulgenzio, 85,98,
   369,370,396,460,479,481
Michel, Paul Henry, 163,
   546
Migne, Jacques Paul, 195,
   249,546
Millefiorini, Pietro, xix
Millini Garcìa, Cardinal,
   217,218,261,268
Mirto, Placido, 299
Monachino, Vincenzo, xvii,
   525
Monte, Francesco del,
   Cardinal, 162,213,
   224,228, 245
Monte, Guidobaldo del, 53,
   54,59,63,92,103
Morandi, Orazio, 168,336,
   372,382,486
Morpurgo-Tagliabue, Guido,
   222,260,546
Müller, Adolf, 523,546
Müller, Nikolaus, 29
Muzzarelli, Giovanni, 513

Napoléon, Bonaparte, 44,
   240,499,519,521,522
Napolitani, Pier Daniele,

162,266,483,533
Naudé, Gabriel, 485
Neugebauer, Otto, 36,547
Newman, John Henry, xiii,
xiv,534
Newton, Isaac, 108,237,
383,493,517
Niccolini, Caterina, see
Riccardi, Caterina
Niccolini, Francesco, 335,
338,341-343,371,373,396-
403,407-420,426,429,433,
435,436,440-442,457,461-
463,468-472,475,477,478,
491,492,514
Noailles, François de, 511
Nonis, Pietro, 524,547
Norlind, Wilhelm, 41,91,
98,547
Nozzolini, Tolomeo, 137,
163

Olivieri, Maurizio
Benedetto, 388,497,
520,521
Orbaan Johannes, A.F.,
160,547
Oreggi (Oregius), Agostino,
361,402,426,463-466
Oresme, Nicole, 38,39
Orsini, Alessandro,
Cardinal, 215-217,228,
246, 257,272,302,327,328,
365,367,368
Orsini, Francesco, Cardinal,
41
Orsini, Paolo, 330,332,367
Osiander, Andreas, 23,25,
40,41,243,263

Pagano, Sergio Maria, 240,
253,258,260,365,508,514,
519,521,522,531,532,547
Pagnoni, Silvestro, 102
Papazzoni, Flaminio, 136
Parente, Pietro, 505,506,
526,529
Paschini, Pio, 42,157,160,
161,242,243,265,266,270,
299,300,456,457,468,483,
503-506,511,515,523-527,
529,530,534,544,547
Pasqualigo, Zaccaria, 427,
463
Pastor, Ludwig von, 458,
461,547
Paul III, 24-26,35,190,226
Paul V, 84,96,104,130,203,
219,226,227,230-232,257-
259,262,263,271,284,293,
313,377
Paul VI, 203,219,226,227,
230-232,257-259,262,263,
377,505,528-531
Pedersen, Olaf, xviii,36-40,
89,548
Peiresc, Nicolas Claude
Fabri de, 132,299,330,
417, 471,484,485
Pereyra, Benito, 247,248
Pesce, Mauro, 177,240,243,
246,253,548
Peucer, Kaspar, 29
Philoponus, Joannes, 38
Philosophical Transactions,
493
Picchena, Curzio, 213-216,
225,226,228,254,255,265,
302,320,362

Piccolomini, Ascanio, 487, 532

Pietro, Giovanni, 41

Pihl, Mogens, 36-40,89,548

Pineda, Juan, 42,124

Pinelli, Giovanni Vincenzio, 63,73,85,93,126

Pius VII, 499

Pius IX, 44,501,522

Pius XI, xiv,523

Pius XII, 504,505,525

Plato, 40,50,156,293,536, 538

Plutarch, 123

Pontifical Academy of Sciences, 503,504,506, 507, 510,523,525,526,527, 529,530,539,543,547

Poppi, Antonino, 96,102, 548

Porta, Giovanni Battista della, 149,160

Poupard, Paul, Cardinal, 508,536,543,546,548

Premoli, Orazio M., 248, 548

Ptolemy, 1,5-8,16-19,22,28, 32,33,55,56,61,67-69,71, 79-81,97,111,112,120, 122,132,151,156,180,182, 189,235,238,242,297,310, 311,315,329,350,352,353, 359,375,381,442,529

Querengo, Antonio, 213, 266

Ramus, Pierre (de la Ramée), 29

Ratzinger, Joseph, Cardinal, xvii

Record, Robert, 29

Redondi, Pietro, 159,258, 301,313,315,317,363-365, 457,458,460,463,483,531, 549

Reinhold, Erasmus 28,

Remo, Giovanni, 276,280, 302,308,310

Renier, Zeno, 461

Renieri, Vincenzo, 391

Restiglian, Marco, 515,549

Rheticus, Georg Joachim, 27,40

Riccardi, Caterina, 335,340

Riccardi, Niccolò, 253,262, 285,297,313,334,335,337- 344,372-374,376,377, 389,393-396,398,399, 401,402,406,407,413, 414,434,435,453,456, 457,459-467,469,486

Ricci, Ostilio, 50,54,89

Richelieu, Armand, Jean du Plessis, Cardinal, 337, 483

Ridolfi, Nicolò, 313

Rinuccini, Giovanni Battista, 275,276

Rinuccini, Tommaso, 316

Rocco, Berlinzone, 85

Roman College, 52,53,56-58, 90-92,95,98,120,126-129, 131-134,145,146,157,160- 162,166,230-232,264,267, 274-276,278-281,283, 285,300-303,306,307,311- 313,317,326,361,363,454,

481,537

Roman Inquisition, *see*
Holy Office
Ronan, Colin A., 149,549
Roncalli, Angelo, *see* John
XXIII
Ronchi, Vasco, 150,549
Ronchitti, Cecco di, 77,79,
81
Rosen, Edward, 41,549
Royal Society, 159

Sacrobosco (Holywood),
John, 30,50,58,67,89
Sagredo, Gianfrancesco, 85,
86,141,142,156,266,311,
347,348,355-357,382
Salviati, Filippo, 80,136,
145,156,171,347-355,357,
358,360,363,378,379,381,
382,387,398
Salviati, Giuseppe,
Cardinal, 41
Salviucci, Pietro, 525,526
Santarelli, Antonio, 483
Santillana, Giorgio de, 18,
128,129,158,162,213,215,
220-222,224,225,232,237,
238,241-243,260,261,266-
269,273,282,314,361,362,
366,367,395,402,404,421-
425,428,431,432,435-438,
440,443,445,446,460,466,
478,479,483,486,549
Sarpi, Paolo, 68,84,85,98,
103,104,108,109,117,150,
154,156,253,369,536
Sarsi, Lotario, *see* Grassi
Scaglia, Desiderio,

Cardinal, 415,471,472,
478
Scandaletti, Paolo, 524,550
Scheiner, Christoph
(Apelle), 138-148,154,
163,164-168,308,275,280,
281,300,308,309,327,330,
353,367,382,327,328,330-
332,353,365,367-369,373,
380,382,392,391,392,454,
455,460,464,465,484,485,
527,539,545
Schönberg (Scommergio),
Nikolaus, Cardinal, 25,
503
Schönmetzer, Adolfus, 248,
503,537
Schoppe, Kaspar, 44
Scorriggio, Lazzaro, 223
Segizzi, Michelangelo, 209,
219,221,222,225,260,261,
361,377,388,402,403,438,
439,448,449,463,480
Segre, Michael, 96,550
Seneca, Lucius, Annaeus,
76,98,279,306,315
Sera, Cosimo del, 470
Serristori, Lodovico, 415,
470,471
Settele, Giuseppe, 496-498,
520,521,545
Settimi, Clemente, 489,513
Sfondrati, Paolo Camillo,
Cardinal, 176,179,209
Shea, William R., 43,304,
305,309-311,315,317,458,
463-465,550
Simoncelli, Paolo, 524,526,
550

Simplicius, 348-351,355,
  357,358,360,374,377,382,
  394,398,486,489,512
Sixtus V, 298
Sizzi, Francesco, 117,125,
  130,168,382
Soccorsi, Filippo, 243,486,
  550
Solomon, 184,185,187
Spina, Bartolomeo, 26,27
Spinelli, Girolamo, 99
Spinola, Fabio, 326,363
Stefani, Giacinto, 340-342,
  373,374
Stelluti, Francesco, 287,
  295,311,330,367
Stunica, see Zuñiga
Sturge, G., 541
Suor Maria Celeste, 87,
  169,335,539

Tartaglia, Niccolò, 58,59
Tartaglia, Pomponio, 247
Tarde (Du Pont de), Jean,
  168
Tasso, Torquato, 312
Tempier, Etienne, 38
Tengnagel, Francesco, 73,
  74
Teruko, Kawasaki-Fantoli,
  xviii
Theodoric of Radzyn, 25,41
Thomas, see Aquinas
Toaldo, Giuseppe, 494-496,
  515-518,549
Toledo, Francisco de, 27,
  42,92
Tolosani, Giovanni Maria,
  26-28,41,42

Torricelli, Evangelista, 89,
  457,464,465,490,512
Tragagliolo, Alberto, 45
Tramontin, Silvio, 524,550
Trent, Council of, 26,186,
  201,202,204,239,240,246,
  364,548
Trismegistus, Hermes, 40
Turiozzi, Fabrizio, 498
Tycho, see Brahe

Urban VIII (see also
  Barberini, Maffeo,
  Cardinal), 131,156,157,
  241, 262,285-287,294,
  319-324,328,335-338,344,
  347,358,361,362,371,372,
  374,376,377,390-393,396-
  401,403-405,408-410,413,
  415,416,418,419,427,429,
  430,433-436,440,441,447,
  453,455-462,465,467-470,
  472,474-476,478,480,483,
  486,487,492,510,511,514

Vale, Giuseppe, 524
Valerio, Luca, 266
Valle (Valla), Paolo della,
  57,92,93,371
Vernet, Juan, 42,550
Verospi, Fabrizio, Cardinal,
  471,477
Vesalius, Andreas, 66
Viganò, Mario, 270,515,551
Villoslada, Ricardo, 90,551
Vinta, Belisario, 94,113,
  119,157
Visconti, Raffaele, 338,339,
  342,372,467

Vitelleschi, Muzio, 309,316, 317,483

Viviani, Vincenzio, 50,62, 66,89,94,96,105,152,490, 493,513,514,516,550

Waard de, Cornelius Jr., 149,551

Wallace, William A., 37,56, 57,89,92-97,386,534,538, 540,551

Wedderburn, Johannes, 119

Welser, Markus, 139-145, 148,164,170,256,299,331

Westfall, Richard S., 159, 238,239,242,365,367,458, 509,551

Westmann, Robert S., 456, 552

Widmanstadt, Johann Albrecht von, 24,25,41

Wisan, Winifred Lovell, 94, 552

Wohlwill, Emil, 260,552

Ximenes, see Cimenes

Yates, Frances A., 157,552

Zacchia, Laudivio, Cardinal, 467,471,480

Zagar, Francesco, 384,552

Zapata y Cisneros, Antonio, Cardinal, 377,471,472

Zollern (Zoller), Frederick, Cardinal, 321,324

Zuñiga, Diego de, 27,42, 202,223,261-263,265,497, 516,521,533

Życiński, Jozef, 535,536

VATICAN PRESS